AN INTRODUCTION TO PUBLIC INTERNATIONAL LAW

Written for students working in a range of disciplines, this textbook provides an accessible, balanced, and nuanced introduction to the field of public international law. It explains the basic concepts and legal frameworks of public international law while acknowledging the field's inherent complexities and controversies. Featuring numerous carefully chosen and clearly explained examples, it demonstrates how the law applies in practice, and public international law's pervasive influence on world affairs, both past and present. Aiming not to over-emphasize any particular domestic jurisprudence or research interest, this textbook offers a global overview of public international law that will be highly valuable to any student new to the study of this very significant field.

D0746545

AN INTRODUCTION TO PUBLIC INTERNATIONAL LAW

CECILY ROSE
Leiden University

NIELS BLOKKER
Leiden University

DANIËLLA DAM-DE JONG
Leiden University

SIMONE VAN DEN DRIEST
Dutch Council of State

ROBERT HEINSCH
Leiden University

ERIK KOPPE
Pels Rijcken

NICO SCHRIJVER
Dutch Council of State

CAMBRIDGE
UNIVERSITY PRESS

University Printing House, Cambridge CB2 8BS, United Kingdom

One Liberty Plaza, 20th Floor, New York, NY 10006, USA

477 Williamstown Road, Port Melbourne, VIC 3207, Australia

314–321, 3rd Floor, Plot 3, Splendor Forum, Jasola District Centre,
New Delhi – 110025, India

103 Penang Road, #05–06/07, Visioncrest Commercial, Singapore 238467

Cambridge University Press is part of the University of Cambridge.

It furthers the University's mission by disseminating knowledge in the pursuit of
education, learning, and research at the highest international levels of excellence.

www.cambridge.org
Information on this title: www.cambridge.org/highereducation/isbn/9781108421454
DOI: 10.1017/9781108377232

© Cecily Rose, Niels Blokker, Daniëlla Dam-de Jong, Simone van den Driest, Robert Heinsch, Erik Koppe,
and Nico Schrijver 2022

First published 2022

Printed in the United Kingdom by TJ Books Limited, Padstow Cornwall 2022

A catalogue record for this publication is available from the British Library.

ISBN 978-1-108-42145-4 Hardback
ISBN 978-1-108-43262-7 Paperback

Contents

Part II The Branches of Public International Law

Author Biographies

Niels Blokker

Niels Blokker is Professor of International Institutional Law (Schermers Chair) at the Grotius Centre for International Legal Studies of Leiden University. He has worked at the Ministry of Foreign Affairs of the Netherlands as a Senior Legal Counsel and Deputy Legal Adviser for over thirteen years.

Daniëlla Dam-de Jong

Daniëlla Dam-de Jong is associate professor of Public International Law and Director of the LL.M. Regular Programme at the Grotius Centre for International Legal Studies of Leiden University.

Simone van den Driest

Simone van den Driest works at the Advisory Division of the Council of State of the Netherlands, where she advises on legislative matters of foreign affairs, justice and security, and defence among others. Prior to this, she was assistant professor of Public International Law at the Grotius Centre for International Legal Studies of Leiden University.

Robert Heinsch

Robert Heinsch is associate professor of Public International Law at the Grotius Centre for International Legal Studies, and the Director of its Kalshoven-Gieskes Forum on International Humanitarian Law at Leiden University. He is also the founder of the Leiden and Bochum International Humanitarian Law Clinics.

Erik Koppe

Erik Koppe is an associate at the Civil Litigation and Arbitration department of Pels Rijcken in The Hague, the Netherlands. Prior to joining Pels Rijcken, he was Assistant Professor of Public International Law at the Grotius Centre for International Legal Studies of Leiden University.

Cecily Rose

Cecily Rose is assistant professor of Public International Law at the Grotius Centre for International Legal Studies of Leiden University. She also works as a consultant for the United Nations and other international organizations. Cecily previously worked at the International Court of Justice, the Special Court for Sierra Leone, and in private practice.

Nico Schrijver

Nico Schrijver is Professor Emeritus of Public International Law and former Academic Director of the Grotius Centre for International Legal Studies of Leiden University. Currently, he serves as State Councillor at the Council of State in the Netherlands and as a judge ad hoc in the Special Chamber of the International Tribunal for the Law of the Sea in the case of *Dispute concerning delimitation of the maritime boundary between Mauritius and Maldives in the Indian Ocean (Mauritius/Maldives)*. He is a member and former president of the Institute of International Law.

Foreword

I am delighted to contribute a Foreword to this book which is designed as an introduction to international law not only for law students but for students from a wide range of disciplines. The great strength of this book is that it sets out to place international law in a broader context. As Cecily Rose says in her Introduction, "public international law represents the legal architecture of international affairs." It is no dry, technical subject but something central to an understanding of the world in which we live. The authors of the present work are able to set international law in that broader context because, as well as being distinguished teachers of the subject, they have a wide experience of the practice of international law.

The result is a thoughtful – and thought-provoking – book which combines a clear explanation of the different parts of the subject with examples ranging from decisions of the International Court of Justice and numerous other courts and tribunals to the correspondence, speeches, and reports of diplomats, ministers, and parliamentarians that so often slip from view in a classical legal text. This approach not only makes the work a far more interesting one for those studying international law, it also has the advantage of showing how an understanding of international law can give new insights into the news stories of the day.

Dame Rosalyn Higgins, a former President of the International Court of Justice, concluded her book *Problems and Process: International Law and How We Use It* with the observation that international law "is a great and exciting adventure."

This book is an excellent starting point for those embarking on this adventure.

Christopher Greenwood
December 2021

Preface

The idea for this book was born in the autumn of 2015, over lunchtime conversations among colleagues at the law faculty in Leiden and, if memory serves me right, at a lively reception following a PhD defence. All of the authors of this book were at the time involved in teaching public international law at an introductory level, and the lead author of this book still is. As a group, we have taught first- and third-year bachelor students in Leiden, liberal arts students at Leiden University College in The Hague, and master students in international relations at the Social Sciences Faculty in Leiden. Each of us felt that our experiences as teachers had given us a strong sense of what we wanted to see in an introductory-level textbook, and yet none of us was satisfied with the books available to us at that time (most of which were written for a more advanced audience). So, we embarked on our own textbook project, with a view towards producing a text that would present the law in a lucid, balanced, and objective way, with the benefit of fully developed examples that students could really understand. We hoped that our diverse range of expertise would also enhance the book, which was conceived of, from the beginning, as a co-authored work.

As the years have passed, much has changed for nearly all of us, both personally and professionally. It was not originally the idea that one author would write half of the book, but this gradually became the path by which we brought this project to a successful conclusion. The composition of the team also changed somewhat in the intervening years, but Cambridge University Press graciously accommodated these adjustments. We hope that the final product will suit not only our own students in Leiden and The Hague, but students everywhere studying public international law in English for the first time.

Cecily Rose
Leiden
20 July 2021

Acknowledgements

This textbook was a collective project in many ways. We are deeply grateful to our colleagues, friends, and even one family member who provided valuable comments on draft chapters: Michael A. Becker, Massimo Lando, Brian McGarry, Federica Paddeu, Daniel Peat, Vid Prislan, Jonathan Rose, and Sara Wharton. The anonymous reviewers of our sample chapters also provided very helpful comments in the early stages of this project. During the final months leading up to the submission of the manuscript, Joëlle Zonjee meticulously polished the manuscript, while also providing priceless feedback on the entire text. Without her help, we could not have completed this project when we did. We are also grateful to Caitlin Lisle, Marianne Nield, and Nicola Chapman, our patient and supportive editors at Cambridge University Press; Joseph Shaw, who meticulously copy-edited the manuscript; and James M. Diggins, who produced the index and table of cases. Many thanks also to Gayathri Tamilselvan and Malini Soupramanian of Integra, who oversaw the very smooth production of this book.

Table of Cases

Regional Courts and Tribunals

National Courts

1

Introduction

Cecily Rose

Public international law represents the legal architecture of international affairs. Often this architecture is hidden behind world events, such as a prime minister's apology to another state, a foreign minister's assertion that the military acted proportionately, or claims by foreign investors that they have been treated unfairly by the states where they operate. Sometimes; however, the language of international law is in plain view, such as when individuals assert their human right to a fair trial, or when one state accuses the other of violating the laws governing international trade. Much of international affairs, including front-page news, can only be fully understood with a knowledge of public international law.

The treatment of the Rohingya in Myanmar, for example, is a matter of great international concern and media attention, in part because recent developments have given rise to serious violations of public international law, and have led to litigation before international courts. The Rohingya are an ethnic Muslim minority population in Myanmar, and have long faced discrimination and persecution in Myanmar, where the vast majority of the population is Buddhist. In 2016 and 2017, matters escalated dramatically when Myanmar security forces undertook 'clearance operations' against the Rohingya, purportedly in order to eliminate the terrorist threat posed by the Rohingya. The ensuing violence and destruction of villages resulted in approximately 10,000 deaths, and a massive flow of more than 700,000 Rohingya refugees, mostly to neighbouring Bangladesh. These events must be understood not only from the perspective of history and politics, for example, but also in legal terms, as public international law provides the framework necessary for capturing the egregiousness of these 'clearance operations', and for holding both the state and individual leaders legally responsible.

While the International Court of Justice (ICJ) is currently hearing a case that will require it to determine whether Myanmar bears legal responsibility for a genocide against the Rohingya, the International Criminal Court (ICC) is investigating whether crimes against humanity have taken place, for which individuals may bear criminal responsibility.[1] The severity of the conduct of the Myanmar security forces cannot be fully captured by domestic crimes, such as murder and arson, nor are domestic institutions in Myanmar likely to provide

---

[1] ICJ *Application of the Convention on the Prevention and Punishment of the Crime of Genocide (The Gambia v Myanmar)*; in November 2019, a Pre-Trial Chamber of the ICC authorized the prosecutor to investigate the situation in Bangladesh/Myanmar.

any real form of accountability. The terms 'genocide' and 'crimes against humanity' originate in public international law and date back to the Nuremberg trials in Germany following the Second World War. By labelling conduct as a genocide or a crime against humanity, other states and international prosecutors acknowledge the extent to which fundamental norms, common to all states, have been transgressed. While litigation before international courts is no panacea, it opens up possibilities for legal accountability, including the criminal punishment of individuals, which would otherwise likely be entirely out of reach.

The goal of this book is to enable a deeper understanding of international affairs and world events through a knowledge of public international law. This chapter begins by introducing a number of foundational concepts, which serve as the starting point in the field of public international law. Section 1 of this chapter begins with the notion that states are sovereign equals, which must consent to be bound by international law. This section also introduces the critical distinction that international law makes between states and 'non-state actors'. Section 2 of this chapter discusses the inevitable comparison of public international law with domestic legal systems, and the significant limitations of this analogy as a means for understanding the field of public international law. Section 3 concludes by explaining this book's overarching structure as well as the approach of this book to the introduction of public international law.

1   Basic Features of International Law

a   *Sovereignty*

Public international law is premised, in part, on the idea that states are 'sovereign equals', meaning that one state may not exercise power over another state. This quite abstract concept goes back many centuries, to the days when monarchs were regarded as sovereign, meaning that they had supreme power, subject to the power of no one. As the state itself came to be seen as separate from the head of state; however, the sovereign status of states emerged as a foundational premise of public international law. Sovereign equality has never meant that states are equal to one another with respect to territorial size, political influence, economic strength, or military power. States are indeed not equal to one another in factual terms, just as individuals are not always equal to one another, factually speaking. Instead, sovereign equality means that states are equal to one another in a legal rather than a factual sense, just as individuals are equal to each other before the law. Broadly speaking, sovereign equality means that each state has, as a matter of principle, the inherent power to make its own decisions about how to order its affairs, with the result that one state may not force its will upon another.

Sovereign equality has important practical implications for public international law and the way that states are bound to interact with each other. First, sovereignty is, as a matter of principle, limited to the territory of the state, which means that each state has supreme authority within its own borders. A state's sovereign powers are generally limited to its territory, which could be delimited by a land and/or a maritime border, depending on the geographical circumstances. As a consequence of the inherently territorial character of sovereignty, one state may not send its police force into the territory of another state in order to arrest a suspect or to gather evidence, at least not without violating that state's sovereignty. Instead, states have to rely on international law for such matters.[2]

The idea that one state may not force another state to submit to its will has other important practical implications, especially with respect to the exercise of military force. The invasion or occupation by one state of the territory of another state is a violation of one of the most basic rules of public international law, the prohibition on the threat or use of force in international relations, as contained in the United Nations Charter.[3] The United Nations (UN) as an organization is explicitly based on the principle of the sovereign equality of all of its members, which now include virtually all states in the world.[4] All UN members must accordingly refrain from threatening or using force against the territorial independence or political integrity of another state. This rule represents a cornerstone of public international law, and states typically attempt to excuse violations of this rule by reference to a small number of exceptions, including the use of force in self-defence.

The principle of sovereign equality has other important practical implications, as states must respect not only each other's territorial integrity and political independence, but also each other's political and economic systems. Within certain bounds, which are now established by international law, in particular human rights law, each state may decide for itself whether or not to embrace a representative democracy or to pursue an economic system based on capitalism, socialism, or communism.[5] These are ideological and political decisions that each sovereign state has the authority to take for itself, without interference, for example, from neighbouring states or regional or global powers. Although capitalist and communist states have long been at odds with each other, as the history of the Cold War amply demonstrates, the fact remains that international law maintains the sovereign equality of all states, regardless of their political and economic orders.

In light of their status as sovereign equals, states must find ways of governing their internal affairs and conducting international relations when also respecting the sovereignty of other states.[6] Public international law can thereby be seen, in very broad terms, as a legal framework that allows sovereign states not only to coexist with one another, but also to cooperate with one another.[7] Friction and conflict inevitably arise between states with clashing interests and ideologies, but these states must nevertheless find ways to coexist

---

[2] In practice, states typically request the surrender of suspects and convicted persons on the basis of extradition treaties and they request evidence on the basis of mutual legal assistance treaties. See Chapter 6 on jurisdiction.

[3] Charter of the UN (adopted 26 June 1945, entered into force 24 October 1945) 1 UNTS XVI (UN Charter) art 2(4). See Chapter 11 on the use of force.

[4] UN Charter arts 2(1), 18(1). Such equality is reflected, for example, in the fact that each member of the UN has one vote in the General Assembly.

[5] See, for example, the International Covenant on Civil and Political Rights, according to which every citizen has the right 'to take part in the conduct of public affairs, directly or through freely chosen representatives'. International Covenant on Civil and Political Rights (adopted 16 December 1966, entered into force 23 March 1976) 999 UNTS 171, art 25(a).

[6] See, *The Island of Palmas Case (or Miangas) (United States v The Netherlands)* (Award of the Tribunal) (1928) PCA Case 1925–01.

[7] Wolfgang Friedmann, *The Changing Structure of International Law* (Columbia University Press 1964) 60–3; Wolfgang Friedmann, 'General Course in Public International Law' (1969) 127 Collected Courses of the Hague Academy of International Law.

with one another in the international community. In addition, certain global problems that cross borders, such as transnational crime and climate change, require states to cooperate with each other in order to find solutions.

Public international legal rules could, thereby be categorized as falling under the scope of either the international law of coexistence or the international law of cooperation, or both in some cases. The law on the use of force, for example, could be seen as constituting part of the international law of coexistence, as it requires states to respect each other's territorial integrity and political independence by refraining from the threat or use of force in their relations with each other. The international law of coexistence could also be seen as encompassing international legal rules that govern the extent of a state's power to enact and enforce domestic laws (the law of jurisdiction); the extent of a state's maritime zones and its rights within those zones (the law of the sea); the circumstances under which a state is responsible for a violation of an international legal rule (law of state responsibility); and the methods by which states can resolve disputes between them (international dispute settlement). For its part, the international law of cooperation could be seen as encompassing international legal rules that govern international organizations; foreign investment and international trade (international economic law); and the protection of the environment (international environmental law). The dividing line between the law of coexistence and the law of cooperation will not always be clear; however, and a given international agreement may serve both ends.[8] Ultimately, this dichotomy may be most usefully employed not so much as a classification device, but as a tool for identifying and distinguishing the two main functions of public international law.

Membership in international organizations, such as the UN and the European Union (EU), allows states to cooperate with each other and also to structure their coexistence. In becoming members of international organizations, states voluntarily limit the exercise of their sovereign powers, such that they no longer have complete freedom to order their affairs however they so choose. In becoming members of the UN, for example, states agree to carry out the binding resolutions that the UN Security Council has the capacity to adopt. States voluntarily surrender parts of their sovereign decision-making authority to international organizations because membership in international organizations enables levels of coexistence and cooperation that would be unattainable otherwise.

In recent years; however, international organizations have experienced something of a backlash, which has entailed not only the United Kingdom's exit from the EU (Brexit), but also tension between African states and the ICC and between the United States and the World Trade Organization (WTO), in particular its Appellate Body.[9] These episodes have all involved serious friction between international organizations and their member states, which may be experiencing a form of 'buyer's remorse'. Although states consent to being members of international organizations and to being bound by their decisions, they cannot fully anticipate what this will entail in the future, and how limiting the

---

[8] Parts of the law of the sea, for example, may be regarded as forming part of the international law of cooperation, in particular the rules governing the exploitation of the deep sea area, which falls beyond the jurisdiction of all states (see Chapter 15).

[9] See Chapter 8 on international organizations.

exercise of their sovereign authority may conflict with domestic politics years down the road. For the most part; however, states accept and abide by the obligations that they assume by virtue of becoming members of international organizations, as they have voluntarily consented to membership and all that comes with that status.

b   *Consent*

In the famous *Lotus* case between France and Turkey, the Permanent Court of International Justice[10] (PCIJ) explained in its 1927 judgment that:

International law governs relations between independent States. The rules of law binding upon States therefore emanate from their own free will as expressed in conventions or usages generally accepted as expressing principles of law and established in order to regulate the relations between these co-existing independent communities or with a view to the achievement of common aims. Restrictions upon the independence of States cannot therefore be presumed.[11]

The Court's reference in this passage to the 'free will' of states must be understood as a reference to the notion of consent, which is a foundational concept in the field of public international law. The term 'consent' in the context of public international law refers to the act of agreeing to be bound by an international legal rule or by the authority of another entity, such as an international organization. In the *Lotus* case, the Court explained that states must consent to be bound by conventions (i.e., treaties) or by unwritten customary rules, which the Court described as 'usages generally accepted as expressing principles of law'.[12] The distinction between the international law of coexistence and the international law of cooperation also underlies this passage, as the Court explained that states may be motivated to give such consent either for the purpose of achieving coexistence, or for the purpose of pursuing 'common aims' through cooperation.

By virtue of being sovereign entities with full powers, states have the authority or capacity to limit their exercise of some of those powers by consenting to be bound by international legal rules. By consenting to a treaty, for example, a state may agree to be bound by laws that require it to refrain from certain conduct (i.e., the use of force in international relations), or laws that require it to engage in certain conduct (i.e., the protection of the environment). States cannot be forced to abide by international legal rules to which they did not consent, as consent is a necessary condition in order for an international legal norm to come into existence. Because of their sovereign status, states must agree to submit themselves to international law, or to the authority of international organizations.

All of public international law is, therefore the product of state consent, to one degree or another, although the link between a state's consent, and its corresponding legal obligation is

---

[10] The PCIJ is the predecessor institution to the ICJ, which is the principal judicial organ of the UN.
[11] *The Case of the S.S. Lotus (France v Turkey)* (Judgment) (1927) PCIJ Rep Series A No 10, para 44.
[12] See Chapter 2 on sources of international law.

admittedly tenuous in certain circumstances. As noted previously, this is true in the context of international organizations, where membership entails consent to submit to the authority of the organization, including future binding decisions reached by the organization, which may or may not enjoy unanimous support among all members. Consent can also be remote in the context of customary international law, which refers to unwritten international legal rules that emerge through the practice of states that is performed out of a sense of legal obligation.[13] Customary international law evolves organically over time through state practice that may not be truly universal. The consent of some or many states to a given customary norm may ultimately be assumed, as states are deemed to have consented to a given norm through passive, silent acceptance of the emerging customary rule. Thus, while consent represents a foundational concept in the field of public international law, state consent may sometimes have a remote or passive character. State consent nevertheless remains explicit and relatively straightforward with respect to treaties, which represent the main source of international law. Where a state has consented to become a party to a treaty, the rules embodied in the treaty accordingly emanate from the state's own free will. Withdrawal from a treaty, which is in practice a relatively infrequent occurrence, is also subject to a state's free will.[14]

c   *States and Non-state Actors*

This introductory chapter has, thus far, dealt mainly with states because only states enjoy sovereignty and, therefore the power to consent to international law. International law is inescapably state-centred because states are the only actors with the capacity to consent to the creation of the international legal rules that bind them. Non-state actors like individuals and multinational corporations do not possess sovereignty, and they do not consent to be bound by international law or otherwise participate directly in the creation of laws that bind states. From an international legal perspective, then, the world may be seen as consisting of two categories of actors: states, and non-state actors.[15] The 'catch-all' category of non-state actors encompasses all entities that are not states, including individuals, companies, non-governmental organizations (NGOs), international organizations, as well as entities that would like to be states, but have not (yet) achieved this status. The term non-state actor, thus refers to a hugely diverse range of actors that are united only by virtue of the fact that they are not states.

While this dichotomy between states and non-state actors is perfectly logical from the perspective of international law, which privileges sovereign states, the reality of international affairs is often far less state-centred. Large multinational corporations, for example, sometimes outmatch small countries in both economic terms and with respect to their political influence. In addition, armed rebel groups may not be state organs, but they can participate in armed conflicts just as the regular armed forces of a state do. The role that

---

[13] See Chapter 2 on sources of international law.
[14] Vienna Convention on the Law of Treaties (adopted 23 May 1969, entered into force 27 January 1980) 1155 UNTS 331, arts 54, 56.
[15] For a discussion of this dichotomy from a human rights perspective, see Philip Alston, 'The "Not-a-Cat" Syndrome: Can the International Human Rights Regime Accommodate Non-State Actors?' in Philip Alston (ed), *Non-State Actors and Human Rights* (Oxford University Press 2005).

non-state actors play in international society is, therefore sometimes at odds with the basic structure of public international law, which mainly consists of a body of rules that are created by states, largely for the purpose of governing their own relations and conduct. To a much more limited extent, public international law governs the relationships between states and non-state actors, and in some instances between non-state actors.

International law; therefore, has a largely 'horizontal' character, in that it governs relations between states, which are all sovereign equals, and thus have the same status and exist on the same level, figuratively speaking. Under international trade law, for example, states have agreed not to create barriers to imports and exports of goods, through tariffs or quotas or other means.[16] Although non-state actors, such as businesses, stand to benefit from the rules that states have created in order to ensure free trade, they generally enjoy no direct rights or obligations under international trade law. States have concluded trade agreements between themselves, and only states enjoy rights and obligations under these laws. The same is true of most areas of public international law: states have created rules that govern relations between them, and although non-state actors may be impacted by or benefit from these rules, they are not parties to these agreements.

Public international law is not; however, entirely horizontal in character. To a limited extent, international law does create rights and duties for certain non-state actors, in particular persons (both natural and legal persons), such that it can also be seen as having a 'vertical' dimension. The relationship between individuals and the state is, for example, governed by human rights law, under which states bear obligations and individuals enjoy rights. Although only states are parties to human rights treaties, these agreements create rights for individuals, who, in certain circumstances, can assert their rights before domestic courts and regional or international bodies. The same is true with respect to investors, who enjoy certain rights under international investment law, and in some situations can pursue their claims before international tribunals. Individuals can also bear obligations, as opposed to rights, under public international law, in particular under international humanitarian law, which regulates conduct during armed conflicts, and international criminal law, which prohibits certain conduct, such as war crimes, crimes against humanity, and genocide. Individuals can now be held criminally liable for international crimes before international criminal courts and tribunals. Public international law is thus best understood as a largely horizontal field of law, created by and for states, but with some important exceptions that involve vertical relationships between states and non-state actors.[17]

2   The Domestic Law Analogy

Lawyers are trained, in part, to think by analogy. Law students are taught, for example, to consider how one case compares with another one, and whether the legal outcomes are likely

---

[16] General Agreement on Tariffs and Trade 1994 (as annexed to the WTO Agreement) (adopted 15 April 1994, entered into force 1 January 1995) 1867 UNTS 187.

[17] See Chapters 12 and 13 on international humanitarian law and international criminal law, respectively.

to be, or should be, the same or different. Seen from this perspective, the fact that students (and sometimes scholars) of international law tend to draw analogies between domestic and international law is therefore unsurprising. Given that many students follow a course on the subject of public international law during their law studies, which mainly focus on domestic law, this sort of analogizing is very much to be expected. To a certain extent, comparing domestic legal systems with public international law brings into relief some of the unique and fundamental features of international law, including the centrality of sovereign equality of states, who must consent to the law that governs their relations with each other. But the utility of the domestic law analogy has its limits, as it tends to give rise to unnuanced accounts of how international law functions, or does not function, as the case may be. Ultimately, it is best to strive for an appreciation of public international law on its own terms, as a legal system that is fundamentally distinct from that of domestic legal systems.

A number of fundamental structural differences separates domestic and international law. Whereas domestic legal systems tend to consist of distinct branches, such as the legislature, the executive, and the judiciary, the same cannot be said of public international law. There is no international legislative body that promulgates rules with which states are obliged to comply. While the UN General Assembly now includes representatives from nearly all states in the world, it can hardly be described as a legislative body, in part because it lacks the capacity to adopt binding decisions.[18] Instead, law-making in the international legal system is highly decentralized. States conclude international agreements as they see fit and where they are able to come to a satisfactory agreement, and the practice of states can also give rise to unwritten customary rules. Because states are both the creators of international law, and the subjects of the law that they create, international law-making somewhat resembles legal relations between private parties within domestic legal systems, such as when individuals conclude private contracts. Domestic legislatures, in contrast, are centralized bodies that enact laws that regulate the relationship between the state and the people. The legislators are often democratically elected, and therefore, represent their constituencies. The international legal system, however, is not inherently democratic, as international law-making is not a representative process. States do not necessarily represent constituencies when they conclude treaties, for example, although domestic political resistance to or support for an international agreement may indeed influence the government's pursuit of such an agreement. The rules adopted by international organizations may; however, take on a democratic quality where they are adopted by a vote among members of the organization.

The international legal system also lacks a judicial or other body that has the capacity to enforce all rules of public international law, and with respect to all states. International courts and tribunals cannot be seen as the enforcers of public international law, nor do they exist for this purpose. Within the UN system, the Security Council is the political body with certain enforcement powers in the context of the maintenance of international peace and security. The ICJ in contrast, was designed for the purpose of settling disputes when states

---

[18] UN Charter arts 11–13.

so desire, and it was not conceived with a view towards playing an explicit role in the enforcement of the law. There are, in fact, no central enforcement bodies that enjoy the authority to compel states to comply with international law in general, for the simple reason that states have declined to create such a system of law.

Although the ICJ is the 'principal judicial organ' of the UN, its jurisdictional competence is far more limited that this phrase might suggest.[19] The ICJ only has the capacity to render binding judgments in inter-state cases when both states have explicitly consented to the Court's jurisdiction over them. The need for state consent a function of state sovereignty, and the fact that states cannot be forced to submit to the will of a judicial body. This means, in practice, that relatively few disputes are litigated before the ICJ, or before other international courts and tribunals, although a steady stream of cases – some of which are quite high profile – has been brought before the ICJ since the 1990s.[20] This picture remarkably different from domestic legal systems, where persons do not have the capacity to decline to consent to the jurisdiction of a court, whether in the context of civil or criminal litigation. In addition, domestic courts benefit from the capacity of the state to enforce their decisions, whether through arrests or the seizure of property, for example, whereas no such parallels exist in the field of public international law.

When viewed from the perspective of domestic law, the absence of compulsory enforcement mechanisms in the field of public international law begs the question: do states comply with international law, and if so, why? Do states refrain from conduct that international law prohibits, and do they engage in the conduct that international law requires? To assume that compliance is low on account of the absence of compulsory enforcement mechanisms would be to miss all the nuanced reasons why states do indeed comply with international law much of the time, but for reasons other than the prospect of a legal sanction for non-compliance.[21] In addition to the sheer force of a given legal commitment, ethics, politics, economics, and reputational concerns can all play roles in bringing about compliance. But to insist that compliance with international law is always exemplary would, of course, paint an overly rosy picture. In the context of governmental decision-making concerning international affairs, for example, public international law provides the legal architecture and helps to guide assessments, but other factors sometimes weigh in favour of outcomes that are ultimately non-compliant, or very belatedly compliant. Moreover, states may not always appreciate the long-term consequences of non-compliance with international law. If approached from the perspective of domestic law, such issues concerning the enforcement of and compliance with international law can seem to bring the whole system of public international law into question. International law is best approached and understood on its own terms, with an openness to the different levers and tools that bring about compliance in this particular context.

---

[19] UN Charter art 92.

[20] See, for example, *Case concerning Application of the Convention on the Prevention and Punishment of the Crime of Genocide (Bosnia and Herzegovina v Serbia and Montenegro)* (Judgment) [2007] ICJ Rep 43; *The Gambia v Myanmar* (n 1).

[21] Louis Henkin, *How Nations Behave* (2nd edn, Columbia University Press 1979) 47: '[A]lmost all nations observe almost all principles of international law and almost all of their obligations almost all of the time'.

3   The Approach and Structure of This Book

This book is composed of two main parts: the first part covers the foundations of public international law (Chapters 2–9), while the second part introduces a number of branches of this field of law. The chapters covering foundational subjects deal with the building blocks of this field, beginning with the sources of international law (Chapter 2) and subjects, statehood, and self-determination (Chapter 3). These two chapters explain what international law is, what qualifies as a state, and how new states emerge. The foundational part of this book also covers the law of international obligations, namely the bodies of law that govern treaties (Chapter 4) and state responsibility (Chapter 5). These are the rules that govern the creation and operation of treaties, which are the primary source of international law, and the rules that allow us to determine when a state has violated international law and what the legal consequences of violations are. Jurisdiction and immunities (Chapters 6 and 7) are also foundational subjects, as they govern the extent of a state's sovereign powers, and the circumstances in which the exercise of those powers is barred for reasons relating to sovereign equality and the furtherance of international relations. The last two foundational topics are international organizations (Chapter 8) and international dispute settlement (Chapter 9). Because of the role that international organizations now play in facilitating coexistence as well as cooperation, an introduction to the law of international organizations is essential for an understanding of the field of public international law. Finally, the settlement of international disputes represents another cross-cutting subject, as all international disputes must be settled through recourse to peaceful means of dispute settlement, with litigation before international courts and tribunals representing just one of these means.

The second part of the book covers what the authors of this book consider to be the most significant sub-fields or branches of public international law, at least for the purposes of an introduction to the field. Many of these branches developed into discrete and robust sub-fields only after the Second World War, typically through the conclusion of treaties. It begins with human rights law (Chapter 10) and then covers bodies of law that cover the prohibition on the use of force (Chapter 11), international humanitarian law (also known as the law of armed conflict), which governs the conduct of hostilities during times of armed conflict (Chapter 12), and international criminal law, which provides for individual criminal responsibility (Chapter 13). These four chapters can be seen as related to each other as armed conflicts represent one of the greatest threats to the enjoyment of human rights, and also tends to result in calls for international criminal justice. International human rights law; however, covers many features of the relationship between a state and individuals, and thus has a scope of application extending well beyond times of armed conflict. The last three chapters of this book cover the sub-fields of international economic law (Chapter 14), the law of the sea (Chapter 15), and international environmental law (Chapter 16). These three bodies of law may also be seen as related to each other insofar as they all relate to questions of sustainable development, namely how economic development, including the exploitation of marine resources, can be balanced with the protection of the environment.

While this book covers a great deal, it also omits a number of subjects and branches that the authors consider to be less essential for an introduction to public international law. The history of international law, for example, is covered to an extent in many of the chapters that follow, but it is not covered at length as the subject of a dedicated chapter. Likewise, the philosophy of international law is also omitted, as this is a subject best explored after a solid understanding of the foundations and branches of the field. Although fascinating subjects in their own right, the topics of refugee law, international labour law, cultural heritage law, and air and space law are also omitted, as most courses on public international law can only cover so much. Finally, this book also does not touch on private international law, which is an altogether different field of law that governs situations where there are conflicts between the domestic laws of different states, such that a choice of law is required.

In introducing the field of public international law, this book – like many other textbooks in the field – adopts a traditional, positivist approach. In the context of public international law, positivism refers to the idea that international law is an objective set of rules that emanate from the free will of states, which are the main subjects of this body of law.[22] This book takes sovereignty and consent as fundamental premises, and proceeds on this basis. Such an approach necessarily entails a focus on what the law *is* and why, but involves relatively little exploration of what the law *should* or *ought* to be, when considered from extra-legal perspectives, such as ethics, politics, and economics. International law can; however, be approached from a significant range of theoretical perspectives, and also from other academic disciplines, such as political science and international relations.[23] While these perspectives have much to offer, a positivist approach, which proceeds from within the discipline of international law, is arguably the best place to begin.

Recommended Reading

Samantha Besson and John Tasioulas (eds), *The Philosophy of International Law* (Oxford University Press 2010).
James Crawford, *Change, Order, Change: The Course of International Law* (Brill/Nijhoff 2014).
Vaughan Lowe, *International Law* (Oxford University Press 2007).
Anthea Roberts, *Is International Law International?* (Oxford University Press 2017).

---

[22] Andrea Bianchi, *International Law Theories: An Inquiry into Different Ways of Thinking* (Oxford University Press 2016) 21.
[23] ibid.

Part I

The Foundations of Public International Law

2

Sources of International Law

Cecily Rose

1   Introduction

Law-making in the international legal field has grown exponentially since the Second World War. Rules of public international law now span a very wide range of topics and govern many global problems that were formerly left entirely to states, from human rights, to the protection of the environment, to money laundering. This chapter seeks to explain how this ever-growing body of law emerges and develops, and where we can look for rules of public international law.

A source of public international law is a process by which international legal norms are created, modified, or annulled, and it is also a place where such norms may be found.[1] The term 'source of international law', therefore has two meanings, as it refers to: (1) legal processes as well as; (2) the location of the norms that are the result of these processes. Textbooks covering domestic law typically would not even need to mention this subject, let alone devote a chapter to it. At the domestic level, constitutions usually specify the sources of law, and the resulting legal norms may be located without any real difficulty. Criminal law, for example, may be created, modified, or annulled through statutes enacted by the legislature, and by the judgments of domestic courts in common law systems. Domestic criminal lawyers seeking to find the law concerning murder or corruption would look, for example, in the criminal code and in published volumes containing court decisions.

In the field of public international law; however, identifying the sources of public international law involves more uncertainty for practitioners and more room for debate. Unlike domestic legal systems, the field of public international law is fundamentally decentralized, as it lacks a constitution as well as a legislature. In the absence of a central law-making body, public international law is mostly created by states themselves. States are; therefore, both the creators of public international law, and the subjects of public international law, meaning that they create the law that then applies to them. States mainly create public international law through treaties and customary law. Because customary law is unwritten law, locating it is inherently more challenging than finding criminal statutes or court judgments in domestic legal systems.

---

[1] Samantha Besson, 'Theorizing the Sources of International Law' in Samantha Besson and John Tasioulas (eds), *The Philosophy of International Law* (Oxford University Press 2010) 169–70.

This chapter begins by explaining why international lawyers typically begin discussions about the sources of public international law by referencing Article 38 of the Statute of the International Court of Justice (ICJ) (Section 2). It then introduces treaties and custom, which are the two main sources of law in this field (Sections 3–4), before discussing other sources, namely general principles of law, decisions of international organizations, unilateral declarations, as well as judicial decisions and the teachings of international legal experts (Sections 5–6). The chapter ends with a discussion of non-binding instruments, which do not contain binding legal rules, but are nonetheless significant in the international legal field, as they contain norms that impact the behaviour of states (Section 7).

2   Article 38 of the Statute of the ICJ

Article 38(1) of the ICJ Statute[2] provides that:

The Court, whose function is to decide in accordance with international law such disputes as are submitted to it, shall apply:

a. international conventions, whether general or particular, establishing rules expressly recognized by the contesting states;
b. international custom, as evidence of a general practice accepted as law;
c. the general principles of law recognized by civilized nations;
d. subject to the provisions of Article 59, judicial decisions and the teachings of the most highly qualified publicists of the various nations, as subsidiary means for the determination of the rules of law.

This provision lists, in total, five different sources of public international law: 'conventions' (which are also known, among other things, as treaties); customary international law; general principles of law; judicial decisions; and 'the teachings of the most highly qualified publicists of the various nations'. As will be explained, treaties, custom, and general principles represent processes for law-making, while judicial decisions and teachings, as well as treaties, represent places where international legal norms may be found.

Article 38 is typically the starting point for discussing the sources of international law because it is the most authoritative and comprehensive list of sources in the field. Because the ICJ is the principal judicial organ of the United Nations (UN), and the oldest standing international judicial body, the list of sources in Article 38 carries special weight and acts as a reference point for other international courts and tribunals. Although Article 38 often serves as a starting point for discussing the sources of public international law in the field as a whole, the purpose of this provision is just to establish the competence or jurisdiction of the ICJ. According to Article 38, the ICJ has jurisdiction over 'disputes', and in deciding these disputes, it is bound to apply the sources listed in paragraph 1 – unless the parties indicate otherwise.

---

[2] Statute of the ICJ (as annexed to the Charter of the UN) (adopted 26 June 1945, entered into force 24 October 1945) USTS 993 (ICJ Statute).

As a starting point for studying the sources of public international law, the list contained in Article 38(1) is neither exhaustive nor ideally formulated. While this list of sources is the most comprehensive list in the field, it is not complete. Article 38 makes no reference, for example, to the decisions of international organizations and unilateral declarations, both of which are now generally regarded as sources of public international law.[3] Moreover, paragraph 1(b) contains a flawed description of custom, which will be discussed in Section 4, and paragraph 1(c) contains antiquated language, namely the term 'civilized nations', which reflects the statute's origins in the 1920s. A provision similar to Article 38 originally appeared in the Statute of the Permanent Court of International Justice (PCIJ), the predecessor to the ICJ, which was established in 1920 after the First World War and was associated with the League of Nations. In 1945, at the end of the Second World War, when states established the UN and the ICJ, the drafters of the ICJ Statute incorporated this provision with few changes. In cases before the ICJ, and in the field of public international law at large, there is no hierarchy between the first three sources listed in Article 38 (e.g., conventions, custom, and general principles). In practice; however, the ICJ and other international courts and tribunals typically look first to treaty law before custom and general principles, because treaty law tends to be the most specific.

3   Treaty Law

Treaty law is the main method for creating, modifying, and annulling public international law. Treaties are written agreements between states, between states and international organizations, or between international organizations, which are governed by public international law.[4] Article 38(1)(a) refers to 'international conventions', but the generic term in English is 'treaty', and there are many other equivalent terms for treaties, including convention, protocol, agreement, charter, joint communiqué, and pact.[5]

In addition to this wide range of terminology, treaties themselves vary greatly in form and function.[6] Treaties may, for instance, be bilateral (between two states) or multilateral (between three or more states). States tend to conclude bilateral treaties concerning their maritime and land boundaries and bilateral treaties have also been an important form of law-making in the field of international investment law, which currently boasts nearly 3,000 bilateral investment treaties.[7] Multilateral treaties may be regional or universal in scope, and are often negotiated under the auspices of an international organization. Since the end

---

[3] Alain Pellet, 'Article 38' in Andreas Zimmerman et al (eds), *The Statute of the International Court of Justice: A Commentary* (2nd edn, Oxford University Press 2012) para 90.

[4] Vienna Convention on the Law of Treaties (23 May 1969, entered into force 27 January 1980) 1155 UNTS 332 (VCLT) art 2(1) (a); VCLT between States and International Organizations or between International Organizations (adopted 21 March 1986, not yet in force) UN Doc A/CONF.129/15, art 2(1)(a).

[5] Malgosia Fitzmaurice, 'Treaties' in *Max Planck Encyclopedia of Public International Law* (last updated February 2010) para 16; Pellet (n 3) para 800.

[6] Similarly, in domestic legal systems, instruments of private law vary greatly, and include a lease or rental agreement between a landlord and a tenant (bilateral agreement), a shareholders agreement (multilateral agreement), and articles of association (constitutive agreement).

[7] Marc Jacob, 'Investments, Bilateral Treaties' in *Max Planck Encyclopedia of Public International Law* (last updated June 2014).

of the Second World War, multilateral treaties have been the engine for the development of entire branches of public international law, including international human rights law, international environmental law, and transnational criminal law. Treaties can also function as 'constitutive instruments', which constitute or establish international organizations and international courts. The UN Charter is the constitutive instrument of the UN, for example, and the Rome Statute is the founding document of the International Criminal Court. Finally, treaties can also take the form of 'framework' agreements that lay out general rights and obligations, which are subsequently supplemented or developed through the conclusion of more detailed protocols that fall under the umbrella of the original framework treaty. In the field of international environmental law, for example, framework agreements like the 1992 UN Framework Convention on Climate Change have been an important method for law-making.[8]

Treaties are a source of public international law in both senses of the term, as they represent a process for creating and changing the law, as well as a place (a written document) where the law may be located. States have nearly complete freedom in the treaty-making process, as they may conclude agreements concerning whatever they wish, so long as the treaty does not contravene peremptory norms of public international law. Legal norms that are 'peremptory' or *jus cogens* are hierarchically above other legal norms, as they are norms from which no state may deviate or 'derogate'.[9] *Jus cogens* norms embody fundamental moral principles, such as the prohibitions on genocide and slavery.[10] This chapter omits any further discussion of *jus cogens* norms (which will be taken up in Chapters 4 and 5 on treaty law and state responsibility, respectively), because they do not represent a source of public international law, but instead concern the legal character of international norms. In other words, *jus cogens* norms are a type of norm rather than a process of law creation or a place where legal norms may be found.

The process of treaty-making consists of a number of phases, the first being the negotiation and conclusion of a text that is formally adopted.[11] Treaties are typically negotiated by delegations from states, but international organizations, non-governmental organizations, and individuals may also be involved in this phase. The second stage involves states (or international organizations) expressing their consent to be bound by the treaty. When states express their consent to be bound they usually seek some form of approval at the domestic level, often from the legislative branch.[12] Entry into force takes place at the third stage, typically when a certain number of states, as stipulated in the treaty, have expressed their consent to be bound.[13] Once treaties enter into force they are binding on the parties to them and must be performed by them in good faith, as captured by the maxim *pacta sunt servanda* ('agreements must be kept').[14] Treaties that have entered into force are not, however, binding on any third parties that have not consented to be bound.[15] In the fourth stage, treaties become

---

[8] UN Framework Convention on Climate Change (adopted 9 May 1992, entered into force 21 March 1994) 1771 UNTS 107.
[9] VCLT art 53. [10] Vaughan Lowe, *International Law* (Oxford University Press 2007) 50.
[11] Rüdiger Wolfrum, 'Sources of International Law' in *Max Planck Encyclopedia of Public International Law* (last updated May 2011) para 17.
[12] VCLT art 11. [13] VCLT art 24. [14] VCLT art 26. [15] VCLT art 36.

living instruments, which may be interpreted, amended or modified, and implemented by states at the domestic level through changes to domestic law, if this is necessary.[16] In their final stage, treaties may cease to exist through termination or due to invalidity, and they may also be suspended.[17] Each of these stages is governed by public international law concerning treaties, which takes the form of both the VCLT and customary international law, and will be covered in depth in Chapter 4.

4 Customary International Law

Customary international law is the process by which unwritten international laws are made, changed, and annulled. Whereas treaty law may be easily found in published treaty texts, customary international law is more difficult to identify, as it is based on the general practice and beliefs of states, and in some cases international organizations.[18] While certain areas of international law are now dominated by extensive networks of treaty law, customary international law remains an important source of law in some areas, such as the law governing the immunity of states and high-level state officials in foreign court proceedings. The importance of customary international law in the international legal field contrasts with many contemporary domestic legal systems, where custom plays a less significant role than in the past.

Customary international law consists of two elements, both of which are necessary for the formation of a customary rule. The first element is 'general practice' among states (and in some cases among international organizations). The second element is the acceptance by, or the conviction of states (or international organizations) that this practice is required by law. Such acceptance is known by the Latin phrase *opinio juris sive necessitatis* ('an opinion of law or necessity') or simply *opinio juris* ('an opinion of law'). Article 38(1)(b) of the ICJ Statute captures these two elements, as it describes 'international custom, as evidence of a general practice accepted as law'.[19] In practice, finding evidence that customary international law exists is challenging, and as a result the content and scope of customary international law tends to be less determinate and more contestable than treaty law. Both elements of customary international law merit further explanation.

a *General Practice*

General practice is the objective element of customary international law, which may be found in the words and actions of states. In some cases, inaction or omissions by states may

---

[16] VCLT pts 3, 4.   [17] VCLT pt 5.

[18] This chapter focuses; however, on customary international law generated by states rather than by international organizations. For more on how international organizations contribute to the creation or expression of customary international law, see International Law Commission (ILC), 'Fourth Report on Identification of Customary International Law by Michael Wood, Special Rapporteur, 68th Session' (8 March 2016) UN Doc A/CN.4/695; Jed Odermatt, 'The Development of Customary International Law by International Organizations' (2017) 66 International and Comparative Law Quarterly 491.

[19] The formulation is imperfect; however, as it suggests that international custom is itself evidence of a general practice ('international custom, *as evidence of* a general practice accepted as law'). In fact, the reverse is true: the existence of international custom is *evidenced by* a general practice accepted by states.

also be evidence of a general practice concerning prohibitory rules, such as the prohibition against torture.[20] In practice, determining what states do or what they say can be difficult in part because of the sheer number of states: there are nearly 200 states, and together they have the potential to generate a very large amount of practice. In addition, states are not unitary entities, meaning that they consist of various branches (executive, legislative, and judicial), all staffed by individuals. When international lawyers assess the general practice of states, they are actually evaluating the practice of a potentially wide range of organs, departments, and individuals within the state. Such practice may take many forms, but in particular: domestic legislation and regulations; domestic court judgments; internal memoranda within ministries, such as the ministry of foreign affairs; diplomatic correspondence; declarations or comments made in international fora like the UN General Assembly; and operational conduct 'on the ground'.[21] While some states publish, or formerly published, collections of their state practice in yearbooks of international law, most do not or have not done so.[22]

As this list of examples illustrates, general practice tends to take the form of words rather than actions. The term 'operational conduct on the ground', however, refers to physical actions rather than spoken or written statements. This term encompasses a range of actions, including 'law enforcement and seizure of property, as well as battlefield or other military activity, such as the movement of troops or vessels, or deployment of certain weapons'.[23] An example of operational conduct on the ground may be found in the United States Freedom of Navigation Program (FON), which dates back to 1979.[24] Every year, the United States conducts military operations in response to what it views as excessive maritime claims by coastal states. The United States currently carries out operations that are designed to challenge the claims of more than twenty states that it views as restricting rights, freedoms, and uses of the sea and airspace, which are guaranteed under the law of the sea (which will be covered in Chapter 15). In the South China Sea, for instance, the United States Navy sails within relatively close proximity to maritime features that are the subject of what may be regarded as excessive claims by China. By conducting such operations, the United States seeks to contribute to a body of state practice that evidences customary rules of international law concerning freedom of the seas.

The term 'general practice' means that the relevant practice does not hinge on the words or actions of just a few major powers, but instead involves practice that is 'sufficiently widespread and representative, as well as consistent'.[25] Determining whether relevant practice qualifies as general is not a science; however, and is not susceptible to a more

---

[20] ICL, 'Report of the International Law Commission, 68th session' (2 May–10 June and 4 July–12 August 2016) UN Doc A/71/10, ch 5, 'Identification of Customary International Law' 86.

[21] Tullio Treves, 'Customary International Law' in *Max Planck Encyclopedia of Public International Law* (last updated November 2006); ILC, 'Identification of Customary International Law' (n 20) conclusion 6.

[22] For a list of available digests, see Sir Michael Wood and Omri Sender, 'State Practice' in *Max Planck Encyclopedia of Public International Law* (last updated January 2017).

[23] ILC, 'Identification of Customary International Law' (n 20) 92.

[24] US Department of Defense, 'Freedom of Navigation (FON) Program' (28 February 2017) <http://policy.defense.gov/Portals/11/DoD%20FON%20Program%20Summary%2016.pdf?ver=2017-03-03-141350-380>.

[25] *North Sea Continental Shelf Cases (Federal Republic of Germany v Denmark; Federal Republic of Germany v Netherlands)* (Judgment) [1969] ICJ Rep 3, paras 73–4; ILC, 'Identification of Customary International Law' (n 20) conclusion 8.

concrete or absolute standard. Practice is sufficiently widespread when it is large or extensive, but not necessarily universal. The amount of practice needed to demonstrate a customary rule depends on the frequency of practice to be expected in the given circumstances. More extensive state practice might be expected, for example, in the field of diplomatic relations, as virtually all states are engaged in diplomatic relations. But somewhat less extensive practice might be expected concerning certain aspects of the law of the sea, as not all states have coasts, navies, or fishing fleets. In addition, practice must not only be widespread, but also representative, meaning that states from various geographical regions, and with various interests, must engage in the practice.[26] Representative state practice may also hinge, in part, on the practice of states specially affected by the customary norm, such as coastal states with respect to the law of the sea.

The requirement of consistency is not an absolute one.[27] When practice is varied, then there is likely no general practice that could support a customary rule. But some inconsistent practice may not undermine the existence of a general practice, in particular when the inconsistent practice is viewed as a breach of the rule, or when the state engaged in the inconsistent practice appeals to excuses or justifications within the rule itself.[28] In its 1986 judgment in *Military and Paramilitary Activities in and against Nicaragua (Nicaragua v United States of America)*, for example, the ICJ noted that perfect conformity by states with the rules prohibiting the use of force and intervention in internal affairs could not be expected. The Court instead deemed it 'sufficient that the conduct of States should, in general, be consistent with such rules, and that instances of State conduct inconsistent with a given rule should generally have been treated as breaches of that rule, not as indications of the recognition of a new rule'.[29]

When a given customary rule is in the process of forming, a state that persistently objects to the rule may be exempt from its application.[30] Such 'persistent objectors', as they are known, must express their objections clearly, make them known to other states, and maintain them persistently during and after the formation of the customary rule.[31] Once a customary rule has crystallized, however, then it is too late for a state to exempt itself by objecting to a given customary rule.[32] The persistent objector principle reflects the fundamental premise that states must consent to (customary) international law before it can be binding upon them, and therefore, may not be subject to rules that they have consistently opposed.

An example of persistent objection may be found in the study conducted by the International Committee of the Red Cross (ICRC) concerning customary international humanitarian law (which will be covered in Chapter 12).[33] On the basis of significant state practice and *opinio juris*, the ICRC found that a norm of customary international law

---

[26] ILC, 'Identification of Customary International Law' (n 20) 95.
[27] *Case Concerning Military and Paramilitary Activities in and against Nicaragua (Nicaragua v United States of America)* (Merits) [1986] ICJ Rep 14, para 186.
[28] ibid.   [29] ibid.   [30] ILC, 'Identification of Customary International Law' (n 20) conclusion 15, para 1.
[31] ibid, conclusion 15, para 2.   [32] ibid 113.
[33] Jean-Marie Henckaerts and Louise Doswald-Beck, *Customary International Humanitarian Law, Volume I: Rules* (Cambridge University Press 2005).

prohibited 'the use of methods or means of warfare that are intended, or may be expected, to cause widespread, long-term and severe damage to the natural environment'.[34] Three states – France, the United Kingdom, and the United States – may; however, be regarded as persistent objectors to the application of this rule, as they have all indicated that they accept this rule's application to conventional weapons, but not to nuclear weapons.[35] According to these three states, this rule does not prohibit the use of nuclear weapons – although their use can still be unlawful on the basis of other rules, such as the prohibition on indiscriminate attacks and the principle of proportionality. France and the United Kingdom clarified their positions when they entered reservations upon ratifying the Additional Protocol I to the Geneva Conventions, a treaty which contains rules that prohibit causing widespread, long-term and severe damage to the natural environment.[36] In addition, the United Kingdom clarified its position in its *Law of Armed Conflict Manual*, and the United States did so in its *Air Force Commander's Handbook*.[37]

General practice must also evolve over a period of time, though this period need not be lengthy. While there is no absolute minimum amount of time that must pass before a rule of customary international law may emerge, this requirement seems to exclude the possibility of 'instant' custom, which comes into existence without the passage of any period of time.[38]

In practice, when the ICJ seeks to determine whether a customary rule exists, or to determine the specific content of an existing rule, its examinations of general practice are more limited than what all of these requirements might suggest. In its 2012 judgment in a case brought by Germany against Italy (*Jurisdictional Immunities of the State*), for instance, the Court undertook a somewhat limited examination of state practice concerning state immunity. In this case, Germany claimed that Italy had violated the law on state immunity because Italian courts had allowed Italian citizens to bring civil claims against the state of Germany. These civil claims concerned violations of international humanitarian law by Germany during the Second World War.[39] In the absence of any treaty provisions that are in force between Germany and Italy, and that govern the exact legal questions raised by this dispute, the Court based its decision on customary international law.

The Court considered state practice in the form of national legislation and national court judgments in reaching its determination that customary international law on state immunity indeed prohibits domestic courts from allowing such civil claims to proceed. The Court's analysis; however, was limited to the national laws of ten states, dating back to the mid 1970s (Argentina, Australia, Canada, Israel, Japan, Pakistan, Singapore, South Africa, the United Kingdom, and the United States), and court decisions in eleven states (Belgium,

---

[34] ibid 152, rule 45.   [35] ibid 154–5.

[36] ibid; Protocol Additional to the Geneva Conventions of 12 August 1949, and Relating to the Protection of Victims of International Armed Conflicts (Protocol I) (adopted 8 June 1977, entered into force 7 December 1978) 1125 UNTS 3, arts 35(3) and 55(1). For more information on reservations, see Chapter 4 on treaty law.

[37] Henckaerts and Doswald-Beck (n 33) 154.

[38] *North Sea Continental Shelf* cases (n 25) para 74; ILC, 'Identification of Customary International Law' (n 20) 96; but see Bin Cheng, 'United Nations Resolutions on Outer Space: 'Instant' International Customary Law?' (1965) 5 Indian Journal of International Law 23.

[39] *Jurisdictional Immunities of the State (Germany v Italy: Greece intervening)* (Judgment) [2012] ICJ Rep 99.

Brazil, Egypt, France, Germany, Ireland, Italy, the Netherlands, Poland, Slovenia, and the United Kingdom).[40] The Court's examination, thereby covered the relevant indicators of state practice stretching over a considerable period of time, from 1976 to 2012, which it found to be consistent. But the body of state practice examined by the Court cannot; however, be described as extensive, and the judgment itself does not indicate why the Court limited its analysis in this manner, though its approach was most likely shaped by the evidence presented by the parties.

While the substantive decision reached by the Court in *Jurisdictional Immunities of the State* is widely viewed as sound, the Court's examination of state practice appears to have been less than comprehensive. Yet, this is often the case whenever the ICJ, or other national or international courts and tribunals, undertake assessments of customary international law. In practice, assessments of custom tend to fall somewhat short of what the concept of custom would theoretically require. Comprehensive assessments of general practice may ultimately be nearly unachievable, given the challenges involved in collecting such evidence. But this has not prevented courts and tribunals from nevertheless determining the existence or content of customary international law, as this case illustrates.

b *Opinio Juris*

Opinio juris is the second, subjective element of customary international law. The term *opinio juris* means that states (or international organizations) engage in a given practice out of a sense of legal obligation. In other words, states recognize or hold a conviction or belief that international law requires, prohibits, or allows a particular practice.[41] Ascertaining the subjective belief of a state is inherently challenging given that states are legal rather than natural persons, and they act through an array of agents. But on occasion states do clearly indicate that their actions are motivated by an understanding that a particular course of conduct is in accordance with public international law. The United States, for instance, asserts that its operations under the FON Program are in keeping with what public international law allows, namely customary international law as reflected in the UN Convention on the Law of the Sea, to which the United States is not a party.[42] Even though the United States is not a party to the UN Convention on the Law of the Sea, it considers itself to be obliged to abide by the customary law equivalents of its provisions.[43]

More often than not, however, *opinio juris* must be inferred from the relevant state practice, due to the absence of any explicit statement about why a state has engaged in a particular practice. This means that *opinio juris* may be best conceptualized as a way of understanding existing practice, rather than as an element supported by its own evidence.

---

[40] ibid paras 70–9.
[41] ILC, 'Identification of Customary International Law' (n 20), conclusion 9; Wood and Sender (n 22), para 2.
[42] US Department of Defense 'FON Program' (n 24).
[43] UN Convention on the Law of the Sea (adopted 10 December 1982, entered into force 16 November 1994) 1833 UNTS 397.

Vaughan Lowe has written that because *opinio juris* is typically described as a component of customary international law, it is easy to assume that it is like an ingredient in a recipe, when in fact it is more akin to a way of cooking the ingredients of state practice.[44] While the existence of *opinio juris* must be analyzed separately from general practice, the same evidence may support both assessments.[45] A separate analysis of *opinio juris* is necessary, however, as a way of maintaining a distinction between general practice that evidences a legal rule, as opposed to general practice that stems from courtesy, habit, or convenience.[46]

In the United States, for instance, when foreign leaders visit the capital, Washington, DC, the president typically holds a photography session in the Oval Office of the White House so that reporters can capture the moment. Many other countries engage in equivalent conduct upon the visit of a foreign leader. But this general practice cannot be taken as evidence of a customary international legal rule requiring photography sessions, because states engage in this conduct not out of a sense of a legal obligation or *opinio juris*, but out of habit and because it is polite and diplomatic to do so.

The concept of *opinio juris* is complicated by the question of how customary international law changes. If *opinio juris* requires that states engage in a given practice out of a sense of legal obligation, then the emergence of a new legal norm would seemingly require states to engage in a new practice on account of a mistaken conviction that this practice is already legally obliged by a customary norm. The better view; however, is that states engage in a new practice not out of a mistaken belief that a rule already exists, but instead with the intention of bringing about the development of a new customary rule, which other states accept as custom in advance of the norm's actual solidification as a customary rule.[47] The question, then, is how to distinguish between a new practice that contributes to the emergence of a new norm of customary international law, and a new practice that simply breaches an existing legal norm that is not in the process of changing. The distinction between these two scenarios will very much depend on the circumstances.

A classic example of the emergence of a new customary rule is the 1945 proclamation of US President Truman concerning the continental shelf – a term that refers to the seabed and subsoil that lie beyond the territorial sea.[48] Before President Truman's proclamation of 28 September 1945, there was no customary international law governing the rights of a state over the seabed and subsoil beyond its territorial sea, which currently extends only twelve miles from the baselines that usually run along the coast. At that time; however, governments and companies in the extractive industries had a growing interest in exploring and exploiting natural resources, such as oil and gas, on and below the seabed. President Truman declared that the US government regarded the natural resources of the seabed and subsoil of the continental shelf to be under its jurisdiction and control. In making this claim, Truman described the policy as 'reasonable' and 'just', but he did not claim that this

[44] Lowe (n 10) 51.   [45] ILC, 'Identification of Customary International Law' (n 20) 87.   [46] ibid 97.   [47] Lowe (n 10) 39.
[48] UN Convention on the Law of the Sea art 76(1); James Crawford, 'Chance, Order, Change: The Course of International Law, General Course on Public International Law' (2013) 365 Collected Courses of the Hague Academy of International Law 13, 61–7; Michael P Scharf, *Customary International Law in Times of Fundamental Change: Recognizing Grotian Moments* (Cambridge University Press 2013) 107–22.

proclamation reflected public international law at that very moment.[49] Afterwards, the proclamation did not meet with opposition, and in fact, other states made similar claims, some going even further than the United States had. By the mid-1950s, this norm of customary international law had crystalized, as the notion that states have jurisdiction over the continental shelf had come to be well accepted, and codified in the 1958 Geneva Convention on the Continental Shelf.[50]

c *Particular Customary International Law*

Customary international law may also be 'particular' as opposed to 'general', meaning that it binds only certain states rather than all states. In such instances, a rule of customary international law applies only to a limited number of states that are linked to each other by belonging to the same region, sub-region, or through some other non-geographical tie.[51] Like general custom, particular custom consists of general practice among the states concerned and *opinio juris*. An example of particular custom can be found in the case of *Right of Passage over Indian Territory (Portugal v India)*.[52] In its 1960 judgment in this case, the ICJ considered the question of whether Portugal had a right of passage, through Indian territory, for the exercise of sovereignty to enclaves that were then Portuguese territories, and that were completely surrounded by Indian territory. The Court rejected India's assertion that local custom could not be established by just two states, and concluded that a 'constant and uniform practice' had permitted free passage by Portugal for well over a century, both before and after India's independence from Great Britain.[53] But this right extended only to private persons, civil officials, and goods, and not to armed forces, armed police, arms, and ammunition.[54]

d *The Relationship between Treaty Law and Customary International Law*

Treaty law and customary international law exist in parallel, such that the same rule may be found in both sources of law. A treaty rule may relate to a rule of customary law in at least three different ways.[55] First, a treaty rule may codify a customary rule that already existed at the time of the treaty's conclusion. Such treaty rules are 'declaratory' because they set forth customary rules that already exist. The law on the use of force in self-defence, for example, was codified in the UN Charter of 1945, but the rules governing self-defence pre-date the

---

[49] Proclamation 2667, 'Policy of the United States with Respect to the Natural Resources of the Subsoil and Sea Bed of the Continental Shelf' (28 September 1945) 10 Fed Reg 12305.
[50] Convention on the Continental Shelf (adopted 29 April 1958, entered into force 10 June 1964) 499 UNTS 311, art 2.
[51] ILC, 'Identification of Customary International Law' (n 20), conclusion 16.
[52] *Case concerning Right of Passage over Indian Territory (Portugal v India)* (Merits) [1960] ICJ Rep 6. In contrast, in its judgment in the 1950 *Colombian-Peruvian Asylum* case, the ICJ declined to find that a particular custom existed concerning diplomatic asylum, although the Court acknowledged the possibility of a 'regional or local custom peculiar to Latin-American States'. *Asylum Case (Colombia v Peru)* (Judgment) [1950] ICJ Rep 266, 276-77.
[53] *Right of Passage over Indian Territory* case (n 52) 39-40.   [54] ibid 42-3.
[55] ILC, 'Identification of Customary International Law' (n 20), conclusion 11.

Charter and continue to exist alongside it.[56] A second possible relationship between treaty and custom involves a treaty rule leading to the crystallization of a rule of customary law that was in the process of emerging prior to the treaty's conclusion. Finally, a treaty rule may itself generate a new customary rule. In practice, this last possibility is especially difficult to trace, in good part because of the need to show that states have undertaken a particular practice out of a sense of legal obligation that is independent from the treaty obligation.[57] In other words, demonstrating the requisite *opinio juris* is difficult when states are already bound by a treaty rule.[58]

5   Other Sources of International Law

While treaty law and customary international law comprise the two main sources of public international law, they are by no means the only sources of public international law, as Article 38 of the ICJ Statute makes clear. Other, less significant sources of public international law include general principles of law, decisions of international organizations, and unilateral declarations.

a   *General Principles of Law*

General principles of law are unwritten legal norms of a broad character that play a gap-filling role in the international legal field. The drafters of the Statute of the PCIJ (which formed the basis for the ICJ Statute, as mentioned in Section 2) included general principles of law to ensure that the PCIJ could have recourse to legal principles in the absence of specific rules in treaty or customary law. General principles of law, in other words, can help to fill any gaps in the law that might be left by treaty law, customary international law, or another source of public international law. Since the drafting of the PCIJ Statute, the process by which general principles of law come into existence has been a matter of debate among international lawyers. There are two different understandings of this source, which are not mutually exclusive.

First, general principles of law may be understood as a source of law that derives from principles that are common in all domestic (or 'municipal') legal systems and transposable to the international level.[59] Unlike customary international law, which derives from the practice *among* states (accompanied by *opinio juris*), general principles of law derive from the practice *within* states: the fundamental principles of domestic legal systems.[60]

---

[56] Charter of the UN (adopted 26 June 1945, entered into force 24 October 1945) 1 UNTS XVI (UN Charter) arts 2(4), 51; *Nicaragua* case (n 27), paras 176–7. A lively academic debate persists about whether customary law and treaty law are the same or different with respect to the use of force in self-defence.

[57] *North Sea Continental Shelf* cases (n 25), paras 71–4.

[58] The ICRC's study on customary international humanitarian law has been criticized in this respect. See, for example, Daniel Bethlehem, 'The Methodological Framework of the Study' in Elizabeth Wilmshurst and Susan Breau (eds), *Perspectives on the ICRC Study on Customary International Humanitarian Law* (Cambridge University Press 2007).

[59] Pellet (n 3), paras 267–9.

[60] Charles T Kotuby Jr and Luke A Sobota, *General Principles of Law and International Due Process: Principles and Norms Applicable in Transnational Disputes* (Oxford University Press 2017) 9.

Examples of general principles of international law that derive from municipal legal systems include the principle of good faith, and the principle of *res judicata*, which means that a legal matter may not be litigated again, once it has been judged on the merits (literally a 'matter (already) judged').[61]

Another example of a general principle of law deriving from domestic legal systems may be found in the ICJ's earliest case. When the ICJ had recourse to circumstantial evidence in its judgment in the *Corfu Channel* case in 1949, it noted that such 'indirect evidence is admitted in all systems of law, and its use is recognized by international decisions'.[62] The Court noted that where there is no direct evidence of a given fact, domestic (and international) courts may have recourse to circumstantial evidence in order to make a factual finding by linking together a series of facts that 'lead logically to a single conclusion'.[63] While the Court did not explicitly refer to circumstantial evidence as a general principle of law in this case, its characterization of this type of evidence suggests that the Court viewed it as a general principle. As the ICJ Statute makes no reference to circumstantial evidence, the Court was filling a gap in public international law, in particular the law governing dispute settlement at the ICJ, by applying a general principle of law derived from municipal legal systems.

Second, general principles of law may also be understood as fundamental principles grounded in the international legal system. While general principles of law have tradition-ally been conceived of as principles derived from domestic legal systems, this source of law has been increasingly recognized as also encompassing principles based in public interna-tional law.[64] The principle of *uti possidetis* is an example of a general principle of law that derives, in its modern meaning, not from municipal legal systems, but from international relations among states.[65] In its 1986 judgment in the *Frontier Dispute* case between Burkina Faso and Mali, the ICJ applied the principle of *uti possidetis*, which refers to the intangibility of frontiers inherited from colonization.[66] The Court described *uti possidetis* as a 'general principle' whose 'obvious purpose is to prevent the independence and stability of new States being endangered by fratricidal struggles provoked by the challenging of frontiers following the withdrawal of the administering power'.[67] Other possible examples of general principles of law that stem from the international level are the precautionary and preventive principles in international environmental law (see Chapter 16 on international environmental law).[68]

---

[61] *Nuclear Tests Case (New Zealand v France)* (Judgment) [1974] ICJ Rep 457, para 49 ('One of the basic principles governing the creation and performance of legal obligations, whatever their source, is the principle of good faith'); *Effect of Awards of Compensation Made by the United Nations Administrative Tribunal* (Advisory Opinion) [1954] ICJ Rep 47, 53 ('According to a well-established and generally recognized principle of law, a judgment rendered by such a judicial body is res judicata and has binding force between the parties to the dispute').

[62] *Corfu Channel Case (UK v Albania)* (Merits) [1949] ICJ Rep 4, 18.   [63] ibid.

[64] Giorgio Gaja, 'General Principles of Law' in *Max Planck Encyclopedia of Public International Law* (last updated April 2020), paras 17–20; Erik V Koppe, 'The Principle of Ambituity and the Prohibition against Excessive Collateral Damage to the Environment during Armed Conflict' (2013) 82 Nordic Journal of International Law 53, 61–2.

[65] The principle of *uti possidetis* originates; however, in Roman law. See Giuseppi Nesi, 'Uti possidetis Doctrine' in *Max Planck Encyclopedia of Public International Law* (last updated February 2018), para 1.

[66] *Case Concerning the Frontier Dispute (Burkina Faso v Republic of Mali)* (Judgment) [1986] ICJ Rep 554, para 20.

[67] ibid.

[68] Koppe (n 64) 62. See also the general principles of the law of the international civil service, in particular the principle of independence, ILO Administrative Tribunal, Judgment 2232, 95th Session (16 July 2003).

b   *Decisions of International Organizations*

While Article 38 of the ICJ Statute does not include any reference to decisions of international organizations as a source of public international law, they are widely considered to form another source of law in the international legal field. The absence of any reference to such decisions in Article 38 may be taken as a reminder that the list of sources in this provision is not exhaustive and perhaps even outdated. International organizations play a far greater role in contemporary international relations than was the case when the statutes of the PCIJ and ICJ were drafted. If Article 38 were to be revised today, decisions of international organizations would likely be included.

International organizations range enormously, and include entities such as the UN, the European Union, the World Trade Organization, and the Organisation for Economic Co-operation and Development (OECD) (see Chapter 8 on international organizations). Despite their variation, international organizations do have defining characteristics, in particular they are established by treaty (or another instrument governed by public international law), and they possess their own legal personality, separate from their member states.[69] In some cases, the constituent treaty or instrument that establishes an international organization grants an organ within the organization the capacity to make decisions that bind all member states. Article 25 of the UN Charter, for example, specifies that the decisions of the Security Council are binding on all UN member states.[70] Likewise, the regulations, decisions, and directives adopted by European Union institutions are binding on the member states of the European Union.[71] While the binding character of decisions by an international organization derives from the organization's constituent treaty or instrument, such decisions nevertheless constitute an independent source of public international law, separate from treaty law. The process by which the Security Council reaches a binding decision is quite distinct, for example, from the process by which states conclude treaties. The fifteen members of the Security Council vote on the adoption of resolutions, which require at least nine affirmative votes.[72] In addition, the five permanent members of the Council have the power to veto resolutions in particular circumstances.[73]

In some instances, the decisions of international organizations have taken on a legislative character, insofar as they contain obligations pertaining to general issues or threats, rather than obligations pertaining to a discrete situation in a specific geographical area, for instance. As sources of public international law, decisions of international organizations have particular significance when they have a legislative character because of their potentially far-reaching effects, which can mirror those of treaty or customary law. Some of the Security Council's decisions on counter-terrorism measures illustrate the manner in which its decision-making has, in some cases, taken on a legislative quality.

---

[69] ILC, 'Draft Articles on the Responsibility of International Organizations' (2011) UN Doc A/66/10, art 2(a). See also Henry G Schermers and Niels M Blokker, *International Institutional Law: Unity within Diversity* (5th edn, Martinus Nijhoff 2011), para 33.
[70] Article 25 of the UN Charter provides that 'the Members of the United Nations agree to accept and carry out the decisions of the Security Council in accordance with the present Charter'.
[71] Consolidated Version of the Treaty on the Functioning of the European Union [2012] OJ C326/49, art 288.
[72] UN Charter art 27.   [73] UN Charter art 27.

After the Al Qaeda terrorist attacks on 11 September 2001 in the United States, the Security Council responded by adopting a number of wide-ranging decisions in Resolution 1373 (2001).[74] This resolution obligated states to take a series of actions to combat the financing of terrorist activities and to prevent terrorism in general.[75] The required measures against terrorist financing were inspired by, though not as detailed as, provisions in the International Convention for the Suppression of the Financing of Terrorism, which had been recently concluded but had not yet come into force at this time.[76] Similarly, in Resolution 1540 (2004), the Security Council obliged all states to take measures to prevent the proliferation of nuclear, chemical, or biological weapons and their means of delivery.[77] As with Resolution 1373, the measures set out in Resolution 1540 are similar to those contained in a number of treaties.[78] In fact, both resolutions may be understood partly as efforts to ensure that particular rules found in treaty law bind all UN member states, regardless of whether they are parties to these treaties.

c   *Unilateral Declarations*

Unilateral declarations of states represent another source of public international law not found in Article 38 of the ICJ Statute. Unilateral declarations of states, made publicly (whether orally or in writing), may in certain limited circumstances create binding legal obligations for the declaring state, upon which other concerned states are entitled to rely.[79] Whether a unilateral declaration by a state constitutes a political commitment, or a legally binding obligation, depends on the content of the declaration, the circumstances surrounding it, and the reactions to the declaration by other concerned states.[80] The process by which a unilateral declaration becomes a source of law is therefore highly fact-specific, and has to be determined on a case-by-case basis. Unilateral declarations that create binding legal obligations must be made by state officials who unquestionably have the authority to do so, namely heads of state or government and ministers of foreign affairs.[81]

   A series of statements made in 1974 on behalf of the French government concerning nuclear tests constitutes one of the most prominent examples of binding unilateral declarations made by a state.[82] From the mid-1960s to the mid-1970s, France carried out atmospheric tests of nuclear devices in the South Pacific region, which, according to New Zealand, caused radioactive fallout to be deposited on its territory.[83] After unsuccessful

---

[74] José E Alvarez, *International Organizations as Law-makers* (Oxford University Press 2005) 196–8; Stefan Talmon, 'The Security Council as World Legislature' (2005) 99 American Journal of International Law 175.

[75] UNSC Res 1373 (28 September 2001), paras 1–2.

[76] International Convention for the Suppression of the Financing of Terrorism (adopted 9 December 1999, entered into force 10 April 2002) 2178 UNTS 197.

[77] UNSC Res 1540 (28 April 2004), para 3.

[78] Treaty on the Non-Proliferation of Nuclear Weapons (adopted 1 July 1968, entered into force 5 March 1970) 729 UNTS 161; Convention on the Prohibition of the Development, Production, Stockpiling and Use of Chemical Weapons and on their Destruction (adopted 3 September 1992, entered into force 29 April 1997) 1974 UNTS 45; The Convention on the Prohibition of the Development, Production and Stockpiling of Bacteriological (Biological) and Toxin Weapons and on Their Destruction (adopted 10 April 1972, entered into force 26 March 1975) 1015 UNTS 163.

[79] ILC, 'Guiding Principles Applicable to Unilateral Declarations of States Capable of Creating Legal Obligations, with Commentaries Thereto' (2006) UN Doc A/61/10, guiding principle 1.

[80] ibid, guiding principle 3.   [81] ibid, guiding principle 4.   [82] *Nuclear Tests* case (n 61), paras 35–44.   [83] ibid 17–18.

diplomatic efforts to bring about an end to France's atmospheric nuclear testing in the region, New Zealand eventually filed proceedings against France before the ICJ in 1973. In its 1974 judgment, the Court examined a number of statements made by the French president and the French embassy in Wellington, New Zealand, and found that they conveyed to New Zealand the intention of France to cease testing in the atmosphere following the conclusion of a series of atmospheric tests in 1974, and to proceed to underground testing.[84] Based on the substance of these statements, and the circumstances surrounding them, the Court determined that the French president had made an undertaking, with binding legal effect, to the international community as a whole.[85]

6   Subsidiary Means for the Determination of International Law

The term 'subsidiary means for the determination of international law', found in Article 38(1)(d) of the ICJ Statute, refers to places where rules of public international law may be found, as opposed to processes for the development of public international law. Judicial decisions and 'the teachings of the most highly qualified publicists of the various nations' are 'subsidiary' sources of public international law in the sense that they only serve as evidence of the existence or the content of rules of public international law, but not as a means for their creation. They are like a warehouse where treaty law, customary international law, general principles, decisions of international organizations, and unilateral declarations are stored.[86]

While the ICJ and other international and domestic courts and tribunals have played important roles in the development of the international legal field, they fundamentally do not create international law – this is what states do (and international organizations, to a limited extent). Article 59 of the ICJ Statute serves as a reminder of this point, and is accordingly referenced as a sort of caveat at the beginning of Article 38(1)(d). Article 59 provides that '[t]he decision of the Court has no binding force except between the parties and in respect of that particular case'. In other words, the Court's decisions do not create public international law, nor do the decisions of any other international court or tribunal. Moreover, the ICJ's decisions do not create binding legal precedents, as is the case for domestic court decisions in common law domestic jurisdictions. In common law systems, the principle of *stare decisis* (literally 'to stand by decided matters') requires courts to abide by precedents, in particular the case law of higher courts. While the ICJ is not bound by its previous decisions, in practice it strives to avoid contradicting statements made in prior decisions, and judgments typically include many references to its earlier judgments and those of the PCIJ.[87]

In practice, while international courts and tribunals do not create the law, they have contributed considerably to the elucidation of the law. In elucidating the law, courts and

---

[84] ibid, para 53.   [85] ibid.
[86] Shabtai Rosenne, *The Law and Practice of the International Court, 1920–2005*, vol 3 (4th edn, Martinus Nijhoff 2006) 1551.
[87] The Court does not; however, as a general rule, reference the decisions of other international courts or tribunals, or secondary literature.

tribunals have an important consolidating effect in the international legal field, in which the law develops partly through decentralized and unwritten customary international law. Decisions of courts and tribunals serve as a key means for identifying customary rules. In addition, the jurisprudence of the ICJ has fed into the work of the ILC – a UN body tasked with codifying and progressively developing international law. In its work on topics such as the law on state responsibility, the ILC has drawn heavily from the jurisprudence of the ICJ and arbitration tribunals (and they, in turn, tend to refer back to the work of the ILC).

The 'teachings of the most highly qualified publicists of the various nations' is a phrase that refers to secondary literature, as well as audiovisual materials, produced by prominent scholars in the international legal field. As a subsidiary source of international law, such teachings are today of somewhat lesser importance than judicial decisions. Nevertheless, monographs, textbooks, journal articles, and the UN's Audiovisual Library of International Law are all examples of teachings that elucidate the law—in addition to criticizing it and theorizing about it.[88] The work of organizations devoted to international law also qualifies as 'teachings of the most highly qualified publicists', in particular the work of the ILC, but also the Institute of International Law (better known by its French name *Institut du droit international*) and the International Law Association. The thirty-four members of the ILC may be considered 'publicists' in their official capacity as commission members who are required to be 'persons of recognized competence in international law'.[89] Even though they are elected by the UN General Assembly on the basis of geographical distribution, the members serve as individual experts rather than as representatives of their states of nationality.[90]

7   Non-binding International Instruments

This chapter has, thus far, dealt with sources of public international *law* – that is, international norms that create binding legal obligations. But international norms may also be non-binding, and in fact, non-binding instruments play an important role in the development of the international legal field, even though they do not qualify as sources of international law.[91] Non-binding instruments embody political or moral commitments, rather than legal obligations. Such non-binding instruments take a wide range of forms, including resolutions, declarations, recommendations, guidelines, and standards adopted within the framework of international organizations and intergovernmental organizations generally.

---

[88] UN, 'Audiovisual Library of International Law' <www.un.org/law/avl/>.
[89] Statute of the ILC (adopted 21 November 1947) UNGA Res 174(II) art 2(1).
[90] UNGA Res 36/39 (19 November 1981), para 3.
[91] For a range of views on this subject, see Jean d'Aspremont, 'Softness in International Law: A Self-Serving Quest for New Legal Materials' (2008) 19 European Journal of International Law 1075; Christine Chinkin, 'The Challenge of Soft Law: Development and Change in International Law (1989) 38 International and Comparative Law Quarterly 850; Jan Klabbers, 'The Redundancy of Soft Law' (1996) 65 Nordic Journal of International Law 167; Joost Pauwelyn, 'Is it International Law or Not and Does It Even Matter?' in Joost Pauwelyn, Ramses A Wessel, and Jan Wouters (eds), *Informal International Lawmaking* (Oxford University Press 2012).

International lawyers often refer to such non-binding instruments as 'soft law'. This chapter avoids this term; however, and instead uses the term 'non-binding instrument', in part because non-binding international instruments do not constitute law or legal norms at all, and therefore should not be characterized as a 'soft' form of law. The term 'soft law' is therefore misleading, and best avoided.

Non-binding instruments play a role in many areas of the international legal field, such as international environmental law, international financial law, and the law governing corruption and money laundering. There are three main ways in which non-binding instruments contribute to these areas of international law. First, non-binding instruments may contribute to the development of a binding norm, such as those found in treaties and customary international law. The Universal Declaration on Human Rights (UDHR), for example, is a non-binding instrument adopted by the UN General Assembly in 1948, in reaction to the atrocities that took place during the Second World War.[92] The birth of contemporary international human rights law may be traced back to the UDHR, which sets out a relatively extensive set of political, civil, social, economic, and cultural rights. While the UDHR represents an authoritative statement of human rights, it remains a non-binding instrument. But the UDHR gave rise to two binding treaties, the 1966 International Covenant on Civil and Political Rights and the International Covenant on Social, Economic and Cultural Rights[93], both of which elaborate upon the norms set out in the declaration. The UDHR is thus an example of a non-binding instrument which led to the creation of international legal norms in the form of treaty law. In addition, many of the human rights set out in the UDHR are now considered to be customary international law.

Second, non-binding norms may also follow treaties, and serve as a means by which treaty rules are expanded or updated. Following the conclusion of the 1997 Anti-Bribery Convention of the OECD, for example, states parties have concluded recommendations and guidelines that have addressed certain issues that were omitted from the treaty.[94] For instance, the Convention itself does not address the controversial issue of the tax deductibility of bribes paid by businesses to foreign public officials. But in light of the growing consensus among states parties that such deductions are unacceptable, recommendations adopted by states parties in 2009 urge states parties to disallow such deductions.[95] While these recommendations are non-binding, they nevertheless represent an important means by which anti-bribery norms have continued to develop, even after the conclusion of the 1997 Anti-Bribery Convention.

---

[92] UDHR (adopted 10 December 1948) UNGA Res 217 A(III).

[93] International Covenant on Civil and Political Rights (adopted 16 December 1966, entered into force 23 March 1976) 999 UNTS 171; International Covenant on Economic, Social and Cultural Rights (adopted 16 December 1966, entered into force 3 January 1976) 993 UNTS 3.

[94] OECD, 'Convention on Combating Bribery of Foreign Public Officials in International Business Transactions' (adopted 17 December 1997, entered into force 15 February 1999) 37 ILM 1.

[95] OECD, 'Recommendation of the Council for Further Combating Bribery of Foreign Public Officials in International Business Transactions' (26 November 2009, amended 18 February 2010) C(2009)159/Rev1/FINAL, C(2010)19; OECD, 'Recommendation of the Council on Tax Measures for Further Combating Bribery of Foreign Public Officials in International Business Transactions' (25 May 2009) C(2009)64.

Finally, non-binding norms and instruments may have an independent life of their own, distinct from any binding rules of public international law. Some non-binding instruments have a normative impact in their own right, and cannot or should not be primarily understood by virtue of their relationship to binding norms. The ILC's 2001 'Articles on the Responsibility of States for Internationally Wrongful Acts', for example, take the form of a non-binding instrument that both codifies and progressively develops the law of state responsibility.[96] These Articles on State Responsibility, which will be discussed at length in Chapter 5; therefore contain a mix of norms, some of which were already customary norms in 2001, and others which may, or may not, become customary norms in the future. While some of the ILC's work on international legal topics forms the basis for treaties, this has not been, and is unlikely to be, the case for the Articles on State Responsibility.[97] The importance of these non-binding articles, however, lies in their written articulation of norms of state responsibility, which international courts and tribunals, and states in general, frequently consult on questions of state responsibility.[98] The articles may be described as forming 'part of the fabric of general international law', if not a source of international law.[99]

8   Concluding Remarks

In the international legal field, lawyers and judges regularly face the challenge of determining whether a given international legal norm exists, and if so, what its content is. Lawyers and judges often look first to treaty law, which has the advantages of being more precise than custom, and in written form, and thus relatively easily located. But customary international law still plays an important role in the field. In some branches of public international law, customary rules exist alongside treaty rules, and bind those states that are not parties to particular treaties. In addition, treaty law has left some important areas untouched, such that customary rules may be the only or the primary source of law. Ascertaining the existence or content of a customary rule requires separate assessments of general practice and *opinio juris*, though these two elements are often found in the same set of evidence. Where treaty and customary rules leave an apparent gap in the applicable law, lawyers and judges may also turn to general principles of international law, which may be derived from the principles common to domestic legal systems, or from fundamental principles at the international level, or both.

Other possible sources of public international law include decisions of international organizations and unilateral declarations of states, despite the fact that Article 38 of the ICJ Statute omits any reference to them. As 'subsidiary' sources of public international law,

---

[96] ILC, 'Draft Articles on the Responsibility of States for Internationally Wrongful Acts' (2001) UN Doc A/56/10.

[97] See, for example, VCLT (n 4); Vienna Convention on Diplomatic Relations (adopted 18 April 1961, entered into force 24 April 1964) 500 UNTS 95; Vienna Convention on Consular Relations (adopted 24 April 1963, entered into force 19 March 1967) 596 UNTS 261.

[98] James R Crawford, 'State Responsibility' in *Max Planck Encyclopedia of Public International Law* (last updated September 2006) paras 64–9.

[99] ibid, para 69.

judicial decisions and the teachings of international legal experts represent not processes by which law may be developed, but places where the law may be located. Finally, non-binding instruments, sometimes also misleadingly known as 'soft law', do not represent sources of public international law at all. Instead, non-binding instruments are sources of political commitments, which can nevertheless play an important role in the development of public international law and the field as a whole.

Recommended Reading

Samantha Besson, "Theorizing the Sources of International Law" in Samantha Besson and John Tasioulas (eds), *The Philosophy of International Law* (Oxford University Press 2010) 163–85.

James Crawford, "Chance, Order, Change: The Course of International Law, General Course on Public International Law" (2013) 365 Collected Courses of the Hague Academy of International Law 13, pt 1, 27–135.

Vaughan Lowe, "How International Law is Made" in *International Law* (Oxford University Press 2007) 34–99.

Alain Pellet, "Article 38" in Andreas Zimmerman and others (eds), *The Statute of the International Court of Justice: A Commentary* (2nd edn, Oxford University Press 2012) 731–870.

Prosper Weil, "Towards Relative Normativity in International Law?" (1983) 77 American Journal of International Law 413.

3

Subjects, Statehood, and Self-Determination

Simone van den Driest

1   Introduction

The international legal system has its own entities to which it applies. These entities are generally referred to as the 'subjects of international law'. The question of which entities qualify as such is of fundamental importance in order to understand to whom substantive norms of international law pertain. Sovereign states are the main subjects of international law and traditionally, they were considered to be the only subjects in this respect. As Oppenheim noted in 1912: '[s]ince the law of nations is based on the common consent of individual States, and not of individual human beings, States solely and exclusively are the subjects of international law'.[1] Seen from this perspective, international law is made by and for states, while individuals and other entities do not participate in the international legal system. In the course of the twenty-first century; however, the circle of subjects has expanded and today, various other entities, such as international (governmental) organizations, individuals, and peoples are also recognized as subjects of international law.

This chapter will first discuss the main subjects of international law and explain their principal features. Second, this chapter will zoom in on states, the traditional and principal actors in the international legal system. It will discuss the criteria for statehood under international law, the role that recognition plays in this respect, and explain how new states emerge. Finally, this chapter will turn to an analysis of the right to self-determination, a notion that plays an important role in the creation of states and is considered to be the most prominent right of one of the subjects of international law: peoples.

2   Subjects of International Law

A subject of international law is an entity that is capable of possessing rights, duties, and/or competences under international law. In this regard, one may think of the right of international organizations not to pay taxes, the duty of states to refrain from the threat or use of force in their international relations, and the competence of individuals to file a complaint before an international court or committee. Not all subjects of international law; however,

---

[1] Lassa Oppenheim, *International Law: A Treatise* (Hersch Lauterpacht ed, 8th edn, Longmans, Green & Co 1955) 19.

have the same powers on the international legal plane. As the International Court of Justice (ICJ) observed in the *Reparation for Injuries* case, '[t]he subjects of law in any legal system are not necessarily identical in their nature or in the extent of their rights'.[2] In this respect, a distinction should be made between subjects with full capacity and subjects with partial legal capacity. States are the only subjects that have full legal capacity, which reflects their prominent position in the international legal system. Their full legal capacity means that as a matter of principle, they have all rights, duties, and competences under international law. All other subjects of international law possess partial legal capacity, meaning that they only have some international legal rights, duties, and competences. International organizations, for instance, do not have the same rights and competences that states have. Instead, as will be explained in more detail later, they merely have those powers that are necessary for the exercise of their functions. This is often referred to as 'functional personality'. Similar limitations apply to the legal capacity of individuals, who are granted rights under international law and have certain duties and competences, but cannot conclude treaties, for example. Which specific powers the various subjects have and what this means in practical terms, is to be determined on a case-by-case basis.

The subsequent sections will present the main subjects of international law. In doing so, their key characteristics and their main rights, duties, and competences, stemming from their international legal personality, will be highlighted.

a   *States*

States are the traditional subjects of international law. Following the Peace of Westphalia, which concluded the Thirty Years' War in 1648, the sovereign nation state, rather than the pope or emperor, became the principal actor in international relations. Today, states are still the main subjects of international law. The prominent and long-standing position of states in the international legal system is reflected in the fact that states are still the only subjects of international law that enjoy full legal capacity. A state has the most encompassing catalogue of rights, duties, and competences under international law. Examples are the right of the state to enjoy immunity before the national judge of another state, the obligation to refrain from the threat or use of force in their relations with other states, and the competence to conclude treaties. These legal powers will be further explained in the subsequent chapters of this book.

With only roughly fifty states at the start of the twentieth century, the number of states increased over the course of the century. Primarily as a result of the decolonization process in the 1950s and 1960s and the collapse of states following the end of the Cold War, the number grew rapidly. At present, 193 states are members of the United Nations (UN), with South Sudan (2011) being the latest addition. The criteria for statehood in international law, how new states are created, and the role of self-determination in this respect are discussed in Sections 3 and 4 of this chapter.

---

[2] *Reparation for Injuries Suffered in the Service of the United Nations* (Advisory Opinion) [1949] ICJ Rep 174, 178.

b   *International Organizations*

In addition to states, international organizations play a prominent role in international law as well.[3] Examples of such entities are the UN, the European Union (EU), the African Union, the North Atlantic Treaty Organization, the World Trade Organization, the Organization for the Prohibition of Chemical Weapons, the International Civil Aviation Organization, the International Telecommunication Union, and the International Network on Bamboo and Rattan. These examples illustrate that international organizations exist in many shapes and are created for a wide range of purposes. Yet, they do share some key characteristics: international organizations are usually established by states and by means of a treaty, for the purpose of exercising certain public tasks. An authoritative definition was developed by the International Law Commission (ILC), which described an international organization as 'an organization established by a treaty or other instrument governed by international law and possessing its own international legal personality. International organizations may include as members, in addition to states, other entities'.[4]

It is important to distinguish these international organizations from non-governmental organizations (NGOs), such as Amnesty International, Greenpeace, and the International Olympic Committee, which are established by private actors and not by means of a treaty, and are governed by national rather than international law. Since they do not possess international legal personality, NGOs do not have rights and obligations under international law.[5] This is not to say, however, that NGOs do not play any role in the international legal system.[6] First, NGOs may be granted observer status within various international organizations. This observer status means that they are permitted to attend meetings of the organization and in some instances, they are allowed to speak, but they do not have a right to vote. Second, NGOs may influence states, for instance by pressuring them to observe certain norms of international law, or by encouraging them to conclude particular treaties. Consequently, NGOs may indirectly contribute to the development and enforcement of international law, but at present, they do not possess international legal personality.

Chapter 8 elaborates on the law pertaining to international organizations and the main features of the UN – the most important international organization at present – are discussed throughout the various chapters of this book. At this stage, it suffices to make some general remarks on the legal personality of these organizations and the scope of their legal capacity. International organizations may obtain international legal personality either explicitly or implicitly. Often, the constituent instrument of the organization (the treaty that created the organization) will explicitly accord international legal personality. Article 4(1) of the Rome Statute of the International Criminal Court (ICC), for instance, specifies that '[t]he Court

---

[3] See also Chapter 8. The leading study on the law of international organizations is Henry G Schermers and Niels M Blokker, *International Institutional Law: Unity within Diversity* (5th edn, Martinus Nijhoff 2011).

[4] ILC, ' Draft Articles on the Responsibility of International Organizations' (2011) UN Doc A/66/10, art 2(a).

[5] The International Committee of the Red Cross (ICRC) poses an exception in this respect, as its mandate is based in international conventions (i.e., the Geneva Conventions). See Chapter 12.

[6] See Anna-Karin Lindblom, *Non-Governmental Organizations in International Law* (Cambridge University Press 2005).

shall have international legal personality'.[7] Where the constituent instrument of the organization remains silent on this matter, international legal personality may be obtained implicitly. In the *Reparation for Injuries* advisory opinion, for instance, the ICJ had to determine whether the UN possessed international legal personality. In the absence of a provision on this in the UN Charter, the ICJ deduced the UN's international legal personality from the intentions of the founders and the functions of the organization as specified in the UN Charter. The Court argued:

[The UN] is at present the supreme type of international organization, and it could not carry out the intentions of its founders if it was devoid of international personality. It must be acknowledged that its Members, by entrusting certain functions to it, with the attendant duties and responsibilities, have clothed it with the competence required to enable those functions to be effectively discharged.[8]

The fact that international organizations such as the UN possess international legal personality is not to say that they possess general rights, obligations, and competences under international law in the way that states do.[9] In general, international organizations only have those powers that are attributed to them by their members and that are necessary for the exercise of their functions. The scope of these powers thus differs from organization to organization. As the ICJ noted in the *Reparation for Injuries* case, the rights and duties of an international organization 'depend upon its purposes and functions as specified or implied in its constituent documents and developed in practice'.[10] The powers of an international organization may thus be expounded in the constituent instrument of the organization, or may be derived from the functions of the organization and its operation in practice. The latter is referred to as 'implied powers'.

c   ***Individuals***

Traditionally, the legal position of individuals was considered to be an internal matter of the sovereign state, which was free to treat its nationals as it pleased. States were only required to respect some basic principles with respect to the nationals of other states ('aliens'). These obligations; however, were not owed to the individuals themselves, but to their state of nationality. The rationale behind this was that the interests of the state were affected by the ill treatment of its nationals abroad. The state of nationality was then entitled to exercise diplomatic protection by bringing a claim against the state that had acted wrongfully against its nationals. Individuals were, thus not considered to have direct rights, or to be able to enforce rights themselves: international law centred on the rights, obligations, and competences of states, which could have implications for individuals. This changed after the Second World War, as the existence of direct rights, obligations, and competences for

---

[7] Rome Statute of the ICC (adopted 17 July 1998, entered into force 1 July 2002) 2187 UNTS 3.

[8] *Reparation for Injuries* advisory opinion (n 2) 179.

[9] *Legality of the Use by a State of Nuclear Weapons in Armed Conflict* (Advisory Opinion) [1996] ICJ Rep 66, para 25.

[10] *Reparation for Injuries* advisory opinion (n 2) 180.

individuals was acknowledged. Two major developments, which are essentially two sides of the same coin, deserve to be highlighted in this respect.

The first concerns the emergence of international human rights law. In the context of the UN and beyond, a significant number of human rights treaties on a wide range of topics have been concluded. International law grants rights to individuals. These rights also come with certain competences, as individuals have access to various international courts and committees to enforce these rights. Chapter 10 addresses this development in more detail. While individual rights on the international plane primarily stem from human rights law, this is not the only source. In the *LaGrand* case, for instance, the ICJ found that Article 36(1) of the Vienna Convention on Consular Relations (VCCR) not only creates rights for the state, but individual rights as well. It concluded that by detaining two German nationals without informing them of their rights to consular assistance under the VCCR, the United States had not only violated its obligations towards Germany, but also the rights of German nationals.[11] In other words: individuals do not only have rights through their state, but also on their own, as human beings.

In addition to rights and competences, individuals also have certain obligations under international law. Norms have emerged that prohibit torture, terrorist activities, war crimes, crimes against humanity, genocide, and other international crimes. This brings us to the second development, which is the emergence of international criminal law. When individuals do not live up to their obligations, they may be held accountable under international law. International courts and tribunals have been established to effectuate individual criminal responsibility for international crimes. The most prominent example in this respect is the ICC, which is discussed in Chapter 13.

d   *Groups of Individuals*

International law accords rights to certain groups of individuals as well. Peoples, for instance, have attained an important place in the international legal system. While there is no clear definition of what constitutes a people, it is generally agreed that peoples are groups of individuals that share a common territory, history, language, and culture.[12] A people is first and foremost the entire population of a sovereign state, for instance, the Dutch people.[13] In addition, groups within a state (or various states) may also qualify as a people because of their distinct yet common characteristics. Examples in this respect are the Kurds and the Tibetans. This means that a state may also consist of a number of peoples. As will be explained in more detail in Section 4, the most important right granted to peoples under international law is the right to self-determination.[14]

---

[11] *LaGrand Case (Germany v United States of America)* (Judgment) [2001] ICJ Rep 466, para 77.
[12] See, for instance, UNESCO, 'International Meeting of Experts on Further Study of the Concept of the Rights of Peoples: Final Report and Recommendations' (22 February 1990) SHS-89/CONF.602/7, para 22.
[13] *Reference re Secession of Quebec* [1998] 2 SCR 217 (Supreme Court of Canada), para 124.
[14] See James Summers, *Peoples and International Law* (2nd rev edn, Brill/Nijhoff 2014).

Indigenous peoples are another example of a collective entity that holds certain rights under international law. Due to the diversity of Indigenous peoples worldwide and the interests of sovereign states, is has proved difficult to formulate a definition that meets with general approval among states. Nonetheless, in essence, these communities are considered Indigenous because of their special relationship with ancestral lands and their self-identification as Indigenous.[15] Examples in this respect are the Aboriginal and Torres Strait Islander people in Australia, the Māori people in New Zealand, and the Sámi people in Finland. In many states, the ancestral lands and accompanying natural resources of Indigenous communities, as well as their traditional knowledge and culture, are at risk, primarily as a consequence of economic development and environmental damage. A number of international instruments seek to protect these Indigenous interests, such as the Indigenous and Tribal Peoples Convention of the International Labour Organization (ILO)[16] and the UN Declaration on the Rights of Indigenous Peoples, which was adopted by the General Assembly in 2007.[17] However, as the Indigenous and Tribal Peoples Convention has been ratified by only a limited number of states,[18] and the UN Declaration is not legally binding, protection on the regional level is important. In parti-cular, the jurisprudence of the Inter-American Court of Human Rights has become funda-mental for protecting the rights of Indigenous peoples.[19]

Similar to peoples and Indigenous peoples, minorities are sub-state groups that have also attained international legal personality to a certain extent. They hold rights relating to the protection of their culture, religion, language, or other characteristics that distinguish them from the majority and dominant part of the population of the state.[20] An important difference with the rights accorded to peoples and Indigenous peoples; however, is that the rights of minorities are generally articulated as individual rather than collective rights. They can only be invoked by an individual member of a minority group, not by the community as a whole. An example is Article 27 of the International Covenant on Civil and Political Rights (ICCPR), which gives 'persons belonging to such minorities … the right, in community with the other members of their group, to enjoy their own culture, to profess and practise their own religion, or to use their own language'.[21] The distinction between individual and collective rights is elaborated upon in Chapter 10.

A collective entity of a somewhat different nature, which holds both rights and obliga-tions, is the armed opposition group. As is explained in Chapter 12, under the laws of armed conflict, these groups have certain fundamental rights and obligations in the context of what is commonly referred to as a civil war, or in legal terminology a non-international armed

---

[15] ILO Convention 169 concerning Indigenous and Tribal Peoples in Independent Countries (adopted 27 June 1989, entered into force 5 September 1991) 1659 UNTS 383, art 1(2).
[16] ibid.   [17] Declaration on the Rights of Indigenous Peoples (adopted 13 September 2007) UNGA Res 61/295.
[18] By April 2021, only twenty-three states had ratified this convention.
[19] See, for instance, Inter-American Court of Human Rights, *Case of the Saramaka People v Suriname* (2007) Series C 172.
[20] See UN Commission on Human Rights (Sub-Commission on the Prevention of Discrimination and Protection of Minorities), 'Study on the Rights of Persons Belonging to Ethnic, Religious and Linguistic Protection of Minorities by Special-Rapporteur Francesco Capotorti' (1991) UN Doc E/CN.4/Sub.2/384/Add.1–7, para 568.
[21] ICCPR (adopted 16 December 1966, entered into force 23 March 1976) 999 UNTS 171.

conflict. Beyond the context of armed conflict, these groups do not have rights, obligations, or competences under international law. For instance, they do not have the capacity to conclude treaties.[22] Consequently, peace agreements concluded between armed opposition groups and states, such as the 2016 peace accord signed between the Revolutionary Armed Forces of Colombia and the Colombian government, do not qualify as treaties and are, therefore not regulated by international law.[23]

e   *Multinational Corporations*

The international legal personality of multinational corporations (MNCs), such as Shell and Primark, is subject to much debate. Traditionally, these corporations merely enjoyed legal personality within the domestic legal system of the state of seat or registry. Over the past decades, however, multinational corporations have gained a position in the international legal system as well. As is demonstrated in Chapter 14, MNCs are bestowed with certain rights under international economic law, primarily in order to protect foreign investments against expropriation, discriminatory regulations, and other actions that may harm the economic value of the investment.

   In addition to rights, it is increasingly argued that MNCs have obligations under international law as well, in particular with respect to human rights and the protection of the environment. After all, multinational corporations are capable of impacting human rights, for instance by employing children or using materials made by forced labour. Moreover, their business activities may damage the environment, thereby affecting people's health or even their means of subsistence. To date; however, international law does not yet entail legally binding obligations for multinational corporations.[24] In 2011, the UN Human Rights Council adopted the Guiding Principles on Businesses and Human Rights,[25] which aims to prevent, address, and remedy human rights abuses caused by business activity. The Guiding Principles stipulate, among other things, the responsibility of corporations to respect human rights, which implies that 'they should avoid infringing on the human rights of others and should address adverse human rights impacts with which they are involved'.[26] While the Guiding Principles have attracted widespread support from states, civil society, and businesses alike, it should be emphasized that they are legally non-binding in nature. The same goes for other instruments that have been drafted on this matter, such as the Organization for Economic Co-operation and Development (OECD) Guidelines for Multinational Enterprises.[27]

---

[22] See, for instance, Special Court for Sierra Leone (Appeals Chamber) *Prosecutor v Morris Kallon* (Decision on Challenge to Jurisdiction: Lomé Accord Amnesty) [2004] SCSL 4, paras 45–8.

[23] See also Christine Bell, *On the Law of Peace: Peace Agreements and the Lex Pacificatoria* (Oxford University Press 2008).

[24] See, for instance, Surya Deva and David Bilchitz (eds), *Human Rights Obligations of Business: Beyond the Corporate Responsibility to Respect?* (Cambridge University Press 2013).

[25] UN Human Rights Council Res 17/4, 'Human Rights and Transnational Corporations and Other Business Enterprises' (16 June 2011) UN Doc A/HRC/17/L.17/Rev.1.

[26] UN Human Rights Council Report of the Special-Representative of the Secretary-General on the Issue of Human Rights and Transnational Corporations and Other Business Enterprises, John Ruggie, 'Guiding Principles on Business and Human Rights: Implementing the United Nations 'Protect, Respect and Remedy' Framework' (2011) UN Doc A/HRC/17/31, Principle 11.

[27] OECD 'Guidelines for Multinational Enterprises' (2011) <www.oecd.org/daf/inv/mne/48004323.pdf>.

3   Statehood

Despite the expansion of the circle of international legal subjects and the increasing role that other actors play in the international arena today, states are still the main subjects of international law. In view of their prominence, they merit a more detailed analysis. This section will, therefore, explain sovereignty as a key feature of states, discuss the criteria for statehood under international law, and expound on how states are created and cease to exist.

a   State Sovereignty

Sovereignty is an important notion in international law and a key feature of states. The term is derived from the medieval Latin notions of *superanitas* or *suprema potestas*, which mean as much as supreme power or authority. In the *Island of Palmas* arbitration – a case involving a territorial conflict between the United States and The Netherlands – Judge Huber observed that:

Sovereignty in the relation between States signifies independence. Independence in regard to a portion of the globe is the right to exercise therein, to the exclusion of any other State, the functions of a State. . . . Territorial sovereignty involves the exclusive right to display the activities of a State.[28]

The sovereignty of the state has two dimensions. The first dimension is an internal one and implies that a state is the highest authority within its territory and has the exclusive right to exercise public authority over this territory and the population inhabiting it. A state can issue laws and regulations, it can adjudicate suspects of violating those laws and regulations, and it can arrest and detain those that have committed a crime. In legal terms, states have jurisdiction over their territory. The scope and limitations of the state's (internal) jurisdiction is further explained in Chapters 6 and 7. The second dimension of state sovereignty is external in nature and refers to the position of the state within the international community. It means that a state cannot be submitted to the authority of another state without its consent, as all states are considered to be legally equal. This principle of sovereign equality of states (in Latin: *par in parem non habet imperium*) is reflected in Article 2(1) of the UN Charter, which reads: 'The Organization is based on the principle of the sovereign equality of all its Members'.[29] So while some states are more powerful, wealthier, or developed than others, in legal terms, all states are considered to be equal. This is also reflected in the fact that all states have one vote in the UN General Assembly.[30] At the same time; however, the political or economic inequality of states is mirrored in international law as well. The veto power of the five permanent members of the UN Security Council is probably the clearest example in this regard, echoing the balance of power shortly after the Second World War.[31]

---

[28] *Island of Palmas Case (United States v Netherlands)* (1928) 2 RIAA 829, 838.
[29] Charter of the UN (adopted 26 June 1945, entered into force 24 October 1945) 1 UNTS XVI (UN Charter).
[30] UN Charter art 18(1).
[31] UN Charter art 27(3). These five permanent members are China, France, Russia, the United Kingdom, and the United States.

b   *Criteria for Statehood*

Having explained sovereignty as a key attribute of the state, we now turn to the question of what qualifies as a state under international law. In the absence of a universally adopted treaty that defines statehood, the Montevideo Convention on the Rights and Duties of States provides the most authoritative set of criteria. While concluded in 1933 as a regional treaty between various American states, Article 1 of this Convention is generally seen to reflect customary international law. It stipulates that:

> The state as a person of international law should possess the following qualifications: a) a permanent population; b) a defined territory; c) a government; and d) the capacity to enter into relations with the other states.[32]

The criteria listed in the Montevideo Convention are often viewed to be inconclusive and incomplete. It is sometimes argued that additional elements should also be taken into consideration, such as the commitment to international norms and a certain degree of civilization.[33] As these factors are not yet generally accepted as formal criteria for statehood, the following sections will primarily focus on the classic standards stipulated in the Montevideo Convention.

i   *Permanent Population*

The first requirement of statehood listed in the Montevideo Convention is that of a permanent population. A certain minimum size is not prescribed. A small island with about 10,000 inhabitants only, such as Tuvalu, may thus qualify as a state in the same way as China does. What does matter, is that there is a (core) population that inhabits the territory on a permanent basis. This population can be comprised of different ethnicities, minorities, and peoples. Moreover, the criterion of a population does not relate to the nationality of the population, meaning that the inhabitants of a state may be of different nationalities. The nationality of a population depends upon statehood, but statehood does not depend upon the nationality of its inhabitants.[34]

ii   *Defined Territory*

The requirement of a permanent population strongly relates to the second criterion of statehood. Being a territorial entity, it is clear that a state cannot exist without a certain territory. As US Ambassador Jessup observed, when arguing for Israel's admission to the UN in 1949:

> The reason for the rule that one of the necessary attributes of a state is that it shall possess territory is that one cannot contemplate a state as a kind of disembodied spirit . . . . [T]here must be some portion of the earth's surface which its people inhabit and over which its Government exercises authority.[35]

In legal terms, the state's territory encompasses the landmass, internal waters (e.g., canals, rivers, lakes, and ports), territorial sea (i.e., for coastal states only), and the air space above

---

[32] Convention on the Rights and Duties of States (adopted 26 December 1933, entered into force 26 December 1934) 165 LNTS 19 (Montevideo Convention) art 1.

[33] See James R Crawford, *The Creation of States in International Law* (2nd edn, Oxford University Press 2006) 89–95.

[34] ibid 52.   [35] Quoted in ibid 48.

the land and territorial sea.[36] There is no rule of international law, however, that prescribes the minimum size of such territory. Consequently, so-called microstates such as Monaco and Liechtenstein[37] qualify as states under international law in the same way as the Russian Federation and China do. Important, however, is that the physical boundaries of the territory are defined. This is by no means to say that this territory should be completely fixed and its boundaries entirely undisputed. Boundary disputes occur between many states and do not affect statehood.[38] Even more controversial claims do not necessarily prevent an entity from qualifying as a state. This is illustrated by the example of Israel, which is recognized as a sovereign state by most other states and is a member state of the UN, while some of its boundaries and claims of title to certain territory – in particular the West Bank and Gaza Strip – are disputed to date.

iii   Effective Government

The Montevideo Convention prescribes that a state should have a government. There must be an entity that is in charge of the territory and its population and to which other states can turn. A state without any form of government will disappear after a while. In 1920, the International Committee of Jurists concluded that Finland could not be considered a sovereign state, 'until a stable political organization had been created, and until the public authorities had become strong enough to assert themselves throughout the territories of the state without the assistance of foreign troops'.[39] It is generally considered that an *effective* government is required.[40] This means that for an entity to qualify as a state, it must possess a government that (more or less) effectively exercises public power over its territory and population. The government must be able to do so to the exclusion of other entities and without being dependent on other states.

Some governments, however, have proved unable to control parts of the state's territory, to maintain law and order, and to provide for the basic needs of their population. This may be the result of, for instance, insurgence, civil war, or foreign occupation. In this context, the term fragile or failing state is often used.[41] A good example concerns Somalia, which has lacked a functioning government since dictator Siad Barre was overthrown in 1991. Armed warlords subsequently ruled the country for years. Since the 2012 elections, the Somali government has been struggling to regain control over the territory, but the state remains fragile. Other contemporary examples of fragile states are, for example, Syria, Afghanistan, South Sudan, and Yemen.[42] It should be emphasized; however, that once a state exists, the ineffectiveness

---

[36] This will be discussed further in Chapter 15.

[37] Monaco has a territory of no more than 2.02 km², while Liechtenstein covers an area of 160 km².

[38] *North Sea Continental Shelf Cases (Federal Republic of Germany v Denmark; Federal Republic of Germany v Netherlands)* (Judgment) [1969] ICJ Rep 3, para 46.

[39] 'Report of the International Commission of Jurists entrusted by the Council of the League of Nations with the Task of Giving an Advisory Opinion upon the Legal Aspects of the Aaland Islands Question', League of Nations Official Journal, Spec Supp 3 (1920) 3.

[40] See Crawford (n 33) 55–61.

[41] See George Barrie, 'Failed States: The New Challenge to International Law' (2015) 40 *South African Yearbook of International Law* 103.

[42] For an overview of fragile or failing states, see the annual Fragile States Index powered by the Fund for Peace <https://fragilestatesindex.org>.

of its government – whether that is temporary or protracted – does not affect its statehood. In other words: once established, a state does not cease to exist due to the fact that the authorities do not function properly, but it will continue to enjoy legal personality under international law. The rationale behind this is that the government may, at least in theory, always be able to regain authority over the territory. The question of the effective functioning of a government is thus of importance for the establishment of a new state and the recognition thereof by third states, but not for its continuity as a subject of international law.[43]

At present, international law does not prescribe a specific governmental system or state structure. As the ICJ noted in its *Western Sahara* advisory opinion, 'no rule of international law ... requires the structure of a State to follow any particular pattern, as is evident from the diversity of forms found in the world today'.[44] Consequently, democracies as well as dictatorships may meet the criteria of statehood. This is not to say, however, that states are completely free to determine their internal structure. In fact, international law increasingly contains norms that reflect features of a (liberal) democracy,[45] such as the rights of political participation that are stipulated in the Universal Declaration on Human Rights and the ICCPR.[46]

iv   Capacity to Enter into International Relations

The fourth and final criterion listed in the Montevideo Convention concerns the capacity to enter into relations with other states. It is often contended that this capacity is a consequence rather than a precondition for statehood and depends on recognition by other states as well. While this may well be true in practical terms, what this criterion boils down to in legal terms is that an entity should have the ability to act and enter into international relations without legal interference from other states.[47] It requires a sense of independence as well. The origin of this criterion may be understood against the backdrop of colonialism. Colonized territories were often granted a significant degree of autonomy, but they were generally not entitled to enter into international relations with other states without the consent of the colonizer, the metropolitan state. Beyond the context of decolonization, this criterion precludes state-like entities, such as Scotland from meeting all criteria for statehood. While it is beyond doubt that Scotland has a permanent population, a defined territory, and an effective government seated in Edinburgh, it is still part of the United Kingdom and does not have the ability to enter into international relations in its own right.

c   Recognition of States

An important yet contentious question concerns the role of recognition in the establishment of a new state. The question arises whether recognition operates as an additional

---

[43] The issue of recognition will be further explained in Section 3(c).
[44] *Western Sahara* (Advisory Opinion) [1975] ICJ Rep 12, para 94.
[45] See, for instance, James R Crawford, 'Democracy and the Body of International Law' in Gregory H Fox and Brad R Roth (eds), *Democratic Governance and International Law* (Cambridge University Press 2000) 91–113.
[46] On international human rights law, see Chapter 10.   [47] Crawford (n 33) 62.

requirement for statehood. Two competing theories are generally discerned: the constitutive theory and the declaratory theory.[48] The constitutive theory posits that the existence of a state depends upon formal recognition by other states. According to this theory, a state does not exist as long as other states have refrained from recognizing it. This theory was dominant in the past, when the international legal community was a closed community of primarily European states, and it was for this community as a whole to decide whether other states were admitted. At present, this theory causes problems, as it leads to uncertainty for two reasons. First, it grants states broad discretion to decide whether or not to recognize and, hence, whether or not a state has emerged. Second, difficulties occur when an entity is recognized by some, but not by others. This leads to the question of how many and which states should recognize an entity before it qualifies as a state under international law.

Today, the constitutive theory has generally been abandoned and most scholars view recognition as declaratory in nature. According to the declaratory theory, recognition by a state merely implies the acknowledgement that the entity meets the criteria for statehood and the acceptance of this state in bilateral relations. The declaratory view of recognition is echoed in Article 6 of the Montevideo Convention, which stipulates that '[t]he recognition of a state merely signifies that the state which recognizes it accepts the personality of the other with all the rights and duties determined by international law'.[49] Recognition primarily serves as a political instrument and the lack of recognition does not necessarily imply that no state – as a subject of international law – has emerged. This is also reflected in the practice of recognition. Often, states that refuse to recognize an entity as a state for political reasons consider that entity to be bound by norms of international law that apply to states anyway. An example is the refusal of various Arab states to recognize Israel, while nonetheless expecting Israel to respect international law at the same time.

While recognition is, thus primarily a political instrument relevant to the bilateral relations between states, it can certainly have legal implications. First and foremost, recognition is important for a new state to actually operate as such within the international legal community, since without recognition, diplomatic or treaty relations will usually not be established. In other words, when recognition remains forthcoming, it is difficult for a state to exercise its rights, duties, and competences under international law. Second, recognition is relevant when it is unclear whether an entity meets the criteria for statehood. Widespread recognition is often seen as evidence that an entity does indeed fulfil these criteria. Conversely, when an entity does not (yet) meet these criteria, recognition may have a corrective effect. The case of Kosovo illustrates this. Dozens of states recognized the Republic of Kosovo soon after its declaration of independence on 17 February 2008, while it was questionable whether the requirement of effective government was met, as the authorities were still heavily dependent on international assistance by, for instance, the UN Interim Administration Mission in Kosovo and the EU Rule of Law Mission in Kosovo. By recognizing and subsequently establishing diplomatic relationships with Kosovo and supporting its authorities, these states

---

[48] See generally, Hersch Lauterpacht, *Recognition in International Law* (Cambridge University Press 2012).
[49] Montevideo Convention (n 32) art 6.

contributed to the consolidation of an effective and independent government. It should be noted though, that premature recognition is considered to violate the principle of non-intervention and is; therefore, unlawful towards the state on whose territory the new state aims to establish itself. Also in more practical terms, premature recognition is not without risks. States that lack an effective government often become weak states. The Republic of South Sudan, for instance, which declared independence from Sudan on 9 July 2011 and was soon admitted to the UN as its 193rd member state and recognized by individual states, has suffered from internal armed conflict since its independence and is seen as one of today's most fragile states in the world.

South Sudan's admission to the UN brings us to the next issue. While recognition generally involves a unilateral act that affects the bilateral relations between states, recognition may also occur collectively, by a group of states in the framework of an international organization. Today, admission to membership of the UN is increasingly viewed as an act similar to collective recognition.[50] However, such admission should not be equated with individual recognition by all UN member states or universal recognition, as admission to membership of the UN requires the approval of a two-thirds rather than absolute majority of the UN member states (including the five permanent members of the Security Council).[51] This means that various individual member states may, nonetheless, refrain from recognizing the state concerned. Illustrative in this regard is Israel's membership of the UN. While Israel was admitted to the UN in 1949, as noted earlier, various Arab states refuse to recognize the state of Israel to this very day.

On a final note, it is important not to conflate the recognition of states with the recognition of governments, as the latter does not have implications for questions of statehood under international law.[52] As the formal recognition of governments of other states may be interpreted as an expression of legitimacy and support, most states prefer not to do so as a matter of policy. An exceptional situation, however, was the recognition of the Libyan National Transitional Council as the legitimate government authority of Libya in 2011 by a large group of states, even before the regime of Colonel Gadaffi was definitively overthrown later that year.

d   *Illegality and Non-recognition*

States enjoy considerable freedom in assessing new claims to statehood and deciding whether or not to recognize an entity as a sovereign state. The criteria listed in the Montevideo Convention will generally be used as a point of departure, although political considerations may also play a role. There are; however, exceptional circumstances in which the emergence of a new state is considered to be unlawful, even when this entity meets the criteria of the Montevideo Convention. As the ICJ observed in its *Kosovo*

---

[50] See John Dugard, *Recognition and the United Nations* (Grotius Publications 1987).

[51] See the admission procedure enshrined in UN Charter art 4.

[52] On this topic, see generally, Stefan Talmon, *Recognition of Governments in International Law: With Particular Reference to Governments in Exile* (Oxford University Press 2001).

advisory opinion, attempts to create a new state are considered to be illegal when they are connected with serious violations of norms of general international law, in particular (peremptory) norms of *jus cogens*.[53] A clear example is the establishment of Southern Rhodesia (now Zimbabwe), which was proclaimed in November 1965 by a white minority government. The Security Council adopted a resolution condemning 'the usurpation of power by a racist settler minority in Southern Rhodesia and [regarding] the declaration of independence by it as having no legal validity'. It subsequently called upon states 'not to recognize this illegal racist minority regime'.[54] Another example is the Turkish Republic of Northern Cyprus (TRNC), which was proclaimed in December 1983 following Turkey's military occupation of the northern part of Cyprus. The Security Council adopted various resolutions in which it condemned the events, declared that the creation of the TRNC was unlawful and called upon states not to recognize the TRNC.[55]

As these two examples indicate, the (attempted) establishment of a state in violation of the right to self-determination or through the unlawful use of force will generally be illegal and prevent an entity from achieving statehood under international law. This corresponds with the principle of *ex injuria jus non oritur*, which means that no rights may arise from illegality. Accordingly, unlawful attempts to create a new state will result in an obligation for third states to withhold recognition. This is reflected today in Article 41(2) of the Draft Articles on the Responsibility of States for Internationally Wrongful Acts, which stipulates that '[n]o State shall recognize as lawful a situation created by a serious breach ... nor render aid or assistance in maintaining that situation'.[56] The principle of non-recognition has also been expressed in various resolutions of the Security Council, as was the case with respect to Southern Rhodesia and the TRNC. A more recent example concerns General Assembly Resolution 68/262, which was adopted following the annexation of Crimea by the Russian Federation in March 2014 and called upon states as well as international organizations 'not to recognize the alteration of the status of the Autonomous Republic of Crimea and the city of Sevastopol on the basis of the ... referendum and to refrain from any action or dealing that might be interpreted as recognizing such altered status'.[57]

e   *Creation and Extinction of States*

Having explained what conditions should be met for acquiring statehood under international law and the role that recognition plays, it is important to turn to the question of how new states are created and how states cease to exist. As already noted, many (relatively) young independent states emerged during the decolonization process. Beyond this context, changes in statehood have occurred as well, most importantly through secession, dissolution, and

---

[53] See *Accordance with International Law of the Unilateral Declaration of Independence in Respect of Kosovo* (Advisory Opinion) [2010] ICJ Rep 403, para 81.
[54] See UNSC Res 216 (12 November 1965).   [55] See UNSC Res 541 (18 November 1983); UNSC Res 550 (11 May 1984).
[56] See ILC, 'Draft Articles on the Responsibility of States for Internationally Wrongful Acts' (2001) UN Doc A/56/10, art 41. See also Crawford (n 33) 158–62.
[57] UNGA Res 68/262 (27 March 2014), para 6.

union or merger. These contemporary modalities of state creation and extinction deserve some further discussion here.

Secession refers to the separation of part of a territory of an existing state to establish a new state. The so-called parent state continues to exist with the same name and legal personality, but with a territory and population that are reduced in size. In some instances, secession occurs with the prior consent of the parent state. If the Scottish people had voted for independence from the United Kingdom during the referendum held in September 2014, then this would have qualified as an example of consensual secession, as the UK government had approved the referendum and committed itself to respect the outcome of the vote.[58] In such a situation, domestic rather than international law governs the secession. Secession may also be based on a provision in the domestic constitution that grants specific groups or entities a right to secede, although such constitutional provisions are rarely effective.[59] More contested; however, are attempts to secede in the absence of parent state consent or a constitutional basis, which are generally referred to as unilateral secession. Examples are the separation of Bangladesh from Pakistan in the early 1970s and Kosovo's secession from Serbia in 2008. As will be seen in the context of the right to self-determination, no general right to unilateral secession exists, because international law primarily prioritizes the protection of existing state's territorial integrity and political unity.

New states may also emerge as a consequence of the dissolution of an existing state. A key characteristic of dissolution is the complete collapse of the state, without any of the new states emerging from it continuing the legal personality of the former state. In other words, the former state ceases to exist in legal terms. As will be explained, this has implications for treaty obligations and membership of international organizations, for example. It must be noted, however, that the distinction between dissolution and secession is sometimes blurred. As the break-up of the Socialist Federal Republic of Yugoslavia (SFRY) in the early 1990s demonstrates, a series of attempts to secede may ultimately lead to the dissolution of a state. In this case, the process of dissolution started with the secession of the republics of Croatia and Slovenia, after which other republics followed and ultimately, the SFRY ceased to exist.

A third modality for creating new states that deserves to be highlighted here is that of (re)unification or merger, by which two or more existing states join to form one single state. Existing states may merge into a completely new state, as in the case of Tanzania, which emerged in 1964 as a result of the merger of Tanganyika and Zanzibar. Another manifestation is the absorption of a state into an already existing state. The most commonly known example in this respect is the absorption of the German Democratic Republic (East Germany) into the Federal Republic of Germany (West Germany) in 1990, following the fall of the Berlin Wall, to form a single, reunited Germany.

---

[58] On the international legal consequences of Scotland's (hypothetical) secession, see James Crawford and Alan Boyle, *Annex A. Opinion: Referendum on the Independence of Scotland – International Law Aspects* (2012) <www.gov.uk/government/uploads/system/uploads/attachment_data/file/79408/Annex_A.pdf>.

[59] An example of a situation in which a constitutional arrangement has actually led to the creation of a new state, is South Sudan's secession from Sudan in 2011. It should be noted; however, that the constitution providing for a right to secession was drafted in the context of peace negotiations.

f   *State Succession*

The break-up of existing states and the creation of new states by means of secession, (re) unification, or merger raise complex questions concerning the rights, obligations, and competences of states. For instance, do existing treaties concluded by the parent state automatically bind the new state in case of secession? When a state dissolves, what happens to membership of international organizations, or to its property and debts? And what nationality do individuals possess when the state on whose territory they live ceases to exist? The most pressing questions of state succession are usually addressed in a treaty concluded between the states concerned. When such treaty does not exist, for instance where the change in statehood was not consensual or peaceful, general rules concerning state succession apply. Relevant treaties are the 1978 Vienna Convention on Succession of States in Respect of Treaties[60] and the 1983 Vienna Convention on Succession of States in Respect of State Property, Archives and Debts.[61] Only a limited number of states; however, are party to the former Convention, while the latter has not yet entered into force. The significance of these conventions thus primarily lies in the fact that many of their provisions reflect customary international law. The rules on state succession, however, are complex and span various branches of international law. Therefore, only two issues deserve to be highlighted at this stage.

First, international law distinguishes between situations in which there is an entity that qualifies as the legal continuation of the previous state (i.e., the successor state), and those in which the change in statehood has resulted in one or more entirely new states. In the case of the fragmentation of the Union of Soviet Socialist Republics (USSR), for instance, the Russian Federation continued the legal personality of the former state. The USSR's membership of the UN and its seat on the Security Council (as a permanent member with a right of veto) were transferred to the Russian Federation. In contrast, when the SFRY dissolved, the Federal Republic of Yugoslavia (Serbia and Montenegro at present) was not regarded as the legal continuation of the SFRY. The Federal Republic of Yugoslavia was; therefore, forced to apply for UN membership. There is; however, no rule of law determining whether or not a new entity can be considered as a successor state. As the examples of the USSR and SFRY also seem to suggest, this primarily depends on a political decision by third states.

Second, it is important to note that with respect to succession to treaties, international law generally does not consider a new state bound by treaties that were concluded by the predecessor state. This is referred to as the 'clean slate' principle and was initially applied in the context of decolonization. Former colonies were not bound by the legal obligations of their colonial powers, but were able to decide for themselves to which treaties they wished to accede.[62] In the contemporary context, there are some exceptions to the 'clean slate'

---

[60] Vienna Convention on Succession of States in Respect of Treaties (adopted 23 August 1978, entered into force 6 November 1996) 1946 UNTS 3.

[61] Vienna Convention on Succession of States in Respect of State Property, Archives and Debts (adopted 8 April 1983, not yet in force) 22 ILM 306.

[62] Vienna Convention on Succession of States in Respect of Treaties art 17.

principle. Geographical boundaries determined by treaty or other 'territorial regimes', for instance, are not affected by state succession and remain in force.[63] This was confirmed in the *Territorial Dispute* case, as the ICJ found that 'a boundary established by treaty ... achieves a permanence which the treaty itself does not necessarily enjoy. The treaty can cease to be in force without in any way affecting the continuance of the boundary'.[64] International law aims to protect the stability of borders. Moreover, it is often argued that human rights treaties should remain in force on the territory as well, in order to prevent individuals from losing the acquired protection under such treaties following a change in statehood.[65] However, while the continued application of human rights treaties in cases of state succession may well be desirable from a moral perspective, a customary norm of international law has not emerged yet in this respect.

4   Right to Self-Determination

In the process of state creation, the right to self-determination plays a prominent role. As was noted before, many of today's independent states have emerged during the decolonization process or as a result of the dissolution of states. It was also explained that some new states have been created by means of secession, either with or without the consent of the parent state. In all instances, the right to self-determination of peoples is relevant.[66] Common Article 1(1) of the ICCPR and the International Covenant on Economic, Social and Cultural Rights stipulates that by virtue of this right, all peoples are entitled to 'freely determine their political status and freely pursue their economic, social and cultural development'.[67] The significance of the right to self-determination, however, is by no means limited to the creation of new states. The right has two dimensions: one external, the other internal. While the external dimension was most prominent in the context of decolonization, today, the right to self-determination first and foremost must be implemented internally, within the borders of a sovereign state.

a   *Decolonization Process*

The UN Charter refers to 'the principle of equal rights and self-determination of peoples' as one of the principal purposes of the UN.[68] Although the inclusion of the principle in the UN Charter was an important step in the development of the notion,[69] its legal status and

---

[63] Vienna Convention on Succession of States in Respect of Treaties arts 11–12.

[64] *Case concerning the Territorial Dispute (Libyan Arab Jamahiriya v Chad)* (Judgment) [1994] ICJ Rep 6, para 73.

[65] See, for instance, Human Rights Committee 'General Comment 26: Continuity of Obligations' (1997) UN Doc. CCPR/C/Rev.1/Add.8/Rev.1, para 4. On this topic more in general, see Menno T Kamminga, 'State Succession in Respect of Human Rights Treaties' (1996) 7 European Journal of International Law 469.

[66] See, in general, Antonio Cassese, *Self-Determination of Peoples: A Legal Reappraisal* (Cambridge University Press 1995).

[67] International Covenant on Economic, Social and Cultural Rights (adopted 16 December 1966, entered into force 3 January 1976) 993 UNTS 3.

[68] UN Charter arts 1(2), 55.

[69] For an early reference to the notion of self-determination in the context of the Aaland Islands, see 'Report of the International Commission of Jurists' (n 39).

content remained ambiguous. Light was shed on this matter in the context of decolonization. The 1960 Declaration on the Granting of Independence to Colonial Countries and Peoples, adopted by the General Assembly in Resolution 1514 (XV), made it clear that the right to self-determination granted all colonized people the right to independence from their metropolitan state (i.e., the colonial power).[70] The ICJ confirmed this in its *South West Africa* advisory opinion, as it held the existence of the right to self-determination as a norm of international law and noted that colonial rule constituted a violation of this right.[71] Moreover, in the *East Timor* case, the ICJ acknowledged that the right to self-determination is one of the fundamental principles of international law and has an *erga omnes* character.[72] This means that the obligation to respect the right to self-determination is owed towards the international community as a whole, and that all states can therefore invoke the norm.[73]

The right to self-determination functioned as an important tool during the decolonization process in the 1960s and 1970s, when more than eighty former colonies gained independence. It even acquired customary law status during this process as a result of the strong *opinio juris* on the matter and widespread practice. At present, there are seventeen remaining territories that are still to be decolonized on the basis of the right to self-determination, including Western Sahara and the Falkland Islands.[74]

b   *Contemporary Meaning*

Beyond the context of decolonization, many groups around the world have invoked the right to self-determination. Examples are the Catalans, the Kosovo-Albanians, the Kurds, and the Scots. An important question, thus concerns the meaning of the right to self-determination outside the colonial context. Does it actually imply a right to establish an independent state for non-colonial peoples, as is often claimed? In *Reference re Secession of Quebec*, the Supreme Court of Canada explained the contemporary meaning of the right to self-determination.[75] In doing so, it distinguished between an internal and an external dimension of this right.

The Supreme Court of Canada observed that '[t]he recognized sources of international law establish that the right to self-determination of a people is normally fulfilled through internal self-determination – a people's pursuit of its political, economic, social and cultural development within the framework of an existing state'.[76] The right to self-determination should, thus first and foremost be realized in the relationship between peoples and their government. This essentially requires two elements: first, the presence of a government that

---

[70] Declaration on the Granting of Independence to Colonial Countries and Peoples (adopted 14 December 1960) UNGA Res 1514 (XV).
[71] *Legal Consequences for States of the Continued Presence of South Africa in Namibia (South West Africa) notwithstanding Security Council Resolution 276 (1970)* (Advisory Opinion) [1971] ICJ Rep 16, 31.
[72] *Case Concerning East Timor (Portugal v Australia)* [1995] (Judgment) ICJ Rep 90, para 29. See also *South West Africa* advisory opinion (n 71); *Legal Consequences of the Construction of a Wall in the Occupied Palestinian Territory* (Advisory Opinion) [2004] ICJ Rep 136, para 88.
[73] *Case concerning the Barcelona Traction, Light and Power Company, Limited (Belgium v Spain)* (2nd Phase) [1970] ICJ Rep 3, para 33.
[74] For a list of these non-self-governing territories, see <www.un.org/dppa/decolonization/en/nsgt>.
[75] See *Reference re Secession of Quebec* (n 13).   [76] ibid, para 126.

represents the people inhabiting the territory without any distinction, and second, participation of the people in the political decision-making process of the state.[77] Federalism and arrangements for autonomy are instruments that may be used to facilitate this, as they offer a degree of self-government for groups within the state.[78]

The right to external self-determination; however, 'only arises in the most extreme of cases and, even then, under carefully defined circumstances'.[79] It applies to peoples subjected to alien subjugation, domination, or exploitation. For these groups, the right to external self-determination may lead to the creation of an independent state, but they may also choose to associate or integrate with an existing state, or opt for any other political status that is based on the free will of the people. This follows from the 1970 Declaration on Principles of International Law concerning Friendly Relations and Co-operation among States in Accordance with the Charter of the UN (Friendly Relations Declaration), which reflects customary international law.[80] This declaration refers to a right to self-determination that is not limited to the context of decolonization. It was with this more general notion of self-determination in mind that the ICJ concluded in its advisory opinion on the *Legal Consequences of a Wall in the Occupied Palestinian Territory* that Israel's occupation of the Palestinian territory violated the right to self-determination of the Palestinian people.[81]

c *Remedial Secession*

Whether the right to external self-determination also applies to peoples who are not subjected to alien subjugation, domination, or exploitation, is highly questionable. International law generally prioritizes the protection of the state's territorial integrity and political unity over the right to self-determination of peoples. This is also reflected in the so-called safeguard clause of the Friendly Relations Declaration, which stipulates:

Nothing in the foregoing paragraphs [concerning the right to self-determination] shall be construed as authorizing or encouraging any action, which would dismember or impair, totally or in part, the territorial integrity or political unity of sovereign and independent States conducting themselves in compliance with the principle of equal rights and self-determination of peoples as described above and thus possessed of a government representing the whole people belonging to the territory without distinction as to race, creed or colour.[82]

This clause generally confines the implementation of the right to self-determination to its internal dimension. No general right to (unilateral) secession exists under international law.

---

[77] See 'Conference on Security and Co-operation in Europe: Final Act' (1 August 1975) 14 ILM 1292, Principle VII.
[78] On various arrangements, see Marc Weller, *Escaping the Self-Determination Trap* (Martinus Nijhoff 2009).
[79] *Reference re Secession of Quebec* (n 13), para 126.
[80] Declaration on Principles of International Law concerning Friendly Relations and Co-operation among States in Accordance with the Charter of the UN (24 October 1970) UNGA Res 2625 (XXV), Principle V.
[81] *Legal Consequences of the Construction of a Wall in the Occupied Palestinian Territory* advisory opinion (n 72), paras 115–22.
[82] Declaration on Principles of International Law concerning Friendly Relations and Co-operation among States (n 80), Principle V, para 7. A similar clause can be found in Vienna Declaration and Programme of Action (as adopted by the World Conference on Human Rights) (12 July 1993) UN Doc A/CONF.157/23, pt 1, para 2.

Yet, it is increasingly argued that a right to external self-determination may arise in situations where a people suffers from serious injustices committed by its own government, such as severe oppression and gross human rights violations. In those exceptional circumstances, a right to external self-determination would emerge as a remedy of last resort. This contested idea is referred to as the doctrine of 'remedial secession'[83] and is mainly based on a reversed (*a contrario*) reading of the safeguard clause.

There are only a few judicial opinions in which the question of a right to remedial secession has been addressed. In the aforementioned *Reference re Secession of Quebec* case, the Supreme Court of Canada was asked whether the Canadian province of Quebec would have a right to secede unilaterally from Canada under international law. The Court acknowledged that in literature, it had been contended that 'when a people is blocked from the meaningful exercise of its right of self-determination internally, it is entitled, as a last resort, to exercise it by secession'. The Court determined that such a right would only apply to the most extreme cases, but also stressed that it remains 'unclear whether this ... actually reflects an established international law standard'.[84] A more recent example of a case in which the question of a right to remedial secession was touched upon, is the *Kosovo* advisory opinion.[85] In this case, the UN General Assembly had asked the ICJ whether Kosovo's declaration of independence of 17 February 2008 was in accordance with international law. The Court interpreted the question put before it restrictively and avoided expressing itself on the legal consequences of the declaration and whether or not Kosovo had become a state under international law. It also avoided any clarification of the contemporary meaning of the right to self-determination and the existence of a right to remedial secession under international law, as it merely noted that states taking part in the advisory proceedings had expressed 'radically different views' on these issues.[86] Likewise, state practice does not display much evidence for the existence of such a right. So, while perhaps appealing from a moral perspective, a right to remedial secession is not accepted under present-day international law.[87]

5   Concluding Remarks

In the course of the twenty-first century, the circle of international legal subjects has expanded to include actors other than states. International organizations, (groups of) individuals, and even multinational corporations have obtained certain capabilities under international law and the inclusion of additional subjects in the future is by no means precluded. These developments do not mean; however, that states have lost their

---

[83] This idea was first coined by Lee Buchheit and Antonio Cassese. See Lee C Buchheit, *Secession: The Legitimacy of Self-Determination* (Yale University Press 1978) 221–2; Cassese (n 66) 118.

[84] *Reference re Secession of Quebec* (n 13), paras 132–5.

[85] For an in-depth discussion of various aspects of this advisory opinion, see Marko Milanović and Michael Wood (eds), *The Law and Politics of the Kosovo Advisory Opinion* (Oxford University Press 2015).

[86] *Kosovo* advisory opinion (n 53), para 82.

[87] See also Simone F van den Driest, 'Crimea's Separation from Ukraine: An Analysis of the Right to Self-Determination and (Remedial) Secession in International Law' (2015) 62 *Netherlands International Law Review* 329, 340–9.

prominence in the international legal system. On the contrary: states are still the main subjects of international law and the only subjects with full legal capacity. Many of today's states emerged in the context of the decolonization process and as a result of the dissolution of states following the end of the Cold War. Over the past decade, such landslides in the landscape of sovereign states have ceased and new states only emerge incidentally. While the composition of the international community of states is by no means static, it has stabilized to a certain extent. This stability, of course, is only relative. As ethnic conflict flares in various corners of the world and nationalist movements continue to strive for more self-government, there will always be groups seeking to establish new, independent states. With a contemporary focus on internal self-determination, limits posed on the exercise of external self-determination, and no acceptance of a right to remedial secession at present, however, international law does not necessarily grant such groups a legal right to create a state. Yet, while not a right, secession is in principle not prohibited under international law either.[88] As long as (aspirant) states are not created in violation of fundamental norms of international law, such as the prohibition on the use of force, are granted widespread recognition by third states, and are possibly even admitted to the UN, these entities may well be able to successfully function as states within the international legal system, with all the rights, obligations, and competences that are attached to this status.

Recommended Reading

Andrea Bianchi (ed), *Non-State Actors and International Law* (Ashgate 2009).
James R Crawford, *The Creation of States in International Law* (2nd edn, Oxford University Press 2006).
Hersch Lauterpacht, *Recognition in International Law* (Cambridge University Press 2012).
Marko Milanović and Michael Wood (eds), *The Law and Politics of the Kosovo Advisory Opinion* (Oxford University Press 2015).
Janne E Nijman, *The Concept of International Legal Personality: An Inquiry into the History and Theory of International Law* (TMC Asser Press 2004).
James Summers, *Peoples and International Law* (2nd rev edn, Brill/Nijhoff 2014).
Christian Walter, Antje von Ungern-Sternberg, and Kavus Abushov (eds), *Self-Determination and Secession in International Law* (Oxford University Press 2013).

---

[88] See Crawford (n 33) 390; Lauterpacht (n 48) 8.

4

Law of Treaties

Cecily Rose

1   Introduction

Treaties are international agreements that create legal obligations for states, as well as other actors like international organizations. The growth of treaties in the field of public international law has been particularly extensive since the end of the Second World War, when international law and international institutions were seen, in part, as ways to prevent future wars. Certain branches of the field, such as international environmental law and international investment law, are now dominated by a substantial collection of treaties, while customary international law plays a relatively minor or secondary role. Treaties in the field of public international law also range enormously. They can take the form of bilateral agreements between two states, or multilateral agreements, in which most or nearly all states participate. They can be regional in character, or limited to members of a particular international organization. Treaties can also deal with an endless variety of subject matters, including climate change, maritime boundaries, human rights, organized crime, and diplomatic immunity. In addition, treaties can play a range of functions. They may have a primarily law-making function, which involves developing the law or codifying existing customary law. But treaties may also establish a legal framework for future law-making, or create an international organization for future cooperation.

Although public international law consists of a vast body of treaties that range enormously, all treaties are governed by certain fundamental rules, known as the law of treaties. The law of treaties may determine, for example, when a treaty comes into force, its scope of application, the interpretation of its language, and when its operation ceases. The law of treaties does not contain substantive or 'primary rules' on the environment or human rights, for example, but instead embodies the ground rules or 'secondary rules' that apply to treaties. The law of treaties is therefore general in character, meaning that the same rules apply to all treaties, regardless of their character, subject matter, or function. This chapter focuses on the rules set out in the 1969 Vienna Convention on the Law of Treaties (VCLT), which is the most important, though not the only, instrument that deals with the law of treaties.[1] The provisions of the VCLT represent the most useful focal point for this

---

[1] VCLT (adopted 23 May 1969, entered into force 27 January 1980) 1155 UNTS 331 (VCLT). See also VCLT between States and International Organizations or between International Organizations (adopted 21 March 1986, not yet in force) 25 ILM 543;

introduction to the law of treaties because much of the VCLT reflects customary international law, which is binding on all states, even those not party to the VCLT; and the VCLT formed the basis for subsequent, more specific instruments governing treaty law.

This chapter begins with the concept of a treaty (Section 2), before discussing treaty-making, with a particular focus on the conclusion of treaties, their entry into force, and reservations to treaties (Section 3). The chapter then delves into how treaties operate, namely their scope of application and their interpretation (Section 4). Finally, this chapter looks at the invalidity, suspension, and termination of treaties (Section 5).

2   What Is a Treaty?

Treaties are a source of public international law. Article 38 of the Statute of the International Court of Justice (ICJ) lists not only 'international conventions' (i.e., treaties), but also customary international law and general principles of international law, as well as 'judicial decisions and the teachings of the most highly qualified publicists of the various nations', which form subsidiary sources of public international law (see Chapter 2). While no hierarchy exists among treaties, custom and general principles as sources of international law, much of the field of public international law is now dominated by treaty law, which can therefore be seen as the most significant source of law in practice. In some branches of public international law, such as human rights law or the law on the use of force, treaty law exists parallel to customary rules, which may or may not be identical to the corresponding treaty law.[2]

The definition of a treaty set out in the VCLT is narrower than the actual range of treaties in practice. This chapter nevertheless focuses on the VCLT's conception of a treaty, because of the central role that this Convention has played in codifying and progressively developing the law on treaties and because its relatively narrow definition provides a useful starting point for studying the law of treaties. According to the VCLT, the term treaty 'means an international agreement concluded between States in written form and governed by international law, whether embodied in a single instrument or in two or more related instruments and whatever its particular designation'.[3] Each element of this definition merits some discussion.

First, in order for a treaty to fall within the scope of the VCLT, it must be between states. All states possess the capacity to enter into treaties, regardless of their size or power.[4] The VCLT's definition of a treaty excludes agreements that are concluded between a state and a non-state actor, such as an international organization or a rebel group, or between two non-state actors. Treaties do indeed exist between states and international organizations, or between international organizations, but they are regulated by a different set of rules that are

Vienna Convention on Succession of States in Respect of Treaties (adopted 23 August 1978, entered into force 6 November 1996) 1946 UNTS 3.
[2] *Case concerning Military and Paramilitary Activities in and against Nicaragua (Nicaragua v United States of America)* (Merits) [1986] ICJ Rep 14, para 178.
[3] VCLT art 2(1)(a).   [4] VCLT art 6.

specific to treaties between states and international organizations or between international organizations.[5]

Second, treaties within the scope of the VCLT must be written as opposed to oral agreements. While an oral agreement could constitute a treaty in certain circumstances, such an agreement would be governed not by the VCLT, but by customary rules. Third, the VCLT applies only to international agreements that are 'governed by international law', as opposed to domestic law. When two states conclude an agreement whereby one state purchases property in the territory of the other state, to be used for a diplomatic mission, for example, such an agreement would be governed by the domestic laws of the state in which the property is purchased, like other real estate transactions between private actors.[6]

Fourth, the VCLT does not require treaties to take a particular form, but instead adopts a flexible approach whereby a treaty may be 'embodied in a single instrument or in two or more related instruments'. The VCLT's flexibility with respect to the form of treaties was litigated before the ICJ in a case between Qatar and Bahrain, both of which are parties to the VCLT.[7] The dispute between Qatar and Bahrain concerned sovereignty over certain islands and shoals in the Arabian/Persian Gulf, and the delimitation of their maritime boundary. In 1990, the Foreign Ministers of Bahrain, Qatar, and Saudi Arabia signed minutes that recorded their consultations, including their agreement as to the circumstances in which the dispute between Qatar and Bahrain could be submitted to the ICJ.[8] In litigation before the Court, however, Bahrain contended that the minutes did not constitute an international agreement (i.e., a treaty). The Court rejected this argument and found that the minutes did not just record discussions between the foreign ministers, but also set out the legal commitments to which the parties had consented.[9] The minutes, thereby constituted an international agreement that created rights and obligations under international law.[10] In addition, the Court noted that a 1987 exchange of letters also constituted an international agreement creating rights and obligations for Qatar and Bahrain.[11] This case shows that under the VCLT, the form of written agreements is unimportant, so long as the agreement embodies a legal, as opposed to a political commitment, and otherwise meets the VCLT's definition of a treaty.

Finally, the VCLT also takes a flexible approach with respect to the title or 'designation' of instruments that fall within its scope. An international agreement may qualify as a treaty under the VCLT regardless of 'its particular designation'. In practice, states use a wide range of designations to refer to treaties, including the terms convention, protocol, charter, pact, agreement, concordat, memorandum of understanding, and joint communiqué.[12] As the case between Qatar and Bahrain demonstrates, in some instances a treaty may have no

---

[5] These rules are embodied in the VCLT between States and International Organizations or between International Organizations (n 1), which adapts the VCLT's provisions to international organizations. This convention is not yet in force, but much of it represents customary international law. Anthony Aust, 'Vienna Convention on the Law of Treaties (1969)' in *Max Planck Encyclopedia of Public International Law* (last updated June 2006), paras 8–9.

[6] Malgosia Fitzmaurice, 'Treaties' in *Max Planck Encyclopedia of Public International Law* (last updated February 2010), para 19.

[7] *Case concerning Maritime Delimitation and Territorial Questions between Qatar and Bahrain (Qatar v Bahrain)* (Jurisdiction and Admissibility) [1994] ICJ Rep 112.

[8] ibid, para 20.   [9] ibid, para 25.   [10] ibid, para 25.   [11] ibid, para 30.   [12] Fitzmaurice (n 6), para 16.

particular designation, such as in circumstances where an exchange of letters constitutes a treaty.

While the VCLT takes a flexible approach to matters of form and titles, many international agreements will, nevertheless, fall outside its scope. Oral agreements, agreements between states and non-state actors or between non-state actors, and agreements governed by domestic law may constitute treaties, but they are not, technically speaking, governed by the VCLT. In addition, treaties that predate the VCLT's entry into force in 1980 also fall outside its scope, as the VCLT does not apply retroactively to treaties concluded before its entry into force.[13] Yet, because many of the VCLT's provisions reflect customary international law, its provisions still represent useful touchstones for judges, lawyers, and others involved in applying treaty law in practice.

3 Treaty Making

The creation of a treaty typically begins with negotiations, which can take the form of small, informal discussions; large, formal international conferences; and everything in between these extremes. Negotiations can be conducted orally or in writing, or through some combination thereof.[14] While states themselves may act as the 'drivers' behind treaty negotiations, international organizations sometimes play key roles in preparing draft treaty provisions.[15] In addition, an important role has historically been played by the International Law Commission (ILC), which was created in 1947 by the United Nations (UN) General Assembly for the purposes of codifying and progressively developing international law.[16] The ILC, which consists of thirty-four members who have been nominated by states and elected by the General Assembly, has prepared draft treaty texts on a number of subjects, including the law of treaties.[17] While non-governmental organizations (NGOs) do not formally participate in treaty negotiations or in the treaties themselves, in some instances NGOs have played important roles in supporting and influencing treaty negotiations.[18] After negotiations have concluded, the states that participated in negotiations then adopt the text of the treaty – a step that is distinct from expressing consent to be bound by the treaty.[19]

a Expressing Consent to Be Bound by a Treaty

Once treaty negotiations have yielded a final text upon which all parties agree, each state must express its consent to be bound by the treaty.[20] The importance of consent in the

---

[13] VCLT art 4. [14] Fitzmaurice (n 6), para 31.

[15] ibid, paras 32, 35. See, for example, the World Bank's drafting of the International Convention on the Settlement of Investment Disputes (ICSID) between States and Nationals of other States (adopted 18 March 1965, entered into force 14 October 1966) 575 UNTS 159.

[16] Statute of the International Law Commission (adopted 21 November 1947) UNGA Res 174(II), art 1(1).

[17] See VCLT; Statute of the ILC arts 2–3.

[18] See, for example, 'Ottowa' Convention on the Prohibition of the Use, Stockpiling, Production and Transfer of Anti-Personnel Mines and on their Destructions (adopted 18 September 1997, entered into force 1 March 1999) 2056 UNTS 211.

[19] VCLT art 9. [20] VCLT art 11.

context of treaty-making is a function of state sovereignty, and in particular the idea that states cannot be bound by a treaty to which they never consented. Article 11 of the VCLT provides for the expression of consent through a wide range of methods, namely 'signature, exchange of instruments constituting a treaty, ratification, acceptance, approval or accession, or by any other means if so agreed'.[21] By providing various methods for expressing consent, the VCLT allows states to determine which method of consent best suits their interests.[22] Article 11 provides for the swift conclusion of treaties by signature, where this is desired by states, while also providing for the involvement of domestic legislative bodies in approving treaties, where this is important for reasons of democratic legitimacy.

In some cases, a signature by a state representative is a sufficient expression of the state's consent to be bound by the treaty.[23] A signature to a treaty represents the simplest and quickest way for a state to express its consent to be bound by an agreement, without, for example, the need for subsequent ratification by a legislative body, a process which can be cumbersome and time-consuming.[24] Although state representatives regularly express consent through signature, it is only available as a method for expressing consent where the treaty or the parties so provide, or where the parties intended for this to be the case.[25] The term 'executive agreement' is used in some domestic legal systems to refer to treaties to which the state has consented through a signature, without the involvement of the domestic legislature in ratifying the treaty.[26] In the United States, for example, executive agreements play an important role because the ratification of treaties by the US Senate requires a supermajority of two-thirds of the Senate, which can represent a serious impediment to the ability of the United States to become a party to treaties.[27] As a result, consent by signature is commonly used by the US executive branch, and this practice has been acknowledged by the legislature, and even specifically authorized by it in the case of trade agreements.[28]

In contrast to signature as a method for consent, ratification allows domestic legislative bodies to play a key role in consenting to a treaty that has been negotiated by the state. Ratification as a method for consent thereby privileges the involvement of legislators over simplicity or speed. According to the VCLT, the term 'ratification' refers to an 'international act' through which a state establishes 'on an international plane its consent to be bound by a treaty'.[29] Such an international act could involve, for example, depositing an

---

[21] VCLT art 11. An exchange of instruments could entail an exchange of letters, as in the exchange of letters between Qatar and Bahrain. See Section 2.

[22] Jan Klabbers, 'Treaties, Conclusion and Entry into Force' in *Max Planck Encyclopedia of Public International Law* (last updated September 2006), para 5.

[23] See VCLT art 7 on full powers.

[24] Cédric Van Assche, 'Article 12: Consent to Be Bound by a Treaty Expressed by Signature' in Olivier Corten and Pierre Klein (eds), *The Vienna Conventions on the Law of Treaties: A Commentary* (Oxford University Press 2011) 201–11.

[25] VCLT art 12.

[26] Fred Morrison, 'Executive Agreements' in *Max Planck Encyclopedia of Public International Law* (last updated May 2007), para 2.

[27] US Constitution art II.

[28] 1972 Case-Zablocki Act, 1 US Code s 112b. From the perspective of US domestic legal system, the 2015 Paris Agreement on climate change is an executive agreement. Paris Agreement (adopted 12 December 2015, entered into force 4 November 2016) registration no 54113.

[29] VCLT art 2(1)(b).

'instrument of ratification' with the depository for the treaty, which could be another state or an international organization.[30] The process leading up to the 'international act' of ratification involves domestic procedures, such as those through which a legislative body consents to a treaty that has been negotiated by the executive branch. Though ratification is, by definition, an international act, it hinges on domestic procedures for consent, which each State determines for itself. In common parlance, the term ratification is often used in reference to these domestic procedures, even though the VCLT specifically defines it as an 'international act'. Approval and acceptance are similar to ratification, but represent less common methods for consent, which the VCLT lists in Article 14, but otherwise does not specifically define.[31]

Along with signature and ratification, accession constitutes a principal method for expressing consent to be bound.[32] Accession is applicable where a state wishes to become a party to a treaty at a relatively late stage, after the prescribed period for signature and/or ratification has expired, which will typically be the case by the time the treaty has come into force.[33] Accession as a method of consent for such latecomers allows for consent through a single act, instead of the two-step signature and ratification process that may have been followed by the states that participated in the negotiations and became parties within the time-period prescribed by the treaty. It usually happens after the treaty has entered into force.

b   *Entry into Force*

By expressing their consent to be bound by a treaty, states give binding force to their agreement. In other words, a treaty only enters into force once states have consented to be bound by it. A treaty's entry into force is often governed by provisions specifically set out in the treaty itself.[34] Where this is not the case, then the treaty enters into force 'as soon as consent to be bound by the treaty has been established for all the negotiating States', in accordance with Article 24 of the VCLT.[35] Multilateral treaties typically require a certain number of ratifications for their entry into force. For example, the 2004 UN Convention on Jurisdictional Immunities of States and Their Property provides that thirty instruments of ratification, acceptance, approval, or accession must be deposited with the Secretary-General of the UN in order for the Convention to enter into force.[36] To date, only twenty-two states have deposited such instruments, with the result that the treaty still has not

---

[30] VCLT art 16.

[31] VCLT art 14(2); Rafãa Ben Achour, Imed Frikha and Mounir Snoussi, 'Article 14' in Corten and Klein (eds) (n 24) 295. Frank Berman and David Bentley, 'Ratification, Accession, Acceptance and Approval, Treaty Succession' in Sir Ivor Roberts (ed), *Satow's Diplomatic Practice* (7th edn, Oxford University Press 2016), sub-s 34.31.

[32] VCTL art 15; Jean-François Marchi, 'Article 15: Consent to Be Bound by a Treaty Expressed by Accession' in Corten and Klein (n 24) 309.

[33] See, for example, UN Convention on the Jurisdictional Immunities of States and Their Property (adopted 2 December 2004, not yet in force) UN Doc A/59/508, arts 28–29; James Devaney, 'Article 28' in Roger O'Keefe and Christian J Tams (eds), *The United Nations Convention on Jurisdictional Immunities of States and Their Property: A Commentary* (Oxford University Press 2013) 395–6.

[34] VCLT art 24(1).   [35] VCLT art 24(2).

[36] UN Convention on the Jurisdictional Immunities of States and Their Property art 30.

entered into force, nearly twenty years after its adoption, for reasons that remain open to speculation.[37] Although the Convention has not yet entered into force, it has nevertheless played a significant role in clarifying and crystalizing customary international law on state immunities.[38]

As the UN Convention on Jurisdictional Immunities of States and Their Property demonstrates, the period between the adoption and signature of a treaty and its entry into force can be prolonged. Although some multilateral treaties enter into force just a few years after they are adopted and opened for signature,[39] the entry into force of key multilateral treaties in some branches of public international law has been delayed by a decade or longer.[40] States may face domestic political resistance to ratifying the treaty at issue, they may be waiting for a critical mass of states to participate in the treaty before doing so themselves, or they may be concerned about whether a given treaty corresponds with customary international law or domestic laws on the subject. Where a treaty requires states parties to amend or enact new domestic legislation or regulations, the time needed to make such legislative or regulatory changes could also help to explain delays in a treaty's entry into force.

Article 18 of the VCLT anticipates such delays, and provides that states have an obligation not to defeat the object and purpose of a treaty prior to its entry into force. This obligation to refrain from acts that run contrary to a treaty's object and purpose applies, for example, when a state has signed a treaty subject to consent through ratification. In addition, this obligation applies when a state has expressed consent to be bound to a treaty that has not yet entered into force, due, for example, to an insufficient number of ratifications. The United States signing and subsequent 'unsigning' of the 1998 Rome Statute of the International Criminal Court (ICC) provides an infamous example of Article 18's practical implications. The United States actively participated in the drafting of the Rome Statute, despite domestic opposition to the prospect of members of the US military possibly being prosecuted by the ICC. Although the United States signed the Rome Statute in December 2000, at the end of the Clinton administration, the executive branch never sent it to the US Senate for its approval, which would very likely not have been forthcoming. In 2002, the Bush administration 'unsigned' or renounced the Rome Statute, thereby signalling its intention not to ratify it.

This act of 'unsigning' also freed the United States from its obligation under Article 18 of the VCLT not to defeat the Rome Statute's object and purpose, which could be described as 'ending impunity for the perpetrators of the most serious crimes of concern to the international community'.[41] After 'unsigning', the United States 'launched a worldwide campaign' to conclude bilateral treaties that obliged other states not to surrender or transfer

---

[37] For a detailed discussion of the various possible explanations, see Roger O'Keefe and Christian J Tams, 'General Introduction' in O'Keefe and Tams (n 33) XL–XLI.

[38] ibid XLI.

[39] See, for example, Rome Statute of the ICC (adopted 17 July 1998, entered into force 1 July 2002) 2187 UNTS 3.

[40] See, for example, International Covenant on Civil and Political Rights (adopted 16 December 1966, entered into force 23 March 1976) 999 UNTS 171 (ICCPR); UN Convention on the Law of the Sea (adopted 10 December 1982, entered into force 16 November 1994) 1833 UNTS 3.

[41] Rome Statute, preamble, para 5.

US nationals facing an ICC arrest warrant to the ICC (or to a third country for the purpose of surrender to the ICC), but instead to extradite such US nationals to the United States.[42] The United States ultimately concluded more than 100 of these bilateral immunity agreements.[43] Had the United States remained a signatory to the Rome Statute, then this campaign would have brought the United States into conflict with its obligation not to defeat the object and purpose of the Rome Statute, as these agreements were aimed at preventing the ICC from gaining custody of and prosecuting accused persons of US nationality.

c   *Reservations*

At the stage when a state expresses its consent to be bound by a treaty, reservations allow the state to limit the extent to which it commits to be bound by the treaty's provisions. Such reservations can exclude or modify the effect of a treaty provision for that state. The VCLT's provisions on reservations attempt to strike a balance between universality and integrity.[44] On the one hand, the VCLT's provisions work towards ensuring wide or even universal participation in treaties by permitting reservations through which states can 'carve out' provisions to which they do not wish to be bound. On the other hand, the VCLT seeks to ensure that reservations do not undermine the treaty's integrity, which could be threatened where states have 'carved out' provisions that are essential for the goals of the treaty. The VCLT defines a reservation as a 'unilateral statement, however phrased or named, made by a State when signing, ratifying, accepting, approving or acceding to a treaty, whereby it purports to exclude or modify the legal effect of certain provisions of the treaty in their application to that State'.[45] In practice, states can enter reservations regarding a wide range of substantive treaty provisions, such as provisions concerning the treaty's scope of application, as well as procedural provisions, such as dispute settlement clauses that provide for the submission of disputes about the treaty's interpretation or application to an international court or tribunal.

According to the VCLT's definition of a reservation, the designation that a state gives to a unilateral statement does not determine whether or not the statement constitutes a reservation. Instead, the substance of the statement is determinative. In some instances, statements that have been labelled by a state as a 'declaration' or an interpretive 'statement' have been found to constitute reservations, because they had the effect of excluding or modifying a treaty provision.[46] Normally, such declarations or interpretive statements are meant to be explanatory in character. Instead of excluding or modifying the effect of a treaty provision, as a reservation does, a declaration explains how the state understands its treaty obligation.[47] A state might enter a declaration for the purpose of advocating a particular

---

[42] Eszter Kirs, 'Bilateral Immunity Agreements' in *Max Planck Encyclopedia of Public International Law* (last updated January 2019), para 3.
[43] ibid, para 14.   [44] Fitzmaurice (n 6), para 59.   [45] VCLT art 2(1)(d). The VCLT does not govern declarations.
[46] *Belilos v Switzerland* App no 10328/8 (ECtHR, 29 April 1988).
[47] ILC, 'Guide to Practice on Reservations to Treaties' (2011) UN Doc A/66/10, guideline 1.3.

interpretation of a given treaty provision, or in order to inform other states parties of the position it would take in any future dispute about a given provision.[48]

Generally speaking, states are free to enter reservations to treaties, but this general rule is subject to a number of exceptions, set out in Article 19 of the VCLT. First, a treaty could explicitly prohibit a reservation, such as a reservation to a dispute settlement or treaty monitoring provision. Second, a treaty could implicitly prohibit a reservation by permitting only specified reservations, not including the reservation at issue. Finally, a reservation could be incompatible with the treaty's object and purpose. When treaties, such as the 1948 Genocide Convention, do not include any rules that establish which reservations are prohibited or permitted, the exception concerning incompatibility with the treaty's object and purpose takes on particular significance, which in the case of the Genocide Convention is to 'prevent and to punish' the international crime of genocide.[49] The ILC's 2011 Guide to Practice on Reservations to Treaties contains non-binding guidelines that both clarify the existing custom and seek to progressively develop the law with respect to the issue of impermissible reservations, such as those that are incompatible with the treaty's object and purpose.[50]

One fundamental issue addressed by the ILC guide concerns the identification of a treaty's object and purpose – the benchmark for assessing whether a reservation is permissible. According to the ILC's guide, a treaty's object and purpose 'is to be determined in good faith, taking account of the terms of the treaty in their context, in particular the title and the preamble of the treaty'. In addition, those involved in assessing the compatibility of reservations (e.g., judges or government lawyers), may also have recourse to the *travaux préparatoires* (the drafting history of the treaty), the circumstances of the treaty's conclusion, and, where appropriate, the parties' subsequent practice.[51] The ILC has further explained that a reservation is incompatible with a treaty's object and purpose 'if it affects an essential element of the treaty that is necessary to its general tenour, in such a way that the reservation impairs the *raison d'être* of the treaty'.[52] Reservations concerning procedural provisions on dispute settlement or treaty monitoring may, for example, be incompatible with a treaty's object and purpose if these procedural provisions are critical for the efficacy of the treaty's substantive provisions.[53]

Another fundamental issue with respect to reservations concerns their legal consequences. The VCLT deals with the issue of legal effect by allowing other states parties to accept or object to a reservation. While states are, as a general rule, free to make reservations to treaties, other states parties are not obliged to accept such reservations. The response of other states parties to a reservation may determine whether the reservation

---

[48] Iain Cameron, 'Treaties, Declarations of Interpretation' in *Max Planck Encyclopedia of Public International Law* (last updated March 2007), para 8.

[49] Convention on the Prevention and Punishment of the Crime of Genocide (adopted 9 December 1948, entered into force 12 January 1951) 78 UNTS 277; *Reservations to the Convention on the Prevention and Punishment of the Crime of Genocide (Advisory Opinion)* [1951] ICJ Rep 15.

[50] The ILC's guide (n 47) was the subject of work by the ILC between 1993 and 2011.

[51] ILC (n 47), guideline 3.1.5.1. Subsequent practice refers to the application of the treaty by states parties which establishes their agreement regarding its interpretation. VCLT art 31(3)(b).

[52] ILC (n 47), guideline 3.1.5.   [53] ibid, guideline 3.1.5.7.

has its intended effect of excluding or modifying a given provision. The possible responses to a treaty reservation can be negative or positive, and explicit or implicit. In the context of a multilateral treaty, a reservation made by one state can be met with silence or with explicit rejection or acceptance by one or more states parties. According to Article 20(5) of the VCLT, silence by other states may be deemed acceptance at the end of a twelve-month period.[54] In the case of acceptance, a reservation has the legal effect of modifying the provision of the treaty to which the reservation relates, as soon as at least one other state has accepted the reservation.[55] Such a modification of the treaty; however, exists only in the relations between the state that has made the reservation and the state that accepts the reservation, not between the accepting states themselves.[56]

If, for example, Kenya enters a reservation with respect to a multilateral treaty and all other states parties to the treaty accept the reservation (whether implicitly or explicitly), then the reservation has the effect of modifying the treaty provision as between Kenya and the other parties to the treaty. If the Kenyan reservation provides that Kenya is not bound by a particular treaty provision, then the other states that have accepted this reservation are also not bound by that same treaty provision, but only in their relations with Kenya, not in their relations with each other.[57] The reservation, thus applies reciprocally in the relations between Kenya and the states that have accepted it. In situations where some states accept a reservation and others object, then a reservation can create differentiated or 'bilateral' obligations between the state that has entered the reservation, and the other states parties to the treaty, depending on whether they have accepted or rejected the reservation.[58]

In the case of an objection, a reservation will not have its intended legal effect as between the objecting state and the reserving state. As a general rule, an objection to a reservation does not prevent a treaty's entry into force between the state that has made the reservation and the state that has objected to the reservation.[59] Instead, the treaty's entry into force between the reserving and the objecting state would only be precluded when the objecting state has 'definitely expressed' its intention to preclude the treaty's entry into force as between itself and the state that has entered the reservation.[60] This rule, set out in Article 20 of the VCLT, has the consequence of privileging participation in treaties, over the integrity of treaties. States can participate in a treaty while at the same time 'carving out' provisions of the treaty through reservations, and the legal effect of an objection is limited. The provision to which the objection relates does not come into force as between the state that has made the reservation and the state that has objected to it, but the treaty as a whole does come into force between them.

The VCLT does not cover the issue of reservations exhaustively. Questions have persisted, for example, about the legal effect of an invalid reservation—apart from the question of acceptance or rejection by other parties. In other words, what is the legal effect of a reservation that is incompatible with the treaty's object and purpose, or otherwise

---

[54] VCLT art 20(5). The twelve-month period is measured from the date on which the other states received notification or the date on which the accepting state expressed its consent to be bound by the treaty, whichever is later.
[55] VCLT art 20(4)(c).   [56] VCLT art 21(1).   [57] VCLT art 21(2).   [58] Fitzmaurice (n 6), para. 57.   [59] VCLT art 20(4)(b).
[60] VCLT art 20(4)(b).

prohibited by the treaty? The ILC has offered a solution to this issue in its guide, which provides that the state that has entered an invalid reservation remains a party to the treaty, without the benefit of the invalid reservation, unless the state expressly indicates a contrary intention (i.e., an intention not to be bound by the treaty without the benefit of the reservation).[61] The state that has entered the reservation, thus remains a party to the treaty without the benefit of the reservation, or ceases to be bound by the treaty altogether. The ILC envisions treaty monitoring bodies playing a role in assessing whether a given reservation is invalid.[62] Objections by other parties may signal that a given reservation is impermissible, but they do not determine the legal effect of the reservation as valid or invalid.

Qatar's relatively recent accession to the 1966 ICCPR illustrates how the VCLT's rules on reservations operate in practice. In 2018, Qatar became only the third Gulf state to become a party to the ICCPR, a treaty that has otherwise been widely ratified.[63] Qatar's accession to the ICCPR was accompanied by two reservations and five interpretative statements, four of which may be considered reservations because they purport to modify or exclude the effect of provisions of the ICCPR. Qatar's reservations and statements aim, in particular, at modifying or excluding the effect of treaty provisions that conflict with its constitution, Sharia (Islamic) law, and its domestic legislation. Twenty-one states parties to the ICCPR objected to one or more of Qatar's reservations in the year following Qatar's accession to the treaty. Twenty of the twenty-one states parties that entered objections did so because they considered that Qatar's reservations were incompatible with the Covenant's object and purpose, and therefore, invalid.

One of Qatar's reservations, for example, purports to exclude the effect of Article 23(4) of the ICCPR, which concerns the 'equality of rights and responsibilities of spouses as to marriage, during marriage and at its dissolution'. Qatar's reservation provides only that this provision of the ICCPR 'contravenes the Islamic Sharia [law]'. This reservation strikes at one of the core aims of the ICCPR, which is non-discrimination on the basis of sex, as well as other grounds.[64] In seeking to ensure the continued application of Sharia law, Qatar's reservation affects an essential element of the treaty, and may therefore, be regarded as incompatible with its object and purpose. The Human Rights Committee, which is the treaty body that monitors compliance with the ICCPR, can be expected in the future to play a decisive role in determining whether Qatar's reservations and statements do indeed conflict with the object and purpose of the ICCPR, as asserted by twenty of the objecting states parties.[65] If the Human Rights Committee determines that the reservations and statements are invalid, then the question remains whether Qatar will be content to remain a party to the ICCPR without the benefit of these reservations and statements.

---

[61] ILC (n 47), guideline 4.5.3.   [62] ibid.
[63] Kuwait and Bahrain became parties in 1996 and 2006, respectively. As of May 2021, the ICCPR had 173 states parties.
[64] ICCPR art 2(1).   [65] ILC (n 47), guideline 4.5.3.4.

4   Treaties in Operation

a   The Performance and Scope of the Application of Treaties

When a treaty comes into force, the states that have consented to be bound by the treaty are legally obliged to give effect to its provisions. The title of Article 26 of the VCLT reiterates this basic proposition with the Latin maxim *pacta sunt servanda*, meaning 'agreements must be kept'. Article 26 provides that '[e]very treaty in force is binding upon the parties to it and must be performed by them in good faith'. The performance of a treaty could involve many different types of actions (or omissions) by a party, depending on the content of the treaty concerned. States parties may perform their treaty obligations by, for example; implementing or amending domestic legislation, regulations or policies; by executing a transboundary infrastructure project; by extraditing suspects; by training police forces not to torture persons in police custody; or by demarcating a land boundary.

Japan's good faith compliance with the 1946 International Convention on the Regulation of Whaling (ICRW) was at the heart of a case brought to the ICJ in 2010 by Australia against Japan.[66] Australia alleged, among other things, that Japan's scientific whaling programme did not represent a good faith application of Article VIII of the ICRW, which creates an exception to the moratorium on the killing of whales for commercial purposes that was instituted under the ICRW in the 1980s. Soon after the moratorium took effect in 1986, Japan instituted a scientific whaling programme that involved the killing of hundreds of minke whales each year. Although suggestions of bad faith permeated the case, the ICJ's decision that Japan's scientific whaling programme violated its obligations under the Convention was grounded in treaty interpretation and scientific evidence.

States are obliged to perform their treaty obligations regardless of the state of their domestic law. If a state's domestic legislation is in conflict with a treaty obligation, then the state is obliged to repeal, amend, or replace the domestic legislation at issue. According to Article 27 of the VCLT, 'internal law' or domestic legislation that conflicts with a given treaty obligation cannot serve as a justification for the non-performance of an obligation. States are meant to make any necessary legislative changes before their treaty obligations enter into force. Otherwise, a state risks breaching its treaty obligations and engaging its state responsibility (see Chapter 5).[67] In practice; however, domestic law reform efforts may lag behind a state's consent to be bound by a treaty, or the treaty's entry into force. Moreover, assessing whether or not a state is in full compliance with its treaty obligations may be no simple matter. Many treaties; therefore, create a treaty body that is responsible for assessing implementation, and making recommendations about how parties can and should bring themselves into full compliance.[68] In addition to the problems of delayed or partial compliance, ensuring that domestic legislation conforms with international treaty obligations can be especially challenging for federal states in which provinces or states have

---

[66] *Whaling in the Antarctic (Australia v Japan: New Zealand Intervening)* (Judgment) [2014] ICJ Rep 226.
[67] Anthony Aust, 'Pacta Sunt Servanda' in *Max Planck Encyclopedia of Public International Law* (last updated February 2007), para 13.
[68] See, for example, ICCPR's Human Rights Committee.

their own legislative bodies, independent from the federal legislature. According to Article 27 of the VCLT, however, the constitutional or political problems involved in ensuring that provincial laws comply with international treaty obligations cannot serve as a justification for non-compliance.

In principle, the scope of application of a treaty is limited both temporally and territorially. With respect to a treaty's temporal scope of application, Article 28 of the VCLT provides that treaties do not apply retroactively, unless the treaty indicates otherwise. In other words, a treaty does not bind a party with respect to acts, facts, or situations that predate the treaty's entry into force for that party. The ICC's Rome Statute, for example, does not bind a state party before the entry into force of the Rome Statute for that party. The ICC; therefore, cannot exercise jurisdiction over situations that predate the Rome Statute's entry into force in 2002 or that predate the statute's entry into force for a state that became a party after 2002.[69] With respect to the territorial scope of a treaty's application, Article 29 of the VCLT provides that 'a treaty is binding upon each party in respect of its entire territory', unless the treaty indicates a different intention. In other words, states' treaty obligations usually extend only to their own territory, though exceptions exist. Some human rights treaties, for example, protect the rights of people not only in their territory, but also 'under their jurisdiction', a phrase which gives some human rights instruments a limited extraterritorial application (see Chapter 10).[70] In addition, international humanitarian law treaties, which govern the conduct of armed forces, apply regardless of where a state party's armed forces are engaged in combat (see Chapter 12).

The application of a treaty is also limited in the sense that it does not apply to third parties that have not consented to be bound by the treaty at issue. Under Article 34 of the VCLT, a treaty cannot create rights or obligations for a third state that is not a party, at least not without its consent. This rule can be considered the converse of the rule of *pacta sunt servanda*: states that have not consented to a treaty are not bound by it. A right or an obligation for a third party arises only when the parties to the treaty intend for the provision to accord such a right or obligation to a third state, and when the third state consents.[71] Whereas a third state must expressly accept an obligation in writing, the assent of a third state to a right can be presumed, unless the treaty provides otherwise, and 'so long as the contrary is not indicated'.[72]

The 2013–2014 Riyadh Agreements provide an example of a set of treaties that create rights for a third party, in this case Egypt. The Riyadh Agreements consist of three concise treaties that were concluded between the members of the Gulf Cooperation Council, which includes Bahrain, Kuwait, Oman, Qatar, Saudi Arabia, and the United Arab Emirates. The Riyadh Agreements oblige the parties to refrain from interfering not only in each other's internal affairs, but also in the affairs of Egypt, which is not a party to the treaties. The agreements oblige the parties to refrain, in particular, from supporting media activity

---

[69] Rome Statute art 11.
[70] See, for example, Convention for the Protection of Human Rights and Fundamental Freedoms (adopted 4 November 1950, entered into force 3 September 1953) 213 UNTS 221 (European Convention on Human Rights, ECHR) art 1.
[71] VCLT arts 35–6.   [72] VCLT arts 35–6.

directed against Egypt, with special reference to the activities of Al-Jazeera, the media outlet that is based in Qatar. In addition, the Riyadh Agreements oblige the parties to refrain from supporting the Muslim Brotherhood, which they describe as a group that threatens the security and stability of Egypt. Although all parties to the Riyadh Agreements bear these obligations, the Agreements' underlying aim is to curtail Qatar's purported interference in Egypt's internal affairs. Egypt has accordingly argued that while it is not a party to the Riyadh Agreements, it is the intended beneficiary of the obligations assumed by the parties to the treaties, thereby making Egypt a third party bearing rights under the agreements.[73]

b   *The Interpretation of Treaties*

The interpretation of a treaty may be thought of as an art, rather than a science. The VCLT's provisions on treaty interpretation may give the impression that treaty interpretation is typically conducted in a methodical, step-by-step manner, but this is often not entirely the case.[74] Treaty interpretation is carried out by various actors, including government lawyers, officials at international organizations, and judges of domestic and international courts and tribunals. When approaching the task of treaty interpretation, lawyers, officials, and judges tend to gravitate towards one of three main schools of thought on treaty interpretation, all of which are reflected in the VCLT, to varying degrees.[75] One school of thought emphasizes the subjective intention of the parties that drafted the treaty. Another school of thought entails an objective or textual approach, which focuses on the ordinary meaning of the treaty language. Yet another school of thought involves a teleological approach, which focuses on the object and purpose of the treaty. Each of these approaches is reflected in the VCLT's provisions on treaty interpretation, although the objective and teleological approaches are favoured, with the subjective approach playing a secondary role.[76]

The VCLT's provisions on treaty interpretation begin with Article 31(1), which provides that: 'A treaty shall be interpreted in good faith in accordance with the ordinary meaning to be given to the terms of the treaty in their context and in the light of its object and purpose.' The objective or textual approach to treaty interpretation is reflected in this provision's reference to 'the ordinary meaning to be given to the terms in their context'. In addition, the teleological approach to treaty interpretation is reflected in this provision's reference to the treaty's 'object and purpose'. Article 32 of the VCLT assigns the parties' subjective intentions a distinctly secondary or supportive role in treaty interpretation. Treaty interpreters may have recourse to 'supplementary means of interpretation, including the preparatory work of the treaty and the circumstances of its conclusion', but only for certain purposes. Such recourse is limited either to confirming the meaning that results from the

---

[73] *Appeal Relating to the Jurisdiction of the ICAO Council Under Article 84 of the Convention on International Civil Aviation (Bahrain, Egypt, Saudi Arabia and United Arab Emirates v Qatar)* (Judgment) [2020] ICJ General List 173; *Appeal Relating to the Jurisdiction of the ICAO Council Under Article II, Section 2 of the 1944 International Air Services Transit Agreement (Bahrain, Egypt and United Arab Emirates v Qatar)* (Judgment) [2020] ICJ General List 174, paras 23, 38.
[74] VCLT arts 31–2.   [75] Fitzmaurice (n 6), para 87.
[76] Matthias Herdegen, 'Interpretation in International Law' in *Max Planck Encyclopedia of Public International Law* (last updated March 2013), paras 6, 26.

application of Article 31, or to determining the meaning of treaty language when interpretation under Article 31 '(a) leaves the meaning ambiguous or obscure; or (b) leads to
a result which is manifestly absurd or unreasonable'. In other words, the parties intentions
are only meant to confirm or to help clarify the meaning of treaty language, and should not
be the first or primary consideration.

The VCLT's reference to the 'ordinary meaning' of treaty language understood in
'context' reflects the view that where the meaning of words is clear or unambiguous,
then treaty interpreters need not and should not look further.[77] Sometimes this objective
approach to treaty interpretation is carried out in part by confirming that the dictionary
definition of the word or words at issue corresponds with use of the word in the treaty
provision.[78] By further considering the relevant context, interpreters can ensure that the
connection between different parts of a treaty is understood and factored into the interpretation of the language at issue.[79] The relevant context consists not only of a treaty's
preamble and any annexes, but also, for example, any agreement relating to the treaty that
was made by all of the parties in connection with the treaty's conclusion.[80] In addition, the
relevant context may include subsequent agreements and practice among the parties to the
treaty.[81] Article 31(3) refers specifically to subsequent agreements between the parties
regarding the interpretation or application of the treaty, as well as subsequent practice in the
application of the treaty that establishes an agreement among the parties as to its
interpretation.[82] Finally, the relevant context can extend beyond agreements and practice
directly connected to the treaty, to include 'any relevant rules of international law applicable in the relations between the parties'.[83]

The teleological approach to treaty interpretation, which is reflected in the phrase 'object
and purpose', is geared towards ensuring that the interpretation of the language at issue is in
keeping with the larger goal of the treaty. In English, the words 'object and purpose' are
widely regarded as synonymous with each other, and thus do not refer to distinct aspects of
the treaty.[84] Ascertaining a treaty's object and purpose could involve a review of the treaty's
title, its preamble, a particular treaty provision, and/or its drafting history.[85] The teleological approach to treaty interpretation encompasses two more specific approaches to treaty
interpretation, namely the principle of effectiveness and dynamic interpretation. The
principle of effectiveness tends to play an important role in the interpretation of treaties

---

[77] *Competence of the General Assembly for the admission of a State to the United Nations* (Advisory Opinion) [1950] ICJ Rep 4,
para 8.

[78] See, for example, WTO, *United States: Measures Affecting the Cross-Border Supply of Gambling and Betting Services—Report
of the Appellate Body* (7 April 2005) WT/DS285/AB/R, paras 163–7 (use of dictionary definition as a starting point for
interpretation).

[79] Herdegen (n 76), para 12.

[80] VCLT art 31(2)(a). The context may also include 'any instrument which was made by one or more parties in connection with the
conclusion of the treaty and accepted by the other parties as an instrument related to the treaty'. VCLT art 31(2)(b).

[81] VCLT art 31(3)(a), (b).

[82] See, for example, the subsequent practice of member states of the UN with respect to art 27(3) of the Charter of the United
Nations (adopted 26 June 1945, entered into force 24 October 1945) 1 UNTS XVI. *Legal Consequences for States of the
Continued Presence of South Africa in Namibia (South West Africa) notwithstanding Security Council Resolution 276 (1970)*
(Advisory Opinion) [1971] ICJ Rep 16, para 22.

[83] VCLT art 31(3)(c). See, for example, *Case concerning Oil Platforms (Islamic Republic of Iran v United States of America)*
(Merits) [2003] ICJ Rep 161, para 41.

[84] But note that the two terms are not considered to have the same meaning in French. Fitzmaurice (n 6), para 90.   [85] ibid.

that provide a framework for long-term cooperation, such as treaties that create an inter-national organization.[86] The principle of effectiveness favours interpretations that help to ensure that the goals of an international organization, for example, can be carried out in an effective manner. The dynamic interpretation of a treaty involves the interpretation of treaty language in situations that may not have been foreseen by the parties that drafted the treaty.[87] By relying on the object and purpose of the treaty in such situations, dynamic interpretation may depart from the subjective intention of the treaty drafters.

The ICJ has relied on the principle of effectiveness in interpreting its own statute, which dates back to 1945, and creates a long-term framework for the functioning of this judicial institution. In the *LaGrand Case (Germany v United States)*, the Court considered the meaning of Article 41 of its statute, a provision that gives it the power to order emergency or 'provisional' measures while a case is pending before the Court, in order to preserve the rights of the parties before the Court delivers its final judgment on the merits of the dispute.[88] Article 41 provides that '[t]he Court shall have the power to indicate, if it considers that circumstances so require, any provisional measures which ought to be taken to preserve the respective rights of either party'. This provision had been the subject of long-standing controversy, because it does not explicitly give the Court the power to order binding provisional measures, with which the parties to the dispute are obliged to comply.[89] In its 2001 judgment in *LaGrand* the Court brought an end to this debate by interpreting Article 41 in keeping with the principle of effectiveness. The Court determined that the statute's object and purpose was the judicial settlement of international disputes through binding decisions, and that the Court's ability to carry out this function would be hampered if it did not have the power to preserve the rights of the parties by indicating binding provisional measures.[90] The Court's decision in this case confirmed that the United States had indeed been bound by the Court's earlier provisional measures order not to execute two German nationals on death row in the United States – an order that the United States had violated when the case was pending before the Court.

The *Whaling in the Antarctic* case between Australia and Japan illustrates some of the challenges involved in treaty interpretation.[91] This case illustrates, in part, the limitations of the teleological approach to treaty interpretation, which loses its force as an interpretive approach where the object and purpose of a treaty cannot be satisfactorily ascertained. In *Whaling in the Antarctic,* the Court was focused on the interpretation and application of Article VIII of the ICRW, which permits states parties to grant special permits authorizing the killing of whales 'for purposes of scientific research ... '. In interpreting this provision, the

---

[86] For example, the UN Charter.

[87] Herdegen (n 76), paras 14, 48; *Dispute regarding Navigational and Related Rights (Costa Rica v Nicaragua)* (Judgment) [2009] ICJ Rep 213.

[88] *LaGrand Case (Germany v United States of America)* (Judgment) [2001] ICJ Rep 466.

[89] Art 41, for example, uses the word 'ought' rather than 'must'. Statute of the ICJ (as annexed to the Charter of the UN) (adopted 26 June 1945, entered into force 24 October 1945) USTS 993.

[90] *LaGrand* case (n 88), para 102.

[91] Although the VCLT technically does not govern the ICRW, which was concluded in 1946, well before the VCLT's entry into force in 1980, the parties and the ICJ, nevertheless, referenced the VCLT's provisions on treaty interpretation, which reflect customary international law.

Court was unable to rely on the treaty's object and purpose, because the ICRW's preamble references the conflicting aims of conservation and sustainable exploitation of whales.[92] Counsel for Australia argued that Article VIII should be interpreted restrictively, in light of the preamble's language on conservation, while counsel for Japan argued that this provision should be interpreted expansively, in light of the preamble's language on exploitation. Because these goals are arguably in tension with each other, the teleological approach to treaty interpretation in this case was unhelpful, and the Court found that these arguments supported neither a restrictive nor an expansive interpretation. Instead, the Court found that Article VIII pursued a separate purpose, namely the promotion of 'scientific knowledge', rather than the aims of conservation and/or sustainable exploitation.[93] The Court supported this interpretation of Article VIII by reference to the provision's context, in particular subsequent agreements between the parties in the form of guidelines issued by the International Whaling Commission, a treaty body established by the ICRW.[94] The Court ultimately embraced a highly textual reading of the provision, which allowed the Court to focus on whether Japan's whaling programme was '*for the purposes of* scientific research' (emphasis added). The Court ultimately concluded that Japan's permits were not for the purposes of scientific research, because the research programme's design and implementation did not have a reasonable relationship to its stated objectives.[95]

5   Invalidating, Terminating, and Suspending Treaties

The law of treaties favours the stability of treaty relations.[96] While the VCLT includes relatively extensive rules concerning the invalidity, termination, and suspension of treaties, in practice these rules tend to privilege the continuity of treaty relations, rather than their disruption. While the rules on the invalidity, termination, and suspension of treaties may resemble the rules of contract law in some domestic legal systems, their application in the context of treaty law is not comparable. In the context of domestic contract law, it is sometimes said that 'contracts are made to be broken'. On the international plane; however, quite the opposite could be said: treaties are made to be kept. This section briefly reviews the grounds for invalidity, before coming to the subjects of termination and suspension.

a   Invalidity

Treaties are presumptively valid, meaning that their validity must be 'impeached' or challenged by reference to certain rules of treaty law[97]. The rules on invalidity fall into

---

[92] *Whaling in the Antarctic* case (n 66), paras 56–8.   [93] ibid, para 58.

[94] ibid, para 83. The Court clarified that such guidelines may not be considered a 'subsequent agreement' as to the interpretation of art VIII (within the meaning of VCLT art 31(3)) if they were agreed upon by only some, but not all of the state parties to the convention. In other words, subsequent agreements must represent a consensus among all of the parties to the treaty.

[95] ibid, para 227.

[96] Fitzmaurice (n 6), para 66; *Case concerning the Gabčíkovo-Nagymaros Project (Hungary v Slovakia)* (Judgment) [1997] ICJ Rep 7, para 114.

[97] VCLT art 42(1).

two categories, which are distinguishable based on the effects that they produce. Under one set of rules on invalidity, a treaty is voidable, and therefore, remains valid until a state successfully invalidates it on the basis of a circumstance surrounding its conclusion. A treaty may be voidable where there is a lack of consent, error, fraud, or corruption.[98] Under the other set of rules on invalidity, a treaty is simply void, and has been from the moment of its purported conclusion (i.e., void *ab initio*). A treaty is void from the beginning where its conclusion involved coercion of the state or its representative, or the treaty conflicts with a *jus cogens* norm, from which no derogation is permitted (e.g., the prohibitions on the use of force, genocide, slavery, and torture).[99] Although the VCLT includes a relatively extensive set of rules concerning treaty invalidity, these rules have limited contemporary application and therefore lack great practical significance.

b   *The Suspension and Termination of Treaties*

Although the law of treaties favours the stability of treaty relations, the obligations that states assume by becoming parties to treaties do not necessarily persist indefinitely or without interruption. Parties may, under certain circumstances, terminate or suspend their treaty obligations. While termination brings treaty obligations to an end, suspension refers to a temporary state of affairs, in which the operation of the treaty is 'paused', while the treaty itself continues to exist. Depending on the circumstances, the treaty itself could be suspended or terminated, or one or more states parties could suspend or terminate their own treaty obligations, leaving the treaty operational for the other parties. Suspension and termination may be governed by the terms of the treaty, or by the default rules set out in the VCLT, which represent customary international law.[100]

Treaties often include provisions that specifically govern the withdrawal of a party from the treaty.[101] Provisions on withdrawal typically include a notice period, which gives the other states parties warning that a state will no longer be bound by the treaty after a certain period of time (e.g., six months or one year). This warning period could also, potentially, serve as an opportunity for the other states parties to attempt to persuade the state to remain a party to the treaty. The ICRW, for example, provides that states parties may withdraw by giving notice on or before 1 January of any given year, with the withdrawal taking effect six months later on 30 June of that same year. Japan made use of this provision on withdrawal after the ICJ's 2014 judgment in *Whaling in the Antarctic*, which required Japan to revoke existing permits for the killing of whales under its scientific whaling programme, and to refrain from granting any further permits under its programme.[102] In late 2018, Japan announced its intention to withdraw from the ICRW, a decision that came into effect on 30 June 2019. While the withdrawal of a party from a multilateral treaty may be regarded as

---

[98] VCLT arts 46–50.   [99] VCLT arts 8, 51–3.
[100] VCLT arts 42(2), 54. Anthony Aust, 'Treaties, Termination' in *Max Planck Encyclopedia for Public International Law* (last updated June 2006), para 18.
[101] See for example, Rome Statute art 127(1); ICSID Convention art 71. Aust (n 100), para 1.
[102] *Whaling in the Antarctic* case (n 66), para 247(7).

a loss for a treaty regime, especially one that aspires to universal participation, it can also be seen as the legally preferred outcome in situations where a state's actual conduct would likely continue to be in tension with its treaty obligations. In circumstances where conventions reflect customary international law, the withdrawal of a party may not have any practical impact, because the withdrawing party will still be bound to comply with its obligations under customary international law.[103] The same is true in the event of suspension.[104]

Not all treaties are capable of withdrawal, meaning that it may not be possible for states parties to terminate their treaty obligations, or to bring a treaty to an end. As a general rule, treaties that lack provisions on termination do not permit withdrawal. Exceptions, however, exist where it can be shown that the parties intended to allow for withdrawal, or such a right 'may be implied by the nature of the treaty'.[105] Certain categories of treaties tend to be incapable of withdrawal, such as peace treaties, disarmament treaties, human rights treaties, and treaties establishing permanent regimes, such as those governing the Suez and Panama canals.[106] In contrast, treaties concerning alliances, commerce and trade, and cultural relations all tend to be capable of withdrawal.[107] The ICCPR serves as an example of a human rights treaty that does not contain a provision for withdrawal, and which, by its nature, does not permit withdrawal, as has been confirmed by the ICCPR's treaty body, the Human Rights Committee. The ICCPR does not have a temporary character typical of treaties that permit withdrawal.[108] Instead, the rights accorded under the ICCPR to the people living in the territory of a state belong to the people, and remain with them, even when fundamental features of the state or government change.[109]

Compared with withdrawal and termination, the suspension of a treaty – or of obligations owed by one or more parties under a treaty – is relatively rare.[110] The operation of a treaty may be suspended either in accordance with the terms of the treaty, or by consent of all parties, following consultation.[111] Some human rights treaties, for example, allow certain provisions to be suspended unilaterally in certain circumstances, such as in times of public emergency which threaten the life of a nation.[112] Suspension could be a unilateral act of just one party, or it could be agreed upon by some or all parties. Where all parties to a treaty agree to suspend their treaty obligations, then the treaty itself would be suspended. Where one or only some parties suspend their treaty obligations, then the treaty remains in operation for the other states parties that have not suspended their obligations. During a period of suspension, parties are required to refrain from acts that would tend to obstruct the resumption of the treaty's operation.[113]

In addition to these basic rules on termination and suspension, the law of treaties provides a number of specific grounds upon which a party could suspend or terminate its

---

[103] VCLT art 43.   [104] VCLT art 43.   [105] VCLT art 56.   [106] Aust (n 100), para 19.   [107] ibid.

[108] Human Rights Committee, 'General Comment 26: Continuity of Obligations' (8 December 1997) UN Doc CCPR/C/21/Rev.1/Add.8/Rev.1, para 3.

[109] ibid, paras 3–5.

[110] Iain Cameron, 'Treaties, Suspension' in *Max Planck Encyclopedia of Public International Law* (last updated February 2007), para 13.

[111] VCLT art 57.   [112] ICCPR art 4; ECHR art 15.   [113] VCLT art 72(2).

obligations under a treaty. These grounds for suspension or termination include material breach, supervening impossibility of performance, and fundamental change of circumstance, among others.[114] Under Article 60 of the VCLT, a breach of a treaty provision by a state party qualifies as a 'material breach' where it 'radically changes the position of every party with respect to the further performance of its obligations under the treaty'.[115] In the case of a bilateral treaty, a material breach by one party would entitle the other party to suspend or terminate the treaty in whole or in part.[116] In the case of a multilateral treaty, a material breach entitles the other parties to suspend or terminate the treaty in whole or in part, either among all parties, or just between the defaulting party and the other parties.[117]

Supervening impossibility of performance, under Article 61 of the VCLT, has a limited scope of application, as it may only be invoked where the impossibility results from 'the permanent disappearance or destruction of an object indispensable for the execution of the treaty'.[118] A temporary impossibility could serve as grounds for suspension, rather than termination.[119] In addition, a party may not invoke impossibility if the impossibility results from its own breach, either of the treaty at issue or of another international obligation that it owes to a party to the treaty.[120] Examples of situations in which supervening impossibility of performance could potentially be invoked include the submergence of island, the disappearance of a river due to drought, or the destruction by fire of a subject of the treaty.

Fundamental change in circumstances, under Article 62 of the VCLT, has an especially narrow scope, as it may not be invoked unless certain conditions are met. First, the existence of the given circumstances must have 'constituted an essential basis of the consent of the parties to be bound by the treaty'. Second, the effect of the change must 'radically transform the extent of the obligations still to be performed under the treaty'. Finally, in certain circumstances, a party may not invoke fundamental change of circumstances, including where the change results from a breach by the party invoking it. Although parties in disputes before international courts and tribunals have repeatedly invoked fundamental change in circumstances, no court or tribunal has yet found that the conditions for its application have been met.[121]

These grounds for termination and suspension may be illustrated by a case between Hungary and Slovakia concerning the Gabcikovo-Nagymaros project.[122] This case demonstrates the extent to which the practical application favours the stability rather than the disruption of treaties. This case concerned a 1977 bilateral treaty between Hungary and Slovakia (then Czechoslovakia), which governed the two states joint construction and operation of a system of locks on the Danube River, which forms the boundary between the two states.[123] The purpose of the project was to produce hydroelectricity, to improve navigation in part of the Danube River, and to protect certain areas along the banks of the river from flooding.[124] The parties also agreed, among other things, not to harm the River's water quality.[125] Joint work on the project began in 1978, but by the late 1980s, the Hungarian government faced intense public criticism of the project, particularly with

---

[114] VCLT arts 60–2. [115] VCLT art 60(2)(c). [116] VCLT art 60(1). [117] VCLT art 60(2)(a). [118] VCLT art 61(1).
[119] VCLT art 61(1). [120] VCLT art 61(2). [121] Aust (n 100), para 39. [122] *Gabčíkovo-Nagymaros Project* case (n 96).
[123] ibid, paras 15–16. [124] ibid, para 15. [125] ibid.

respect to its environmental consequences.[126] In October 1989, the Hungarian government abandoned the works at Nagymaros, on the Hungarian side of the Danube River.[127] Slovakia responded by devising and then implementing a unilateral diversion of the Danube, known as 'Variant C'.[128] Hungary considered Variant C to be in violation of the treaty, and in May 1992 it informed Slovakia that it was terminating the treaty.[129] The dispute between the parties concerned whether Hungary had a legal basis for terminating the treaty. Ultimately, the ICJ decided that Hungary's termination of the treaty did not have a legal basis, and that Hungary's abandonment of the project in 1989 was itself a violation of the treaty.

One by one, the Court rejected Hungary's arguments about its termination of the treaty based on the grounds of impossibility of performance, fundamental change in circumstances, and material breach. First, with respect to impossibility of performance, Hungary argued that the essential object of the treaty had disappeared and it was; therefore, impossible to perform. The essential object, according to Hungary, was 'an economic joint investment which was consistent with environmental protection' and which was operated jointly by the parties.[130] The Court; however, noted that the joint exploitation of the investment was no longer possible because Hungary itself had not carried out most of the works for which it was responsible. Moreover, the treaty contained provisions that would have enabled the parties to rebalance economic and ecological imperatives.

Second, with respect to fundamental change in circumstances, Hungary argued, in part, that since the treaty's conclusion in 1977, a number of fundamental circumstances had changed, including political changes and the project's economic viability.[131] In the period since 1977, Hungary and Slovakia had both emerged from communist regimes, and had become market economies. The Court; however, found that the parties' political conditions and economic systems were not so closely linked to the object and purpose of the treaty that they constituted an essential basis for consent. Moreover, while the project's profitably had diminished since 1977, it had not diminished to such an extent that the parties' obligations were 'radically transformed'.

Finally, with respect to material breach, Hungary argued that Slovakia's implementation of Variant C violated the treaty and constituted a material breach.[132] The Court rejected this argument because it found that Hungary's suspension of works in 1989 had contributed to a situation that was not conducive to fruitful negotiations between itself and Slovakia.[133] According to the Court, Slovakia's construction of Variant C did not, in itself, violate the treaty (though the actual operation of Variant C would have violated the treaty). Because Slovakia had not actually breached the treaty as of Hungary's notice of termination in May 1992, Hungary was not entitled to terminate the treaty on the ground of material breach. In other words, Hungary's termination was premature, as Slovakia's operation of Variant C only took place after this, in October 1992.[134] This case highlights the extent to which the law of treaties prioritizes stability or continuation, rather than the suspension or

---

[126] ibid, para 22.   [127] ibid.   [128] ibid, para 23.   [129] ibid.   [130] ibid, para 103.   [131] ibid, para 104.
[132] ibid, para 105.   [133] ibid, para 107.   [134] ibid, para 108.

termination of treaties in existence. In this case, the Court's judgment suggests that the parties should have returned to the negotiating table to work out their differences and adjust their obligations as needed, and as provided for in the terms of the treaty.

6   Concluding Remarks

Flexibility is a key feature of the law of treaties, which provides a general set of rules that govern all treaties, regardless of their subject matter, function, or number of state parties. Treaties, may for example, take many different forms and may bear various titles. While the rules on treaty interpretation may appear, at first glance, to provide a step-by-step methodology for understanding treaty language, their application in practice is far from rigid and tends to accommodate the preferences of treaty interpreters. In addition to its flexibility, the law of treaties seeks to achieve a balance between fostering participation in treaties and maintaining their integrity. While states are free to enter reservations, the law of treaties seeks to contain the extent to which such reservations damage the object and purpose of the treaty. Finally, while the law of treaties encompasses an extensive set of rules on invalidity, termination, and suspension, these rules ultimately tend towards the maintenance rather than the disruption of existing treaty relations.

Recommended Reading

Anthony Aust, *Modern Treaty Law and Practice* (3rd edn, Cambridge University Press 2013).

James Crawford, "The Current Political Discourse Concerning International Law" (2018) 81 The Modern Law Review 1.

Megan Donaldson, "The Survival of the Secret Treaty: Publicity, Secrecy, and Legality in the International Legal Order" (2017) 111 American Journal of International Law 575.

Malgosia Fitzmaurice, "Concept of a Treaty in Decisions of International Courts and Tribunals" (2018) 20 International Community Law Review 137.

Laurence R Helfer, 'Terminating Treaties' in Duncan B Hollis (ed), *The Oxford Guide to Treaties* (2nd edn, Oxford University Press 2020).

5

Law of State Responsibility

Cecily Rose

1   Introduction

Every state is bound by a vast web of international legal obligations, based in treaties, and customary international law. These substantive international legal rules, which concern the behaviour of states, govern everything from protection of the environment to diplomatic immunity, are known as the 'primary rules' of public international law. Because each state is party to a different combination of bilateral and multilateral treaties, each state is bound by a unique set of primary rules. The rules governing state responsibility are; however, common to every state, and are part of the 'secondary rules' of public international law.[1] The secondary rules on state responsibility provide the legal framework for determining when a state has breached an international legal obligation, what the legal consequences are, and who can invoke responsibility. In other words, the secondary rules of state responsibility govern the operation of the many primary rules of international law. The law of treaties, which was the subject of the previous chapter, also comprises an important body of secondary rules in the field of public international law (see Chapter 4).

The rules of state responsibility are set out in the International Law Commission's (ILC) Articles on the Responsibility of States for Internationally Wrongful Acts (ARSIWA or the Articles on State Responsibility), which will be referenced throughout this chapter. The ILC's work on the Articles on State Responsibility spanned many decades, beginning in 1956 and concluding in 2001, when the United Nations (UN) General Assembly took note of the articles.[2] The articles themselves are non-binding, although many of the provisions reflect customary international law, and are therefore binding on all states. In addition, the Articles on State Responsibility are highly authoritative and are regularly referenced and relied upon by international courts and tribunals as well as governments. The ILC's articles could have formed the basis for a treaty on state responsibility, much like the 1969 Vienna Convention on the Law of Treaties (VCLTs), which is also based on the work of the ILC. But some states were opposed to negotiating a treaty on the secondary rules of state responsibility out of

---

[1] Eric David, 'Primary and Secondary Rules' in James Crawford, Alain Pellet, and Simon Olleson (eds), *The Law of International Responsibility* (Oxford University Press 2010) 27–33.

[2] ILC, 'Draft Articles on the Responsibility of States for Internationally Wrongful Acts' (2001) UN Doc A/56/10 (ARSIWA); UNGA Res 56/83 (12 December 2001).

concern that the compromises struck during the forty-five years of work at the ILC would be reopened, and that the articles would be weakened.[3]

This chapter introduces the basic features of the ILC's Articles on State Responsibility, beginning with an explanation of what constitutes an internationally wrongful act (Section 2). The following section discusses the circumstances precluding wrongfulness that may be invoked by states seeking to avoid responsibility for an internationally wrongful act (Section 3). The chapter then covers the aftermath of an internationally wrongful act, which can involve legal consequences, such as reparations (Section 4), as well as counter-measures (Section 5). This chapter focuses specifically on the responsibility of states, rather than the responsibility of international organizations or individuals, topics that are covered in Chapters 8 and 13, respectively.

2 Internationally Wrongful Act

A state bears international responsibility for its 'internationally wrongful acts', a term of art which refers to a breach of an international legal obligation by the state.[4] Through the use of this somewhat cumbersome term, the ILC avoided characterizing unlawful acts of states as either international crimes or international torts (or delicts), concepts which do not exist in the international legal field. The term internationally wrongful act is therefore a generic term that applies to breaches of all types of international legal obligations, regardless of whether those breaches concern violations by the state of the rules on the use of force, the law of the sea, or human rights law, for example. The term also covers both acts and omissions, even though the term itself refers only to acts.[5] Breaches of internal or domestic law do not give rise to an internationally wrongful act, which must be a violation of international law. In some instances, a breach of an international legal rule may actually be required by and in conformity with internal law.[6]

An internationally wrongful act consists of two elements: attribution and breach.[7] The given act or omission must first be attributable to the state and it must secondly breach an international legal obligation of the state. If the act or omission is attributable only to non-state actors or is lawful under international law, then it cannot constitute an internationally wrongful act under the Articles on State Responsibility. Damage is not a necessary element of an internationally wrongful act, in that a breach does not need to have caused harm to another state in order to qualify as an internationally wrongful act.[8] Even though a state's failure to implement

---

[3] For a detailed discussion of the historical background of the ILC's Articles on State Responsibility, see James Crawford, *State Responsibility: The General Part* (Cambridge University Press 2013) 35–44; see further Federica Paddeu, 'To Convene or Not to Convene? The Future Status of the Articles on State Responsibility: Recent Developments' (2017) 21 Max Planck Yearbook of United Nations Law 83.

[4] ARSIWA art 1.

[5] ARSIWA art 2 chapeau; *The Corfu Channel Case* (Merits) [1949] ICJ Rep 4, 22–3 (The Court held that Albania was responsible under international law due to its failure to warn British warships of a minefield in its waters).

[6] ARSIWA art 3. Pierre-Marie Dupuy, 'Relations between the International Law of Responsibility and Responsibility in Municipal Law' in Crawford, Pellet, and Olleson (eds) (n 1) 173–83; See for example, the United States Foreign Sovereign Immunities Act 1976, which creates an exception to state immunity where the defendant state is alleged to have engaged in state-sponsored terrorism. This exception in US domestic law is widely regarded as violating international law on state immunity.

[7] ARSIWA art 2.   [8] ARSIWA Commentary art 2, para 9.

a particular treaty obligation in its domestic legislation, for example, may not result in any harm to another state, it nevertheless, represents an internationally wrongful act.

a   *Attribution*

As a general rule, acts or omissions of states, rather than non-state actors, give rise to an internationally wrongful act. This seemingly obvious rule is complicated by the fact that states are legal constructs that can only act through natural persons – human beings. The challenge often lies in determining which persons or entities may be equated with the state, and which acts or omissions qualify as the conduct of the state. The matter of attribution is further complicated by a number of exceptions to the general rule. In relatively rare circumstances, the conduct of private actors may be attributed to the state. The following begins by elaborating upon the 'core' forms of attribution, which involve the conduct of the state, before delving into some of the exceptional circumstances in which the conduct of non-state actors may be attributed to the state.

i   *Core Forms of Attribution*

State Organs: *De Jure* and *De Facto* The first core form of attribution provides for the attribution of the conduct of 'state organs', a concept that has a potentially vast scope.[9] According to Article 4 of the Articles on State Responsibility, state organs may exercise legislative, executive, judicial, or other functions, and may form part of the central government or a territorial unit of the state.[10] The term 'state organs'; therefore, covers all branches of government, as well as all levels of government, from federal to provincial to local. The parliament, a prime minister, a judge, the military, a local policeman, and a mayor all qualify as state organs whose conduct is capable of engaging state responsibility. State organs may be identified as such according to the 'internal law' of the state, such as a constitution, in which case the person or entity may be described as a *de jure* state organ.[11] But *de facto* state organs are also a possibility, meaning that a person or an entity may qualify as a state organ based on internal practice rather than internal law. For a person or entity to qualify as a *de facto* state organ, the person or entity must be 'completely dependent' on the state, a threshold that entails a very high level of state control.[12]

Even in the case of *de jure* organs, such as branches of the military, the attribution of conduct may be quite challenging from an evidentiary perspective. In the case of the downing of Malaysia Airlines Flight MH17 on 17 July 2014, for example, the attribution of the conduct at issue has been the source of a significant dispute between Russia and several other states, including the Netherlands and Australia. This commercial passenger flight, travelling from Amsterdam to Kuala Lumpur, was shot down by a missile over

---

[9] Djamchid Momtaz, 'Attribution of Conduct to the State: State Organs and Entities Empowered to Exercise Elements of Governmental Authority' in Crawford, Pellet, and Olleson (eds) (n 1) 237–46.
[10] ARSIWA art 4(1).   [11] ARSIWA art 4(2).
[12] *Case concerning Application of the Convention on the Prevention and Punishment of the Crime of Genocide (Bosnia and Herzegovina v Serbia and Montenegro)* (Judgment) [2007] ICJ Rep 43, paras 392–3. See also *Case concerning Military and Paramilitary Activities in and against Nicaragua (Nicaragua v United States of America)* (Merits) [1986] ICJ Rep 14, paras 109–110.

Ukraine, killing all 298 persons on board. The downing took place in eastern Ukraine, a region that was in the midst of an armed conflict between the government of Ukraine and pro-Russian Ukrainian separatists. On the basis of extensive satellite imagery as well as social media postings, a Joint Investigation Team led by the Netherlands[13] determined that the plane was shot down by a type of missile system that belonged to a particular brigade of the Russian army.[14] Moreover, the missile system had been delivered from Russia to eastern Ukraine shortly before the downing of MH17. In May 2018, on the basis of these factual findings, the Netherlands and Australia announced that they considered Russia to be responsible for the downing of Flight MH17. The Netherlands and Australia were able to reach this conclusion, in part, because the evidentiary record showed that the downing could be attributed to a *de jure* organ of the Russian state, namely the Russian army.[15] Though inter-state negotiations between the Netherlands and Russia concerning the downing of Flight MH17 broke down in 2020, Dutch courts are currently presiding over related but separate criminal proceedings against three Russian officials and one Ukrainian individual, whom Dutch prosecutors have accused of perpetrating the downing.

Persons or Entities Exercising Elements of Governmental Authority The second core form of attribution concerns the conduct of persons or entities that exercise elements of governmental authority. Article 5 of the Articles on State Responsibility addresses situations in which a person or entity is not an organ of the state (either *de jure* or *de facto*) but is, nevertheless, empowered by the law of the state to exercise elements of governmental authority. In such circumstances, the conduct of the person or entity is attributable to the state, provided that the conduct at issue may be characterized as governmental activity, rather than private or commercial activity.[16] The ILC intended Article 5 to cover former state corporations that have been privatized, as well as parastatal entities (e.g., state-owned companies).[17] Article 5 has great contemporary relevance, as states commonly and increasingly outsource traditional government functions through the privatization of public entities, the creation of state owned corporations, and through contracts with private companies.[18] For example, airlines exercise control over immigration and companies run prisons and military detention centres.[19] The determination of what constitutes 'governmental authority' is quite fact-specific, and depends on factors such as the content of the powers, how the state has conferred the powers to the entity, the purpose for which the powers will be exercised, and the extent to which the government is accountable for the exercise of the powers.[20]

---

[13] The Joint Investigation Team consisted of law enforcement from Australia, Belgium, Malaysia, the Netherlands, and Ukraine.

[14] Netherlands Public Prosecution Service, 'Update in Criminal Investigation MH17 Disaster' (24 May 2018) <www.prosecutionservice.nl/topics/mh17-plane-crash/news/2018/05/24/update-in-criminal-investigation-mh17-disaster>.

[15] Government of the Netherlands, 'MH17: The Netherlands and Australia hold Russia Responsible' (25 May 2018) <www.government.nl/latest/news/2018/05/25/mh17-the-netherlands-and-australia-hold-russia-responsible>. Radio Free Europe, 'Russia Agrees to Talks with Netherlands on Downing of MH17' (8 February 2019) <www.rferl.org/a/russia-agrees-to-talks-with-netherlands-on-mh17-shootdown/29759629.html>.

[16] ARSIWA Commentary art 5, para 5.   [17] ARSIWA Commentary art 5, para 1.   [18] Crawford (n 3) 127.

[19] ibid 127–8; Chia Lenhardt, 'Private Military Companies' in *Max Planck Encyclopedia of Public International Law* (last updated May 2011); James Cockayne, 'Private Military and Security Companies' in Andrew Clapham and Paola Gaeta (eds), *The Oxford Handbook of International Law in Armed Conflict* (Oxford University Press 2014).

[20] ARSIWA Commentary art 5, para 6; Crawford (n 3) 129–32.

Organs Placed at the Disposal of a State by Another State A third core form of attribution concerns the conduct of organs that one state has placed at the disposal of another state. According to Article 6, when state A places one of its state organs at the disposal of state B, then the conduct of the organ of state A shall be considered the conduct of state B if the organ is exercising elements of state B's governmental authority. This form of attribution is highly relevant in the context of contemporary military operations. Drone strikes carried out by the US military in Pakistan, Somalia, Yemen, Iraq, and Syria, for example, have involved significant assistance from a number of European states, including the provision of intelligence, metadata, operational, and logistical support.[21] Some of this assistance may be attributable to the United States itself, through Article 6 of the Articles on State Responsibility. UK Royal Air Force pilots have, for instance, arguably been 'placed at the disposal' of the United States, as they have operated under the command of a wing of the US Air Force that conducts drone operations.[22] Where UK personnel have been embedded in US operations, their conduct could arguably be attributable to the United States as opposed to the United Kingdom. The United Kingdom itself could also bear state responsibility for aid or assistance to the United States, which constitutes another form of state responsibility.[23]

Conduct *Ultra Vires* Finally, conduct attributable to the state includes *ultra vires* (unauthorized) conduct by a state organ or an entity or person empowered to exercise elements of governmental authority. According to Article 7, as long as the organ, person, or entity is exercising state authority, then the conduct is attributable to the state, even if it exceeds the authority or contravenes instructions. In other words, attribution hinges not on whether the conduct conformed with an internal law or instructions given, but whether the conduct was carried out in an official capacity.[24] For example, when a government official solicits a bribe from a person or a company in exchange for issuing a licence or granting a procurement contract, the conduct of the government official is attributable to the state because the official is issuing the licence or granting the contract in his or her official capacity.[25] The fact that internal laws prohibit the government official from soliciting bribes, such that this conduct is *ultra vires*, does not prevent the attribution of this conduct to the state.

ii   An Exceptional Form of Attribution: Private Conduct Instructed, Directed, or Controlled by the State

The core forms of attribution considered so far have concerned the attribution of the conduct of state organs, or persons or entities empowered to exercise governmental authority. As a general rule, the conduct of private persons or entities is not attributable

---

[21] Amnesty International, 'Deadly Assistance: The Role of European States in US Drone Strikes' (2018). For a fictional depiction of military cooperation between the United Kingdom, the United States and Kenya in the context of a drone strike, see the film *Eye in the Sky* (2015).

[22] Letter from UK Ministry of Defence (8 September 2015) <https://assets.publishing.service.gov.uk/government/uploads/system/uploads/attachment_data/file/462375/20150908-UK_Personnel_stationed_Creech_Air_Force_Base.pdf>.

[23] ARSIWA art 16. Aid and assistance fall outside the scope of this chapter.   [24] Crawford (n 3) 136–7.

[25] Aloysius P Llamzon, *Corruption in International Investment Arbitration* (Oxford University Press 2014) ss 10.49–10.62.

to the state.[26] In a number of specific – and, in practice, quite rare – circumstances; however, the conduct of purely private actors may be attributed to the state.[27] The most significant exception, found in Article 8 of the Articles on State Responsibility, provides for the attribution of the conduct of a person or group of persons that is 'acting under the instructions of, or under the direction or control of, that State in carrying out the conduct'. This exception prevents states from avoiding international responsibility by simply delegating wrongful acts to private actors.[28]

The ILC intended for the three terms, 'instructions', 'direction', and 'control' to be disjunctive, meaning that they were meant to signify three distinct forms of attribution, but in practice, the terms 'direction and control' have been interpreted as a single form of attribution.[29] Thus, under Article 8, the conduct of private actors may be attributed to the state in two circumstances: first, where the state issues instructions to private person(s) to act on its behalf; and second, where the state directs or controls private person(s). The first situation typically entails a state hiring, recruiting, or instigating private actors to supplement the actions of the state's police or military.[30] When a state gives instructions to a private security company, for example, the conduct that follows may be attributable to the state.[31] In the *Nicaragua* and *Bosnia Genocide* cases, the International Court of Justice (ICJ) interpreted 'instruction' to mean instruction with respect to each operation undertaken by the private person(s).[32] General instructions concerning the overall actions to be taken by the private actors would therefore fall short of the required threshold under Article 8. Similarly, the second situation involves the state's 'effective control' over each operation, rather than the overall actions taken by the private actors.[33]

As interpreted by the ICJ, the threshold for attribution under both strands of Article 8 is very high, thereby preventing the attribution of private conduct that the state supports, plans, or influences in a more general sense.[34] In the *Nicaragua* case, for example, the ICJ examined the conduct of the Contras, a guerrilla insurgency movement that was opposed to the Sandinista regime in Nicaragua in the early to mid-1980s. During the proceedings before the ICJ, Nicaragua argued that the Contras' alleged violations of international humanitarian law were attributable to the United States, on account of the United States relatively extensive involvement with them. The United States participated in funding, organizing, training, supplying, and equipping the Contras, as well as planning and target selection.[35] Yet, the Court determined that this level of involvement did not entail the United States effective control over the Contras, as the evidence did not support the contention that the United States had 'directed or enforced the perpetration' of conduct that violated international law.[36] According to the Court, the Contras could have committed

---

[26] Olivier de Frouville, 'Attribution of Conduct to the State: Private Individuals' in Crawford, Pellet, and Olleson (eds) (n 1) 261–4.

[27] ARSIWA arts 8–11.   [28] Crawford (n 3) 141.   [29] ARSIWA Commentary art 8, para 7; Crawford (n 3) 146.

[30] ARSIWA Commentary art 8, para 2.   [31] Lenhardt (n 19); Cockayne (n 19); Crawford (n 3) 145.

[32] *Bosnia Genocide* case (n 12), para 400.   [33] ARSIWA Commentary art 8, para 3.

[34] Alexander Kees, 'Responsibility of States for Private Actors' in *Max Planck Encyclopedia of Public International Law* (last updated March 2011), para 14.

[35] *Nicaragua* case (n 12), para 115.   [36] ibid.

such acts without the control of the United States, despite their high degree of dependence on the United States, in general.[37]

This high threshold has, however, generated some controversy, resulting in an often cited example of the 'fragmentation' of international law.[38] In 1999, the Appeals Chamber of the International Criminal Tribunal for the former Yugoslavia (ICTY) departed from the 'effective control' test, which it did not consider to be applicable in all circumstances.[39] Instead, the ICTY adopted a lower threshold for attribution, which requires only that private actors are under the 'overall control' of the state, without the need for each operation to have been instructed, directed, or controlled by the state.[40] In 2007, in the *Bosnia Genocide* case; however, the ICJ upheld the threshold set out in *Nicaragua*, and noted that the ICTY's '"overall control" test is unsuitable, for it stretches, almost to the breaking point, the connection which must exist between the conduct of a State's organs and its international responsibility'.[41] The Court further held that the threshold was not met in this case, as there was no evidence that the government of Serbia (then the Federal Republic of Yugoslavia) had instructed or effectively controlled the decision taken by the Bosnian Serb Army (Army of the Republika Srpska) to kill the adult male population in Srebrenica, a town in Bosnia and Herzegovina.[42]

By upholding a high threshold under Article 8, the ICJ has greatly limited the applicability of this exceptional form of attribution, at least in proceedings before the Court. A more liberal interpretation of this form of attribution, in keeping with *Tadic*, would arguably undermine the integrity of the general rule that the conduct of private actors is not attributable to the state. The application of the ICJ's strict approach can, however, result in seeming injustices, as a state may not bear responsibility for the egregious conduct of private actors, despite having provided them with relatively significant support. Yet, in both the *Nicaragua* and *Bosnia Genocide* cases, the Court ultimately held that the respondent states (the United States and Serbia, respectively), bore responsibility for their own conduct, that is, the conduct of the states themselves. Article 8, in other words, represents only one of many forms of attribution under the Articles on State Responsibility.

iii   *Other Exceptional Forms of Attribution*

A number of other highly exceptional forms of attribution concerning the conduct of private actors merit brief mention. Article 9 of the Articles on State Responsibility concerns the conduct of private actors who exercise public powers in the midst of a power vacuum. During or after a revolution, armed conflict, or foreign occupation, for example, private actors may exercise elements of governmental authority 'in the absence or default of the official authorities'.[43] Despite the many examples of governmental authorities dissolving or disintegrating in the midst of violent upheaval, the exercise of public power by private

---

[37] ibid.

[38] ILC, 'Fragmentation of International Law: Difficulties Arising from the Diversification and Expansion of International Law' (13 April 2006) UN Doc A/CN.4/L.682, paras 49–52.

[39] *Prosecutor v Duko Tadic* (Judgment) IT-94-1-A (15 July 1999) (ICTY Appeals Chamber), para 117.   [40] ibid, para 20.

[41] *Bosnia Genocide* case (n 12), para 406.   [42] ibid, para 413.   [43] ARSIWA Commentary art 9, para 1.

actors in such circumstances appears to be more unusual, or has, at least, generated very little practice by states and courts or tribunals.[44]

Article 10 addresses a related but distinct scenario in which an insurgency either replaces the existing government of the state, or forms the government of a new state.[45] As a general rule, states are not responsible for the conduct of insurrectional movements fighting against them, as this would run contrary to both common sense and the general rule of attribution, whereby the conduct of private actors is not attributable to the state. But in the exceptional circumstance where an insurrectional movement succeeds in forming the new government of an existing state or of a new state, then the successful insurgents are prevented from escaping responsibility for their conduct during the insurgency.

Finally, Article 11 covers the situation in which the state adopts the conduct of a private actor after the fact, or *ex post facto*. Even if the conduct of private actors is not attributable to the state under any of the other rules on attribution, it may nevertheless be attributable 'if and to the extent that the State acknowledges and adopts the conduct in question as its own'. The Tehran hostage crisis remains one of the best examples of this rare phenomenon. During the Iranian revolution in 1979, Iranian militants seized the US embassy in Tehran and held US diplomatic and consular agents hostage. The leader of the revolution and the founder of the Islamic Republic of Iran, Ayatollah Khomeini, explicitly 'approved and maintained' the actions of the militants.[46] The Ayatollah announced that the Iranian government would maintain the situation for the purpose of exerting pressure on the United States, and other Iranian authorities repeated these statements. The ICJ held that his words had the effect of transforming the conduct of the militants, who were non-state actors, into the acts of the Iranian state.[47]

b   Breach

If conduct is attributable to the state, through the application of one of the rules of attribution discussed in Section 2(a), then the next question is whether the act of the state breaches an international obligation held by the state.[48] If conduct is attributable to the state but does not actually breach any international obligations, then of course no state responsibility will result. The term 'breach' is synonymous with the term 'violation', and means that the act is not in conformity with what an international obligation requires of the state.[49] The determination of whether or not the act of a state breaches an international obligation is based on primary rules of international law, the source of which may be treaty law, customary law, or general principles of international law. Primary rules vary hugely in character.[50] While some rules require states to take or refrain from taking certain actions (positive or negative obligations, respectively), other rules require states to prevent or punish certain conduct by private actors

---

[44] Crawford (n 3) 168.

[45] Gerard Cahin, 'Attribution of Conduct to the State: Insurrectional Movements' in Crawford, Pellet, and Olleson (eds) (n 1) 247–55. Patrick Dumberry, 'New State Responsibility for Internationally Wrongful Acts by an Insurrectional Movement' (2006) 17 European Journal of International Law 605.

[46] ARSIWA Commentary art 11, para 4. *Case concerning United States Diplomatic and Consular Staff in Tehran* (Judgment) [1980] ICJ Rep 3, paras 71–3.

[47] *US Diplomatic and Consular Staff in Tehran* case (n 46), para 74.   [48] ARSIWA art 12.

[49] ARSIWA Commentary art 12, para 7.   [50] Crawford (n 3) 219.

(obligations of prevention and repression, respectively). Furthermore, some rules require states to achieve a particular result, while others only require the state to engage in a certain course of conduct without necessarily achieving a particular result (obligations of result and conduct, respectively). The determination of whether an act of the state breaches an international obligation is therefore always specific to the obligation under consideration.

A few secondary rules of state responsibility apply to all breaches, regardless of the source or the character of the primary rule under consideration. These general, secondary rules concern temporal aspects of a breach of an international obligation.[51] Most significantly, in order for a breach to occur, the state has to have been bound by the obligation at the time that the act took place.[52] If an act of a state conflicts with a provision of a treaty that had not yet come into force for the state at the time that the act took place, for example, then there can be no breach. While determining when a treaty came into force for a given state is usually fairly straightforward, determining when a rule of customary international law came into existence is often much more complex, as these rules typically develop and coalesce over time.

The ICJ dealt with this problem in the context of its 2019 advisory opinion concerning the *Legal Consequences of the Separation of the Chagos Archipelago from Mauritius in 1965* case. In this case, the Court faced the question of whether the United Kingdom had breached the customary rule of self-determination when it separated the Chagos Archipelago from Mauritius in 1965, before Mauritius gained independence from the United Kingdom in 1968. Since the independence of Mauritius, the Chagos Archipelago has remained under the administration of the United Kingdom. Based in part on a number of UN General Assembly resolutions from the early 1950s to the mid-1960s, in particular Resolution 1514 of 1960, the Court determined that by 1960 the right to self-determination was a customary norm, which entailed a non-self-governing territory's right to territorial integrity.[53] According to the Court, the detachment of part of a non-self-governing territory by an administering power without 'the freely expressed and genuine will' of the people in the territory violates the people's right to self-determination.[54] This rule of customary law had coalesced before the United Kingdom detached the Chagos Archipelago from Mauritius in 1965. The United Kingdom had; therefore, breached the right of the people of Mauritius to self-determination during the process of decolonization of Mauritius, as the detachment was not based on the 'free and genuine expression of the will of the people' of Mauritius.[55]

3   Circumstances Precluding Wrongfulness

When conduct is both attributable to the state and in breach of an international obligation, then the state bears international legal responsibility for an internationally wrongful act,

---

[51] ARSIWA arts 13–15. ARSIWA arts 14 and 15, which are not covered here, deal with instantaneous and continuous acts (art 14) and composite acts, meaning a series of acts or omissions (art 15).

[52] ARSIWA art 13.

[53] *Legal Consequences of the Separation of the Chagos Archipelago from Mauritius in 1965* (Advisory Opinion) [2019] ICJ Rep 95, para 150.

[54] ibid, para 160.   [55] ibid, para 172.

unless one of the six circumstances precluding wrongfulness is applicable.[56] The term 'circumstance precluding wrongfulness' is unique to public international law, and encompasses what may be classified as justifications as well as excuses.[57] Unlike many domestic legal systems, the Articles on State Responsibility do not distinguish between justifications, which preclude the wrongfulness of an act altogether, and excuses, which preclude only the legal consequences of a wrongful act, but not the wrongfulness of the act itself. Under the law of state responsibility, all circumstances precluding the wrongfulness have the effect of 'shielding' or protecting the state from bearing responsibility for what would otherwise be a 'well-founded claim for the breach of an international obligation'.[58] Circumstances precluding wrongfulness do not; however, act as a sword, meaning that they do not terminate the obligation itself.[59] States remain bound by the relevant international obligation, and once the circumstance precluding wrongfulness no longer exists, the state must resume compliance with the obligation at issue.[60] Circumstances precluding wrongfulness; therefore, have a different effect than the grounds for invalidating or terminating a treaty, which act as a sword because they bring the treaty obligation to an end (see Chapter 4).[61] The following introduces and illustrates each of the six circumstances precluding wrongfulness, namely: consent; self-defence; countermeasures; force majeure; distress; and necessity.[62]

a   *Consent*

When one state provides 'valid consent' to an act committed by another state, then the wrongfulness of that act is precluded in relation to the state providing consent, but only 'to the extent that the act remains within the limits of that consent'.[63] One state could, for example, consent to the police officers or military of another state operating on its territory in circumstances that would otherwise violate the sovereignty and territorial integrity of the state providing consent.[64] The term 'valid' consent means that the state giving consent must have done so freely, out of its own will, and the consent must also have been expressed clearly.[65] Consent that has been coerced or only presumed will not qualify as 'valid' consent. Consent also has a temporal component, in that states must give consent before or during the commission of what would otherwise be a wrongful act.[66]

---

[56] ARSIWA arts 20–5.
[57] See generally Federica Paddeu, *Justification and Excuse in International Law: Concept and Theory of General Defences* (Cambridge University Press 2018); Vaughan Lowe, 'Precluding Wrongfulness or Responsibility: A Plea for Excuses' (1999) 10 European Journal of International Law 405.
[58] ARSIWA Commentary ch V, para 1.   [59] ARSIWA Commentary ch V, para 2.
[60] ARSIWA art 27 ('The invocation of a circumstance precluding wrongfulness . . . is without prejudice to (a) compliance with the obligation in question, if and to the extent that the circumstance precluding wrongfulness no longer exists').
[61] VCLTs (adopted 23 May 1969, entered into force 27 January 1980) 1155 UNTS 331, pt V.   [62] ARSIWA arts 20–5.
[63] ARSIWA art 20; Affef Ben Mansour, 'Circumstances Precluding Wrongfulness in the ICL Articles on State Responsibility: Consent' in Crawford, Pellet, and Olleson (eds) (n 1) 439–47.
[64] *Case concerning Armed Activities on the Territory of the Congo (Democratic Republic of the Congo v Uganda)* (Judgment) [2005] ICJ Rep 168.
[65] ARSIWA Commentary art 20, para 6.
[66] ARSIWA art 45 ('The responsibility of a State may not be invoked if: the injured State has validly waived the claim; (b) the injured State is to be considered as having, by reason of its conduct, validly acquiesced in the lapse of the claim').

b   *Self-Defence*

States may invoke self-defence as a circumstance precluding wrongfulness 'if the act constitutes a lawful measure of self-defence taken in conformity with the Charter of the United Nations'.[67] This secondary rule of state responsibility is somewhat unusual in that it fully incorporates a primary rule of international law, namely Article 51 of the UN Charter.[68] The lawfulness of an act of self-defence is therefore determined by reference to Article 51, which provides for 'the inherent right of individual or collective self-defence if an armed attack occurs' against a UN member. Although Article 51 does not itself indicate that acts of self-defence must be necessary or proportionate, these requirements exist in customary international law, which is referenced by the term 'inherent right' to self-defence in Article 51 (see Chapter 11).[69]

The distinction between the secondary rule of self-defence, as set out in the Articles on State Responsibility, and the primary rule of self-defence, as set out in the UN Charter, is significant because of its implications for the scope of application of self-defence as a circumstance precluding wrongfulness. Article 51 of the UN Charter is a primary rule which provides for the right of self-defence. The exercise of this right does not result in a breach of Article 2(4) of the Charter, which prohibits the threat or use of force in international relations.[70] Instead, the right to self-defence forms an exception to the prohibition on the use of force under Article 2(4). As a result of how these two primary rules relate to each other, self-defence cannot preclude the wrongfulness of a violation of Article 2(4) of the UN Charter, as this provision has not been not violated in the first place. But self-defence can preclude the wrongfulness of a violation of other international obligations, besides Article 2(4) of the UN Charter. A lawful act of self-defence could, for example, give rise to breaches of international obligations concerning economic or consular relations between the aggressor state and the state acting in self-defence. Such breaches could potentially be justified under the rule of self-defence as a circumstance precluding wrongfulness.[71]

The scope of application of self-defence as a circumstance precluding wrongfulness is further limited with respect to two bodies of law that are expressly designed to govern situations in which a state acts in lawful self-defence. International humanitarian law (IHL) governs the conduct of hostilities between states, including one state's lawful use of force in self-defence against another state (see Chapter 12). Responsibility for violations of IHL; therefore, cannot be precluded in circumstances where a state has acted in lawful self-defence. In addition, under human rights law, states cannot derogate from certain human rights obligations, such as the right to life, during 'times of public emergency' (see Chapter 10). These rights remain non-derogable during public emergencies that involve the state's use of force in lawful self-defence against another state.[72]

---

[67] ARSIWA art 21; Jean-Marc Thouvenin, 'Circumstances Precluding Wrongfulness in the ICL Articles on State Responsibility: Self-Defence' in Crawford, Pellet and Olleson (eds) (n 1) 455–67.
[68] Crawford (n 3) 189.   [69] *Nicaragua* case (n 12), para 176.   [70] ARSIWA Commentary art 20, para 1.
[71] *Case concerning Oil Platforms (Islamic Republic of Iran v United States of America)* (Judgment) [2003] ICJ Rep 161.
[72] International Covenant on Civil and Political Rights (adopted 16 December 1966, entered into force 23 March 1976) 999 UNTS 171, art 4.

c **Countermeasures**

Countermeasures represent a tool for bringing about compliance with international obligations. Resort to countermeasures is possible because they qualify as a circumstance precluding wrongfulness.[73] In situations where one state is responsible for an internationally wrongful act, the injured state may, under certain conditions, direct countermeasures against the responsible state through non-compliance with an obligation owed to the responsible state. Provided that such non-compliance meets the criteria for countermeasures, its wrongfulness will be precluded. Because the conditions governing countermeasures are relatively elaborate and primarily concern the implementation of state responsibility, they will be discussed separately, at the end of this chapter.[74]

d **Force Majeure**

Force majeure is a circumstance precluding wrongfulness that covers situations in which a state involuntarily engages in conduct that breaches an international obligation.[75] The Articles on State Responsibility define force majeure as 'the occurrence of an irresistible force or of an unforeseen event, beyond the control of the State, making it materially impossible in the circumstances to perform the obligation'.[76] This circumstance precluding wrongfulness is inapplicable; however, if the situation is due at least in part to the conduct of the state invoking force majeure, or if the state assumed the risk of the situation occurring.[77]

This definition contains three elements. First, the conduct of the state must be due to 'an irresistible force' or an 'unforeseen event', which could be a natural disaster (such as an earthquake, flood, or drought), or a man-made event (such as an insurrection or some other military activity) or both.[78] The word 'irresistible' indicates that the state must be unable to 'avoid or oppose' the force by its own means, while the word 'unforeseen' indicates that the state must not have been able to predict that such an event would occur.[79] The second element requires that the force or event is beyond the control of the state, meaning that the state must not have caused or induced the situation, whether intentionally or through negligence. Finally, the third element requires that compliance by the state with its international obligation is 'materially impossible', which means that it is not just difficult, but physically impossible.[80] Investment arbitration tribunals have held that a political or economic crisis would typically make a state's compliance with international investment law difficult or burdensome, but not materially impossible.[81] The first and the third

---

[73] ARSIWA art 22; Hubert Lesaffre, 'Circumstances Precluding Wrongfulness in the ICL Articles on State Responsibility: Countermeasures' in Crawford, Pellet, and Olleson (eds) (n 1) 469–73.

[74] ARSIWA arts 49–54.

[75] ARSIWA Commentary art 23, para 1; Sandra Szurek, 'Circumstances Precluding Wrongfulness in the ICL Articles on State Responsibility: *Force Majeure*' in Crawford, Pellet, and Olleson (eds) (n 1) 475–80.

[76] ARSIWA art 23(1).   [77] ARSIWA art 23(2).

[78] See eg, *Gould Marketing, Inc v Ministry of National Defense of Iran* (Interlocutory Award) (1983) 3 Iran-US CTR 147.

[79] ARSIWA Commentary art 23, para 2.   [80] ARSIWA Commentary art 23, para 3.

[81] ARSIWA Commentary art 23, para 3.

elements are causally related to each other in that the material impossibility must have been caused by the irresistible force or the unforeseen event.[82]

e   Distress

A state may invoke distress in order to preclude the wrongfulness of conduct that is voluntary, and taken in the midst of an emergency situation.[83] In a situation of distress, the state is capable of complying with the international obligation, unlike a situation involving force majeure, where compliance is materially impossible. But while compliance remains possible in a situation of distress, non-compliance represents the only 'reasonable way ... of saving the author's life or the lives of other persons entrusted to the author's care'.[84] The term 'author' refers to a government official or other actor whose conduct is attributable to the state. Distress as a circumstance precluding wrongfulness has been inspired by cases involving a ship or an aircraft that breaches an international obligation due to an emergency situation caused, for example, by foul weather or a mechanical failure that forces it to dock or land in foreign territory without prior consent. Human lives are at stake in situations of distress, although this circumstance precluding wrongfulness has also arguably been applied more to situations involving a serious health risk.[85] As with force majeure, if the emergency situation arose due to the conduct of the state invoking distress, then this circumstance precluding wrongfulness is inapplicable.[86] In addition, the conduct of the state invoking distress must not create a peril that is comparable to or greater than the peril that caused the distress in the first place.[87]

f   Necessity

In situations of necessity, the state engages in voluntary conduct that is inconsistent with an international obligation on account of an emergency concerning the life of the state, rather than human life.[88] An act of necessity must be 'the only way for the State to safeguard an essential interest against a grave and imminent peril'.[89] In addition, the act of necessity must not 'seriously impair an essential interest of the State or States towards which the obligation exists or of the international community as a whole'.[90] The essential interests of the state engaged in an act of necessity must therefore be balanced against the essential interest of the state(s) or international community, to whom the obligation is owed.[91] States have historically abused the concept of necessity by invoking self-preservation in order to

---

[82] ARSIWA Commentary art 23, para 2.

[83] Sandra Szurek, 'Circumstances Precluding Wrongfulness in the ICL Articles on State Responsibility: Distress' in Crawford, Pellet, and Olleson (eds) (n 1) 481–9.

[84] ARSIWA art 24.

[85] ARSIWA Commentary art 24, para 6; *Case concerning the difference between New Zealand and France concerning the interpretation or application of two agreements, concluding on 9 July 1986 between the two States and which related to the problems arising from the Rainbow Warrior Affair* (1990) XX RIAA 215, paras 78–88.

[86] ARSIWA art 24(2).   [87] ARSIWA art 24(2).

[88] ARSIWA art 25; Sarah Heathcote, 'Circumstances Precluding Wrongfulness in the ICL Articles on State Responsibility: Necessity' in Crawford, Pellet, and Olleson (eds) (n 1) 491–501.

[89] ARSIWA art 25(1)(a).   [90] ARSIWA art 25(1)(b).   [91] Crawford (n 3) 312–13.

justify occupations of other states.[92] As a result, the Articles on State Responsibility define necessity narrowly, and emphasize the exceptional character of this circumstance precluding wrongfulness by phrasing this article in the negative: 'necessity may *not* be invoked by a State as a ground for precluding the wrongfulness of an act not in conformity with an international obligation of that State *unless* ... '.[93] Situations involving an 'essential interest' could, for example, concern the existence of the state, the protection of the environment, or the safety of the civilian population.[94] As with distress and force majeure, the conduct of the state invoking necessity must not have contributed to creating the situation of necessity.[95] In the context of investment arbitration, states have relatively frequently invoked necessity with respect to regulatory measures taken in the midst of economic emergencies, but this plea has met with almost no success to date.[96]

4   Legal Consequences of an Internationally Wrongful Act

When conduct is attributable to a state and breaches an international obligation and none of the circumstances precluding wrongfulness are applicable, then the state bears international responsibility for its conduct. International responsibility for a wrongful act involves a number of general legal consequences, namely, the obligations to cease the wrongful conduct and to make full reparation for the injury caused by the wrongful act.[97] In certain circumstances, assurances or guarantees of non-repetition may also be appropriate.[98] In addition to these general legal consequences, a 'serious breach' of a peremptory or *jus cogens* norm entails further, exceptional legal consequences.[99] This section covers these general and exceptional legal consequences in turn.

a   General Legal Consequences

i   Cessation and Non-repetition

The general legal consequences of a wrongful act involve obligations that are both forward-looking and backward-looking. The forward-looking legal consequences involve the obligations to cease wrongful conduct and to offer appropriate assurances and guarantees of non-repetition, while the backward-looking consequences involve the obligation to make reparation.[100] If a wrongful act is ongoing, or 'continuing', then the state has a forward-looking obligation to cease such conduct. The obligation of cessation is geared towards bringing about future compliance with the international obligation being breached and it

---

[92] ibid 305–6.   [93] ARSIWA art 25 chapeau (emphasis added).
[94] Julia Pfeil, 'The Torrey Canyon' in *Max Planck Encyclopedia of Public International Law* (last updated December 2006).
[95] ARSIWA art 25(2).
[96] See, for example, *Sempra Energy International v Argentine Republic* (28 September 2007) ICSID Case No ARB/02/16; *Enron Corporation and Ponderosa Assets LP v Argentine Republic* (22 May 2007) ICSID Case No ARB/01/3; *CMS Gas Transmission Company v Argentine Republic* (12 May 2005) ICSID Case No ARB/01/8.
[97] ARSIWA arts 28, 30–1.   [98] ARSIWA art 30.   [99] ARSIWA arts 40–1.
[100] ARSIWA art 30. Olivier Corten, 'The Obligation of Cessation' in Crawford, Pellet and Olleson (eds) (n 1) 545–49; Sandrine Barbier, 'Assurances and Guarantees of Non-Repetition' in Crawford, Pellet, and Olleson (eds) (n 1) 551–61.

can be characterized as a 'negative' obligation because the state must refrain from certain conduct (whether an act or an omission).[101] Cessation also has a broader function concerned with the interests of the international community in preserving the rule of law. The cessation of a wrongful act not only brings about future compliance, but also contributes more generally to upholding the 'validity and effectiveness' of the primary rule at issue.[102]

Assurances and guarantees of non-repetition are also forward-looking legal consequences, in that their function is to prevent future violations, and thereby restore the injured states' confidence in future compliance.[103] Assurances and guarantees of non-repetition can be characterized as positive, rather than negative obligations because the state that has engaged in the wrongful conduct must take steps to reinforce its future compliance.[104] An injured state typically seeks assurances or guarantees in circumstances where cessation alone may not provide adequate protection against future non-compliance, such as in situations where there is a risk of repetition or the breach would be serious.[105] An assurance of non-repetition would normally involve a verbal act, such as a promise given by legal counsel during the course of court proceedings, while a guarantee would involve preventive measures geared towards avoiding future breaches, such as modification or repeal of domestic legislation.[106]

The *Mauritius* advisory opinion, discussed in Section 2(b), provides an example of how the obligation of cessation operates in practice. The Court in this case determined that the United Kingdom's continued administration of the Chagos Archipelago constituted an unlawful act of a continuing character.[107] Since the separation of the Chagos Archipelago from Mauritius in 1965, the United Kingdom has administered this territory in violation of Mauritius' right to self-determination. The Court further determined that the United Kingdom was; therefore, 'under an obligation to bring an end to its administration of the Chagos Archipelago as rapidly as possible', so that Mauritius can complete its process of decolonization in keeping with its right to self-determination.[108] The United Kingdom's obligation to cease its administration of the Chagos Archipelago is forward-looking because it concerns the United Kingdom's future compliance with its obligation to respect Mauritius' right to self-determination, rather than the past harm to Mauritius caused by the United Kingdom's failure to comply with this obligation. The Court's decision concerning the United Kingdom's obligation of cessation also has special significance for the international rule of law given the importance of self-determination as a primary rule of human rights law (see Chapter 3).

ii   Reparations

The general legal consequences of an internationally wrongful act also include the backward-looking obligation to make 'full reparation'. The term 'full reparation' means that the

---

[101] ARSIWA Commentary art 30, para 1.   [102] ARSIWA Commentary art 30, para 5.
[103] ARSIWA Commentary art 30, paras 1, 9.   [104] ARSIWA Commentary art 30, para 1.
[105] ARSIWA Commentary art 30, para 1. Barbier (n 100) 557.
[106] ARSIWA Commentary art 30, para 12. *LaGrand Case (Germany v United States of America)* (Judgment) [2001] ICJ Rep 466, para 128(6).
[107] *Mauritius* advisory opinion (n 53), para 177.   [108] ibid, para 178.

state bearing responsibility must wipe out the consequences of the illegal act and re-establish the situation that would exist today had the wrongful act not been committed.[109] The obligation to make full reparation is backward-looking because it focuses on addressing the damage caused by a wrongful act, and on the situation that existed prior to the breach. In cases where a wrongful act has not caused any damage, then reparations may or may not be necessary; cessation alone may suffice. Reparation may take three different forms: restitution, compensation, or satisfaction. Depending on the character of the injury caused by the wrongful act, these forms of reparation may be applied 'singly or in combination', meaning that one, two or all three forms of reparation may be applicable in a given case. Injuries may be classified according to whether they cause material damage or moral damage. On the one hand, material damage refers to 'damage to property or other interests of the State and its nationals which is assessable in financial terms'. On the other hand, moral damage refers to 'individual pain and suffering, loss of loved ones or personal affront associated with an intrusion on one's home or private life'. Moral damage is not considered to be 'financially assessable' under the law of state responsibility.[110]

The three forms of reparation bear a particular relationship to one another in that restitution has primacy over compensation and satisfaction, and compensation, in turn, has primacy over satisfaction. The term restitution refers to re-establishing the situation that existed prior to the wrongful act.[111] This could involve the restoration or return of property, persons, or territory, or the annulment or amendment of a judicial or legislative act.[112] A person, for example, could be released from detention, security forces could withdraw from occupied territory, or an arrest warrant could be annulled.[113] In many cases; however, restitution is 'materially impossible', such as where property or lives have been destroyed.[114] In addition, restitution is possible but inapplicable where it would involve a burden that is disproportionate to the benefit that would derive from restitution rather than compensation.[115]

Because restitution is often either impossible or inappropriate, monetary compensation is common in practice, particularly in the context of international investment arbitration.[116] Where restitution is impossible, disproportionate, or would not provide full reparation, then compensation may be paid, either in lieu of or alongside restitution.[117] Compensation usually takes the form of a monetary payment and is limited to 'financially assessable damage including loss of profits'.[118] Compensation thereby includes material damage, but excludes moral damage, which is instead dealt with through satisfaction. The function of compensation is 'to address the actual losses' resulting from the wrongful act, and not to

---

[109] ARSIWA art 31. *Case concerning the Factory at Chorzów (Germany v Poland)* (Merits) (1928) PCIJ Rep Series A No 17, 29 ('reparation must, as far as possible, wipe out all the consequences of the illegal act and reestablish the situation which would, in all probability have existed if that act had not been committed').

[110] ARSIWA Commentary art 36, para 1. [111] ARSIWA art 35; Commentary art 35, para 2.

[112] ARSIWA Commentary art 35, para 5.

[113] *US Diplomatic and Consular Staff in Tehran* case (n 46); *Case concerning the Temple of Preah Vihear (Cambodia v Thailand)* (Merits) [1962] ICJ Rep 6, second para of dispositif; *Case concerning the Arrest Warrant of 11 April 2000 (Democratic Republic of the Congo v Belgium)* (Judgment) [2002] ICJ Rep 3, para 78(3).

[114] *Bosnia Genocide* case (n 12), para 460. [115] ARSIWA art 35(b).

[116] Attila Tanzi, 'Restitution' in *Max Planck Encyclopedia of Public International Law* (last updated January 2021), para 14.

[117] ARSIWA art 36(1). [118] ARSIWA art 36(2); Commentary art 36, para 4.

punish the responsible state.[119] A state incurs compensable losses, for example, when its ships are attacked and damaged or destroyed, when its consulates or embassies come under attack, and when its territory is polluted.[120]

Finally, satisfaction is applicable as a form of reparation only to the extent that restitution and compensation do not provide full reparation.[121] In cases involving injuries to the state where the resulting moral damage is not financially assessable, compensation is not a possibility. Symbolic injuries result, for example, from violations of a state's sovereignty or territorial integrity, such as when one state's military jet violates the airspace of another state. Satisfaction may take many different forms, including the responsible state's acknowledgement of a breach, expression of regret, or formal apology.[122] Another common form of satisfaction, known as declaratory relief, takes the form of a declaration of wrongfulness by a court or tribunal, such as the ICJ.[123] Further possible forms of satisfaction include an investigation by a responsible state into an incident that resulted in injury to another state, and domestic criminal prosecution of individuals whose conduct gave rise to the wrongful act.[124] In the *Bosnia Genocide* case, for example, the ICJ determined that appropriate satisfaction included its declaration that Serbia had failed to comply with the obligation to prevent the crime of genocide and to comply with its outstanding obligations to transfer persons accused of genocide to the ICTY.[125] As satisfaction can take so many different forms, and is applicable in circumstances when restitution and compensation are either inapplicable or ineffective, satisfaction can be seen as a sort of 'catch-all' category of reparation. Satisfaction is limited, however, insofar as it may not impose a burden on the responsible state that is disproportionate to the injury, nor may it take a form that is humiliating to the responsible state.[126]

b   *Legal Consequences of a Serious Breach of a Peremptory Norm*

As noted at the beginning of this chapter, the law on state responsibility does not make any distinction between torts (delicts) and crimes; violations of the entire range of primary rules are qualified as internationally wrongful acts and are subject to the same secondary rules of state responsibility. In the case of 'serious breaches of peremptory norms'; however, some further legal consequences apply, in addition to the general legal consequences already discussed.[127] Peremptory norms (also known as *jus cogens* norms) are a special category of international obligations from which no derogation is possible.[128] This means, for example, that states may not conclude treaties that purport to permit or require breaches of peremptory norms, such as the prohibition on torture or slavery. These rules have a special status because they concern conduct that the international community views as 'intolerable'. Peremptory norms concern a relatively limited set of conduct that poses a threat 'to the survival of States and their peoples and the most basic human values'.[129] Examples of international obligations that are widely accepted as peremptory include the prohibitions on

[119] ARSIWA Commentary art 36, para 4.   [120] ARSIWA Commentary art 36, para 8.   [121] ARSIWA art 37(1).
[122] ARSIWA art 37(2).   [123] ARSIWA Commentary art 37, para 6.   [124] ARSIWA Commentary art 37, para 5.
[125] *Bosnia Genocide* case (n 12), paras 463, 465.   [126] ARSIWA art 37(3).   [127] ARSIWA Commentary ch III, para 7.
[128] VCLT art 53.   [129] ARSIWA Commentary art 40, para 3.

slavery and the slave trade, aggression, genocide, racial discrimination, apartheid, and torture, as well as the right to self-determination.[130]

Under the law of state responsibility, a breach of a peremptory norm gives rise to special legal consequences only when the breach is 'serious'. The Articles on State Responsibility define a 'serious breach' of a peremptory norm as one that 'involves a gross or systematic failure by the responsible State to fulfill the obligation'.[131] The word 'gross' indicates that the conduct and its effects must amount to a 'direct and outright assault on the values protected by the rule'.[132] The word 'systematic' indicates that the conduct must be carried out in an organized and deliberate manner.[133] By defining 'serious breach' as gross or systematic, the Articles on State Responsibility seek to distinguish between relatively small-scale and large-scale violations of peremptory norms.[134]

A serious breach of a peremptory norm results in two particular legal consequences for all states.[135] First, all states have a positive duty to cooperate to bring to an end any serious breach, through lawful means.[136] This duty will often entail cooperation within the framework of an international organization like the UN, but cooperation outside of the framework of an international organization is also conceivable.[137] In the *Mauritius* advisory opinion, for example, the Court determined that all UN member states have a duty to cooperate with the UN to bring about the decolonization of Mauritius.[138] The United Kingdom's continued administration of the Chagos Archipelago thereby gives rise to a legal obligation on all UN member states to cooperate with the General Assembly in whatever steps it decides to take to ensure the completion of Mauritius' decolonization process.

Second, states have a negative duty not to recognize as lawful a situation created by a serious breach, or to render aid or assistance in maintaining such a situation.[139] The obligation of non-recognition is relevant, for example, in situations where one state has occupied the territory of another state or denied the right of self-determination of peoples, and it serves to prevent gradual acquiescence by the international community.[140] As this obligation of non-recognition applies to all states in the event of a serious breach of a peremptory norm, it is meant to bring about 'collective non-recognition' of a situation created by a serious breach.[141] The obligation not to render aid or assistance, however, goes beyond non-recognition, by requiring all states not to lend support, such as through the supply of weapons, to a state that is, for example, engaging in genocide or violating the right to self-determination.

5 Countermeasures

Countermeasures are a form of self-help for states, which operate in a highly decentralized international legal system that offers few dispute settlement mechanisms that are

---

[130] ARSIWA Commentary art 40, paras 4–5.   [131] ARSIWA art 40(2).   [132] ARSIWA Commentary art 40, para 8.
[133] ARSIWA Commentary art 40, para 8.   [134] ARSIWA Commentary art 40, para 7.
[135] ARSIWA Commentary ch III, para 7.   [136] ARSIWA art 41(1).   [137] ARSIWA Commentary art 41, paras 2–3.
[138] *Mauritius* advisory opinion (n 53), paras 180–2.   [139] ARSIWA art 41(2).
[140] See, for example, the 2014 Russian occupation of Crimea.   [141] ARSIWA Commentary art 41, para 8.

compulsory.[142] Countermeasures represent a method by which states can nevertheless vindicate their rights and repair relationships that have been disrupted by a wrongful act.[143] When one state breaches the rights of another state, a dispute between the responsible state and the injured state typically arises. The dispute might arise, for example, because the responsible state contends that it has not actually breached an international obligation. Even if the two states agree that a wrongful act has occurred, they might still disagree on the legal consequences for the responsible state. They might dispute the level of compensation required or the need for assurances or guarantees of non-repetition, for example. Disputing parties can resolve such disagreements through any of the dispute settlement methods discussed in Chapter 9, including negotiations, but also litigation at an international court or tribunal, such as the ICJ. When states have attempted and failed to resolve their differences through negotiations, countermeasures represent one possible next step for the injured state. Instead of referring the dispute to a third party, such as the ICJ, countermeasures allow injured states to take matters into their own hands, in a manner that is potentially more efficient, but also open to abuse. The following introduces the concept of countermeasures as well as the substantive and procedural rules that are designed to prevent abuse of this form of self-help.

Countermeasures are unilateral measures adopted by an injured state in response to a breach of its rights due to the wrongful act of another state.[144] Countermeasures entail the injured state's temporary non-compliance with its own international obligations towards the responsible state.[145] The illegality or wrongfulness of such conduct by the injured state is precluded, as countermeasures constitute one of the circumstances precluding wrongfulness, discussed in Section 3.[146] If the injured state's countermeasures result in non-compliance with its obligations towards other third states, then the wrongfulness of its conduct towards these other states will not be precluded.[147] The purpose of countermeasures is to induce compliance by the responsible state, not to punish the responsible state for its wrongful conduct.[148] An injured state may also attempt to induce compliance through unfriendly but lawful conduct, but this constitutes a different form of self-help, known as retorsion.[149]

The existence of a wrongful act is a precondition for resort to countermeasures. Because countermeasures are self-help measures, a state that resorts to countermeasures must rely on its own, unilateral assessment of the situation, and it bears the risk of an incorrect determination that a wrongful act exists.[150] A state that purports to resort to counter-measures, on the basis of an incorrect assessment, may therefore engage in wrongful

---

[142] The term countermeasures is the term of art, which has replaced the terms reprisal and sanction.
[143] ARSIWA Commentary pt III, ch II, para 1.
[144] Federica Paddeu, 'Countermeasures' in *Max Planck Encyclopedia of Public International Law* (last updated September 2015). ARSIWA art 49(1).
[145] ARSIWA art 49(2).   [146] ARSIWA art 22.   [147] ARSIWA Commentary art 49, para 4.
[148] ARSIWA art 49(1); Commentary art 49, para 1.
[149] The Financial Action Task Force (FATF) requires its members to impose limitations on financial transactions with certain 'blacklisted' states whose anti-money laundering laws do not meet FATF's standards. Such limitations do not violate any international legal obligations, though they are unfriendly acts, and thus constitute a form of retorsion, rather than counter-measures (though FATF refers to them as countermeasures).
[150] ARSIWA Commentary art 49, para 3.

conduct itself. Assuming the existence of a wrongful act, a state's resort to countermeasures is governed by a number of substantive and procedural requirements that are designed to safeguard against abuse of countermeasures.

Substantively, certain primary rules may not be impaired by countermeasures.[151] Some primary rules are excluded from the scope of countermeasures because of their fundamental character, namely the prohibition on the use of force, fundamental human rights, humanitarian rules, and peremptory norms.[152] Countermeasures also do not extend to dispute settlement procedures and the rules on the inviolability of diplomatic and consular agents, premises, archives and documents (see Chapters 7 and 9). These rules on inviolability are not of a fundamental character, but they are critical for the maintenance of communications between disputing states, and the resolution of disputes.[153] Finally, a state that takes countermeasures is further bound by the substantive requirement of proportionality.[154] This involves a consideration of the gravity of the injury suffered on account of the wrongful act and the rights of both the injured state and the responsible state (i.e., the state taking the countermeasures and the state that bears responsibility for the wrongful act to which the countermeasures respond).[155] Countermeasures that entail non-compliance with an obligation that is the same as or similar to the obligation that was originally violated by the responsible state are more likely to be considered to be proportionate.[156]

Countermeasures are also subject to a number of procedural requirements that are partly geared towards ensuring that other forms of dispute settlement, such as negotiations and litigation, can run their course before an injured state resorts to countermeasures. An injured state must first call on the responsible state to comply with its legal obligations and to provide reparation,[157] and it must also notify the responsible state of its decision to pursue countermeasures and offer to negotiate.[158] These procedural requirements help to ensure that the responsible state has an opportunity to cease its wrongful conduct and repair its relationship with the injured state before the injured state pursues potentially damaging countermeasures against it.[159] In addition, countermeasures are incompatible with litigation before a court or tribunal that has the authority to take a binding decision concerning the dispute. Pending litigation thereby precludes an injured party from taking countermeasures, and the initiation of litigation would also require the injured party to suspend any existing countermeasures.[160]

The procedural requirements also ensure that countermeasures are both temporary and reversible. Countermeasures may continue for only as long as the wrongful conduct persists and the responsible state has not made reparation.[161] Once the responsible state ceases and makes reparation for its wrongful conduct, then the injured state must terminate its countermeasures.[162] In addition, countermeasures must be reversible 'as far as possible',

---

[151] ARSIWA art 50(1).   [152] ARSIWA art 50.   [153] ARSIWA Commentary art 50, para 2.   [154] ARSIWA art 51.
[155] ARSIWA Commentary art 51, para 6.
[156] Paddeu (n 144), para 24. See, for example, *Air Services Agreement of 27 March 1946 between the United States of America and France* (1978) XVIII RIAA 417, para 83.
[157] ARSIWA art 52(1)(a).   [158] ARSIWA art 52(1)(b).   [159] ARSIWA Commentary art 52, para 4.
[160] ARSIWA art 52(3)(b).   [161] ARSIWA art 49(2).   [162] ARSIWA art 53.

so that the state taking countermeasures can resume its compliance with its obligations as soon as the termination of the countermeasures is required.[163]

The issue of countermeasures arose in the context of a contemporary dispute between Qatar, on the one hand, and Bahrain, Egypt, Saudi Arabia and the United Arab Emirates (the 'Quartet'), on the other hand.[164] In June 2017, following years of tension between the Quartet and Qatar, the Quartet imposed a series of aviation restrictions on Qatar. These restrictions barred all Qatar-registered aircraft from landing at or departing from the airports of Bahrain, Egypt, Saudi Arabia, and the United Arab Emirates, and the restrictions also denied Qatar-registered aircraft the right to fly over their territories.[165] The measures taken by the Quartet conflicted with their obligations under two civil aviation treaties,[166] but the Quartet argued that their conduct was not wrongful because it could be characterized as lawful countermeasures.[167] According to the Quartet, they had imposed aviation restrictions in response to Qatar's violations of the Riyadh Agreements of 2013 and 2014, to which both Qatar and the Quartet are parties.[168] The Riyadh Agreements required Qatar to take certain measures to counter terrorism and non-interference in the internal affairs of the Quartet, as well as Egypt. The Quartet objected, in particular, to Qatar's continued support for the media outlet Al-Jazeera, which, according to the Quartet, disseminates the hate speech of terrorists. In the course of litigation before the ICJ concerning separate but related legal issues, the Quartet claimed that Qatar had failed to comply with its obligations under the Riyadh Agreements, such that its aviation restrictions constituted lawful countermeasures.

The dispute that came before the ICJ did not require the Court to rule on the issue of the lawfulness of the countermeasures taken by the Quartet. If the Court had ruled on this issue, however, the Court may very well have found that these countermeasures were unlawful under the law on state responsibility, in light of the substantive and procedural requirements that govern countermeasures. With respect to the substantive requirement of proportionality, the Quartet's aviation restrictions entailed non-compliance with civil aviation obligations, which are not the same as or similar to the obligations assumed by the Quartet under the Riyadh Agreements, which concern counter-terrorism and non-interference. In addition, the Quartet's aviation restrictions could arguably be seen as disproportionate given the importance of Qatar's rights with respect to civil aviation. The restrictions were, for example, imposed by the Quartet suddenly, while flights were mid-air, thereby disrupting all air traffic on certain routes.[169] Because the airspace of the

---

[163] ARSIWA art 49.

[164] *Appeal Relating to the Jurisdiction of the ICAO Council under Article 84 of the Convention on International Civil Aviation (Bahrain, Egypt, Saudi Arabia and United Arab Emirates v Qatar)* (Judgment) ICJ General List No 173 [2020]; *Appeal Relating to the Jurisdiction of the ICAO Council under Article II, Section 2, of the 1944 International Air Services Transit Agreement (Bahrain, Egypt and United Arab Emirates v Qatar)* (Judgment) ICJ General List No 174 [2020] (*Appeals Relating to the Jurisdiction of the ICAO Council*).

[165] *Appeals Relating to the Jurisdiction of the ICAO Council*, para 21.

[166] Convention on International Civil Aviation (adopted 7 December 1944, entered into force 4 April 1947) 15 UNTS 295; International Air Services Transit Agreement (adopted 7 December 1944, entered into force 30 January 1945) 84 UNTS 389.

[167] *Appeals Relating to the Jurisdiction of the ICAO Council*, paras 41–3.   [168] ibid, para 21.

[169] *Appeals Relating to the Jurisdiction of the ICAO Council*, CR 2019/15 (verbatim record), Al-Khulaifi, paras 4–7.

Quartet geographically surrounds the airspace of Qatar, the aviation restrictions also had the long-term effect of greatly restricting the ability of Qatari aircraft to fly into and out of Qatar. In proceedings before the ICJ, Qatar asserted that the restrictions had disrupted air navigation, flight safety and efficiency, trade, commerce, and communication.[170] With respect to the procedural requirements governing the imposition of countermeasures, the Quartet also did not suspend the countermeasures after Qatar instituted litigation before the Council of the International Civil Aviation Authority.

This dispute illustrates the extent to which the imposition of countermeasures is constrained by both substantive and procedural requirements, which significantly restrict the scope of countermeasures, and the manner in which a state may pursue them. In the case of Qatar and the Quartet, it appears that these self-help measures went beyond the bounds established by the law on state responsibility.

6 Concluding Remarks

This chapter introduced the law on state responsibility, with a particular focus on the ILC's Articles on State Responsibility, many of which reflect customary international law. The law on state responsibility provides a legal framework for determining whether a state has violated an international legal obligation, and the legal consequences of such a violation. The first lines of inquiry involve assessments of whether the conduct at issue is attributable to the state, and whether a breach of an international legal obligation has occurred. As a general rule, only the conduct of state organs can be attributed to the state, although a number of exceptions to this rule allow for the attribution of the conduct of private actors in circumstances that are, in practice, relatively rare. The breach of an international obligation does not necessarily give rise to an internationally wrongful act on account of a number of circumstances precluding wrongfulness, which act as general defences in the law of state responsibility. When none of these circumstances precluding wrongfulness applies, which will often be the case, then the legal consequences of the wrongful act may include cessation, a guarantee of non-repetition, and reparation, which can entail restitution, compensation, and satisfaction. In certain circumstances, states that have been affected or injured by the wrongful act of another state can take matters into their own hands by resorting to countermeasures, though this self-help mechanism is subject to a number of limitations in order to prevent abuse. Although these rules on state responsibility govern the operation of much of the primary rules of public international law, they can be displaced through rules that are more specialized or specific (i.e., *lex specialis*).[171] The default rules; however, are embodied in the Articles on State Responsibility, which remain the touchstone in this area.

---

[170] ibid, para 7.
[171] The Dispute Settlement Understanding of the World Trade Organization, for example, contains a body of special rules on countermeasures, which displace the general rules of state responsibility (*lex generalis*).

Recommended Reading

Daniel Costelloe, "Legal Consequences in the Law of International Responsibility" in *Legal Consequences of Peremptory Norms in International Law* (Cambridge University Press 2017).

James Crawford, Alain Pellet, Simon Olleson (eds), and Kate Parlett (ass ed), *The Law of International Responsibility* (Oxford University Press 2010).

Vladyslav Lanovoy, *Complicity and Its Limits in the Law of International Responsibility* (Hart 2016).

André Nollkaemper, Ilias Plakokefalos (eds), and Jessica NM Schechinger (ass ed), *Principles of Shared Responsibility in International Law: An Appraisal of the State of the Art* (Cambridge University Press 2014).

Federica Paddeu, *Justification and Excuse in International Law: Concept and Theory of General Defences* (Cambridge University Press 2018).

6

Jurisdiction

Erik Koppe[*]

1   Introduction

In Chapter 3, we established that states are the main subjects of public international law. Each state enjoys full sovereignty over its territory and therefore has, in principle, full jurisdiction over events and persons within its territory.[1] Jurisdiction is derived from the Latin word '*ius*', which means 'law' or 'authority', and the Latin word '*dicere*', which means to 'speak' or 'determine'. The term 'jurisdiction' is often associated with the power of a court to hear a case,[2] but judicial or adjudicative jurisdiction is just one of three manifestations of jurisdiction. The exercise of jurisdiction is also manifested in the authority of states to prescribe rules (legislative or prescriptive jurisdiction) and the power of states to enforce rules (enforcement jurisdiction). In other words, jurisdiction encompasses all exercises of governmental power.[3]

Although the power of states to exercise jurisdiction follows from the principle of sovereignty, which attributes '*suprema potestas*' (full governmental power) and independence to each state,[4] this power is not unlimited. After all, each state has to respect the personality and sovereign equality of other states,[5] and overstepping this boundary entails a violation of public international law. This limitation is most pertinent when a state exercises jurisdiction *outside* its own territory, for example when it enforces domestic legislation outside of its territory or when it extends the application of its domestic laws to people, property, or events outside of its own territory. But public international law also limits the exercise of jurisdiction by states *within* their own territories; for example, in relation to foreign states and their property, foreign state officials, and international organizations. After all, foreign states generally enjoy immunity from the adjudicative

---

[*] The views and opinions expressed in this chapter do not purport to reflect the views or opinions of Pels Rijcken or its clients.

[1] *Jurisdictional Immunities of the State (Germany v Italy: Greece Intervening)* (Judgment) [2012] ICJ Rep 99, para 57. The link between jurisdiction and territory is of relatively recent origin. Lowe writes that '[j]urisdiction almost certainly began as a personal, rather than a territorial, link'. Vaughan Lowe, *International Law* (Oxford University Press 2007) 174.

[2] See, for example, the discussion relating to the jurisdiction of international courts and tribunals, such as the International Court of Justice (ICJ) (Chapter 9) and the International Criminal Court (ICC) (Chapter 13).

[3] See Michael Akehurst, *A Modern Introduction to International Law* (6th edn, Routledge 1987) 104. Lowe and Staker only distinguish between prescriptive and enforcement jurisdiction. See Lowe (n 1) 171; Christopher Staker, 'Jurisdiction' in Malcolm D Evans (ed), *International Law* (4th edn, Oxford University Press 2014) 313.

[4] See *The Island of Palmas Case (or Miangas) (United States v The Netherlands)* (Award of the Tribunal) (1928) PCA Case 1925-01, 8.

[5] According to the General Assembly, one of the elements of sovereign equality is that '[e]ach State has the duty to respect the personality of other States'. UNGA Res 2625 (XXV) (24 October 1970).

jurisdiction of another state and their property which is, as a matter of principle, inviolable and not subject to the enforcement jurisdiction of another state.

This chapter discusses the scope of the jurisdiction of states when states exercise enforcement, prescriptive, and adjudicative jurisdiction in relation to persons, property, and acts *outside* of their own territory. The following chapter will discuss the scope of the jurisdiction of states when they exercise jurisdiction *within* their own territories, in light of the immunity of states, state officials, and international organizations.

2   Enforcement Jurisdiction

Enforcement means the exercise of jurisdiction by the government of a state, namely the executive branch of government. The executive branch is that branch of government that is responsible for the enforcement of regulations and the maintenance of public order. The most obvious state officials exercising enforcement jurisdiction are therefore those officials who are authorized to use force, such as police officers and military personnel.

The exercise of enforcement jurisdiction is the most intrusive manifestation of jurisdiction by a state and would therefore be the most likely to interfere with the sovereign rights of other states. The exercise of enforcement jurisdiction outside a state's territory is therefore, in principle, prohibited under public international law. The Permanent Court of International Justice (PCIJ) held in the *S.S. Lotus* case: '[T]he first and foremost restriction imposed by international law upon a State is that – failing the existence of a permissive rule to the contrary – it may not exercise its power in any form in the territory of another State'.[6]

In practice this means that state officials may not exercise any form of enforcement jurisdiction in the territory of another state. Neither police officers nor security agents may make an arrest in the territory of another state, even when they are in hot pursuit.[7] They are also not allowed to conduct any criminal investigations in another state, and they are not even allowed to accompany immigrants across the border.[8] State officials are not allowed to enter the land registers (whether these land registers are in paper or digital format) of other states to establish whether their residents, who receive social security benefits, own any real estate in another state,[9] or enforce any administrative orders like the closing of a workplace because of violations of labour or environmental laws. Bailiffs are also not allowed to serve a writ of summons in the territory of another state and they cannot attach property in the territory of another state to enforce a judgment.

---

[6] *The Case of the S.S. 'Lotus' (France v Turkey)* (Judgment) (1927) PCIJ Rep Series A No 10, 18.
[7] Hot pursuit of a foreign ship is, under certain conditions, allowed under Article 111 of the United Nations Convention on the Law of the Sea (adopted 10 December 1982, entered into force 16 November 1994) 1833 UNTS 3 (UNCLOS). See also Chapter 15.
[8] On 22 September 2016, two Belgian police officers were arrested in France after they had escorted thirteen immigrants across the border into France. See BBC News, 'France Arrests Belgian Police in Migrant Border Row' (22 September 2016) <www .bbc.com/news/world-europe-37442328>. Similarly, on 18 September 2015, the Hungarian police reportedly arrested and disarmed thirty-six Croatian police officers who escorted a group of approximately 1,000 immigrants by train from Croatia to Austria over Hungarian territory. See Aljazeera, 'Hungary Seizes Refugee Train Arriving from Croatia' (19 September 2015) <www.aljazeera.com/news/2015/09/hungary-seizes-refugee-train-arriving-croatia-150919003810139.html>.
[9] See *De Volkskrant*, 'Kadaster in Marokko open voor attache' (2 March 2002) <www.volkskrant.nl/nieuws-achtergrond/kada ster-in-marokko-open-voor-attache~b5364ce1>.

The exercise of enforcement jurisdiction in the territory of another state is only allowed if the other state has consented to the exercise of jurisdiction. After all, consent precludes the wrongfulness of an act to the extent that the act remains within the limits of that consent (Article 20 of the Articles on State Responsibility).[10] Such consent may be given after the wrongful act has already occurred[11] but consent can also be given in advance, for example, by means of a treaty. In that case, the state exercising enforcement jurisdiction, may rely on a 'permissive rule' of public international law. For example, the twenty-six states parties to the 1990 Schengen Convention allow, under specific conditions, the police officers of other states parties to continue their pursuit of individuals who have been caught in the commission of or participation in particular crimes in their territory, without prior authorization.[12] In 1991, the United Kingdom and France concluded a treaty pursuant to which British and French customs and immigration officers are allowed to operate on each other's territory in relation to the Channel Tunnel.[13] And in 2009 and 2015 the Netherlands concluded treaties with Belgium and Norway pursuant to which the Netherlands allowed both states to carry out or execute Belgian and Norwegian prison sentences in the Netherlands.[14]

Also, court judgments cannot be enforced in the territory of another state without the permission of that state.[15] Such permission can generally be provided by means of a general statute enacted by the other state or by means of a treaty or international instrument concluded between the two (or more) states. Such treaties or instruments have been concluded, for example, on the enforcement of criminal judgments,[16] on the mutual recognition of financial penalties,[17] and on the recognition of judgments in civil and commercial matters within the European Union[18] (EU) and globally.[19]

---

[10] See Chapter 5.

[11] A state may also decide not to pursue the matter any further and acquiesce in the violation of its territorial sovereignty. See Staker (n 3) 332.

[12] See Convention Implementing the Schengen Agreement of 14 June 1985 between the Governments of the States of the Benelux Economic Union, the Federal Republic of Germany and the French Republic on the Gradual Abolition of Checks at Their Common Borders [1985] OJ L239, art 41. Lowe refers to agreements concluded in the Caribbean relating to drug trafficking on the basis of which extra-territorial law enforcement is permitted under certain conditions. See Lowe (n 1) 184. See also Staker (n 3) 332.

[13] Protocol between the Government of the United Kingdom of Great Britain and Northern Ireland and the Government of the French Republic Concerning Frontier Controls and Policing, Co-operation in Criminal Justice, Public Safety and Mutual Assistance Relating to the Channel Fixed Link (25 November 1991) UKTS 70 (1993).

[14] Verdrag tussen het Koninkrijk der Nederlanden en het Koninkrijk België over de terbeschikkingstelling van een penitentiaire inrichting in Nederland ten behoeve van de tenuitvoerlegging van bij Belgische veroordelingen opgelegde vrijheidsstraffen (Agreement between the Kingdom of the Netherlands and the Kingdom of Belgium on the Use of a Prison in the Netherlands for the Purpose of the Execution of Belgian Sentences of Imprisonment) (31 October 2009) Trb 2009, 202; Agreement between the Kingdom of the Netherlands and the Kingdom of Norway on the Use of a Prison in the Netherlands for the Purpose of the Execution of Norwegian Sentences of Imprisonment (2 March 2015) Trb 2015, 37.

[15] See, for example, arts 430 and 431 of the Dutch Code of Civil Procedure, which provide, in short, that civil judgments of Dutch courts can be enforced within the whole territory of the Netherlands while civil judgments of foreign courts cannot be enforced in the Netherlands. An unofficial translation is available through <www.dutchcivillaw.com/civilprocedureleg.htm>. Art 2 of the Dutch Enforcement of Criminal Judgments (Transfer) Act provides that criminal judgments cannot be enforced in the Netherlands, except on the basis of a treaty.

[16] Convention on the Transfer of Sentenced Persons (adopted 21 March 1983, entered into force 1 July 1985) ETS 112.

[17] Council (EC) Framework Decision 2005/214/JHA of 24 February 2005 on the Application of the Principle of Mutual Recognition to Financial Penalties [2005] OJ L76/16.

[18] Regulation (EU) No 1215/2012 of the European Parliament and of the Council of 12 December 2012 on Jurisdiction and the Recognition and Enforcement of Judgments in Civil and Commercial Matters [2012] OJ L351/01 (Brussels I Regulation (recast)).

[19] Also, in 2019, the Hague Conference on Private International Law (HCCH) Convention on the Recognition and Enforcement of Foreign Judgments in Civil or Commercial Matters (2 July 2019) was concluded within the framework of the HCCH. The HCCH is an international organization that aims to progressively unify the rules of private international law. The first meeting of

These treaties and international instruments must be distinguished from mutual legal assistance treaties (MLATs) that are defined as 'treaty-based reciprocal obligations to provide legal assistance, developed as evidence-gathering tools in regard to specific transnational crimes',[20] and have been concluded both multilaterally and bilaterally. Multilateral MLATs have been concluded, for example, by the members of the Council of Europe[21] and the members of the EU.[22] Bilateral MLATs have been concluded by, for example, the United States and Switzerland[23] and the Netherlands and Canada.[24] Similar treaties have been concluded to facilitate civil (as opposed to criminal) litigation. In 1965, for example, the HCCH adopted the Convention on the Service Abroad of Judicial and Extrajudicial Documents in Civil or Commercial Matters[25] and in 1970 the Convention on the Taking of Evidence Abroad in Civil or Commercial Matters.[26]

Finally, the exercise of enforcement jurisdiction by a state outside its territory is not only generally prohibited when it is exercised on the territory of another state, but also when it is exercised at sea in an area that is subject to the sovereignty of another coastal state or in an area in which a coastal state may exercise sovereign rights. As will be discussed in Chapter 15 of this book, the 1982 UNCLOS attributes sovereignty to a coastal state over an area known as the territorial sea extending to a maximum of twelve nautical miles from its land territory (Article 2 UNCLOS). It also attributes sovereign rights to coastal states over additional maritime zones for public order and economic reasons.[27] The exercise of enforcement jurisdiction by a state in these maritime zones, or in the high seas against ships flying the flag of another state, without prior authorization from the coastal state or flag state, would, in principle, conflict with the sovereign rights of the coastal state or flag state and would therefore not be in conformity with public international law.

3   Prescriptive Jurisdiction

a   *Introduction*

In most states, multiple branches of government are involved in legislation or prescription. While most constitutions attribute the general power to legislate to parliament, a parliamentary

---

the Hague Conference was convened in 1893 by the Netherlands upon the initiative of TMC Asser, who was awarded the Nobel Peace Prize in 1911.

[20] Neil Boister, *An Introduction to Transnational Criminal Law* (2nd edn, Oxford University Press 2018) 313.

[21] European Convention on Mutual Assistance in Criminal Matters (adopted 20 April 1959, entered into force 12 June 1962) ETS 030.

[22] Council Act of 29 May 2000 Establishing in Accordance with Article 34 of the Treaty on EU the Convention on Mutual Assistance in Criminal Matters between the Member States of the European Union [2000] OJ C197/01.

[23] Treaty between the United States of America and the Swiss Confederation on Mutual Assistance in Criminal Matters (signed 25 May 1973) 27 UST 2019.

[24] Treaty between the Kingdoms of the Netherlands and Canada on Mutual Assistance in Criminal Matters (1 May 1991) Trb 1991, 85.

[25] HCCH Convention on the Service Abroad of Judicial and Extrajudicial Documents in Civil or Commercial Matters (15 November 1965).

[26] HCCH Convention on the Taking of Evidence Abroad in Civil or Commercial Matters (18 March 1970).

[27] See further Chapter 15.

assembly or jointly to parliament and the government (the executive branch), many constitutions also allow that some of these legislative powers are delegated to other state organs, such as the government or individual ministers. The terms 'prescription' and 'legislation' refer to the prescription of rules that are generally applicable to an unspecified number of addressees but prescription and legislation may also include specific decisions addressed to a limited number of people or entities.

The exercise of prescriptive jurisdiction is, just like the exercise of enforcement jurisdiction, generally limited to the territory of the prescribing state. After all, the jurisdiction of states follows from the principle of sovereignty and sovereignty is linked to the territory of a state. Most, if not all states, however, also extend the scope of some of their rules to persons, property, and acts outside of their own territory. The exercise of prescriptive jurisdiction is less intrusive than the exercise of enforcement jurisdiction (which generally involves the presence of enforcement authorities or the carrying out of physical acts by state agents in a foreign state) and for that reason public international law allows states a large measure of discretion to extend the scope of their legislation outside their territories.

The PCIJ held in 1927 in the *S.S. Lotus* case that public international law does not prohibit states from exercising jurisdiction in their own territories 'in respect of any case which relates to acts which have taken place abroad'.[28] The Court explained that:

> Far from laying down a general prohibition to the effect that States may not extend the application of their laws and the jurisdiction of their courts to persons, property and acts outside their territory, it leaves them in this respect a wide measure of discretion, which is only limited in certain cases by prohibitive rules; as regards other cases, every State remains free to adopt the principles which it regards as best and most suitable.[29]

Already in 1927, the PCIJ observed that in practice, states had adopted a great variety of rules 'without objections or complaints on the part of other States'. 'In these circumstances, all that can be required of a State is that it should not overstep the limits which international law places upon its jurisdiction; within these limits, its title to exercise jurisdiction rests in its sovereignty'.[30]

Although public international law allows states a large measure of discretion to extend the scope of their legislation outside their territories, the PCIJ observed that the jurisdiction of states is not unlimited. After all, by extending the scope of their legislation to persons, property, and acts outside their own territory, states can exert significant influence outside their territory, which may interfere with the sovereign rights of other states. This is particularly true when a state extends the application of its public laws outside of its territory, such as its criminal laws, its tax laws, and its administrative laws, including its financial and economic laws.[31] Such public laws are 'quintessentially manifestations of the state's sovereign power, rather than laws that lay down the ground rules for the creation of

---

[28] *S.S. Lotus* case (n 6) 19.   [29] ibid.   [30] ibid.

[31] See also Lowe (n 1). Lowe illustrates the scope of the prescriptive jurisdiction of states by reference to criminal law, but 'the principles apply to all 'public' laws that make up the public order of the state including, for example, tax and competition laws'. Lowe (n 1) 171–2.

rights and duties between individuals, in the way that, say, contract, family, and land law do'.[32]

The US Supreme Court has; therefore, adopted a general presumption against the extra-territorial application of its domestic legislation because it wants to ensure that its inter-pretations of US law do not have unintended and unwarranted foreign policy consequences.[33] The Supreme Court held in 2013 that this presumption protects against 'unintended clashes' between US laws and the laws of other states, which could 'result in international discord'. The Supreme Court further explained that for the judiciary to interfere in the 'delicate field of international relations', the Congress must have clearly expressed such an intention. According to the Supreme Court, '[t]he presumption against extra-territorial application helps ensure that the Judiciary does not erroneously adopt an interpretation of U.S. law that carries foreign policy consequences not clearly intended by the political branches'.[34]

While public international law does not explicitly permit the exercise of prescriptive jurisdiction, it does appear to require a genuine link between a state exercising prescriptive jurisdiction outside its own territory and the persons, property, or acts affected by such legislation.[35] There should be a link or nexus with the territory of the prescribing state,[36] a link on the basis of nationality with the prescribing state, a link with the vital interests of the prescribing state, or a link with universal interests.

State practice shows that many, if not most states explicitly extend the scope of some of their legislation to persons, property, or acts outside their own territory by relying in some form on territoriality, nationality, or the protection of vital or universal interests. We could even speak of legislative principles used by legislators or courts to justify the extra-territorial application of legislation. In practice, four principles can be identified: the territoriality principle, the nationality or personality principle, the protective principle, and the universality principle.

b   *The Territoriality Principle*

The territoriality principle justifies the extra-territorial application of domestic legislation in case of a genuine link between the person, property, or act affected by the legislation and the territory of the prescribing state. On the basis of the territoriality principle, for example, a state's criminal code (the most intrusive branch of public law) may extend to persons,

---

[32] Staker (n 3) 331. Some laws are difficult to classify, however. According to Staker, tort law, which is essentially private law, 'may also be viewed as laws by which the State prescribes rules of conduct for society, in the same way that it does in its criminal law, but leaving the enforcement of those rules up to private parties. This duel nature of tort law is most evident in US antitrust laws, where those injured by unlawful anticompetitive practices are enabled to recover treble damages, as an incentive to act as "private attorneys general" in the enforcement of the laws. For that reason, English courts have refused to enforce US antitrust laws'. Staker (n 3) 331–2.

[33] Also, under English law there is a presumption against extra-territoriality of legislation. See Lowe (n 1) 175.

[34] *Kiobel et al v Royal Dutch Petroleum Co et al* 569 US 108 (2013) (US Supreme Court) 116–17.

[35] UNCLOS (n 7) for example, attributes sovereign rights to coastal states in maritime zones extending beyond their territorial sea. See Chapter 15.

[36] Similarly, Staker (n 3) 315.

property, or acts outside the prescribing state's territory if a particular crime or element of this crime occurred in or can somehow be localized in the prescribing state.

If an Israeli soldier is shot dead by a Lebanese sniper from across the border, the crime can be localized both in Lebanon and in Israel.[37] If someone operates a drone to deliver abortion pills from Germany into Poland across the River Oder, then the operator may still be subjected to Polish criminal law even though he or she was not present on Polish territory.[38] And a German farmer who tried to avoid criminal responsibility for violating the Netherlands' export prohibitions to Germany in 1914 by pulling a horse on a rope from the Dutch side to the German side of a border channel, all when standing on the German side himself, was found guilty for violating the aforementioned ban, because the Supreme Court of the Netherlands established that the crime had occurred in the Netherlands.[39]

These examples show that some crimes have transboundary elements and can been seen as taking place (or localized) in multiple states. This is particularly true in the case of border incidents,[40] but may also be true in the case of cybercrime, where computers and computer servers located in one state may be accessed (hacked) by people who operate another computer on the other side of the world.

Because some crimes may take place in multiple states,[41] one generally distinguishes between those states that may exercise prescriptive jurisdiction on the basis of the subjective territoriality principle and those states that may exercise prescriptive jurisdiction on the basis of the objective territoriality principle. The subjective territoriality principle justifies the application of domestic criminal law (and thus the exercise of prescriptive jurisdiction) in relation to a crime that is instigated (or begun) on the territory of that particular state but that is subsequently completed in another state. The objective territoriality principle then justifies the application of domestic criminal law by the state where such crime is completed, even though the crime was instigated in another state. So, for example, in the case of the killing of the Israeli soldier in Israel by a Lebanese sniper operating from Lebanese territory, the application of Israeli criminal law would be justified on the basis of the objective territoriality principle and the application of Lebanese criminal law would be justified on the basis of the subjective territoriality principle.

The territoriality principle also justifies extra-territorial application of other public laws, such as tax law. The Dutch Income Tax Act, for example, applies to anyone who receives income from the Netherlands, irrespective of nationality or country of residence. This is

---

[37] See 'Israeli Soldier Killed by Shots from Lebanon', BBC News, 16 December 2013 <www.bbc.com/news/world-middle-east -25395226>.

[38] See Nadia Khomami, '"Abortion Drone" to Fly Pills across Border into Poland', *The Guardian*, 24 June 2015 <www .theguardian.com/world/2015/jun/24/abortion-drone-border-poland-germany-women-on-waves> and 'Dutch Campaigners Fly Abortion Pills into Poland', BBC News, 27 June 2015 <www.bbc.com/news/world-europe-33299660>.

[39] HR 6 April 1915 (Azewijnse paard) ECLI:NL:HR:1915:BG9430 (Supreme Court of the Netherlands) 427.

[40] The border between the Netherlands and Belgium at Baarle-Nassau/Baarle-Hertog, for example, is particularly problematic since it consists of a patchwork of Belgian enclaves surrounded by Dutch territory. In 1957, the Netherlands and Belgium requested the ICJ to settle a dispute between both states regarding the sovereignty over two plots of land at Baarle-Nassau /Baarle-Hertog. In 1959, the Court held that sovereignty over both plots of land belonged to Belgium. *Case concerning Sovereignty over certain Frontier Land (Belgium v Netherlands)* (Judgment) [1959] ICJ Rep 209.

[41] See for a discussion of the difficulties of localizing acts, Staker (n 3) 328–9.

known as taxation of domestic-source income. This tax rule, which applies irrespective of the nationality or country of residence, is well established in international (tax) law.[42]

Some states have also justified the extra-territorial application of financial and economic laws, such as antitrust laws, on the basis of the territoriality principle.[43] The United States, for example, extended its antitrust laws to foreign corporations outside its territory because the conduct of these corporations had an adverse effect in the territory of the United States. In the absence of any tangible link with the territory of the prescribing states, such extra-territorial application of domestic law is controversial.[44]

c   The Nationality Principle

Public international law further allows states to extend the application of their domestic legislation outside their territory to regulate or protect their nationals abroad. The bond between a state and its nationals has traditionally been viewed as a sufficiently genuine link to justify extra-territorial application of domestic legislation.[45]

On the basis of the nationality principle (also sometimes referred to as the personal or personality principle), a state may choose to extend the application of some of its criminal laws to its nationals abroad who are actively committing a crime (the so-called active nationality principle) and to anyone committing crime against one of its nationals (the so-called passive nationality principle).[46] The Dutch legislator, for example, chose to extend the application of a limited number of provisions of the Dutch criminal code to Dutch nationals outside the Netherlands[47] and to anyone committing one of the indicated crimes against a Dutch national outside the Netherlands.[48] Similar provisions can be found in the criminal codes of Denmark,[49] Japan,[50] and New Zealand.[51]

---

[42]   See Reuven S Avi-Yonah, *International Tax as International Law* (Cambridge University Press 2007) 27.

[43]   The application of domestic legislation to persons, property, or acts outside the territory of a state must be distinguished from the application of domestic legislation within the territory of the prescribing state, but which has an extra-territorial effect. Mills calls this 'extra-territorial projection' of legislation. A state may, for example, 'condition entry of goods into its territory on the state of origin's compliance with human rights law, environmental regulation, or labour standards'. See Alex Mills, 'Private Interests and Private Law Regulation in Public International Law Jurisdiction' in Stephen Allen et al (eds), *The Oxford Handbook of Jurisdiction in International Law* (Oxford University Press 2019) 335. Extra-territorial projection of legislation may lead to disputes under international trade law as was illustrated by the dispute between India, Malaysia, Pakistan, and Thailand on the one hand and the United States on the other hand, within the framework of the World Trade Organization (WTO). See WTO, *United States: Import Prohibition of Certain Shrimp and Shrimp Products—Report of the Appellate Body* (12 October 1998) WT/DS58/AB/R. See further Chapter 14.

[44]   See Lowe (n 1) 173, who writes that although the so-called effects doctrine has been controversial, there appears to be increasing acceptance of the need for such exercise of extra-territorial jurisdiction. See also Staker (n 3) 317–18.

[45]   Indeed, as indicated earlier, jurisdiction almost certainly begins as a bond between an individual and his or her sovereign. Lowe (n 1) 174.

[46]   The passive nationality principle used to be regarded as controversial although states increasingly justify the extra-territorial scope of their legislation on the basis of this principle. See Staker (n 3) 326–7.

[47]   See, for example, Dutch Criminal Code art 7. An unofficial translation in English of a previous version of the Dutch Criminal Code can be found through <www.legislationline.org>.

[48]   See, for example, Dutch Criminal Code art 5.

[49]   See, for example, Danish Criminal Code s 7 (active nationality principle) and s 8(3) (passive nationality principle). An unofficial translation in English can be found through <www.legislationline.org>.

[50]   See, for example, Penal Code of Japan art 3(1) (active nationality principle) and art 3(2) (passive nationality principle). An unofficial translation in English can be found through <www.japaneselawtranslation.go.jp>.

[51]   See, for example, New Zealand Crimes Act s 7A(1)(a)(i) (active nationality principle) and s 7A(1)(c)(i) (passive nationality principle).

The nationality principle also justifies the extra-territorial application of tax laws to nationals living abroad[52] and to corporations established under the law of the prescribing state (and therefore qualify as 'corporate nationals')[53] in relation to activities carried out in other countries. Corporations established under Dutch law, for example, are required to pay corporate tax in the Netherlands in relation to all their activities, including activities carried out outside the Netherlands.[54]

d   The Protective Principle

In addition to the territoriality and nationality principles, which justify the extra-territorial application of domestic legislation because of a tangible or genuine link between the prescribing state and the persons, property, or acts outside its territory, public international law also allows states to extend the application of their domestic legislation to persons, property, and acts outside its territory in order to protect their vital interests, such as the protection of the state and the protection of the head of state. The protective principle justifies the extra-territorial application of domestic legislation in relation to persons who do not possess the nationality of the prescribing state and in relation to conduct that takes place outside of the territory of the prescribing state, without any territorial link. The extra-territorial application of domestic legislation under these circumstances is only justified because the vital interests of the state are at stake and it appears that this is only applied in relation to domestic criminal laws.

For example, the Netherlands has chosen to extend the application of a limited number of provisions of the Dutch criminal code to anyone outside the Netherlands who is involved in activities that touch upon the country's vital interests, such as conspiracy against the state and forgery of currency.[55] Similar examples can be found in the criminal codes of Germany,[56] Sweden,[57] and Russia.[58]

e   The Universality Principle

Finally, in a number of exceptional cases, public international law allows states to extend their domestic legislation to persons, property, or acts outside their territories in the absence of any link with the prescribing state. Similar to the protective principle, the universality principle

---

[52] All US nationals, for example, are subject to United States federal income tax legislation, irrespective of country of residence.
[53] The 'nationality' of corporations has been a subject of discussion. Some states accord nationality to corporations on the basis of the place of incorporation; other states accord nationality on the basis of the corporation's seat. See Staker (n 3) 319.
[54] The application of domestic sanctions against branches of domestic corporations that operate outside a state's territory appears to be more problematic; however. Lowe refers to the sanctions imposed by the United States against Libya in 1986, which included a freeze on Libyan assets held by US persons and corporations including their overseas branches. The freezing order led to court proceedings in the United Kingdom in relation to monies held in an account of the London branch of an American bank. See Lowe (n 1) 175.
[55] See, for example, Dutch Criminal Code art 4.
[56] See, for example, German Criminal Code art 5. An unofficial translation in English can be found through <www.legislationline.org>.
[57] See, for example, Swedish Penal Code, ch 2, s 3(4). An unofficial translation in English can be found through <www.legislationline.org>.
[58] See, for example, Russian Criminal Code art 12(3). An unofficial translation in English can be found through <www.legislationline.org>.

justifies the extra-territorial application of domestic legislation in relation to persons who do not possess the nationality of the prescribing state and in relation to conduct that takes place outside the territory of the prescribing state and in the absence of any territorial link. However, the universality principle must be distinguished from the protective principle because it aims to protect different interests. While the protective principle aims to protect the vital (national) interests of the prescribing state, the universality principle aims to protect universal values and universal interests.

In practice states rely on the universality principle to extend their domestic criminal legislation to persons, property, or acts outside their territory only in relation to international crimes that concern humanity as a whole. All states, for example, have an interest in combating piracy since it affects global trade and often occurs in areas beyond national jurisdiction, which allows pirates to evade the jurisdiction of any state.[59] States may; therefore, choose to extend the application of their domestic criminal law to anyone involved in the crime of piracy anywhere in the world and many states have indeed done so.[60] Article 381 of the Dutch Criminal Code, which criminalizes piracy, is applicable to anyone involved in such crimes, anywhere in the world.[61] The Dutch Criminal Code does not require a link between the Netherlands and the act of piracy, the pirate him- or herself or his or her victims.

Further, many states have chosen to extend their domestic criminal legislation to anyone outside their territories who has been involved in the commission of international crimes, such as war crimes, crimes against humanity, and genocide. In the interest of mankind or humanity, all states may extend their criminal legislation to anyone outside their territories so that no one involved in such crimes may go unpunished.

The establishment of the International Criminal Court (ICC) in 2002 provided a strong impetus for states to adopt criminal legislation in relation to international crimes, namely, genocide, crimes against humanity, war crimes, and the crime of aggression. In the preamble to the Rome Statute,[62] states parties affirmed 'that the most serious crimes of concern to the international community as a whole must not go unpunished and that their effective prosecution must be ensured by taking measures at the national level and by enhancing international cooperation'. They were determined 'to put an end to impunity for the perpetrators of these crimes and thus to contribute to the prevention of such crimes' and recalled that 'it is the duty of every State to exercise its criminal jurisdiction over those responsible for international crimes'.

Although the Rome Statute does not specifically require the ICC's member states to include the crimes set out in the Rome Statute in their domestic legislation, these pre-ambular declarations have generally been interpreted by ICC member states as a call to establish prescriptive jurisdiction in relation to these crimes and to extend the scope of their domestic legislation to cover crimes committed by anyone outside their territories. After all,

---

[59] In ancient times, pirates were already qualified as the enemies of mankind ('*hostes humani generis*'). See also Staker (n 3) 322.
[60] States also have a right to seize a pirate ship on the high seas or in any other areas beyond national jurisdiction and arrest the people on board. This form of enforcement jurisdiction has been codified in UNCLOS art 105. See also Chapter 15.
[61] See Dutch Criminal Code art 4(e), which extends the applicability of art 381 to anyone committing the crime of piracy outside the territory of the Netherlands.
[62] Rome Statute of the ICC (adopted 17 July 1998, entered into force 1 July 2002) 2187 UNTS 3.

every state has a duty under the Rome Statute to exercise criminal jurisdiction over those responsible for international crimes and the primary responsibility for the exercise of criminal jurisdiction lies with the member states. Although Article 1 of the Rome Statute provides that the ICC has jurisdiction over persons 'for the most serious crimes of international concern, as referred to in this Statute', its jurisdiction is only complementary to national criminal jurisdictions. Therefore, a case may only be admissible before the ICC if a (member) state that has jurisdiction is unable or unwilling to genuinely carry out an investigation or prosecution (Article 17 of the Rome Statute).[63]

The Netherlands, for example, adopted the comprehensive International Crimes Act (ICA) following its ratification of the Rome Statute, by which the Netherlands established criminal jurisdiction in relation to the crimes codified in the Rome Statute, even if these crimes are committed outside the territory of the Netherlands. Pursuant to Article 2(1)(a) ICA, the ICA applies to anyone who has committed any of the crimes laid down in the ICA outside the territory of the Netherlands, provided; however, that the person suspected of these crimes is in fact present on the territory of the Netherlands. The language of this provision indicates that this scope-rule is a manifestation of the principle of universality.[64]

Although a large number of states have opted to establish universal criminal jurisdiction in relation to international crimes, the exercise of universal criminal jurisdiction in the absence of a multilateral treaty that requires the establishment of universal jurisdiction[65] has been controversial.[66] On 14 February 2002, the International Court of Justice (ICJ) rendered its judgment in a dispute between the Democratic Republic of the Congo (DRC) and Belgium. The dispute related to the question to what extent a Belgian arrest warrant against the then incumbent minister for foreign affairs of the DRC, Yerodia, was wrongful towards the DRC. Yerodia was charged in Belgium with offences constituting war crimes and crimes against humanity during the civil war in the DRC in the 1990s. Yerodia was prosecuted on the basis of a Belgian statute, which provided for universal jurisdiction in relation to war crimes and crimes against humanity (among other crimes), and thus irrespective of a territorial link with Belgium or a link on the basis of nationality.

The DRC initially argued that the scope of the Belgian statute on the basis of which Yerodia was prosecuted constituted a violation of public international law. It stated that '"[t]he universal jurisdiction that the Belgian State attributes to itself under Article 7 of the

---

[63] See Chapter 13 on international criminal law.

[64] Pursuant to ICA art 2(1)(c), the ICA also applies to Dutch nationals who have committed any of the crimes laid down in the ICA outside the territory of the Netherlands and pursuant to art 2(1)(b), the ICA also applies to anyone who has committed any of these crimes against a Dutch national, a Dutch civil servant, or a Dutch vehicle, ship, or aircraft outside the territory of the Netherlands. The provisions are, respectively, manifestations of the active and passive nationality principles, which justify the extra-territorial application of domestic legislation outside the territory of a state.

[65] This is called treaty-based jurisdiction. States parties to those treaties are obliged to assert jurisdiction over the crimes regulated by these treaties. See for example the Geneva Convention (IV) relative to the Protection of Civilian Persons in Time of War (adopted 12 August 1949, entered into force 21 October 1950) 75 UNTS 287, art 146, which provides, in short, that all contracting parties must implement legislation to allow for prosecution of anyone accused of war crimes, irrespective of nationality, and anywhere in the world. Similar requirements can be found in treaties relating to various kinds of terrorism and organized crime.

[66] The exercise of universal jurisdiction in criminal matters must be distinguished from the exercise of universal jurisdiction in civil matters, which will be discussed in Section 4.

Law in question" constituted a "[v]iolation of the principle that a State may not exercise its authority on the territory of another State and of the principle of sovereign equality among all Members of the United Nations, as laid down in Article 2, paragraph 1, of the Charter of the United Nations'".[67] During the proceedings, however, the DRC did not pursue this argument any further and did not include it in its final submissions.[68] The ICJ therefore refrained from deciding on the legality of Belgian's exercise of prescriptive jurisdiction[69] and did not otherwise discuss the issue in its reasoning.

A number of judges, however, issued separate opinions to the judgment in this case,[70] in which they discussed the legality of the exercise of universal criminal jurisdiction, including the exercise of universal criminal jurisdiction in the absence of the accused.[71] On the one hand, Judge Guillaume was of the opinion that the exercise of universal criminal jurisdiction, without a legal basis in a multilateral treaty, was not in conformity with public international law. In his view there was insufficient state practice to persuade him that states had a right to extend the scope of their legislation to persons, property, or acts outside their territories in the absence of a genuine link with the prescribing state.[72] On the other hand, Judge Higgins, Judge Kooijmans, and Judge Buergenthal were of the opinion that the exercise of universal criminal jurisdiction was not contrary to public international law. Although they acknowledged that there was insufficient state practice to support the view that states had a customary right to exercise universal criminal jurisdiction in the absence of a treaty obligation to do so, states may still be entitled to do so.[73] Subsequently, they indicated that if a state would exercise or assert universal criminal jurisdiction this could only be done in relation to the most serious crimes that are damaging to the interests of all.[74]

The scope and application of the principle of universal jurisdiction (or the universality principle) has been on the agenda of the (Sixth Committee of) the UN General Assembly since 2009.[75] From the reports submitted to it on the subject matter, it appears that many UN member states have meanwhile asserted universal criminal jurisdiction in relation to international crimes, in particular in relation to piracy, war crimes, crimes against humanity, and genocide.[76]

---

[67] *Case Concerning the Arrest Warrant of 11 April 2000 (Democratic Republic of the Congo v Belgium)* (Judgment) [2002] ICJ Rep 3, para 17.

[68] The DRC stated that 'its interest in bringing these proceedings [was] to obtain a finding by the Court that it [had] been the victim of an internationally wrongful act, the question whether this case [involved] the "exercise of an excessive universal jurisdiction" being in this connection only a secondary consideration'. *Arrest Warrant* case, para 42.

[69] *Arrest Warrant* case, para 43.

[70] A separate opinion of a judge of the ICJ is a document that is attached to the judgment of the ICJ that reflects the personal views of that judge on the case. Pursuant to ICJ Statute art 57, any judge is entitled to deliver a separate opinion if the judgment does not represent in whole or in part the unanimous opinion of the judges. Statute of the ICJ (as annexed to the Charter of the UN) (adopted 26 June 1945, entered into force 24 October 1945) USTS 993.

[71] The requirement that the accused is present on the territory of the prescribing state for the exercise of universal criminal jurisdiction appears to be related to international treaties, such as the 1949 Geneva Conventions and the Convention against Torture, which require the contracting parties to establish universal criminal jurisdiction and either prosecute or extradite the accused. This form of universal jurisdiction allows for the possibility to prosecute an accused if the state that has a genuine link with the case is unable or unwilling to do so.

[72] *Arrest Warrant* case (n 67), Separate Opinion of President Guillaume, para 16. See also para 9.

[73] ibid, Joint Separate Opinion of Judges Higgins, Kooijmans, and Buergenthal, paras 45–6.   [74] ibid, paras 60–1.

[75] UNGA Res 64/117 (16 December 2009).

[76] See, for example, UNGA Res 74/192 (18 December 2019) and the reports mentioned therein.

f   **Concurrent Jurisdiction**

In view of the freedom of states to extend their legislation to persons, property, and acts outside their territories, there is a reasonable chance that a person, a property, or an act is subject to the jurisdiction of multiple states. This phenomenon is called concurrence of jurisdiction and there are no general rules of public international law that determine which rules take precedence under those circumstances.

In case of concurrence of criminal legislation, for example, the relevant states often determine, among themselves, which state will assume responsibility for the prosecution of the accused. The availability of evidence may under such circumstances be a relevant factor. If no agreement is reached among the relevant states, then the accused must rely on general principles of criminal law that prevent him or her from being prosecuted twice for the same crime.[77]

Dependent on the severity and the scope of the case, an agreement between states that have criminal jurisdiction in relation to a particular crime may be laid down in a treaty. For example, the individuals responsible for the downing of flight MH17 on 17 July 2014 are subject to the jurisdiction of multiple states, including Ukraine and the Netherlands. They are subject to Ukrainian criminal law because the downing of flight MH17 occurred in the territory of Ukraine, which includes the airspace above it. They are also subject to Dutch criminal law because, as mentioned earlier, the Netherlands chose to extend the scope of a number of provisions of the Dutch Criminal Code to anyone committing such crimes against Dutch nationals anywhere in the world, an extension that is justified by the passive nationality principle.[78] Since the large majority of the people who were killed in 2014 had Dutch nationality, the states that have jurisdiction to investigate this crime (Australia, Belgium, the Netherlands, Ukraine, and Malaysia) agreed that the Netherlands would take the lead in conducting criminal investigations into the downing of flight MH17. When the establishment of an international criminal tribunal by the Security Council proved to be impossible (the draft Security Council resolution was vetoed by the Russian Federation), these states decided on 5 July 2017 that the people responsible for the downing of flight MH17 were to be prosecuted and tried in the Netherlands, on the basis of Dutch criminal law.[79] The trial against four identified suspects started on 9 March 2020, before the District Court of The Hague.

---

[77] According to Akehurst, international law is silent on this point. Concurrent jurisdiction may then result in 'great hardship'. Akehurst (n 3) 106.

[78] See Dutch Criminal Code art 5, which provides, in short, that the Dutch Criminal Code is also applicable to anyone committing a crime against, among others, a Dutch national, if such crime is punishable with a prison sentence of at least eight years and the crime is also punishable in the state where the crime was committed.

[79] See for more information De Rechtspraak, 'The MH17 trial' <www.courtmh17.com/en> (information about the trial from the Dutch judiciary) and Netherlands Public Prosecution Service 'MH17 plane crash' <www.prosecutionservice.nl/topics/mh17-plane-crash> (information about the trial from the Netherlands Public Prosecution Service) and generally Government of the Netherlands, 'MH17 incident' <www.government.nl/topics/mh17-incident> (information about the downing of flight MH17 from the Dutch government). The Netherlands and Ukraine concluded a separate agreement on legal cooperation, which, among other things, provided for Dutch jurisdiction in relation to the killing of all 283 passengers, irrespective of nationality, the transfer of criminal proceedings, the extradition of suspects, the conducting of video conferencing technology, and the transfer of enforcement of prison sentences.

States try to prevent concurrence of domestic tax legislation by concluding bilateral or multilateral tax treaties. These treaties regulate, among other things, which state is entitled to tax someone's income or property and prevent double taxation.[80]

In order to prevent concurrence of domestic civil law, states have developed so-called conflict rules under domestic law, which determine which domestic law is applicable to resolve a dispute between individuals and/or corporations with an international or trans-boundary character. These conflict rules are part of a branch of domestic civil law that is called private international law. Such rules determine, for example, which domestic civil law applies to a dispute between Dutch (greenhouse) farmers and a French mining company about the level of pollution of the water of the Rhine river.[81] If the parties to a particular dispute have not made a choice for a domestic legal system to govern their mutual relationship, then these conflict rules will determine, on the basis of a number of factors, which domestic law will be applicable. These factors include a link with the territory of a particular state or a link with a particular state on the basis of nationality.

In order to increase legal certainty, states have increasingly chosen to unify their domestic private international law by means of international instruments. Within the EU, for example, Regulation (EC) No 593/2008 ('Rome I') regulates which law should apply to contractual obligations in case of a conflict of laws in civil and commercial matters and Regulation (EC) No 864/2007 ('Rome II') regulates which law should apply to non-contractual obligations involving more than one country. Within the HCCH, forty-one conventions and instruments have been concluded on a wide variety of topics, including on the law applicable to traffic accidents, on the law applicable to maintenance obligations (family law), and the law applicable to contracts for the international sale of goods.[82]

4   Adjudicative Jurisdiction

Adjudication is the exercise of jurisdiction by a court of a state, in particular the judicial branch of government. The exercise of adjudicative jurisdiction is a manifestation of governmental power and derives from the principle of sovereignty. In practice, the term jurisdiction is often associated with the power of a court to hear a case.

Similar to enforcement and prescription, the exercise of adjudicative jurisdiction is, in principle, limited to the territory of a state. Courts are organs of the state and adjudication generally occurs within the territorial boundaries of a state.[83] Only under exceptional circumstances are courts allowed to exercise their judicial function outside the territory

---

[80] Some tax treaties also regulate the exchange of information between tax authorities, which is a form of mutual legal assistance intended to help enforcement of tax laws.

[81] See HR 23 September 1988 ECLI:NL:HR:1988:AD5713 (Supreme Court of the Netherlands).

[82] See HCCH, 'Conventions, Protocols and Principles' <www.hcch.net/en/instruments/conventions>.

[83] See, for example, ILC, 'Draft Articles on the Responsibility of States for Internationally Wrongful Acts' (2001) UN Doc A/56/10, art 4, which provides that the 'conduct of any State organ shall be considered an act of that State under international law, whether the organ exercises legislative, executive, judicial or any other functions, whatever position it holds in the organization of the State, and whatever its character as an organ of the central government or of a territorial unit of the State'.

of their state. For example, on 18 September 1998, the Netherlands and the United Kingdom concluded a treaty under which the Netherlands allowed a Scottish court to try two Libyan nationals in the territory of the Netherlands.[84] The two men were charged with the bombing of Pan Am flight 103 that crashed near the Scottish town of Lockerbie, killing all 259 passengers on board. Further, the exercise of adjudicative jurisdiction is generally limited to persons and property that are present in the territory of the state, or to events that have occurred in the territory of that state. It is not uncommon for states; however, to extend the authority of their courts to persons, property, or acts outside their territory. Indeed, similar to the exercise of prescriptive jurisdiction outside the territory of a state, public international law allows states a large measure of discretion to extend the scope of their adjudicative power outside their territories. In the *S.S. Lotus* case, the PCIJ not only held that states have a large measure of discretion to extend the scope of their legislation outside their territories, but also to extend the scope of the jurisdiction of their courts. The PCIJ observed that in practice, states had adopted a great variety of rules relating to the application of their laws and the jurisdiction of their courts 'without objections or complaints on the part of other States'.[85]

Similar to the exercise of prescriptive jurisdiction, public international law requires a genuine link between a state exercising adjudicative jurisdiction in relation to persons, property, and acts outside its territory. After all, a state may not only exert significant influence outside its territory by means of legislation, but also by means of adjudication and such influence may interfere with the sovereign rights of another state.[86] If a domestic court exercises jurisdiction that would be regarded as excessive or exorbitant, a state whose interests are adversely affected by such an act could invoke the responsibility of that state.[87] The Netherlands and the United Kingdom stated in their *amici curiae* brief in the *Kiobel v Royal Dutch Petroleum Co.* case in the US Supreme Court that both states have 'maintained over a long period of time their opposition to overly broad assertions of extraterritorial civil jurisdiction arising out of aliens' claims against foreign defendants for alleged activities in foreign jurisdictions that caused injury'.[88]

Although public international law does not explicitly attribute jurisdiction to the courts of a particular state,[89] a link is generally required for a domestic court to assert adjudicative

---

[84] Agreement between the Government of the Kingdom of the Netherlands and the Government of the United Kingdom of Great Britain and Northern Ireland concerning a Scottish trial in the Netherlands (18 September 1998) Trb 1998, 237.

[85] ibid, emphasis added.

[86] See, for example, HR 17 July 2020 ECLI:NL:HR:2020:1280 (Supreme Court of the Netherlands), para 3.6. The case related to the meaning and scope of art 5 of the International Convention Relating to the Arrest of Seagoing Ships (adopted 10 May 1952, entered into force 24 February 1956) 439 UNTS 193, which attributes jurisdiction to the courts of the state where a ship has been arrested to release the ship upon sufficient bail or other security being furnished. In this case, the Court held that art 5 of the convention attributed exclusive jurisdiction to the courts of the state where a particular ship was arrested, including exclusive jurisdiction with respect to issues related to the seizure of that ship. According to the Court, it would be inappropriate to circumvent such exclusive jurisdiction if one of the parties involved would be ordered by a court of another state party to the convention to adopt a particular position. If a court would give such an injunction, it would exert unacceptable influence on the court that has exclusive jurisdiction on the basis of art 5 of the convention.

[87] See Akehurst (n 3) 104–5. See Mills (n 43) 344–5 for examples of grounds of adjudicative jurisdiction, which are sometimes described as 'exorbitant'. It is rare, however, for states to criticize each other's exercise of adjudicative jurisdiction.

[88] *Kiobel et al v Royal Dutch Petroleum Co et al* (n 34); Brief of the Governments of the United Kingdom of Great Britain and Northern Ireland and the Kingdom of the Netherlands as *Amici Curiae* in Support of the Respondents No 10-1491, 2.

[89] See, for example, Convention Relating to the Arrest of Seagoing Ships (n 87) art 5.

jurisdiction in relation to persons, property, and acts outside the territory of the state, both in criminal and in civil and commercial matters.[90]

It appears that in matters of public law, courts always apply their own laws.[91] Their jurisdiction is; therefore, always determined by the relevant public laws. In criminal proceedings, the jurisdiction of the courts of a particular state is generally determined by the scope of the criminal code of the relevant state. This means that the adjudicative jurisdiction of a state in criminal proceedings is intrinsically linked with the prescriptive jurisdiction of that state. Articles 2–8 of the Dutch Criminal Code, for example, establish the territorial scope of the Dutch Criminal Code. If someone is subject to the Dutch Criminal Code on the basis of these provisions, then Article 2 and other provisions of the Dutch Code of Criminal Procedure indicate which courts are authorized to try the accused.[92] Similarly, Chapter 2, Section 1 of the Swedish Criminal Code provides that offences committed in Sweden shall be judged under Swedish law and in a Swedish court.[93]

In civil and commercial proceedings, however, the adjudicative jurisdiction of a state and the prescriptive jurisdiction of a state are not intrinsically linked. A Dutch civil court may have to apply foreign law if the relevant rules of private international law so dictate, and a German civil court may have to decline jurisdiction to hear a case if the parties have agreed to submit their disputes before a foreign court, even though the relationship between the parties is governed by German civil law.

Most states have incorporated the rules attributing jurisdiction in civil and commercial cases in their codes of civil procedure or similar statutes. In the Netherlands, for example, these rules have been laid down in Articles 1–14 of the Dutch Code of Civil Procedure (DCCP) and in the Republic of Korea these rules have been laid down in Article 2 of the Korean Private International Act (KPIA) in connection with the Korean Code of Civil Procedure (KCCP).[94] Generally, Dutch and Korean courts have jurisdiction in civil and commercial matters if the defendant resides in the Netherlands or Korea (Article 2 DCCP and Article 2 KPIA in connection with Article 2 KCCP) or if the subject matter of the dispute is sufficiently connected with the Netherlands or Korea.[95]

Most states require a genuine link between either the parties to the dispute or the subject matter of the claim and the so-called 'forum' state.[96] States have only asserted adjudicative jurisdiction in civil and commercial matters without a genuine link with the forum state

---

[90] It appears that the exercise of adjudicative jurisdiction in administrative legal proceedings is inherently restricted to the territory of the state involved.

[91] Mills (n 43) 344.

[92] An unofficial translation of a previous version of the Dutch Code of Criminal Procedure is available through <www .legislationline.org>.

[93] An unofficial translation of the Swedish Criminal Code is available through <www.legislationline.org>.

[94] See the HCCH Permanent Bureau, 'Comparative Tables on Grounds of Jurisdiction' (29 September 2014) <https://assets .hcch.net/docs/6d2ee48f-9661-49dd-90a5-40fd0920615f.pdf>. Unofficial translations of the KPIA and the KCCP can be accessed through <https://elaw.klri.re.kr/eng_mobile/main.do>.

[95] See, for example, DCCP art 6(a), which attributes adjudicative jurisdiction to Dutch courts in civil matters if the disputed contractual obligation has been performed in the Netherlands or had to be performed in the Netherlands. See also KPIA art 2, in connection with KCCP arts 8 and 18.

[96] According to Akehurst, a genuine link is not required for the exercise of adjudicative jurisdiction in civil and commercial cases: 'Apart from cases of sovereign and diplomatic immunity, and so on … international law does not seem to impose any restrictions on the jurisdiction of courts in civil cases; it restricts jurisdiction only in criminal cases'. Akehurst (n 3) 105.

under exceptional circumstances. Some states assert adjudicative jurisdiction in civil and commercial matters without a genuine link if it appears to be impossible to submit a civil or commercial claim before the courts of another state. This ground of jurisdiction is known as the ground of *forum necessitatis* (forum of necessity).[97] Other states assert adjudicative jurisdiction in civil and commercial matters if the interest of the parties dictates that the case be heard before the courts of that state, which is known as the ground of *forum conveniens* (forum of convenience).[98]

Only one state has asserted universal civil jurisdiction in relation to alleged human rights violations: the United States' Alien Tort Statute (ATS). The ATS provides that '[t]he district courts shall have original jurisdiction of any civil action by an alien for a tort only, committed in violation of the law of nations or a treaty of the United States'.[99] In practice, the scope of the ATS has been significantly reduced. In 2004 the US Supreme Court ruled that the ATS only provided for jurisdiction for a private cause of action in relation to norms of public international law that are sufficiently specific, universal, and obligatory to create a federal remedy.[100] In 2013, the Supreme Court ruled that the presumption against extra-territorial application of statutes also applies to claims under the ATS and that nothing in the ATS rebutted that presumption.[101] Therefore, the ATS may only provide for a cause of action for violation of the law of nations occurring within the territory of a sovereign state other than the United States under exceptional circumstances,[102] when the claims touch upon or concern the territory of the United States to a sufficient degree.[103]

Similar to other branches of private international law, the rules attributing adjudicative jurisdiction in civil and commercial matters have increasingly been codified in international instruments, just like the codification of other areas of private international law. Within the EU, Regulation (EU) No 1215/2012 ('Brussels I Regulation (recast)') not only regulates the recognition and enforcement of judgments in civil or commercial matters, as mentioned in Section 2, but also the adjudicative jurisdiction of EU member states in civil and commercial matters.[104]

---

[97] See DCCP art 9(b), which provides that Dutch courts have jurisdiction to hear a civil claim if its jurisdiction cannot be based on any of the other grounds and legal proceedings outside the Netherlands appear to be impossible. See also Mills (n 43) 342.

[98] See, for example, DCCP art 3(c), which provides that Dutch courts have jurisdiction to hear *ex parte* petitions (as opposed to claims directed against a respondent) if the case is sufficiently connected with the Netherlands. See also Mills (n 43) 340. Under the new Dutch Act on Collective Damages Claims (Wet Afwikkeling Massaschade in Collectieve Actie), which entered into force on 1 January 2020, a sufficient connection between the claim and the Netherlands is used as an admissibility criterion rather than a ground for jurisdiction (see Dutch Civil Code art 3:305a(3)(b)).

[99] Alien Tort Statute 28 US Code §1350. The ATS was adopted as part of the 1789 Judiciary Act.

[100] *Sosa v Alvarez-Machain* 542 US 692 (2004) (US Supreme Court) 695, 732 and 738.

[101] *Kiobel et al v Royal Dutch Petroleum Co et al* (n 34) 117, 124.

[102] The Supreme Court was conscious of the foreign policy considerations of attributing jurisdiction in civil and commercial matters to the courts of the United States. In relation to the offense of piracy, for example, which would be an actionable tort under the ATS, it held that 'although the offense of piracy normally occurs on the high seas, beyond the territorial jurisdiction of the United States or any other country, applying U.S. law to pirates does not typically impose the sovereign will of the United States onto conduct occurring within the territorial jurisdiction of another sovereign, and therefore carries less direct foreign policy consequences'. It further held that 'there is no indication that the ATS was passed to make the United States a uniquely hospitable forum for the enforcement of international norms'. ibid 109 and 110.

[103] ibid 125.

[104] In preambular para 15 and 16 of Brussels I Regulation (recast) (n 18), the EU legislator indicates the grounds of jurisdiction for the courts of member states of the European Union in civil and commercial matters and the rationale behind unification: 'The rules of jurisdiction should be highly predictable and founded on the principle that jurisdiction is generally based on the defendant's domicile. Jurisdiction should always be available on this ground save in a few well-defined situations in which the subject-matter of the dispute or the autonomy of the parties warrants a different connecting factor. The domicile of a legal person must be defined autonomously so as to make the common rules more transparent and avoid conflicts of jurisdiction. In

In 2019 the HCCP decided to study the scope of the adjudicative jurisdiction of states in civil and commercial matters.[105]

Finally, as a matter of principle, the judgments of domestic courts and tribunals are only recognized and only have legal effect within the territory of the forum state.[106] This applies both to judgments in criminal cases and to judgments in civil and commercial matters. As was discussed in Section 2, the enforcement of a judgment in the territory of another state requires permission of that state, for example on the basis of an international instrument, like the Brussels I Regulation (recast) or the 2019 Hague Convention on the Recognition of and Enforcement of Foreign Judgments in Civil or Commercial Matters.

5   Concluding Remarks

The exercise of jurisdiction entails the authority of states to prescribe rules (legislative or prescriptive jurisdiction), the power of states to enforce rules (enforcement jurisdiction), and the power of states to adjudicate (adjudicative jurisdiction). In other words, jurisdiction encompasses all exercises of governmental power. Although the power of states to exercise jurisdiction follows from the principle of sovereignty, this power is not unlimited. Each state has to respect the personality and sovereign equality of other states, and overstepping this boundary entails a violation of public international law. This limitation is most pertinent when a state exercises jurisdiction outside of its own territory.

While the exercise of enforcement jurisdiction outside of a state's territory is generally prohibited under public international law, public international law allows states a large measure of discretion to extend the application of their laws (prescriptive jurisdiction) and the jurisdiction of their courts (adjudicative jurisdiction) outside their territories. Although the exercise of extra-territorial prescriptive or adjudicative jurisdiction is not explicitly permitted under public international law, a genuine link is required between a state exercising such jurisdiction and the persons, property, or acts affected by such legislation or adjudication.

This chapter discussed the scope of the jurisdiction of states when states exercise enforcement, prescriptive, and adjudicative jurisdiction in relation to persons, property, and acts *outside* of their own territory. The following chapter will discuss the scope of the jurisdiction of states when they exercise jurisdiction *within* their own territories, in light of the immunity of states, state officials, and international organizations.

---

addition to the defendant's domicile, there should be alternative grounds of jurisdiction based on a close connection between the court and the action or in order to facilitate the sound administration of justice. The existence of a close connection should ensure legal certainty and avoid the possibility of the defendant being sued in a court of a Member State which he could not reasonably have foreseen. This is important, particularly in disputes concerning non-contractual obligations arising out of violations of privacy and rights relating to personality, including defamation'.

[105] See HCCH, 'Jurisdiction Project' <www.hcch.net/en/projects/legislative-projects/jurisdiction-project>.
[106] See also Mills (n 43) 346.

Recommended Reading

Stephen Allen et al (eds), *The Oxford Handbook of Jurisdiction in International Law* (Oxford University Press 2019).

André de Hoogh and Gelijn Molier, 'Jurisdictie' in Nathalie Horbach, René Lefeber, and Olivier Ribbelink (eds), *Handboek Internationaal Recht* (TMC Asser Press 2007).

Frederick A Mann, 'The Doctrine of Jurisdiction in International Law' (1964) 111 Collected Courses of the Hague Academy of International Law 1–162.

Cedric Ryngaert, *Jurisdiction in International Law* (2nd edn, Oxford University Press 2015).

Christopher Staker, 'Jurisdiction', in Malcolm D Evans (ed), *International Law* (5th edn, Oxford University Press 2014).

7

Immunities

Cecily Rose

1 Introduction

International law on immunities consists of a body of fundamentally procedural rules that set limits on when a state may exercise jurisdiction within its very own territory. International law; therefore governs not only the extent to which a state's exercise of jurisdiction may have extraterritorial implications (see Chapter 6), but it also governs a state's exercise of jurisdiction within its own borders. These procedural rules could prevent a domestic court, for example, from exercising jurisdiction in a case involving a foreign state, an official of a foreign state, as well as an international organization. These rules could also prevent a police officer from exercising jurisdiction by, for example, arresting and detaining a foreign diplomat or a minister of foreign affairs. International law bars the exercise of jurisdiction in such situations either because the exercise of jurisdiction would threaten the equality of sovereign states or because the capacity of the individual or organization to carry out their functions would be compromised. In essence, the law on immunities enables international relations to run their course, undisrupted by domestic court litigation and local law enforcement. These rules do not govern situations where, for example, a state or a state official is the subject of litigation in its own domestic courts, but instead only apply where the state or the official face the prospect of being subject to the jurisdiction of a foreign state.

While the exact rationales for these rules on immunity vary, depending on the beneficiary of the immunity and the circumstances, the effect is the same: the exercise of jurisdiction by domestic actors is barred. The law on immunity notably acts only as a procedural impediment to the exercise of jurisdiction, and does not affect the substantive laws at issue, which remain in force and continue to apply. This body of rules; therefore has the effect of diverting the resolution of certain legal issues away from domestic courts, and towards other dispute settlement methods, such as negotiation, mediation, and arbitration. Disputes involving states, state officials, or international organizations therefore typically have to be resolved through means other than domestic litigation. The diversion of certain types of legal issues away from domestic courts, particularly those involving serious crimes, has proved to be quite controversial, especially since the late 1990s, but the law has been slow to evolve with respect to possible exceptions to immunity in such circumstances.

This chapter begins with the law on state immunity, which has evolved over the centuries from an absolute doctrine to a more restrictive one, which permits exceptions, in particular when states engage in commercial activities (Section 2). The following section introduces the immunities that apply to all individuals who serve as state officials, whether they serve as relatively low-level civil servants or as the president or prime minister (Section 3). The next sections deal with two special regimes, one governing diplomatic and consular agents who serve abroad, and the other governing international organizations (Sections 4 and 5).

2   State Immunity

a   *State Immunity's Basic Function and Legal Bases*

The law on sovereign or state immunity is grounded in the fundamental principle of sovereign equality, which holds that one state may not exercise power over another. This concept is captured by the Latin maxim *par in parem non habet imperium*, meaning 'an equal has no authority over an equal'. In the context of state immunity, this means that the courts of the Netherlands, for example, may not exercise adjudicatory jurisdiction over another state that is the subject of a claim in Dutch courts. In other words, a court in the Netherlands, which is the 'forum state' in this scenario, may not assert adjudicatory jurisdiction for the purpose of determining whether another state has violated international or domestic laws. Likewise, the Dutch police may not exercise enforcement jurisdiction over another state by seizing property in the Netherlands that is owned by another state. Immunity from enforcement jurisdiction is also referred to as 'inviolability'. These limitations on the exercise of jurisdiction stem not from politeness or comity, but from a legal obligation under international law. The judicial and executive branches do not voluntarily decline to exercise jurisdiction, but instead do so because they are required to by the law on state immunity, the breach of which may give rise to an internationally wrongful act under the law on state responsibility (see Chapter 5).

The law on state immunity may be distinguished from other rules that require domestic courts to decline to hear a case concerning the conduct of a foreign state, such as the act of state doctrine.[1] While the law on state immunity forms part of customary international law and therefore applies to all states, the act of state doctrine is a rule of domestic law that exists in only some legal systems. With respect to state immunity, the courts of the forum state must decline to exercise jurisdiction because the respondent, in the case of civil litigation, is a state. In other words, the sovereign status of the respondent creates a bar to the exercise of jurisdiction, such that the forum state is not an appropriate forum for the settlement of the dispute. With respect to the act of state doctrine, by contrast, the very subject matter of the case, rather than the identity of the respondent, creates a bar to judicial

---

[1] Hazel Fox and Philippa Webb, *The Law on State Immunity* (3rd edn, Oxford University Press 2013) 53–72. A forum state may also lack jurisdiction in a case involving the conduct of a foreign state on account of the political question doctrine and the plea of non-justiciability.

review. The act of state doctrine, which originated in the US and UK legal systems, bars a domestic court from passing judgment on the validity of an act taken by a foreign government in its own territory. Domestic courts may apply the act of state doctrine even in cases where the foreign government is not a litigant in the court case, but the legal issues before the court would, nevertheless, require it to rule on the conduct of a foreign state, such as its expropriation of a foreign investment.[2] While the act of state doctrine and the law on immunity are related in that both create bars to the exercise of jurisdiction, the act of state doctrine concerns the subject matter of the dispute, whereas immunity concerns the identity of the litigant (i.e., personal jurisdiction).

The law on state immunities is one of the oldest branches of public international law, and also one of the remaining areas of the field that is still dominated by customary international law. Through the centuries, customary rules have emerged by means of state practice consisting of domestic legislation, executive acts, and judicial decisions. Although a number of important treaties on the subject of state immunities have been concluded by states, custom continues to play an important role because these treaties have not attracted widespread participation. In 1972, for example, the European Convention on State Immunity was concluded under the auspices of the Council of Europe, which consists of forty-seven member states.[3] Although the Convention entered into force in 1976, it still has only eight states parties.[4] More recently, in 2004, the United Nations (UN) Convention on Jurisdictional Immunities of States and Their Property was concluded on the basis of work carried out on the subject of state immunity by the International Law Commission (ILC).[5] The UN Convention on Jurisdictional Immunities has not yet entered into force; however, as it is yet to attract the necessary number of ratifications (or acceptances, approvals, or accessions).[6]

Even though these treaties have not attracted widespread participation, they neverthe-less, serve as important reference points for states and international and domestic courts because many of their provisions represent a codification of customary international law. As for why states have been reluctant or unwilling to become parties to these instruments given their close relationship with customary international law, this remains a subject of speculation.[7] Some states may consider ratification to be unnecessary given that the treaties codify the existing custom to a large extent. Other states may prefer to defer ratification until a significant number of states have become parties, perhaps due in part to the elements of the treaties that represent a progressive development of the law, rather than a codification of existing custom.

---

[2] See, for example, *Banco Nacional de Cuba v Sabbatino* 376 US 398 (1964) (US Supreme Court); *Kuwait Airways Corporation v Iraqi Airways Company* [2002] UKHL 19 (UK House of Lords).

[3] European Convention on State Immunity (adopted 16 May 1972, entered into force 11 June 1976) 1495 UNTS 181.

[4] Austria, Belgium, Cyprus, Germany, Luxembourg, the Netherlands, Switzerland, and the United Kingdom.

[5] UN Convention on Jurisdictional Immunities of States and Their Property (adopted 2 December 2004, not yet in force) UN Doc A/59/508 (UN Convention on Jurisdictional Immunities).

[6] UN Convention on Jurisdictional Immunities art 30; as of July 2021, twenty-two states had become parties to the convention, which requires thirty parties in order for the treaty to come into force.

[7] For a detailed discussion of the various possible explanations, see Roger O'Keefe and Christian J Tams, 'General Introduction' in Roger O'Keefe, Christian J Tams (eds), and Antonios Tzanakopoulos (ass ed), *The United Nations Convention on Jurisdictional Immunities of States and Their Property: A Commentary* (Oxford University Press 2013) XL–XLI.

b   Scope of State Immunity

The law on state immunity applies to all organs of the state as well as state property, and it acts as a bar to the exercise of adjudicatory as well as enforcement jurisdiction by a foreign state.[8] The law on state immunity does not; however, extend to individuals who represent the state, whether as prime minister or as a diplomat, for example. Individuals are instead the beneficiaries of other laws on immunity, based in both custom and treaties (see Sections 3 and 4 of this chapter). Historically, the law on state immunity had an absolute character because it completely barred any exercise of jurisdiction by one state over another state. In other words, no exceptions to this rule existed. The doctrine of absolute immunity was developed in the 1800s by US and UK courts, which upheld the immunity of state-owned ships from arrest and judicial process when docked in the port of a foreign state.[9] As a consequence of the absolute character of state immunity, disputes between states or between states and private actors, such as foreign investors, could not be resolved in domestic courts without state consent, and instead had to be resolved through recourse to diplomatic means of dispute settlement such as negotiation.

As the twentieth century progressed; however, this absolute approach to state immunity could no longer be sustained due to the increasing involvement of states in trade and commerce, financial matters (such as the issuance of bonds) and in the acquisition of industries. State immunity from jurisdiction and enforcement could no longer be justified where states behaved more like private investors or companies than sovereign powers. Where states engaged in conduct identical to that of private actors, the absolute doctrine of state immunity permitted abuses and was therefore untenable, as states could avoid legal responsibility for conduct such as a failure to repay a debt or to perform a contractual obligation. A distinction therefore began to emerge in domestic jurisprudence and legislation between sovereign or public acts that only a state can perform (*acta jure imperii*) and commercial acts that private persons can perform (*acta jure gestionis*).[10] According to the restrictive doctrine of immunity, which began to emerge in the 1970s, state immunity applies to sovereign acts, but not to commercial acts. The application of this seemingly simple, logical distinction between *acta jure imperii* and *act jure gestionis* has, however, proven to be challenging in practice.

The 2004 UN Convention on Jurisdictional Immunities codifies this distinction between sovereign and commercial acts and provides a basic methodology for drawing the line between the two in practice. The Convention codifies an exception to state immunity for commercial transactions,[11] which it defines as including commercial 'contracts' or 'transactions' for the sale of goods or the supply of services, as well as contracts for 'a loan or

---

[8] UN Convention on Jurisdictional Immunities art 5.

[9] For an overview of this history, see Hazel Fox, 'The Restrictive Rule of State Immunity: The 1970s Enactment and its Contemporary Status' in Tom Ruys', Nicolas Angelet and Luca Ferro (eds), *The Cambridge Handbook of Immunities and International Law* (Cambridge University Press 2019). For two leading cases that adopt an absolute approach to state immunity, see *The Schooner Exchange v McFaddon* 11 US 116 (1812) (US Supreme Court); *The Parlement Belge* [1879] PD 120, 187 (UK Probate, Divorce, and Admiralty Division).

[10] See, for example, Singapore, State Immunity Act 1985; United Kingdom, State Immunity Act 1978; United States, Foreign Sovereign Immunities Act 1976.

[11] UN Convention on Jurisdictional Immunities art 10.

other transaction of a financial nature'.[12] Because the Convention defines the term 'commercial transaction' in part by using the word 'commercial', this definition has a circular character and is therefore of limited utility in determining what is and is not 'commercial' in the first place. The Convention does, however, address this issue by providing that the commercial character of a contract or transaction should be determined primarily by reference to its 'nature'.[13] A contract or transaction may be considered to have a commercial nature if it concerns activities in which private actors can engage. Examples of contracts or transactions with a commercial nature include the purchase of a fishing vessel by a state and a contract concluded by a state for the supply of lumber for a foreign air force base.[14] Examples of financial transactions of a commercial nature include the assumption of mortgage obligations by a state and the sale by a state of certificates of deposit.[15] The commercial nature of an activity does not depend on whether the state was motivated by the desire to make a profit, although a 'profit motive' could be an indicator that a contract or transaction has a commercial nature.[16]

The 'purpose' of the contract or transaction plays a secondary role, according to the Convention, as it should be taken into account only if the parties to the contract or transaction so agree, or if purpose is relevant according to the domestic practice of the forum state.[17] The Convention thereby accommodates domestic legal systems that have embraced a purpose-based approach to determining whether a transaction is commercial.[18] In the context of civil litigation, such an approach tends to be favourable to states, because essentially all transactions or contracts entered into by a state can be seen as serving a sovereign purpose, and as therefore worthy of immunity, though the relationship between the conduct and the sovereign purpose may be quite attenuated or remote.[19] In contrast, the application of the 'nature' criterion tends to favour the actors that have concluded contracts or engaged in transactions with states. According to the nature approach, as long as the state is engaged activities in which a private actor can also engage, then the contract or transaction has a commercial nature and does not attract immunity, regardless of whether the contract or transaction ultimately serves a sovereign purpose. In practice, whether domestic judiciaries adopt an approach based on 'nature' or 'purpose', they necessarily have to make relatively fact-intensive and case-by-case determinations as to whether a contract or transaction is commercial in character. At times, courts have drawn very fine lines between commercial and non-commercial (i.e., sovereign) activities.[20]

---

[12] UN Convention on Jurisdictional Immunities art 2(1)(c). This provision also includes a 'catch-all' provision that provides that a commercial transaction also means 'any other contract or transaction of a commercial, industrial, trading or professional nature, but not including a contract of employment of persons'. Art 2(1)(c)(iii).

[13] UN Convention on Jurisdictional Immunities art 2(2).

[14] Stephan Wittich, 'Article 2: Use of Terms' in O'Keefe, Tams, and Tzanakopoulos (eds) (n 7) 63–4.   [15] ibid 64–5.

[16] ibid 61–2.   [17] ibid.

[18] See, for example, *Borri v Argentina* Case No 11225 88 Rivista di Diritto Internazionale 856 (2005) (Supreme Court of Cassation of Italy) (granting sovereign immunity to Argentina in a case concerning Argentina's rescheduling of the repayment of its bonds during an economic emergency).

[19] Yas Banifatemi, 'Jurisdictional Immunities of States: Commercial Transactions' in Ruys, Angelet, and Ferro (eds) (n 9) 141.

[20] See, for example, *UNC Lear Services Inc v Kingdom of Saudi Arabia* 581 F.3d 210 (5th Cir 2009) (US Court of Appeals) (the court concluded that a services contract that provided for the integration of personnel with the Saudi Air Force was not commercial in nature, but a contract for the provision of spare parts and equipment was commercial in nature).

The commercial activities exception constitutes the most important exception to state immunity, but it is by no means the only exception. The restrictive doctrine of immunity, as codified by the UN Convention on Jurisdictional Immunities, enumerates various exceptions relating to non-sovereign conduct. The law on state immunity does not apply, for example, to certain employment contracts between a state and an individual, for work to be performed at least partly in the territory of the forum state.[21] This exception ensures that the forum state can, in certain circumstances, exercise jurisdiction over another state with respect to its compliance with public laws and policies on labour relations, and the treatment of employees. The law on state immunity also does not apply to personal injuries and damage to property that are attributable to a state, and which took place at least partly in the forum state.[22] This exception, which is also known as the 'territorial tort' exception, does not necessarily relate to non-sovereign activities. Instead, this exception to state immunity is designed to cover situations such as traffic accidents, including those that occur in the course of government business. Other exceptions to state immunity cover non-sovereign activities related to real estate or property in the forum state, intellectual property in the forum state, participation in foreign companies based in the forum state, state-owned or state-operated ships, and arbitration awards.[23] In addition to these exceptions, states may also waive their immunity by expressly consenting to the jurisdiction of the forum state.[24]

Neither customary international law nor the treaties on state immunity include an exception that deprives a state of its immunity because of its alleged participation in serious violations of human rights law or international humanitarian law (IHL). Powerful policy arguments may be advanced in favour of such an exception, but state practice does not, at present, support the existence of a rule depriving states of immunity in such circumstances.[25] The absence of any such exception in customary international law was confirmed by a 2012 judgment of the International Court of Justice (ICJ) in the *Jurisdictional Immunities* case between Germany and Italy.[26] This dispute between Germany and Italy arose out of events that took place during the Second World War. During Germany's occupation of Italy between 1943 and 1945, German forces massacred civilians and also deported large numbers of civilians for use as forced labour.[27] In addition, German forces also denied prisoner of war status to members of the Italian armed forces, and deported them to Germany or German-occupied territories for use as forced labour.[28]

Although Germany had enacted compensation laws for war victims, and Germany and Italy had also concluded peace agreements that provided for compensation, many victims fell outside the scope of these legal instruments and never received compensation. Luigi Ferrini was one such victim. He was an Italian civilian who was arrested by German forces in 1944, deported to Germany, and subjected to forced labour in a munitions factory until

---

[21] UN Convention on Jurisdictional Immunities art 11.   [22] UN Convention on Jurisdictional Immunities art 12.
[23] UN Convention on Jurisdictional Immunities arts 13–17.   [24] UN Convention on Jurisdictional Immunities art 7(1).
[25] Roger O'Keefe, 'State Immunity and Human Rights: Heads and Walls, Hearts and Minds' (2011) 44 Vanderbilt Journal of Transnational Law 999.
[26] *Jurisdictional Immunities of the State (Germany v Italy: Greece Intervening)* (Judgment) [2012] ICJ Rep 99. See also *Jones v Ministry of Interior of the Kingdom of Saudi Arabia* [2006] UKHL 26 (UK House of Lords).
[27] *Jurisdictional Immunities* case, para 21.   [28] ibid.

the end of the war. Decades later, Ferrini pursued civil proceedings against the State of Germany, in Italian courts, and in 2011 he prevailed when the Court of Appeal of Florence held that the law on state immunity does not apply in cases involving acts that constitute crimes under international law.[29] This judgment, and other judgments in related cases in Italy as well as Greece, were highly controversial from an international legal perspective.[30]

In 2008, in response to these ongoing civil proceedings in Italian courts, Germany brought a case to the ICJ against Italy. Germany claimed that Italian courts—and therefore the Italian state—were violating its right to state immunity from the jurisdiction of Italian courts, not only in the *Ferrini* case, but others as well. In its 2012 judgment, the ICJ determined that the gravity of the state conduct at issue did not affect the applicability of the law on state immunity. Based on its survey of state practice and *opinio juris*, the ICJ concluded that customary international law, as of 2012, did not deprive a state of immunity because the accusations against it concern serious violations of human rights law or international humanitarian law (IHL).[31] The ICJ also determined that this conclusion would be the same even if the human rights and IHL norms at issue had a *jus cogens* character, which would mean that no derogation from them is possible.[32] As the ICJ explained, the rules on immunity, which are procedural in character, do not conflict with *jus cogens* norms concerning human rights and IHL, which are substantive in character. International law on state immunity is procedural in that it stipulates whether the courts of one state may exercise jurisdiction with respect to another state. These procedural rules do not bear on whether the conduct at issue was lawful, and therefore do not conflict with or derogate from substantive *jus cogens* norms. Rules on state immunity therefore have the effect of diverting disputes concerning state conduct away from foreign domestic courts, towards other, diplomatic methods of settlement.[33] The ICJ in this case noted, in *obiter dictum*,[34] that the question of Germany's obligation to provide Italian war victims with reparation remained an issue and could be the subject of further negotiations between the two states, with a view towards resolving this dispute.[35]

c   *State Immunity from Enforcement Jurisdiction*

State immunity not only bars one state from exercising adjudicatory jurisdiction over another state, but it also bars one state from exercising enforcement jurisdiction over another state. While a significant number of exceptions now exist with respect to immunity from jurisdiction, the same cannot be said with respect to immunity from enforcement jurisdiction. Whereas the restrictive doctrine of immunity includes numerous exceptions

---

[29] ibid, para 27.   [30] ibid, paras 28–36.   [31] ibid, para 91.

[32] The ICJ assumed, for the sake of its analysis, that the human rights and IHL norms at issue have a *jus cogens* character, but did not determine that this was the case. These norms concern the prohibition of the murder of civilians in occupied territory, the deportation of civilian inhabitants to slave labour, and the deportation of prisoners of war to slave labour. ibid, para 93.

[33] Hazel Fox, 'In Defence of State Immunity: Why the UN Convention on State Immunity is Important' (2006) 55 International and Comparative Law Quarterly 399, 405.

[34] The Latin phrase *obiter dictum* literally means 'other thing said'. In the context of a judgment, this means that a given passage sets out the judges' opinion on a particular issue that is not essential for the decision taken.

[35] *Jurisdictional Immunities* case (n 26), paras 100, 104.

for non-sovereign activities that take place in the forum state, immunity from enforcement jurisdiction has largely retained its absolute character, although a few limited exceptions do exist. Before the emergence of the restrictive doctrine of immunity, the distinction between adjudicatory and enforcement jurisdiction had relatively little practical significance in the context of state immunity, as the law on state immunity imposed an absolute bar on the exercise of jurisdiction, regardless of the type of jurisdiction.[36] But now that states may be subject to the adjudicatory jurisdiction of other states in some circumstances, the distinction has taken on more significance. As a consequence, even where the courts of one state may exercise adjudicatory jurisdiction over another state, it is unlikely that the authorities of the forum state will be able to enforce the judgment by, for example, ordering property to be seized and used to pay the debt of the foreign state.

As a general rule, the property of a state is immune with respect to measures of constraint that another state might seek to take against it. In this context, the term 'property' has an expansive scope and refers to all state assets, including movable property (e.g., equipment, ships), immovable property (e.g., land, buildings), intellectual property rights and bank accounts. The term 'measure of constraint' refers to measures that may be taken both before and after a judgment (pre-judgment and post-judgment). Pre-judgment measures, such as the attachment or seizure of a building or the arrest of a ship, aim to restrain the use or disposal of property before a final judgment can be handed down.[37] Post-judgment measures refer not only to attachment and arrest, but also to execution, which could involve the actual possession of the property of a foreign state by the forum state.[38] The dispute between Germany and Italy in the *Jurisdictional Immunities* case, for example, partly concerned the unlawful, post-judgment measures of constraint that Italy took against German property located in Italy, namely Villa Vigoni, which was used by Germany to promote cultural exchanges between itself and Italy.[39]

The rationale behind the largely absolute character of immunity from enforcement jurisdiction stems from the fact that measures of constraint represent a greater interference with state sovereignty than court procedures. The actual seizure of property represents a more significant intrusion on a state's ability to order its own affairs than being subjected to court proceedings.[40] The practical consequence of this general rule providing for state immunity from enforcement jurisdiction is that a domestic court judgment that orders a foreign state to pay compensation must normally be dealt with out of court, through diplomatic means that ideally result in a settlement between the litigants.[41]

The exceptions to state immunity from enforcement jurisdiction are narrow, and have been codified in the UN Convention on Jurisdictional Immunities. The first two exceptions apply in the context of both pre- and post-judgment measures of constraint. First, states may expressly consent to such measures being taken by the forum state.[42] A state's waiver of

---

[36] Peter-Tobias Stoll, 'State Immunity' in *Max Planck Encyclopedia of Public International Law* (last updated 2011), paras 50–1.
[37] UN Convention on Jurisdictional Immunities art 18. Chester Brown and Roger O'Keefe, 'Article 18' in O'Keefe, Tams, and Tzanakopoulos (eds) (n 7) 300–1.
[38] UN Convention on Jurisdictional Immunities art 19. Chester Brown and Roger O'Keefe, 'Article 19' in O'Keefe, Tams, and Tzanakopoulos (eds) (n 7) 316–17.
[39] *Jurisdictional Immunities* case (n 26), paras 109–20.   [40] Fox and Webb (n 1) 481.   [41] ibid.
[42] UN Convention on Jurisdictional Immunities arts 18(a), 19(a).

immunity from adjudicatory jurisdiction may not, however, be taken as implicit consent to enforcement jurisdiction.[43] Such consent must be given separately and expressly.[44] Second, states can specifically allocate or earmark property to be used for the satisfaction of a claim that is the subject of court proceedings.[45] Finally, measures of constraint may be taken against a state's property which is located in the forum state and used for purposes 'other than government non-commercial purposes'.[46] In other words, property may be subject to enforcement jurisdiction where the intended or actual use of the property is for commercial purposes.[47] In addition, such property must have a connection with the object of the proceedings.[48] In the case of Germany's Villa Vigoni, none of these exceptions applied. The Villa was a cultural centre that served the non-commercial purpose of promoting cultural exchanges between Germany and Italy. Germany had neither consented to the measure of constraint taken against it nor had it allocated Villa Vigoni for the satisfaction of legal claims against it.[49]

3 Immunity of State Officials

The individuals who serve as state officials also benefit from immunity from the jurisdiction of foreign states. From a practical perspective, if state officials did not enjoy such immunities, then legal claims against sovereign states could simply be reformulated and redirected as claims against those individuals who serve as state officials. As with state immunity, individuals who represent states enjoy immunity from the adjudicatory jurisdiction of foreign states, which means that they may not be subject to civil proceedings, criminal prosecution or extradition proceedings, or summoned to appear as a witness.[50] State representatives also enjoy immunity from enforcement jurisdiction, which in this context is referred to as 'inviolability' and encompasses measures that involve physical constraint or other interference, such as the arrest, detention, or search of an individual.[51] The term 'state official' or 'representative' is used in this section to refer to all government officials, whether low-level civil servants, ministers, or heads of state or government. Such individuals are the beneficiaries of immunities that belong not to them, but to the state, with the consequence that only the state has the capacity to waive such immunities. The question of whether state representatives enjoy immunity in their domestic legal systems remains a question for domestic law. International law on immunity only governs the scenario in which one state seeks to exercise its jurisdiction with respect to the representative of another state.

---

[43] UN Convention on Jurisdictional Immunities art 7(2).   [44] UN Convention on Jurisdictional Immunities art 20.
[45] UN Convention on Jurisdictional Immunities arts 18(b), 19(b).
[46] UN Convention on Jurisdictional Immunities arts 18(c), 19(c)
[47] Art 21 of the UN Convention on Jurisdictional Immunities specifies, which categories of property cannot be considered commercial.
[48] UN Convention on Jurisdictional Immunities art 19(c); Brown and O'Keefe (n 38) 323.
[49] *Jurisdictional Immunities* case (n 26), para 119.
[50] *Case concerning Certain Questions of Mutual Assistance in Criminal Matters (Djibouti v France)* (Judgment) [2008] ICJ Rep 177.
[51] On the distinction between immunity and inviolability, see Roger O'Keefe, *International Criminal Law* (Oxford University Press 2015) 409.

a   ***Functional and Personal Immunities***

Individuals may benefit from two different types of immunities, which may be distinguished on the basis of their underlying rationales, their scopes of application, and their legal bases. On the one hand, all state officials may benefit from subject matter or functional immunity, which is also known as immunity *ratione materiae*. On the other hand, a small number of very high-level state officials may benefit from status or personal immunity, which is also known as immunity *ratione personae*. This chapter uses the terms 'functional immunity' and 'personal immunity', which, along with their Latin equivalents, are used most frequently in practice and in scholarship.

Functional immunities derive from state immunity and are grounded in the same rationale that underlies state immunity, namely, the sovereign equality of states.[52] The fundamental principle of sovereign equality precludes a state from exercising jurisdiction over not only the state itself, but also its officials, to the extent that they are acting in an official capacity. The scope of functional immunities is therefore limited to conduct performed in an official capacity by a state official. A state official's private conduct, which is not carried out in the course of his or her official capacity, does not benefit from immunity from the jurisdiction of a foreign state in civil or criminal proceedings. The scope of functional immunities is unlimited in a temporal sense because it covers all acts carried out in an official capacity, and continues to apply when the official leaves office, such that a state official cannot be prosecuted after leaving office for acts that were performed in an official capacity. Private acts committed during or before an official's time in office do not, however, fall within the scope of functional immunity. In summary, functional immunities apply to all serving and former state officials and cover only conduct carried out in their official capacity. The law governing functional immunity is based in customary international law and treaty law, in particular the 1963 Vienna Convention on Consular Relations (VCCR) (see Section 4 of this chapter).[53]

Unlike functional immunities, personal immunities do not derive from state immunity. Instead, a different, inherently pragmatic rationale underlies personal immunities, namely the importance of enabling very high-level state officials to carry out their functions on behalf of states. Heads of state or government, for example, must be able to travel to meetings abroad without fear of being arrested, detained, or otherwise subject to court proceedings in foreign states. Personal immunity guarantees that international relations can be carried out at the highest levels, without interference by foreign police officers, prosecutors, etc. Whereas all state officials benefit from functional immunities, a very select group of high-level officials benefit from personal immunity. According to current state practice, heads of state, heads of government, and ministers of foreign affairs are widely regarded as benefitting from personal immunity. In addition, some state practice further indicates that ministers of defence and ministers of commerce may also benefit from personal immunity, although a widespread consensus has not yet emerged on this

---

[52] *Certain Questions of Mutual Assistance in Criminal Matters* case (n 50), para 188.
[53] VCCR (adopted 24 April 1963, entered into force 19 March 1967) 596 UNTS 261.

point.[54] Customary international law governs personal immunities for heads of state or government and ministers of defence, and could, at least in theory, evolve in the future to include a broader group of individuals. Diplomatic agents and certain members of special missions also benefit from a version of personal immunities, but their immunities are governed by a separate legal regime consisting, in particular, of the 1961 Vienna Convention on Diplomatic Relations (VCDR) and the 1969 Convention on Special Missions (see Section 4).[55]

While functional immunity covers only conduct carried out in an official capacity, personal immunity covers all conduct, but only for the duration of the official's time in office. In other words, conduct carried out in both an official and a private capacity falls within the scope of personal immunity, but the official ceases to benefit from personal immunity when he or she leaves office. The extension of personal immunity to acts committed in a private capacity reflects the underlying rationale of personal immunity, which holds that very high-level officials must be able to conduct international relations without being hindered by the possibility of being subjected to the jurisdiction of foreign states. The temporal scope of personal immunity is limited because these officials no longer require such protection once they have left office. After leaving their posts, these very high-level officials continue to benefit from functional immunity, which applied alongside personal immunity during their time in office. Very high-level officials; therefore, enjoy immunity for conduct carried out in their official, as opposed to private capacity, even after leaving office. In summary, personal immunities apply to a very limited range of state officials, and cover all conduct, whether carried out in a public or private capacity, but only for the duration of the official's time in office.

b   *Immunities and International Crimes*

As the law stands at present, both functional and personal immunities continue to apply, even where the state official has allegedly engaged in conduct that could be characterized as an international crime, such as a war crime or a crime against humanity (see Chapter 13). The existence of exceptions that would remove immunity in such circumstances has been the subject of domestic and international litigation, and has also been intensely debated by states and scholars.[56] This section describes the state of the law at present, while acknowledging that the law may change, and arguably should change, in the future. The current state of the law on immunity is unsatisfactory from the perspective of ethics and politics, which counsel in favour of holding accountable those who have committed the most serious

---

[54] O'Keefe (n 51) 420–1.

[55] VCDR (adopted 18 April 1961, entered into force 24 April 1964) 500 UNTS 95; Convention on Special Missions (adopted 8 December 1969, entered into force 21 June 1985) 1400 UNTS 231.

[56] See, for example, Antonio Cassese, 'When May Senior State Officials Be Tried for International Crimes? Some Comments on the *Congo v Belgium* Case' (2002) 13 European Journal of International Law 853; Rosanne van Alebeek, *The Immunity of States and Their Officials in International Criminal Law and International Human Rights Law* (Oxford University Press 2008); Zachary Douglas, 'State Immunity for the Acts of State Officials' (2012) 82 British Yearbook of International Law 281; Andrew Sanger, 'Immunity of State Officials from the Criminal Jurisdiction of a Foreign State' (2013) 62 International and Comparative Law Quarterly 193.

crimes of international concern. International law, however, balances the international community's interest in fighting impunity with the importance of ensuring sovereign equality (in the case of functional immunity) and the smooth functioning of international relations (in the case of personal immunity). At present, state practice still tips in favour of personal and functional immunity and does not support the proposition that immunities cease to apply to individuals when international crimes are at stake. In the case of functional immunities, however, state practice may be in the process of very slowly gravitating towards the creation of an exception with respect to international crimes. This section begins with the state of the law with respect to personal immunity, which was clarified in the *Arrest Warrant* case, and then discusses the ongoing debate with respect to functional immunities.

i   *Personal Immunity*

In 1999, Belgium amended its laws to allow Belgian courts to exercise jurisdiction over violations of international humanitarian law, without the need for any link between Belgium and the alleged conduct, the accused persons, or the victims.[57] The new Belgian law thereby allowed for the exercise of universal jurisdiction, and it led to a number of controversial criminal investigations in the years that followed.[58] In April 2000, for example, a Belgian investigating judge issued an international arrest warrant against Abdulaye Yerodia, who was at that time the minister of foreign affairs of the Democratic Republic of Congo (DRC).[59] The Belgian investigating judge alleged that in August 1998, in the midst of an armed conflict in the DRC, Yerodia had made speeches that incited racial hatred and provoked massacres of Tutsi civilians, in violation of international humanitarian law.[60] In the *Arrest Warrant* case that the DRC subsequently brought to the ICJ against Belgium, the DRC argued, in part, that Belgium's issuance and circulation of the arrest warrant against Yerodia violated his right to immunity.[61] Because the existing treaties on immunity do not cover the immunity of high-ranking state officials, such as the minister of foreign affairs, the ICJ had to consider whether Yerodia was entitled to personal immunity under customary international law.[62]

In its 2002 judgment, the ICJ determined that state practice does not support the existence of an exception to immunity from criminal jurisdiction in situations where the accused person is suspected of having committed international crimes, such as war crimes

---

[57] *Case concerning the Arrest Warrant of 11 April 2000 (Democratic Republic of the Congo v Belgium)* (Judgment) [2002] ICJ Rep 3, para 15; Belgium, 1993 Act Concerning Punishment for Grave breaches of the International Humanitarian Law, as amended in 1999 to include genocide and crimes against humanity.

[58] See, for example, the charges brought by Belgium prosecutors against the Israeli prime minister, Ariel Sharon, and the former US president, George HW Bush.

[59] *Arrest Warrant* case, para 15.   [60] ibid.

[61] ibid, para 62. The DRC also alleged that the issuance and circulation of the arrest warrant violated Yerodia's right to inviolability and the Court found that both rights were violated, though without dealing with the distinction between immunity and inviolability. This description of the case focuses on the issue of immunity, as the issuance and circulation of the arrest warrant are best understood as having violated Yerodia's right to be free from judicial process, which is an issue of immunity. The mere issuance and circulation of the arrest warrant did not amount to a physical interference with Yerodia's person, which would be necessary in order for an issue of inviolability to arise. See *Arrest Warrant* case, Dissenting Opinion of Judge van den Wyngaert, para 75.

[62] *Arrest Warrant* case, para 52.

or crimes against humanity.[63] The Court explained that the immunities enjoyed by ministers of foreign affairs help to ensure their effective performance of their functions, which require them to travel internationally and to represent the state in international negotiations and intergovernmental meetings.[64] According to the Court, the risk of exposure to arrest and legal proceedings could deter travel for such official functions and could therefore prevent a minister of foreign affairs from performing his or her duties.[65] The ICJ; therefore, determined that the issuance and international circulation of the arrest warrant violated Yerodia's right to immunity, and it ordered Belgium to cancel the arrest warrant and to inform the authorities to whom it was circulated of its cancellation.[66]

The Court evidently anticipated dissatisfaction with the outcome in this case, as it included a passage, as *obiter dictum*, in which it explained that immunity does not equate with 'impunity', meaning exemption from punishment.[67] The Court noted that international law on immunities does not bar the prosecution of a minister of foreign affairs in all circumstances, and it outlined four conceivable scenarios in which a minister of foreign affairs could be lawfully subject to criminal court proceedings.[68] First, a minister of foreign affairs could be prosecuted in the state which he or she represents. International law on immunity, after all, only governs the exercise of jurisdiction by foreign states, not by the state that the individual represents. Second, the state that the foreign minister represents could waive his or her immunity. Third, acts committed in a private capacity before, during and after his or her time in office may be the subject of domestic court proceedings after he or she leaves office. Finally, a minister of foreign affairs may be subject to proceedings before an international criminal court, such as the International Criminal Court (ICC). This passage highlights the possibilities, at least in theory, for holding high-level officials, such as ministers of foreign affairs, criminally liable despite their right to personal immunity in foreign jurisdictions. Whether these possibilities represent realistic options is; however, an open question. Major domestic political shifts may be necessary before a state is willing to prosecute its own high-level officials or waive their immunity in a foreign jurisdiction, and international criminal courts like the ICC suffer from both limited jurisdiction and limited capacity (see Chapter 13).

ii   Functional Immunity

While the *Arrest Warrant* judgment brought clarity with respect to personal immunity and the absence of any exception in cases involving international crimes, this issue has continued to be debated with respect to functional immunity. Legal debates have revolved, in part, around questions of legal reasoning, such as whether international crimes may be characterized as conduct carried out in an official capacity and whether the law on immunities conflicts with *jus cogens* norms.[69] Ultimately; however, the state of the law with respect to functional immunity hinges on developments in state practice, and accompanying *opinio juris*.

---

[63] ibid, para 58.   [64] ibid, para 53.   [65] ibid, para 54–5.   [66] ibid, para 70–1.   [67] ibid, para 60.   [68] ibid, para 61.
[69] For a discussion of such arguments, see O'Keefe (n 51) 447–53.

The *Pinochet* case in the United Kingdom initially raised questions about the possible existence of an exception to functional immunity in cases involving international crimes. As the head of state of Chile between 1973 and 1990, Augusto Pinochet Ugarte was infamous for the extra-judicial execution, torture, and forced disappearance of political opponents. After he stepped down as president of Chile, he served as commander-in-chief of the Chilean army until 1998, when he retired. At this point, a number of European states issued international arrest warrants for Pinochet, including Spain, which charged him with torture, among other things.[70] When Pinochet travelled to the United Kingdom for medical treatment in 1998, following his retirement, he was arrested and subjected to proceedings for his extradition to Spain. This gave rise to a number of extradition proceedings in UK courts, which culminated in a 1999 House of Lords judgment which is known as *Pinochet (No 3)* because this was the third panel of the House of Lords to deal with this extradition case.[71]

A majority of the Law Lords rejected Pinochet's claim to immunity with respect to charges of torture.[72] Although the reasoning set forth by the various Law Lords differs, the majority decision converges on the specifics of the Convention against Torture, which was at issue in this case.[73] The reasoning centred around the fact that if state officials suspected of torture were entitled to immunity, then the Convention against Torture would lose its effect. The Convention is fundamentally premised on states parties (like the United Kingdom and Spain) exercising universal jurisdiction over state officials who commit torture, and either extraditing or prosecuting such individuals suspected of torture when they are present in their territory. Despite this decision, Pinochet was ultimately never extradited to Spain because he was deemed unfit to stand trial due to his state of health. But *Pinochet (No 3)*, nevertheless, ignited debate about whether state practice supported the existence of a wider exception to functional immunity in cases involving allegations of international crimes.

Although the ICJ has since heard a number of cases concerning immunities, and possible exceptions thereto, it has never had to rule specifically on whether an exception with respect to functional immunities exists in customary international law.[74] The ILC has; however, addressed this issue, but its proposed codification has not been without controversy. In 2017, as a part of its work on 'draft articles on immunity of state officials from foreign criminal jurisdiction', the ILC adopted a draft article concerning crimes with respect to which functional immunity does not apply.[75] The enumerated offences are crimes of genocide, crimes against humanity, war crimes, the crime of apartheid, torture,

---

[70] Belgian, French, and Swiss magistrates also issued arrest warrants for Pinochet.

[71] The first judgment (Pinochet (No 1)) was set aside because one of the Law Lords was later disqualified (Pinochet (No 2)) and a new panel delivered the judgment in the third instance (Pinochet (No 3)). See generally Andrea Gattini, 'Pinochet Cases' in *Max Planck Encyclopedia of Public International Law* (last updated June 2007).

[72] *Regina v Bow Street Metropolitan Stipendiary Magistrate, Ex Parte Pinochet Ugarte* (No 3) [1999] UKHL 17, [2000] 1 AC 147 (1999) (UK House of Lords).

[73] Convention against Torture and Other Cruel, Inhuman or Degrading Treatment or Punishment (adopted 10 December 1984, entered into force 26 June 1987) 1465 UNTS 85, arts 5, 7.

[74] See, for example, *Arrest Warrant* case (n 57); *Jurisdictional Immunities* case (n 26).

[75] ILC, 'Report of the International Law Commission on the Work of the 69th Session' (2017) UN Doc A/72/10.

and enforced disappearance.[76] In its commentary on this draft article, the ILC explained that it had identified a 'discernible trend' in state practice 'towards limiting the applicability of immunity from jurisdiction *ratione materiae* in respect of certain types of behavior that constitute crimes under international law'.[77] The ILC also cited the importance of balancing respect for the sovereign equality of states (i.e., the rationale that underpins functional immunity), with the need to end impunity for the most serious international crimes.[78] Not all of the commissioners of the ILC agreed with this conclusion; however, as some considered there to be insufficient state practice as of 2017 to support such a conclusion.[79]

It remains to be seen how state practice will evolve on this issue, and whether a sufficient body of domestic court decisions and domestic legislation will develop to provide robust support for the existence of an exception with respect to international crimes. Such a body of state practice could, in part, emerge out of the ongoing investigations being conducted in states such as France and Germany, where former Syrian officials face charges concerning the widespread torture of detainees in Syria during the armed conflict there.[80] The ILC's draft articles on the immunity of state officials from foreign criminal jurisdiction could also aid the progressive development of the law on this issue, should domestic practice increasingly come into alignment with the views of the ILC.

4   Diplomatic and Consular Immunities

Diplomats and consular agents are a sub-set of officials who represent states, and they benefit from a special legal regime that has been codified in the 1961 Vienna Convention on Diplomatic Relations (VCDR) and the 1963 Vienna Convention on Consular Relations (VCCR), both of which reflect customary international law.[81] These instruments contain a detailed set of rules concerning not only immunity, but also inviolability and privileges. The rules governing the immunity and inviolability of diplomatic and consular agents are procedural in character, in that they bar the adjudication or enforcement of substantive laws that remain applicable to them. Privileges are, however, distinct from immunities as they are substantive rather than procedural in character. Privileges provide for an exemption from or modification of the substantive law, so that the substantive, domestic law is altered in relation to diplomatic and consular agents. Privileges often take the form of exemptions from taxes as well as customs duties, among other things. The beneficiaries of these rules are not only diplomatic and consular agents but also, to varying and lesser extents, their family members and members of technical and administrative staff at embassies and consulates.[82] Individuals

---

[76] ibid 176, art 7.   [77] ibid 178–9, Commentary to Art 7, para 5.   [78] ibid 181, Commentary to Art 7, para 6.
[79] See, for example, Sean D Murphy, 'Immunity Ratione Materiae of State Officials from Foreign Criminal Jurisdiction: Where is the State Practice in Support of Exceptions?' (2018) 112 American Journal of International Law Unbound 4. Scholars who are not members of the ILC have also been critical. See also Roger O'Keefe, 'An International Crime Exception to the Immunity of State Officials from Foreign Criminal Jurisdiction: Not Currently, Not Likely' (2015) 109 American Journal of International Law Unbound 167.
[80] See eg, the arrest warrant issued of General Jamil Hassan in Germany.   [81] VCDR (n 55); VCCR (n 53).
[82] VCDR art 37; VCCR art 43.

who represent states on temporary missions, such as special envoys who lead peace processes, for example, also benefit from immunity and inviolability, though they are covered not by the Vienna Conventions, but by the 1969 Convention on Special Missions.[83]

The existence of diplomatic and consular immunities may be explained by reference to a pragmatic rationale, namely the development and maintenance of friendly relations among states.[84] Diplomatic and consular agents must be able to carry out their functions in an efficient manner, unhindered by the 'receiving state', meaning the state to which the diplomatic or consular agent has been sent by his or her 'sending state'.[85] International relations depend on diplomatic and consular agents who facilitate inter-state communication and negotiations, as well as commercial, economic, scientific, and cultural relations. Broadly speaking, the functions of diplomats are relatively high-level and potentially sensitive politically, as they involve, among other things, representing the sending state, protecting its interests, and negotiating with the receiving state.[86] Diplomats include ambassadors, who head missions, as well as lower-level diplomatic agents.[87] The functions of consular agents tend to involve more practical and administrative matters (e.g., the issuance of passports and visas), as well as more interaction with local actors such as businesses, the cultural sector, and police and prisons.[88] Because diplomatic and consular agents carry out their functions in the receiving state, they are especially vulnerable, and events in recent years have shown that in the most extreme situations, they sometimes risk their lives.[89] For the most part; however, compliance with this body of rules is quite high, as each state sends as well as receives diplomatic and consular agents, and therefore, has a reciprocal or mutual interest in ensuring that these laws are upheld.

Diplomatic and consular agents both benefit from immunities, although diplomats benefit from fuller protection from the adjudicative and administrative jurisdiction of the receiving state. The law provides fuller protection for diplomatic, as opposed to consular agents, because diplomatic functions involve more sensitive, political, high-level matters that heighten their vulnerability. Diplomatic agents; therefore, enjoy personal immunity, which means that the activities that they carry out in both official and personal capacities are protected from criminal and civil litigation as well as administrative proceedings in the receiving state. The personal immunity of diplomatic agents is subject to very limited exceptions, one of which concerns professional or commercial activities.[90] A UK court has, for example, interpreted the commercial activities exception to mean that a diplomat's involvement in human trafficking, which is a commercial activity, albeit an illegal one, is not covered by personal immunity.[91] In contrast with diplomats, consular agents enjoy

---

[83] Convention on Special Missions (n 55).   [84] VCDR, preambular para 3; VCCR, preambular para 4.
[85] VCDR, preambular para 4; VCCR, preambular para 5.   [86] VCDR art 3.   [87] VCDR art 14.
[88] VCCR art 5. On the distinctions between diplomatic and consular functions, see Sanderijn Duquet, 'Immunities of Diplomatic and Consular Personnel: An Overview' in Ruys, Angelet and Ferro (eds) (n 9) 413.
[89] See, for example, the 2012 attack on the US consulate in Benghazi, Libya, which resulted in the death of the US ambassador to Libya, among others; the 2021 ambush of a World Food Programme convoy in the DRC, which resulted in the death of the Italian ambassador to the DRC.
[90] VCDR art 31. The other exceptions relate to private immovable property (e.g., land) that is located in the territory of the sending state (unless the agent holds it on behalf of the sending state for the purposes of the mission) and matters of succession, where the diplomatic agent is involved, but not on behalf of the sending state.
[91] *Reyes v Al-Malki* [2017] UKSC 61 (2017) (UK Supreme Court).

more limited protection, in the form of functional immunity, which covers only acts carried out in an official capacity, and is also subject to some exceptions.[92]

Both diplomatic and consular agents are also entitled to inviolability, which requires the receiving state to refrain from subjecting them to its enforcement jurisdiction through arrest, detention, or search.[93] The VCCR does; however, set out an exception with respect to the inviolability of a consular officer suspected of a 'grave crime', in which case a consular officer may be arrested and detained.[94] In addition to the negative obligation not to infringe the inviolability of diplomatic and consular agents by subjecting them to its enforcement jurisdiction, the receiving state also bears a positive obligation to prevent attacks on their 'person, freedom or dignity'.[95] In other words, the receiving state must take preventive measures to ensure that diplomatic and consular agents remain inviolable, and are not subject to attacks on their physical integrity, including by private actors, such as militant groups. In addition, the diplomatic mission is itself inviolable, which means that agents of the receiving state cannot enter the mission without the consent of the head of mission.[96] The receiving state is further obliged to 'take all steps' to protect the premises of diplomatic and consular missions against intrusion or damage, and to prevent 'any disturbance of the peace of the mission or impairment of its dignity'.[97] Inviolability also extends to the archives and documents of the mission as well as official correspondence and the diplomatic bag.[98]

The *Tehran Hostages* case arose out of one of the most infamous violations of this obligation to prevent infringements of the inviolability of diplomatic and consular agents and the premises of missions.[99] In November 1979, during the Iranian Revolution, mass demonstrations outside of the United States embassy in Tehran were triggered by a decision by the US government to permit the former Shah of Iran to enter the United States for medical treatment. Over the course of three hours, the embassy in Tehran was overrun by a group of several hundred militants who breached the premises, and took diplomatic and consular personnel hostage.[100] Over fifty diplomatic and consular personnel were ultimately held hostage for more than a year, until January 1981. As the embassy was being overrun, Iranian security personnel reportedly 'disappeared from the scene', and despite repeated requests from the United States for help, Iran did not send police or security forces to protect the embassy, nor did Iran make an effort to rescue the hostages or to persuade the militants to withdraw.[101] The ICJ determined that Iran's inaction during this episode constituted a 'clear and serious violation' of numerous obligations held by Iran under the VCDR and the VCCR, including the obligation to prevent attacks on diplomatic and consular agents, and to protect the premises of the embassy.[102]

Such infringements on the inviolability of diplomatic and consular agents and the premises of embassies and consulates are unfortunately not just a matter of historical

---

[92] VCCR arts 43, 45(3).   [93] VCDR art 29; VCCR arts 40–1.   [94] VCCR art 41(1).   [95] VCDR art 29, VCCR arts 40.
[96] VCDR art 22(1). Consular missions enjoy inviolability to a somewhat lesser extent. See VCCR art 31.
[97] VCDR art 22(2).   [98] VCDR arts 24, 27.
[99] *Case concerning United States Diplomatic and Consular Staff in Tehran (United States of America v Iran)* (Judgment) [1980] ICJ Rep 3.
[100] ibid, para 17.   [101] ibid, paras 17–18.   [102] ibid, para 67.

interest.[103] These incidents must be understood, however, as rare instances of non-compliance with the law on diplomatic and consular immunities, which generally attracts relatively high levels of compliance for the reasons noted in this section.

5   Privileges and Immunities of International Organizations

In addition to states and individuals, international organizations also benefit from immunity from domestic jurisdictions in certain circumstances. The term 'international organization' refers to a framework for cooperation that is established by a treaty or another instrument governed by international law and possesses its own international legal personality (see Chapter 8). The UN, the European Union (EU), and the World Bank are all examples of international organizations. Because international organizations only became a real phenomenon after the Second World War, the law on the immunity of international organizations is also of a newer vintage than the law on the immunity of states and state officials. International organizations benefit from immunity from the adjudicatory jurisdiction of states in both criminal and civil proceedings, as well as immunity from enforcement jurisdiction. The officials of international organizations also benefit from immunity and inviolability, which varies in its protection depending on the status of the individual.[104] In addition to immunity and inviolability, international organizations and their officials are also entitled to certain privileges, which involve exemptions from or modifications of substantive domestic laws such as taxes and customs duties.

Because of the inherent differences between states and international organizations, distinct rationales underly the immunities and privileges of international organizations and their officials.[105] Unlike states, international organizations are not sovereign and do not possess any territory over which they exercise supreme authority. Instead, international organizations enjoy only those limited powers that have been granted to them by their member states. Moreover, international organizations are inevitably based in the territory of a state. Because of these fundamental differences between states and international organizations, sovereign equality, which is the rationale underlying state immunity, has no relevance with respect to international organizations. The immunity and privileges of international organizations are instead premised on the pragmatic rationale of functional necessity.

According to the principle of functional necessity, international organizations must be able to carry out their essential functions without interference on account of the exercise of jurisdiction by states. Because international organizations are based in and operate in states, they are vulnerable to interference by those states. The independence and smooth functioning of international organizations could be threatened where the organization is,

---

[103] See n 89.
[104] Convention on the Privileges and Immunities of the UN (adopted 13 February 1946, entered into force 17 September 1946) 1 UNTS 15, arts 18–20.
[105] Fox and Webb (n 1) 571.

for example, subject to local court proceedings, where property is seized, or where the organization must pay taxes to the host state in which it is based. This rationale of functional necessity is reflected in Article 105 of the UN Charter, which provides that the UN 'shall enjoy in the territory of each of its members such privileges and immunities as are necessary for the fulfillment of its purposes'.[106] This underlying rationale determines the scope of application of the immunities of international organizations and their officials, as organizations are only entitled to immunity with respect to activities that fall within the scope of their functions. If a given activity is necessary for the effective functioning of the organization or its capacity to fulfil its mandate, then immunity applies.

The law governing the immunities and privileges of international organizations and their officials consists of treaties and, to a lesser extent, domestic laws that implement these international agreements. Unlike state immunity and the immunity of state representatives, the law on the immunities and privileges of international organizations is not based in customary international law, though some treaty rules may have become rules of custom.[107] Various types of treaties govern the privileges and immunities of international organizations, including constituent instruments, such as the UN Charter; multilateral agreements, such as the 1946 Convention on the Privileges and Immunities of the UN;[108] and bilateral agreements, such as the headquarter agreement that the UN concluded with the United States, as the UNs headquarters are located in New York.[109] This area of law has not; however, benefited from a successful effort to codify general rules governing privileges and immunities with respect to all international organizations. The ILC dropped its work on the topic of the relations between states and international organizations in 1992, with the result that an equivalent to the UN Convention on Jurisdictional Immunities never took shape.

The law on the immunities of international organizations naturally poses an obstacle for parties that wish to pursue claims against them, though international organizations may, at least in theory, waive their immunity to adjudicatory and enforcement jurisdiction. Just as states must waive enforcement jurisdiction explicitly and separately from any waiver of adjudicatory jurisdiction, the same is true for international organizations. A waiver by an international organization with respect to adjudicatory jurisdiction does not imply a waiver with respect to enforcement jurisdiction.[110] In the absence of a waiver, parties to disputes with international organizations must rely on alternative dispute settlement methods, beyond domestic court systems. The Convention on the Privileges and Immunities of the

---

[106] Charter of the UN (adopted 26 June 1945, entered into force 24 October 1945) 1 UNTS XVI.

[107] Mirka Möldner, 'International Organizations or Institutions, Privileges and Immunities' in *Max Planck Encyclopedia for Public International Law* (last updated May 2011), para 11.

[108] See also Convention on the Privileges and Immunities of the Specialized Agencies (adopted 21 November 1947, entered into force 2 December 1948) 33 UNTS 261.

[109] Agreement between the UN and the United States of America regarding the Headquarters of the UN, UNGA Res 169(II) (31 October 1947); see also the status of forces agreements that the UN concludes with respect to its peacekeeping operations.

[110] Convention on the Privileges and Immunities of the UN art II s 2, art V s 20.

UN obliges the UN, for example, to provide for appropriate dispute settlement mechanisms.[111] Without such mechanisms, the immunities of international organizations could give rise to serious injustices, as claimants would lack any way of seeking remedies. Disputes with international organizations that arise out of contracts may, for example, be settled through negotiation, conciliation, or arbitration, while disputes that arise out of employment relationships may be resolved through a range of informal and formal procedures. Within the UNs, employment-related disputes may be handled through a formal two-tiered internal system which allows recourse, at first instance, to the UN Dispute Tribunal, followed by an appeal to the UN Appeals Tribunal.[112]

The immunity of international organizations from jurisdiction can come into tension with the human right to access to justice.[113] This tension was illustrated by court proceedings that arose out of the conduct of the Dutch peacekeepers, known as Dutchbat, who served in the former Yugoslavia during the armed conflict there in the mid-1990s.[114] Dutchbat was present in Srebrenica, a town in Bosnia and Herzegovina, during its siege in 1995 by the Bosnian Serb army, which carried out a genocide of more than 8,000 Bosniak Muslim men and boys. Dutchbat was a small, lightly-armed infantry that had neither the mandate nor the capability needed to prevent the Srebrenica massacre. Its role in the events that unfolded resulted in major political fallout in the Netherlands, as well as civil litigation brought by victims against both the UN and the Netherlands. Following years of civil litigation in Dutch courts, this case ultimately came before the European Court of Human Rights (ECtHR), which ruled that the UN was indeed entitled to immunity in the Dutch courts.[115]

The ECtHR held that the immunity that had been granted to the UN by the Dutch court served a legitimate purpose and did not result in a disproportionate restriction on the right of access to justice. The ECtHR explained that granting immunity to international organizations allows them to function properly, 'free from unilateral interference by individual governments', such as the Netherlands. According to the ECtHR, if domestic courts were permitted to rule on peacekeeping operations authorized by the UN Security Council, then this could result in individual states interfering with the Security Council's fulfilment of its key mission, which is the maintenance of international peace and security. The ECtHR also noted that immunity serves the interest of the good functioning of international organizations, to which states have increasingly resorted for the purpose of international cooperation. This case illustrates, in part, the extent to which the immunities of international organizations remain applicable, even in the face of mass atrocities involving international crimes. The human right to access to justice is not an absolute right, as the ECtHR noted, and it may be subject to limitations, such as those resulting from the immunity of international organizations in domestic jurisdictions.

---

[111] Convention on the Privileges and Immunities of the UN art V s 21, art VIII s 29.

[112] UNGA Res 63/253 (17 March 2009).

[113] Convention for the Protection of Human Rights and Fundamental Freedoms (adopted 4 November 1950, entered into force 3 September 1953) ETS 5 (ECHR) art 6(1).

[114] *Stichting Mothers of Srebrenica and Others v The Netherlands* App no 65542/12 (ECtHR, 11 June 2013).

[115] See HR 19 July 2019 (The Netherlands v Stichting 'Mothers of Srebrenica) ECLI:NL:HR:2019:1223 (Supreme Court of the Netherlands) (apportioning liability to the Dutch state based on its participation in peacekeeping operation).

6   Concluding Remarks

This chapter has introduced a body of procedural rules that bar states from exercising jurisdiction over foreign states; the state officials of foreign states, including diplomatic and consular agents; and international organizations. While state immunity and the functional immunity of state officials are grounded in the equality of sovereign states, personal immunities and the immunities of diplomatic and consular agents and international organizations have a more pragmatic foundation, namely the importance of enabling these actors to perform their functions. In order to protect the integrity of international relations, the law on immunity results in the diversion of legal issues involving these actors away from foreign legal systems, towards other, international means of dispute settlement. At times, the operation of the law on immunity can result in outcomes that seem unjust and undesirable, especially where a domestic court lacks jurisdiction with respect to a case that involves allegations of serious international crimes. In these instances, state practice continues to privilege the maintenance of international relations through immunities, over the quest to end impunity through means involving domestic litigation in foreign states. These are among the situations that currently challenge the boundaries of this body of law, which has been in the process of evolving and developing for many centuries, and will no doubt continue to do so.

Recommended Reading

Dapo Akande and Sangeeta Shah, "Immunities of State Officials, International Crimes, and Foreign Domestic Courts" (2010) 21 European Journal of International Law 815.

Rosanne van Alebeek, *The Immunity of States and Their Officials in International Criminal Law and International Human Rights Law* (Oxford University Press 2008).

Antonio Cassese, "When May Senior State Officials Be Tried for International Crimes? Some Comments on the *Congo v. Belgium* Case" (2002) 13 European Journal of International Law 853.

Hazel Fox and Philippa Webb, *The Law of State Immunity* (3rd edn, Oxford University Press 2013).

Adil Ahmad Haque, "Immunity and Impunity" in Kevin Jon Heller et al (eds), *The Oxford Handbook of International Criminal Law* (Oxford University Press 2020).

Roger O'Keefe, Christian J Tams (eds), and Antonios Tzanakopoulos (ass ed), *The United Nations Convention on Jurisdictional Immunities of States and Their Property: A Commentary* (Oxford University Press 2013).

Sir Arthur Watts, "The Legal Position in International Law of Heads of States, Heads of Governments and Foreign Ministers" (1994) 247 Collected Courses of the Hague Academy of International Law 9.

Xiaodong Yang, *State Immunity in International Law* (Cambridge University Press 2012).

8

International Organizations

Niels Blokker

1   Introduction

International organizations play an important role in the international community. While the state continues to be the supreme form of political organization in the world, it has become generally recognized that international organizations are indispensable for coping with the consequences of globalization and increasing interdependence. Global problems, such as international armed conflicts, climate change, and infectious diseases require global solutions and cooperation within a permanent international framework. Nowadays, the United Nations (UN), the International Monetary Fund and the World Bank, the World Trade Organization (WTO), and the World Health Organization (WHO) are often front-page news. The outbreak of the coronavirus responsible for COVID-19 in December 2019 not only demonstrated that it is for each state to decide on a lockdown or other measures, but it also showed that cooperation between international organizations is necessary to deal with this pandemic and its economic and financial implications most effectively.

The need for cooperation at the regional level has resulted in the establishment of regional international organizations such as the European Union (EU), the Organization of American States, the African Union, and the Association of South East Asian Nations. In addition, there are hundreds of other international organizations. Some are well known (e.g., North Atlantic Treaty Organization, the Organization of the Petroleum Exporting Countries (OPEC), and the International Criminal Court (ICC)). Others are less well known, but they may, nonetheless play an important role in a particular part of the world or in a particular technical field. Examples are the World Meteorological Organization and the International Renewable Energy Agency. Organizations, such as regional space organizations (e.g., the European Space Agency and the Asia-Pacific Space Cooperation Organization) have been created because 'the magnitude of the human, technical and financial resources' required for activities in the space field is far beyond the capacities of the individual member states.[1] In short, international

---

[1] See the preambles of the Convention for the Establishment of a European Space Agency (adopted 30 May 1975, entered into force 30 October 1980) 1297 UNTS 161 and the Convention of the Asia-Pacific Space Cooperation Organization (adopted 28 October 2005, entered into force 12 October 2006) 2423 UNTS 127.

organizations perform activities in areas in which states can no longer operate effectively in isolation, and in which there is a common interest in cooperation within a permanent international framework.

International organizations may be defined as frameworks for cooperation, established by treaty or other instrument, governed by international law, and possessing their own international legal personality. International organizations may include as members, in addition to states, other international organizations.[2] In practice, almost all international organizations are established by treaty. This characteristic distinguishes them from more informal frameworks for cooperation and from non-governmental organizations (NGOs). An example of an informal framework for cooperation is the Group of 20, better known as the G20, which brings together the nineteen most powerful economic states and the EU to coordinate their policies. NGOs organizations are normally created under the domestic laws of a state, not by treaty. The requirement that international organizations possess their own international legal personality is included in order to make clear that they must have their own identity in the international legal order, separate from that of their members. Traditionally, only states were members of international organizations. However, increasingly also international organizations have become members, as will be discussed in Section 3. For example, the EU is a member of the WTO, together with its member states.

This chapter will examine international organizations primarily from a legal perspective. Each organization has its own laws: its basic rules (laid down in the treaty by which it is created), the more detailed rules governing its internal functioning, its binding or non-binding decisions, its agreements with states or other international organizations, etc. However, this chapter will not discuss the law of particular international organizations. Rather, it aims to present a general overview of the law of international organizations, considering that there are an increasing number of rules applicable to all international organizations, that many rules of international organizations resemble each other, and that it is possible to distil certain underlying principles. This chapter will first discuss the legal status, privileges, and immunities of international organizations (Section 2). Subsequently, it will deal with membership issues (Section 3), powers (Section 4), and institutional structures (Section 5). Next, we will look at decisions of international organizations: the way in which they are taken and the different types of decisions (Section 6). Section 7 will briefly examine the finances of international organizations. There has been an exponential increase of activities of international organizations over the years. Not all of these activities have been successful, however, and there have been failures and wrongdoings. In recent years, a much-debated issue is to what extent international organizations and/or their members may be held responsible for such failures and wrongdoings. This is briefly examined in Section 8, followed by some concluding observations in Section 9.

---

[2] This definition largely follows the one adopted by the International Law Commission in 2011 (ILC), see ILC, 'Draft Articles on the Responsibility of International Organizations' (2011) UN Doc A/66/10 (ARIO) art 2(a).

2   Legal Status, Privileges, and Immunities

a   *Legal Status*

International organizations were first created in the nineteenth century. Examples are the Central Commission for the Navigation of the Rhine (1815), the International Telegraph Union, now called the International Telecommunication Union (1865), and the Universal Postal Union (1874). At the time, the precise legal status of these organizations was far from clear. States were the only entities entitled to bear rights and obligations under international law. Should international organizations also have this status, even though it is clear that they are not states? Only during the twentieth century did the position of international organizations in the international and the national legal order become clearer.

To be a legal person is to have the capacity to bear rights and obligations within a particular legal order. To be an international legal person is to have the capacity to bear rights and obligations under international law. This entails the possibility to conclude treaties. Specific examples of such rights and obligations under international law are laid down, for example, in headquarters agreements (concluded between international organizations and their host states). Such agreements normally state that the organization is entitled to certain tax privileges and that authorities of the host state may not enter the premises of the organization without the latter's permission. An example of obligations of international organizations is the obligation to cooperate with the authorities of the member states (including the host state) to facilitate the proper administration of justice, secure the observance of police regulations, and prevent the occurrence of any abuse of privileges and immunities.

It has long been accepted that international organizations are legal persons within the domestic legal order of their member states. This status allows them to conclude contracts under the domestic laws of the member states, for example to rent offices. However, for a long time it was much more controversial whether international organizations should also be able to operate as *international* legal persons, just like states. In the nineteenth and early twentieth centuries, the status of international legal person was reserved for states only. But following the establishment of large and important international organizations, such as the League of Nations and the International Labour Organization (ILO), it became increasingly clear that such organizations would not be able to perform their functions on the international plane – for example by concluding treaties and sending and receiving delegations – without enjoying international legal personality, separately from their members. Not having their own territory (like states), they needed to conclude treaties with their host states to guarantee their independent functioning, in the interest of all member states, and they needed to be able to receive representatives from member states, even if the host would normally be reluctant to have these representatives on its territory. The old order started to change. Key moments in this process of gradual change were the foundation of the UN in 1945 and the *Reparation for Injuries* advisory opinion of the International Court of Justice (ICJ) in 1949.

The legal status of the UN was debated during the negotiation of the UN Charter in 1945. The negotiating states decided not to include an explicit provision in the Charter by which international legal personality would be given to the new world organization. The fifty negotiating states did not want to give the impression they were creating something like a 'superstate'.[3] They only agreed that the UN 'shall enjoy in the territory of each of its members such legal capacity as may be necessary for the exercise of its functions and the fulfilment of its purposes'.[4] But this provision of the UN Charter only deals with the less controversial issue of the status of the UN at the national level, within the domestic legal orders of the member states. The UN's legal status in the international legal order remained unsettled.

While the fifty states negotiating the UN Charter were perfectly free to leave this issue open, at the same time it was clear that the issue would not go away. The UN member states wanted the organization to carry out a wide variety of functions, which could hardly be performed without an appropriate international legal status: to achieve important aims, conduct many activities, take decisions, etc. Not long after the UN was created, it appointed Count Folke Bernadotte from Sweden as a UN mediator for the conflict in Palestine/Israel. On 17 September 1948, Count Bernadotte was murdered in Jerusalem by members of the militant Zionist group Lehi. After this event, the question arose whether the UN could bring a claim against Israel – after all, it was the UN on whose behalf Count Bernadotte was carrying out his mission, and he was killed on Israeli territory. On 3 December 1948, the UN General Assembly decided to request an advisory opinion from the ICJ about this question. The opinion was given on 11 April 1949. The Court stated the following:

In order to answer this question, the Court must first enquire whether the Charter has given the Organization such a position that it possesses, in regard to its Members, rights which it is entitled to ask them to respect. In other words, does the Organization possess international personality?[5]

The Court noted that the provisions of the Charter are silent about this question, and it examined what characteristics the Charter intended to give the UN:

The subjects of law in any legal system are not necessarily identical in their nature or in the extent of their rights, and their nature depends upon the needs of the community. Throughout its history, the development of international law has been influenced by the requirements of international life, and the progressive increase in the collective activities of States has already given rise to instances of action upon the international plane by certain entities which are not States. This development culminated in the establishment in June 1945 of an international organization whose purposes and principles are specified in the Charter of the United Nations. But to achieve these ends the attribution of international personality is indispensable.[6]

---

[3] This term is used in the report to the US president on the results of the 1945 San Francisco Conference establishing the UN (see C Wilfred Jenks, 'The Legal Personality of International Organizations' (1945) 22 British Yearbook of International Law 267, 270). The same word is also used in the explanatory report on the UN Charter by the Dutch Government ('superstaat', see *Kamerstukken II* 1945, dossiernr 3, ondernr 3, 18).

[4] Charter of the UN (adopted 26 June 1945, entered into force 24 October 1945) 1 UNTS XVI (UN Charter) art 104.

[5] *Reparation for Injuries Suffered in the Service of the United Nations* (Advisory Opinion) [1949] ICJ Rep 174, 178.   [6] ibid.

Next, in a few sentences only, the Court further analyzed the Charter and the early practice of the UN. It considered that the UN was not created to function only as a forum where member states could meet and discuss issues of common interest. The Charter also created a number of organs that were given the power to take decisions, some of which the member states would have to accept as binding. The Charter also provided for the conclusion of agreements between the organization and its members. These and other characteristics brought the Court to the following conclusion:

[T]he Organization was intended to exercise and enjoy, and is in fact exercising and enjoying, functions and rights which can only be explained on the basis of the possession of a large measure of international personality and the capacity to operate upon an international plane. It is at present the supreme type of international organization, and it could not carry out the intentions of its founders if it was devoid of international personality.[7]

Having drawn the conclusion that the UN is an international legal person, the Court addressed, in the following way, the political sensitivities surrounding the issue:

Accordingly, the Court has come to the conclusion that the Organization is an international person. That is not the same thing as saying that it is a State, which it certainly is not, or that its legal personality and rights and duties are the same as those of a State. Still less is it the same thing as saying that it is 'a super-State', whatever that expression may mean. It does not even imply that all its rights and duties must be upon the international plane, any more than all the rights and duties of a State must be upon that plane. What it does mean is that it is a subject of international law and capable of possessing international rights and duties, and that it has capacity to maintain its rights by bringing international claims.[8]

This is why and how the ICJ drew the conclusion that the UN is an international legal person. This was the conclusion that the fifty states that negotiated the Charter had not wanted to draw explicitly, less than four years earlier when they created the UN.

The *Reparation for Injuries* advisory opinion is important not only because it resolved the issue of the international legal status of the UN. It is also important because the same reasoning has subsequently been followed in relation to other international organizations.[9] The Court demonstrated that in order to enjoy international legal personality, treaties creating a new international organization would not need to include an explicit provision to this effect. Such a status could also be granted *implicitly* to an international organization, and this is how international organizations for a long time obtained international legal personality. This started to change only in the 1990s, when it became more common for a treaty establishing a new international organization to *explicitly* provide that the newly established organization has this status. For example, Article XIII(A) of the 2009 Statute of the International Renewable Energy Agency provides that 'the Agency shall have international legal personality'.[10]

---

[7] ibid 179. [8] ibid.
[9] See further Henry G Schermers and Niels M Blokker, *International Institutional Law* (6th edn, Brill/Nijhof 2018), para 1565 ff.
[10] Statue of the International Atomic Energy Agency (adopted 26 October 1956, entered into force 29 July 1957) 276 UNTS 3.

In sum, international organizations may now obtain international legal personality either explicitly (by treaty) or implicitly (following the *'Reparation for Injuries* reasoning'). It may be useful to emphasize that being an international legal person only means that an international organization has the *capacity* to have rights, duties, and powers of its own. Being a legal person does not mean in and of itself having a particular set of powers (see Section 4).

b   *Privileges and Immunities*

In order to be able to perform their functions, international organizations and their staff require privileges and immunities. Even though the notion of 'privileges and immunities' is used as one single concept, privileges and immunities are distinct from each other. The word 'privilege' refers to situations in which local legislation is not applicable or has been modified with respect to the international organization. An example is the exemption from direct taxation. The direct taxing of an organization and its staff would impact the organization's independence, as it would unduly favour the host state and would disadvantage other member states, which would not be willing to raise the host state's tax revenue in this way. International organizations and their staff are therefore normally exempted from direct taxation by the host state. The word 'immunity' is used here to mean 'immunity from jurisdiction'. It refers to situations where local legislation is applicable (thus: no privileged position is granted by the member states) but where local courts are not allowed to apply this in specific cases.[11] International organizations belong to all members, therefore a court of one member state is ill-placed to exercise its jurisdiction over an international organization if a case is brought against the organization in its courts. Consequently, many treaties provide that the organization concerned shall enjoy 'immunity from every form of legal process';[12] in other words, absolute immunity. Immunities may be waived by the organization concerned in specific cases. Such a waiver must always be given explicitly. If a case is brought against an international organization before a national court and the organization sends a letter to the court in which it invokes its immunity, this does not constitute an implicit waiver of immunity, but instead represents an explicit assertion of the right to immunity.

The rationale for privileges and immunities of international organizations and their staff is fundamentally different from that of privileges and immunities in the relations between states and their representatives. As discussed in Chapter 7, the main traditional rationale of state immunity, *par in parem non habet imperium* (states are equally sovereign, and therefore may not exercise jurisdiction over each other), does not exist for international organizations. The immunity of international organizations is based on the need to exercise their functions (often referred to as 'functional necessity').[13] In addition, the classic

---

[11] Schermers and Blokker (n 9), para 323 ff.

[12] See, for example Convention on the Privileges and Immunities of the UN (adopted 13 February 1946, entered into force 17 September 1946) 1 UNTS 15, s 2; Agreement on the Privileges and Immunities of the ICC (adopted 9 September 2002, entered into force 22 July 2004) 2271 UNTS 3, art 6(1).

[13] See Chapter 7.

distinction between *acta iure gestionis* (commercial acts, for which no immunity is given) and *acta iure imperii* (governmental, non-commercial acts, for which immunity is recognized) is generally accepted for state immunity,[14] but hardly or not at all accepted for the immunity of international organizations.

Privileges and immunities are usually given to international organizations in three types of treaties: the constituent instrument of the organization, a multilateral agreement on privileges and immunities, and a bilateral agreement concluded between the organization and its host state (often called a 'headquarters agreement'). Normally, rules on privileges and immunities in the organization's constituent instrument are rather general. For example, Article 105(1) of the UN Charter provides that the UN 'shall enjoy in the territory of each of its Members such privileges and immunities as are necessary for the fulfilment of its purposes'. The rules in the other two types of treaties are much more specific. For example, according to Article II, Section 3 of the 1946 Convention on the Privileges and Immunities of the UN (a multilateral agreement), '[t]he premises of the United Nations shall be inviolable. The 'property and assets of the United Nations, wherever located and by whomsoever held, shall be immune from search, requisition, confiscation, expropriation and any other form of interference, whether by executive, administrative, judicial or legislative action'. Another example is Article 9(1) of the headquarters agreement concluded between the Netherlands and the ICC, which provides that '[t]he competent authorities shall secure, upon the request of the Registrar or a member of staff of the Court designated by him or her, on fair and equitable conditions, the public services needed by the Court such as, but not limited to, postal, telephone, telegraphic services, any means of communication, electricity, water, gas, sewage, collection of waste, fire protection and cleaning of public streets including snow removal'.[15]

3   Membership

Most treaties establishing international organizations contain provisions on membership. Such provisions may deal with the conditions for membership and the procedure for admission. For example, Article 4 of the UN Charter provides the following:

1. Membership in the United Nations is open to all other peace-loving states which accept the obligations contained in the present Charter and, in the judgment of the Organization, are able and willing to carry out these obligations.
2. The admission of any such state to membership in the United Nations will be effected by a decision of the General Assembly upon the recommendation of the Security Council.

The conditions for membership of the UN are laid down in Article 4(1). It is clear that only states, and not for example other international organizations, may be members of the UN.

---

[14] ibid.
[15] Headquarters Agreement between the ICC and the Host State (adopted 7 June 2007, entered into force 1 March 2008) ICC-BD/ 04-01-08.

They may only be admitted if they are 'peace-loving', if they accept the obligations contained in the UN Charter, and if they are, in the judgment of the UN, able and willing to carry out these obligations. Article 4(2) contains the admission procedure: only after the Security Council has recommended admitting a particular state may the General Assembly take a decision to this effect. On the basis of these provisions nearly all states have joined the UN since 1945; it can truly claim to be a universal organization. Since South Sudan became a member in 2011, the UN has 193 member states.[16]

Other international organizations have different provisions dealing with the admission of new members. In some cases, their founding treaties provide that not only states but also international organizations may become members. For example, Article II.3 of the constitution of the Food and Agriculture Organization (FAO) provides that regional economic integration organizations may become members.[17] On this basis the European Community (now the EU) was admitted to the FAO in 1991. Some constituent instruments of international organizations lay down specific or general conditions for membership. In other cases there are no such conditions and it is simply left to the organization to admit new members. Several organizations only admit new members that belong to a particular group. For example, only *European* states may become members of the EU, and only countries with a substantial net export of crude petroleum and interests fundamentally similar to those of member countries may join OPEC.[18]

It may also happen that a member leaves an international organization. The initiative for bringing membership to an end may be taken by the member (withdrawal), but sometimes also by the organization (expulsion). Many constituent instruments of international organizations explicitly provide that members may withdraw. For example, Article 127(1) of the Statute of the ICC provides that:

A State Party may, by written notification addressed to the Secretary-General of the United Nations, withdraw from this Statute. The withdrawal shall take effect one year after the date of receipt of the notification, unless the notification specifies a later date.

So far, two countries have withdrawn from the ICC Statute: Burundi (27 October 2017) and the Philippines (17 March 2019). Likewise, according to Article 50 of the Treaty on European Union, member states may withdraw from the EU. Following the procedure laid down in Article 50(2), the United Kingdom notified the European Council in March 2017 of its intention to withdraw. Since 1 February 2020, the United Kingdom is no longer a member state of the EU. The constituent instruments of some international organizations do not contain an explicit provision on withdrawal, and in such circumstances the 'default' provisions on withdrawal, contained in the Vienna Convention on the Law of Treaties, will apply.[19]

---

[16] The Holy See and the State of Palestine are, for example, non-member states that participate as observers in the General Assembly.

[17] Constitution of the UN Food and Agriculture Organization (adopted and entered into force 16 October 1945).

[18] Consolidated Version of the Treaty on EU [2008] OJ C115/13, art 49; Statute of the Organization of the Petroleum Exporting Countries (OPEC) (1965) 4 ILM 1175, art 7(c).

[19] For example, the UN Charter. In 1949 and 1950, ten members withdrew from the WHO, even though the constitution of this organization does not have a provision on withdrawing. After a few years, these countries re-joined the WHO.

Some international organizations may expel members. According to Article 6 of the UN Charter, upon the recommendation of the Security Council, the General Assembly may expel a member that has persistently violated the principles contained in the Charter. Even though one could argue that there have been cases where members have persistently violated Charter principles, no member has ever been expelled from the UN.[20] This may partly be explained by the fact that expelling a member would not bring the violation of Charter principles to an end; on the contrary, the organization would close the door to influencing the member concerned. It could also be argued that expelling a member is at odds with the aim of universal membership of the UN. Finally, if a procedure to expel a particular member were ever initiated, it is likely that one of the permanent members of the Security Council would use its veto, because states usually maintain good relationships with at least one of the five permanent members.

Membership provisions are usually related to the aims of a particular organization, as is clear from some of the examples just given. In practice it has so far been much more common for states to join than to leave international organizations. Obviously states may decide to leave an international organization. However, this in itself will not stop the processes of globalization and interdependence, which earlier prompted them to join.

Membership decisions are highly political. But at the same time the relevant rules of international organizations define the legal limits within which such decisions must be taken. Such rules explain why Palestine has been admitted as a member of the United Nations Educational, Scientific, and Cultural Organisation (UNESCO) but not as a member of the UN. Mainly, the right of veto of the five permanent members of the Security Council explains why the Council has not been able to adopt a positive recommendation to admit Palestine, as required by Article 4(2) of the UN Charter. In particular the United States does not recognize Palestine as a state and is against admitting Palestine as a member of the UN. A right of veto does not exist within UNESCO, and Palestine was admitted because the necessary majority of members of the relevant UNESCO organs was in favour.

4   Powers

International organizations – in contrast to states – only have those powers that have been given to them by their members, normally in their constituent instruments. Exceptionally, these instruments specify areas in which an organization may *not* exercise any powers.[21]

---

[20] For example, South Africa, by maintaining its policy of apartheid until 1990. In 1974, a draft resolution was presented in the Security Council recommending to the General Assembly 'the immediate expulsion of South Africa from the United Nations', mainly because of the policy of apartheid (UNSC, Kenya, Mauritania and United Republic of Cameroon: Draft Resolution (1974) UN Doc S/11543). However, this draft resolution was not adopted (three votes against by permanent members (France, the United Kingdom, and the United States), two abstentions – see UNSC, 1808th meeting (30 October 1974) UN Doc S/PV.1808, 18).

[21] See, for example, Statute of the Council of Europe, ETS 1, art 1(d): 'Matters relating to national defence do not fall within the scope of the Council of Europe'.

Powers not given to an international organization remain with the member states.[22] In the words of the ICJ:[23]

> The Court need hardly point out that international organizations are subjects of international law which do not, unlike States, possess a general competence. International organizations are governed by the 'principle of speciality', that is to say, they are invested by the States which create them with powers, the limits of which are a function of the common interests whose promotion those States entrust to them.

This principle of speciality is also called the principle of attribution, or the principle of conferred powers. *Prima facie* this key principle governing powers of international organizations seems to be simple and clear: in order to be able to act, international organizations must be able to show that the members have conferred upon them the necessary powers. However, as is often the case, this principle is in practice more complex.

A distinction must be made between explicit and implied powers. The former are those powers that have been attributed explicitly to an international organization. For example, Article 41 of the UN Charter empowers the Security Council to adopt 'measures not involving the use of armed force' binding upon the member states – for example, economic sanctions. Implied powers are powers that have not been explicitly attributed to international organizations, but that are considered necessary for the exercise of their functions or their explicit powers.

All international organizations have implied powers, for two main reasons. First, it is simply impossible to specify, in detail, all the powers that an organization must have to be able to perform its functions. While Article 41 of the UN Charter empowers the Security Council to adopt 'measures not involving the use of armed force', it does not attribute a specific power to impose financial sanctions on individuals and to establish the Office of the Ombudsperson to the Islamic State (ISIL) and Al-Qaida Sanctions Committee, who reviews requests by individuals seeking to be removed from the sanctions list. Even though such a specific power is not mentioned, it is generally accepted by the member states that the Security Council has such powers. Second, and more fundamentally, it is impossible to foresee the unforeseeable. International organizations are by definition established for an unknown future. While it may be clear at the time of their creation what powers these international organizations need to realize the agreed aims, such powers may not be adequate in later years, following societal, political, economic, and other developments. A treaty creating an international organization may be amended to attribute additional powers to the organization. This sometimes happens,[24] but it is usually a cumbersome process and it may not always be possible to reach agreement among member states. More often, the organization is able to adapt to changing realities by implying certain powers. As the ICJ has observed:[25]

---

[22] As is explicitly stated twice in the Treaty on European Union arts 4(1), 5(2).

[23] *Legality of the Use by a State of Nuclear Weapons in Armed Conflict* (Advisory Opinion) [1996] ICJ Rep 66, 78.

[24] For example, the Treaty on EU was amended in 2007 to include the power of the EU to accede to the European Convention for the Protection of Human Rights and Fundamental Freedoms.

[25] *Legality of the Use by a State of Nuclear Weapons in Armed Conflict* advisory opinion (n 24) 79.

The powers conferred on international organizations are normally the subject of an express statement in their constituent instruments. Nevertheless, the necessities of international life may point to the need for organizations, in order to achieve their objectives, to possess subsidiary powers which are not expressly provided for in the basic instruments which govern their activities. It is generally accepted that international organizations can exercise such powers, known as 'implied' powers.

What may or may not be implied is often in the eyes of the beholder. Member states often disagree about the scope of implied powers. Whether or not organs of the organization are able to take the necessary decisions in such cases depends on the specific voting rules and practices of each individual organization (see Section 6). For instance, in 1993 and 1994 the UN Security Council established two ad hoc criminal tribunals, the International Criminal Tribunals for the former Yugoslavia (ICTY) and for Rwanda. But it was not beyond doubt for all members of the Security Council that it had the power to do so. The UN Charter does not explicitly confer such a power upon the Security Council. More generally, the Council does not have specific powers in the field of international criminal justice. During the Security Council meeting where the resolution creating the Rwanda Tribunal was adopted the representative of Brazil stated the following:[26]

As we stated in the case of the Tribunal for the former Yugoslavia, Brazil is not convinced that the competence to establish and/or exercise an international criminal jurisdiction is among the constitutional powers of the Security Council.

However, at the end of the day there was sufficient support in the Security Council for the establishment of these ad hoc criminal tribunals. The resolution creating the ICTY was adopted unanimously; the resolution creating the Rwanda Tribunal was adopted by thirteen votes in favour, one vote against (Rwanda) and one abstention (China).[27] When objections were raised by defence counsel against the legality of the creation of the ICTY in the *Tadić* case, the ICTY's Appeals Chamber concluded in 1995 that 'the establishment of the International Tribunal falls squarely within the powers of the Security Council under Article 41 [of the UN Charter]'.[28]

Sometimes the judicial organs of international organizations give guidance in these situations, as some further examples will illustrate. A first example is the 1996 advisory opinion of the ICJ given at the request of the WHO. In this opinion, the Court concluded that the power to address the legality of nuclear weapons was not within the powers of the WHO.[29] The Court considered that the WHO has the power to deal with the effects on health of the use of nuclear weapons irrespective of the answer to the question whether such use is lawful or not. The Court also considered that the WHO is a *specialized agency*, vested with sectoral powers, in contrast to the UN with its powers of general scope.[30]

---

[26] UNSC 'The situation concerning Rwanda' (1994) UN Doc S/PV.3453, 9.   [27] ibid 3.

[28] *Prosecutor v Dusko Tadic a/k/a 'Dule'* (Decision on the Defence Motion for Interlocutory Appeal on Jurisdiction) IT-94-1-A72 (2 October 1995) (ICTY Appeals Chamber), para 36.

[29] *Legality of the Use by a State of Nuclear Weapons in Armed Conflict* advisory opinion (n 24), para 25 ('such competence could not be deemed a necessary implication of the Constitution of the Organization in the light of the purposes assigned to it by its member States').

[30] The answer of the Court in this case should also be seen in the context of the advisory opinion that it gave on the same day, 8 July 1996, at a largely similar request about the legality of the use of nuclear weapons by the UN General Assembly: *Legality of the Threat or Use of Nuclear Weapons* (Advisory Opinion) [1996] ICJ Rep 226.

A second example comes from the European Court of Justice. In 1994, the Court was asked by the EU Council whether the European Community (now succeeded by the EU) had the power to become a party to the European Convention on Human Rights. The Court answered in 1996: '[a]s Community law now stands, the Community has no competence to accede to the European Convention for the Protection of Human Rights and Fundamental Freedoms'.[31] Since the Court did not see room for an implied power to join the European Convention, the only alternative was to attribute such a power by treaty amendment. This is what happened with the 2007 Lisbon Treaty. Article 6(2) of the Treaty on EU now explicitly provides that '[t]he Union shall accede to the European Convention for the Protection of Human Rights and Fundamental Freedoms'.

These two examples deal with the question of whether *an international organization* has specific (implied) powers. This must be distinguished from the question whether or not *a specific organ* of an organization has certain powers. This question was addressed by the ICJ in its 1962 *Certain Expenses* advisory opinion.[32] In 1956, the UN General Assembly created a peacekeeping force, the UN Emergency Force (UNEF).[33] It was never questioned whether *the UN* had the power to do so. The key question in this case was whether, within the UN, *the General Assembly* had the power to create this force, or whether only the Security Council could do so. France and the Soviet Union (both permanent members of the Security Council with the right of veto) argued that it was exclusively for the Security Council to create such a peacekeeping force and refused to pay their share of the costs involved. The ICJ concluded; however, that such a view was too narrow, that the establishment of this force served to fulfil the purposes of the UN (in particular, the maintenance of international peace and security), and that the relevant expenses were expenses of the UN that must be borne by its members.[34]

5   Institutional Structure

A treaty creating an international organization normally lays down the institutional structure of the new organization. The relevant provisions establish the specific organs which the organization needs to perform its functions. They determine how these organs are composed, their powers, and decision-making rules. While each organization has its own institutional structure, these structures have a number of common characteristics.

Almost all international organizations have a plenary organ, composed of representatives of all the members (in most cases representatives from governments). The most well-known example is the UN General Assembly. These plenary organs usually have the power

---

[31] *Opinion 2/94 of the Court (Accession by the Community to the European Convention for the Protection of Human Rights and Fundamental Freedoms)* (admissibility of the request for an Opinion) ECR 1996 I-01759, I-1790.

[32] *Certain Expenses of the United Nations (Article 17, paragraph 2, of the Charter)* (Advisory Opinion) [1962] ICJ Rep 151.

[33] Arising out of the Suez Crisis, UNEF's mandate was to secure and supervise the cessation of hostilities between France, Israel, the United Kingdom, and Egypt and to supervise the ceasefire between Israel and Egypt.

[34] *Certain Expenses of the UN* advisory opinion.

to take the main policy-decisions of the organization. For example, the plenary organ of the International Labour Organization (ILO) is the ILC, which adopts labour conventions and recommendations. In addition, these organs usually take membership decisions (i.e., a decision to admit a new member) and adopt the budget of the organization (see Section 8).

All international organizations need a secretariat. These secretariats are usually composed of independent international civil servants, who do not represent their home state and exclusively work under the leadership of the head of the secretariat (secretary-general, director-general, executive director, etc.). Members of the organization may; therefore, not exercise any influence or pressure on their nationals working in international secretariats. *Vice versa*, international civil servants may not seek or receive instructions from outside the organization (including from their home state).[35] These are fundamental requirements: '[T]he independence of international civil servants is an essential guarantee, not only for the civil servants themselves, but also for the proper functioning of international organizations'.[36]

Almost all universal organizations (as well as other organizations that have many members) have one or more non-plenary organs (organs in which not all the members are represented). Decision-making in such organs is easier and faster than decision-making in plenary organs, in which 150 to 195 states may be represented. The most well-known example is the UN Security Council, composed of 15 of the 193 UN member states. The members of these non-plenary organs are usually elected by the plenary organ of the organization for a particular period of time, taking into account certain criteria. Such elections are dominated by politics. Candidates for a non-permanent seat in the Security Council may campaign for more than ten years before the elections take place. However, legal elements may also play a role in elections for non-plenary organs. For example, in 1959 the Assembly of the International Maritime Consultative Organization (IMCO, the predecessor of the International Maritime Organization) did not elect Liberia and Panama as members of the Maritime Safety Committee. These two countries objected, because they are very large ship-owning nations, and IMCO's constituent instrument provides that at least eight of the largest ship-owning nations should be members of this Committee. The Assembly requested an advisory opinion from the ICJ. The Court answered in 1960 that the Assembly, by electing neither Liberia nor Panama, had failed to comply with IMCO's constituent instrument.[37]

In addition to the three types of organs just mentioned, some international organizations have judicial and/or parliamentary organs. Parliamentary organs differ from plenary bodies in that the representatives are elected and therefore represent people more than states. Examples are the courts and parliamentary organs of regional organizations, such as the EU, the Andean Community and the East African Community. During the last few decades,

---

[35] See, for example, UN Charter art 100. Many constituent instruments of international organizations contain provisions similar to those in art 100.

[36] ILO Administrative Tribunal, Judgment 2232, 95th Session (16 July 2003), para 16.

[37] *Constitution of the Maritime Safety Committee of the Inter-Governmental Maritime Consultative Organization* (Advisory Opinion) [1960] ICJ Rep 150.

many of such judicial and parliamentary organs have been created. In particular when important powers are attributed to international organizations, members feel the need to provide for the necessary judicial and political checks and balances.

Apart from the organs mentioned in this section, international organizations may create subsidiary organs. The UN Charter contains an explicit power to do so, both in general and for specific principal organs.[38] This power is often used; examples are the criminal tribunals for the former Yugoslavia and for Rwanda.

6   Decision-Making and Decisions

Each international organization has its own rules dealing with decision-making and with the different types of decisions that may be adopted. The following general observations may be made concerning these rules.

a   *Decision-Making*

Originally, when the first international organizations were established, it was required that all or most decisions were taken unanimously. The agreement of all members obviously facilitates proper implementation of these decisions. At the same time, the main disadvantage is that it may be impossible or very difficult, and in any case take considerable time, before compromises can be reached that satisfy all members. Gradually it was accepted that an increasing number of decisions could be taken by majority vote, and therefore involve overruling some (sovereign!) members. First, this happened in particular in the 1920s and 1930s with regard to procedural decisions. This is hardly surprising: would it really be necessary to decide unanimously when, for example, the next session of an organ should take place? In addition, it became acceptable to adopt certain non-binding decisions by majority vote.

A number of new universal organizations were created during and immediately after the Second World War, such as the UN and its specialized agencies. When establishing these organizations, states often accepted that organs of these organizations could take decisions by majority vote. As one observer wrote at the time: '[T]he battle to substitute majority decision for the requirement of unanimity in international organization has now been largely won'.[39] The UN Charter even gives the Security Council the power to take binding enforcement measures by majority vote (on the condition that no permanent member would use its veto power).

However, in practice, another trend has prevailed. While many international organizations nowadays may take many of their decisions by majority vote, in practice decisions are mostly taken by consensus. This means that the chair of a meeting of an organ proposes to

---

[38] UN Charter art 7(2) (general). For specific principal organs, see, for example, arts 22 (General Assembly) and 29 (Security Council).
[39] C. Wilfred Jenks, 'Some Constitutional Problems of International Organizations' (1945) 22 British Yearbook of International Law 11, 34.

adopt a draft decision. If no delegation objects, the decision is adopted. Taking decisions by consensus is different from taking decisions unanimously. In case of the former, there is <u>no</u> formal voting; a draft decision is prepared in informal consultations and is considered adopted if there is no formal objection. If decisions are taken unanimously, there <u>is</u> a vote, and all participants in the decision-making agree to the proposed decision (or abstain from voting, depending on the applicable voting rules). Decisions are taken by consensus when this is prescribed by the rules of the organization. An example is Article 15(4) of the Treaty on EU: 'Except where the Treaties provide otherwise, decisions of the European Council shall be taken by consensus'. However, decisions may also be taken by consensus if this is not explicitly required. For example, according to Article 18 of the UN Charter, the General Assembly takes its decisions 'on important questions' by two-thirds majority of the members present and voting and its decisions 'on other questions' by a majority of the members present and voting. However, for decades the General Assembly has taken most of its (important and other) decisions not by vote, but by consensus.

Therefore, in order to find out how decisions are taken in a particular organ of an international organization, it is necessary to not only look at the organization's rules, but also at its practice. This may be further illustrated by the decision-making rules and practice of the UN Security Council. According to Article 27(2) of the UN Charter, '[d]ecisions of the Security Council on procedural matters shall be made by an affirmative vote of nine members'. According to Article 27(3), '[d]ecisions of the Security Council on all other matters shall be made by an affirmative vote of nine members including the concurring votes of the permanent members'. What if one (or more) of the permanent members does not vote in favour but abstains (refrains from voting 'yes' or 'no'), in the case of a substantive (non-procedural) decision? The text of Article 27(3) seems to require that all five permanent members must vote in favour ('affirmative vote of nine members *including* the concurring votes of the permanent members' (italics added)). However, as early as the late 1940s, a practice started to develop whereby one or more permanent members abstained when a draft decision of the Security Council (on a substantive, non-procedural matter) was put to the vote. In a case before the ICJ, South Africa questioned the lawfulness of this practice. The case concerned a request by the Security Council for an advisory opinion from the Court. South Africa argued that Resolution 284 (in which the request was made) was invalid as it was not adopted in accordance with Article 27(3) of the UN Charter, since two of the permanent members had abstained from voting. The Court rejected this view, in the following carefully formulated way:[40]

However, the proceedings of the Security Council extending over a long period supply abundant evidence that presidential rulings and the positions taken by members of the Council, in particular its permanent members, have consistently and uniformly interpreted the practice of voluntary abstention by a permanent member as not constituting a bar to the adoption of resolutions. By abstaining, a member does not signify its objection to the approval of what is being proposed; in order to prevent

---

[40] *Legal Consequences for States of the Continued Presence of South Africa in Namibia (South West Africa) notwithstanding Security Council Resolution 276 (1970)* (Advisory Opinion) [1971] ICJ Rep 16, 22.

the adoption of a resolution requiring unanimity of the permanent members, a permanent member has only to cast a negative vote. This procedure followed by the Security Council, which has continued unchanged after the amendment in 1965 of Article 27 of the Charter, has been generally accepted by Members of the United Nations and evidences a general practice of that Organization.

This demonstrates the importance of taking into account the practice of international organizations in interpreting its rules. The rule is that Security Council decisions on substantive matters may be adopted while one or more of the permanent members abstain from voting, even though the text of Article 27(3) of the UN Charter seems to suggest otherwise.[41]

b   *Decisions*

Decisions of international organizations may or may not be legally binding. Most of the so-called internal decisions are legally binding. These are decisions concerning the internal functioning of the organization. An example is the appointment of someone as the chair of an organ, but also the decision to adopt the budget of the organization. External decisions are decisions directed towards the members, recommending or requiring them to do or not to do something. They may be binding in some cases, such as many sanction resolutions of the UN Security Council.[42] But often they are recommendations. Nevertheless, it should be empha-sized that the lack of binding legal effect does not at all make recommendations irrelevant or without any legal, moral, or political effect. Members of the General Assembly; therefore, often negotiate hard to add or remove sentences or words in paragraphs of draft resolutions. The ICJ has stated the following regarding the normative value of resolutions of the UN General Assembly, as evidence of an existing or emerging rule of custom:[43]

The Court notes that General Assembly resolutions, even if they are not binding, may sometimes have normative value. They can, in certain circumstances, provide evidence important for establishing the existence of a rule or the emergence of an *opinio juris*. To establish whether this is true of a given General Assembly resolution, it is necessary to look at its content and the conditions of its adoption; it is also necessary to see whether an *opinio juris* exists as to its normative character. Or a series of resolutions may show the gradual evolution of the *opinio juris* required for the establishment of a new rule.

An example of a recommendation that has had significant effect in practice is the recom-mendation by the World Health Assembly (the plenary organ of the WHO), pursuant to which the International Code of Marketing of Breast-milk Substitutes was adopted in 1981. In practice, most governments have given effect to at least parts of this code through legally enforceable measures.[44]

---

[41] See Chapter 4.4.b on treaty interpretation for more on the importance of subsequent practice.

[42] See, for example, UNSC Res 2551 (12 November 2020) on the arms embargo on Somalia.

[43] *Legality of the Threat or Use of Nuclear Weapons* advisory opinion (n 31) 254–5. The quoted observation was repeated in 2019: *Legal Consequences of the Separation of the Chagos Archipelago from Mauritius in 1965* (Advisory Opinion) [2019] ICJ Rep 95, 132.

[44] For details and references, see Schermers and Blokker (n 9), para 1220.

7   Finances

Each international organization has its own detailed financial rules and regulations governing its expenditure and the collection of its income. Each international organization also has its own budget, the size of which depends on the type of activities performed. The budgets of organizations such as the European Space Agency (launching satellites) and the World Bank are much, much larger than those of the Universal Postal Union and the OAS. In order to give some perspective, it may be useful to mention the following figures (budgets for 2020):

Regular budget of the UN (excluding peacekeeping): $3.1 billion (approximately €2.6 billion)[45]

Budget of the EU: €169 billion[46]

Budget of the Kingdom of the Netherlands: €323 billion[47]

Budget of the City of Amsterdam: €6.3 billion[48]

These figures may put discussions about the expenditures of international organizations into some perspective. The size of the budget of the EU is impressive, but is still much lower than that of the Netherlands, a medium-sized EU member state. The size of the budget of the UN (excluding peacekeeping) is less than half the size of the budget of the city of Amsterdam.

The power to adopt the organization's budget is normally attributed to the plenary organ. This is only fair, since all members need to pay so they all should be involved in what is included in the budget. How much each individual member must pay is usually also decided by the plenary organ. These are binding decisions, without which an international organization cannot function. It is therefore unlawful for a member not to pay its (compulsory) contribution. Sometimes a member threatens to do so because it strongly objects to certain activities or decisions of the organization, but in practice almost all members of almost all international organizations almost always pay their compulsory contribution.[49] As a sanction for non-payment, many organizations may suspend the voting rights of the member concerned if, for instance, the amount in arrears (i.e., owed) is equal to or exceeds the amount of the contributions that it owes for the preceding two years.[50]

In only a few international organizations, each member pays the same compulsory contribution. Examples are OPEC, the East African Community, and Mercosur (South American common market). However, in most organizations each member's capacity to pay is taken into account, and the plenary organ may decide that some members pay (much) more than others. For example, in the UN the United States pays 22 per cent of the regular

---

[45] UNGA Res 74/264 (15 January 2020).

[46] Definitive adoption (EU, Euratom) 2020/227 of the EU's general budget for the financial year 2020 [2020] OJ L57/13.

[47] See Rijksoverheid, 'Miljoenennota 2020' <www.rijksbegroting.nl/2020/kamerstukken,2019/1/1/kst264817_5.html>.

[48] See Gemeente Amsterdam, 'Begroting 2020' <www.amsterdam.nl/bestuur-organisatie/financien/begroting-2020>.

[49] This sentence is inspired by Henkin, who wrote: 'Almost all nations observe almost all principles of international law and almost all of their obligations almost all of the time'. Louis Henkin, *How Nations Behave: Law and Foreign Policy* (2nd edn, Cambridge University Press 1979) 47.

[50] See, for example, UN Charter art 19.

budget (this is higher than any other member); whereas the thirty-two least developed members pay 0.001 per cent of the budget.[51] Even though all members of the UN General Assembly have one vote (UN Charter, Article 17(1)), the 'power of the purse' gives considerable influence to the members that pay most.

Apart from compulsory contributions, many organizations also receive voluntary contributions. In particular, in recent years a shift has taken place. More than before, activities of international organizations are paid from voluntary contributions by states, which give members more control over these activities. If they no longer wish to pay, they can unilaterally decide to stop paying.

8   Responsibility

Over the years, the number of activities of international organizations has grown exponentially. It is unavoidable that sometimes things go wrong, for many different reasons. Third parties (states, individuals, or others) may suffer and there may be considerable damage. For example, in the 1980s, the International Tin Council collapsed. This international organization was established to stabilize tin prices. When tin prices fell, the organization's buffer stock manager was obliged to buy tin, but in the end, he ran short of funds, having incurred liabilities of £900 million to a number of banks and tin brokers. In 1989, an overall settlement of £182.5 million was arrived at between the International Tin Council and its creditors. Other examples are the genocides in Rwanda and in Srebrenica (former Yugoslavia) in the 1990s, which the UN was unable to prevent, even though its peace-keepers were present on the ground.

Whenever this happens, it is always important to carefully distinguish between the organization and its members. In some cases, it is clear that severe mistakes have been made by the secretariat (secretary-general or officials), while in other cases, mistakes have been made by member states. Questions often emerge concerning the responsibility for such mistakes or failures. These questions have political, moral, and also legal dimensions.

When the ILC of the UN was in the process of preparing rules on state responsibility, the members of the ILC discussed whether these rules should also cover the responsibility of international organizations. In 1963, ILC member Roberto Ago (at the time the rapporteur for this topic) stated that it was 'questionable whether such organizations had the capacity to commit internationally wrongful acts'; international organizations 'were too recent a phenomenon and the question of a possible international responsibility by reason of alleged wrongful acts committed by such organizations was not suited to codification'.[52]

When the ILC adopted its Articles on State Responsibility in 2001, these rules did not cover the activities of international organizations. At this time; however, the ILC and

---

[51] UN Doc ST/ADM/SER.B/1023 (7 January 2021).

[52] 'Documents of the fifteenth session including the report of the Commission to the General Assembly' (1963) II Yearbook of the ILC 1, 229, 234.

General Assembly decided that the topic of responsibility of international organizations was ripe for codification.[53] Preparations started and resulted in the adoption by the ILC, in 2011, of the ARIO.[54] These articles are not legally binding. Moreover, unlike the Articles on State Responsibility, a considerable number of these articles are not considered by states and scholars to reflect customary international law, but rather the progressive development of the law. Nevertheless, the ARIO is often used in practice, because it is the only available set of rules that has been thoroughly prepared by the ILC, with the involvement of states in the (Legal Committee of the) UN General Assembly.

The substance of the ARIO resembles, to some extent, the articles on the responsibility of states. This is particularly true for the structure and the main rules of the ARIO. For example, the two main elements of an internationally wrongful act of states and international organizations are similar: there is an internationally wrongful act of an international organization when conduct consisting of an action or omission: (a) is attributable to that organization under international law; and (b) constitutes a breach of an international obligation of that organization.[55] However, a number of other articles of the ARIO do not have a 'sister article' in the state responsibility articles. This is particularly true for articles involving the relationship between international organizations and their members.[56]

A key rule of the ARIO is that it is, in principle, the international organization itself (as an independent international legal person) that is responsible for its own wrongful acts.[57] Only in a few exceptional situations may the members be responsible for wrongdoings of 'their' organization.[58] Nevertheless, in practice claims may be brought against one or more members, even if the issue is an alleged wrongdoing of the organization. In the absence of domestic courts or other internal remedial mechanisms within international organizations, injured parties may try to establish some responsibility of the member(s), for the wrongful act of the organization or for the lack of legal remedies. So far, national courts have dealt differently with such claims.[59] A major hurdle is the fact that the wrongful act concerned is often attributable to the organization, not to its member(s). It is not an alternative to bring the claim (also) against the organization, as the organization will normally enjoy immunity.

In the end, in such cases, a feeling of injustice may prevail, due to what is often referred to as the 'lack of accountability' of international organizations. Does the right to a remedy only exist *vis-à-vis* states, and not *vis-à-vis* an international organization, even though the wrongdoing and the harm are the same? It is for the members of the organizations facing such issues to improve the situation, for example by creating adequate remedial mechanisms, such as the Ombudsperson to the ISIL and Al-Qaida Sanctions Committee

---

[53] See UNGA Res 56/82 (18 January 2002), para 8.   [54] See UNGA Res 66/100 (27 February 2012).   [55] ARIO art 4.

[56] For example, ARIO arts 17, 18, 32(2), 40, 58–62.

[57] See ARIO art 3: 'Every internationally wrongful act of an international organization entails the international responsibility *of that organization*' (italics added). Thus, members are not responsible for wrongdoings of the organizations merely because they are members.

[58] See ARIO, pt 5 (arts 58–63).

[59] For examples, see the ICL, 'Text of the Draft Articles with Commentaries Thereto' (2011) UN Doc A/66/10, 69–172. See also *Mothers of Srebrenica v The Netherlands* (ECtHR) (n 15).

(mentioned in Section 4). Otherwise support for cooperation within the organization concerned may decrease.

9 Concluding Remarks

This chapter has given a bird's eye view of international organizations, mainly from a legal perspective. They have not been created as part of some long-term masterplan for the development of a 'world state' or a 'world government'. Rather they have been created during the last two centuries, and in particular since the 1940s, in response to the challenges posed by globalization and interdependence. It became increasingly difficult for states to perform 'the functions of the state' individually and it became increasingly necessary, and in their common interest, to cooperate within permanent frameworks. Today there is hardly any area of human activity in which no role is played by one or more international organizations. As Mosler wrote in 1974, they 'now form a kind of superstructure over and above the society of states'.[60]

Due to the rise in the number and activities of international organizations, new questions have emerged over time. To what extent are members willing to attribute the (explicit and implied) powers and financial resources necessary to achieve the agreed objectives? How to better coordinate the activities of international organizations? To what extent are international organizations and their members able and willing to 'update' international organizations to face growing demands for accountability, for example by setting up remedial mechanisms in international organizations that may cause damage? The way in which these and other questions are addressed will influence the support for international organizations and the effectiveness of their activities.

Recommended Reading

Chittharanjan Felix Amerasinghe, *Principles of the Institutional Law of International Organizations* (2nd edn, Cambridge University Press 2005).

Catherine Brölmann, *The Institutional Veil in Public International Law: International Organisations and the Law of Treaties* (Hart 2007).

Jan Klabbers, *An Introduction to International Organizations Law* (3rd edn, Cambridge University Press 2015).

Evelyne Lagrange and Jean-Marc Sorel, *Droit des organisations internationales* (LGDJ 2013).

Matthias Ruffert and Christian Walter (eds), *Institutionalised International Law* (Bloomsbury 2015) (or the original German edition: *Institutionalisiertes Völkerrecht* (CH Beck 2009)).

Philippe Sands and Pierre Klein, *Bowett's: Law of International Institutions* (6th edn, Sweet & Maxwell 2009).

---

[60] Hermann Mosler, 'The International Society as a Legal Community' (1974) 140 Collected Courses of the Hague Academy of International Law 1, 189.

Henry G Schermers and Niels M Blokker, *International Institutional Law* (6th edn, Brill/ Nijhof 2018).

Ignaz Seidl-Hohenveldern and Gerhard Loibl, *Das Recht der Internationalen Organisationen, einschließlich der Supranationalen Gemeinschaften* (7th edn, Heymanns 2000).

Nigel D White, *The Law of International Organisations* (3rd edn, Manchester University Press 2017).

9

International Dispute Settlement

Cecily Rose

1   Introduction

Disputes are a common feature of societies, both domestic and international. At the international level, disagreements between states, and also between states and non-state actors, are to be expected given the frequency with which states interact with each other, and also with individuals, corporations, non-governmental organizations, and international organizations. Disagreements can arise about any number of subjects, from the course of a land or maritime boundary, to state sponsorship of terrorism, to a state's treatment of a foreign investor. International law requires states to settle their disputes in a peaceful manner, without recourse to the use of force, but states have considerable freedom to choose the method of dispute settlement – or to choose not to settle a dispute at all. Most of the chapters of this book discuss disputes settled by international courts and tribunals, such as the International Court of Justice (ICJ). This could give the misleading impression that states generally settle their disputes through judicial bodies like the ICJ. In fact, such 'legal' methods of dispute settlement are the exception rather than the rule, as states turn more frequently to 'diplomatic' forms of dispute settlement, such as negotiations and mediation.[1]

This chapter begins by elaborating on the concept of a dispute, before providing an historical perspective on the evolution of the requirement to settle disputes peacefully. The chapter then explores diplomatic as well as legal methods of dispute settlement. The focus of this chapter will be on the settlement of inter-state disputes, as opposed to disputes between states and non-state actors or between non-state actors. There is much to be said about the settlement of disputes between states and individuals with human rights claims, as well as disputes between states and foreign investors. But these topics are better left to the chapters on human rights and international economic law, respectively. Non-state actors play a prominent role in international relations and they also have access to certain international dispute settlement mechanisms, but our focus here is on the settlement of disputes between states.

---

[1] Shirley Scott, 'Litigation versus Dispute Resolution through Political Processes' in Natalie Klein (ed), *Litigating International Law Disputes: Weighing the Options* (Cambridge University Press 2014).

a   ***The Concept of a Dispute***

The word 'dispute' is a term of art in the field of international dispute settlement, and should be distinguished from the word 'conflict'.[2] A dispute is a specific disagreement that relates to legal rights or obligations, facts, or policies, which the parties pursue through claims, counterclaims, refusals, denials, etc.[3] A conflict, in contrast, involves a general grievance or state of hostility between parties. A conflict may or may not stem from or give rise to disputes. Since Iran's Islamic Revolution of 1979, for example, the relationship between the United States and Iran has been mired in conflict, relating in part to historic grievances held by Iran about American involvement in Iranian politics, and, more recently, American opposition to Iran acquiring nuclear weapons and supporting terrorism. But this conflict has also involved discrete disputes about issues such as the expropriation of the property of American investors by Iran following the Islamic Revolution, and the Iranian detention of American diplomatic and consular staff who were held as hostages from November 1979 to January 1981.

The range of potential disputes is vast, but disputes may be categorized in a number of useful ways. First, a basic distinction may be made between factual and legal disputes. Some disputes are primarily factual in character, insofar as states disagree about what happened in a given incident or over the course of series of incidents. In the late 1990s, for example, Uganda and the Democratic Republic of Congo (DRC) disagreed in part about whether, and for how long, the DRC had consented to the Ugandan military presence in its territory in the late 1990s.[4] This factual disagreement arose out of a complex armed conflict that engulfed the DRC as well as many neighbouring states and rebel groups from 1998 to 2003. Other disputes are primarily legal in character, in that states may agree about what happened, but disagree about the law – what the content of the law is, whether a particular rule even exists in the first place, or how the law should be applied. In *Jurisdictional Immunities of the State (Germany v Italy: Greece intervening)*, for example, the parties disagreed about whether the law on state immunity had evolved so as to include an exception that would allow civil claims to be brought against a state for violations of international humanitarian law. The ICJ held that no such exception existed.

A second distinction exists between bilateral and multilateral disputes. Bilateral disputes involve two states, whereas multilateral disputes involve three or more states. Many disputes about the immunities of state officials are essentially bilateral, in that they concern the treatment of one state's official by another state. But given the dense web of international relations today, and the geographical proximity of many states to each other, many disputes are inherently multilateral, even if states might pursue their resolution in a bilateral manner, via arbitration or judicial proceedings. The *North Sea Continental Shelf* cases, for instance, involved a multilateral dispute between Germany, the Netherlands, and Denmark

---

[2] See also John Collier and Vaughan Lowe, *The Settlement of Disputes in International Law: Institutions and Procedures* (Oxford University Press 1999) 1.

[3] See also JG Merrills, *International Dispute Settlement* (5th edn, Cambridge University Press 2011) 1.

[4] *Case concerning Armed Activities on the Territory of the Congo (Democratic Republic of the Congo v Uganda)* (Judgment) [2005] ICJ Rep 168, paras 42–54.

about the course of their maritime boundaries in the North Sea. The three states initially filed two separate cases (one filed by Germany and the Netherlands, the other by Germany and Denmark), but the Court ultimately joined the proceedings and issued a single judgment.

Such categorizations serve not only as a way of organizing what can seem like a chaotic world of international relations, but they can also help us to make sense of why states would choose one dispute settlement method over others. As will be discussed in Section 2 of this chapter, fact-intensive disputes may be best suited to commissions of inquiry, for instance. A state's pursuit of a particular method to settle a given dispute will often be the result of a strategic decision that takes into account characteristics such as the ones mentioned here (factual v legal, bilateral v multilateral, etc.).

Finally, in light of this chapter's focus on the settlement of disputes, it would be easy to lose sight of the fact that some disputes may be best left unsettled for political or strategic reasons. The study of international dispute settlement could give the mistaken impression that all international disputes ought to be settled. In fact, states may have good reasons for letting low-level disputes continue indefinitely, due, for example, to the risks involved in losing a claim, or uncertainty about the state of the law. This is acceptable from a legal standpoint, as states have no general obligation under international law to resolve their disputes, though when states do pursue the settlement of their disputes, they must do so peacefully.

b   *Dispute Settlement from the Covenant of the League of Nations to the United Nations Charter*

States have not always been obligated to settle their disputes in a peaceful manner. In fact, resort to armed force was a permissible means of settling disputes under international law in the era pre-dating the United Nations (UN) Charter.[5] The first multilateral treaty that pointed states towards peaceful dispute settlement was the 1899 Hague Convention on the Pacific Settlement of International Disputes, which obligated states to avoid recourse to force 'as far as possible' by using their 'best efforts to insure the pacific settlement of international differences'.[6] With the subsequent adoption of the Covenant of the League of Nations in 1919, states did not outlaw war altogether, but instead imposed a series of conditions on the resort to war.[7] Resort to war remained a lawful option for states that had exhausted certain peaceful dispute settlement procedures. The first outright ban on the resort to war did not come into existence until the 1928 Kellogg-Briand Pact, a brief treaty that specifically condemned recourse to war 'for the settlement of international

---

[5] Stephen C Neff, *War and the Law of Nations: A General History* (Cambridge University Press 2005).
[6] Convention for the Pacific Settlement of International Disputes (Hague, I) (adopted 29 July 1899, entered into force 4 September 1900) 187 CTS 410 (1899 Convention) art 1.
[7] Covenant of the League of Nations (adopted 28 June 1919, entered into force 10 January 1920) 108 LNTS 188, arts 12, 13, 15. Prior to the Covenant, the 1907 Drago-Porter Convention had outlawed recourse to armed force specifically with respect to the recovery of contractual debts. Convention Respecting the Limitation of the Employment of Force for the Recovery of Contract Debts (signed 18 October 1907, entered into force 26 January 1910) 36 Stat 2241.

controversies' and provided that only 'pacific means' were available to states parties seeking the settlement of their disputes or conflicts.[8] But by prohibiting war, rather than the use of force in general, the Pact did not go as far as it might have, and thereby allowed states parties to the pact to pursue arguments that their military actions fell short of war and therefore did not violate international law (see Chapter 11).

The failure of the League of Nations and the Kellogg-Briand Pact to prevent the Second World War ultimately led to a renewed attempt to outlaw war, this time in the form of the Charter of the UN, concluded in 1945. But unlike the Covenant of the League of Nations and the Kellogg-Briand Pact, the UN Charter does not use the term 'war'. Instead, the UN Charter prohibits the 'threat or use of force' in international relations, which represents a broader ban on military force.[9] This prohibition on the threat or use of force is complemented by the requirement in the Charter that all members shall 'settle their international disputes by peaceful means in such a manner that international peace and security, and justice, are not endangered'.[10]

Chapter VI of the UN Charter sets out a framework for the peaceful or 'pacific' settlement of disputes, mostly involving non-binding measures by the Security Council that are designed to support peaceful dispute settlement by disputing parties. Article 33 of Chapter VI is a particularly important provision for our purposes, as it sets out a range of possible dispute settlement methods that may be recommended by the Security Council, or pursued by member states on their own accord, with no direction from the Security Council. Article 33(1) provides that:

The parties to any dispute, the continuance of which is likely to endanger the maintenance of international peace and security, shall first of all, seek a solution by negotiation, enquiry, mediation, conciliation, arbitration, judicial settlement, resort to regional agencies or arrangements, or other peaceful means of their own choice.

Although this list of dispute settlement methods is quite comprehensive, it does not purport to be exhaustive, as indicated by the final phrase, which provides that states may pursue 'other peaceful means of their own choice'. Good offices, a dispute settlement technique similar to mediation (explained in Section 2(b)), is indeed missing from this list.

In addition, there is no hierarchy among the various methods listed in Article 33, meaning that states need not pursue negotiations first, before proceeding on to inquiry, mediation, etc. But the six dispute settlement methods listed in Article 33 – negotiation, inquiry, mediation, conciliation, arbitration, and judicial settlement – do not appear in a random order. Instead, they fall along a spectrum, with negotiations involving no third-party participation, and judicial settlement involving maximum third-party participation. Between negotiations and judicial settlement, the degree of third-party involvement increases incrementally. Many disputes will involve the use of more than one method.

---

[8] General Treaty for Renunciation of War as an Instrument of National Policy (adopted 27 August 1928, entered into force 25 July 1929) 94 LNTS 57, arts I–II.
[9] Charter of the UN (adopted 26 June 1945, entered into force 24 October 1945) 1 UNTS XVI (UN Charter) art 2(4).
[10] UN Charter art 2(3).

Negotiations can, for example, lead to recourse to adjudication, which may then be followed by mediation to bring about compliance with the judgment.[11]

Article 33 is also not an entirely homogenous list, insofar as it includes 'regional agencies or arrangements', which represent not a method of dispute settlement, like negotiations and judicial settlement, but institutions capable of supporting dispute settlement in various ways. The Organization of American States (OAS) is an example of a regional entity designed in part to facilitate the peaceful settlement of regional disputes. One of the foundational treaties of the OAS, the American Treaty on Pacific Settlement (widely known as the Pact of Bogotá), obligates states parties to pursue dispute settlement peacefully, and aims to bring about dispute settlement through the same means listed in Article 33 of the UN Charter.[12]

Finally, the methods of dispute settlement listed in Article 33 may be divided into two categories: diplomatic or political methods, and legal or judicial methods. Negotiations, inquiry, mediation, and conciliation represent diplomatic means, while arbitration and judicial settlement represent legal means. These categories partly distinguish between the different bases for dispute settlement. While a negotiated or mediated settlement will often be based on political considerations (though legal rules may also be taken into consideration), arbitration awards and court judgments are based on legal rules. These two categories also differ with respect to the outcome of the dispute settlement procedure. Diplomatic methods result in non-binding outcomes, which the disputing parties may choose to transform into binding legal commitments. Legal methods, however, culminate in binding outcomes, which are legally enforceable and require compliance by the disputing parties.

Diplomatic and legal methods of dispute settlement do, however, have one very important element in common: disputing parties must consent to each of these forms of dispute settlement. Because states are sovereign entities, they are not subject to any higher authority or body of law without their consent (see Chapter 1). States; therefore; cannot be forced to enter into negotiations or to submit a dispute to arbitration. The following sections will elaborate on the characteristics of the various forms of diplomatic and legal dispute settlement, with a view towards understanding why states might choose to consent to one form of dispute settlement over another.

2   Diplomatic Methods of Dispute Settlement

a   *Negotiations*

Negotiations may be defined as the process by which states seek to achieve a common understanding or agreement.[13] Within the international legal field, negotiations have two

---

[11] See, for example, *Case concerning the Land and Maritime Boundary between Cameroon and Nigeria (Cameroon v Nigeria: Equatorial Guinea intervening)* (Judgment) [2002] ICJ Rep 303.

[12] American Treaty on Pacific Settlement (Pact of Bogotá) (adopted 30 April 1948, entered into force 6 May 1949) 30 UNTS 55.

[13] Kari Hakapää, 'Negotiation' in *Max Planck Encyclopedia of Public International Law* (last updated May 2013), para 1; see also Michael Waibel, 'The Diplomatic Channel' in James Crawford and Alain Pellet (eds), *The Law of International Responsibility* (Oxford University Press 2010) 1087.

distinct functions. States may pursue negotiations for the settlement of their disputes, but they may also pursue negotiations for the purpose of codifying or progressively developing international law itself. This distinction is significant because negotiations geared towards developing international law through a treaty, for example, do not generally entail the resolution of a concrete dispute, and therefore fall outside of the scope of this chapter.

When seeking to resolve their disputes, states turn most frequently to negotiations.[14] A number of key characteristics can make negotiations an optimal method of dispute settlement for both major or highly sensitive disputes, as well as more minor or less sensitive disputes. Negotiations offer parties maximum control and flexibility, with the potential for confidentiality and relatively low costs. First, negotiations generally do not involve third parties, which means that the disputing parties retain full control over the process. The disputing parties also avoid the possibility of being legally bound by an unsatisfactory outcome formulated by a third party.

Control over the process and outcome is related to the second characteristic: flexibility. Negotiations are the most flexible form of dispute settlement – they do not need to adhere to any particular procedure or timeline, nor do they need to produce any particular type of outcome. Negotiations can take place in a range of settings, including both formal summits and informal meetings. Moreover, communication between disputing parties need not be in-person, as negotiations may also be carried out through correspondence, phone calls, and video conferences. Discussions may proceed as slowly or quickly as the parties desire, and may be paused and taken up again as convenient. The outcome of negotiations can range from a joint statement or press communiqué by the parties, to an agreement that could even take the form of a binding treaty. The outcome of negotiations could also be a decision to pursue another form of dispute settlement, such as arbitration or adjudication.

Third, negotiations allow for confidentiality. Because publicity may hinder the resolution of highly sensitive disputes, states may prefer to conduct negotiations outside of the public eye. Negotiations within the context of high-level summit meetings would therefore only be appropriate when the parties consider confidentiality to be less important, or publicity to be useful (as when publicity puts pressure on one or both parties to find a solution). Finally, negotiations are relatively low cost. The disputing parties do not need to pay for the assistance of third parties, though negotiations that take the form of high-level summit meetings between heads of state or ministers of foreign affairs will, of course, be more costly than negotiations carried out through lower-level, informal meetings. For example, the Iran nuclear negotiations, which came to a conclusion in July 2015, were negotiated at ministerial level. High-level officials from Iran, six world powers (China, France, Germany, Russia, the United Kingdom, and the United States), and the European Union(EU) agreed on a deal to limit Iran's nuclear program to peaceful purposes in exchange for the lifting of related international sanctions against Iran.

Despite the advantages of negotiations, this method of dispute settlement may be ineffective or undesirable in certain circumstances. When the disputing parties hold widely

---

[14] Waibel (n 13) 1085.

disparate positions and cannot even agree on an agenda for discussions, for example, negotiations are unlikely to be an effective means of reaching a solution. A significant power imbalance between disputing parties may also make negotiations undesirable for the less powerful party, which may have a weaker bargaining position, and may enhance the appeal of other forms of dispute resolution that involve third parties who can help to ensure a settlement. When negotiations result in a deadlock, disputing parties may decide to pursue another form of dispute settlement. Under many treaties, recourse to arbitration or adjudication may be available, but only on the condition that the parties have attempted negotiations for a reasonable period of time without success.[15] Parties can always decide to resume negotiations during arbitral or court proceedings, and in fact, it is not uncommon for states engaged in litigation to reach an 'out-of-court' settlement and withdraw a case.[16]

b   *Mediation*

Mediation is the process by which disputing parties seek to resolve a dispute with the active participation of a third party that helps the disputing parties reach a solution. Mediation is distinct from good offices, which involves a third party that merely helps the disputing parties initiate or continue negotiations that will then take place without the involvement of the third party. Mediation however, entails the active involvement of the third party in the talks, after the parties have come together.[17] The distinction between good offices and mediation is commonly blurred in practice. For instance, the UN Secretary-General's former Special Envoy for Syria, Staffan de Mistura, was formally responsible for providing good offices, but in practice he was actively involved in talks to end the Syrian conflict between the Assad regime and opposition groups.

Like negotiations, mediation benefits from certain features that make it well suited for disputing parties seeking to resolve major or highly sensitive international disputes. First, the disputing parties still retain a high degree of control over the process and the outcome, even though mediation involves the participation of a third party. The parties may select the mediator of their choice, they are free to accept or reject the mediator's proposals, and they are not bound by the outcome of the mediation process. Second, confidentiality is also typically a feature of mediation—while the existence of mediation efforts might be publicly known, the substance would not be.

Third, mediation, like negotiation, is also a highly flexible form of dispute settlement, with no prescribed procedures, timeline, or outcome. This flexibility can be seen partly in the range of possible functions of the mediator. Depending on the needs of the disputing parties, a mediator may facilitate communication between the parties; provide advice, suggestions or proposals; help each side better appreciate the strengths and weaknesses

---

[15] UN Convention against Corruption (adopted 31 October 2003, entered into force 14 December 2005) 2349 UNTS 41, art 66; International Convention on the Elimination of All Forms of Racial Discrimination (adopted 7 March 1966, entered into force 4 January 1969) 660 UNTS 195, art 22.

[16] See, for example, *Aerial Herbicide Spraying (Ecuador v Colombia): Case removed from the Court's List at the request of the Republic of Ecuador*, ICJ Press Release 2013/20 <www.icj-cij.org/public/files/case-related/138/17526.pdf>.

[17] Collier and Lowe (n 2) 27.

of their arguments; engage in fact-finding; and assist with implementation of the settlement. The role taken on by a mediator may be tailored to the situation. When an inability to even agree on an agenda prevents parties from meeting with one another, for example, a mediator may help bring parties to the table by facilitating communication as an intermediary, and by proposing an agenda. When both parties show an unwillingness to make concessions, a mediator may propose a compromise solution. In order to be able to carry out these functions, mediators typically must be seen by the parties as independent, impartial, and trustworthy. In addition, expertise in the subject matter of the dispute may give mediators further credibility. Mediators can be distinguished individuals, such as former diplomats or the pope, or officials representing one or more states or international organizations, such as the UN.

Mediation played a role, for example, in resolving a major, highly complex armed conflict that took place in Bosnia and Herzegovina in the early to mid-1990s, following the dissolution of the former Yugoslavia.[18] This armed conflict partly entailed the ethnic cleansing of Bosnian Muslims by Serb authorities and paramilitaries. After a number of unsuccessful mediation efforts led by the European Community and the UN, a US-led mediation effort took hold in 1995, with US diplomat Richard Holbrooke at the helm. A 'contact group', which included France, Germany, Russia, and the United Kingdom also participated in the talks. Holbrooke engaged in 'shuttle diplomacy' by acting as an intermediary who travelled back and forth between Bosnia, Croatia, and Serbia, where he met with high-level officials. His efforts continued during talks hosted by the United States over the course of three weeks in November 1995 at a US Air Force base in Dayton, Ohio. The resulting Dayton Agreement was concluded between the Republic of Bosnia and Herzegovina, the Republic of Croatia, and the Federal Republic of Yugoslavia (now Serbia). The Agreement set out, among other things, the new constitution of Bosnia and Herzegovina, and it also provided for international assistance in implementing and monitoring the peace deal.[19]

c   *Inquiry*

Inquiry is a process for clarifying facts through impartial investigation. Inquiries are carried out by permanent or ad hoc entities, which may be known as commissions of inquiry, panels, or fact-finding bodies. An inquiry is most useful and appropriate as a dispute settlement method when the dispute between the parties originates, at least in part, in different perceptions or understandings of certain facts. These facts might relate to a particular incident, such as a use of force against a fishing boat or an assassination, or to a series of events, such as a brief armed conflict. Inquiries often facilitate other forms of

---

[18] Melanie C Greenberg and Margaret E McGuinness, 'From Lisbon to Dayton: International Mediation and the Bosnia Crisis' in Melanie C Greenberg, John H Barton, and Margaret McGuiness (eds), *Words Over War: Mediation and Arbitration to Prevent Deadly Conflict* (Rowman & Littlefield 2000).

[19] The General Framework Agreement for Peace in Bosnia and Herzegovina with Annexes (adopted and entered into force 14 December 1995) 35 ILM 75.

dispute settlement that cannot be pursued effectively by the parties until they have agreed upon the facts. Inquiries culminate in reports that do not bind the parties but may, for instance, serve as the basis for subsequent negotiations between the disputing parties on issues such as reparations.

Inquiries as a dispute settlement method have historical origins in the 1899 and 1907 Hague Conventions for the Pacific Settlement of International Disputes.[20] The drafters of the 1899 Hague Convention conceived of commissions of inquiry as entities that would conduct 'impartial and conscientious' investigations of disputed facts, with the exception of disputes involving 'honor' and 'vital interests'.[21] Under the Convention, reports produced by commissions were to be limited to statements of facts, as opposed to legal conclusions, and were to be non-binding.[22] The drafters of the 1907 Hague Convention further aimed to facilitate and encourage the use of commissions of inquiry by providing a relatively elaborate set of rules or guidelines covering a wide range of procedural issues.[23] The procedures set out in the 1907 Hague Convention highlight the fact that inquiry is typically a less flexible, more formal method of dispute settlement as compared with negotiations and mediation.

In practice, the 1899 and 1907 Hague Conventions met with only limited success in bringing about more extensive use of commissions of inquiry by disputing parties. Incidents involving vessels at sea gave rise to the first commissions under these conventions, beginning with the Dogger Bank inquiry of 1904–5.[24] This incident involved a Russian warship that fired at a British fishing fleet that it mistook for torpedo boats. Despite the limits on inquiries, as envisaged by the drafters of the 1899 Convention, this commission dealt with matters of 'honor' and 'vital interests' by virtue of its investigation of the mistaken use of military force. In addition, the parties requested that the commission deal with factual as well as legal issues concerning responsibility and 'blame'. To this day, inquiries continue to depart from the limited approach envisaged in the Hague Conventions, as they sometimes deal with sensitive subjects, and they make legal findings when directed to do so by the parties.[25]

The creation of commissions of inquiry within the framework provided by the 1899 and 1907 Hague Conventions may be considered a relatively short-lived phenomenon of the past. In addition, although the Hague Conventions inspired the conclusion of a series of other treaties providing for the creation of commissions of inquiry, these treaties have been almost untouched in practice.[26] Inquiries have not, however, fallen out of use, although they

---

[20] 1899 Convention (n 6); Convention for the Pacific Settlement of International Disputes (Hague, II) (adopted 18 October 1907, entered into force 26 January 1910) 205 CTS 277 (1907 Convention).

[21] 1899 Convention art 9.   [22] 1899 Convention art 14.   [23] 1907 Convention arts 9–36.

[24] The International Commission of Inquiry between Great Britain and Russia Arising out of the North Sea incident, 'Finding of the International Commission of Inquiry Organized under Article 9 of the Convention for the Pacific Settlement of International Disputes' (1908) 2 American Journal of International Law 929.

[25] See, for example, *Dispute Concerning Responsibility for the Deaths of Letelier and Moffitt (United States, Chile)* (1992) XXV RIAA 1.

[26] See, for example, Treaty for the Advancement of General Peace, concluded between the United States and Chile (adopted 24 July 1914, entered into force 19 January 1916) 14 USTS 621 (Bryan-Suárez Mujica Treaty). See also Protocol Additional to the Geneva Conventions of 12 August 1949, and Relating to the Protection of Victims of International Armed Conflicts (Protocol I) (adopted 8 June 1977, entered into force 7 December 1978) 1125 UNTS 3, art 90. The Council of the League of Nations did; however, establish a number of commissions of inquiry. UNGA, 'Report of the Secretary-General on Methods of Fact-Finding' (1964) UN Doc A/5694.

exist outside of the framework provided by the Hague Conventions and they frequently serve functions other than dispute settlement.[27] Fact-finding bodies are, for example, frequently established by UN bodies such as the Security Council, the General Assembly, the Secretary-General, and the Human Rights Council (a subsidiary body of the General Assembly) for the purpose of investigating a range of matters, including human rights violations, assassinations, and frontier incidents.[28] The Independent International Commission of Inquiry on the Syrian Arab Republic, for instance, was created in 2011 by the Human Rights Council for the purpose of investigating human rights violations in Syria and identifying those most responsible for the perpetration of crimes.[29] Such UN-led inquiries commonly focus on violations of human rights and international humanitarian law, and tend to be geared more towards publicizing and condemning atrocities and perhaps stimulating action by the UN Security Council, rather than defusing and resolving a dispute.[30] Understanding the relatively limited role of inquiries in contemporary dispute settlement therefore requires us to differentiate between inquiries that are designed to facilitate the bilateral settlement of disputes, and inquiries that serve some other purpose.

Although inquiries expressly geared toward facilitating dispute settlement are somewhat infrequent today, examples may be found.[31] For instance, the UN Secretary-General established a Panel of Inquiry following the 2010 'Mavi Marmara' incident, which gave rise to a dispute between Israel and Turkey.[32] The Mavi Marmara incident involved the use of force by the Israel Defence Forces (IDF) against a flotilla of six vessels carrying people and humanitarian supplies to the Gaza strip in the Palestinian territories. A Turkish humanitarian organization played a leading role in planning the flotilla, and most of the passengers were Turkish. When the flotilla attempted to breach a naval blockade imposed by Israel to prevent weapons from entering Gaza by sea, the IDF responded with the use of force, which resulted in the death of nine passengers and injuries to many others. In its report on the incident, the panel concluded that the flotilla had acted recklessly in attempting to breach the naval blockade, and that the Israeli response was excessive and unreasonable. The panel recommended that Israel offer a statement of regret and payment for the benefit of the deceased and injured victims and their families. The panel also recommended ways to avoid such incidents in the future – an aspect of its mandate that went beyond dispute settlement between Israel and Turkey. In addition to its factual findings and recommendations, the panel also made some legal determinations about issues such as the legality of the naval blockade. This panel report thus demonstrates that, like the early inquiries established under the framework of the

---

[27] In addition, they may operate without the consent of the parties that are the subject of the inquiry.

[28] See, for example, the UN Secretary-General's report with respect to the fall of Srebrenica during the conflict in the former Yugoslavia. UNGA, 'Report of the Secretary-General pursuant to General Assembly Resolution 53/55: The Fall of Srebrenica' (1999) UN Doc A/54/549.

[29] Human Rights Council. 'The Human Rights Situation in the Syrian Arab Republic (2011) UN Doc A/HRC/S-17/1.

[30] Larissa J van den Herik, 'An Inquiry into the Role of Commissions of Inquiry in International Law: Navigating the Tensions between Fact-Finding and Application of International Law' (2014) 13 Chinese Journal of International Law 507.

[31] In addition, some multilateral treaties require state parties to resort to inquiry. See, for example, Convention on the Law of the Non-navigational Uses of International Watercourses (adopted 21 May 1997, entered into force 17 August 2014) UNGA Res 51/229, art 33.

[32] Report of the Secretary-General's Panel of Inquiry on the 31 May 2010 Flotilla Incident (September 2011).

1899 and 1907 Hague Conventions, contemporary inquiries continue to make legal assessments as well as factual findings, and touch on 'vital interests', such as security matters.

d   Conciliation

Conciliation is a procedure by which a third party examines all aspects of a dispute, and makes recommendations that the parties can accept or reject.[33] Because conciliation commissions or panels may be expressly designed to deal with the facts, law, as well as other considerations, conciliation could be regarded as lying somewhere in between diplomatic and legal dispute settlement methods. But conciliation is most appropriately classified as a form of diplomatic dispute settlement because of the non-binding status of conciliation reports and the fact that the commissions may take non-legal factors, such as equity or fairness into consideration. These represent fundamental distinctions between conciliation and legal methods of dispute settlement, which result in binding arbitral awards or judicial decisions based on the law.

Conciliation allows disputing parties more flexibility than arbitration or adjudication, in that conciliation results only in recommendations, which the disputing parties are not bound to accept. In contrast with negotiations and mediation, however, conciliation is considerably less flexible, as it can entail more formal, court-like proceedings. While disputing parties exercise a fair amount of control over conciliation proceedings, the degree of control is again less than with negotiations or mediation. Disputing parties that pursue conciliation choose the panellists or participate in their selection, and they also confer a mandate on the panel, thereby defining the scope of the panellists' work.

Conciliation has proven to be an uncommon method of dispute settlement since its introduction in the 1920s, during the inter-war period. Since this time, disputing parties have resorted to conciliation commissions about twenty times in total, with only a handful of commissions since the 1920s.[34] Although a significant number of bilateral and multilateral treaties provide for conciliation, in practice states have not pursued this form of dispute settlement under these treaties.[35] States have occasionally turned to conciliation commissions not for the settlement of major disputes, but for the resolution of more technical matters of secondary importance.[36]

One of the more recent conciliation commissions, which was active in the early 1980s, contributed to the settlement of a dispute between Iceland and Norway with respect to the dividing line for the continental shelf between Iceland and Jan Mayen, a Norwegian island

---

[33] See, generally, Sven MG Koopmans, *Diplomatic Dispute Settlement: The Use of Inter-State Conciliation* (TMC Asser Press 2008) 44–8.

[34] Nadine Susani, 'Conciliation and Other Forms of Non-Binding Third Party Dispute Settlement' in James Crawford and others (eds), *The Law of International Responsibility* (Oxford University Press 2010) 1099, 1102; Jean-Pierre Cot, 'Conciliation' in *Max Planck Encyclopedia of Public International Law* (last updated April 2006), para 35.

[35] See, for example, Convention on Biological Diversity (adopted 5 June 1992, entered into force 29 December 1993) 1760 UNTS 79, art 27; United Nations Convention on the Law of the Sea (adopted 10 December 1982, entered into force 16 November 1994) 1833 UNTS 3 (UNCLOS) art 284; Convention on the Settlement of Investment Disputes Between States and Nationals of Other States (adopted 18 March 1965, entered into force 14 October 1966) 575 UNTS 159, arts 28–35.

[36] See generally Jean-Pierre Cot, *International Conciliation* (Europa Publications 1968).

in the Arctic Ocean.[37] In keeping with its mandate, the commission based its recommenda-tions not only on the law of the sea, but also non-legal considerations, such as Iceland's strong economic interest in the area, geographical, and geological factors. The commission ultimately recommended the adoption of a joint development agreement between Norway and Iceland that would substantially cover all of the area that offered a significant prospect of hydrocarbon production, and the two states subsequently reached an agreement on the basis of these recommendations. In its report, the commission thereby went beyond the strict application of the law of the sea, which would have suggested a maritime delimitation rather than a joint development zone. Because conciliation is a non-binding form of dispute settlement, it may be optimal for disputes that are most suitable for resolution on the basis of non-legal factors. While parties could, in theory, direct an arbitral tribunal or a judicial body to apply equitable considerations, known as *ex aequo et bono*, parties would be under-standably reluctant to commit themselves in advance to a binding decision on these grounds.[38]

3 Legal Methods of Dispute Settlement

a Arbitration

Arbitration is a procedure for the binding settlement of a dispute through the application of legal rules by decision-makers selected by and with the participation of the disputing parties. Inter-state arbitration dates back centuries, and involves relatively formal legal procedures, such as written submissions by the parties and oral hearings, followed by the issuance of an arbitral award by the arbitrators deciding the case. A number of key characteristics distinguish arbitration from diplomatic methods of dispute settlement as well as judicial settlement. First, arbitration tribunals generally settle disputes through the application of the law, as opposed to political or other considerations (although disputing parties could, in theory, direct arbitral tribunals to take non-legal considerations into account). Second, the outcome of arbitration is a binding and final award, meaning that the parties are legally obliged to comply with the award and may not appeal the tribunal's decision.

   Third, the disputing parties exercise a degree of control over the process, as they participate in the selection of at least some of the decision-makers, and may specify which procedural rules the arbitrators should apply. A typical arbitration tribunal is comprised of three or five arbitrators, of whom two are party-appointed (each party normally appoints one arbitrator). The disputing parties or the party-appointed arbitrators then reach agreement on the remaining arbitrator(s) or, in the case of a disagreement, refer this decision to a neutral third party. The ability to participate in the selection of arbitrators

---

[37] *Conciliation Commission on the Continental Shelf area between Iceland and Jan Mayen: Report and recommendations to the governments of Iceland and Norway* (1981) XXVII RIAA 1. See also *In the Matter of the Maritime Boundary Between Timor-Leste and Australia (The 'Timor Sea Conciliation')* (Report and Recommendations of the Compulsory Conciliation Commission Between Timor-Leste and Australia on the Timor Sea) (2018) PCA Case No 2016-10.

[38] Cot (n 34), para 36.

gives disputing parties a greater degree of control over the composition of the tribunal than is possible before judicial bodies that have fixed benches of judges. The disputing parties also exercise more control over procedural matters, including the level of confidentiality. The parties themselves may decide, for example, whether to open the oral proceedings to the public or to publish the parties' written submissions.

Finally, arbitral tribunals are temporary or ad hoc, which again distinguishes them from permanent judicial institutions like the ICJ or the International Tribunal for the Law of the Sea (ITLOS). Arbitral tribunals can be established for the resolution of a single dispute, or a class of disputes. The Iran–United States Claims Tribunal, for example, was established by Iran and the United States in 1981 to resolve a class of disputes – claims arising out of Iran's Islamic Revolution. Following a decade of economic difficulties and growing social discontent in Iran, a popular uprising in 1978–79 culminated in the overthrow of the Shah's regime, and the declaration of an Islamic Republic by the religious leader Ayatollah Khomeini. The revolution led to a crisis in relations between the United States and Iran due to the hostage-taking of US diplomats by Iran, the subsequent freezing of Iranian assets by the United States, as well as outstanding commercial claims by both states' nationals against the other state. The claims tribunal is still in operation, and has dealt with nearly 4,000 claims over the course of the last thirty-five years. It has, thus taken on the appearance of a permanent institution, though it will one-day complete its work and cease to exist.

Inter-state arbitration, or arbitration between states, is only one possible form of arbitration. 'Mixed arbitration' involves the settlement of disputes between states and private actors, such as private investors, while 'commercial arbitration' involves the settlement of disputes between private actors on the basis of domestic law. Our focus in this chapter is on inter-state arbitration, which has a relatively long history, going back to the 1794 John Jay Treaty between Great Britain and the United States.[39] Following the American War of Independence, Great Britain and the United States concluded the Jay Treaty for the purpose of settling outstanding disputes, in part through arbitral commissions comprised of British 'subjects' and American citizens. The first such commission resolved a dispute regarding the north-east boundary between the United States and Canada (which was then part of Great Britain).[40] The decisions reached by these commissions, which dealt with both inter-state and mixed claims, represent the first prominent example of arbitrators issuing reasoned awards based on the law.[41]

The United States and Great Britain resorted to arbitration once again following the American Civil War (1861–65) for the settlement of sensitive claims regarding Great Britain's proclamation of neutrality. The United States argued that Great Britain had violated the law of neutrality during the war by allowing the construction and supply of warships in British ports for the Confederate States, which had fought unsuccessfully to secede from the United States. The 1871 Treaty of Washington between Great Britain and the United States established a tribunal to deal with the 'Alabama Claims', named after one

---

[39] Treaty of Amity, Commerce and Navigation between His Britannick Majesty and the United States of America (adopted 19 November 1794, entered into force 29 February 1796).

[40] Treaty of Amity, Commerce and Navigation art 5.

[41] Charles H Brower II, 'Arbitration' in *Max Planck Encyclopedia of Public International Law* (last updated February 2007), para 17.

of the warships.[42] The five-member tribunal was the first prominent example of a tribunal with a minority of party-appointed arbitrators, a feature that enhanced its independence and judicial character.[43] The tribunal ultimately held Great Britain responsible for acts committed by certain vessels, and ordered it to pay the United States $15.5 million in gold as compensation, an enormous sum in its day (approximately £4.4 billion today).[44] Great Britain complied with the award.

The Alabama Claims arbitration inspired the further development of arbitration as a method of dispute settlement through the establishment of the Permanent Court of Arbitration (PCA) in 1899. By this time, arbitration had become a popular method of dispute settlement, although one which frequently involved difficult negotiations between disputing parties about the applicable procedures and the selection of arbitrators. The drafters of the 1899 Hague Convention therefore aimed to facilitate recourse to arbitration by providing states with a standard set of procedures and a list of potential arbitrators.[45] These efforts resulted in the PCA, an institution that bears a misleading name, as it is neither a court, nor a permanent arbitral body. Instead, the PCA is an intergovernmental organization, based in Peace Palace in The Hague, which facilitates the formation of ad hoc, or temporary, arbitral tribunals, and supports the proceedings, both written and oral. In other words, the PCA does not itself arbitrate disputes; instead, tribunals created and operated under its auspices carry out this task.

During the first two decades of the PCA's existence, the majority of inter-state arbitrations took place under its auspices. But following the establishment of the Permanent Court of International Justice in 1922 after the First World War, the PCA fell into disuse and entered an extended period of dormancy.[46] By the mid-1990s; however, the PCA had entered a period of resurgence. Since this time, a dramatic increase in both inter-state and mixed arbitrations being administered by the PCA may be attributed to a range of factors, including increased interest in legal methods of dispute settlement, the flexibility of the PCA's procedural rules, and the status of arbitration as the default dispute settlement method under the UN Convention on the Law of the Sea.[47] As a forum for the settlement of inter-state disputes on the basis of law, the PCA now rivals the ICJ, and has in recent years enjoyed a particularly steady stream of cases relating to the law of the sea.[48]

b   *Adjudication*

Judicial settlement or adjudication is a procedure for the binding settlement of a dispute through the application of legal rules by adjudicators who are members of a permanent institution. Like

---

[42] See generally, Tom Bingham, 'The *Alabama* Claims Arbitration' (2005) 54 International and Comparative Law Quarterly 1.
[43] ibid, para 22.   [44] *Alabama claims of the United States of America against Great Britain* (1871) XXIX RIAA 125.
[45] 1899 Convention (n 6) arts 20–9.   [46] The Permanent Court of International Justice is the predecessor of the ICJ.
[47] UNCLOS art 287(1).
[48] See, for example, *Arbitration Between the Republic of Croatia and the Republic of Slovenia* (Final Award) (2017) PCA Case 2012-04; *The Arctic Sunrise Arbitration (Netherlands v Russian Federation)* (Merits) (2015) PCA Case 2014-02; *Bay of Bengal Maritime Boundary Arbitration between Bangladesh and India* (Award) (2014) PCA Case 2010-16; *Chagos Marine Protected Area Arbitration (Mauritius v United Kingdom)* (Award) (2015) PCA Case 2011-03; *The South China Sea Arbitration (The Republic of Philippines v The People's Republic of China)* (Award) (2016) PCA Case 2013-19. The PCA currently acts as the registry in eight inter-state proceedings.

arbitration, adjudication may be distinguished from diplomatic methods of dispute settlement by virtue of the fact that judicial settlement entails the application of the law in the context of a binding judgment from which no appeal is available.[49] Unlike arbitration; however, adjudication allows the disputing parties to exercise only a minimal degree of control over the selection of the decision-makers and the applicable procedural rules. In fact, adjudication represents the least flexible form of dispute settlement, and states may therefore perceive the initiation of judicial proceedings against them as an unfriendly act.

International adjudication is carried out by standing judicial bodies that have fixed benches of judges, much like domestic courts. The ICJ and the ITLOS, for example, have fixed benches with fifteen and twenty-one members, respectively.[50] Unlike arbitrators, who settle disputes on an ad hoc basis, judges who are members of standing institutions may approach dispute settlement with greater concern for certain institutional or systemic issues, such as the consistency of its jurisprudence. The extent to which the disputing parties can affect the composition of either bench by selecting particular judges to settle their case is extremely limited. Each party can appoint one ad hoc judge if a judge of its nationality is not already sitting on the bench.[51] While the fixed membership of the ICJ and ITLOS greatly diminishes the capacity of states to select their own decision-makers, this may be of little consequence for states that value the convenience of a fixed bench, and perhaps also the cost-savings involved. The parties themselves do not pay the salaries of judges at standing judicial bodies like the ICJ and ITLOS, whereas arbitrators' fees are covered by the parties.[52]

The permanence of judicial bodies also diminishes the capacity of the disputing parties to determine their own procedural rules, but this too, may be regarded as convenient and desirable by some states. Permanent judicial institutions like the ICJ, ITLOS, and the World Trade Organization's (WTO) Appellate Body have their own fixed procedural rules with which litigants must comply, with relatively little room for deviation.[53] The standard procedures and working methods of the ICJ, for example, result in a relatively high degree of transparency with respect to both written and oral proceedings, in contrast with the confidential character of many inter-state arbitral proceedings.[54]

Judicial institutions in the international legal field have a somewhat shorter history than arbitral tribunals.[55] The first universal judicial institution, the Permanent Court of

---

[49] Statute of the ICJ (as annexed to the Charter of the UN) (adopted 26 June 1945, entered into force 24 October 1945) USTS 993 (ICJ Statute) arts 59–60.
[50] ICJ Statute art 3(1); Statute of the ITLOS (as annexed to the United States Convention on the Law of the Sea) (adopted 10 December 1982, entered into force 16 November 1994) 1833 UNTS 561 (ITLOS Statute) art 2(1).
[51] ICJ Statute art 31; ITLOS Statute art 17.
[52] The UN bears the costs of the salaries of ICJ judges (ICJ Statute art 32); States Parties to UNCLOS bear the costs of the salaries of ITLOS judges (ITLOS Statute arts 18–19); See also PCA Optional Rules for Arbitrating Disputes Between Two States (1992) arts 38–40.
[53] See the ICJ's Rules of Court (1978) and Practice Directions (2001); ITLOS Rules of the Tribunal (1997); WTO Understanding on Rules and Procedures Governing the Settlement of Disputes (1996) and WTO Working Procedures for Appellate Review (2010).
[54] ICJ Statute art 46; ICJ Rules of Court art 53; PCA Optional Rules for Arbitrating Disputes Between Two States arts 25(4), 32(5).
[55] For a timeline, see 'Annex 1, International Judicial Bodies: Recapitulation' in Cesare PR Romano, Karen J Alter and Yuval Shany (eds), *The Oxford Handbook of International Adjudication* (Oxford University Press 2014).

International Justice (PCIJ), was established by states in 1922 in association with the League of Nations. The PCIJ was based in the Peace Palace in The Hague, a home that it shared with the PCA. In 1946, following the Second World War, the PCIJ was succeeded by the ICJ, which serves as the 'principal judicial organ of the United Nations', alongside the other principal organs of the UN, such as the General Assembly and the Security Council.[56] The ICJ adopted both the home of the PCIJ in The Hague, as well as the PCIJ's statute, with minimal changes.[57]

As stipulated in its statute, the ICJ is composed of fifteen judges who are nominated by 'national groups' created by UN member states, and then elected to the bench by an absolute majority of votes in the UN General Assembly and Security Council.[58] Together, the fifteen judges represent the 'main forms of civilization' and the 'principal legal systems of the world'.[59] In practice, the composition of the bench follows an established geographical distribution, with three seats reserved for judges from Africa, two for Latin America and the Caribbean, three for Asia, five for Western Europe and other states[60], and two for Eastern Europe. The permanent five members of the Security Council – China, France, Russia, the United Kingdom, and the United States – have almost always had a judge of their nationality on the bench.[61] Though the bench is designed to ensure geographical diversity, the members of the Court do not represent their home governments, but instead serve in their individual capacity, as independent judges. The judges serve nine-year terms, which are staggered, such that no more than one third of the bench changes over every three years, with each election.[62] Judges may serve more than one term, and many do.

Taken together, the jurisprudence of the ICJ and the PCIJ has played an important role in the development of the international legal field, as can be seen throughout the chapters of this book. For many decades the ICJ was the only permanent international judicial institution available for the settlement of inter-state disputes.[63] In the mid-1990s, two other standing bodies came into existence, namely ITLOS and the Appellate Body of the WTO.[64] But the ICJ remains the only international judicial body with general jurisdiction, meaning that it has the competence to adjudicate a very wide range of disputes between states under international law, from disputes concerning maritime delimitation, to the use of force, to the law of immunities. ITLOS is; however, limited to disputes concerning the UNCLOS, and the WTO Appellate Body, which is currently not in operation, is confined to international trade disputes (see chapters 14 and 15). Despite its relatively long line of jurisprudence and its unique position among international judicial institutions, the importance of the ICJ should not be overstated. The frequency with which states submit their disputes to the ICJ has fluctuated over time, and the Court generally decides only a few

---

[56] ICJ Statute art 1.   [57] The ICJ is, in fact, the only principal organ of the UN based outside of UN headquarters in New York.
[58] ICJ Statute arts 3–4, 10.   [59] ICJ Statute art 9.
[60] The 'Western Europe and Others Group' is one of the five unofficial regional groupings in the UN.
[61] The United Kingdom's seat on the bench went to India following the 2017 elections.   [62] ICJ Statute art 13(1).
[63] A number of other permanent judicial institutions also have competence over inter-state disputes, including the European Court of Justice and the European Court of Human Rights, but they may be considered regional as opposed to universal institutions.
[64] The WTO's first stage of judicial settlement involves 'panels', which cannot be described as standing judicial bodies, as the WTO's Dispute Settlement Body selects a different set of panellists for each dispute.

disputes each year. In contrast, the WTO's Dispute Settlement Body, which consists of Panels and previously also the Appellate Body, has become a hive of activity over the past two decades (see Chapter 14).

c   *Methods for Consenting to Arbitration and Adjudication*

All methods of dispute settlement, whether diplomatic or legal, require the consent of the disputing parties. In other words, one state cannot be compelled by another state, against its will, to submit to a particular form of dispute settlement, from negotiations to judicial settlement. But consent is especially important in the context of legal forms of dispute settlement, because the disputing parties are bound by the outcome. Consent in the context of arbitration and adjudication is therefore especially formal, so as to ensure that the disputing states have actually agreed to grant arbitrators or judges the authority to render a binding decision.

In the case of the ICJ, for example, states do not consent to the Court's 'contentious jurisdiction' simply by virtue of becoming a party to its statute. All UN member states are automatically parties to the ICJ's statute, which forms an integral part of the UN Charter. But UN membership only gives states access to the Court, as the statute further requires states to explicitly consent to the settlement of specific disputes by the Court through more formal mechanisms.[65] The term 'contentious jurisdiction' refers to the Court's competence to decide legal disputes between states that have consented to its jurisdiction. The Court's contentious jurisdiction is notably restricted to states alone, thus excluding non-state actors such as international organizations and individuals.[66] The ICJ's 'advisory jurisdiction', by contrast, involves the resolution of legal questions, rather than legal disputes, and access is restricted to the UN General Assembly, Security Council, and UN specialized agencies, thus excluding states.[67] The Court's advisory jurisdiction allows it to provide non-binding advice on legal questions, in the form of advisory opinions, to these UN bodies upon their request.

States can consent to the arbitration or adjudication of a dispute in any one or more of the following ways. First, disputing parties may conclude a special agreement or *compromis*, by which they consent to the jurisdiction of an arbitral tribunal or a judicial institution over an existing dispute.[68] Special agreements may be regarded as backward looking or retrospective insofar as parties conclude them after a dispute has arisen. Special agreements are advantageous in cases in which the parties would like to direct the court or tribunal towards specific issues, or provide for the application of a particular body of law.[69] In other words, special agreements allow the parties

---

[65] UN Charter arts 92–3.   [66] UN Charter art 34(1).   [67] UN Charter art 96.

[68] See, for example, *Case concerning the Gabčíkovo-Nagymaros Project (Hungary v Slovakia)* (Judgment) [1997] ICJ Rep 7.

[69] See, for example, *Frontier Dispute (Burkina Faso v Niger)* (Judgment) [2013] ICJ Rep 44; *North Sea Continental Shelf Cases (Federal Republic of Germany v Denmark; Federal Republic of Germany v Netherlands)* (Judgment) [1969] ICJ Rep 1969 3.

to exercise a degree of control over the court's or tribunal's legal approach to the dispute.

Second, disputing parties may consent to the jurisdiction of a specific court or tribunal over future disputes by becoming a party to a treaty with a compromissory clause. A compromissory clause is a dispute resolution provision in a treaty that provides for recourse to arbitration and/or adjudication for the settlement of disputes concerning the interpretation or application of the treaty, to which both states must be parties.[70] An example may be found in Article IX of the Convention on the Prevention and Punishment of the Crime of Genocide, which provides that:

Disputes between the Contracting Parties relating to the interpretation, application or fulfilment of the present Convention, ... shall be submitted to the International Court of Justice at the request of any of the parties to the dispute.[71]

In contrast with special agreements, compromissory clauses are forward-looking or prospective. By becoming a party to a treaty with a compromissory clause, states consent to the litigation of disputes that may arise many years or decades in the future. Respondent states may not, however, anticipate (or desire) that a treaty signed long ago could one day be invoked by another state as the basis for its consent to adjudication. Cases brought under compromissory clauses therefore tend to prompt challenges to the Court's jurisdiction by respondent states claiming that the dispute does not actually concern the interpretation or application of the given treaty.

The terms 'special agreement' and 'compromissory clause' are terms of art used by international lawyers to signify distinct methods of consent, even though this specific language does not actually appear in the statutes of the ICJ or ITLOS, or in other treaties that confer jurisdiction on these institutions. For example, Article 36 of the ICJ's statute, which sets out the various methods of consent to the Court's jurisdiction, does not actually use the terms 'special agreement', '*compromis*', or compromissory clause. Instead, these terms have been 'read into' the language in the statute. The first paragraph of Article 36 stipulates that '[t]he jurisdiction of the Court comprises all cases which the parties refer to it and all matters specifically provided for in the Charter of the United Nations or in treaties and conventions in force'. The phrase 'all cases which the parties refer to it' signifies special agreements, while the phrase 'all matters specifically provided for ... in treaties and conventions in force' refers to compromissory clauses.

Two other methods of consent are specific to the ICJ. The first and most important method may be found in Article 36(2) of the Court's statute, which allows states to make what are known as 'optional clause declarations'. Such a declaration allows a state to accept the jurisdiction of the Court over all of its disputes, or a particular class of disputes, regardless of any relevant compromissory clauses. The only condition is that the other

---

[70] See, for example, UN Convention against Transnational Organized Crime (adopted 15 November 2000, entered into force 29 September 2003) 2225 UNTS 209, art 35. Equatorial Guinea recently invoked this compromissory clause in a case that it brought against France concerning immunity in June 2016. *Immunities and Criminal Proceedings (Equatorial Guinea v France)* (Merits) [2020] ICJ General List 163.

[71] Convention on the Prevention and Punishment of the Crime of Genocide (adopted 9 December 1948, entered into force 12 January 1951) 78 UNTS 277.

disputing party has also made such a declaration. Again, the term 'optional clause declaration' appears nowhere in Article 36(2), which stipulates that:

The states parties to the present Statute may at any time declare that they recognize as compulsory *ipso facto* and without special agreement, in relation to any other state accepting the same obligation, the jurisdiction of the Court in all legal disputes concerning:

(a) the interpretation of a treaty;
(b) any question of international law;
(c) the existence of any fact which, if established, would constitute the breach of an international obligation;
(d) the nature or extent of the reparation to be made for the breach of an international obligation.

The drafters of the PCIJ's statute, which included identical language, anticipated that optional clause declarations would constitute the primary method for consent to the Court's jurisdiction. In practice, however, this has not been the case for the PCIJ nor the ICJ.[72] Out of the 193 parties to the ICJ's statute, only 73 (more than one-third) have deposited declarations accepting the compulsory jurisdiction of the Court.

In addition, many of the existing declarations include reservations, which can significantly limit the applicability of a declaration. In this context, reservations are unilateral statements by which states modify the legal effect of their optional clause declarations.[73] States are free, for example, to include reservations that exclude certain types of disputes from the jurisdiction of the Court. For instance, Australia has excluded disputes concerning maritime delimitation, and the United Kingdom has excluded disputes with former or current Commonwealth states. The effect of such reservations can be significant, because the reservations apply reciprocally, by virtue of the fact that states making declarations only accept the Court's jurisdiction 'in relation to any other state accepting the same obligation' (Article 36(2)). This means that a respondent state that is the subject of a claim may invoke a reservation made by the applicant state. In other words, a reservation included by an applicant state in its optional clause declaration applies reciprocally to the respondent state, which may invoke it to preclude the Court's jurisdiction. If an applicant state has, for example, excluded maritime delimitation disputes from the Court's jurisdiction, then the respondent state may effectively adopt this reservation as its own, even if its own declaration accepts the Court's jurisdiction unconditionally. The respondent state has, after all, only accepted the Court's jurisdiction 'in relation to any other state accepting the same obligation', which means that its acceptance is not unconditional in relation to states with more limited declarations.

The final method of consent to the Court's jurisdiction is *forum prorogatum*, an obscure mechanism that allows a would-be respondent state to accept the Court's jurisdiction after an applicant state has filed a case against it in circumstances in which there is no other basis for jurisdiction. In other words, the applicant state files an application in the hope that the

---

[72] Christian Tomuschat, 'Article 36' in Andreas Zimmerman and others (eds), *The Statute of the International Court of Justice: A Commentary* (2nd edn, Oxford University Press 2012), para 69.
[73] For more on reservations, see Chapter 4 on treaty law.

would-be respondent state accepts the invitation to litigate before the Court. The term *forum prorogatum* again appears nowhere in the Court's statute or the Rules of Court, but Article 38(5) of the rules does provide the basis for this form of consent:

When the applicant State proposes to found the jurisdiction of the Court upon a consent thereto yet to be given or manifested by the State against which such application is made, the application shall be transmitted to that State. It shall not however be entered in the General List, nor any action taken in the proceedings, unless and until the State against which such application is made consents to the Court's jurisdiction for the purpose of the case.

The General List, which is the Court's docket of cases, thus excludes cases filed by applicant states in the hope of obtaining consent through *forum prorogatum*. This procedural rule is designed to avoid creating the impression that the Court actually has jurisdiction, when in fact jurisdiction awaits consent by the would-be respondent. In practice, a number of cases have been filed in the hope of obtaining consent through *forum prorogatum*, but consent has been granted in this manner only twice, in *Certain Criminal Proceedings in France (Republic of the Congo v France)* and *Certain Questions of Mutual Assistance in Criminal Matters (Djibouti v France)*.[74] In the latter case, the Court explained that the consent of the respondent state must be explicit or capable of being 'clearly deduced' from the State's conduct, a standard which was met when France expressly accepted the Court's jurisdiction by letter.[75]

d   The 'Monetary Gold Principle' and the Consent of Third Parties

Legal dispute settlement methods are primarily designed to settle bilateral disputes between just two states – an applicant or claimant, and a respondent. As acknowledged at the beginning of this chapter; however, some disputes are best characterized as multilateral rather than bilateral. Moreover, many disputes have at least some multilateral elements. While interventions by third parties are possible at the ICJ, for example, this is relatively rare and tightly controlled by the Court.[76] More commonly, a single applicant state might bring separate but related proceedings against a number of respondent states, which the Court may join.[77] The multilateral character of a dispute can, however, cause problems for courts and tribunals, even in cases where there is no doubt that both the applicant and respondent states have consented to the jurisdiction of the judicial body. An admissibility problem may arise, in particular, when the settlement of a dispute between an applicant and

---

[74] Recent unsuccessful attempts include a case filed by Equatorial Guinea against France in 2012 (*The Republic of Equatorial Guinea seeks to institute proceedings against France before the International Court of Justice. It requests France to accept the Court's jurisdiction,* ICJ Press release 2012/26) and a case filed by Argentina against the United States in 2014 (*The Argentine Republic seeks to institute proceedings against the United States of America before the International Court of Justice. It requests US to accept the Court's jurisdiction,* ICJ Press release 2014/25).

[75] *Case concerning Certain Questions of Mutual Assistance in Criminal Matters (Djibouti v France)* (Judgment) ICJ Reports 2008 177, paras 62, 65. France's letter informed the Court that it 'consent[ed] to the Court's jurisdiction to entertain the Application pursuant to, and solely on the basis of . . . Article 38, paragraph 5' of the Rules of Court. ibid, para 4.

[76] ICJ Statute arts 62–3.

[77] ICJ Rules of Court art 47; see, for example, *Jurisdictional Immunities of the State (Germany v Italy: Greece intervening)* (Judgment) [2012] ICJ Rep 99.

a respondent requires the Court to rule on the rights or obligations of a third state that does not wish to intervene and has not consented to the Court's jurisdiction.

The rule governing such situations is known as the 'Monetary Gold principle', because the ICJ first articulated the rule in *Monetary Gold Removed from Rome in 1943 (Italy v France, United Kingdom of Great Britain and Northern Ireland and the United States)*. This dispute arose out of Germany's seizure during the Second World War of gold that was held in a bank in Rome, but belonged to the National Bank of Albania. After the War, the distribution of such monetary gold fell to the allied powers, France, the United Kingdom, and the United States. Italy and the United Kingdom made competing claims to the monetary gold, which both states sought as compensation for outstanding legal claims that they held against Albania. Italy pressed its claim to have priority over the gold by instituting proceedings before the ICJ against France, the United Kingdom, and the United States. The Court; however, held that it could not decide the dispute because Italy's claims required it to rule on the lawfulness of actions by Albania, which had not consented to the Court's jurisdiction. According to the Court, adjudicating Italy's claim without Albania's consent would 'run counter to a well-established principle of international law embodied in the Court's Statute, namely, that the Court can only exercise jurisdiction over a State with its consent'.[78]

The Monetary Gold principle may, thus be summarized as follows: The Court may not decide a dispute between states A and B if state C's 'legal interests would not only be affected by [the] decision, but would form the very subject matter of the decision', in circumstances where state C has not given its consent to the jurisdiction of the Court in that case.[79] Since the *Monetary Gold* case in 1954, parties have objected to the Court's jurisdiction on this basis in numerous cases, but with limited success.[80]

4 Concluding Remarks

Resort by states to dispute settlement procedures, and in particular legal methods of dispute settlement, has grown exponentially in the last decades. Since the 1990s, the ICJ has had an increasingly active docket of cases, and in addition, the PCA has undergone a sort of renaissance. But international dispute settlement must also be understood as typically or commonly involving the resort to diplomatic or non-legal forms of dispute settlement, which can be attractive to disputing parties that may, for example, wish to retain greater control over the dispute settlement process, or to avoid binding outcomes. Finally, it must also be acknowledged that in many instances, disputing parties do not pursue dispute

---

[78] *Case of the Monetary Gold Removed from Rome in 1943 (Preliminary Question) (Italy v France, United Kingdom of Great Britain and Northern Ireland and United States of America)* (Judgment) [1954] ICJ Rep 19, 32.

[79] ibid.

[80] See, for example, *Case concerning Certain Phosphate Lands in Nauru (Nauru v Australia)* (Preliminary objections) [1992] ICJ Rep 240; *Case concerning Application of the Convention on the Prevention and Punishment of the Crime of Genocide (Croatia v Serbia)* (Preliminary objections) [2008] ICJ Rep 412; but see *Case concerning East Timor (Portugal v Australia)* (Judgment) [1995] ICJ Rep 90.

settlement procedures at all, and this is not only permissible under international law, but also to be expected, given the realities of international politics.

Recommended Reading

Jacob Bercovitch and Richard Jackson, *Conflict Resolution in the Twenty-first Century: Principles, Methods, and Approaches* (University of Michigan Press 2009).

Chester Brown, *A Common Law of International Adjudication* (Oxford University Press 2007).

John Collier and Vaughan Lowe, *The Settlement of Disputes in International Law: Institutions and Procedures* (Oxford University Press 1999).

Duncan French, Matthew Saul, and Nigel D White (eds), *International Law and Dispute Settlement: New Problems and Techniques* (Hart 2010).

John G Merrills, *International Dispute Settlement* (5th edn, Cambridge University Press 2011).

Part II

The Branches of Public International Law

10

International Human Rights Law

Simone van den Driest

1   Introduction

As was explained in Chapter 3, international law traditionally centres on the rights, obligations, and competences of states. The legal position of individuals was perceived by states as
a domestic affair of the sovereign state, which could effectively treat its citizens as it pleased.
It was not until after the Second World War that this fundamentally changed and international
law began to grant individuals rights to protect them from the state. As such, the emergence of
human rights law should be viewed against the backdrop of a development that is often called
the 'humanization of international law'[1] and refers to the evolution of international law from
a primarily state-centred system towards a more human-centred system, in which states are no
longer the sole actors and which is increasingly aimed at respecting and promoting the
interests of human beings. While various other developments – such as the emergence of
international criminal law[2] and the establishment of the International Criminal Court (ICC),[3]
the endorsement of the Responsibility to Protect,[4] and the doctrine of remedial secession[5] –
may also be seen against this backdrop, the 'humanization of international law' is probably
most visible in the field of international human rights law.

This chapter will start by briefly sketching the development of international human rights
law. Then, it will present the main categories or generations of human rights and discuss their
key characteristics. This chapter will subsequently turn to several matters concerning the scope
of human rights norms, including their addressees, their territorial scope of application, and the
circumstances under which human rights may be restricted by the state. Finally, this chapter
will explain how human rights are monitored and enforced under international law.

2   Development of International Human Rights Law

Prior to the end of the Second World War, the legal position of individuals and their
protection was considered to be an internal matter of the state. This is not to say that

---

[1] See Theodor Meron, *The Humanization of International Law* (Martinus Nijhoff 2007).
[2] This will be explained in Chapter 13.
[3] Rome Statute of the ICC (adopted 17 July 1998, entered into force 1 July 2002) 2187 UNTS 3.
[4] UNGA Res 60/1 '2005 World Summit Outcome' (24 October 2005) 138–40.
[5] This concept was explained in Chapter 3, para 4(c).

individuals did not enjoy any rights at all. Various states had included some individual rights in their domestic laws, such as the English Magna Carta of 1215, the American Bill of Rights of 1776, the French Déclaration des Droits de l'Homme et du Citoyen of 1789, and the Dutch Constitution of 1814. On the international level; however, states were only obliged to respect some basic principles with respect to the nationals of other states ('aliens'). In the eighteenth century, an international minimum standard for the protection of 'aliens' developed, as Western states wished to protect their nationals living in overseas territories. The international minimum standard therefore provided for the protection of property, a right to non-discrimination in relation to the nationals of these states, and access to a judge in the host state. It should be emphasized though, that this standard only protected 'aliens', and did not benefit the nationals of these states.[6]

This system, in which the protection of human beings was essentially left to the domestic legal order of sovereign states, first started to change after the First World War. As the map of Europe was redrawn, new minorities emerged within the altered boundaries. To protect these minorities, the Allied Powers concluded a series of treaties with various states – such as Czechoslovakia, Greece, Poland, Romania, and Turkey – in the context of the League of Nations.[7] The horrors of the Second World War subsequently sparked a growing awareness that respect for human rights is important for maintaining international stability and peaceful relations between states. How a state treats its nationals, thus gradually came to be viewed as a matter of international concern rather than a mere domestic affair.

The importance of human rights was subsequently reflected in the United Nations (UN) Charter,[8] Article 1(3) of which stipulates that one of the purposes of the UN is 'to achieve international cooperation ... in promoting and encouraging respect for human rights and for fundamental freedoms for all without distinction as to race, sex, language, or religion'. Article 55 of the UN Charter refers to respect for human rights as necessary conditions for peaceful and friendly relations amongst states, and pursuant to Article 56, all UN member states 'pledge themselves to take joint and separate action' to achieve this purpose. Notwithstanding the importance of these provisions, the UN Charter does not impose any concrete human rights obligations upon UN member states. Rather, these provisions provide a legal basis for the UN to act and formulate human rights policies. It was on this basis that the Universal Declaration on Human Rights (UDHR) was drafted and adopted by UN member states in 1948.[9] This milestone document contains thirty provisions listing fundamental human rights, ranging from the right to life (Article 3) and freedom from torture (Article 5) to the right to a nationality (Article 15) and the more aspirational right to an adequate standard of living (Article 25). As a resolution adopted by the UN General Assembly, the UDHR is not legally binding, but it nevertheless, has significant authority and has influenced the development of the field. Some of the rights enshrined in the UDHR now reflect customary international law. Moreover, the rights of the UDHR have subsequently been codified and developed in various

---

[6] The international minimum standard is also explained in Chapter 14.
[7] See Anna Meijknecht, 'Minority Protection System Between Word War I and World War II' in *Max Planck Encyclopedia of Public International Law* (last updated October 2010).
[8] Charter of the UN (adopted 26 June 1945, entered into force 24 October 1945) 1 UNTS XVI (UN Charter).
[9] UDHR (adopted 10 December 1948) UNGA Res 217 A(III) (UDHR).

legally binding human rights instruments, most prominently the 1966 International Covenant on Civil and Political Rights (ICCPR)[10] and the 1966 International Covenant on Economic, Social and Cultural Rights (ICESCR).[11] As of July 2021, the ICCPR has 173 states parties, while 171 states are party to the ICESCR. Together with the UDHR, these instruments are often referred to as the 'International Bill of Rights'.

A myriad of treaties elaborating upon the rights provided for in the International Bill of Rights has been created since 1948. Some treaties are aimed at the protection of particular categories of individuals that are considered to be vulnerable, such as the 1979 Convention on the Elimination of All Forms of Discrimination Against Women (CEDAW),[12] the 1989 Convention on the Rights of the Child (CRC),[13] the 1990 Convention on the Protection of the Rights of All Migrant Workers and Members of Their Families (ICRMW),[14] and the 2006 Convention on the Rights of Persons with Disabilities (CRPD).[15] Other treaties focus on the protection of individuals against specific human rights violations, such as the 1948 Convention on the Prevention and Punishment of the Crime of Genocide,[16] the 1984 Convention Against Torture and Other Cruel, Inhuman or Degrading Treatment or Punishment (CAT),[17] and the 2006 International Convention for the Protection of All Persons from Enforced Disappearance.[18]

Next to these instruments on the international level, human rights treaties have been created in the regional sphere as well. Examples in this respect are the 1950 European Convention on Human Rights and Fundamental Freedoms (ECHR),[19] the 1969 American Convention on Human Rights (ACHR),[20] the 1981 African Charter on Human and Peoples' Rights (ACHPR),[21] and the 2004 Arab Charter on Human Rights.[22] No legally binding human rights treaty has been established by states in the Asian region to date, although a declaration was adopted in 2012.[23] Individuals in Asia

---

[10] ICCPR (adopted 16 December 1966, entered into force 23 March 1976) 999 UNTS 171.

[11] ICESR (adopted 16 December 1966, entered into force 3 January 1976) 993 UNTS 3.

[12] CEDAW (adopted 18 December 1979, entered into force 3 September 1981) 1249 UNTS 1.

[13] CRC (adopted 20 November 1989, entered into force 2 September 1990) 1577 UNTS 3.

[14] ICRMW (adopted 18 December 1990, entered into force 1 July 2003) 2220 UNTS 3.

[15] CRPD (adopted 13 December 2006, entered into force 3 May 2008) 2515 UNTS 3.

[16] Convention on the Prevention and Punishment of the Crime of Genocide (adopted 9 December 1948, entered into force 12 January 1951) 78 UNTS 277 (Genocide Convention).

[17] CAT (adopted 10 December 1984, entered into force 26 June 1987) 1465 UNTS 85.

[18] International Convention for the Protection of All Persons from Enforced Disappearance (adopted 20 December 2006, entered into force 23 December 2010) 2716 UNTS 3.

[19] ECHR (adopted 4 November 1950, entered into force 3 September 1953) 213 UNTS 221.

[20] ACHR (adopted 22 November 1969, entered into force 18 July 1978) 1144 UNTS 123.

[21] ACHPR (adopted 27 June 1981, entered into force 21 October 1986) 1520 UNTS 217.

[22] Arab Charter on Human Rights (adopted 22 May 2004, entered into force 15 March 2008) 12 International Human Rights Report 893. Notably, in 2008, the then UN high commissioner for human rights expressed concerns that various provisions of the Arab Charter were incompatible with international human rights standards, in particular those concerning the application of the death penalty to children and the treatment of women and non-citizens. See UN Press Release, 'Arab Rights Charter Deviates from International Standards, Says UN Official' (30 January 2008) <https://news.un.org/en/story/2008/01/247292-arab-rights-charter-deviates-international-standards-says-un-official>.

[23] Association of South East Asian Nations (ASEAN) Human Rights Declaration (adopted 18 November 2012). Here as well, the then UN high commissioner for human rights expressed concerns that the declaration contains language that is inconsistent with international human rights standards. See UN Press Release, 'UN Official Welcomes ASEAN Commitment to Human Rights, but Concerned over Declaration Wording' (19 November 2012) <https://news.un.org/en/story/2012/11/426012#.Wk0M9BR0Z6C>.

remain protected by international human rights treaties – at least to the extent that the state concerned is party to these instruments. While the content of regional human rights treaties overlaps with international instruments to a considerable extent, their added value should not be underestimated. Not only do they generally better suit the particular situation in the region concerned, states have also been more willing to create stronger enforcement mechanisms in a regional context.[24] Combined with the 'proximity' of these enforcement mechanisms, regional treaties have practically become the most important instruments in protecting human rights.

All in all, the emergence of international and regional human rights law has ensured that the protection of individuals no longer depends on the domestic legal order, but has become a legitimate matter of international concern.[25]

3   Categories of Human Rights

Human rights are generally organized in three categories or generations: (a) civil and political rights; (b) economic, social and cultural rights; and (c) collective rights. This section will explain these categories of human rights and their main characteristics. The distinction between the various categories of human rights is primarily relevant for understanding the nature of the principal obligations they involve for states. There is no hierarchy between the various categories and they are interdependent and interrelated.[26] For instance, the right to stand for elections is practically futile for those who are illiterate, while the right to education is of little use for those who are not protected against torture and arbitrary killings. Moreover, each human right is seen to entail obligations for states to respect, to protect and to fulfil. This is sometimes referred to as the tripartite typology of human rights. The obligation to respect requires states to refrain from interfering with the enjoyment of human rights. The obligation to protect means that states must prevent others from interfering with the enjoyment of human rights. The obligation to fulfil requires states to take action to facilitate the enjoyment of human rights. As such, the distinction between the various categories of human rights is not as sharp as it first appears.

a   *Civil and Political Rights*

The oldest category of human rights is comprised of civil and political rights, which are therefore referred to as first generation human rights. Their aim is essentially twofold: protecting the individual from the state and enabling the individual to

---

[24] This will be explained in Section 5.
[25] See Vienna Declaration and Programme of Action (as adopted by the World Conference on Human Rights) (12 July 1993) UN Doc A/CONF.157/23, 4.
[26] UNGA Res 63/176 (18 December 2008), Preamble.

participate in the political life of the state. Examples are the right to life,[27] the prohibition against torture,[28] the right to a fair trial,[29] the freedom of expression,[30] and the right to vote and to be elected.[31] These rights are enshrined in general human rights instruments, such as the UDHR, ICCPR, and the ECHR, and principally require the state to abstain from interfering with the enjoyment of these rights. Such obligations are generally referred to as 'negative obligations' for states. The effective enjoyment of these rights, however, will often require more than state abstention only. A certain degree of positive action by the state is called for as well. The right to life, for instance, not only obliges state officials not to kill citizens arbitrarily, but also means that the state must criminalize homicide in its domestic legislation and ensure effective police investigations.[32] Another important characteristic of civil and political rights is that they require immediate realization by states. This is reflected in the wording of Article 2 of the ICCPR, which embodies an immediate obligation for each state party 'to respect and to ensure' the rights recognized in the Covenant. These rights thus contain an obligation of (instant) result. As will be explained, this is quite a fundamental difference with the second category of human rights.

b   *Economic, Social, and Cultural Rights*

The second category or generation of human rights concerns economic, social, and cultural rights. These rights are aimed at safeguarding the socio-economic well-being of the individual and his or her cultural identity and freedom. Examples are the right to work and adequate working conditions,[33] the right to social security,[34] the right to education,[35] and the right to an adequate standard of living, including adequate food, clothing, and housing.[36] These second-generation rights are, among others, included in the ICESCR and the European Social Charter.[37] In contrast to civil and political rights, these rights entail primarily 'positive obligations' for states. This means that states are expected to actively promote economic, social, and cultural rights, for instance by adopting relevant laws and policies. Yet, these second-generation rights may sometimes call for abstention by states as well. The right to strike, for example, requires states to refrain from interfering.[38] Moreover, it is important to emphasize that economic, social, and cultural rights generally permit progressive rather than immediate realization. They entail an obligation of conduct (i.e., states must undertake certain steps) rather than an obligation of result (i.e., states must attain a particular outcome). This is reflected, for instance, in Article 2(1) of the ICESCR, which stipulates that:

---

[27] See, for example, ICCPR art 6 and ECHR art 2.   [28] See, for example, ICCPR art 7 and ECHR art 3.
[29] See, for example, ICCPR art 14 and ECHR art 6.   [30] See, for example, ICCPR art 19 and ECHR art 10.
[31] See, for example, ICCPR art 25.
[32] See, for instance, *McCann and Others v the United Kingdom* App no 18984/91 (ECtHR, 27 September 1995) 151–64; *Osman v the United Kingdom* App no 23452/94 (ECtHR, 28 October 1998) 11.
[33] See, for example, ICESCR arts 6–7.   [34] See, for example, ICESCR art 9.   [35] See, for example, ICESCR arts 13–14.
[36] See, for example, ICESCR art 11.
[37] European Social Charter (adopted 3 May 1996, entered into force 1 July 1999) ETS 163.   [38] See ICESCR art 8(1)(d).

Each State Party to the present Covenant *undertakes to take steps*, individually and through international assistance and co-operation, especially economic and technical, *to the maximum of its available resources, with a view to achieving progressively the full realization of the rights recognized* in the present Covenant by all appropriate means, including particularly the adoption of legislative measures.[39]

Second-generation rights allow for their progressive realization for two reasons. First, states – in particular developing countries – may have certain resource constraints, which could hamper the fulfilment of, for example, the right to adequate food. In addition, given the nature of the rights involved, full implementation of these rights may take time.[40] Yet, states cannot delay action indefinitely. Article 2(1) of the ICESCR makes clear that states have an obligation to take legislative and other measures to ensure the enjoyment of the rights articulated in the Covenant 'within a reasonably short time'.[41] Moreover, economic, social, and cultural rights do impose some obligations on states that are of immediate effect. Article 2(2) of the ICESCR, for example, stipulates that states guarantee that these rights 'will be exercised without discrimination'.[42]

c   *Collective Rights*

In addition to civil and political rights, and economic, social, and cultural rights, collective rights have emerged. This category is often referred to as the third-generation of human rights. Collective rights generally belong to certain groups that are considered to be vulnerable and in need of special protection. The most prominent example of a collective right is the right to self-determination of peoples,[43] which was already expounded in Chapter 3. Other examples include land rights for Indigenous peoples,[44] the right to a healthy environment,[45] and the somewhat intangible right to development.[46] It is important to bear in mind that collective rights belong to a group collectively and, in principle, cannot be claimed by individual members of that group but only by (representatives of) the group as a whole. Minority rights, strictly speaking, do not involve collective rights, as they are generally articulated as entitlements for individuals who are part of a group.[47] Conversely, some human rights that are essentially collective in nature are sometimes invoked as individual rights in practice. For example, individuals have invoked the right to a healthy environment on the basis of, among others, the right to life.[48] This is what happened in the *Urgenda* case, where the Dutch Supreme Court upheld the decision that the

---

[39] Emphasis added.
[40] See UN Committee on Economic, Social and Cultural Rights 'General Comment No 3: The Nature of States Parties' Obligations (Art. 2, Para. 1, of the Covenant)' (1990) UN Doc E/1991/23.
[41] ibid, para 2.   [42] ibid, para 1.   [43] ICCPR art 1(1) and ICESCR art 1(1).
[44] On the issue of land rights, see Jérémie Gilbert, *Indigenous Peoples' Land Rights Under International Law: From Victims to Actors* (2nd edn, Brill/Nijhoff 2016).
[45] See Chapter 16.   [46] Declaration on the Right to Development (adopted 4 December 1986) UNGA Res 41/128.
[47] See, for example, ICCPR art 27.
[48] See Malgosia Fitzmaurice and Jill Marshall, 'The Human Right to a Clean Environment–Phantom or Reality? The European Court of Human Rights and English Courts Perspective on Balancing Rights in Environmental Cases' (2007) 76 Nordic Journal of International Law 103.

state should reduce its greenhouse gas emissions in line with its human rights obligations under the ECHR.[49]

4   Scope of Human Rights Norms

Having explained the three categories or generations of human rights as they are enshrined in various treaties and conventions, it is important to consider certain matters concerning the scope of human rights norms. Who are bound by these norms? When and where are individuals protected by human rights norms? Must all human rights be respected under all circumstances? These issues will be explained in this section.

a   Addressees of Human Rights Norms

As human rights norms initially emerged in order to protect the individual against the (arbitrary) exercise of public authority by the state, human rights are traditionally addressed to sovereign states. This is reflected in the language of human rights treaties, as they expressly impose obligations on states parties. Article 2(1) of the ICCPR, for instance, refers to the obligations of '[e]ach State Party to the present Covenant'. Likewise, Article 1 of the ECHR refers to '[t]he High Contracting Parties'. Yet, states are not the only actors on the international plane that can affect the human rights of individuals. It is therefore relevant to ask whether other subjects of international law may also hold human right obligations.[50]

International organizations, for instance, increasingly affect human rights in a manner similar to states. A pertinent example concerns the decisions of the UN Security Council to list suspected terrorists and terrorist groups and to freeze their financial assets, which raises issues concerning the right to a fair trial.[51] Another example concerns the failure of UN authorized troops to carry out the necessary de-mining activities in Kosovo after the 1999 North Atlantic Treaty Organization (NATO) airstrikes. Following the detonation of a cluster bomb that was left after the bombings, a boy was killed and his younger brother seriously injured.[52] The International Court of Justice (ICJ) has indeed recognized that as subjects of international law, international organizations 'are bound by any obligations incumbent upon them under general rules of international law', and hence human rights that are part of *customary* international law.[53] However, international organizations generally are not party to human rights *treaties* and are thus technically not bound by these treaty norms. An exceptional case in this respect concerns the European Union (EU), which is

---

[49] HR 20 December 2019 (*The State of the Netherlands v Urgenda Foundation*) ECLI:NL:HR:2019:2007 (Supreme Court of the Netherlands).
[50] See Andrew Clapham, *Human Rights Obligations of Non-State Actors* (Oxford University Press 2006).
[51] See, for instance, UNSC Res 1373 (28 September 2001). See also UNSC Res 1989 (17 June 2011).
[52] See *Behrami and Behrami v France and Saramati v France, Germany and Norway* App nos 71412/01 and 78166/01 (ECtHR, 2 May 2007).
[53] *Interpretation of the Agreement of 25 March 1951 between the WTO and Egypt* (Advisory Opinion) [1980] ICJ Rep 73, para 37.

expected to accede to the ECHR *as per* Article 6 of the Treaty on the EU.[54] With respect to the UN, however, no such developments are taking place so far.

In addition to international organizations, multinational corporations (MNCs) are capable of affecting the human rights of individuals and groups alike. As was already noted in Chapter 3, MNCs may be engaged in child labour or use materials produced by forced labour. Their business activities may also cause environmental damage, which may impact people's health or their means of subsistence. For example, the pollution caused by the oil industry in the Niger Delta affected the food supply and livelihood of the Ogoni population inhabiting the region. While various instruments stipulating the responsibility of multinational corporations with respect to human rights have been adopted in the context of the UN and beyond, no legally binding obligations under international law exist to date.[55] As a result, corporations are governed only by domestic laws, private contracts and self-imposed codes of conduct.

b   *Territorial Scope of Human Rights Norms*

Human rights treaties govern the conduct of the state in relation to individuals on its territory, and also subject to its jurisdiction, which can extend beyond the state's territory in exceptional circumstances.[56] The scope of application of the ECHR is set out in Article 1, which provides that states parties 'shall secure to everyone within their jurisdiction the rights and freedoms defined in [the] Convention'. In a similar vein, Article 2(1) of the ICCPR stipulates that states parties must respect and ensure 'to all individuals within its territory and subject to its jurisdiction the rights recognized in the ... Covenant'. These jurisdictional clauses mean that these treaties apply to every individual on the territory of a state party, irrespective of their nationality and status. Nationals of the state, as well as stateless people, asylum seekers, migrant workers and other persons present on the territory of a state party may invoke the rights enshrined in the treaty concerned.[57] The references to individuals subject to the jurisdiction of a state party also imply that the application of these treaties is not necessarily limited to those present on the territory of a state party, for states sometimes exercise jurisdiction on foreign soil as well. As the drafters of human rights treaties 'did not intend to allow States to escape from their obligations when they exercise jurisdiction outside their national territory',[58] international courts and human rights bodies[59] have generally recognized that human rights treaties may, in exceptional circumstances, apply extraterritorially.[60]

---

[54] See, for instance, Vasiliki Kosta, Nikos Skoutaris, and Vassilis P Tzevelekos (eds), *The EU Accession to the ECHR* (Hart 2014). In late 2014; however, the European Court of Justice identified problems regarding the Draft Accession Agreement of the EU to the ECHR and gave a negative opinion. See Case C-2/13 *Opinion 2/13 of the Court (Full Court)* (18 December 2014) ECLI:EU:C:2014:2454.

[55] See Section 2(e) of Chapter 3.   [56] On the jurisdiction of states, see Chapter 6.

[57] See, for instance, UN Human Rights Committee, 'General Comment No 31: The Nature of the General Legal Obligation Imposed on States Parties to the Covenant' (2004) UN Doc CCPR/C/21/Rev.1/Add.13, para 10.

[58] *Legal Consequences of the Construction of a Wall in the Occupied Palestinian Territory* (Advisory Opinion) [2004] ICJ Rep 136, para 109.

[59] These bodies and their role in the monitoring and enforcement of human rights law will be discussed in Section 5.

[60] On this issue, see Marko Milanovic, *Extraterritorial Application of Human Rights Treaties: Law, Principles, and Policy* (Oxford University Press 2011).

An extraterritorial exercise of jurisdiction occurs, for example, when the state exercises 'effective control' over (part of) a foreign territory. Scholars have described such an extraterritorial exercise of jurisdiction as having a 'spatial' character because it is based on control over territory (i.e. spatial model of jurisdiction).[61] States most obviously exercise effective control in situations of foreign occupation. In its advisory opinion on *The Legality of the Construction of a Wall in the Occupied Palestinian Territory*, for instance, the ICJ concluded that various human rights instruments applied to Israel's conduct in the Occupied Palestinian Territory.[62] The ICJ has also endorsed the criterion of 'effective control' over foreign territory beyond the context of foreign occupation. In the *Case concerning Armed Activities on the Territory of the Congo (Democratic Republic of the Congo v. Uganda)*, it held Uganda responsible for human rights violations committed by its military forces and rebel groups in the Democratic Republic of Congo.[63] On the regional level, the European Court of Human Rights (ECtHR)[64] has adopted a similar approach to the extraterritorial application of the rights protected under the ECHR.[65]

States may; however, still be bound by their human rights treaty obligations when they are involved in (military) operations abroad that do not meet the threshold of 'effective control' over (part of) a territory. Examples of situations that fall short of territorial control could include the airstrikes against Islamic State (ISIL) in Syria executed by a coalition of states, drone attacks by the United States on Pakistani soil, and surveillance activities by Dutch troops contributing to the UN peacekeeping mission in Mali (MINUSMA). Some human rights courts and bodies have acknowledged the extraterritorial application of human rights treaties in situations where a state exercises authority or control over an *individual* rather than (part of) a *territory*. Scholars have described such an extraterritorial exercise of foreign jurisdiction as having a personal character because it is based on control over a person (i.e., personal model of territorial jurisdiction).[66] It is the position of the UN Human Rights Committee, which monitors compliance with the ICCPR,[67] that 'a State Party must respect and ensure the rights laid down in the Covenant to anyone within the power or effective control of that State Party, even if not situated within the territory of that State Party'.[68] This may include situations in which state agents abroad use deadly force or take an individual into custody. In the case of *Lopez Burgos v Uruguay*, for instance, the Committee concluded that Uruguay violated its obligations under the ICCPR as its security forces kidnapped a Uruguayan national on Argentinian soil and held him in *incommunicado* detention there.[69] On a number of occasions, the European Court of Human Rights has likewise recognized the extraterritorial application of the ECHR 'whenever the State

---

[61] ibid.   [62] *Legality of the Construction of a Wall in the Occupied Palestinian Territory* advisory opinion (n 58), paras 109–13.
[63] *Case concerning Armed Activities on the Territory of the Congo (Democratic Republic of the Congo v Uganda)* (Judgment) [2005] ICJ Rep 168, paras 179, 216–17.
[64] For an explanation of the role of the ECtHR in monitoring and enforcing human rights, see Section 5(c)(i).
[65] The landmark case in this respect is *Loizidou v Turkey* (preliminary objections) App no 15318/89 (ECtHR, 23 March 1995), para 62. On effective control over foreign territory beyond the context of foreign occupation, see, for instance, *Bankovic and Others v Belgium and Others* App no 52207/99 (ECtHR, 12 December 2001), para 80.
[66] See Milanovic (n 60).   [67] For a more elaborate discussion of the UN Human Rights Committee, see Section 5(b).
[68] UN Human Rights Committee, 'General Comment No 31' (n 57), para 10.
[69] *Sergio Ruben Lopez Burgos v Uruguay* (1981) Comm no R.12/52, UN Doc Supp no 40 (A/36/40) 176, para 12.3.

through its agents exercises control and authority over an individual, and thus jurisdiction'.[70] It should be noted, however, that the Court's case law is not entirely consistent in applying this principle to similar factual situations.

c   *Restrictions to Human Rights*

Some human rights are considered to be so fundamental that they must be respected at all times, such as the prohibition on torture and inhuman or degrading treatment. These rights are generally referred to as absolute rights[71] and may not be balanced with other rights or interests, not even in the context of what is often referred to as the 'War on Terror'. Even when torture might lead to information that could be crucial for preventing a terrorist attack – often called the 'ticking bomb-scenario' – it would still be unlawful. Most human rights, however, are not absolute and may be restricted under certain circumstances. This system of restrictions will be explained in this section.

i   *Derogation in Time of Public Emergency*

Human rights treaties may allow states to temporarily suspend some of their human rights obligations in a situation of public emergency. This is referred to as derogation and is permitted under, for instance, Article 4(1) of the ICCPR and Article 15(1) of the ECHR. Over the past few years, various states have attempted to derogate from their human rights obligations for a certain period of time. Ukraine, for instance, announced in June 2015 that it would take measures derogating from the right to liberty and security, the right to a fair trial, the right to respect for private and family life, and the right to an effective remedy under both the ECHR[72] and the ICCPR[73] in relation to the conflict in Eastern Ukraine. Later that year, France proclaimed a state of emergency following the terrorist attacks in Paris and announced that some of the emergency measures could involve derogation from its obligations under the ECHR.[74] France ended the state of emergency on 1 November 2017.

For states to derogate lawfully from their human rights obligations, various procedural as well as substantive requirements have to be met. These requirements are stipulated in the derogation clauses of the treaty at hand and may vary from treaty to treaty.[75] In general; however, human rights treaties condition a valid derogation on the existence of a public emergency that threatens the life of the nation. This is a high threshold, as it implies that 'not every disturbance or catastrophe' will qualify as such.[76] According to the ECtHR, it must concern 'an exceptional situation of crisis or emergency which . . . constitutes a threat to the

---

[70] *Al-Skeini and Others v United Kingdom* App no 55721/07 (ECtHR, 7 July 2011), para 137.
[71] Absolute rights generally qualify as *jus cogens* norms, but *jus cogens* norms are not limited to human rights.
[72] ECHR arts 5, 6, 8, 13.   [73] ICCPR arts 2(3), 9, 12, 14, 17.
[74] Remarkably, France did not specify which specific provisions it would potentially derogate from.
[75] For derogation under the ICCPR, see UN Human Rights Committee, 'General Comment No. 29: Article 4: Derogations during a State of Emergency' 2001 UN Doc CCPR/C/21/Rev.1/Add.11; 'The Siracusa Principles on the Limitation and Derogation Provisions in the ICCPR' (1985) 7 Human Rights Quarterly 3; Richard B Lillich, 'The Paris Minimum Standards of Human Rights Norms in a State of Emergency' (1985) 79 American Journal of International Law 1072.
[76] UN Human Rights Committee, 'General Comment No 29 – Article 4' (n 75), para 3.

organized life of the community of which the state is composed'.[77] The ECtHR found that such a threat was posed by, for example, the serious risk of terrorist attacks committed by Al-Qaida in the United Kingdom immediately after 9/11 and the attempted military coup in Turkey in July 2016.[78]

When states take certain measures derogating from their human rights obligations, various substantive requirements must be met as well. First, the measures concerned must be 'strictly required by the exigencies of the situation'. This requirement encapsulates the principles of necessity and proportionality. It considers, among other things, the nature, duration, and impact of the measures taken, in light of the facts concerning the state of emergency.[79] This may be illustrated by the case of *Aksoy v Turkey*, in which the ECtHR was not convinced that the *incommunicado* detention of an individual who was suspected of aiding and abetting the PKK and being a member of the organization was strictly necessary for 'the fight against terrorism in South East Turkey'. Moreover, it concluded that the 'exceptionally long' period of the unsupervised detention was disproportionate, as it rendered the individual vulnerable to torture.[80] Other factors may be taken into account as well. In the case of *A. and Others v United Kingdom*, for instance, the ECtHR found British derogation measures to have been disproportionate, as they authorized preventative detention of suspected terrorists of non-British nationality only, thereby unjustifiably discriminating between nationals and non-nationals.[81]

A second substantive requirement reflected in most derogation clauses is that the measures taken may not be inconsistent with the state's other obligations under international law, including customary international law. In particular, states may never derogate in a manner that would violate a *jus cogens* norm. In addition, in the event of a public emergency that qualifies as an armed conflict, rules of international humanitarian law[82] are simultaneously applicable (see Chapter 12).[83] Third, derogation measures taken by states may never affect non-derogable rights. Derogation clauses typically list certain fundamental rights and freedoms that are protected from derogation, such as the right to life, the prohibition on torture, and the prohibition on slavery.[84] The Human Rights Committee has also listed additional provisions that may not be derogated from under the ICCPR, as it considers these rights to be connected to the non-derogable rights listed in Article 4(2) of the Convention. An example is the right to the humane treatment of detainees, which is closely related to the prohibition of torture and cruel, inhuman, or degrading treatment.[85] Finally, derogation clauses generally entail an international notification requirement: states must immediately inform the treaty depositary of the derogation measures taken and the reasons therefore.[86]

---

[77] *Lawless v Ireland (no 3)* App no 332/57 (ECtHR, 1 July 1961), para 28.
[78] See, for instance, *A. and Others v the United Kingdom* App no 3455/05 (ECtHR, 19 February 2009), paras 177–81; *Mehmet Hasan Altan v Turkey* App no 13237/17 (ECtHR, 20 March 2018), paras 88–94.
[79] See UN Human Rights Committee, 'General Comment No. 29 – Article 4' (n 75), para 4.
[80] *Aksoy v Turkey* App no 21987/93 (ECtHR, 18 December 1996), para 78.   [81] *A and Others v UK* (n 78), paras 182–90.
[82] On the law of armed conflict, see Chapter 12.
[83] See UN Human Rights Committee, 'General Comment No. 29 – Article 4' (n 75), paras 9–10.
[84] See, for example, ICCPR art 4(2) and ECHR art 15(2).
[85] UN Human Rights Committee, 'General Comment No. 29 – Article 4' (n 75), paras 8–16.
[86] See, for example, ICCPR art 4(3) and ECHR art 15(3).

ii   Other Restrictions

Many human rights provisions also contain so-called limitation clauses, permitting states to restrict those rights under certain conditions that are unrelated to situations of public emergency. Even the right to life is not absolute and may be limited in particular circumstances. Article 2(1) of the ECHR, for instance, indicates among other things that 'no one shall be deprived of his life intentionally save in the execution of a sentence of a court following his conviction of a crime for which this penalty is provided by law'. In a similar vein, Article 5(1) of the ECHR specifies that the right to liberty is not infringed by, among other things, 'the lawful detention of a person after conviction by a competent court'.

Most limitation clauses, however, are phrased in more general terms. Examples can be found with respect to the right to private and family life (Article 8 ECHR), the freedom of thought, conscience, and religion (Article 9 ECHR and Article 18 ICCPR), the freedom of expression (Article 10 ECHR and Article 19 ICCPR), and the freedom of assembly (Article 11 ECHR and Articles 21–2 ICCPR). General limitation clauses typically stipulate three cumulative conditions for lawfully restricting the rights concerned. First, restrictions must be prescribed by law or in accordance with the law. This condition stems from the principle of legality and prevents the state, for example, from prohibiting a protest march in the absence of a legal basis in domestic law. Legal bases for restrictions must be sufficiently clear and accessible, in order to be foreseeable for individuals.[87] The second condition is that restrictions must serve one of the legitimate aims that are listed in the limitation clause at hand. Legitimate aims may include, for instance, national security, public safety, public order, the prevention of disorder or crime, the protection of health or morals, and the protection of the rights and freedoms of others. General limitation clauses may, thus allow the state, in principle, to prohibit the operation or existence of a fascist party for the purpose of protecting public order, or to limit the freedom of expression of one individual in order to protect the right to privacy of another individual.[88] However, as a third condition, general limitation clauses also typically require restrictions to be 'necessary in a democratic society'. This condition generally requires that the restriction responds to a pressing social or public need, and is proportionate to the legitimate aim pursued.[89] As this threshold is more difficult to meet than the previous two, this final condition is often decisive in determining whether a particular restriction is lawful under international human rights law.

5   Monitoring and Enforcement of Human Rights

Having explained the categories and matters concerning the scope of human rights, the question arises of how to supervise the observance of these norms and how to address

---

[87] See, for example, *Sunday Times v The United Kingdom (no 1)* App no 6538/74, (ECtHR, 26 April 1979), paras 47–9.

[88] The ECtHR generally accepts the existence of a legitimate aim quite easily. See, for instance, *Leyla Sahin v Turkey* App no 44774/98 (ECtHR, 10 November 2005), para 99. For a more elaborate assessment, see *Vintman v Ukraine* App no 28403/05 (ECtHR, 23 October 2014), paras 94–9.

[89] See, for instance, *Sunday Times v The United Kingdom* (n 87), para 59.

alleged violations of human rights. For this purpose, states have devised monitoring and enforcement systems. At the UN, a distinction can be made between so-called Charter-based mechanisms that find their basis in the UN Charter and treaty-based mechanisms that are created by specific human rights treaties. Both categories are discussed in Sections 5(a) and (b) respectively, after which the main regional systems for the protection of human rights will be addressed.

a   *Charter-Based Mechanisms*

The Charter-based mechanisms include various institutions. The Office of the High Commissioner for Human Rights is endowed with the primary responsibility for the promotion and protection of human rights. The tasks of the high commissioner for human rights include providing states with technical assistance in the field of human rights, strengthening international cooperation, and improving the ratification and implementation of human rights treaties.[90]

Another prominent institution is the Human Rights Commission, which was established by the Economic and Social Council in 1946 on the basis of Article 68 of the UN Charter, but no longer exists today. The Commission played an important part in the development of human rights instruments, including the UDHR and the 1966 Human Rights Covenants. From the 1960s onwards, the Commission dealt with human rights violations. It developed so-called 'special procedures' to monitor compliance with and investigate alleged violations of human rights. However, as the Human Rights Commission was composed of state representatives rather than independent experts, it was highly politicized and rather weak. Members with a questionable human rights track record themselves, such as China and Zimbabwe, were able to block decisions concerning their own behaviour or that of their allies, while Israel was a consistent target of the Commission. States; therefore, decided to replace the Commission with the Human Rights Council (HRC). One may wonder; however, whether this HRC is actually less politicized and more effective than its predecessor.

The HRC was established in 2006 as a subsidiary body of the General Assembly and is composed of forty-seven representatives of states who are divided regionally and elected by secret ballot by an absolute majority of the General Assembly.[91] All states are eligible for election, including states with a problematic human rights track record themselves, such as Saudi Arabia, the Philippines, and the Democratic Republic of the Congo (DRC) – all of which have been represented. An important difference with its predecessor is that the General Assembly can suspend membership of the Council in the case of gross human rights violations. This; however, has only happened once, when Libya's membership was suspended in 2011 in view of the human rights violations committed by the regime of Colonel Kaddafi.[92] Recent calls to suspend the membership of Saudi Arabia in view of the serious human rights violations committed both at home and in Yemen have been to no avail.

---

[90] UNGA Res 48/141 (7 January 1993).   [91] UNGA Res 60/251 (3 April 2006).   [92] UNGA Res 65/265 (1 March 2011).

Whereas the Commission only met once a year, the HRC meets three times annually and has scheduled special sessions to examine urgent issues. The Council retained the system of 'special procedures' already existing under the commission and it has appointed special rapporteurs and established Working Groups, Commissions of Inquiry, and Independent Fact-Finding Missions to examine thematic or country-specific human rights issues and make recommendations in that respect. In March 2017, for instance, the Council established an Independent International Fact-Finding Mission on Myanmar to establish the facts and circumstances concerning the human rights violations allegedly committed by military and security forces there, in particular with respect to the Rohingya minority population in Rakhine State.[93]

A novel mechanism that was established with the creation of the HRC is the Universal Periodic Review. Under this procedure, the human rights compliance of all 193 UN member states is assessed every four years.[94] The Council's evaluation is not only based on the human rights norms enshrined in the human rights treaties to which the state concerned is party, but also the UN Charter, the UDHR, voluntary commitments by the state, and applicable international humanitarian law. As with most international monitoring bodies; however, the Council's outcome reports are non-binding.

In addition to these institutions and mechanisms, other UN bodies also contribute to the protection of human rights. Although the UN Charter does not explicitly grant the Security Council special competences in this respect, it does play a role in practice. First, under Chapter VI of the UN Charter (Articles 33–8), the Security Council may investigate disputes when their continuance is likely to endanger the maintenance of international peace and security, and recommend appropriate measures of adjustment. Human rights violations in a particular state can influence international peace and security, as they may give rise to major refugee flows, instigate disturbances in neighbouring states and potentially lead to the destabilization of an entire region. An example of collective action under Chapter VI of the UN Charter is the UN Observer Mission in El Salvador (ONUSAL) in 1990, which was established by the Security Council and tasked with monitoring the human rights situation in El Salvador, investigating specific cases, and making recommendations to eliminate human rights violations in the country.[95] Second, under Chapter VII of the UN Charter (Articles 39–50), the Security Council may determine the existence of a threat to the peace, breach of the peace, or act of aggression.[96] Upon such a determination, the Security Council may call on member states to apply sanctions, including boycotts and embargoes,[97] or to take military action to restore international peace and security.[98] In response to the gross human rights violations committed in Libya, for instance, the Security Council first adopted Resolution 1970 (2011), which imposed an arms embargo, travel ban, and asset freeze, and referred the situation in Libya to the ICC.[99] One month later, the Security Council adopted Resolution 1973 (2011) authorizing military intervention in Libya 'to protect civilians and civilian populated areas under

---

[93] UNHRC Res 34/22 (3 April 2017).   [94] UNHRC Res 5/1 (7 August 2007).   [95] UNSC Res 693 (20 May 1991).
[96] UN Charter art 39.   [97] UN Charter art 41.   [98] UN Charter art 42.   [99] UNSC Res 1970 (26 February 2011).

threat of attack'.[100] Because the Security Council is a political body, it has however acted inconsistently in responding to human rights violations. With respect to the ongoing crisis in Syria, for instance, no such action has been taken to date, primarily due to vetoes cast by the Russian Federation and China.

b   Treaty-Based Mechanisms

Alongside these UN Charter-based institutions and mechanisms, human rights treaties also create mechanisms to monitor and enforce compliance with human rights. For each of the international human rights treaties a committee has been established that plays a central role in that respect. These committees (or treaty bodies) are composed of independent experts who typically serve for a term of four years in their personal capacity rather than as state representatives. The most well-known committee is the Human Rights Committee, which monitors the implementation of the ICCPR.[101] Which specific tools are at the disposal of each committee depends on the treaty to which they are attached. The procedures most common to the various international human rights treaties are periodic reporting, individual complaints, inter-state complaints, and inquiry. These four procedures are briefly explained in this sub-section.

Almost all of the core international human rights treaties – with the exception of the 1948 Genocide Convention – include a periodic reporting procedure, obliging states parties to submit reports on their compliance under the treaty every four years. As several provisions in the human rights treaties overlap, so do the accompanying reporting obligations for states. Examples of such reporting obligations can be found in Article 40 of the ICCPR and Article 16(1) of the ICESCR. The relevant committee reviews the reports submitted as well as information submitted by other sources, such as non-governmental organizations (NGOs) and national human rights institutions. Although the concluding observations issued by the committee on the basis of its review are not legally binding, they are authoritative and represent a form of sanctioning by 'naming and shaming'.

Several human rights treaties also provide for an individual complaints procedure that allows individuals to file a complaint against a state party before the relevant Committee. This procedure; however, is optional under the international human rights treaties. Individuals may only file such a complaint when the state concerned has accepted the competence of the committee in this respect, either by issuing a declaration[102] or by becoming party to an optional protocol.[103] Another important condition for the individual complaints procedure concerns the so-called 'local remedies rule'.[104] It can be found in most human rights treaties and requires the individual to exhaust all domestic remedies in

---

[100] UNSC Res 1973 (17 March 2011), para 4 (implicitly referring to the Responsibility to Protect).
[101] For an overview of the various committees, see OHCHR.org, 'Human Rights Bodies' <www.ohchr.org/en/hrbodies/Pages/ HumanRightsBodies.aspx>.
[102] See, for instance, CAT art 22.
[103] See, for instance, Optional Protocol to the ICCPR (adopted 16 December 1966, entered into force 23 March 1976) 999 UNTS 171 (Optional Protocol ICCPR) art 1.
[104] See, for instance, Optional Protocol ICCPR art 5; ECHR art 35(1).

the (allegedly) violating state first, before bringing a complaint before the relevant treaty body. The rationale of this rule is to afford national authorities the opportunity to prevent or redress the alleged violations, as it is principally for sovereign states themselves to guarantee that human rights are respected in their territories. In addition, the 'local remedies rule' also makes the procedure more efficient. Although the individual complaints procedure is available under various international human rights treaties, including both the ICCPR[105] and ICESCR,[106] it is most frequently used on the regional level. Regional systems for the protection of human rights, in particular that of the ECtHR, will be elaborated upon in Section 5(c).

The inter-state complaints procedure allows states parties to a human rights treaty to file complaints against one another regarding their alleged human rights violations. Although this procedure is enshrined in a number of human rights treaties, including in Article 41 of the ICCPR and Article 21 of the CAT, it has never actually been used on the international level. Instead, states usually employ diplomatic means or use unilateral (economic) sanctions as a tool to force foreign governments to comply with fundamental human rights norms. In April 2017, for instance, the EU renewed its embargo on providing Myanmar with arms and other equipment that might be used for repression in the country.[107] Moreover, filing a complaint against another state is considered to be an unfriendly act, which may well harm the bilateral relations between the states concerned. To date, examples of inter-state complaints may only be found on the regional level and typically involve states that already have a rather troubled relationship, such as in the case of *Cyprus v Turkey*[108] and that of *Ireland v United Kingdom*.[109]

Finally, the inquiry procedure allows committees to initiate an investigation when it has received reliable information concerning serious, grave, or systematic human rights violations in a state party. This mechanism is somewhat different in nature compared to the ones already mentioned, in that it allows the treaty body to act on its own initiative rather than reacting to a prior report or complaint. Only a few committees, however, have the competence to initiate an inquiry. Examples are the Committee against Torture (Article 20 CAT), the CEDAW (Article 8 of the Optional Protocol to CEDAW), and the Committee on Economic, Social and Cultural Rights (Article 11 of the Optional Protocol to ICESCR). The reports reflecting the outcomes of an inquiry are not legally binding and generally not made public either, save in exceptional situations.

c   *Regional Systems*

Besides the monitoring and enforcement mechanisms provided for with respect to the international human rights obligations of states, regional systems for the protection of

---

[105] Optional Protocol ICCPR arts 1–2.
[106] See Optional Protocol to the ICESCR (adopted 10 December 2008, entered into force 5 May 2013) GAOR 63rd Session Supp 49.
[107] Council Decision (CFSP) 2017/734 of 25 April 2017 amending Decision 2013/184/CFSP concerning restrictive measures against Myanmar/Burma [2017] OJ L108/35.
[108] *Cyprus v Turkey* App no 25781/94 (ECtHR, 10 May 2001).
[109] *Ireland v United Kingdom* App no 5310/71 (ECtHR, 18 January 1978).

human rights have been created. This section will discuss the most well-developed systems, which are those of Europe, the Americas, and Africa.

i   *Europe*

On the European level, the Council of Europe plays a prominent role in the protection of human rights. This organization was founded in 1949 at the original initiative of Sir Winston Churchill with a view to promoting and protecting the rule of law, democracy, and human rights. Numerous treaties have been concluded in the context of the Council of Europe, the most important being the ECHR. This treaty was drafted in tandem with the development of the non-binding UDHR. Yet, with the horrors of the Second World War still fresh, European states sensed the need to make legally binding arrangements for the protection of human rights. In Europe, the ECHR was consequently adopted in 1950, while it was not until 1966 that such a treaty was concluded within the framework of the UN. Initially, the Council of Europe only had thirteen member states, but following the fall of the Berlin Wall many new states acceded to the organization. Today, the Council counts forty-seven member states. These states are all parties to the ECHR, which makes the Convention applicable to more than 800 million individuals. The ECHR protects predominantly civil and political rights, such as the prohibition of torture, the right to a fair trial, the freedom of expression, and the freedom of assembly and association.[110] As such, the Convention protects individuals against interference with these rights by the state. The ECtHR, seated in Strasbourg (France), was established to adjudicate compliance with these rights.[111] It is authorized to deal with inter-state as well as individual complaints.[112] In contrast to the international human rights treaty bodies, this Court issues legally binding judgments. Member states are; therefore, obliged to execute the decisions of the Court, which is monitored by the Committee of Ministers.[113]

Although inter-state cases are sporadic and have only been filed on the regional level, over the past decade, various inter-state complaints against the Russian Federation have been brought before the Court. In 2008, Georgia initiated a case against the Russian Federation claiming that the arrest, detention, and expulsion of Georgian nationals from Russian territory violated Russia's obligations under the ECHR.[114] A second inter-state complaint lodged by Georgia concerned alleged human rights violations committed by the Russian Federation during the 2008 armed conflict in South Ossetia and Abkhazia.[115] Since 2014, Ukraine has also filed various complaints against the Russian Federation. These complaints concern the Russian intervention on the Crimean Peninsula as well as its involvement in the conflict in Eastern Ukraine and alleged human rights violations in that context.[116] In one of these cases, the Court issued an interim measure indicating that the

---

[110] See ECHR arts 2–14.   [111] ECHR art 19.   [112] ECHR arts 34–5.   [113] ECHR art 46.
[114] *Georgia v Russia (I)* App no 1325/07 (ECtHR, 3 July 2014).
[115] *Georgia v Russia (II)* App no 38263/08 (ECtHR, 29 January 2021).
[116] *Ukraine v Russia (I)* App no 20958/14 (ECtHR, 14 January 2021); *Ukraine v Russia (II)* App no 43800/14 (still pending).

Russian government 'should refrain from measures which might threaten the life and health of the civilian population on the territory of Ukraine'.[117]

The individual complaints procedure is provided for in Article 34 of the ECHR and not only grants individuals, but also NGOs or groups of individuals that claim to be victims of a violation of the Convention by one of the states parties the right to file a complaint. Yet, various criteria have to be met before the Court can deal with such complaint. These admissibility criteria are enshrined in Article 35 and include – perhaps most importantly – the 'local remedies rule': the Court may only deal with a case after all domestic remedies have been exhausted.[118]

Additional requirements are that the complaint has been launched within six months after the final decision was taken on the domestic level,[119] and that the complaint is not 'substantially the same as a matter that has already been examined by the Court or has already been submitted to another procedure of international investigation or settlement'.[120] The latter requirement means that an individual cannot lodge a complaint before the Court and an international human rights treaty body simultaneously.

The individual complaints procedure is much more frequently used than the inter-state procedure. As a consequence of an annually increasing number of individual applications, 62,000 cases were still pending by the end of 2020, while the Court had received more than 41,000 new applications over the year.[121] In view of the caseload, the Court has sought to increase its efficiency through various means, for instance by adopting Protocol No. 14 in 2004.[122] This Protocol included a new admissibility criterion that is incorporated in Article 35 of the Convention and provides that cases can be declared inadmissible by the Court when the applicant has not suffered a significant disadvantage.

Alongside the Council of Europe, the EU plays a part in the regional protection of human rights as well. In 2000, the EU proclaimed the Charter of Fundamental Rights of the EU.[123] Initially, it remained without legally binding effect. The entry into force of the Treaty of Lisbon in 2009;[124] however, gave the Charter a legally binding effect. It contains fifty rights, many of which had already been recognized in the jurisprudence of the Court of Justice of the European Union (CJEU) and are also included in the ECHR. Compared with the ECHR; however, the Charter also entrenches economic and social rights in addition to civil and political rights. Moreover, the scope of application of the Charter is fundamentally different from the ECHR, as the Charter is primarily addressed to EU institutions and bodies.[125] This

---

[117] ECtHR Press Release, 'Interim Measure Granted in Inter-state Case Brought by Ukraine against Russia' (13 March 2014) ECHR 073 (2014).
[118] ECHR art 35(1).   [119] ECHR art 35(1).   [120] ECHR art 35(2)(b).
[121] See Council of Europe, *European Court of Human Rights: Statistics 2020 (compared to the same period 2019)* <www .echr.coe.int/Documents/Stats_annual_2020_ENG.pdf>.
[122] Protocol No 14 to the Convention for the Protection of Human Rights and Fundamental Freedoms, amending the control system of the Convention (adopted 13 May 2004, entered into force 1 June 2010) CETS 194.
[123] Charter of Fundamental Rights of the EU (adopted 18 December 2000, entered into force 1 December 2009) OJ C303/01 (Charter of Fundamental Rights).
[124] Treaty of Lisbon amending the Treaty on EU and the Treaty establishing the European Community (adopted 13 December 2007, entered into force 1 December 2009) OJ C306/01 (Treaty on the EU) art 6(1).
[125] Charter of Fundamental Rights art 51(1).

means that the (legislative) work of the European Parliament, the Council of Ministers, and the European Commission must be in conformity with the Charter. The CJEU and the European Commission are tasked with monitoring and enforcing compliance in this respect. It is important to note that the Charter only applies to the authorities of member states when they are implementing EU law, for instance by applying EU regulations or decisions.[126] Beyond the acts concerning the implementation of EU law, domestic constitutional law as well as the ECHR continue to provide for the protection of human rights within EU member states.

ii   The Americas

In the Americas, human rights protection primarily centres around the ACHR Rights,[127] which was adopted by the Organization of American States in 1969 and entered into force in 1979. The Convention has been ratified by most Latin American states – notably, Canada and the United States did not ratify the Convention – and protects civil and political rights as well as economic, social, and cultural rights. The Inter-American Commission of Human Rights and the Inter-American Court of Human Rights ensure compliance with these rights. The Inter-American Commission, for its part, is a quasi-judicial body tasked with promoting and monitoring human rights in the Americas and to that end, it is authorized to receive individual as well as inter-state complaints.[128] The Inter-American Court has a dual function, which is to deal with contentious cases on the one hand, and to issue advisory opinions on the other.[129] But only the Inter-American Commission and member states are entitled to bring cases before the Inter-American Court or request an advisory opinion.[130] In contrast to the European system of human rights protection, individuals may not lodge a complaint directly with the Inter-American Court. Instead, the Inter-American Commission functions as the first instance for individuals alleging violations of human rights protected by the Convention. When the Inter-American Commission concludes that the state concerned has indeed violated its obligations under the Convention, it may issue non-binding recommendations for reparation and measures to be taken in order to prevent violations in the future. In the event that the state does not implement these recommendations but has recognized the jurisdiction of the Inter-American Court – and the majority of states parties has done so – the Inter-American Commission may refer the case to the Inter-American Court, which may in turn issue a legally binding judgment. Although relatively few cases have been brought before the Inter-American Court to date,[131] its role in the protection of human rights should not be underestimated, for instance with respect to the rights of Indigenous peoples.[132]

---

[126] Charter of Fundamental Rights art 51(1).   [127] ACHR (n 20).   [128] ACHR arts 41, 44–5.   [129] ACHR art 64.
[130] ACHR art 61.
[131] In 2020, only twenty-three individual complaints were brought before the Court. See Inter-American Court of Human Rights, 'Annual Report 2020' <www.corteidh.or.cr/docs/informe2020/ingles.pdf>.
[132] See, for instance, Yves Haeck, Oswaldo Ruiz-Chiriboga, and Clara Burbano Herrera (eds), *The Inter-American Court of Human Rights: Theory and Practice, Present and Future* (Intersentia 2015).

iii   Africa

On the African continent, a system of human rights protection has been established as well. In 1981, the Organisation of African Unity (OAU, predecessor of the African Union) adopted the ACHPR.[133] This human rights treaty not only protects civil and political rights and economic, social, and cultural rights, but also covers collective rights. Examples are the right of all peoples to self-determination, their right to freely dispose of wealth and resources, and their right to economic, social, and cultural development.[134] Similar to the inter-American system of human rights protection, both a commission and a court play a role in ensuring compliance with the rights provided for in the Charter. The African Commission is a quasi-judicial body mandated with the promotion and protection of human rights in Africa.[135] In this capacity, it may review inter-state complaints[136] as well as complaints from individuals and NGOs alleging that rights enshrined in the Charter have been violated.[137] The inter-state complaints procedure; however, has only been utilized once to date.[138] The African Commission is complemented by the African Court on Human and Peoples' Rights, to which it may refer cases.[139] The African Commission will typically do so when the state concerned fails to implement the commission's non-binding recommendations, but it may also do so when it deems intervention by the African Court on Human and Peoples' Rights necessary, for instance, in cases of massive human rights violations. The Court may also receive complaints directly from states that are party to the protocol to the Charter.[140] Individuals and NGOs; however, only have direct access to the Court when the state against which they are complaining has recognized the jurisdiction of the Court by issuing a declaration in this respect.[141] By 2021, no more than six states had done so.

6   Concluding Remarks

The adoption of the UDHR in 1948 marked the emergence of contemporary international human rights law. Since its adoption, a myriad of human rights instruments and accompanying enforcement mechanisms has been created, both at the international and regional levels, aiming to protect specific rights and freedoms or particular categories of individuals that are considered to be vulnerable. While in theory, the net of protection offered by these systems essentially covers the globe, in practice, international (human rights) law has been insufficiently powerful to prevent and effectively address gross human rights violations on various occasions. The ongoing crisis in Syria is a striking example in this respect, but

---

[133] ACHPR (n 21).   [134] See ACHPR arts 20–4.   [135] ACHPR art 55.   [136] ACHPR arts 48–9.   [137] ACHPR art 55.

[138] *Democratic Republic of Congo v Burundi, Rwanda, Uganda,* African Commission on Human and Peoples' Rights Comm No 227/99 (29 May 2003). In its communication to the Commission, the DRC claimed that the armed forces of Burundi, Rwanda, and Uganda had been occupying its eastern provinces and committing grave and massive violations of human rights and international law there.

[139] Protocol to the ACHPR on the Establishment of an African Court on Human and People's Rights (adopted 10 June 1998, entered into force 25 January 2004) OAU Doc OAU/LEG/AFCHPR/PROT (III) (Protocol to the ACHRP) arts 1–2.

[140] By May 2021, the Protocol had thirty-one states parties.   [141] Protocol to the ACHRP art 34(6).

humanitarian tragedies have unfortunately unfolded in different corners of the world in the decades since these instruments were concluded. Admittedly, the system of international human rights law deserves to be strengthened, in particular on the level of the UN. Although the creation of the HRC along with the Universal Periodic Review is an important step, it remains to be seen whether the Council will actually be more effective and less politicized compared to its predecessor. In contrast, regional systems have proved capable of playing an important role in the protection of human rights. Various factors may explain the success of regional systems, in particular the ECHR. States have appeared more willing to create comprehensive systems in a regional context, as they operate with like-minded states and the system can be better tailored to the particular situation in the region concerned. This has resulted in the establishment of independent, legally binding, and accessible enforcement mechanisms on the regional level, as opposed to the often politicized, non-binding, and more distant mechanisms available on the international plane. As such, regional systems may be seen to provide for the most promising context for the further development and strengthening of international human rights law.

Recommended Reading

Philip Alston (ed), *Non-State Actors and Human Rights* (Oxford University Press 2008).
Pieter van Dijk et al (eds), *Theory and Practice of the European Convention on Human Rights* (5th edn, Intersentia 2018).
Jack Donnelly, *Universal Human Rights in Theory and Practice* (3rd edn, Cornell University Press 2013).
Sarah Joseph and Melissa Castan, *The International Covenant on Civil and Political Rights: Cases, Materials and Commentary* (3rd edn, Oxford University Press 2013).
Paul Gordon Lauren, *The Evolution of International Human Rights: Visions Seen* (3rd edn, University of Pennsylvania Press 2011).
Marko Milanovic, *Extraterritorial Application of Human Rights Treaties: Law, Principles and Policy* (Oxford University Press 2011).
Daniel Moeckli, Sangeeta Shah, and Sandesh Sivakumaran (eds), *International Human Rights Law* (3rd edn, Oxford University Press 2017).

11

Law on the Use of Force

Niels Blokker and Daniëlla Dam-de Jong

1   Introduction

The rules on the use of force in the international legal order are not unlike those in the national legal order. As a rule, within domestic societies, the modern state enjoys a monopoly on the use of force. Only the state may lawfully use or authorize physical force. At the same time, there is one main exception to this state monopoly: individuals are allowed to use force in self-defence under certain circumstances. If we are attacked, no matter whether this is in the streets of Amsterdam, Beijing, Moscow, or New Delhi, we may protect and defend ourselves. In international society, essentially the same fundamental rule and exception apply. The use of force by states, even the threat to use force, is prohibited, unless this is authorized by the United Nations (UN). At the same time, states enjoy an inherent right of self-defence. In spite of this similarity, the way in which these rules on the use of force are implemented and enforced in our international society differs from how this works at the national level. This can be explained by the differences between the centralized national legal order and the decentralized international legal order. There is no world government with a monopoly on the use of force. However, this does not imply that each state can decide for itself whether, where, and when to use force in its international relations. Gone are the days of Carl von Clausewitz, the Prussian general, who some 200 years ago defined war as 'a mere continuation of policy by other means'.[1] At present, in our globalized world, with the existence of weapons of mass destruction, such a view would be a threat to all and a recipe for war. It is in the common interest of all states that the rules governing the use of force are clear and restrictive.

This chapter introduces the *jus ad bellum*: the rules of law determining when states may resort to war or, more broadly, the use of armed force. These rules must be distinguished from the *jus in bello*: these are the rules of law that apply *in* armed conflict (known as international humanitarian law, see Chapter 12). In order to put the current *jus ad bellum* rules into perspective, the chapter begins by introducing the concept of collective security and demonstrating how this was applied during the League of Nations era (Section 2). The following sections set out the relevant rules of the UN Charter on the prevention and

---

[1] Carl von Clausewitz, *On War* (JJ Graham tr; new, rev edn by FN Maude, first published 1832, Kegan Paul, Trench, Trubner & Co 1918), vol 1, ch 1, para 24.

regulation of recourse to the use of force (Section 3), with a particular focus on the prohibition on the threat or use of force (Section 4). Section 5 discusses the collective use of force, meaning the use of force authorized by the Security Council, while Section 6 concentrates on the unilateral use of force in self-defence. Section 7 examines whether new exceptions to the prohibition of the use of force are emerging, in particular humanitarian intervention and the responsibility to protect.

2   Collective Security and the League of Nations

The UN system for the maintenance of international peace and security 'has often been termed a collective security system, since a wronged state was to be protected by all, and a wrongdoer punished by all'.[2] A collective security system is an arrangement providing for peace and security for those states that participate in it. It implies the recognition by the participating states that it is in their common interest to protect themselves against external threats and attacks, and to punish a state that is responsible for such a threat or attack. The implications of establishing an effective collective security system are therefore consider-able. Making it work requires a continuous commitment to world peace. It is; therefore, not surprising that states would only be willing to create a collective security system and to submit themselves to the obligations involved in such a system after experiencing the horrors of war. This moment came after the end of the First World War: a war by accident, with some 20 million victims, the battlefields of Ypes (Belgium) and Verdun (France) and the use of biological and chemical weapons. To prevent this from happening again the League of Nations was established in 1920 by forty-two states.[3]

The concept of collective security was implemented by the Covenant of the League of Nations, which recognized, first, that war was a matter of concern to the whole League, not only to individual states.[4] If a member of the League resorted to war in disregard of its obligations under the Covenant, 'it shall ipso facto be deemed to have committed an act of war against all other members of the League, which hereby undertake immediately to subject it to' a number of specific economic (not military) sanctions.[5] It was for each member state, individually, to decide whether a member of the league had resorted to war (and whether, therefore, it was obliged to impose economic sanctions). The role envisaged for the League itself was rather limited: it could not impose binding enforcement measures but it could *recommend* what military measures should be taken.[6] Second, in case of a dispute between member states, the Covenant stipulated that 'they will submit the matter either to arbitration or judicial settlement or to enquiry by the Council, and they agree in no case to resort to war until three months after the award by the arbitrators or the judicial decision, or the report by the Council'.[7] After this 'waiting period' the Covenant did not

---

[2] Malcolm N Shaw, *International Law* (7th edn, Cambridge University Press 2014) 897–8.
[3] Covenant of the League of Nations (adopted 29 April 1919, entered into force 10 January 1920) [1919] UKTS 4 (Cmd 153).
[4] Covenant of the League of Nations art 11.   [5] Covenant of the League of Nations art 16.
[6] Covenant of the League of Nations art 16.   [7] Covenant of the League of Nations art 12.

forbid recourse to military force to settle the dispute. The Covenant therefore did not contain a comprehensive prohibition on the use of force.

The British lawyer, parliamentarian, and cabinet minister, Robert Cecil, who was involved in the creation of the league and participated in its work, later referred to it as 'a great experiment'.[8] It was the first experiment in maintaining universal peace by implementing the concept of collective security within the framework of an international organization. Since the League, collective security has been 'associated with international organization as ham is with eggs'.[9] However, it is clear that this first experiment failed: the League and its members did little or nothing following the Japanese invasion of Manchuria in 1931, the Italian invasion of Abyssinia in 1935, and the German aggression from the late 1930s onwards. The Second World War started in 1939, less than two decades after the Covenant entered into force.

Overall, the League of Nations system of collective security was a rather decentralized system. It was mostly for the member states themselves to make it work, as only limited powers were attributed to organs of the League. One of the lessons learned from this first 'experiment' was the need to strengthen the system: to lay down stricter obligations for states, together with much stronger powers for the organization that would succeed the League.

3   UN Charter Framework

This part sets out the principal features of the UN Charter framework for collective security. These concern, first, the twin pillars of peaceful dispute settlement and the prohibition of the use of force and, second, the primary responsibility of the Security Council for the maintenance of international peace and security. Lastly, this part examines the role of non-military measures (sanctions) imposed by the Security Council as a means of de-escalating threats to or breaches of the peace.

a   *Obligation to Settle Disputes Peacefully and Prohibition of the Use of Force*

The UN was established with the primary aim 'to save succeeding generations from the scourge of war'.[10] It is therefore unsurprising that the maintenance of international peace and security takes a prominent position in the UN Charter. Having learned from the failures of the League of Nations system, the drafters of the UN Charter gathered in San Francisco between April and June 1945 to devise a centralized system for the maintenance of international peace and security. This system is based on two pillars, which are reflected in Article 1(1) of the UN Charter, namely the peaceful settlement of disputes and effective

---

[8] Robert Cecil, *A Great Experiment: An Autobiography* (Oxford University Press 1941).
[9] Inis L Claude Jr, *Swords into Plowshares: The Problems and Progress of International Organization* (4th edn, Random House 1971) 246.
[10] Charter of the UN (adopted 26 June 1945, entered into force 24 October 1945) 1 UNTS XVI (UN Charter), preambular para 1.

collective (as opposed to unilateral) measures to prevent or remove threats to the peace, breaches of the peace, or acts of aggression.

Pursuant to the first pillar, states are obliged to settle their disputes in a peaceful manner as a matter of conflict prevention. This obligation is set out in Article 2(3) and Chapter VI of the UN Charter, which deals with pacific settlement of disputes.[11] The second pillar involves a prohibition on states using force in their relations, as found in Article 2(4) of the UN Charter. Armed force is to be used only 'in the common interest',[12] when authorized by the Security Council (Article 42 of the UN Charter). There is only one other exception to the prohibition on the use of force. Article 51 of the UN Charter sets out the right of states to act in self-defence when they become the victim of an armed attack. These two exceptions to the prohibition of the use of force are discussed in more detail in Sections 5 and 6 of this chapter.

b   Roles of the Security Council and General Assembly

Pursuant to Article 24(1) of the UN Charter, UN member states have conferred primary responsibility for the maintenance of international peace and security on the Security Council and have agreed that the Council, in carrying out its duties under this responsibility, acts on their behalf. In practice, the five permanent members of the Security Council (China, France, the Russian Federation, the United Kingdom, and the United States) have a decisive influence on the decisions that the Council takes. This is because Article 27(3) of the UN Charter determines that '[d]ecisions of the Security Council ... shall be made by an affirmative vote of nine members including the concurring votes of the permanent members'. This provision effectively creates a veto right for the permanent members.[13]

The Security Council has been given wide-ranging powers to adopt coercive measures, including the use of force, to maintain or restore international peace and security. Pursuant to Article 25 of the UN Charter, UN member states have furthermore agreed to accept and carry out the decisions of the Security Council. In this way, the UN Charter has effectively created an organ with supranational competences that can take decisions on behalf of all UN member states and whose decisions are legally binding upon all of these states. This gives considerable weight to the decisions of the Security Council, which makes it pertinent to understand what constitutes a decision, as opposed to a non-binding recommendation. Unfortunately, the UN Charter does not provide a clear answer to this question. It merely distinguishes between decisions and recommendations adopted by the Security Council.[14] The most relevant example of a provision making this distinction is Article 39, according to which the Security Council 'shall determine the existence of any threat to the peace, breach of the peace, or act of aggression and shall make *recommendations*, or *decide* what measures shall be taken in accordance with Articles 41 and 42, to maintain or restore

---

[11] This pillar is discussed in Chapter 9 of this book.   [12] UN Charter, preamble.

[13] See Chapter 8 on the law of international organizations for a more extensive discussion of the Security Council's structure and working methods.

[14] See, for example, UN Charter arts 36(1), 41.

international peace and security'.[15] In the *Namibia* advisory opinion, the International Court of Justice developed a test to determine whether the Security Council has exercised its powers under Article 25 of the UN Charter to issue binding decisions. According to the Court, this 'is to be determined in each case, having regard to the terms of the resolution to be interpreted, the discussions leading to it, the Charter provisions invoked and, in general, all circumstances that might assist in determining the legal consequences of the resolution of the Security Council'.[16] A given resolution adopted by the Security Council can include binding, non-binding, or even a combination of binding and non-binding measures. Whether particular measures are to be considered binding is to be determined on a case-by-case basis, by interpreting the text of the resolution within its broader context.

The UN Charter assigns 'primary' responsibility to the Security Council for the maintenance of international peace and security. This responsibility exists alongside the subsidiary responsibility of the General Assembly for the maintenance of international peace and security. Pursuant to Article 14 of the UN Charter, the General Assembly 'may recommend measures for the peaceful adjustment of any situation'. It must; however, refrain from doing so 'while the Security Council is exercising in respect of any dispute or situation the functions assigned to it in the present Charter'.[17] Two observations can be made with respect to the relationship between the Security Council and the General Assembly as set out in this provision.

First, according to Article 14, the General Assembly only has the capacity to make recommendations. It is therefore not in a position to authorize states to use force to address situations that threaten international peace and security. Nevertheless, this authority to issue recommendations can be useful, especially in situations in which the Security Council is paralyzed due to tensions between its permanent members. For example, in 2012, former UN Secretary-General, Kofi Annan, was appointed as special envoy by the General Assembly and the League of Arab States to devise a peace plan for Syria.[18] This initiative was taken in response to a dead-lock in the Security Council, which was utterly divided due to diametrically opposed views of the United States and the Russian Federation on the approach to be taken to end the violence in Syria. Ultimately, the peace plan was not successful, but Annan did manage to garner the support of the Security Council for his plan, thereby providing a new impetus to attempts to resolve the armed conflict in Syria.[19]

Second, Article 14 of the UN Charter restrains the competence of the General Assembly to address situations of which the Security Council is seized, meaning situations on the Council's agenda. This provision should, however, not be taken too literally. In its *the Legal Consequences of the Construction of a Wall in the Occupied Palestinian Territory* advisory opinion, the International Court of Justice stated that 'there has been an increasing tendency over time for the General Assembly and the Security Council to deal in parallel with the same matter concerning the maintenance of international peace and security. . . . It is often

---

[15] Emphasis added.
[16] *Legal Consequences for States of the Continued Presence of South Africa in Namibia (South West Africa) notwithstanding Security Council Resolution 276 (1970)* (Advisory Opinion) [1971] ICJ Rep 16, para 114.
[17] UN Charter art 12.   [18] UNGA Res 66/253 (16 February 2012).   [19] See UNSC Res 2054 (29 June 2012).

the case that, while the Security Council has tended to focus on the aspects of such matters related to international peace and security, the General Assembly has taken a broader view, considering also their humanitarian, social and economic aspects'.[20] The General Assembly may; therefore, address situations concerning the maintenance of international peace and security that are on the Security Council's agenda, as long as it does not interfere directly with the core peace and security issues for which the Security Council has primary responsibility.

c   *Measures Not Involving the Use of Force*

Though the Security Council has been given wide-ranging powers to adopt coercive measures, including the use of force, to maintain or restore international peace and security, the UN Charter makes it clear that measures involving the use of force should remain exceptional. Article 42 explicitly stipulates that the Security Council may only take measures involving the use of force when it considers 'that measures provided for in Article 41 [i.e., not involving the use of force] would be inadequate or have proved to be inadequate'. The Security Council should therefore first impose (or at least consider imposing) non-military measures to de-escalate a situation, before resorting to measures involving the use of force.

Article 41 of the UN Charter provides the Security Council with ample choice on the types of non-military measures it may impose to give effect to its decisions. The provision contains a non-exhaustive list of measures, including measures of an economic and diplomatic nature. Article 41 has served as the legal basis for a great variety of measures adopted by the Security Council, even including the establishment of ad hoc international criminal tribunals, such as the International Criminal Tribunals for the Former Yugoslavia and Rwanda (see Chapter 8).[21] Most importantly; however, Article 41 constitutes the bedrock of the Council's sanctions practice. The primary purpose of sanctions is to compel particular actors, whether these are states, armed groups, or individuals, to change their behaviour. This behaviour does not necessarily have to be contrary to international law. The benchmark for Security Council action is not whether the conduct is unlawful, but rather whether the targeted behaviour contributes to a threat to the peace, breach of the peace, or act of aggression.

Sanctions can take various forms, depending on their context and objectives. The most far-reaching sanctions involve comprehensive financial and trade measures, which effectively paralyze the economy of states against which they are imposed. These types of sanctions have become rare in recent decades, due to increasing recognition of their devastating impact on the population of the affected state. The '661 sanctions regime' that was imposed against Iraq in the 1990s, first to bring Iraq's invasion and occupation of Kuwait to an end and later to address Iraq's possession of weapons of mass destruction, is

---

[20] *Legal Consequences of the Construction of a Wall in the Occupied Palestinian Territory* (Advisory Opinion) [2004] ICJ Rep 136, para 27.
[21] See UNSC Res 827 (25 May 1993); UNSC Res 995 (8 November 1994).

generally considered a turning-point in the Council's sanctions practice.[22] The introduction of humanitarian exemptions through the 'Oil for Food programme' allowed Iraq to export fixed quantities of oil to fulfil the primary needs of its population, but the sanctions regime, nevertheless, put a heavy toll on the Iraqi people. This created an important impetus for the Security Council to reform its sanctions practice.

Although quasi-comprehensive sanctions regimes are still sometimes imposed, for example currently against North Korea in relation to its nuclear proliferation programme,[23] they are now used as an option of last resort. Instead, the Security Council has shifted its attention to specific actors or commodities deemed responsible for maintaining situations that pose a threat to the peace, taking account of the potential impact of sanctions on vulnerable groups.[24] These so-called 'smart' sanctions can be either 'selective', 'targeted', or a combination thereof. Examples of selective sanctions include restrictions on trade in specific commodities such as the infamous 'blood diamonds' used to fund armed conflicts in Africa. Targeted sanctions are imposed against particular persons or groups of persons and often consist of travel bans and asset freezes. This 'individualization' of sanctions has created problems of its own,[25] most notably with respect to due process guarantees for persons placed on sanctions lists: they are not always given reasons for their listing and they do not necessarily have an opportunity to appeal the decision or to request removal from the list.[26] Although important innovations in the listing and delisting procedures have been introduced in recent years to ensure minimal due process guarantees, these still do not apply generally across sanctions regimes.[27]

Targeted sanctions enable the Security Council to bring a wide range of actors directly within the reach of its measures. Whereas comprehensive sanctions can only be imposed against states, targeted sanctions have been imposed against a variety of state and non-state actors, including senior government officials, members of terrorist organizations and armed groups as well as against corporations providing support to sanctioned groups and individuals. Sometimes, resolutions containing targeted sanctions refer to specific persons against whom sanctions are imposed. For instance, Resolution 1970 (2011) on Libya contains two annexes including the names of senior Libyan officials, amongst whom were members of the ruling Kaddafi family. These sanctions were imposed to put an end to gross and systematic violations of human rights ordered by these senior officials, including the repression of peaceful demonstrators. Usually; however, the Security Council formulates abstract criteria and leaves it to separate sanctions committees to designate specific individuals and entities based on these criteria. Such sanctions committees are subsidiary bodies established by the Security Council pursuant to Article 29 of the UN Charter and typically have the same membership as the Security Council itself.

---

[22] This sanctions regime was introduced by UNSC Res 661 (6 August 1990).   [23] See UNSC Res 2397 (22 December 2017).

[24] David Cortright and George A Lopez (eds), *Smart Sanctions: Targeting Economic Statecraft* (Rowman and Littlefield 2002).

[25] See Larissa van den Herik, 'The Individualization and Formalization of UN Sanctions' in Larissa van den Herik (ed), *Research Handbook on UN Sanctions and International Law* (Edward Elgar 2017) 1–16.

[26] The lack of basic due process guarantees has led to a clash with the European Court of Justice. See Joined Cases C–402/05 P and C–415/05 P *Kadi and Al Barakaat International Foundation v Council and Commission* [2008] ECR I–6351.

[27] See Kimberly Prost, 'Security Council Sanctions and Fair Process' in Van den Herik (n 25) 213–35.

During most of its existence, the Security Council has imposed sanctions in response to threats that are geographically and temporally defined (i.e., in relation to specific (conflict) situations). This is indeed what the drafters of the UN Charter had in mind: the Security Council was supposed to use its powers to respond to emergency situations. In recent years however, the Security Council has started to address generic threats as well. The most notable example concerns terrorism. In the aftermath of the terrorist attacks on New York and Washington, DC on 11 September 2001, the Security Council adopted several resolutions in which it determined that terrorism, and activities related to terrorism, constitute a threat to the peace.[28] In these resolutions, the Security Council called upon states to become parties to relevant terrorism suppression conventions and to adopt domestic legislation to suppress (the financing of) terrorism. In addition, it imposed targeted sanctions on individuals associated with terrorism. These sanctions have a global reach. Resolution 1373, for example, states that 'all States shall ... [f]reeze without delay funds and other financial assets or economic resources of persons who commit, or attempt to commit, terrorist acts or participate in or facilitate the commission of terrorist acts'. This open formulation may raise interpretation issues in practice, such as when can it be said that someone facilitates terrorist acts.

Proper implementation of sanctions ultimately depends on how states interpret and apply the sanctions regime. If a state does not implement Article 41 sanctions imposed by the Security Council, then other states may only enforce such sanctions by using armed force if the Security Council has issued an authorization to this effect. Enforcement measures can for instance consist of cargo inspections of vessels at sea to prevent sanctioned goods, such as weapons, from reaching or leaving the state against which sanctions have been imposed.[29] The legal basis for such an authorization is Article 42, as Article 41 only empowers the Security Council to take measures 'not involving the use of armed force'.

4   Prohibition of the Threat or Use of Force (Article 2(4))

A key pillar of the UN collective security system is the prohibition of the threat or use of force, laid down in Article 2(4) of the Charter: 'All Members shall refrain in their international relations from the threat or use of force against the territorial integrity or political independence of any state, or in any manner inconsistent with the Purposes of the United Nations'.[30] This is a far-reaching obligation, which is much more prohibitive than the relevant provisions of the Covenant of the League of Nations. Article 2(4) not only prohibits the *use*, but also the *threat* of force. Furthermore, the prohibition on the use of force applies permanently; it is not limited to a 'waiting period' of three months, when attempts should be made to resolve the dispute peacefully.

---

[28] See, for example, UNSC Res 1373 (28 September 2001), 1377 (12 November 2001) and 2178 (24 September 2014).

[29] See, for example, UNSC Res 221 (9 April 1966), para 5; 665 (25 August 1990), para 1 and 1973 (17 March 2011), para 13.

[30] The International Court of Justice (ICJ) referred to art 2(4) as 'a cornerstone of the United Nations Charter' in the *Case concerning Armed Activities on the Territory of the Congo (Democratic Republic of the Congo v Uganda)* (Judgment) [2005] ICJ Rep 168, para 148.

The prohibition of the threat or use of force, as laid down in Article 2(4), is also a rule of customary international law,[31] which therefore also binds the very few states that are not parties to the UN Charter. Moreover, the fundamental nature of this prohibition is underlined by the many states and scholars who regard it also as a rule of *jus cogens*.[32]

The precise scope of this prohibition depends on the interpretation of a number of its elements. First, pursuant to Article 2(4), all members shall refrain 'in their international relations' from the threat or use of force. These words make clear that Article 2(4) does not cover the threat or use of force by states *internally*, on their own territory. It only covers the threat or use of force abroad, outside a state's own territory. If a state uses force against part of its own population, in the event of a coup d'état or for other reasons, this may be a violation of international law, but it is not a violation of Article 2(4).

Second, all members shall refrain in their international relations from the 'threat' of 'force'. The drafters of the Charter, in their attempt 'to save succeeding generations from the scourge of war',[33] did not limit the prohibition covered by Article 2(4) to the *actual* use of force, but also considered it necessary to prohibit state conduct that typically precedes the use of force, namely the *threat* to do so. It demonstrates how determined the founders of the UN were to avoid, by all means, that history would repeat itself. In practice, however, it is not uncommon for political or military leaders of states to express threats to use force against other states, and such expressions do not necessarily violate Article 2(4). For example, Iranian leaders have repeatedly threatened to destroy Israel. In 2017 and 2018, North Korea and the United States both threatened to attack each other, more or less explicitly. To the extent that such threats are political rhetoric of a general nature, they are generally not seen as violations of Article 2(4), unless the threat becomes sufficiently specific.[34]

The third element goes to the heart of Article 2(4): 'All Members shall refrain in their international relations from the . . . use of force'. This general wording might suggest that it could not only cover military but also *economic* force. It is conceivable that an economically powerful state could exert considerable pressure on another state that is economically heavily dependent on it, and this could perhaps endanger international peace and security. However, even though Article 2(4) was intended to be broad in scope, the *travaux préparatoires*, subsequent practice and the general view in writings show that only military (armed) force is covered.[35]

---

[31] See further Bruno Simma et al (eds), *The Charter of the United Nations: A Commentary* (3rd edn, Oxford University Press 2012) 229–31 (with further references).

[32] See further ibid 231–2 (with further references). But see James A Green, 'Questioning the Peremptory Status of the Prohibition of the Use of Force' (2011) 32 Michigan Journal of International Law 215.

[33] UN Charter, preambular para 1.

[34] However, *specific* threats to use force are not by definition violations of art 2(4). An example is a specific threat in reaction to an armed attack. A threat to use force preceding a lawful exercise of self-defence would itself be lawful. See further Anne Lagerwall and Francois Dubuisson, 'The Threat of the Use of Force and Ultimata' in Marc Weller (ed), *The Oxford Handbook of the Use of Force in International Law* (Oxford University Press 2015) 910–24.

[35] During the Charter negotiations, a Brazilian proposal to include economic coercion as a form of 'force' was not accepted. For the relevant *travaux préparatoires*, see Documents of the UN Conference on International Organization (1945) vol 6, Doc 215, 609, and vol 3, Doc 2, 253–4. See further Nico Schrijver, 'The Ban on the Use of Force in the UN Charter' in Weller (n 34) 465–87.

Fourth, the prohibited threat or use of force mentioned in Article 2(4) must be directed 'against the territorial integrity or political independence of any state, or in any other manner inconsistent with the Purposes of the United Nations'. The question is whether these words limit in any way the general prohibition laid down in the preceding part of Article 2(4). The answer generally given to this question is that this is not the case. Therefore, even if troops of a state cross the border of another state only temporarily and in a limited way, without the intention of occupying foreign territory (and thus violating its territorial integrity and political independence), this is generally still seen as a violation of Article 2(4).[36]

The scope of the prohibition laid down in Article 2(4) is broad and serves as the starting point for the Charter system of collective security. This prohibition is much stricter than the League of Nations rules, which left ample room for states to use force. It would not; however, be realistic to assume that states would be ready to comply with such a far-reaching obligation without the existence of strong and reliable guarantees that the organization would protect states if and where they would no longer be allowed to do so themselves. The drafters of the UN Charter; therefore, laid down such guarantees in a number of provisions of Chapter VII, which concerns actions with respect to threats to the peace, breaches of the peace, and acts of aggression.

5 Collective Use of Force: Authorization of the Use of Force by the Security Council

This section introduces the specific collective guarantees that have been laid down in the UN Charter, and how these have been implemented in practice. First, Section 5(a) will analyze in which cases the Security Council may undertake action. Originally, the founders of the UN agreed that the Security Council should have its own military forces. However, the rules laid down in the Charter for the establishment and functioning of such forces have never been implemented. The only UN forces created in practice are UN peacekeeping forces, which are primarily created to *keep* the peace, not to *enforce* it. Mostly, peace-keeping forces only have limited authority to use force (see Section 5(b)). In addition, the Security Council has also authorized the use of force by individual states, ad hoc coalitions of states, or regional organizations (see Section 5(c)).

a Threats to the Peace, Breaches of the Peace, and Acts of Aggression

The most important Security Council powers are laid down in Chapter VII of the UN Charter. The first few words of Article 39, the opening article of Chapter VII, make clear that the UN collective security system is more centralized than that of the League of Nations: '*The Security Council shall determine* the existence of any threat to the peace,

---

[36] See further Simma (n 31) 216; Schrijver (n 35) 471; ILA, 'Final Report on Aggression and the Use of Force' (Sydney Conference 2018) 4–5.

breach of the peace, or act of aggression and shall make recommendations, or decide what measures shall be taken in accordance with Article 41 and 42, to maintain or restore international peace and security'.[37] Ultimately, it is for the Security Council, not for individual member states to determine whether or not a situation exists that requires action to maintain or restore international peace and security. Article 39 (as well as the title of Chapter VII) mentions three types of situations: threats to the peace, breaches of the peace, and acts of aggression. It is these situations, not a violation of the use of force prohibition in Article 2(4), that may trigger Chapter VII action by the Security Council. Thus, the threshold in Article 39 does not strictly mirror the language of Article 2(4) and gives broad leeway to the Security Council to implement its primary responsibility for the maintenance and restoration of international peace and security. In particular the notion of 'threat to the peace' in Article 39 is broader than 'threat or use of force' in Article 2(4).

The three situations mentioned in Article 39 (threats to and breaches of the peace, and acts of aggression) are not defined by the Charter. Nor has the Security Council formulated general definitions of these terms. In practice, the Council determines, on a case-by-case basis, if one of these situations exists.[38] The Council has often determined that a particular situation amounted to a threat to the peace, whereas it has only exceptionally found the existence of an act of aggression or other breach of the peace.[39] The Security Council has, for example, concluded that there was a threat to the peace in situations involving the 'proliferation of nuclear, chemical, and biological weapons, as well as their means of delivery';[40] 'the use of chemical weapons anywhere';[41] 'the deteriorating humanitarian situation in Syria';[42] and the determination 'that terrorism in all forms and manifestations constitutes one of the most serious threats to peace and security'.[43] In 2014, the Security Council even determined that 'the unprecedented extent of the Ebola outbreak in Africa constitutes a threat to international peace and security'.[44]

The Security Council not only determines whether or not there is a threat to the peace, breach of the peace, or act of aggression, but it also makes recommendations or takes measures, in order to maintain or restore international peace and security. These measures may include non-military or military measures, pursuant to Articles 41 and 42 of the UN Charter. Before doing so; however, and '[i]n order to prevent an aggravation of the situation', the Security Council may 'call upon the parties concerned to comply with such provisional measures as it deems necessary or desirable' (Article 40). An example of such a provisional measure is a resolution demanding that the states concerned observe a cease-fire. The Council has regularly adopted such resolutions, sometimes explicitly referring to Article 40, but more often without mentioning this provision.[45]

---

[37] Emphasis added.   [38] See, for example, UNSC Res 2431 (30 July 2018) (concerning Somalia).

[39] Examples of such exceptions are UNSC Res 660 (2 August 1990) concerning the invasion of Kuwait by Iraq (breach of the peace) and Res 573 (4 October 1985) and 611 (5 April 1988) concerning the use of force by Israel against Tunisia (act of aggression).

[40] See, inter alia, UNSC Res 2345 (23 March 2017) and 2397 (22 December 2017), preambles.

[41] For example, UNSC Res 2118 (27 September 2013), para 1.

[42] For example, UNSC Res 2258 (22 December 2015), preamble.

[43] For example, UNSC Res 2253 (17 December 2015), preamble.   [44] UNSC Res 2177 (18 September 2014), preamble.

[45] In UNSC Res 598 (20 July 1987) the Council explicitly referred to arts 39 and 40 when demanding the Islamic Republic of Iran and Iraq to 'observe an immediate ceasefire, discontinue all military actions on land, at sea and in the air, and withdraw all forces to the internationally recognized boundaries without delay'. In UNSC Res 2046 (2 May 2012), the council decided, inter alia, that Sudan and South Sudan shall '[i]mmediately cease all hostilities', without; however, explicitly referring to art 40.

The Security Council may take measures 'not involving the use of armed force' (Article 41) or, in case it considers that such measures 'would be inadequate or have proved to be inadequate', it may decide to 'take such action by air, sea or land forces as may be necessary to maintain or restore international peace and security' (Article 42). Measures taken on the basis of Article 41 (such as economic sanctions) have been discussed in Section 3(c). In order to be able to take military measures itself, the Security Council would need its own armed forces. The Charter lays down rules according to which all members of the UN 'undertake to make available to the Security Council, on its call and in accordance with a special agreement or agreements, armed forces' (Article 43(1)). However, in practice, such agreements have never been concluded. This is partly because of disagreements during the Cold War, in particular among the five permanent members of the Security Council.[46] However, the lack of willingness to conclude Article 43 agreements since the end of the Cold War demonstrates that this cannot be the only reason. The necessary preconditions for implementing a truly supranational collective security system perhaps do not (yet) exist. While a number of elements of the UN collective security system are centralized, implementing the most far-reaching element, a truly supranational military force which is at the disposal of the Security Council, has until now been a bridge too far.

This does not mean, however, that the use of military force by the Security Council has not occurred in practice. As the International Court of Justice stated in 1962, '[i]t cannot be said that the Charter has left the Security Council impotent in the face of an emergency situation when agreements under Article 43 have not been concluded'.[47] In practice, two types of forces have been created: UN peacekeeping forces established by the UN and forces that were not established but 'only' authorized by the Security Council. Even though both types of forces are not fully-fledged substitutes for the supranational force that the founding fathers of the UN envisaged, they have both become important assets in the arsenal of instruments available to the Security Council in carrying out its primary responsibility for the maintenance of international peace and security.

b   UN Peacekeeping Forces

Peacekeeping is among the most prominent and well-known activities of the UN. It was not foreseen in the UN Charter, but originated in UN practice in the 1950s. From supervising the cessation of hostilities and the implementation of peace agreements to assisting in disarmament and demobilization, election monitoring, and other peace-building activities, UN peacekeeping forces have fulfilled a wide variety of tasks. This sub-section further examines if and to what extent UN peacekeeping forces may also be mandated to use force.[48]

---

[46] See further Simma (n 31) 1354–6; Jean-Pierre Cot, Alain Pellet, and Mathias Forteau (eds), *La Charte des Nations Unies* (3rd edn, Economica 2005) 1264.

[47] *Certain Expenses of the United Nations (Article 17, paragraph 2, of the Charter)* (Advisory Opinion) [1962] ICJ Rep 151, 167.

[48] See for more details Scott Sheeran, 'The Use of force in United Nations Peacekeeping Operations' in Weller (n 34) 347–74. The mandate of a peacekeeping force is normally mentioned in the resolution creating the force, or extending its operation.

Originally, peacekeeping forces were only allowed to use force in self-defence; they could not take *the initiative* to use force.[49] However, with respect to the UN operation in the Congo in the 1960s, the UN Secretary-General interpreted self-defence in a broader way, as also including the right to use force in self-defence if the UN force was prevented from performing its mandate.[50] Since 1973, it has become standard for UN peacekeeping forces to possess a mandate to use force in self-defence, in order to resist 'attempts by forceful means to prevent [them] from discharging [their] duties under the mandate of the Security Council', such as the disarmament of armed groups.[51]

In the 1990s, this expanded but still limited scope for the use of force made it difficult or even impossible for some peacekeeping operations to be effective and to offer the necessary protection to civilians.[52] Against this background, a high-level group of experts recommended that peacekeeping should be more robust when necessary, thereby relaxing the distinction between peacekeeping and peace-enforcement.[53] Subsequently, since the beginning of this century, the Security Council has allowed a number of peacekeeping operations to use force to a larger extent than before.

An example of a UN peacekeeping force that has received permission from the Security Council to use force is MINUSMA (the United Nations Multidimensional Integrated Stabilization Mission in Mali). In its resolutions, the Security Council authorized 'MINUSMA to use all necessary means to carry out its mandate, within its capabilities and its areas of deployment'.[54] The phrase 'all necessary means' is generally understood to cover the use of force. The mandate of MINUSMA is detailed in these resolutions and is of considerable scope: it includes, among other things, the support of the disarmament of armed groups, the restoration of state authority in the centre of Mali, protection of civilians, and humanitarian assistance. Other UN peacekeeping forces have been given by the Security Council similarly broad authorization to use force. Perhaps most far-reaching is the UN operation in the Democratic Republic of Congo (DRC). Following the actions of a number of rebel groups in the east of that country, the Security Council decided in Resolution 2098 (2013), 'on an exceptional basis and without creating a precedent or any prejudice to the agreed principles of peacekeeping', to establish an Intervention Brigade within the UN peacekeeping operation, which was authorized 'to carry out targeted offensive operations . . . to prevent the expansion of all armed groups, neutralize these groups, and to disarm them'.[55] This demonstrates that UN peacekeeping forces may now use force in a much wider range of situations than in the 1950s, when the

---

[49] UNGA, 'Report of the Secretary-General A/3943' (9 October 1958), para 178.   [50] Simma (n 31) 1182.

[51] UNSC, 'Report of the Secretary-General on the Implementation of Security Council Resolution 340' (1973) UN Doc S/11052/Rev.1, 3. See further N Blokker, 'The Security Council and the Use of Force: on Recent Practice' in Niels Blokker and Nico Schrijver (eds), *The Security Council and the Use of Force: Theory and Reality – A Need for Change?* (Martinus Nijhoff 2005) 1–29, in particular at 18–19.

[52] See, for example, the experience of the UN peacekeeping mission during the 1995 fall of Srebrenica.

[53] See the UNGA/UNSC, 'Report of the Panel on United Nations Peace Operations' (2000) UN Doc A/55/305 – S/2000/809 ('Brahimi report', named after the Chairman of this Panel) (arguing that UN peacekeeping forces must be more capable of responding to attempts by local parties or forces to undermine a peace agreement, threaten civilians, etc).

[54] See, for example, UNSC Res 2423 (28 June 2018), para 32.

[55] See further Scott P Sheeran, 'A Constitutional Moment? United Nations Peacekeeping in the Democratic Republic of Congo' (2011) 8 International Organizations Law Review 55.

use of force was permitted only in strict cases of self-defence, not at the initiative of the UN force.

c   *Security Council Authorized Coalitions*

The Security Council may also authorize member states to use force. Such operations are conducted not by the UN itself but by ad hoc coalitions of states or (exceptionally) by an individual state. Such operations are different from centralized military enforcement action (as laid down in the UN Charter but never implemented) and from UN peacekeeping. The Security Council 'only' *authorizes* the use of force, meaning that it is delegating the implementation of a military operation. In contrast, peacekeeping operations are UN operations, implemented and financed by the UN, not by an 'outside' coalition of states. This model of enforcement action is not alien to the UN Charter. In Chapter VIII of the Charter (dealing with regional arrangements), Article 53(1) provides that '[t]he Security Council shall, where appropriate, utilize such regional arrangements or agencies for enforcement action under its authority. But no enforcement action shall be taken under regional arrangements or by regional agencies without the authorization of the Security Council'. The Charter does not, however, explicitly provide for the use of this concept outside the context of regional arrangements.

The first case in which such permission to use force was given to member states was the operation by the United States and a number of other countries in Korea in 1950. In its Resolutions 83 and 84 (1950), the Security Council recommended that member states assist South Korea following the armed attack by North Korea and to make their military forces and other assistance available to a unified command under the United States. It was not until the end of the Cold War that the Security Council started to regularly authorize the use of force by ad hoc coalitions, or 'coalitions of the able and willing'. Following the invasion of Kuwait by Iraq in 1990, the Security Council first imposed economic sanctions and took other measures, and subsequently authorized member states cooperating with Kuwait 'to use all necessary means to uphold and implement Resolution 660 (1990) and all subsequent relevant resolutions and to restore international peace and security in the area'.[56] On the basis of this Resolution, Operation Desert Storm was carried out from January to March 1991 to liberate Kuwait, under the command of the United States. As the quoted text of Security Council Resolution 678 reveals, the aim of the operation was couched in very broad terms. It was; therefore, for the United States and other participating states to decide, in practice, what should be done and when 'international peace and security in the area' was restored (so that the operation could be terminated). The Security Council almost gave a *carte blanche* to the ad hoc coalition to use force. This authorization was unlimited in time, and those who were authorized hardly needed to report in detail to the Security Council.

Since then, the Security Council has adopted many resolutions in which it authorized member states to use 'all necessary measures' or 'all necessary means'.[57] This wording is

---

[56] UNSC Res 678 (2 August 1990).
[57] See Niels Blokker, 'Outsourcing the Use of Force: Towards More Security Council Control of Authorized Operations?' in Weller (n 34) 202–26.

generally interpreted to include the use of military force, and the employment of this technique of enforcement has been generally accepted. Nevertheless, in individual cases it has given rise to fundamental disagreements that have made it difficult at times for the Security Council to perform its key role of maintaining international peace and security. For example, when a number of North Atlantic Treaty Organization (NATO) member states used force against Serbia in view of the humanitarian catastrophe in Kosovo in 1999, in the last stages of the war in the former Yugoslavia, some of these NATO member states claimed that the use of such force was authorized by the Security Council.[58] However, the Council had not explicitly authorized the use of all necessary measures in any of the resolutions that it adopted in relation to the situation in Kosovo.[59]

The question of whether or not the Security Council had authorized the use force arose again a few years later in 2002 and 2003, when the United States, the United Kingdom, and other countries started another military operation against Iraq for a mix of reasons including the need to disarm Iraq of weapons of mass destruction and the need to stop the Iraqi government, led by Saddam Hussein, from supporting terrorism. The United States and the United Kingdom claimed that the broad language of a number of resolutions (including Resolution 678 (1990) and Resolution 1441 (2002)) together provided a sufficient legal basis for the use of force. This claim was rejected by many other countries (including China, France, and the Russian Federation), which took the view that the Security Council would need to adopt a new resolution authorizing the use of force.

At present, it is generally accepted that the Security Council may take enforcement action by authorizing the use of' 'all necessary means' or 'all necessary measures'.[60] The adoption of a resolution which only refers to Chapter VII of the UN Charter (without specifically authorizing the use of force) is generally considered insufficient as a legal basis for the use of force. In practice, the Security Council has exercised more control over the implementation of the military operations that it has authorized, by specifying the mandate in more detail (e.g., the purposes for which force may be used), by laying down temporal limitations (e.g., a few months, or one year), and by requiring regular reporting.[61] An example is Resolution 2431 (2018), in which the Security Council authorized AMISOM (the African Union Mission in Somalia) 'to take all necessary measures, in full compliance with participating States' obligations under international law, including international humanitarian law and international human rights law, ... to carry out its mandate'. The mandate of AMISOM is specifically defined as encompassing, among other things, 'the gradual handing over of security responsibilities from AMISOM to the Somali security forces', reducing 'the threat posed by Al Shabaab and other armed opposition groups, including through mitigating the threat posed by improvised explosive devices', and assisting 'the Somali security forces to provide security for the political process at all

---

[58] For example, the Netherlands, letter by the Ministers of Foreign Affairs and Defence to the House of Representatives (*Tweede Kamer*) of the Dutch Parliament, *Kamerstukken II* 1998-99, dossiernr 22181, ondernr 213 (8 October 1998).

[59] UNSC Res 1160 (31 March 1998), 1199 (23 September 1998), and 1203 (24 October 1998).

[60] See, for example, UNSC Res 1973 (17 March 2011), para 4.   [61] See Blokker (n 57) 202–26.

levels'. This is much more specific than the authorization to use force against Iraq in 1990–1, to restore 'international peace and security in the area'.

Security Council authorizations of the use of force, with respect to either UN peace-keeping forces or 'coalitions of the able and willing', have become the way in which the Security Council implements its military enforcement role as defined in the UN Charter. These two alternatives for the truly supranational force that the drafters of the Charter had in mind have become important assets in the arsenal of enforcement instruments available for the Security Council, in particular since the 1990s. Nonetheless, often they have not provided adequate safeguards to protect states in cases of threats to the peace, breaches of the peace, or acts of aggression. On many occasions the Security Council has failed to take the necessary action, in particular because of the veto power held by permanent members of the Council. This has heightened the importance of the other main exception to the prohibition of the use of force, the right to self-defence.

6   Unilateral Use of Force: Self-Defence

The prohibition of the use of force does not preclude states from defending themselves against armed attacks. Even though the principal aim of the system developed in the UN Charter was to ban unilateral force by states and, for that purpose, to vest the authority to decide on the use of force in the Security Council, this system was not intended to abolish the 'inherent' right of states to use force in self-defence. This important exception to the prohibition on the use of force is included in Article 51 of the UN Charter, the concluding provision of Chapter VII. Self-defence can be exercised individually (by the victim state itself) or collectively (by third states on the request of the victim state). The exercise of the right to self-defence is subject to a number of conditions, which underline its emergency character. These are as follows: (1) self-defence is only permitted in response to an armed attack; (2) the exercise of self-defence must be necessary and proportionate; and (3) it must be reported to the Security Council. These conditions will be discussed in the following sub-sections, which will also address the debated question of whether the right to self-defence applies to attacks launched by non-state actors, such as terrorist groups.

a   *Armed Attack*

Article 51 provides that states may use force in self-defence 'if an armed attack occurs'. This requirement raises several questions relevant for determining the scope of the right to self-defence, which have not been settled conclusively. These questions include the threshold for and the author of an armed attack, as well as the question of anticipatory self-defence, that is, self-defence in anticipation of an armed attack, rather than in response to one.

While there are many uncertainties surrounding the notion of 'armed attack' in Article 51, there is; however, general agreement that it has an autonomous meaning compared with the notion 'use of force' in Article 2(4) of the UN Charter. In other words, the terms 'armed attack' and 'use of force' are not interchangeable. In the *Nicaragua* judgment, a landmark case addressing the United States' intervention in the armed conflict in Nicaragua in the early 1980s, the ICJ distinguished 'the most grave forms of the use of force (those constituting an armed attack) from other less grave forms'.[62] Not every use of force necessarily amounts to an armed attack. The Court considered that mere frontier incidents, as well as the provision of weapons or logistical support to armed groups, remain below the gravity threshold required by Article 51.[63] These acts may amount to a threat of or use of force,[64] but they are not sufficient to trigger the right to self-defence. The mining of a single military vessel; however, might suffice in the opinion of the ICJ, depending on the circumstances.[65] The question of whether a particular use of force amounts to an armed attack generally depends on scale and effects, such as the number of casualties and damage to property. There is; however, no clear watermark for distinguishing armed attacks from uses of force that do not give rise to a right of self-defence under Article 51.

Armed attacks must also originate from the territory of another state. This was determined by the ICJ in its advisory opinion on the wall constructed by Israel to protect it against attacks from the Palestinian West Bank (*Wall* advisory opinion). The Court was of the opinion that the cross-border requirement was not satisfied in the circumstances, as the threat against which Israel claimed to defend itself originated from Palestine, which was within the territory where Israel exercised effective control as an occupying power.[66] Related to this issue is the question of whether there are specific requirements as to the author of an armed attack. In the *Israeli Wall* advisory opinion, the Court explicitly stated that the right of self-defence only exists 'in the case of armed attack by one State against another State'.[67] It confirmed this position in its judgment regarding armed activities on the territory of the DRC, where it implicitly stated that in case an armed attack emanates from an armed group, a state can only exercise its right to self-defence if that group operates under the effective control of another state, meaning it can be attributed to a state.[68] This position of the Court has been criticized as being overly restrictive and leaving states without means to respond to attacks launched by terrorist groups.[69]

Another heavily debated question is whether and under what conditions a state can defend itself against an armed attack that has not yet occurred. Article 51 of the UN Charter clearly states that states have a right to self-defence 'if an armed attack occurs', which

---

[62] *Case concerning Military and Paramilitary Activities in and against Nicaragua (Nicaragua v United States of America)* (Judgment) [1986] ICJ Rep 14, para 191.

[63] ibid, para 195.   [64] ibid, para 228.

[65] *Case concerning Oil Platforms (Islamic Republic of Iran v United States of America)* (Merits) [2003] ICJ Rep 161, para 72.

[66] *Legal Consequences of the Construction of a Wall in the Occupied Palestinian Territory* advisory opinion (n 20), para 139.

[67] ibid.   [68] *Armed Activities on the Territory of the Congo* case (n 30), para 146.

[69] See, for example, Sean D Murphy, 'Self-Defense and the Israeli Wall Advisory Opinion: An *Ipse Dixit* from the ICJ?' (2005) 99 American Journal of International Law 62. The Court's position has also been criticized from within. See the separate opinions of Judges Higgins and Kooijmans and the declaration of Judge Buergenthal to the Court's advisory opinion regarding the *Israeli Wall* case (n 20) and the separate opinions of Judges Kooijmans and Simma to the Court's judgment in the *Armed Activities on the Territory of the Congo* case (n 30).

seems to imply that the right to self-defence is triggered only once an armed attack has occurred. However, there is widespread recognition of a right to anticipatory self-defence, as long as the attack is imminent, such that the need to act is 'instant, overwhelming, leaving no choice of means and no moment for deliberation'.[70] The right to act pre-emptively against imminent attacks must be clearly distinguished from preventive action against more distant threats, such as those posed by so-called 'rogue states' possessing weapons of mass destruction.[71] The prohibition of the use of force would lose all its meaning if states were allowed to defend themselves against such potential armed attacks. Instead, states should resort to the UN Security Council with such concerns. A relevant example concerns the diplomatic crisis between the United States and North Korea in 2017, when North Korea threatened to launch an intercontinental nuclear missile at the United States. The United States brought this matter before the Security Council, which strengthened the sanctions regime against North Korea in an attempt to obtain North Korea's consent to nuclear disarmament.[72] While the threat posed by North Korea is still present, this step de-escalated the situation and paved the way for diplomatic talks to come to a more permanent solution.

b *Necessity and Proportionality*

Although not explicitly stated in Article 51 of the UN Charter, every lawful exercise of the right to self-defence must satisfy the conditions of necessity and proportionality. Already in its 1986 judgment in the *Nicaragua* case, the International Court of Justice stated that these conditions are part of customary international law.[73] This was later confirmed in its 2003 judgment in the *Oil Platforms* case.[74] Whether a use of force in response to an armed attack is 'necessary' depends first on the availability of alternative measures that do not involve the use of force but that would enable the victim state to repel the attack. In other words, resort to the use of force in self-defence is a measure of last resort, which only arises when diplomatic attempts have failed or would be futile in light of the circumstances.[75]

Proportionality is about balancing the end with the means. However, there are competing understandings of what this means in practice. In the *Oil Platforms* case, proportionality was interpreted as requiring that the harm that is to be caused by the exercise of self-defence is comparable to the harm that has been caused by the preceding attack. In that case, the Court considered that the bombing of several oil platforms was not proportionate to the harm suffered by the United States, namely damage to a single war ship without loss of life.[76] However, instead of focusing on the harm caused by the preceding attack, proportionality can also be assessed in relation to the broader effects of the armed attack to which it

---

[70] These criteria are, generally, referred to as the *Caroline* test, as formulated by US secretary of state, Daniel Webster, in an exchange of letters between 1841 and 1843 with British diplomat Henry Stephen Fox in response to the burning and sinking of a ship called the *Caroline*.
[71] See 'The National Security Strategy of the United States of America' (September 2002) <https://2009-2017.state.gov/docuuments/organization/63562.pdf>. This strategy attempted to broaden the scope of preemptive self-defence by including preventive measures in its description.
[72] See UNSC Res 2371 (5 August 2017), 2375 (11 September 2017 and 2397 (22 December 2017).
[73] *Nicaragua* case (n 62), para 176.   [74] *Oil Platforms* case (n 65), para 73–7.   [75] Ibid, para 76.   [76] Ibid, para 77.

responds.[77] This approach takes into account strategic advantages that an attack may have, which may call for a greater use of force to repel the attack than would be warranted based on the gravity of the attack itself. Of course, the determination of what is proportionate depends very much on the facts and circumstances of each specific case.

c   *Non-state Actors*

According to Article 51, states may use force in self-defence 'if an armed attack occurs'. The ICJ has interpreted this narrowly as referring exclusively to attacks that are launched by or on behalf of states (see Section 6(a)). However, many attacks today are carried out by armed groups or terrorist organizations acting independently from states. The effects of these attacks can be as devastating as those resulting from attacks carried out by states. This has brought to the fore the question of whether states can invoke their right to self-defence to repel those attacks, even if this means that they would violate the territorial integrity of another state that was not involved in the armed attack.

The first time that this question was considered was in response to the terrorist attacks in New York and Washington, DC on 11 September 2001, which resulted in almost 3,000 casualties. The Security Council adopted two landmark resolutions on threats to international peace and security caused by terrorist acts in response to this event. Resolutions 1368 and 1373 (2001) recognized that states have an 'inherent right of individual or collective self-defence in accordance with the Charter' and that acts of international terrorism constitute threats to international peace and security. These resolutions have been interpreted as recognizing the applicability of the right to self-defence to terrorist attacks, but they do not do so expressly. They merely confirm the right to self-defence as set out in the UN Charter. Nonetheless, there has been significant practice by states invoking the right to self-defence in response to attacks by non-state actors ever since.[78] This practice has not been condemned by the international community. The bone of contention between states in favour of an extensive interpretation of the right to self-defence to cover attacks by terrorist or armed groups, on the one hand, and states arguing for a more restrictive interpretation of the right to self-defence, on the other, seems to be whether and in which circumstances the right of one state to defend itself against cross-border terrorist attacks may lead to a violation of the territorial integrity of another state.

Indeed, it is one thing to recognize the applicability of the right to self-defence to attacks by non-state armed groups, but it is another to allow states to use force on the territory of another state to repel such attacks without the consent of the state in which the non-state actors are present. The right to self-defence must be balanced with respect for the territorial integrity of the state from whose territory the attack has been launched. Pursuant to the

---

[77] See Christopher Greenwood, 'Self-Defence' in *Max Planck Encyclopedia of Public International Law* (last updated April 2011). See also the former legal advisor of the US Department of State's article – William H Taft, 'Self-Defence and the Oil Platforms Decision' (2004) 29 Yale Journal of International Law 295, 305 – criticizing the Court's interpretation of proportionality.

[78] See Christine Gray, *International Law and the Use of Force* (4th edn, Oxford University Press 2018), ch 5 for an overview of (recent) state practice.

requirement of necessity, the victim state will have to explore other options to repel the attack, such as diplomatic negotiations with the state hosting the armed group. Some authors argue that respect for the territorial integrity of the host state can be dispensed with if that state is 'unable or unwilling' to take action.[79] This doctrine has been invoked (either explicitly or implicitly) by several Western states to justify measures against the Islamic State, which operates from Syrian territory, to stop it from launching cross-border attacks on Iraq and planning terrorist attacks on other states.[80] Nevertheless, the 'unable or unwilling' doctrine is controversial and it has been rejected by a great number of other states.[81]

d   Function of the Security Council

Article 51 of the UN Charter emphasizes that the right to self-defence is subordinated to measures taken by the Security Council. First, member states must report measures to the Security Council. Disrespect for this obligation will not render the exercise of self-defence illegal, but it will undermine a state's claim that it was in fact acting in self-defence.[82] Second, the right of self-defence ceases when the Security Council has taken measures necessary to maintain international peace and security. Lastly, the Council retains the authority and responsibility to 'take at any time such action as it deems necessary' independently from the exercise of the right to self-defence. Article 51; therefore, not only lays down the inherent right of states to use force *unilaterally*, in self-defence; it also clearly demonstrates the *collective* nature of the system for the maintenance of international peace and security as laid down in the UN Charter.

7   Humanitarian Intervention and 'Responsibility to Protect'

The system of collective security, as included in the UN Charter, is premised on the Security Council taking an active role in maintaining or restoring international peace and security. However, the Council is a political body, whose members are not always able to reach agreement on a course of action. Disagreement in the Security Council is exacerbated by the veto power of the permanent members, which enables a single member to block the adoption of a resolution on which the majority of the Council agrees. This is particularly

---

[79] See Christian J Tams, 'The Use of Force against Terrorists' (2009) 20 European Journal of International Law 359; Kimberley N Trapp, 'The Use of Force against Terrorists: A Reply to Christian J. Tams' (2010) 20 European Journal of International Law 1049.

[80] See, for example, UNSC, 'Letter Dated 23 September 2014 from the Permanent Representative of the United States of America to the United Nations Addressed to the Secretary-General' (23 September 2014) UN Doc S/2014/695, relying on collective and individual self-defence; and UNSC, 'Letter Dated 10 December 2015 from the Chargé d'affaires a.i. of the Permanent Mission of Germany to the United Nations Addressed to the President of the Security Council' (10 December 2015) UN Doc S/2015/946, relying on collective self-defence.

[81] See, for example, the 'Statement by the Permanent Mission of the El Salvador to the United Nations on Behalf of the Community of Latin American and Caribbean States (CELAC) on Measures to Eliminate International Terrorism' (3 October 2018). CELAC is comprised of thirty-three states.

[82] See *Nicaragua* case (n 62), para 200 ('the absence of a report may be one of the factors indicating whether the State in question was itself convinced that it was acting in self-defence').

difficult for the international community to accept in situations where gross human rights violations are being committed.

The advent of the doctrine of humanitarian intervention can be explained against this background, and in particular against the backdrop of the tragedy of the 1994 genocide in Rwanda and the 1999 NATO intervention in Kosovo. Whereas the international community stood idly by when 800,000 members of the Tutsi minority and politically moderate Hutus were killed by Hutu extremists in Rwanda, NATO decided to intervene in Kosovo to stop the atrocities committed by the Serbs against the Kosovar population. This intervention led to a debate between fervent proponents and opponents of humanitarian intervention. At the core of the debate was the question of whether states have the right to intervene militarily to stop mass atrocities in the face of Security Council paralysis. The dilemma underlying this debate is a clash between the protection of human rights, on the one hand, and respect for the system of collective security as set out in the UN Charter, on the other. Accepting a novel exception to Article 2(4) of the UN Charter would risk undermining the system that had so carefully been built after the end of the Second World War, but allowing atrocities to be committed against people is equally unacceptable.[83] It was clear that the UN needed to find a solution to the problem of humanitarian catastrophes that would be more in line with the system of collective security included in the UN Charter. This solution was found in the concept of 'responsibility to protect' (R2P), which was set out in the outcome document of the 2005 World Summit, a major conference bringing together more than 170 world leaders to reach agreement on goals and principles for the UN and its members in the fields of development, security, and human rights.[84]

This outcome document ties R2P to the commission of four international crimes, namely genocide, war crimes, ethnic cleansing, and crimes against humanity. It formulates a primary responsibility for every state, as part of its sovereignty, to protect its population against the commission of these crimes. In addition, it articulates a complementary responsibility for the international community to help states protect their population through diplomatic, humanitarian and other peaceful means, while reserving the possibility to intervene through the use of military force as an option of last resort. However, very importantly, the Security Council would need to authorize such use of military force.

The General Assembly's outcome document therefore embeds military intervention pursuant to R2P within the UN Charter system of collective security. In this sense, R2P does not solve the problem it was intended to address, namely Security Council paralysis. Its principal contribution to *jus ad bellum* is therefore to confirm that the commission of international crimes may amount to a threat to international peace and security and therefore falls within the ambit of collective security. Thereby, R2P emphasizes the need to protect the security of people and communities, even against their own state.[85]

---

[83] See Alex J Bellamy and Tim Dunne (eds), *The Oxford Handbook of the Responsibility to Protect* (Oxford University Press 2016).
[84] UNGA Res 60/1, '2005 World Summit Outcome' (24 October 2005), paras 138–9.
[85] See Christopher K Penny, 'Human Security' in Thomas G Weiss and Sam Daws (eds), *The Oxford Handbook on the United Nations* (2nd edn, Oxford University Press 2018).

R2P has rarely been used in practice as a legal basis for the authorization of the use of force. It was used in 2011 by the Security Council to stop the Libyan government from committing war crimes and crimes against humanity against its own population.[86] Due to controversies between the permanent members of the Security Council regarding the implementation of this mandate in Libya; however, there have been no subsequent authorizations to use force pursuant to R2P.

8   Concluding Remarks

In 1945, following the atrocities of the Second World War, the international community was able to agree on the UN Charter, which embodies a collective security system that is remarkably centralized. While the pre-existing, decentralized League of Nations system failed within two decades, the UN system is still in place. When there is a threat to the peace, breach of the peace, or act of aggression, it is for the Security Council to take decisions to maintain or restore international peace and security. It would be too simple to attribute the absence of another world war largely to the UN. The Security Council was largely impotent during the Cold War, and has often failed to act in more recent times. Moreover, the UN has not been able to prevent a considerable number of armed conflicts and 'to save succeeding generations from the scourge of war'. Nevertheless, its rules and organs have disciplined the member states. While previously decisions to use force were largely a sovereign prerogative of individual states, they are now embedded in a self-imposed collective security system, though this system can only be effective if it has the necessary support, in particular from the five permanent members of the Security Council. Realizing the ideals of the UN Charter and implementing its collective security system to its full effect and in good faith is a long-term process, to be pursued in the interest of all states.

Recommended Reading

Christine Gray, *International Law and the Use of Force* (4th edn, Oxford University Press 2018).
Christine Henderson, *The Use of Force and International Law* (Cambridge University Press 2018).
Claus Kress, "Major Post-Westphalian Shifts and Some Important Neo-Westphalian Hesitations in the State Practice on the International Law on the Use of Force" (2014) 1 Journal on the Use of Force and International Law 11.
Bruno Simma et al (eds), *The Charter of the United Nations: A Commentary* (3rd edn, Oxford University Press 2012).
Marc Weller (ed), *The Oxford Handbook of the Use of Force in International Law* (Oxford University Press 2015).

---

[86] See UNSC Res 1970 (25 February 2011) and 1973 (26 February 2011).

12

International Humanitarian Law

Robert Heinsch

1 Introduction

International humanitarian law is the field of public international law that regulates the use of force in situations of armed conflict and is therefore also often referred to as *jus in bello,* the law of armed conflict or the law of war.[1] These denominations can be used interchangeably, but we will mainly refer to the generally accepted terminology international humanitarian law (IHL). The most traditional and now somewhat antiquated term is the 'law of war', which comes from a time when the application of IHL depended on the existence of a declaration of war. Many academics and practitioners – especially with a military background – refer to IHL as the 'law of armed conflict'. This is almost a literal translation of the Latin term '*jus in bello*', which is often used to distinguish this body of law from the '*jus ad bello*' in the field of public international law, which deals with the prohibition of the use of force in interstate relations, as reflected in Article 2(4) of the Charter of the United Nations (UN) (see Chapter 11).[2] The term 'international humanitarian law' is most often used by academics and practitioners who have a background or a connection to the Red Cross and Red Crescent Movement (i.e., the International Committee of the Red Cross (ICRC) the International Federation of the Red Cross (IFRC) and the respective national societies), whose mandate it is to disseminate IHL and whose task it is to protect the 'humanitarian' aspects of IHL.

The term 'humanitarian law' stems from the fact that the law of armed conflict deals, in part, with the protection of persons. This branch of law focuses on the individual and establishes limitations on how persons who are not participating in hostilities should be protected from the effects of war. This body of law originates in an initiative by the Swiss merchant Henry Dunant, who in 1857 walked over the battlefield in Solferino, Italy, and was confronted with the terrible suffering of more than 40,000 wounded soldiers. He went on to give the impetus not only for the creation of the ICRC in 1863, but also for the creation of the First Geneva Convention for the 'Amelioration of the Condition of the Wounded and

---

[1] See on this topic also the author's Massive Open Online Course 'International Humanitarian Law in Theory and Practice', which is accessible for free on Coursera at <www.coursera.org/learn/international-humanitarian-law>, and which was partly the basis for this chapter.

[2] Charter of the UN (adopted 26 June 1945, entered into force 24 October 1945) 1 UNTS XVI (UN Charter).

Sick in Armed Forces in the Field' in 1864. At almost the same time in 1863, Abraham Lincoln tasked the German American lawyer, Francis Lieber, with writing the main rules of warfare in a military manual for the Union troops during the American Civil War. This manual, which later came to be known as the 'Lieber Code', was in many ways the forerunner of what would come to be referred to as the 'Hague Law', as laid down in the 1899 and 1907 Hague Conventions, which further codified the rules governing the so-called 'means and methods of warfare'.

IHL has historically been divided into two main branches consisting of rules that regulate the 'means and methods of warfare' and the rules that deal with the 'protection of persons and projects'. These two strands of IHL have their origins in the historical development of the law of armed conflict. The rules governing the means and methods of warfare are known as 'Hague Law' due to the fact that the main treaties governing this field of law were, for a long time, the 1899 and 1907 Hague Conventions and the annexed Hague Regulations.[3] The provisions dealing with the protection of persons and objects *hors de combat* ('out of combat') are known as 'Geneva Law', as these rules can be found in the Four Geneva Conventions of 1949.[4] The strict separation between these two branches of IHL has, however, been more or less abandoned due to the conclusion of the two Additional Protocols of 1977, which cover both norms concerning the means and methods of warfare, as well as those protecting individuals.[5]

This chapter begins with the foundations and the history of IHL (Section 2) before discussing the scope of application of IHL (Section 3) and the law governing the conduct of hostilities, namely the means and method of warfare (Section 4). The final sections discuss the law governing the protection of persons during armed conflict (Section 5) and the implementation and enforcement of IHL (Section 6).

2   IHL's Rationale and Relationships with Other Bodies of Law

a   *Rationale*

The main rationale behind IHL is that certain standards of humanity must be upheld, even at times when enemies are trying to eliminate each other. Thus, IHL tries to find a balance between military necessity and the principles of humanity, and it applies to every armed conflict regardless of whether the prohibition of the use of force, as laid down in Article 2(4)

---

[3] ICRC How does Law Protect in War?, 'Law of the Hague' <https://casebook.icrc.org/glossary/law-hague>.

[4] ICRC How does Law Protect in War?, 'Law of Geneva' <https://casebook.icrc.org/glossary/law-geneva>. Geneva Convention for the Amelioration of the Condition of the Wounded and Sick in Armed Forces in the Field (adopted 12 August 1949, entered into force 21 October 1950) 75 UNTS 31 (First Geneva Convention); Geneva Convention for the Amelioration of the Condition of the Wounded, Sick and Shipwrecked Members of the Armed Forces at Sea (adopted 12 August 1949, entered into force 21 October 1950) 75 UNTS 85 (Second Geneva Convention); Geneva Convention relative to the Treatment of Prisoners of War (adopted 12 August 1949, entered into force 21 October 1950) 75 UNTS 135 (Third Geneva Convention); Geneva Convention relative to the Protection of Civilian Persons in Time of War (adopted 12 August 1949, entered into force 21 October 1950) 75 UNTS 287 (Fourth Geneva Convention).

[5] Protocol Additional to the Geneva Conventions of 12 August 1949, and relating to the protection of victims of international armed conflicts (adopted 8 June 1977, entered into force 7 December 1978) 1125 UNTS 3 (Additional Protocol I); Protocol Additional to the Geneva Conventions of 12 August 1949 and relating to the protection of victims of non-international armed conflicts (adopted 8 June 1977, entered into force 7 December 1978) 1125 UNTS 609 (Additional Protocol II).

of the UN Charter, has been violated.[6] A legal regime that upholds humanity in times of extreme violence and animosity might appear to be paradoxical. Human history; however, has shown that even in times of armed conflict, parties are willing to agree on certain standards, like the distinction between combatants and civilians and the prohibition of means and methods of warfare that create unnecessary suffering. Even in times of war, human beings are connected and guided by the common heritage of humanity. The regulation of conduct during times of armed conflict is almost as old as humankind, and seems to reflect the urge of humans to limit the suffering in armed conflict to what is necessary from a military perspective and to balance this against the principle of humanity. Reciprocity also plays a role in this context, in that each party to an armed conflict has an incentive to treat the prisoners of war of the opposing party decently, in the expectation that their own soldiers, should they be captured, will also enjoy humane treatment. Finally, adherence to certain standards of humanity during armed conflict allows enemies to live together again after a civil war, for example, and to conclude a peace agreement. While other fields of public international law, like human rights law, allow for derogation from certain human rights under special circumstances, IHL norms are non-derogable and many are also regarded as *jus cogens* or peremptory norms, as was indicated by the International Court of Justice (ICJ) in the *Nuclear Weapons* advisory opinion.[7]

b   The Relationship between Jus in Bello and Jus ad Bellum

Some commentators have questioned whether IHL enables armed conflicts by attempting to prevent the most egregious conduct, and thereby making war more acceptable.[8] Some have suggested that the law of armed conflict seems to view war as an 'inevitable social phenomenon'[9] and that it may legitimize the use of force.[10] These arguments overlook the fact that human history has shown that wars are unfortunately waged regardless of whether a legal regime is in place to govern the conduct of hostilities. Few political decision-makers consider IHL when deciding whether or not to go to war. Wars are motivated by the desire to gain territory, resources, or political power, or to destroy an enemy because of political, religious, racial, ethnic, or other reasons. Were it not for the now rather sophisticated system of rules protecting the victims of war and limiting the means and methods of warfare, the impact of armed conflict would be even more disastrous.[11]

---

[6] As early as 1868, the St Petersburg Declaration provided that wars should not be fought with all means available, but only with those that are necessary in order to defeat the enemy, excluding anything which would violate the principle of distinction, the principle of proportionality, or the prohibition of unnecessary suffering (see Section 4). The declaration also acknowledges that at a certain point, military necessity may give way to the principle of humanity. Declaration Renouncing the Use, in Time of War, of Explosive Projectiles Under 400 Grammes Weight (adopted and entered into force 11 December 1868), published in Dietrich Schindler and Jiři Toman, *The Laws of Armed Conflicts* (Martinus Nijhoff 1988) 102.

[7] *Legality of the Threat or Use of Nuclear Weapons* (Advisory Opinion) [1996] ICJ Rep 226, para 83.

[8] See, for example, David Kennedy, 'Lawfare and Warfare' in James Crawford and Martti Koskenniemi (eds), *The Cambridge Companion to International Law* (Cambridge University Press 2012) 181–2.

[9] Gleider Hernandez, *International Law* (Oxford University Press 2019) 378, 405.

[10] See Chris af Jochnick and Roger Normand, 'The Legitimation of Violence: A Critical History of the Laws of War' (1994) 35 Harvard International Law Journal 49; David Kennedy, *Of Law and War* (Princeton University Press 2006).

[11] Illustrations of how IHL protects civilians, wounded soldiers, and other protected persons can be found on the ICRC's 'IHL in Action' website, which presents positive examples of IHL compliance. See <https://ihl-in-action.icrc.org>.

The relationship between IHL and the law on the use of force (*jus in bello* and *jus ad bellum*) is characterized by complete separation.[12] Under IHL, there is no distinction between the aggressor and the victim of aggression, and efforts to deny the aggressor the benefits and protections of the law of armed conflict were rejected during the drafting of the Additional Protocols to the Geneva Conventions.[13] If aggressors were denied the benefits and protections of IHL by virtue of having initiated the conflict, then this would be a practical 'death sentence' for the law of armed conflict, as the humanitarian purpose of this body of law would be undermined. Moreover, experience has shown that it is rarely clear, which party initiated a conflict, or whether the parties had legitimate reasons for entering into an armed conflict. Allowing or obliging commanders and soldiers to decide whether different rules apply to their own forces or to the enemy would make this field of law unworkable. The Preamble to Additional Protocol I accordingly reaffirms that:

... the provisions of the Geneva Conventions of 12 August 1949 and of this Protocol must be fully applied in all circumstances to all persons who are protected by those instruments, without any adverse distinction based on the nature or origin of the armed conflict or on the causes espoused by or attributed to the Parties to the conflict.

A party that is bound by a rule of IHL must comply without reference to whether the attack leading to the application of IHL was legitimate or whether the opposing party is complying with IHL.[14]

c   *The Relationship between IHL and International Human Rights Law*

The question of how IHL and international human rights law relate to each other has been the object of extensive discussion in literature and has been addressed in international and national jurisprudence, all of which highlight the differences and similarities of both regimes.[15] These bodies of law differ, for example, in that IHL permits combatants to kill other combatants, while human rights law prohibits the arbitrary taking of life.[16] In addition, in the context of an international armed conflict, which involves two or more

---

[12] On this topic, see Federica D'Alessandra and Robert Heinsch, 'Rethinking the Relationship Between Jus in Bello and Jus ad Bellum: A Dialogue Between Authors' in Leila Nadya Sadat (ed), *Seeking Accountability for the Unlawful Use of Force* (Cambridge University Press 2018).

[13] See Christopher Greenwood, 'Historical Development and Legal Basis' in Dieter Fleck (ed), *The Handbook of International Humanitarian Law* (Oxford University Press 1995) 101.

[14] ibid, margin note 102; this was already confirmed by the original 1958 ICRC Commentary which states that 'an engagement concluded on the basis of reciprocity, binding each party to the contract only in so far as the other party observes its obligations. It is rather a series of unilateral engagements solemnly contracted before the world as represented by other Contracting parties'. ICRC, *Commentary: Geneva Convention (I)* (ICRC 1958) 25.

[15] See Hans-Joachim Heintze, 'On the Relationship between Human Rights Law Protection and International Humanitarian Law' (2004) 86 International Review of the Red Cross 789; Matthew Happold, 'International Humanitarian Law and Human Rights Law' in Nigel D White and Christian Henderson (eds), *Research Handbook on International Conflict and Security Law* (Edward Elgar 2013); Marko Milanovic, 'Norm Conflicts, International Humanitarian Law and Human Rights Law' and Yuval Shany, 'Human Rights and Humanitarian Law As Competing Legal Paradigms for Fighting Terror' both in Orna Ben-Naftali (ed), *International Humanitarian Law and International Human Rights Law: Collected Courses of the Academy of European Law XIX/1* (Oxford University Press 2010).

[16] International Covenant on Civil and Political Rights (adopted 16 December 1966, entered into force 23 March 1976) 999 UNTS 171, art 6(1); Theodor Meron, 'The Humanization of Humanitarian Law' (2000) 94 American Journal of International Law 239, 240.

states, IHL provides a legal framework for formally equal opponents, whereas human rights law protects the weaker party – the citizen – against the state. These two legal regimes are nevertheless based on the same basic concept: the protection of the individual, and adherence to certain minimum standards, which are derived from the principle of humanity and human dignity.

The question of whether both bodies of law can apply during times of armed conflict is significant, as the regimes do not have the same scope, though some issues, such as the protection of prisoners from torture and other inhumane treatment, are covered by both regimes. International human rights norms were originally seen as being mainly applicable during times of peace, especially because some human rights provisions are derogable under special circumstances like armed conflicts (see Chapter 10). In contrast, IHL was seen as providing protections for situations of armed conflict, which are non-derogable.[17] These two bodies of law are now regarded as enjoying cumulative application, meaning that they may both apply during times of armed conflict.[18] This has been acknowledged by the ICJ, which addressed the relationship between IHL and human rights law in both the *Nuclear Weapons* advisory opinion[19] and the *Wall* advisory opinion.[20] While some rights may be addressed only by IHL, others may be addressed only by human rights law, and yet other rights may be addressed by both bodies of law.

Finally, some situations, known as internal disturbances, may fall into a legal lacuna that is covered neither by IHL nor by the full body of human rights law. Internal disturbances (i.e., riots) refer to situations that do not rise to the level of a (non-international) armed conflict, but that nevertheless involve violence of a certain seriousness or duration. Because these situations do not qualify as (non-international) armed conflicts, IHL does not apply. At the same time, because states may, under certain conditions, derogate from many human rights during such internal disturbances, much of human rights law may not apply either, resulting in a legal gap. The Turku-Declaration on Minimum Humanitarian Standards was drafted in 1990 to try to close this gap, but it has not attracted significant support among states.[21]

3   Scope of Application

The application of IHL depends on the existence of an armed conflict, which may be 'international' or 'non-international' in character.[22] This distinction between international and non-international armed conflicts is significant because all of the rules set out in all four

---

[17] See Hans-Peter Gasser, *International Humanitarian Law: An Introduction* (ICRC 1994).

[18] UNSC, 'Report of the Secretary-General to the Security Council on the Protection of Civilians in Armed Conflict' (1999) UN Doc S/1999/957.

[19] *Legality of the Threat or Use of Nuclear Weapons* advisory opinion (n 7), para 24–5.

[20] *Legal Consequences of the Construction of a Wall in the Occupied Palestinian Territory* (Advisory Opinion) [2004] ICJ Rep 136, paras 102–6.

[21] Declaration of Minimum Humanitarian Standards, adopted by a meeting of experts, organised by the Human Rights Institute of Abo Akademi in Turku/Abo (Finland) (2 December 1990) UN Doc E/CN.4/Sub.2/1991/55.

[22] See Dietrich Schindler, 'The Different Types of Armed Conflicts According to the Geneva Conventions and Protocols' (1979) 163 Collected Courses of The Hague Academy of International Law, 117–63.

Geneva Conventions apply to international armed conflicts, whereas only Common Article 3 of the Geneva Conventions is applicable to non-international armed conflicts. Additional Protocols I and II also apply to international and non-international armed conflicts, respectively, but only with respect to parties to conflicts that are bound by these Protocols, which are less widely ratified than the Geneva Conventions.

Historically, public international law only governed the relationship between sovereign states, with the result that the traditional law of war only applied to conflicts between two or more sovereign states (i.e., international armed conflicts).[23] Non-international armed conflicts were seen as exclusively internal affairs of states, which were unwilling to accept that their own citizens could engage in an armed conflict against them.[24] As a consequence, states did not grant rebels any kind of combatant status, which would have entitled them to immunity from prosecution after the end of the civil war.[25] Before 1949, the law of war only applied to non-international armed conflicts if the state recognized the rebels as belligerents ('recognition of belligerency'),[26] but recognition of belligerency was, in practice, the exception rather than the rule.[27] The fact that the application of IHL to non-international armed conflicts depended on the subjective view of the state engaged in the armed conflict was generally regarded as unsatisfactory.[28]

This problem was partly remedied in 1949, when the first three Geneva Conventions were updated and the Fourth Geneva Convention for the protection of civilians was added to this body of law.[29] While the vast majority of rules contained in all four Geneva Conventions are applicable in international armed conflicts, states also agreed to include a so-called 'mini-convention', which is set out in Common Article 3 of the 1949 Geneva Conventions, and applies to non-international armed conflicts.

a   ***International and Non-international Armed Conflicts in the Geneva Conventions***

Common Article 2 of the Geneva Conventions contains little by way of a definition of the term 'international armed conflict'. Common Article 2 clarifies that a formal declaration of war is not necessary, and that the existence of factual circumstances amounting to an armed conflict between two or more sovereign states results in the application of the Geneva Conventions. The application of IHL is now; therefore, independent of the belligerent parties' will (i.e., a declaration of war), but is instead based on the facts existing on the ground. The Appeals Chamber of the International Criminal Tribunal for the Former

---

[23] Leslie C Green, *The Contemporary Law of Armed Conflict* (2nd edn, Juris 2000) 54.

[24] See Michael Bothe, 'War Crimes in Non-International Armed Conflicts' (1994) 24 Israel Yearbook on Human Rights 241.

[25] See Knut Ipsen, 'Combatants and Non-Combatants' in Fleck (n 13), margin note 301.

[26] See Eibe H Riedel , 'Recognition of Belligerency' in Rudolf Bernhardt (ed), *Encyclopedia of Public International Law*, vol 4 (North Holland 2000) 47 ff; see also Gasser (n 17); Green (n 23) 59, and Knut Ipsen, *Völkerrecht* (Beck 1999), para 65, margin note 12.

[27] Gasser (n 17) 84, gives an example from 1902.   [28] Ipsen (n 26), para 65, margin note 12.

[29] The First Geneva Convention (for the wounded and sick in the field) was concluded in 1864; the Second Geneva Convention (for the wounded, sick, and shipwrecked at sea) was concluded in 1906, and the Third Geneva Convention (for the treatment of prisoners of war) was concluded in 1929.

Yugoslavia (ICTY), in its famous 1995 *Tadić* decision on jurisdiction, further specified that an international armed conflict exists whenever there is 'resort to armed force between States',[30] a definition which has since been seen as an accurate description of the state of the law.

Common Article 3 of the Geneva Conventions, which explicitly applies to non-international armed conflicts, represented a small revolution at the time it was concluded in 1949.[31] Following the cruelties of the Spanish Civil War, which took place between 1936 and 1939 and included the aerial bombing of civilians in the Basque town of Guernica in 1937, states considered it necessary to agree on certain rules applicable to non-international armed conflicts. During the drafting of the 1949 Geneva Conventions, states' delegates were also very much under the strong impressions of the terrible atrocities of the Second World War. Due to the inter-state character of the Second World War; however, states focused mainly on the regulation of international armed conflicts. Nevertheless, the inclusion of Common Article 3 in the Geneva Conventions represented a very important step in the further development of the rules applicable in non-international armed conflicts.[32] In contrast to earlier times, in which the subjective evaluation of the respective state was crucial, Common Article 3's application depends on an objective criterion: the existence of an armed conflict of non-international character. Common Article 3 represents the absolute minimum standard applicable to non-international armed conflicts,[33] and reflects of the most basic considerations of humanity.[34] Common Article 3 is regarded as customary IHL and has also been referred to as a *jus cogens* norm.[35] Like Common Article 2 for international armed conflicts, Common Article 3 also does not clearly define a 'non-international armed conflict', but just speaks of 'armed conflict not of an international character occurring in the territory of one of the High Contracting Parties'.

It was only in 1995 that the ICTY Appeals Chamber, in the aforementioned *Tadić* case, affirmed that Common Article 3 is applicable to non-international armed conflicts 'whenever there is . . . protracted armed violence between governmental authorities and organised armed groups or between such groups within a State'.[36] In 2008, in a judgment in the *Haradinaj* case, an ICTY Trial Chamber further clarified that two factors must be fulfilled in order for this threshold to be met: (A) the armed violence must rise to a certain level of intensity; and (B) the armed group must have a certain level of organization.[37] With regard to the intensity-of-violence threshold, the following non-exhaustive list of factors may be considered: (1) the number, duration and intensity of individual confrontations; (2) the type of weapons and other military equipment used; (3) the number of persons partaking in the

---

[30] *Prosecutor v Dusko Tadić a/k/a 'Dule'* (Decision on the Defence Motion for Interlocutory Appeal on Jurisdiction) IT-94-1-AR72 (2 October 1995) (ICTY Appeals Chamber), para 70.
[31] Greenwood (n 13) margin note 211; Geoffrey Best, *War and Law Since 1945* (Clarendon 1994) 170–1.
[32] See Best (n 31) 168 ff.
[33] *Case concerning Military and Paramilitary Activities in and against Nicaragua* (Merits) [1986] ICJ Rep 14, para 218.
[34] ibid.   [35] Gasser (n 17) 80; see also Greenwood (n 13), margin note 211.
[36] *Prosecutor v Dusko Tadić* (Decision on the Defence Motion for Interlocutory Appeal on Jurisdiction) IT-94-1-AR72 (2 October 1995) (ICTY Appeals Chamber), para 70.
[37] *Prosecutor v Ramush Haradinaj, Idriz Balaj and Lahi Brahimaj* (Judgement) IT-04-84-T (3 April 2008) (ICTY Trial Chamber), paras 50–60.

fighting; (4) the number of casualties; and (5) the extent of material destruction. In addition, a number of indicative factors may be considered in assessing whether an armed group satisfies the organization criterion under Common Article 3. These indicators include, among others: (1) the existence of a command structure; (2) disciplinary rules; (3) a headquarters for the group; (4) territorial control; (5) the ability to access weapons and other military equipment; (6) the capacity to recruit new members; and (7) the ability to provide training.

b   International and Non-international Armed Conflicts in the Additional Protocols

The growing numbers of armed conflicts during the 1960s and 1970s, especially the Vietnam War (1960–73),[38] resulted in the conclusion of Additional Protocol I, which was designed to further protect victims of international armed conflicts.[39] Against the background of these armed conflicts, Additional Protocol I put three very specific types of 'liberation wars' on the same level as traditional international armed conflicts. Thus, while Additional Protocol I applies mainly to traditional international armed conflicts as laid down in Article 1(3) of Additional Protocol I, Article 1(4) expands the concept of international armed conflict to the following situations:

... armed conflicts in which peoples are fighting against colonial domination and alien occupation and against racist régimes in the exercise of their right of self-determination, as enshrined in the Charter of the United Nations and the Declaration on Principles of International Law concerning Friendly Relations and Co-operation among States in accordance with the Charter of the United Nations.

The drafters of this provision had in mind three specific situations: states freeing themselves from colonial regimes, the Israel–Palestine conflict, and the fight against Apartheid in South Africa.

The 1977 Additional Protocol II to the Geneva Conventions was the first treaty that contained rules only for non-international armed conflicts.[40] Some of the delegates to the 1977 Diplomatic Conference wanted to transpose as many rules as possible from the regime governing international armed conflicts to the regime governing non-international armed conflicts.[41] But because of the opposition of some states, especially some developing countries,[42] the conference resulted in relatively rudimentary rules compared to those set out in the much more detailed Additional Protocol I, which covers international armed conflicts. Additional Protocol II nevertheless represents a decisive development in the legal

---

[38] See Best (n 31) 80 ff.
[39] Armed conflicts during this period also took place, for example, in the DCR, Nigeria, and Israel. See Michael Bothe, Karl Josef Partsch, and Waldemar A Solf, *New Rules for Victims of Armed Conflicts: Commentary on the Two 1977 Protocols Additional to the Geneva Conventions of 1949* (2nd edn, Martinus Nijhoff 2013).
[40] See Yves Sandoz, Christophe Swinarski, and Bruno Zimmermann (eds), *Commentary on the Additional Protocols of 8 June 1977 to the Geneva Conventions of 12 August 1949* (Martinus Nijhoff 1987); Bothe, Partsch, and Solf (n 39).
[41] See David P Forsythe, 'Legal Management of Internal War' (1978) 72 American Journal of International Law 272, 280.
[42] ibid 281.

limits on warfare in non-international armed conflicts.[43] It codifies, for example, the prohibition on attacking a civilian population or using force against civilians.[44]

The scope of application of Additional Protocol II is, however, limited in comparison with the scope of application of Common Article 3. According to Article 1(1) of Additional Protocol II, an armed group that fights against a government must fulfil certain criteria, especially the exercise of territorial control, in order for the Protocol to apply.[45] Additional Protocol II also does not apply to non-international armed conflicts between organized armed groups, but instead only governs non-international armed conflicts between a non-state actor and a state.[46] In addition, Additional Protocol II does 'not apply to situations of internal disturbances and tensions, such as riots, isolated and sporadic acts of violence and other acts of a similar nature, as not being armed conflicts'.[47] The definition of a non-international armed conflict under Additional Protcol II is; therefore, much more limited than the one found in Common Article 3, such that Additional Protocol II has a more restricted scope of application.

With regard to the enforcement of IHL rules, neither Common Article 3 nor Additional Protocol II creates individual criminal responsibility for the perpetrators of violations. While the Geneva Conventions and Additional Protocol I established criminal responsibility for so-called 'grave breaches'[48] (i.e., war crimes), a similar provision is missing from both Common Article 3 and Additional Protocol II.[49] The idea of criminal prosecution for war crimes committed in non-international armed conflicts only became a reality in 1994, with the creation of the International Criminal Tribunal for Rwanda, which was established for the purpose of prosecuting those responsible for the Rwandan genocide, which was an internal armed conflict.[50] This development was codified in 1998 in Article 8 of the Rome Statute, which gives the International Criminal Court jurisdiction over war crimes committed in both international and non-international armed conflicts.[51]

4   The Conduct of Hostilities

The so-called 'Hague Law' deals primarily with the limitations on the conduct of hostilities, namely the means and methods of warfare. This body of law is based mainly in the 1907 Hague Regulations, but also provisions of the 1977 Additional Protocols and customary international law.[52] Throughout history, the conduct of hostilities has brought terrible

---

[43] Greenwood (n 13), margin note 211.   [44] Gasser (n 17) 81; see Additional Protocol II art 13.

[45] See Ipsen (n 26), para 65, margin note 2   [46] Greenwood (n 13), margin note 211.

[47] See Additional Protocol II art 1(2).

[48] See James G Stewart (ed), 'The Grave Breaches Regime in the Geneva Conventions: A Reassessment Sixty Years On' (2009) 7 Journal of International Criminal Justice 653.

[49] First Geneva Convention arts 49–50; Second Geneva Convention arts 50–1; Third Geneva Convention arts 129–30; Fourth Geneva Convention arts 146–7.

[50] See Sonja Boelaert-Suominen, 'Grave Breaches, Universal Jurisdiction and Internal Armed Conflict: Is Customary Law Moving Towards a Uniform Enforcement Mechanism for all Armed Conflicts?' (2000) 5 Journal of Conflict and Security Law 63. *Prosecutor v Dusko Tadic* (Decision on the Defence Motion for Interlocutory Appeal on Jurisdiction) IT-94-1-AR72 (2 October 1995) (ICTY Appeals Chamber), para 134.

[51] Rome Statute of the ICC (adopted 17 July 1998, entered into force 1 July 2002) 2187 UNTS 3.

[52] See for more details on the term 'conduct of hostilities' Robert Heinsch, 'Conduct of Hostilities' in Drazan Djukic and Niccolo Pons (eds), *The Companion to International Humanitarian Law* (Brill 2018) 379–83.

suffering to mankind. Thousands of combatants and fighters have been traumatized, injured, or killed. Civilians have lost their property, their loved ones, and their lives. For more than a hundred years, IHL has; therefore regulated the conduct of hostilities for the purpose of minimizing the suffering caused by war. As a result, IHL contains an extensive body of rules on the means and methods of warfare. The 'means of warfare' refer to the types of weapons that are developed, possessed, and used during armed conflict. The 'methods of warfare' concern the ways in which such weapons are used, or in which ways hostilities are conducted.

International humanitarian law either restricts or prohibits certain means and methods of warfare, on the basis of the long-standing rule of limited warfare. Any act of war must balance the concerns of humanity on the one hand, and military necessity, on the other hand. The rule of limited warfare was initially codified in Article 22 of the 1907 Hague Regulations, and later restated in Article 35(1) of Additional Protocol I, which provides that '[t]he right of the Parties to the conflict to choose methods or means of warfare is not unlimited'. This rule undisputedly forms part of customary international law.[53] There are a few important principles that follow from this rejection of total war, namely those of distinction, proportionality and precautions, and the prohibition of unnecessary suffering. Many other rules are built upon these fundamental principles.

a   *The Methods of Warfare*

i   *Principle of distinction*

According to the principle of distinction, the parties to a conflict must at all times distinguish between civilians and combatants, and between civilian objects and military objectives.[54] Attacks may only be directed against combatants and military objectives. Thus, in general, it is prohibited to carry out attacks against civilians and civilian objects. The aim of this principle is to protect the civilian population from the dangers arising from military operations. The principle is codified in Articles 48 and 51(2) of Additional Protocol I and is also considered to form part of customary international law.[55] Having established that the parties to an armed conflict must distinguish at all times between civilians and combatants, and between civilian objects and military objectives, it is now important to explore what these terms actually mean.

Combatants are described by Article 43(2) of Additional Protocol I as the members of the armed forces of a party to an international armed conflict, with the exception of medical and religious personnel. Likewise, Article 4(A)(1) of the Third Geneva Convention defines prisoners of war as '[m]embers of the armed forces of a Party to the conflict, as well as members of militias or volunteer corps forming part of such armed forces' and who have

---

[53] ICRC, Customary IHL Database Rule 17: Choice of Means and Methods of Warfare <https://ihl-databases.icrc.org/customary-ihl/eng/docs/v1_rul_rule17>.

[54] See Robert Heinsch, 'Distinction' in Djukic and Pons (n 52) 307–9.

[55] ICRC, Customary IHL Database Rule 1: The Principle of Distinction between Civilians and Combatants <https://ihl-databases.icrc.org/customary-ihl/eng/docs/v2_rul_rule1> and Rule 7: The Principle of Distinction between Civilian Objects and Military Objectives <https://ihl-databases.icrc.org/customary-ihl/eng/docs/v2_rul_rule7>.

fallen into the hands of the enemy. Thus, IHL recognizes that the rights and duties of war apply not only to regular armed forces, but can also extend to other organized armed groups in an international armed conflict, such as militias or volunteer corps. Members of these other organized armed groups also receive combatant status, provided that they fulfil the following four conditions:

1. They must be commanded by a person responsible for his subordinates;
2. They must have a fixed distinctive sign recognizable at a distance;
3. They must carry arms openly; and
4. They must conduct their operations in accordance with the rules of IHL.[56]

These four conditions ensure that armed groups that receive combatant status effectively resemble regular armed forces. Three legal consequences result from an individual's combatant status. First, as follows from the principle of distinction, combatants are legitimate military objectives or targets, meaning that they may be lawfully attacked at any time during armed conflict. Second, combatants enjoy 'combatant privilege', which means that they have the right to use lawful means and methods of warfare. They may directly participate in hostilities without facing criminal prosecution during or after the conflict. Finally, combatants who fall into the hands of the enemy are entitled to prisoner of war (POW) status, which means that they enjoy certain privileges and protection under the Third Geneva Convention (see Section 4(a)).[57] Article 50(1) of Additional Protocol I defines civilians in a negative manner as persons who are *not* combatants. In case of doubt about a person's status, he or she must be presumed to be a civilian. As a general rule, civilians are protected by the principle of distinction, and as a result they may not be attacked by the parties to a conflict.

An object must meet two cumulative criteria in order to qualify as a military objective pursuant to Article 52(2) of Additional Protocol I, which reflects customary IHL. First, an object must contribute effectively to the enemy's military action by virtue of its nature, location, purpose, or current use. Second, the destruction, capture, or neutralization of such an object must offer the attacker 'a definite military advantage', in the sense that the military advantage must be concrete and perceptible. Examples of military objectives are buildings where enemy combatants and their material and weapons are located, such as military barracks, and means of transportation, such as tanks or fighter jets.

Like civilians, civilian objects are also negatively defined and encompass all objects that are not military.[58] Generally, cities, residential areas, buildings, houses, schools, hospitals, and historic monuments are presumed to be civilian objects.[59] This presumption guarantees the protection of such objects in situations that are not clear-cut. These objects could, however, under certain conditions, also be used by combatants to make an effective contribution to military action. This use would then turn them – at least partly or

---

[56] Fourth Geneva Convention art 4(A)(2).
[57] See Emily Crawford, *The Treatment of Combatants and Insurgents under the Law of Armed Conflict* (Oxford University Press 2010) 238; Gregory P Noone and others, 'Prisoners of War in the 21st Century: Issues in Modern Warfare'; (2004) 50 Naval Law Review 1.
[58] Additional Protocol I art 52(1).   [59] See Additional Protocol I art 52(3).

temporarily – into military objectives. They are then referred to as 'dual-use objects'. In practice, it is crucial for a commander to carry out a case-by-case assessment to determine whether an object is civilian.

ii   Prohibition of Indiscriminate Attacks

The prohibition on indiscriminate attacks, as found in Article 51(4) of Additional Protocol I, derives from the principle of distinction. Indiscriminate attacks are attacks that cannot be directed at specific military objectives and that therefore strike military objectives and civilians and civilian objects without distinction.[60] Examples of indiscriminate attacks are listed in Article 51(5) of Additional Protocol I, and include, for instance, an attack by bombardment that 'treats as a single military objective a number of clearly separated and distinct military objectives located in a city, town, village or other area containing a similar concentration of civilians or civilian objects'. This provision must be understood as a reaction to the so-called 'area bombardments' during the Second World War, which were seen as legal by the Allied powers at that time.[61]

Civilian objects, such as schools, hospitals, and houses, may be closely located to military objectives such as tanks and military barracks, especially since warfare is now often waged in populated urban areas, as has been exemplified by the Battle of Aleppo in Syria (2012–16).[62] Attacking military barracks may also result in the destruction of an adjacent school, for instance, thereby leading to the loss of civilian lives. The fact that a military objective has been identified as such, in accordance with the principle of distinction, is therefore not enough to limit human suffering as much as possible. In this context, two further principles govern the conduct of hostilities: the principle of proportionality and the principle of precautions. These two principles have been built upon the rule of limited warfare and the principle of distinction, and further restrict the available means and methods of warfare in order to spare the civilian population from the consequences of war. Both principles are considered to form part of customary international law.[63]

iii   Principle of Proportionality

Under the principle of proportionality, a lawful attack against a combatant or military objective must always be proportionate to the aim that it seeks to accomplish in relation to the possible resulting civilian damage. Thus, Article 51(5)(b) of Additional Protocol I prohibits attacks that:

> may be expected to cause incidental loss of civilian life, injury to civilians, damage to civilian objects, or a combination thereof, which would be excessive in relation to the concrete and military advantage anticipated.

---

[60] See for more details, Robert Heinsch, 'Indiscriminate Attacks' in Djukic and Pons (n 52) 408–12.

[61] See Stefan Oeter, 'Methods and Means of Combat' in Fleck (n 13) 196.

[62] Laurent Gisel and others, 'Urban warfare: an age-old problem in need of new solutions' (*Humanitarian Law & Policy*, 27 April 2021) <https://blogs.icrc.org/law-and-policy/2021/04/27/urban-warfare/>.

[63] ICRC, Customary IHL Database Rule 14: Proportionality in Attack <https://ihl-databases.icrc.org/customary-ihl/eng/docs/v1_rul_rule14> and Rule 15: Principle of Precautions in Attack <https://ihl-databases.icrc.org/ customary-ihl/eng/docs/v1_rul_rule15>.

The proportionality principle requires that damage caused to civilians by a military attack, also known as 'collateral damage', must not be 'excessive'. IHL does not provide an objective threshold above which collateral damage is excessive, such as a certain number of civilian victims. Rather, the reasonable commander on the ground must make a judgement based upon the circumstances ruling at the time. While this judgement is therefore partially subjective, IHL does provide a few objective guidelines. In particular, the military advantage gained by the attack must be 'concrete and direct', and not just hypothetical. Also, a military advantage must result from a specific operation, not just the war as a whole. The principle of proportionality is not easy to apply in practice and puts a lot of responsibility on the reasonable commander.

iv   *Principle of Precautions*

According to the principle of precautions in attack, '[i]n the conduct of military operations, constant care must be taken to spare the civilian population, civilians and civilian objects'. This means that 'those who plan or decide upon an attack shall ... take all feasible precautions in the choice of means and methods of attack with a view to avoiding, and in any event minimizing, incidental loss of civilian life, injury to civilians and damage to civilian objects'. The principle of precautions is codified in Articles 57(1) and 57(2)(a)(i) of Additional Protocol I, which reflect customary international law.

In general, the term 'feasible' refers to those measures that are practicable, taking into account all circumstances at the time. Article 57(2) of Additional Protocol I provides that precautionary measures must be taken by both the attacking party and, under Article 58(a) of Additional Protocol I, by the attacked party, which must remove the civilian population, individual civilians, and civilian objects under their control from the vicinity of military objectives. In other words, the attacking party must take 'precautions in attack' while the attacked party must take 'precautions against the effects of attack'. With respect to the attacking party, the precautionary measures must be taken before and during an attack. Before an attack, those who plan and decide upon the attack must do everything feasible to verify that their targets are military and not civilian in nature. Furthermore, those who plan the attack must assess whether the attack would cause excessive collateral damage according to the principle of proportionality. If it would, then they must refrain from attack.

Finally, prior to an attack, the attacking party must give effective advance warning to the civilian population if they may be affected by the attack. This can be implemented, for example, by dropping warning leaflets from an aircraft, or by sending warning messages to mobile phones or over the Internet. This has been done, for example, by the Israel Defense Forces during the 2014 and 2021 conflicts in Gaza.[64] While one might assume that this invites pre-emptive counterattacks or takes away the element of surprise, this is usually avoided by the fact that an attacking party only gives such warnings very shortly before the

---

[64] Steven Erlanger and Fares Akram, 'Israel Warns Gaza Targets by Phone and Leaflet', *New York Times* (8 July 2014) <www.nytimes.com/2014/07/09/world/middleeast/by-phone-and-leaflet-israeli-attackers-warn-gazans.html>.

actual attack. During an attack, the attacking party is obliged to cancel or suspend the attack if a target that was identified as being military in nature subsequently appears not to be. Similarly, an attack that is being carried out must be cancelled or suspended if the collateral damage that it is causing appears to be more significant than originally anticipated. Otherwise, the attack would violate the principle of proportionality.

Under Article 58 of Additional Protocol I and customary international law, the attacked party is obliged, to the maximum extent feasible, to take measures to protect the civilian population under their control against military attacks from the enemy.[65] The attacked party must; therefore, remove the civilian population under their control from the vicinity of military objectives, like military headquarters or barracks.[66] They must also avoid locating military objectives within or near densely populated areas, such as city centres.[67] Finally, the attacked party must take other precautions to protect the civilian population where necessary, such as by creating shelters and safe places, distributing information about expected attacks, and evacuating civilians.[68]

b   The Means of Warfare

Weapons are referred to as the 'means of warfare' and are guided by the same fundamental principles as the methods of warfare.[69] Because of their enormous humanitarian consequences, certain types of weapons have been either restricted or prohibited by IHL. Weapons may only be used in armed conflict when they do not cause superfluous injury or unnecessary suffering, and when they can correctly distinguish between civilians and civilian objects on the one hand, and combatants and military objectives on the other hand. In other words, IHL prohibits the use of weapons that cause superfluous injury or unnecessary suffering as well as indiscriminate attacks.

Article 35(2) of Additional Protocol I prohibits parties to a conflict from employing 'weapons, projectiles and material and methods of warfare which are of a nature to cause superfluous injury or unnecessary suffering'. Examples of such weapons include napalm, an incendiary weapon used during the Vietnam war, and Dum-Dum bullets, which produce a larger wound by expanding on impact. The terms 'superfluous injury' and 'unnecessary suffering' are relatively broad, and lack a treaty-based definition. Many states have accepted that a balance must be struck between military necessity and considerations of humanity, an approach that the ICJ affirmed in its 1996 *Nuclear Weapons* advisory opinion. According to the Court, it is unlawful to cause harm to combatants which is 'greater than that unavoidable to achieve legitimate military objectives'.[70] IHL, thereby restricts or prohibits certain weapons that cause severe injury to soldiers and civilians, and that are, at the same time, unnecessary to

---

[65] ICRC, Customary IHL Database Rule 22: Principle of Precautions against the Effects of Attacks <https://ihl-databases.icrc.org/customary-ihl/eng/docs/v1_rul_rule22>.

[66] Additional Protocol I art 58(a).   [67] Additional Protocol I art 58(b).

[68] Additional Protocol I art 58(c); Customary IHL Database Rule 22 (n 65).

[69] See for more details: ICRC, How does Law Protect in War? 'A to Z: Means of Warfare' <https://casebook.icrc.org/glossary/means-warfare>.

[70] *Legality of the Threat or Use of Nuclear Weapons* advisory opinion (n 7), para 78.

'win the war'. While some of these means of warfare have been restricted or prohibited by treaties created specifically for this purpose, such as the Protocol on Blinding Laser Weapons or the Convention on Anti-Personnel Mines,[71] such weapons would already be banned under the general prohibition on causing unnecessary suffering or superfluous injury.

The prohibition of indiscriminate attacks also limits the use of weapons that cannot be directed at specific military objectives. Article 51(4) of Additional Protocol I provides that weapons that cannot be directed at specific military objectives, and which consequently strike military objectives and civilians without distinction, are indiscriminate and therefore prohibited. This includes weapons that are expected to cause excessive collateral damage, as specified in Article 51(5) of Additional Protocol I. A landmine, for example, can be triggered by either a civilian or a combatant, without distinguishing between the two, and is; therefore, an indiscriminate weapon.

Despite the existence of these general prohibitions, reaching a consensus on which specific weapons breach IHL can be challenging because the underlying principles are formulated rather broadly and leave discretion to the person applying the law. Thus, numerous conventions that explicitly restrict or prohibit specific weapons have been adopted, thereby leaving no doubt as to whether these weapons are prohibited.[72] These specific treaties regulate both conventional weapons, such as small arms and light weapons, and weapons of mass destruction, such as chemical, biological, and nuclear weapons.[73] Weapons of mass destruction can cause enormous numbers of casualties, while also destroying entire cities or natural landscapes, such as mountains and forests. As a result of these severe consequences, states have explicitly prohibited the use of certain weapons of mass destruction, like biological and chemical weapons, in separate conventions. The 1972 Biological Weapons Convention[74] and the 1992 Chemical Weapons Convention[75] both state, in absolute terms, that the contracting parties shall 'never under any circumstances' make use of biological and chemical weapons in the conduct of hostilities. More recently, in 2017, states concluded the Treaty on the Prohibition of Nuclear Weapons (TPNW), which entered into force on 22 January 2021, and currently has fifty-four states parties, none of which are among the current nuclear powers.[76]

---

[71] Additional Protocol to the Convention on Prohibitions or Restrictions on the Use of Certain Conventional Weapons which may be deemed to be Excessively Injurious or to have Indiscriminate Effects (Protocol IV, entitled Protocol on Blinding Laser Weapons) (adopted 13 October 1995, entered into force 30 July 1998) 1380 UNTS 370; Convention on the Prohibition of the Use, Stockpiling, Production and Transfer of Anti-Personnel Mines and on Their Destruction (adopted 18 September 1997, entered into force 1 March 1999) 2056 UNTS 211.

[72] See, for example, Convention on the Prohibition of the Development, Production and Stockpiling of Bacteriological (Biological) and Toxin Weapons and on Their Destruction (adopted 10 April 1972, entered into force 26 March 1975) 1015 UNTS 163; Convention on Prohibitions or Restrictions on the Use of Certain Conventional Weapons Which May Be Deemed to Be Excessively Injurious or to Have Indiscriminate Effects (with Protocols I, II, and III) (adopted 10 October 1980, entered into force 2 December 1983) 1342 UNTS 137; Convention on the Prohibition of the Development, Production, Stockpiling and Use of Chemical Weapons and on Their Destruction (adopted 3 September 1992, entered into force 29 April 1997) 1975 UNTS 45; Anti-Personnel Mines Convention (n 71).

[73] Convention on Certain Conventional Weapons, Protocols I, II and III (n 72); Protocol IV (n 71) and Protocol V (adopted 28 November 2003, entered into force 12 November 2006) 2399 UNTS 100; Convention on Cluster Munitions (adopted 30 May 2008, entered into force 1 August 2010) 2688 UNTS 39

[74] Biological and Toxin Weapons Convention (n 72).   [75] Chemical Weapons Convention (n 72).

[76] TPNW (adopted 7 July 2017, entered into force 22 January 2021); see also UN, 'Treaty on the Prohibition of Nuclear Weapons' <www.un.org/disarmament/wmd/nuclear/tpnw/>.

The fact that the nuclear powers have not ratified the TPNW does not mean that as parties to an armed conflict they could lawfully resort to nuclear weapons. In nearly all conceivable scenarios, the use of nuclear weapons would foreseeably violate the principles of distinction and proportionality, as well as the prohibition of superfluous injury or unnecessary suffering. This view was adopted by the ICJ in its 1996 *Nuclear Weapons* advisory opinion, which stated that:

> ... methods and means of warfare, which would preclude any distinction between civilian and military targets, or which would result in unnecessary suffering to combatants, are prohibited. In view of the unique characteristics of nuclear weapons, to which the Court has referred above, the use of such weapons in fact seems scarcely reconcilable with respect for such requirements.[77]

The Court nevertheless did not 'reach a definitive conclusion as to the legality or illegality of the use of nuclear weapons by a state in an extreme circumstance of self-defence, in which its very survival would be at stake'.[78]

IHL also addresses the development of new weapons, such as armed drones, autonomous weapons, and cyber warfare. Article 36 of Additional Protocol I, which is considered by some commentators to reflect customary international law, obliges states parties to conduct a legal review of new weapons.[79] The development and use of new weapons must be restricted or prohibited if their expected use would not comply with the rules of IHL, namely the prohibition of superfluous injury or unnecessary suffering, as well as the prohibition on indiscriminate attacks. At present, armed drones and autonomous weapons, which are at the forefront of modern warfare, are not explicitly prohibited by IHL, though they are the subject of an ongoing debate as to whether they comply with the most fundamental rules of IHL.[80] Because of extensive use of armed drones, especially by the United States in its counter-terrorism measures in locations like Pakistan and Yemen,[81] some have advocated for the total ban of these weapons.[82]

c   Conduct of Hostilities in Non-international Armed Conflicts

Many of the treaty rules governing the conduct of hostilities, particularly those codified in Additional Protocol I, apply only to international armed conflicts. Common Article 3 and the provisions of Additional Protocol II, which are the main rules governing non-international armed conflicts, build upon the same fundamental rules of limited warfare, as found in the Geneva Conventions and Additional Protocol I, but they are much more limited and not as detailed as the treaty law governing international armed conflicts. As a result, a number of

---

[77] *Legality of the Threat or Use of Nuclear Weapons* advisory opinion (n 7), para 95.   [78] ibid.

[79] On this topic, see Natalia Jevglevskaja, 'Weapons Review Obligation under Customary International Law' (2018) 94 International Law Studies 186.

[80] See Terry Gill, Robert Heinsch, and Robin Geiss, 'ILA Study Group: The Conduct of Hostilities and International Humanitarian Law, Challenges of 21st Century Warfare – Interim Report' (2014) 6–9.

[81] See, for example, James Cavallaro, Stephan Sonnenberg, and Sarah Knuckey, *Living Under Drones: Death, Injury, and Trauma to Civilians from US Drone Practices in Pakistan* (International Human Rights and Conflict Resolution Clinic at Stanford Law School and Global Justice Clinic at NYU School of Law 2012).

[82] See, for example, the 'Campaign to Stop Killer Robots' <www.stopkillerrobots.org/>.

specific weapons prohibitions, for instance, only apply to non-international armed conflicts by means of customary international law.[83]

Furthermore, neither Common Article 3 of the Geneva Conventions, nor Additional Protocol II, grant combatant status to so-called 'fighters' against a state's armed forces. Unlike the official combatants of state armies, such fighters cannot lawfully conduct hostilities by killing members of the state's armed forces, and may be prosecuted for such acts during or after the war, under the criminal law of the state of their nationality for offences such as murder and manslaughter. Whereas members of organized armed groups can attain combatant status in the context of international armed conflicts under certain circumstances, this is not the case in the context of non-international armed conflicts, where fighters operating in armed groups remain unlawful.[84]

Such fighters enjoy neither combatant status nor the protections to which civilians are entitled. In the context of non-international armed conflicts, civilians that take up arms as fighters lose their civilian protection 'for such time as they take a direct part in hostilities'.[85] During the time when they are directly taking part in hostilities, they may be lawfully attacked. The relevant treaty law does not provide a clear definition of the phrase 'direct participation in hostilities', though the ICRC has published interpretive guidance on the notion of direct participation in hostilities.[86] According to this guidance, acts by civilians that provide support to an organized armed group that is party to a non-international armed conflict, and that directly harm the enemy, for example by inflicting death, amount to direct participation in hostilities.[87] Acts by civilians that fall short of the threshold of direct participation in hostilities include, for example, merely funding an organized armed group, or helping them to produce a weapon.

In some situations, civilians do not just take part in hostilities on a sporadic basis, but do so on a continuous basis for an organized armed group, in what is known as a *'continuous combat function'*.[88] These civilians are regarded as members of that armed group and are legitimate military targets, and not just 'for such time as they take a direct part in hostilities'. For example, a civilian who joins the organized armed branch of a non-state actor like Daesh/ISIS in the conflict in Syria, receives his weapons and his 'uniform', as well as his instructions from the commanding officers, and does not return on a daily basis to his family. He, thereby assumes a continuous combat function, like a soldier in a regular army, but he does not enjoy the same privileges as combatants in an international armed conflict.

5   The Protection of Persons

The first three Geneva Conventions originally limited their protection to wounded, sick, shipwrecked, and imprisoned members of armed forces. It was only after the Second World

---

[83] See ICRC, Customary IHL Database Rules 70–86 <https://ihl-databases.icrc.org/customary-ihl/eng/docs/v1_rul>.

[84] Fourth Geneva Convention art 4(A)(2).

[85] Additional Protocol II art 13(3), Common art 3; see also Additional Protocol I art 51(3).

[86] Nils Melzer, *Interpretive Guidance on the Notion of Direct Participation in Hostilities under International Humanitarian Law* (International Committee of the Red Cross 2009).

[87] The ICRC Guidance on Direct Participation in Hostilities requires three cumulative conditions: (1) threshold of harm, (2) direct causation, and (3) belligerent nexus, see supra note 86, pp. 46–64.

[88] ibid.

War, with the adoption of the Fourth Geneva Convention in 1949, that states addressed the provision of medical care and special protection for all persons in need, including civilians.

a *Protection of Wounded Persons*

Contemporary IHL protects the wounded and sick in armed conflict through the 1949 First Geneva Convention 'for the Amelioration of the Condition of the Wounded and Sick in Armed Forces', the Second Geneva Convention 'for the Amelioration of the Condition of Wounded, Sick and Shipwrecked Members of Armed Forces at Sea', the Fourth Geneva Convention 'relative to the Protection of Civilian Persons in Time of War'; and the two 1977 Additional Protocols. With the adoption of the 1977 Additional Protocols, the wounded and sick include all persons who, because of trauma, disease, or other physical or mental disorder or disability, are in need of medical assistance or care, and who refrain from any act of hostility.[89] Expectant mothers and babies are also included in the definition.[90] These provisions in the Additional Protocols apply irrespective of the military or civilian status of the wounded and sick persons, although a wounded person who resumes fighting loses his or her protection under IHL.

According to Article 12 of the First Geneva Convention, the wounded and sick must be respected and protected in all circumstances and cared for by the party to the conflict in whose power they may be. In this context, the term 'respected' includes a negative obligation to refrain from attack or other violent acts. The duty to 'protect' entails a positive obligation to safeguard the sick and wounded. The belligerent parties must actively search for and collect the wounded and sick from the zone of hostilities to protect them against pillage and ill-treatment. Finally, the duty of care means that the parties to the conflict must provide the sick and wounded with the necessary medical treatment, without distinction or priority on any grounds other than medical necessity. In other words, the belligerents must not distinguish between sick or wounded persons on the basis of ethnicity, race, political opinion, or any other similar criteria.[91] The sick and wounded also retain other protections to which they might be entitled under IHL. For example, injured civilians continue to benefit from the protections flowing from their civilian status. Articles 24 and 25 of the First Geneva Convention further provide that belligerent parties must also respect and protect medical personnel, the rationale being that the sick and wounded could not be adequately protected if medical personnel were exposed to attacks.[92]

The protection that IHL provides for the sick and wounded also extends to 'medical units' and 'medical transports'.[93] Hospitals are a classic example of medical units, but they also include blood transfusion centres, medical depots, and pharmacies. Examples of medical transports include ambulances, hospital ships, and medical aircraft. Both medical units and medical transports must be respected and protected in all circumstances. They cannot form the object of an attack or be used to shield military objectives from attack. The

---

[89] Additional Protocol I art 8(a). [90] Additional Protocol I art 8(a). [91] First Geneva Convention art 12.
[92] ICRC, *Respecting and Protecting Health Care in Armed Conflicts and in Situations Not Covered by International Humanitarian Law* (April 2021) <www.icrc.org/en/download/file/166987/dp_consult_31_hcid_web.pdf>.
[93] Additional Protocol I art 8(e).

misuse of medical units and transports to harm the enemy results in a loss of special protection. For example, hospitals that serve as military observation posts, or ambulances that are used to transport weapons, lose their special protection under IHL.

In contrast to the extensive regime for international armed conflicts, the protection of the wounded and sick in non-international armed conflicts is only regulated by Common Article 3, which provides that persons taking no active part in hostilities, including members of the armed forces who have laid down their arms as a result of sickness or wounds, should be treated humanely, and that the wounded and sick shall be collected and cared for. Additional Protocol II builds upon this minimum standard of protection, by providing that the wounded and sick, as well as medical personnel, units, and transports, shall be respected and protected. The provisions of Geneva Law applicable to non-international armed conflicts are more rudimentary than for international armed conflicts, but basic guarantees are upheld by the law in both types of armed conflicts.[94] An example of treatment of wounded persons that is in keeping with the Geneva Conventions may be found in the context of the non-international armed conflict between Sri Lanka and the Liberation Tigers of Tamil Eelam. The wounded and sick were successfully evacuated by the Sri Lankan Navy, with support of the ICRC, and the rescued persons were provided with much needed food and medical assistance.[95]

b   *Protection of Prisoners of War*

The detention of combatants and civilians in armed conflict is a common and often lawful occurrence. Such detainees have, however, proven to be extremely vulnerable to abuse, as they are isolated and in the hands of the enemy. International humanitarian law, and more specifically the Third Geneva Convention 'Relative to the Treatment of Prisoners of War' as well as the Fourth Geneva Convention and Additional Protocol II; therefore, govern detention during armed conflict, and set certain boundaries with respect to the treatment of detainees. In situations of armed conflict, detainees benefit from protection under a set of rules that is different from those applicable in peace time, under international human rights law, for example. The application of these rules of IHL depends on the legal status of the detainee, who may fall into one of three categories:

1. Combatants who are deprived of their liberty in international armed conflicts, and benefit from prisoner of war status under the Third Geneva Convention;
2. Civilians detained in international armed conflicts, who are protected under the Fourth Geneva Convention; and
3. Persons detained in non-international armed conflicts, who benefit from the protection of Common Article 3 and Additional Protocol II.

---

[94] For further details, please see Sandesh Sivakumaran, *The Law of Non-International Armed Conflict* (Oxford University Press 2012), ch 8.
[95] IHL-in-Action Database, Case Study by Angèle Jeangeorge, *Sri Lanka: Evacuation of the Wounded and Sick* <https://ihl-in-action.icrc.org/case-study/sri-lanka-evacuation-wounded-and-sick>.

The term prisoner of war, or POW, is defined in Article 4 of the Third Geneva Convention as a combatant who has 'fallen into the power of the enemy'. 'Combatants' are members of the armed forces of a party to an international armed conflict, with the exception of medical and religious personnel. Members of irregular armed forces in international armed conflicts are also entitled to POW status when captured, provided that they fulfil the four requirements to be assimilated to the regular armed forces (see Section 3(a)(i)). Because they carry out belligerent acts, combatants are, in principle, considered to pose a threat to the security of the adverse party, which can therefore lawfully deprive them of their liberty until 'the cessation of active hostilities'.[96] The internment of combatants is a non-criminal, preventive measure taken by the adverse party to protect itself against security threats.[97] POWs can be interned without any specific judicial or administrative procedure and are not entitled to a review of the lawfulness of their internment while hostilities are ongoing, since 'POWs are considered to pose a security threat ipso facto'.[98]

POWs are protected by a number of rules of IHL 'from the time they fall into the power of the enemy and until their final release and repatriation'.[99] Article 13 of the Third Geneva Convention provides that they 'must at all times be humanely treated'. Causing death or seriously endangering the health of a POW is explicitly prohibited.[100] Furthermore, the detaining power must protect POWs against acts of violence or intimidation, and against insults and public curiosity.[101] Measures of reprisal against POWs are also prohibited.[102] The detaining power must also tend to POWs basic needs, free of charge. POWs must receive adequate food, water, clothing, shelter, and medical attention.[103] They must be allowed to freely practice their religion, and to engage in educational and recreational activities.[104] IHL further enables POWs to retain contact with the outside world.[105] The detaining power must allow POWs to communicate with their family, their home state and the ICRC.[106] The US military, for example, adapted their detention policies in Iraq, in the context of the international armed conflict there, in order to accommodate more visits by the families of Iraqi prisoners at Camp Bucca in Umm Qasr.[107]

c *Detention of Civilians in International Armed Conflicts*

Unlike combatants, civilians do not, by definition, pose a threat to the security of the belligerents, because they are not supposed to participate in the hostilities. In some cases; however, for example, in occupied territories, civilians may participate in criminal

---

[96] Third Geneva Convention art 118.   [97] The term 'internment', rather than detention, is used in relation to POWs.
[98] ICRC Opinion Paper, *Internment in Armed Conflict: Basic Rules and Challenges* (November 2014) 4 <www.icrc.org/en/download/file/3223/security-detention-position-paper-icrc-11-2014.pdf>.
[99] Third Geneva Convention art 5.   [100] Third Geneva Convention art 13(1).   [101] Third Geneva Convention art 13(2).
[102] Third Geneva Convention art 13(3).   [103] See Third Geneva Convention arts 15, 26–7 and 30.
[104] Third Geneva Convention art 34.   [105] Third Geneva Convention art 69.   [106] Third Geneva Convention art 71.
[107] IHL-in-Action Database, Case Study by Clara Delarue, Ana-Paula Ilg, Claudia Langianese and Eleanor Umeyor, *Iraq: Reform in Iraqi Detention Facilities Leads to Family Visitation to Detainees in Camp Bucca* <https://ihl-in-action.icrc.org/case-study/iraq-reform-iraqi-detention-facilities-leads-family-visitation-detainees-camp-bucca>.

activities against the occupying power and can be lawfully detained as a result. Civilians may; therefore, be interned when absolutely necessary for security reasons, but only if an appropriate court or administrative board determines that they pose a significant threat to the security of the belligerent party.[108] This is the case when civilians take up arms and directly participate in hostilities, without qualifying as combatants. Like POWs, civilians who are interned by the enemy during an armed conflict must receive adequate protection. Unlike POWs, however, civilians are entitled to a review of their detention by a court or an administrative board. Civilians who are detained should also be released 'as soon as possible', and in any event after the cessation of hostilities.

The law governing non-international armed conflict does not provide an explicit legal basis for the detention of protected persons. Nevertheless, the legal provisions that regulate non-international armed conflicts implicitly refer to the possibility of detention of protected persons, as they provide for a minimum level of protection for persons who have been deprived of their liberty, including humane treatment, provision of basic needs, and contact with the outside world.[109] IHL, thereby ensures that all persons in armed conflict who are deprived of their liberty, whether international or non-international, receive a minimum level of protection.

6   The Implementation and Enforcement of IHL

The implementation of IHL refers to the process of giving effect to international obligations at the national level. States can implement IHL through the adoption of domestic legislation, by instructing military commanders of the armed forces, and through the dissemination of information about IHL among the general public. Enforcement of IHL refers to the mechanisms that ensure that the laws of armed conflict are respected. IHL can be enforced in a number of ways, including through: (1) public opinion; (2) measures taken by the UN Security Council under Chapter VII of the UN Charter (see Chapter 11); (3) judgments or awards of international courts and tribunals in inter-state cases; (4) reparations, such as compensation; (5) the International Humanitarian Fact-Finding Commission under Article 90 of Additional Protocol I; and (6) criminal prosecution of individuals before national and international criminal courts and tribunals (see Chapter 13).

IHL specifically requires states to implement and enforce the rules that govern armed conflict. Common Article 1 of the Geneva Conventions states that the high contracting parties have a duty 'to respect and to ensure respect' for IHL. This rule entails two duties for states: (1) a negative duty to refrain from any violation of IHL (respect); and (2) a positive duty to ensure the implementation and application of IHL (ensure respect).[110] In practice, IHL is sometimes both violated and respected in the same context, though the media tends to focus on the violations.[111]

---

[108] Fourth Geneva Convention arts 42, 43.   [109] Additional Protocol II arts 4–6.
[110] For more details, please see ICRC, *Commentary: Geneva Convention (I)* (2016) art 1 <https://ihl-databases.icrc.org/ihl/full/GCI-commentaryArt1>.
[111] IHL in Action: Respect for the Law on the Battlefield <https://ihl-in-action.icrc.org/>.

Enforcement in the IHL context is challenging because of the absence of a central body or hierarchical institution that is responsible for the enforcement of IHL. Although IHL was created to make situations of armed conflict more humane, the international community has not been prepared to ban all means and methods of war, and has therefore been reluctant to establish efficient enforcement mechanisms. This has been illustrated by the failed attempt of the ICRC to institute a new compliance mechanism for IHL.[112]

The prosecution of individuals for their involvement in the commission of war crimes, along with crimes against humanity and genocide, represents one of the most powerful tools for strengthening respect for IHL (see Chapter 13). War crimes are grave breaches of the Geneva Conventions and the Additional Protocols, as well as other serious violations of IHL that give rise to individual criminal responsibility.[113] As the word 'grave' suggests, only 'serious' violations of IHL constitute war crimes. In other words, not all violations of IHL constitute a criminal offence that gives rise to individual liability. For example, deliberately targeting a civilian population is a serious violation, while mistakenly doing so on the basis of faulty intelligence would not necessarily be a criminal offence. Grave breaches as well as many other serious violations of IHL have now been codified as war crimes in Article 8 of the Rome Statute of the International Criminal Court.

7   Concluding Remarks

International humanitarian law is one of the oldest and most detailed areas of international law, which aims to ensure that during the darkest hours of humankind, the principles of humanity are taken into account, and the weakest and most vulnerable are protected from attack. Challenges to this legal regime have, however, been posed by modern warfare, which has seen increasing numbers of non-international armed conflicts, the proliferation of non-state actors, and the use of modern technologies like autonomous weapons and cyber warfare. Nevertheless, the international community continues to grapple with these challenges, and to strive towards solutions to the challenges of twenty-first century warfare.

Recommended Reading

Emily Crawford and Alison Pert, *International Humanitarian Law* (2nd edn, Cambridge University Press 2020).

Cordula Droege, "The interplay between International Humanitarian Law and International Human Rights Law in Situations of Armed Conflict" (2007) 40 Israel Law Review 310.

Henry Dunant, *A memory of Solferino* (first published 1862, International Committee of the Red Cross 1939, 1959).

---

[112] See Giulio Bartolini, 'The 'Compliance Track' on a Track to Nowhere' (*EJIL Talk*, 22 January 2016) <www.ejiltalk.org/the-compliance-track-on-a-track-to-nowhere>.

[113] Additional Protocol I art 85.

Jean-Marie Henckaerts, "Study on Customary International Humanitarian law: A Contribution to the Understanding and Respect for the Rule of Law in Armed Conflict" (2005) 87 International Review of the Red Cross 175.

Nils Melzer, *International Humanitarian Law: A Comprehensive Introduction* (International Committee of the Red Cross 2019).

13

International Criminal Law

Cecily Rose

1   Introduction

International criminal law is the branch of public international law under which individuals may be held criminally responsible for the offences of genocide, crimes against humanity, war crimes, and the crime of aggression. Within the larger field of public international law, international criminal law is unique in that it imposes legal obligations on individuals, as opposed to states. Individuals were first prosecuted for international crimes, by international judicial institutions, after the Second World War. Only in the 1990s, however, did a robust body of international criminal law emerge, due to the creation of a number of international criminal courts and tribunals, including the International Criminal Tribunals for the former Yugoslavia and Rwanda, and the International Criminal Court (ICC). The ICC will form a focal point in this chapter, in part because it is the only permanent international court that can try individuals for international crimes, and will therefore remain an important judicial body in this area of law.

This chapter forms a complement to the chapters on the law on the use of force and international humanitarian law (IHL) (Chapters 11 and 12), as international crimes often take place during times of armed conflict, though some international crimes may also be committed during peace-time. International criminal law seeks to prevent impunity by holding accountable those individuals who are responsible for serious violations of international criminal law. This chapter begins with the history of international criminal law, starting with the aftermath of the First and Second World Wars, and ending with the creation of a spate of international criminal courts and tribunals in recent decades (Section 2). The chapter then covers substantive aspects of international criminal law, namely the crime of genocide, crimes against humanity, war crimes, and the crime of aggression (Section 3). Finally, the chapter covers key procedural aspects of international criminal law, including the jurisdiction of international courts and tribunals, the admissibility of cases, modes of liability, and immunities (Section 4).

This chapter focuses on international criminal law, to the exclusion of transnational criminal law. Transnational crimes include a wide range of conduct, including terrorism, drug trafficking, human trafficking, piracy, corruption, and organized crime. The term 'transnational criminal law' refers to an extensive body of treaties that require states parties to criminalize certain conduct in their domestic legal systems, and to cooperate with each other in carrying out domestic investigations and prosecutions.[1] Whereas transnational criminal law results in individuals being held criminally accountable under domestic law, international criminal law results in individuals being held liable directly under international law. Transnational criminal law is no less important or worthy of study than international criminal law, but because this chapter can only cover so much, the focus is on international crimes, and the laws and institutions that have evolved for the purposes of holding individuals criminally responsible directly under international law.

2   A History of International Criminal Law

The modern history of international criminal law began following the First World War. The victorious Allied Powers established a commission that was responsible for exploring the possibility of holding the Associated Powers responsible for crimes committed by them during the war.[2] The commission proposed the creation of a High Allied Tribunal, which would try perpetrators of 'violations of law and customs of war and the law of humanity' (e.g., modern day war crimes and crimes against humanity). The commission recommended the prosecution of the former German Emperor, Wilhelm Hohenzollern, for ordering such crimes. Although the Treaty of Versailles, which was concluded between Germany and the Allied Powers after the war, provided for the creation of a special tribunal to try the former Emperor, the tribunal never came into existence and the former Emperor lived the remainder of his life in exile in the Netherlands.[3] Instead, in 1921, Germany itself prosecuted suspected war criminals in what came to be known as the 'Leipzig trials'. Between the First and Second World Wars, some states also pursued the idea of creating an international criminal court for the prosecution of terrorist offences, but this too, never came to fruition.[4]

a   *International Military Tribunals at Nuremberg and Tokyo*

Following the Second World War, the Allied Powers prevailed in their pursuit of international criminal justice. In August 1945, the Allied Powers, consisting of France, the Soviet Union, the United Kingdom, and the United States, concluded the London Agreement, which provided for the prosecution and punishment of the major war criminals of the European Axis (i.e., the leaders of Nazi Germany). The Charter of the International Military Tribunal (the Nuremberg Tribunal) was annexed to the London Agreement and set out the Nuremberg Tribunal's mandate and structure. The Charter provided for the prosecution of

---

[1] See, generally, Neil Boister, *An Introduction to Transnational Criminal Law* (2nd edn, Oxford University Press 2018).

[2] The Commission on the Responsibility of the Authors of the War and on Enforcement of Penalties. During the First World War, the Allied Powers were France, Great Britain, Italy, Japan, Russia, and the United States. The Associated Powers were Germany, Austria-Hungary, the Ottoman Empire, and Bulgaria.

[3] Treaty of Versailles (adopted 28 June 1919, entered into force 10 January 1920) 1920 ATS 1, art 227. See, generally, William A Schabas, *The Trial of the Kaiser* (Oxford University Press 2018).

[4] Manley O Hudson, 'The Proposed International Criminal Court' (1938) 32 American Journal of International Law 549; Michael D Callahan, 'Terrorism Court (1937)' in *Max Planck Encyclopedia of Public International Law* (last updated October 2018).

three substantive crimes: crimes against peace, war crimes, and crimes against humanity.[5] The prosecution of the different counts of the indictment was divided among prosecutors from the four Allied Powers, and each Allied Power appointed one judge of its nationality to the bench.[6] After a ten-month trial, which ran from November 1945 to September 1946, the tribunal acquitted three individuals and convicted nineteen individuals, who were sentenced to death or imprisonment.[7] Of the six organizations that were indicted, three were acquitted and three were found to be criminal.[8]

The Nuremberg Tribunal's legacy was significant and largely positive, despite the critique that it had engaged in victor's justice. The Tribunal's judgment of 1 October 1946 established that individuals could be held liable directly under international law. The Tribunal famously explained that '[c]rimes against international law are committed by men, not by abstract entities, and only by punishing individuals who commit such crimes can the provisions of international law be enforced'.[9] Another important aspect of the tribunal's legacy is its rejection of the argument that the inclusion of crimes against the peace in the London Agreement breached the principle of legality (*nullum crimen sine lege*), according to which criminal responsibility may only be imposed if the crime was clearly established by law at the time of its commission. The Tribunal determined that the principle of legality was not breached by the prosecution of the defendants for crimes against the peace, as at least some of the defendants knew that Germany's invasions and attacks on neighbouring states were in violation of treaties to which Germany was a party.[10]

The pursuit of international criminal justice following the Second World War extended well beyond Nuremberg. The International Military Tribunal for the Far East (Tokyo Tribunal) was established in 1946, not by treaty, but by a Special Proclamation issued by General Douglas MacArthur, the supreme commander for the Allied Powers in Japan.[11] The prosecutors in Tokyo charged Japanese leaders with crimes against peace, murder, war crimes, and crimes against humanity. The bench of judges was relatively large, by comparison to the Nuremberg Tribunal, as each of the nine signatories to Japan's surrender appointed a judge, in addition to two non-signatories.[12] After a trial of nearly two years, which ran from May 1946 to April 1948, the Tokyo Tribunal delivered its judgment in November 1948. The Tokyo Tribunal convicted all twenty-five defendants, and sentenced them to death or imprisonment.[13] The majority judgment

---

[5] Charter of the International Military Tribunal (adopted and entered into force 8 August 1945) 82 UNTS 279 (Nuremberg Charter) art 6.

[6] Nuremberg Charter art 2. Each Allied Power also appointed one alternate judge, in case a judge should fall ill or become otherwise incapacitated.

[7] Out of the twenty-four indicted persons, one committed suicide and one was declared medically unfit to stand trial.

[8] The Nazi leadership, the Gestapo and the *Sicherheitsdienst* (SD), and the *Schutzstaffel* (SS) were found to be criminal organizations; the *Sturmabteilung* (SA), the Reich Cabinet, and the General Staff and High Command of the German Armed Forces were acquitted.

[9] 'International Military Tribunal (Nuremberg) Judgment and Sentences' (1947) 41 American Journal of International Law 172, 221.

[10] ibid 217.

[11] Neil Boister and Robert Cryer (eds), *Documents on the Tokyo International Military Tribunal: Charter, Indictment and Judgments* (Oxford University Press 2008).

[12] The Japanese Instrument of Surrender (2 September 1945) was signed by representatives of Australia, Canada, China, France, the Netherlands, New Zealand, the Soviet Union, the United Kingdom, and the United States. The two non-signatories who appointed judges were India and the Philippines.

[13] Two defendants died during the trial and one was declared unfit to stand trial.

was accompanied by a number of opinions, including the dissenting opinion of Judge Pal of India, who would have acquitted all of the defendants.[14] Like the Nuremberg Tribunal, the Tokyo Tribunal has been criticized as an exercise in victor's justice, but the critiques have also highlighted flaws in the trial procedure as well as the unnuanced understanding of the facts held by the judges in the majority.[15] In addition to the Nuremberg and Tokyo Tribunals, extensive prosecutions of lower-level accused persons also took place in domestic courts in Europe, the Far East, and elsewhere following the Second World War, and were carried out, in part, by prosecutors from the Allied Powers.[16]

The Nuremberg and Tokyo Tribunals gave rise to efforts to codify international criminal law and to create a permanent international criminal court. Progress, however, was slow and halting. In 1946 the United Nations (UN) General Assembly affirmed the principles of international law that were recognized by the Charter of the Nuremberg Tribunal and its judgment and directed the International Law Commission (ILC) to develop a code of offences against the peace and security of mankind.[17] The General Assembly took further action in 1948, after the conclusion of the Convention on the Prevention and Punishment of the Crime of Genocide (Genocide Convention), which envisages the prosecution of acts of genocide by domestic authorities or by an 'international penal tribunal'.[18] The General Assembly directed the ILC to study the possibility of establishing such a tribunal, which it initially conceived of as a criminal chamber of the International Court of Justice (ICJ), rather than an entirely separate judicial body.[19] By 1953, the ILC had produced a draft statute for a judicial body, but the General Assembly postponed consideration of the statute until the ILC's draft code of offences against the peace and security of mankind was complete.[20] The ILC's work on the code, however, proceeded slowly and in two quite separate phases (1947–54 and 1982–96), due, in part, to controversies surrounding the definition of the crime of aggression.[21] In 1996, the ILC finally adopted the code, which the General Assembly brought to the attention of the drafters of the Statute of the ICC.[22]

b   *Ad Hoc Tribunals for the Former Yugoslavia and Rwanda*

After the Nuremberg and Tokyo Tribunals, the next international criminal prosecutions did not take place until the mid-1990s, after the end of the Cold War. The politics of the Cold

---

[14] For a discussion of Pal's dissent, see Neha Jain, 'Radical Dissents in International Criminal Trials' (2017) 28 European Journal of International Law 1163.

[15] Robert Cryer, Darryl Robinson, and Sergey Vasiliev, *An Introduction to International Criminal Law and Procedure* (4th edn, Cambridge University Press 2019) 123–4.

[16] See, for example, Kevin Jon Heller, *The Nuremberg Military Tribunals and the Origins of International Criminal Law* (Oxford University Press 2011); Control Council for Germany, Law No 10 (20 December 1945). See, generally, Johannes Fuchs and Flavia Lattanzi, 'International Military Tribunals' in *Max Planck Encyclopedia of Public International Law* (last updated April 2011), paras 72–7.

[17] UNGA Res 95(I) (11 December 1946).

[18] Convention on the Prevention and Punishment of the Crime of Genocide (adopted 9 December 1948, entered into force 12 January 1951) 78 UNTS 277 (Genocide Convention) art VI.

[19] UNGA Res 260(B) (9 December 1948).

[20] UNGA Res 898(IX) (14 December 1954); UNGA 'Report of the 1953 Committee on International Criminal Jurisdiction' (29 July–20 August 1953) UN Doc A/2645.

[21] ILC Yearbook 1996 vol 2, pt 2, 15.   [22] UNGA Res 51/60 (16 December 1996).

War, in particular the geopolitical struggle between two permanent members of the UN Security Council – the United States and the Soviet Union – had greatly impeded the ability of the Security Council to take action with respect to mass atrocities under Chapter VII of the UN Charter. The 1990s; therefore, represented a time of renewed possibility for the Security Council. During this period, in the early to mid-1990s, mass atrocities unfolded in both the former Yugoslavia and Rwanda.

The conflict in the former Yugoslavia grew out of the break-up of the Socialist Federal Republic of Yugoslavia, a federal state that consisted of six republics and two autonomous regions, and a mix of ethnicities and religions.[23] The break-up of Yugoslavia and the ensuing violence began in 1991, following the declarations of independence by Slovenia and Croatia, which had been two of the federal republics of Yugoslavia.[24] After another republic, Bosnia and Herzegovina, declared independence in 1992, Serbian forces began to carry out a policy of ethnic cleansing, which involved arbitrary killings, destruction of cultural heritage, sexual violence, and the detention of Muslims and Croats in concentration camps.[25]

In the spring of 1993, the Security Council responded by establishing a temporary or 'ad hoc' International Criminal Tribunal for the former Yugoslavia (ICTY) to try persons responsible for violations of laws or customs of war (i.e., war crimes), genocide, and crimes against humanity.[26] Initial controversy about whether the Security Council had the authority to create such an international tribunal was put to rest during the first case prosecuted by the ICTY.[27] The ICTY's temporal jurisdiction was open ended, as it extended from 1 January 1991 onwards. The ICTY was therefore able to prosecutes individuals for crimes committed not only between 1991 and the end of the conflict in Bosnia and Herzegovina in 1995, but also crimes committed during the conflicts in the late 1990s and early 2000s in Kosovo and Former Yugoslav Republic of Macedonia. The tribunal, which was located in The Hague, the Netherlands, had primacy over national courts, whether in the former Yugoslavia or elsewhere.[28] The ICTY thereby had the authority to ask national courts to defer to its jurisdiction, and to transfer cases to it. In 2002, however, due to the Security Council's concerns about the ICTY's completion of its work, the ICTY judges amended the rules of procedure and evidence to allow for the transfer of indictments and cases from the ICTY back to national courts.[29] The Security Council's focus on the ICTY's completion strategy also led it to explicitly require the tribunal to focus on the 'most senior leaders suspected of being the most responsible for crimes' within the ICTY's jurisdiction.[30]

---

[23] The six republics were Bosnia and Herzegovina, Croatia, Macedonia, Montenegro, Serbia, and Slovenia.

[24] Stefan Oeter, 'Dissolution of Yugoslavia' in *Max Planck Encyclopedia for Public International Law* (last updated May 2011), paras 15–19.

[25] ibid, paras 42–3.

[26] UNSC Res 808 (22 February 1993); UNSC Res 827 (25 May 1993). Statute of the ICTY (25 May 1993) UN Doc S/RES/827 (ICTY Statute) arts 3–5.

[27] *Prosecutor v Dusko Tadic a/k/a 'Dule'* (Decision on the Defence Motion for Interlocutory Appeal on Jurisdiction) IT-94-1-A72 (2 October 1995) (ICTY Appeals Chamber), paras 9–48.

[28] ICTY Statute art 9(2).   [29] ICTY Rules of Procedure and Evidence, Rule 11 *bis*.

[30] UNSC Res 1534 (26 March 2004), para 5.

Approximately a year after the Security Council created the ICTY, a genocide rapidly unfolded in Rwanda, which had recently emerged from a civil war that had origins in long-standing tension between the Hutu and Tutsi ethnic groups.[31] In April 1994, the assassination of the Rwandan president Juvénal Habyarimana, a Hutu, triggered the mass slaughter of Tutsis and politically moderate Hutus by soldiers, police, and militia as well as some Hutu civilians. Over the course of approximately 100 days, between April 1994 and July 1994, between 800,000 to 1 million Tutsis and moderate Hutus were killed. The Security Council failed to prevent the genocide. A UN peacekeeping mission, which had been authorized by the Security Council, was on the ground in Rwanda before and during the genocide, but their mandate and capacity left the peacekeepers largely powerless to prevent or stop the mass killings. After the genocide occurred; however, the Security Council moved quickly to establish an ad hoc tribunal that would be equivalent to the tribunal that had been established a year earlier for the former Yugoslavia.[32]

The Security Council mandated the International Criminal Tribunal for Rwanda (ICTR) to prosecute persons responsible for genocide, crimes against humanity, and serious violations of international humanitarian law (i.e., war crimes).[33] The ICTR was located not in Rwanda, but in Arusha, Tanzania and it shared an Appeals Chamber with the ICTY, which was located in The Hague.[34] Until 2003, the ICTY and the ICTR also shared a prosecutor, but concerns about the ICTR's completion of its work led the Security Council to create a separate prosecutor for the ICTR.[35] The Statute of the ICTR largely paralleled the Statute of the ICTY, with some adjustments due to the particularities of the conflict in Rwanda.[36] The ICTR's temporal jurisdiction was not open-ended like the ICTY's, but instead ran for one year, from 1 January 1994 to 31 December 1994.[37]

The ad hoc tribunals both experienced slow, troubled starts. The ICTY initially struggled to gain custody over accused persons. By the mid to late 1990s, however, some accused had voluntarily surrendered and the North Atlantic Treaty Organization (NATO), which had forces in Bosnia and Herzegovina, began arresting suspects.[38] During this early period the ICTY came under criticism for focusing on the prosecution of relatively 'small fish', rather than those persons considered most responsible for the crimes committed during the conflict. The first person tried by the ICTY was Duško Tadić, a local Serb politician who did not have a high-level leadership role during the armed conflict. Yet, because he was the first accused to be tried by the tribunal, the *Tadic* appeal judgment has an outsized

---

[31] Roland Adjovi and Nandor Kunst, 'Rwanda' in *Max Planck Encyclopedia for Public International Law* (last updated September 2010).

[32] UNSC Res 955 (8 November 1994).

[33] Statute of the International Tribunal for Rwanda (8 November 1994) UN Doc S/RES/955 (ICTR Statute) art 1.

[34] ICTR Statute art 13(4).

[35] UNSC Res 1503 (28 August 2003), para 8; ICTR Statute art 15(4) (as amended on 28 August 2003).

[36] Because the genocide in Rwanda qualified as a non-international armed conflict, art 4 of the ICTR Statute does not include grave breaches of the 1949 Geneva Conventions, which apply only in international armed conflicts.

[37] ICTR Statute art 7.

[38] NATO's Stabilization Force in Bosnia and Herzegovina detained twenty-seven persons indicted by the ICTY, see NATO SFOR 'History of the NATO-led Stabilisation Force (SFOR) in Bosnia and Herzegovina-Background' <www.nato.int/sfor/docu/d981116a.htm>.

importance from a legal perspective, as it deals at length with a number of important legal issues and shaped the jurisprudence that followed.[39]

While the ICTR initially had less difficulty in gaining custody over accused persons, it suffered from serious mismanagement in its early years, which was the subject of a UN audit and investigation, and which culminated in the resignations of its registrar and deputy-prosecutor.[40] In addition, cooperation between the government of Rwanda and the ICTR came to an abrupt halt in November 1999, after the Appeals Chamber ordered the release of an accused person, Jean-Bosco Barayagwiza, because his detention had violated his right to a fair trial.[41] The relationship between Rwanda and the ICTR improved after the Appeals Chamber reconsidered and reversed its ruling in March 2000, a move which was itself highly controversial.[42] Barayagwiza was ultimately convicted in 2003 and he died while serving his sentence.

Despite these initial challenges and stumbles, the ad hoc tribunals left important and impressive legacies in the field of international criminal law.[43] The ICTY indicted 161 individuals, and ultimately convicted and sentenced 90, while 18 were acquitted.[44] The ICTR indicted 93 individuals, and ultimately convicted and sentenced 61, while 14 were acquitted.[45] The ICTY's judgments played a particularly important role in the development of many features of international criminal law, such as joint criminal enterprise, a mode of liability discussed in Section 4(c). In addition, both the ICTY and the ICTR achieved important and early convictions for genocide.[46] The ICTR's *Akayesu* case, for example, resulted in the ground-breaking determination that rape and sexual violence may constitute a genocidal act.[47] The ICTY eventually gained custody of high-profile accused persons, including Slobodan Milošević, the president of the Federal Republic of Yugoslavia (now Serbia); Radovan Karadžić, the president of Republika Srpska (a predominantly Serbian region in Bosnia and Herzegovina); and Ratko Mladić, the commander of the main staff of the army of Republika Srpska.[48] The trial of Milošević; however, vividly demonstrated the challenges involved in prosecuting high-profile accused persons who engage in disruptive court room behaviour, at which Milošević excelled. His death before the end of his trial in 2006 was a major blow to the ICTY, which only later gained custody of Karadžić and Mladić.

---

[39] The Tadic Appeals Chamber dealt with the issue of the Security Council's competence to establish the tribunal as well as joint criminal enterprise as a mode of liability.

[40] UN Doc S/1997/868 (13 November 1997), para 57.

[41] *Jean-Bosco Barayagwiza v The Prosecutor* (Decision) ICTR-97–19-AR72 (3 November 1999) (ICTR Appeals Chamber).

[42] *Jean Bosco Barayagwiza v The Prosecutor* (Decision (Prosecutor's Request for Review or Reconsideration)) ICTR-97–19-AR72 (31 March 2000) (ICTR Appeals Chamber). William A Schabas, 'Barayagwiza v. Prosecutor (Decision, and Decision (Prosecutor's Request for Review or Reconsideration)) Case No. ICTR-97–19-AR72' (2000) 94 American Journal of International Law 563.

[43] See, for example, Milena Sterio and Michael P Scharf (eds), *The Legacy of Ad Hoc Tribunals in International Criminal Law: Assessing the ICTY's and the ICTR's Most Significant Legal Accomplishments* (Cambridge University Press 2019).

[44] International Residual Mechanism for Criminal Tribunals Legacy website of the ICTY 'Key Figures of the Cases' <www .icty.org/en/cases/key-figures-cases>. The ICTY eventually gained custody over all indicted persons who were not deceased.

[45] IRMCT Legacy website of the ICTR 'Key Figures of Cases' <unictr.irmct.org/en/cases/key-figures-cases>. Six indicted persons remain at large.

[46] *Prosecutor v Radislav Krsić* (Judgement) IT-98–33-A (19 April 2004) (ICTY Appeals Chamber); *The Prosecutor v Jean-Paul Akayesu* (Judgement) ICTR-96–4 (2 September 1998) (ICTR Trial Chamber).

[47] *Prosecutor v Jean-Paul Akayesu.*

[48] Milošević was arrested and transferred to the ICTY in 2001; Karadžić was arrested and transferred to the ICTY in 2008; Mladić was arrested and transferred in 2011.

The completion of the work of the ad hoc tribunals required far more time and money than the Security Council expected, or was prepared to accept. But after more than twenty years in operation, the ICTR closed at the end of 2015, and the ICTY closed at the end of 2017. In anticipation of these closures, the Security Council created the International Residual Mechanism for Criminal Tribunals (MICT or Mechanism) in 2010.[49] The mechanism has branches in The Hague and Arusha, and is designed to handle the small number of remaining trials and appeals, as well as the ongoing protection of victims and witnesses and administrative matters such as the management of records and archives. The mechanism is essentially a smaller, more efficient, and combined version of the two ad hoc tribunals.

c   *Hybrid or Internationalized Criminal Courts and Tribunals*

The ad hoc tribunals represent the Security Council's first and possibly also its last foray into the field of international criminal justice through the creation of judicial bodies. The time and expense involved in operating the ad hoc tribunals fuelled the Security Council's disinterest in repeating such an exercise. In addition, the creation of a permanent institution, the ICC, reduced the need for such ad hoc bodies. Since the 1990s; however, a range of other 'hybrid' or 'internationalized' criminal courts and tribunals have come into existence. Many of these bodies have been created for the purpose of prosecuting crimes that took place well before the ICC came into existence, and which therefore, fall outside of its temporal jurisdiction. Many of these judicial bodies have been located in the states where the crimes took place, with a view towards increasing legitimacy, facilitating local outreach, and building the capacity of domestic legal systems.

The terms 'hybrid' or 'internationalized' are used loosely to refer to criminal judicial bodies with features that are not entirely domestic or international, but instead involve some combination of domestic and international characteristics.[50] The bench may, for example, represent a mix of national and international judges. The applicable law may provide for the application of domestic and/or international rules on procedure and evidence. In addition, the subject matter jurisdiction may encompass domestic crimes like murder, as well as international crimes.[51] Hybrid or internationalized criminal courts and tribunals have been established not by Security Council resolutions, but through treaties,[52] international transitional administrations,[53] and under domestic laws.[54]

---

[49] UNSC Res 1966 (22 December 2010).   [50] See, generally, Cryer, Robinson, and Vasiliev (n 15), ch 9.

[51] See, for example, Agreement between the UN and the Government of Sierra Leone on the establishment of a Special Court for Sierra Leone (with Statute) (adopted 16 January 2002, entered into force 12 April 2002) 2178 UNTS 137 (SCSL Statute) art 5 (including offences relating to the abuse of girls and arson).

[52] Special Court for Sierra Leone, the Extraordinary Chambers in the Courts of Cambodia, and the Extraordinary African Chambers. The agreement between the UN and Lebanon to create the Special Tribunal for Lebanon was not ratified by Lebanon, and the provisions of the agreement were instead brought into force by UNSC Res 1757 (30 May 2007).

[53] An international transitional administration entails the temporary exercise of governmental functions not by the state, but by another entity such as the UN. Examples include Special Panels and Serious Crimes Unit in East Timor, Regulation 64 Panels in the Courts of Kosovo, War Crimes Chamber of the Court in Bosnia and Herzegovina.

[54] Kosovo Specialist Chambers, Iraqi High Tribunal, the War Crimes Chamber in the Belgrade District Court, Serbia, and the Special Criminal Court for the Central African Republic.

In general, hybrid or internationalized bodies have been relatively limited and less costly endeavours, as compared with the ad hoc tribunals. The Special Court for Sierra Leone, for example, indicted just thirteen individuals, and ultimately prosecuted nine accused, though the conflict in Sierra Leone was prolonged (1991–2002) and extremely violent. While these institutions have been less costly than the ad hoc tribunals, their financing has also been more precarious, as they have relied, in part, on voluntary contributions by the international community. In addition, they have also tended to struggle under the weight of domestic politics, to which they have been more vulnerable due to their mixed domestic and international elements.[55] Hybrid or internationalized bodies are likely to continue to form part of an evolving international criminal justice system and may be seen as a complement to the ICC.

d   The Creation of the ICC

A permanent international criminal court finally came into being in 2002, approximately fifty years after the possibility was first seriously explored following the Second World War. Trinidad and Tobago spurred renewed interest in a court in 1989, by requesting that the topic of a court be placed back on the General Assembly's agenda.[56] Trinidad and Tobago was particularly interested in the international prosecution of drug trafficking, a problem of particular concern in the Caribbean region. The preparatory negotiations that took place in the mid-1990s were aided by the precedent set by the ad hoc tribunals, along with the work of the ILC on a draft statute and a code of offences against the peace and security of mankind. These preparatory negotiations culminated in negotiations over a five-week period in Rome, during the summer of 1998.[57] The Rome Statute of the ICC established a permanent institution with the authority to prosecute 'the most serious crimes of international concern'.[58] The Rome Statute came into force in July 2002, and the Court began operations in The Hague in 2003. At present, the ICC has 123 states parties.

Unlike the ad hoc tribunals, the ICC is not an entity within the UN system, but is instead a separate judicial body whose relationship with the UN is regulated by an agreement.[59] The ICC consists of three organs: the Chambers, the Office of the Prosecutor, and the Registry. With eighteen judges in total, the Chambers consist of a Pre-Trial Division, a Trial Division, and an Appeals Division. The Pre-Trial Division represents an innovative aspect of the Court's design, and reflects the civil law tradition. The Pre-Trial Chamber is responsible, among other things, for authorizing investigations, confirming charges when there is enough evidence for a case to go to trial, and issuing arrest warrants;[60] while the

---

[55] See, for example, John D Ciorciari and Anne Heindel, *Hybrid Justice: The Extraordinary Chambers in the Courts of Cambodia* (University of Michigan Press 2014).

[56] 'Letter Dated 15 September 1989 from the Permanent Representative of Trinidad and Tobago to the United Nations Addressed to the President of the General Assembly' (19 September 1989) UN Doc A/44/532.

[57] Roy S Lee (ed), *The International Criminal Court: The Making of the Rome Statute* (Kluwer Law International 1999).

[58] Rome Statute of the ICC (adopted 17 July 1998, entered into force 1 July 2002) 2187 UNTS 3, art 1.

[59] Rome Statute art 2; Negotiated Relationship Agreement between the ICC and the UN (signed and entered into force 4 October 2004) ICC-ASP/3/Res.1.

[60] Rome Statute arts 56–8.

Trial Chamber is responsible for determining guilt or innocence. The Registry is respon-sible for administrative aspects of the Court's work, and includes a unit devoted to the protection of victims and witnesses. In addition to the Court's three organs, the Rome Statute created an Assembly of States Parties, which consists of a representative from each state party.[61] The Assembly is responsible, among other things, for overseeing the manage-ment of the ICC, and adopting its budget and subsidiary instruments like the Elements of Crimes and the Rules of Procedure and Evidence.[62] In addition, the Assembly elects the judges and the prosecutor. The judges are meant to have particular characteristics, including not only subject matter expertise but also a 'high moral character, impartiality and integrity'.[63] The judges must also be a diverse group that represents different legal systems, geographical regions, and genders.[64]

3   Substantive Aspects of International Criminal Law

Substantive international criminal law consists of what are known as 'core crimes', a term that refers to genocide, crimes against humanity, war crimes, and the crime of aggression. These are the four crimes over which the ICC can exercise jurisdiction. The drafters of the Rome Statute could have given the ICC jurisdiction over 'transnational crimes', such as drug trafficking, but they ultimately did not depart significantly from the precedent established by the ad hoc tribunals and the Nuremberg and Tokyo Tribunals.[65] Each core crime has two main elements that must be proven: the material element (*actus reus*), which refers to the accused person's conduct; and the mental element (*mens rea*), which refers to the accused person's state of mind. As a general rule, the mental element always involves some degree of intent to commit the material element, as well as knowledge of legally relevant circumstances. These elements allow us to distinguish between serious domestic crimes, such as murder, and core international crimes, which must be committed in certain violent contexts, and/or with a particular mental state. As in domestic legal systems, acts committed negligently or recklessly do not satisfy the requisite mental element for criminal acts.

a   Genocide

The development of the concept of genocide was the life's work of Rafael Lemkin, a Polish Jewish lawyer who fled the Austro-Hungarian Empire at the beginning of the Second World War. During the war, as a refugee in the United States, Lemkin wrote a lengthy book in which he coined the term 'genocide' to refer to the destruction of peoples.[66] Lemkin lobbied for the inclusion of the crime of genocide in the Nuremberg Charter and in the arguments

---

[61] Rome Statute art 112.   [62] Rome Statute art 9, 51, 112(b), (d).   [63] Rome Statute art 36(3)(a), (b).

[64] Rome Statute art 36(8)(a).

[65] Neil Boister, 'The Exclusion of Treaty Crimes from the Jurisdiction of the Proposed International Criminal Court: Law, Pragmatism, Politics' (1998) 3 Journal of Conflict and Security Law 27.

[66] Raphael Lemkin, *Axis Rule in Occupied Europe: Laws of Occupation, Analysis of Government, Proposals for Redress* (first published 1944, 2nd edn, The Lawbook Exchange 2008).

put forwards by the American and British prosecutors at Nuremberg, and was partially successful.[67] His efforts really bore fruit in 1948, with the conclusion of the Genocide Convention. The definition of genocide set out in the Convention has been replicated in the Rome Statute, as well as the statutes of the ad hoc tribunals.[68]

'Genocide' refers to certain acts that are 'committed with intent to destroy, in whole or in part, a national, ethnical, racial or religious group, as such'. These acts are exhaustively enumerated in Article II of the Genocide Convention and include:

(a). Killing members of the group;
(b). Causing serious bodily or mental harm to members of the group;
(c). Deliberately inflicting on the group conditions of life calculated to bring about its physical destruction in whole or in part;
(d). Imposing measures intended to prevent births within the group;
(e). Forcibly transferring children of the group to another group.

These genocidal acts comprise the material element of genocide. In order for a given act to qualify as a genocidal act, the victim(s) must be a member of a group defined according to its nationality, ethnicity, race or religion. Although genocide is typically associated with mass violence and armed conflict, a genocide can also take place in times of peace, and a genocidal act does not necessarily entail a killing. The forced sterilization of women in a particular group could, for example, qualify as the genocidal act of 'imposing measures intended to prevent births within a group', provided that the requisite mental element has been met.[69] Furthermore, rape could qualify as a measure intended to prevent births within a group, particularly in patriarchal societies, where the identity of the father, rather than the mother, determines whether a child is a member of the given group.[70]

Unlike other international crimes, the mental element of genocide requires 'special intent' (*dolus specialis*), meaning that the perpetrator must not only intend to commit the given genocidal act, but must do so in order to achieve a particular result, namely the destruction of the group. The mental element distinguishes genocide from mass murder, which involves an intention to kill, but without the special intention to target of members of a specific group, with a view towards destroying that group.[71] The special intent for genocide has a quantitative aspect, as a perpetrator must intend to destroy a 'substantial' part of a particular group.[72] Determining what qualifies as 'substantial' involves case-by-case consideration of the absolute number of victims as well as the number of victims relative to the overall size of the group. Qualitative factors may also be taken into consideration, such as the prominence of the victims within the group.[73] In practice, the

---

[67] Genocide was prosecuted at Nuremberg as the crime against humanity of extermination of a civilian population.
[68] Genocide Convention art II; Rome Statute art 6; ICTY Statute art 4; ICTR Statute art 2.
[69] See, for example, widespread reports of allegedly forced sterilization of women in China who are members of the Uyghur ethnic minority.
[70] *Akayesu* Trial Judgement (n 46), para 507.
[71] Roger O'Keefe, *International Criminal Law* (Oxford University Press 2015) 150.
[72] *Krstić* appeals judgment (n 46), paras 8–13.
[73] *Case concerning Application of the Convention on the Prevention and Punishment of the Crime of Genocide (Bosnia and Herzegovina v Serbia and Montenegro)* (Judgment) [2007] ICJ Rep 43, para 296.

requirement of special intent creates a significant evidentiary challenge for prosecutors appearing before international criminal courts and tribunals and counsel appearing before the ICJ in cases concerning genocide.[74]

Genocide has been referred to as 'the crime of crimes', a description which is potentially misleading.[75] From a legal perspective, the crime of genocide is not hierarchically above the other 'core crimes', nor are genocidal acts necessarily any more atrocious than, for example, crimes against humanity. From a political perspective, however, the term 'genocide' has taken on a heightened significance, as a way to condemn what are considered to be the most serious violations of international criminal law.[76] Given the evidentiary challenges involved in proving genocide; however, such political rhetoric entails serious legal hurtles, at least in cases before international courts and tribunals.

b   *Crimes against Humanity*

'Crimes against humanity' is an umbrella term that encompasses a range of serious crimes that target civilians, as opposed to combatants. Whereas the crime of genocide was omitted from the Nuremberg Charter, crimes against humanity were included, despite questions about whether crimes against humanity actually comprised part of customary international law at the time of the Second World War.[77] Unlike war crimes and genocide, crimes against humanity have never been codified in a dedicated treaty, but they have been included in the statutes of the ad hoc tribunals, the ICC, and the hybrid or internationalized courts and tribunals.[78] Unlike genocide, crimes against humanity do not, by definition, involve the targeting of a particular group, but instead involve the targeting of civilians in general. In practice, this means that the evidentiary burden involved in proving crimes against humanity can be more manageable for prosecutors before international courts and tribunals.

The term 'crimes against humanity' is defined in the Rome Statute as a range of serious crimes 'committed as part of a widespread or systematic attack directed against any civilian population, with knowledge of the attack'.[79] The Rome Statute includes an extensive list of acts that can constitute a crime against humanity, provided that the mental element is also met. The material element of crimes against humanity thus encompasses murder; extermination; enslavement; deportation or forcible transfer of a population; 'imprisonment or other severe deprivation of physical liberty in violation of fundamental rules of international law'; torture; 'rape, sexual slavery, enforced prostitution, forced pregnancy, enforced sterilization, or any other form of sexual violence of comparable gravity'; persecution; enforced disappearance of persons; and apartheid. The Rome Statute also includes 'other

---

[74] See ibid.

[75] See, for example, *Prosecutor v Jean Kambanda* (Judgment and Sentence) ICTR 97-23-S (4 September 1998) (ICTR Trial Chamber), para 16.

[76] See, for example, Advisory Committee on Issues of Public International Law and External Adviser on Public International Law, 'Advisory Report on the Scope for and the Significant and Desirability of the Use of the Term "Genocide" by Politicians' CAVV Advisory Report No 28/EVA Advisory Report (March 2017).

[77] Nuremberg Charter art 6(c); O'Keefe (n 71) 138–9.

[78] ICTY Statute art 5; ICTR Statute art 3; SCSL Statute art 2; Rome Statute art 7.   [79] Rome Statute art 7(1) (chapeau).

inhumane acts', a catch-all category which captures other conduct that is comparable to the enumerated crimes against humanity.[80]

In order for the material element of crimes against humanity to be met, the criminal conduct must occur as part of a 'widespread or systematic attack directed against any civilian population'. An 'attack' is a broad concept which encompasses 'any mistreatment of the civilian population' and does not need to involve the use of armed force.[81] An attack may; therefore, occur in peacetime, outside of the context of an armed conflict. In addition, an attack must be 'widespread or systematic'; only one of these qualifiers must be met. While the term 'widespread' refers to the large-scale of an attack and the number of victims, the term 'systematic' refers to the organized character of the mistreatment.[82] The extensive use of torture in the context of the armed conflict in Syria would, for example, very likely meet the threshold of both 'widespread' and 'systematic'. The armed conflict, which has been ongoing since 2011, has been characterized, in part, by the torture of civilians in detention centres on a massive scale and in a coordinated manner.[83] Finally, the mental element of crimes against humanity requires both intention and knowledge. The perpetrator must not only intentionally commit the specific act, such as torture, but must also do so with knowledge of the attack, and with knowledge that his or her act constitutes part of that attack. In the Syrian example, the requisite mental element would be met if a security official intended to torture a detainee, and did so with the awareness that his or conduct formed part of a larger policy involving the torture of detainees.

c *War Crimes*

The term 'war crimes' refers to violations of IHL that give rise to individual criminal responsibility. Whereas some violations of IHL may give rise only to state responsibility, others may also give rise to individual criminal responsibility.[84] Individual liability for violations of IHL can arise out of a very extensive range of misconduct. The Rome Statute lists, for example, killing, torture, and rape; the pillage of a town or a place, and destruction of property; various forms of mistreatment of prisoners of war; and intentionally directing attacks against the civilian population or civilian objects.[85] The conscription of child soldiers was, for example, a core feature of the armed conflict in Sierra Leone in the 1990s, and was prosecuted as a war crime by the Special Court for Sierra Leone (SCSL).[86]

---

[80] Rome Statute art 7(1)(k) (other inhumane acts must be 'of a similar character intentionally causing great suffering, or serious injury to body or to mental or physical health').

[81] *Prosecutor v Dragoljub Kunarac, Radomir Kovac and Zoran Vukovic* (Judgement) IT-96-23 and IT-96-23/1-A (12 June 2002) (ICTY Appeals Chamber), para 86.

[82] ibid, para 94.

[83] For example, in February 2021, the High Regional Court in Koblenz, Germany convicted Eyad al-Gharib, former Syrian official, of aiding and abetting the crimes against humanity of torture and murder; see further, Anne Barnard, 'Inside Syria's Secret Torture Prisons: How Bashar al-Assad Crushed Dissent', *The New York Times* (11 May 2019).

[84] The United States bore state responsibility under international humanitarian law for its failure to issue notifications or warnings of the presence of mines that it had laid near Nicaraguan ports in the 1980s. *Case concerning Military and Paramilitary Activities in an against Nicaragua (Nicaragua v United States of America)* (Merits) [1986] ICJ Rep 14, para 215.

[85] Rome Statute art 8.

[86] SCSL Statute art 4(c); *Prosecutor v Sam Hinga Norman* (Decision on Preliminary Motion Based on Lack of Jurisdiction) SCSL-2004-14-AR72(E) (31 May 2004) (SCSL Appeals Chamber).

The Rome Statute defines war crimes by reference to the 1949 Geneva Conventions, as well as customary international law. Both 'grave breaches' of the 1949 Geneva Conventions as well as 'other serious violations of the law and customs applicable in armed conflict' give rise to individual criminal responsibility.

The material elements for war crimes require the existence of an armed conflict. Unlike genocide and crimes against humanity, which can take place during peace time, war crimes take place, by definition, during an armed conflict, whether international or non-international. In addition to the existence of an armed conflict, the conduct at issue must be connected to the armed conflict, such that conduct unrelated to the conflict cannot qualify as a war crime.[87] With respect to the requisite mental element, the perpetrator of a war crime must have intended to perform the specific act, such as murder or pillage. In addition, the perpetrator must have knowledge of the 'factual circumstances that established the existence of an armed conflict'.[88] This requirement of knowledge of the existence of an armed conflict does not, however, require the perpetrator to have made a legal evaluation with respect to the existence of an armed conflict, or the character of the conflict as international or non-international. War crimes do not require special intent, like the crime of genocide, nor do they require proof of a 'widespread or systematic attack', like crimes against humanity. Article 8 of the Rome Statute indicates that the Court has jurisdiction over 'war crimes in particular when committed as part of a plan or policy or as part of a large-scale commission of such crimes'. This passage is only meant direct the prosecutor to pursue more serious instances of war crimes, and does not form a definitional requirement for war crimes.[89]

d   Crime of Aggression

The crime of aggression involves individual criminal responsibility for the participation of a leader or policy-maker in an act of aggression by one state, against another state, in violation of the UN Charter.[90] A given act of aggression by a state could, therefore, give rise not only to state responsibility, but also individual criminal responsibility. The crime of aggression has historically been mired in controversy. The crime was included in the Nuremberg and Tokyo Charters as 'crimes against the peace', and both tribunals entered convictions for this form of conduct.[91] But a definition of aggression eluded the ILC, which did not define it in its 1996 Code of Crimes Against the Peace and Security of Mankind.[92] In 1998 the drafters of the Rome Statute also failed to define the term, or to agree on whether the UN Security Council should play a role in deciding that an act of aggression has occurred. Instead, the drafters of the Rome Statute agreed to include a 'placeholder' in it, which provided for future negotiations on the issue.[93] In 2010, to everyone's surprise, the

---

[87] ICC Elements of Crimes (2011), para 4.   [88] Elements of Crimes art 8, introduction.   [89] O'Keefe (n 71) 135.
[90] Cryer, Robinson, and Vasiliev (n 15) 297.
[91] Nuremberg Charter art 6(a); Charter of the International Military Tribunal for the Far East (adopted and entered into force 19 January 1946) TIAS 1589 (Tokyo Charter) art 5(a).
[92] See UNGA Res 3314 (14 December 1974).   [93] Rome Statute art 5(2) (provision was deleted after 2010 amendment).

Assembly of States Parties managed to reach an agreement on the definition of aggression, resulting in an amendment to the Rome Statute.[94]

Article 8*bis* of the Rome Statute defines the 'crime of aggression' as:

The planning, preparation, initiation or execution, by a person in a position effectively to exercise control over or to direct the political or military action of a State, of an act of aggression which, by its character, gravity and scale, constitutes a manifest violation of the Charter of the United Nations.

The term 'act of aggression' is defined by reference to Article 2(4) of the UN Charter, which prohibits 'the use of armed force by a State against the sovereignty, territorial integrity or political independence of another State, or in any other manner inconsistent with the Charter of the United Nations'. Article 8*bis* further provides a non-exhaustive list of acts that qualify as acts of aggression, regardless of whether there has been a formal declaration of war.[95] These acts include, for example, one state's invasion of another state, occupation, bombardment, and blockade, among other acts.[96] In addition to these various acts of aggression, the material elements of aggression require that the perpetrator is in a leadership position within a state, such as a high-level military or political figure.[97] Furthermore, the leader must participate in the act of aggression by planning, preparing, initiating or executing the act of aggression. The act of aggression must also be 'manifest', in light of its 'character, gravity and scale'. The word 'manifest' can be taken to mean 'serious' in this context.[98] The mental elements of the crime of aggression require two forms of knowledge. The perpetrator must have been aware of the factual circumstances that established the illegality of the use of armed force, under the UN Charter, as well as the manifestly illegal character of the violation. The crime of aggression therefore requires an awareness of the legal character of the situation.

Now that the definition of the crime of aggression has been established by the Assembly of States Parties, it remains to be seen whether the ICC will have significant opportunities to develop the crime of aggression in its jurisprudence. Given that contemporary armed conflicts are often internal, and do not involve attacks by one state against another, the ICC's newfound jurisdiction over the crime of aggression may have limited practical consequences. In addition, the Court's jurisdiction over the crime of aggression is subject to a number of jurisdictional limitations that do not apply to the other crimes within the ICC's jurisdiction.[99]

4   Procedural Aspects of International Criminal Law

The procedural aspects of international criminal law govern the circumstances in which an individual may be held responsible for the international crimes described in Section 3. The

---

[94] Article 8*bis* did not take effect until 2018, after the Assembly of States Parties decided to activate the jurisdiction of the Court over the crime of aggression. Res ICC-ASP/16/Res.5 (14 December 2017).
[95] The list of acts of aggression set out in Article 8 *bis* reflects the list set out in UNGA Res 3314 (XXIX) (14 December 1974).
[96] Rome Statute art 8*bis*(2)(a).   [97] Elements of Crimes art 8*bis* element 2.   [98] O'Keefe (n 71) 158–9.
[99] See Rome Statute art 15*bis*.

procedural topics covered in this section include jurisdiction, admissibility, modes of liability, and immunity in the context of the ICC. The topic of defences is omitted because grounds for excluding the criminal responsibility of accused persons have not, to date, featured significantly in the jurisprudence of international criminal courts and tribunals.[100]

a   *Jurisdiction*

The drafters of the Rome Statute constructed a complex solution to the question of jurisdiction, a term that refers to the ICC's competence to investigate situations and to try accused persons. The concept of 'jurisdiction' in the context of international courts and tribunals such as the ICC has two aspects. One aspect of jurisdiction concerns the very existence of jurisdiction, meaning whether the ICC actually has any competence at all. The other aspect of jurisdiction concerns the scope of jurisdiction, meaning the extent to which the ICC can exercise its existing jurisdiction. The existence of jurisdiction at the ICC does not necessarily hinge on whether a state is a party to the Rome Statute, although the ICC has primarily exercised jurisdiction over nationals states parties. When a state becomes a party to the Rome Statute, this means that the state accepts, in principle, the jurisdiction of the ICC with respect to the crimes listed in Article 5 of the Rome Statute: the crime of genocide, crimes against humanity, war crimes, and the crime of aggression.[101] States parties to the Rome Statute therefore accept the possibility that in the future, the ICC could possess jurisdiction over these crimes in certain circumstances, namely when the crimes involve its nationals, or take place on its territory.

The existence of jurisdiction at the ICC requires that one of three possible conditions has been met. First, jurisdiction may exist when a state party refers to the prosecutor a situation involving the apparent commission of one or more of the crimes listed in Article 5 of the Rome Statute.[102] Second, a referral of a situation to the prosecutor by the UN Security Council acting under Chapter VII of the UN Charter could also give the ICC competence to investigate and prosecute. Finally, jurisdiction may exist when the prosecutor itself initiates an investigation.[103]

In practice, the ICC has come to possess jurisdiction in each of these ways. Though it might seem counterintuitive for a state party to ask the prosecutor to investigate and prosecute a situation in its own territory and concerning its own nationals, this has, in fact, been an important source of jurisdiction for the ICC.[104] States may prefer for the ICC to exercise jurisdiction in circumstances where domestic politics or limited judicial capacity could hinder proceedings. The Central African Republic, the Democratic Republic of Congo, Gabon, Mali, Palestine, and Uganda have all referred situations to the prosecutor. The ICC has come under criticism for its heavy focus on situations in Africa, but to a certain

---

[100] Rome Statute arts 31–3 (covering mental incapacity, intoxication, self-defence, duress, necessity, mistake of fact, superior orders); See generally Sara Wharton, 'Defences to Criminal Liability' in Charles C Jalloh et al (eds), *The African Court of Justice and Human and Peoples' Rights in Context* (Cambridge University Press 2019).
[101] Rome Statute art 12(1).   [102] Rome Statute art 14.   [103] Rome Statute art 15.
[104] A state party could also refer a situation in another state party.

extent, this state of affairs has arisen through self-referrals by African states parties to the Rome Statute.[105] The prosecutor itself has also initiated a number of investigations, in particular with respect to Afghanistan, Bangladesh/Myanmar, Burundi, Cote d'Ivoire, Georgia, and Kenya.

Finally, the Security Council has made two referrals to the prosecutor. The Security Council referred the situation in Darfur, Sudan to the prosecutor in 2005, and the situation in Libya in 2011.[106] Security Council referrals have proven to be relatively rare events, as they require the support of the five permanent members of the Security Council, which must refrain from exercising their veto power with respect to a referral, though abstention is permitted.[107] Because the Security Council is an inherently political body, the selection of situations by the Security Council for referral has been driven not only by legal considerations, but also by geopolitics. Like the Libyan revolution of 2011, the armed conflict in Syria has generated calls for a referral to the prosecutor by the Security Council, but such a referral has never garnered the support of all of the permanent members of the Security Council, in particular Russia and China.[108]

The term 'scope of jurisdiction' refers to the extent of the ICC's competence, namely its subject matter jurisdiction, personal jurisdiction, territorial jurisdiction, and temporal jurisdiction. The ICC's subject matter jurisdiction covers the crime of genocide, crimes against humanity, war crimes, and the crime of aggression. No matter how serious a crime might be (i.e., drug trafficking), if it does not qualify as one of these core crimes, then it does not fall within the ICC's jurisdiction. The extent of the ICC's personal and territorial jurisdiction depends on the way in which the ICC came to possess jurisdiction over the situation. When the Security Council refers a situation to the prosecutor, then the ICC's personal and territorial jurisdiction are not limited to parties to the Rome Statute. This means that the Security Council may refer situations to the prosecutor concerning persons who are not nationals of any state party to the Rome Statute, and regarding situations that took place on the territory of a state that is not a party to the Rome Statute. Sudan, for example, is not a party to the Rome Statute, such that the situation in Darfur neither involved nationals of a state party, nor took place on the territory of a state party. The Security Council was, nevertheless, able to refer the situation to the prosecutor because it acted under Chapter VII of the UN Charter, which allows it to take binding decisions with which all UN member states are obliged to comply.[109]

The personal and territorial jurisdiction of the ICC are; however, limited when the basis for the existence of jurisdiction is either a referral by a state party, or a prosecutor-initiated investigation.[110] In each of these scenarios, either the accused person must be a national of a state party, or the conduct must have occurred on the territory of a state party. This means

---

[105] Kamari M Clarke, Abel S Knottnerus, and Eefje de Volder (eds), *Africa and the ICC: Perceptions of Justice* (Cambridge University Press 2016).
[106] UNSC Res 1593 (31 March 2005); UNSC Res 1970 (26 February 2011). Three of the five permanent members of the Security Council are not parties to the Rome Statute: China, Russia, and the United States.
[107] The United States and China abstained with respect to Res 1593 (Sudan). Res 1970 was unanimously adopted.
[108] See, for example, veto of draft Security Council resolution by Russia and China in May 2014.
[109] Charter of the UN (adopted 26 June 1945, entered into force 24 October 1945) 1 UNTS XVI, art 25.
[110] Rome Statute arts 12(2), 13(a), (c).

that an accused person who is not a national of a state party may still be prosecuted if the alleged conduct occurred, at least in part, on the territory of a state party.[111] For example, even though the United States is not a party to the Rome Statute, a US national who served as a member of the armed forces in Afghanistan could, in principle, be prosecuted by the ICC for conduct committed in the territory of Afghanistan, which is a party to the Rome Statute. Conversely, an accused who is a national of a state party may be prosecuted even when the conduct at issue took place on the territory of a state that is not a party to the Rome Statute. For example, even though Iraq is not a party to the Rome Statute, British nationals who served in the armed forces in Iraq could be prosecuted by the ICC because the United Kingdom is a party to the Rome Statute. The scope of the ICC's personal and territorial jurisdiction; therefore, depends on the way in which the ICC came to possess jurisdiction in the first place, whether through a referral by the Security Council, referral by a state party, or initiation by the prosecutor.[112]

Finally, the ICC's temporal jurisdiction is limited insofar as the Rome Statute does not apply retroactively. According to Article 11 of the Rome Statute, the Court's temporal jurisdiction is limited to crimes committed after the statute's entry into force in July 2002.[113] If a state becomes a party to the Rome Statute following its entry into force in 2002, then the ICC's temporal jurisdiction only begins after the entry into force of the Statute for that state. The ICC; therefore, cannot exercise jurisdiction over crimes that occurred before the Statute entered into force, or before a state became a party to the Statute, following its entry into force. An exception to this general rule exists when a state makes an ad hoc declaration specifically accepting the Court's jurisdiction in circumstances where the Court would not otherwise possess jurisdiction.[114] Such declarations act as consent to the ICC's exercise of jurisdiction on a retroactive basis, potentially going as far back as the statute's 2002 entry into force.

b   Admissibility

Even when the ICC possesses jurisdiction, and a given situation falls within the scope of the Court's jurisdiction, it will not necessarily be appropriate for the ICC to proceed with an investigation and prosecution. Questions about the appropriateness of the ICC's actual exercise of jurisdiction are characterized as questions of 'admissibility'. The Rome Statute sets out two circumstances in which the exercise of jurisdiction could be inappropriate, thereby rendering a case inadmissible. First, the exercise of jurisdiction could violate the principle of complementarity. Second, a case might not be of sufficient gravity to justify action by the Court. In addition to providing for these grounds of inadmissibility, the Rome

---

[111] ICC Pre-Trial Chamber III, Decision Pursuant to Article 15 of the Rome Statute on the Authorisation of an Investigation into the People's Republic of Bangladesh/Republic of the Union of Myanmar, ICC-01/19-27 (14 November 2019).

[112] The ICC's personal jurisdiction also excludes persons under the age of eighteen at the time of the alleged commission of the crime. Rome Statute art 26.

[113] Rome Statute art 11(1).

[114] Rome Statute arts 11(2), 12(3). Ukraine, for example, lodged two declarations in 2014 and 2015, under art 12(3), by which it accepted the jurisdiction of the Court over crimes committed on its territory from 21 November 2013 onwards.

Statute also gives the prosecutor the ability to decline to pursue a case on a discretionary basis, where doing so would be in conflict with the interests of justice.[115] The following focuses on the principle of complementarity, which is a fundamental aspect of the ICC's design.

Unlike the ad hoc tribunals, the ICC does not have primacy over national investigations and prosecutions. Instead, the ICC was designed to complement rather than supplant domestic criminal justice systems. In practice, the Rome Statute has indeed brought about legislative reform in many states parties, which now have the capacity to enforce domestic criminal laws concerning international crimes, even where the conduct at issue did not take place on their territory or involve their nationals (i.e., universal jurisdiction).[116] This system of complementarity also reflects pragmatism about what a single international judicial institution can realistically accomplish. The ICC has been able to investigate and prosecute only a small fraction of the serious crimes that have been committed since the Rome Statute's entry into force. Out of necessity, international criminal justice must involve significant enforcement efforts within domestic legal systems.

The Rome Statute provides for complementarity by requiring the Court to determine that a case is inadmissible when the case is currently being investigated and prosecuted by a State that has jurisdiction over it.[117] The ICC must also defer to domestic authorities that have already investigated a case and decided not to prosecute the person concerned.[118] In both of these scenarios, the case would be inadmissible, unless the state is 'unwilling or unable genuinely to carry out' the investigation or prosecution. A domestic prosecution could, for example, lack a 'genuine' character if it is a sham or show trial, designed merely to give the appearance of criminal justice. Furthermore, a state may be considered 'unwilling' to investigate or prosecute where domestic criminal proceedings are for the purpose of 'shielding' someone from the ICC's jurisdiction.[119] Unwillingness could also take the form of an 'unjustified delay' in domestic criminal proceedings, or proceedings that lack independence or impartiality.[120]

In the Libyan situation, for example, the ICC's case against Abdullah Al-Senussi was inadmissible because of ongoing domestic proceedings against him in Libya.[121] After the Security Council referred the situation in Libya to the Prosecutor in 2011, the prosecutor indicted Al-Senussi, who was Libya's long-serving director of military intelligence. The ICC's case against Al-Senussi concerned his involvement in the crimes against humanity of murder and persecution, which took place during the Libyan revolution in early 2011. In April 2012; however, after the Security Council referral, Libyan authorities began investigating Al-Senussi's conduct from the 1980s through the 2011 revolution. The Pre-Trial Chamber held, in part, that even though Libyan authorities had not yet charged Al-Senussi

---

[115] Rome Statute art 53(1)(c), (2)(c).
[116] See, for example, New Zealand, International Crimes and International Criminal Court Act 2000.
[117] Rome Statute art 17(1)(a).   [118] Rome Statute art 17(1)(b).   [119] Rome Statute art 17(2)(a).
[120] Rome Statute art 17(2)(b), (c).
[121] *The Prosecutor v Said Al-Islam Gaddafi and Abdullah Al-Senussi* (Decision on the Admissibility of the Case against Abdulla Al-Senussi) ICC-01/11-01/11 (11 October 2013) (ICC Pre-Trial Chamber); *The Prosecutor v Saif Al-Islam and Abdullah Al-Senussi* (Judgment on the appeal of Mr Abdullah Al-Senussi against the decision of Pre-Trial Chamber I of 11 October 2013) ICC-OI/II-OI/IIOA6 (24 July 2014) (ICC Appeals Chamber).

(or provided him with a defence lawyer), they were taking 'concrete and progressive steps' towards ascertaining Al-Senussi's criminal responsibility for substantially the same conduct that was at issue in the ICC proceedings.[122] The Pre-Trial Chamber further held that Libya was willing to carry out the proceedings, as there was no indication that the proceedings were for the purpose of shielding Al-Senussi from criminal responsibility, and the national proceedings could not be regarded as 'tainted by an unjustified delay'.[123] With respect to Libya's ability to carry out the proceedings, the Pre-Trial Chamber determined that the 'precarious security situation' in Libya had not prejudiced the ability of Libyan authorities to collect evidence and witness testimony.[124] In 2015, the Libyan court proceedings culminated in Al-Senussi's conviction and death sentence.

c   *Modes of Liability*

As a general rule, international criminal courts and tribunals focus on high-level perpetrators who in most cases have not themselves committed the international crimes at issue. While high-level leaders, such as heads of state and military commanders, may not 'pull the trigger' themselves, their involvement takes other forms, such as ordering or facilitating crimes that are committed by their subordinates. Just as in domestic legal systems, international criminal law provides for various 'modes of liability', a term that refers to an individual's level of involvement in a given crime. Under the Rome Statute, the modes of liability include commission; ordering, soliciting, or inducing the commission of a crime; aiding, abetting, or otherwise assisting; contribution to a crime committed by a group of persons acting with a common purpose; command responsibility; and attempt.[125] In addition, the Rome Statute provides for incitement as a separate mode of liability that is specific to genocide.[126] Each mode of liability entails its own material and mental elements, with the result that the elements of both the substantive crime and the mode of liability must be met in order for an accused to be convicted.

Because international crimes are typically carried out by a group of individuals acting together as a collective, modes of liability take on a special importance before international courts and tribunals. The actual perpetrators of international crimes may represent only a small part of a picture that also involves people at higher levels who, for example, encouraged the commission of the crimes or supplied weapons and equipment. The challenges involved in prosecuting high-level accused for crimes carried out by a collective led the ICTY to rely, in good part, on a mode of liability known as 'joint criminal enterprise' (JCE).[127] The ICTY considered that the term 'commission' in Article 7 of its Statute encompassed not only direct commission by a perpetrator, but also participation by an accused in a joint criminal enterprise, which could take one of three forms.[128] JCE I covers situations in which all of the participants in a 'common design' or plan share the same criminal intent to commit a given crime, which one of them actually

---

[122] *Prosecutor v Said Al-Islam Gaddafi and Abdullah Al-Senussi* (Decision on Admissibility) (n 121), para 160.
[123] ibid, para 243.   [124] ibid, para 301.   [125] Rome Statute arts 25(2), (3), 28.   [126] Rome Statute art 25(3)(e).
[127] *Prosecutor v Dusko Tadic* (Judgment) IT-94-1-A (15 July 1999) (ICTY Appeals Chamber).   [128] ICTY Statute art 7(1).

commits.[129] JCE II is a variant on JCE I, which specifically covers participation in a common plan in the context of a concentration camp.[130] Finally, JCE III provides for criminal liability for crimes committed by members of a group where such crimes were outside of the common purpose, but a 'natural and foreseeable consequence' of it.[131] A plan to pillage a village, for example, could foreseeably result in acts of violence against the villagers. The ICTY's understanding of the scope of 'commission' generated controversy, and the most extended form of joint criminal enterprise (JCE III), has been seen as an overly inclusive form of liability. Joint criminal enterprise nevertheless formed a central aspect of the ICTY's jurisprudence, and was consistently upheld by the ICTY and followed by the ICTR.[132]

The drafters of the Rome Statute developed a distinct form of liability to cover participation in a common plan. Article 25(3)(d) of the Rome Statute does not treat this form of liability as a form of commission, as did the ICTY. Instead, the Rome Statute sets out a separate mode of liability for persons who intentionally contribute to the commission, or attempted commission, of a crime by a 'group of persons acting with a common purpose'. The contribution must be made either 'with the aim of furthering the criminal activity or criminal purpose of the group', or 'in the knowledge of the intention of the group to commit the crime'. This mode of liability is not as extensive as JCE because an accused person cannot be held responsible for all crimes that form part of the common purpose, but rather only those crimes to which he or she actually contributed.[133]

The form of liability set out in Article 25(3)(d) of the Rome Statute was first applied by an ICC Chamber in a case against Germain Katanga, a leader of an armed group that carried out an attack on Bogoro, a village in an eastern region of the Democratic Republic of Congo. In 2014, a Trial Chamber found Katanga guilty as an accessory to murder, pillage and destruction of property, and sentenced him to twelve years in prison. The common purpose in this case entailed driving the civilian population from Bogoro, destroying homes in Bogoro, and pillaging the villager's property and livestock, which was essential to their survival.[134] The Trial Chamber found that Katanga made a 'significant contribution' to this common purpose by equipping the armed group with weapons and providing it with logistical support.[135]

d   *Immunity*

International criminal courts and tribunals have played important roles in closing the impunity gap created by the operation of immunities in domestic legal systems.[136] The immunities enjoyed by government officials in the domestic courts of foreign states (see

---

[129] *Prosecutor v Dusko Tadic* (n 127), para 196.   [130] ibid, para 202.   [131] ibid, para 204.
[132] See, Case No 002 (Decision on the Appeals the Co-Investigative Judges Order on Joint Criminal Enterprise (JCE)) D97/15/9 (20 May 2010) (ECCC Pre-Trial Chamber).
[133] *Prosecutor v Germain Katanga* (Judgment) ICC-01/04-01/07 (7 March 2014) (ICC Trial Chamber II), para 1619.
[134] ibid, para 1665.   [135] ibid, para 1680.
[136] *Case concerning the Arrest Warrant of 11 April 2000 (Democratic Republic of the Congo v Belgium)* (Judgment) [2002] ICJ Rep 3, para 61.

Chapter 7) are removed by the statutes of the ad hoc tribunals and the ICC.[137] Article 27(2) of the Rome Statute, for example, provides that the immunities that attach to the official capacity of a person shall not bar the Court from exercising jurisdiction over the person. Thus, government officials are not entitled to immunities before the ICC. This seemingly simple rule has proved to be complicated in practice, because the ICC depends on states to arrest and transfer suspects to it. Article 98 of the Rome Statute deals with the issue of transfers of suspects to the Court, and provides that the ICC cannot request a state to surrender an accused person to it if doing so would require the requested state to violate its obligations under international law with respect to the immunity of the accused person (unless the accused person's state of nationality waives their immunity). In practice, the most significant questions about immunities in the context of the ICC concern how the Court can obtain custody of an accused person without the surrendering state violating the immunity of the accused person. In other words, how do Articles 27(2) and 98(1) interact with each other?

One possible scenario could involve a state surrendering an accused person who is a national of another state that is a party to the Rome Statute. In such a scenario, the accused person would not be entitled to immunity from surrender by the foreign state to the ICC because the accused person's state of nationality has effectively waived his immunity by virtue of becoming a party to the Rome Statute. In other words, by becoming a party to the Rome Statute, and consenting to Article 27(2) of the Rome Statute, states parties implicitly waive the immunity of their officials in the context of surrender by a foreign state.

Another, more controversial scenario involves the surrender of an accused person who is a national of a state that is not a party to the Rome Statute, such as Sudan. For example, would the surrender of Omar Al Bashir, the former Sudanese head of state, to the ICC by a foreign state have the effect of violating Al Bashir's immunity under international law? In 2009 and 2010, the ICC charged Al Bashir with crimes of genocide, crimes against humanity, and war crimes in connection with the situation in Darfur, but Al Bashir has remained at large. The relationship between Articles 27(2) and 98(1) of the Rome Statute has been the subject of numerous proceedings at the ICC, which have arisen out of Al Bashir's visits to foreign states, which are parties to the Rome Statute, and which have declined to transfer him to the ICC, on the grounds that he enjoys immunity from surrender.[138] In each of these proceedings, the ICC Chambers have found that Al Bashir is not entitled to immunity from surrender in foreign states, though the Chambers' reasoning has varied.

A visit by Al Bashir to Jordan in March 2017 gave rise to the Appeals Chamber's most definitive pronouncement to date on the subject of immunity and surrender. The Appeals Chamber upheld the Pre-Trial Chamber's determination that Jordan, a party to the Rome Statute, had failed to comply with its obligation to execute an ICC arrest warrant by arresting and surrendering Al Bashir. The Appeals Chamber's reasoning was based, in

---

[137] ICTY Statute art 7(2); Rome Statute art 27(2).

[138] Al Bashir's visits to Chad, Malawi, the Democratic Republic of Congo, Jordan, and South Africa have all resulted in ICC proceedings.

part, on Security Council Resolution 1593, which referred the situation in Darfur, Sudan, to the ICC.[139] This resolution obliges Sudan to 'cooperate fully' with the ICC.[140] The Appeals Chamber interpreted this to mean that Sudan is subject to the same cooperation regime that applies to states parties to the Rome Statute, a regime that does not recognize immunities. According to the Appeals Chamber, Sudan's obligation of full cooperation precludes it from invoking the immunity of Al Bashir, either in relation to the ICC, or in its 'horizontal relationship' with states parties, namely Jordan. The Appeals Chamber's judgment avoids a conflict between Articles 27(2) and 98(1) of the Rome Statute, as Jordan's arrest and surrender of Al Bashir would not have violated his immunity, which did not exist in these circumstances. While this Judgment is not without controversy, it has likely settled the issue of immunity in the *Al Bashir* case.

5 Concluding Remarks

International criminal law has undergone dramatic growth since the 1990s, due to the creation of a spate of international criminal courts and tribunals, from the ad hoc tribunals, to the ICC and a series of hybrid or internationalized courts and tribunals. Impunity can hardly be said to be a thing of the past, but the persons most responsible for serious international crimes now at least face the prospect of being held accountable before an international court or tribunal. The ICC's first two decades of existence have; however, proven to be disappointing to many, due to its heavy focus on African countries, its slow progress, major evidentiary problems, and the quality of its bench, among a range of issues. While these criticisms are not unfair, perhaps the ICC never could have met the lofty expectations of states, scholars, and activists.[141] It can only be hoped that this institution finds its footing in the years to come.

Recommended Reading

Neil Boister, "Transnational Criminal Law?" (2003) 14 European Journal of International Law 953.

Robert Cryer, Darryl Robinson, and Sergey Vasiliev, *An Introduction to International Criminal Law and Procedure* (4th edn, Cambridge University Press 2019).

Roger O'Keefe, *International Criminal Law* (Oxford University Press 2015).

Leila Nadya Sadat, "Crimes against Humanity in the Modern Age" (2013) 107 American Journal of International Law 334.

Philippe Sands, *East West Street: On the Origins of Genocide and Crimes against Humanity* (Weidenfeld & Nicolson 2016).

Sarah Williams, *Hybrid and Internationalised Criminal Tribunals* (Hart 2012).

---

[139] *The Prosecutor v Omar Hassan Ahmad Al-Bashir* (Judgment) ICC-02/05-01/09 OA2 (6 May 2019 (ICC Appeals Chamber), para 149.

[140] UNSC Res 1593 (31 March 2005), para 2.

[141] Darryl Robinson, 'Inescapable Dyads: Why the International Criminal Court Cannot Win' (2015) 28 Leiden Journal of International Law 323.

14

International Economic Law

Cecily Rose

1   Introduction

International economic law is a field of public international law that regulates cross-border transactions in goods, services, and capital, as well as monetary relations between states.[1] Although states, companies, and individuals have engaged in cross-border economic relations for many centuries, going back to antiquity, much of international economic law as we know it today has developed only since the end of the Second World War. In principle, states are not obligated under international law to conduct economic relations with each other, or to maintain any particular economic system domestically.[2] In practice; however, states have developed a relatively vast body of treaty law that, for instance, effectively obliges them to maintain a market economy and to conduct trade relations in a particular manner.

Present day international economic law can be understood in part as a response to the protectionist economic policies that played a significant role in the Great Depression of the 1930s and the advent of the Second World War. In 1944, before the Second World War had even come to an end, representatives from forty-four states met in Bretton Woods, New Hampshire (United States), to negotiate a post-war framework for international economic cooperation to prevent such a depression in the future, and to help rebuild post-war economies.[3] These negotiations resulted in the creation of what are known as the Bretton Woods institutions, namely the World Bank and the International Monetary Fund (IMF). While the World Bank was created to assist states with post-war reconstruction and to provide financial assistance to developing states, the IMF was established to regulate monetary relations between states. Post-war negotiations also led to the development of a body of international trade law, but the creation of a permanent international organization responsible for regulating international trade did not take place until the mid-1990s, with the establishment of the Geneva-based World Trade Organization (WTO).

---

[1] Matthias Herdegen, *Principles of International Economic Law* (2nd edn, Oxford University Press 2016) 3.
[2] See, for example, *Case concerning Military and Paramilitary Activities in and against Nicaragua (Nicaragua v United States of America)* (Merits) [1986] ICJ Rep 14, paras 258, 276; International Covenant on Civil and Political Rights (adopted 16 December 1966, entered into force 23 March 1976) 999 UNTS 171, art 1(1); International Covenant on Economic, Social and Cultural Rights (adopted 16 December 1966, entered into force 3 January 1976) 993 UNTS 3, art 1(1).
[3] Andreas F Lowenfeld, 'Bretton Woods Conference (1944)' in *Max Planck Encyclopedia of Public International Law* (last updated March 2013).

This chapter focuses on the branches of international economic law that govern international trade and international investment, as the law governing these cross-border activities is now relatively robust, and features quite active international dispute settlement mechanisms. International monetary law will also be covered in brief at the end of the chapter. Branches of international economic law that are omitted from this chapter include competition law, intellectual property law, and international commercial law, as these subjects are of lesser importance for a basic understanding of the field of international economic law.[4] This chapter sets out the historical background, fundamental rules, and dispute settlement systems in the areas of international trade law (Section 2) and international investment law (Section 3), and it concludes by introducing international monetary law (Section 4).

2   International Trade Law

a   Introduction

Contemporary international trade law aims to ensure the free flow of trade by reducing or eliminating barriers to trade and by eliminating discriminatory treatment. The broad goals that the WTO seeks to achieve through trade liberalization include 'raising standards of living, ensuring full employment and a large and steadily growing volume of real income and effective demand, and expanding the production of and trade in goods and services'.[5] The origins of the WTO, which did not come into existence until 1995, may be traced back to the end of the Second World War, when states, in particular the United States and the United Kingdom, were grappling with how to design an international trade system that would help to prevent another great depression in the future. In 1948, a relatively small group of states, led by the United Kingdom and the United States, concluded the Havana Charter, which would have created the International Trade Organization, had the Havana Charter come into force. But because of opposition in the United States, stemming in part from the Charter's ambitious provisions (which covered trade as well as employment, labour standards, economic development and reconstruction, and commodity agreements), the Charter never came into effect.[6] Instead, the General Agreement on Tariffs and Trade (GATT), concluded in 1947, became the de facto framework for international trade, as well as the name of the de facto organization for regulating this area of international law. The term 'GATT' may; therefore, refer to both the treaty governing trade in goods, and to the provisional organization that formerly regulated international trade. As a treaty, GATT aims to minimize restrictions on international trade, and it has provided a legal framework for

---

[4] For a discussion of the scope of the field of international economic law, see Steve Charnovitz, 'What is International Economic Law?' (2011) 14 Journal of International Economic Law 3.

[5] Marrakesh Agreement Establishing the WTO (adopted 15 April 1994, entered into force 1 January 1995) 1867 UNTS 154 (WTO Agreement), preambular para 1.

[6] Giorgio Sacerdoti, 'Havana Charter (1948)' in *Max Planck Encyclopedia of Public International Law* (last updated June 2014), paras 9–10.

multiple rounds of trade negotiations geared towards successively liberalizing international trade.

Between 1947 and the mid-1990s, states parties to GATT conducted multiple rounds of trade negotiations for the purpose of eliminating or reducing tariffs and non-tariff barriers, both of which pose obstacles to free trade. Whereas the term 'tariffs' refers to customs duties imposed on goods when they cross a national border, the term 'non-tariff barrier' refers to other bureaucratic or legal requirements imposed by an importing state that could hinder trade, such as quotas and rules that govern how to label where a product was made (rules of origin). The Uruguay Round, which began in 1986 and concluded in 1994, led in part to a reform of the international trade system and the creation of the WTO, a permanent international organization that replaced GATT, the de facto organization regulating international trade law.[7]

There are currently 164 members of the WTO, including states as well as international organizations, like the European Union (EU), and separate customs territories that are not states, such as Taiwan, Hong Kong, and Macao. Approximately two-thirds of the WTO's members are developing countries. The day-to-day functions of the WTO are carried out by the General Council, a plenary body that consists of representatives from all of the WTO's members, who generally make decisions by consensus.[8] The General Council meets as the Dispute Settlement Body (DSB), which is responsible for the operation of the WTO's dispute settlement system, and it also meets as the Trade Review Policy Body, which is responsible for the surveillance of national trade policies. While the DSB oversees the settlement of trade disputes, the disputes themselves are actually heard by judicial bodies, namely panels and the Appellate Body, which produce judgment-like 'reports' that are subsequently adopted by the DSB (see Section 2(c)).[9]

b   *Fundamental Rules of International Trade Law*

Although GATT, the provisional organization, ceased to exist in 1995, when it was replaced by the WTO, GATT, the treaty governing trade in goods, was updated in 1994 at the end of the Uruguay Round and it remains in force. In discussing a number of fundamental rules of international trade law, this section will focus on GATT, which remains the most significant multilateral trade agreement, even though more than a dozen other multilateral and plurilateral agreements governing goods, services, and intellectual property now exist as well.[10] While multilateral agreements must be ratified by all WTO members, as a condition

---

[7] WTO Agreement art VII(1).   [8] WTO Agreement arts IV, IX.

[9] Understanding on Rules and Procedures Governing the Settlement of Disputes (as annexed to the WTO Agreement) (adopted 15 April 1994, entered into force 1 January 1995) 1869 UNTS 401 (Dispute Settlement Understanding, DSU) art 2.

[10] See WTO Agreement, Annexes 1 and 4. The multilateral agreements on trade in goods include the Agreement on the Application of Sanitary and Phytosanitary Measures (SPS Agreement); the Agreement on Technical Barriers to Trade (TBT Agreement); the Agreement on Trade-Related Investment Measures (TRIMS); the Agreement on Subsidies and Countervailing Measures; and the Agreement on Agriculture. Trade in services is governed by the multilateral General Agreement on Trade in Services (GATS). Trade in intellectual property is governed by the multilateral Agreement on Trade-Related Aspects of Intellectual Property Rights (TRIPS). Plurilateral agreements include the Agreement on Trade in Civil Aircraft and the Agreement on Government Procurement.

of membership, plurilateral agreements are optional for WTO members. The following discusses, in particular, the rules governing most favoured nation treatment, national treatment, and the reduction of tariffs and non-tariff barriers. This section shows that international trade law consists of a balance between fundamental rules, such as non-discrimination, and delimited exceptions to those rules.

i   Reduction of Tariffs and Non-tariff Barriers

GATT promotes free trade in part by requiring contracting parties (i.e., states parties) to reduce tariffs. Under GATT, tariffs remain an acceptable way for states to regulate trade and to protect their domestic industries – but only within prescribed limits. Through successive trade rounds, contracting parties have negotiated tariff concessions, involving fixed upper limits for tariffs. Contracting parties have agreed to abide by 'bound tariffs', which set a ceiling for tariff levels, such that tariffs can be below, but not above this threshold. These tariff levels are listed in a schedule to GATT, which forms an integral part of this agreement.[11]

In addition, GATT imposes a general prohibition on non-tariff barriers or 'quantitative restrictions', such as quotas and import or export licenses.[12] In other words, contracting parties must not impose measures that deter imports by, for example, blocking market access or increasing transaction costs.[13] The ban on quantitative restrictions is not absolute, as narrow exceptions exist, but in general GATT manifests the contracting parties' preference for tariffs as a means for regulating trade and protecting domestic industries.[14] Tariffs, which are set out in schedules and have relatively clear-cut effects, are a more transparent method for regulating trade and are therefore easier to address through trade negotiations.[15] Because successive trade rounds have resulted in reduced tariff levels, however, the regulation of non-tariff barriers has become an increasingly important part of international trade law.

ii   Non-discrimination: Most Favoured Nation Treatment and National Treatment

The principle of non-discrimination, which is fundamental to both international trade law and international investment law, aims to ensure fair competition. In both areas of law, this principle takes the form of two rules: most favoured nation treatment (MFN), and national treatment. In the trade context, these two rules regulate indirect barriers to trade, rather than direct barriers to trade. According to the MFN rule, WTO members that grant a trade advantage to one contracting party must grant the same advantage to all other contracting parties. More specifically, when a contracting party grants 'any favour, privilege or immunity' to any product that originates in or is destined for another country, it must accord the same treatment 'immediately and unconditionally' to 'like products' that

---

[11] GATT 1994 (as annexed to the WTO Agreement) (adopted 15 April 1994, entered into force 1 January 1995) 1867 UNTS 187 (GATT) art II(7).
[12] GATT art XI.   [13] Herdegen (n 1) 233.   [14] GATT arts XI and XII.
[15] Peter-Tobias Stoll, 'World Trade Organization (WTO)' in *Max Planck Encyclopedia of Public International Law* (last updated October 2014), para 29.

originate in or are destined for all other contracting parties.[16] This means, in practice, that a contracting party that lowers the customs duty for a product imported from another contracting party must do the same for similar products from all other contracting parties. In doing so, the contracting party that lowers the customs duty cannot expect that any advantage will be granted in return by other contracting parties, as this rule operates 'unconditionally'.

Two significant exceptions to this fundamental rule exist under GATT. First, preferential trade agreements, such as customs unions and free-trade areas, are permissible.[17] In theory, at least, customs unions and free-trade areas promote free trade, and thus support the overarching goals of the WTO system, if not exactly the MFN rule.[18] There is, however, currently a 'spaghetti bowl' of about 250 bilateral and regional trade agreements, which arguably erode MFN treatment.[19] The EU is an especially prominent example of a customs union and free-trade area. The EU is also a party to a number of preferential trade agreements and is in the process of negotiating others, such as a trade agreement between the EU and MERCOSUR (comprising Argentina, Brazil, Paraguay, and Uruguay).[20]

A second exception to the MFN rule provides for preferences for developing countries. This exception is also in keeping with the overall objectives of GATT, which focus specifically on the need to raise living standards and progressively develop the economies of less-developed contracting parties.[21] The term developing country refers to 'those contracting parties the economies of which can only support low standards of living and are in the early stages of development'.[22] This provision is 'self-judging' in that contracting parties determine for themselves whether they meet this definition. Products originating in less-developed countries are exempted from MFN treatment under GATT, such that these products can benefit from special treatment by other WTO members.[23] In addition, 'least-developed countries', a special category of developing countries, are not legally bound to comply with MFN treatment. Instead, they are 'only required to undertake commitments and concessions to the extent consistent with their individual development, financial and trade needs, or their administrative and institutional capacities'.[24]

The rule of national treatment ensures that contracting parties also refrain from discriminating between domestic and imported products. This rule is; therefore, geared towards creating competitive conditions between domestic and imported products. The requirement of national treatment is based on the recognition that internal taxes and charges, as well as

[16] GATT art I(1). See also inclusion of the MFN rule in provisions on freedom of transit (art V), marks of origin (IX(1)), non-discriminatory administration of quantitative restrictions (art XIII), and state trade enterprises (XVII(1)).

[17] GATT art XXIV(4)–(12).

[18] See Lorand Bartels and Federico Ortino (eds), *Regional Trade Agreements and the WTO Legal System* (Oxford University Press 2006).

[19] Jagdish Bhagwati, *US Trade Policy: The Infatuation with FTAs* (Columbia University Discussion Paper Series No 726, 1995).

[20] See also the EU–Canada Comprehensive Economic Trade Agreement (CETA), which must be ratified in EU states before it takes full effect.

[21] GATT art XXXVI(1).   [22] GATT art XVIII(1).

[23] Differential and More Favourable Treatment, Reciprocity and Fuller Participation of Developing Countries (1979) Tokyo Round Code L/4903.

[24] WTO Agreement art XI(2).

laws, regulations and requirements can afford protection to domestic producers by reducing the competitiveness of imported products.[25] As with MFN treatment, national treatment requires contracting parties to treat imports the same as 'like domestic products' or 'like products of national origin', terms which must be understood in light of the existing jurisprudence on this issue.[26]

National treatment was at issue, for example, in a case brought before the WTO Dispute Settlement Body by Canada, the European Communities, and the United States against Japan (*Japan – Alcoholic Beverages II*).[27] This dispute concerned Japan's taxation of sochu, a Japanese alcohol, in comparison with its taxation of other alcoholic beverages. The three complaining parties (Canada, the European Communities, and the United States) challenged Japan's Liquor Tax Law, which imposed higher taxes on whisky, brandy, other distilled spirits, such as vodka and gin, and liquors compared with sochu. In this case, the WTO DSB emphasized that establishing the 'likeness' of products requires a case-by-case analysis that allows for consideration of various factors, such as the products' physical characteristics, their nature and quality, their end uses, consumers' tastes and habits, and tariff classifications and tariff bindings (which are commitments not to increase customs duty rates above an agreed level).[28] The panel determined that sochu and vodka were like products because they share most physical characteristics, as they are both 'white' or 'clean' spirits that are made of similar raw materials, with the only difference being the media used for filtration.[29] In addition, their end uses are virtually identical and they shared the same classification under Japanese tariffs. In reaching this conclusion, the panel rejected Japan's argument that the two products are unlike each other because its legislation did not have the aim or effect of protecting sochu. With respect to gin and genever; however, the panel found that the use of additives in these spirits made them unlike sochu. In addition, the use of ingredients in rum and the appearance of whisky and brandy also made them unlike sochu.

iii   General Exceptions

A number of general exceptions, set out mainly in Article XX of GATT, allow states to depart from the rules governing trade in goods for certain specified reasons. The fundamental rules on non-discrimination set out in Section 2(b)(ii) of this chapter, for example, do not prevent contracting parties from adopting or enforcing certain measures necessary to protect public order, the environment, and to conserve 'exhaustible natural resources'.[30] Contracting parties must ensure that such measures fall within one of the delimited categories in Article XX of GATT, and they must also refrain from applying these measures in a manner that constitutes 'arbitrary or unjustifiable discrimination between countries where the same conditions prevail, or a disguised restriction on international trade'.[31] In

---

[25] GATT art III(1).   [26] GATT arts III(2), III(4).

[27] WTO, *Japan: Taxes on Alcoholic Beverages – Report of the Panel* (11 July 1996) WT/DS8/R, WT/DS10/R and WT/DS11/R.

[28] ibid, paras 6.21–6.22. WTO, *Japan: Taxes on Alcoholic Beverages – Report of the Appellate Body* (4 October 1996) WT/DS8/AB/R, WT/DS10/AB/R and WT/DS11/AB/R, 20.

[29] *Japan: Taxes on Alcoholic Beverages* report of the panel (n 27), para 6.23.

[30] See also GATT art XXI (security exceptions); GATT art XIX (emergency measures to protect domestic industries).

[31] Lorand Bartels, 'The Chapeau of the General Exceptions in the WTO GATT and GATS Agreements: A Reconstruction' (2015) 109 American Journal of International Law 95.

other words, WTO members must apply these exceptions reasonably, without abusing or misusing the exceptions.

A dispute concerning a United States prohibition on imports of shrimp and shrimp products (*US—Import Prohibition of Certain Shrimp and Shrimp Products*) demonstrates how such exceptions operate in practice, and where WTO panels draw the line between permissible and impermissible measures.[32] In 1987 the US government issued regulations under the Endangered Species Act that required all US shrimp trawling vessels to prevent the incidental capture and death of sea turtles by using approved 'Turtle Excluder Devices' or by restricting their 'tow time'.[33] These regulations also banned imports of shrimps harvested with commercial fishing technology that could negatively impact sea turtles.[34] Four WTO members that are significant exporters of shrimp products (India, Malaysia, Pakistan, and Thailand) brought complaints against the United States concerning this import ban. They argued that the import ban did not fall within the scope of Article XX (g), which provides an exception for 'the conservation of exhaustible natural resources if such measures are made effective in conjunction with restrictions on domestic production or consumption'. The WTO's Appellate Body held that even though the import ban did relate to the conservation of exhaustible natural resources, it was not permissible because it constituted unjustifiable and arbitrary discrimination against shrimp imports from the complainant countries. The regulations amounted to unjustifiable discrimination in part because of their essentially coercive effect on the policy decisions made by other contracting parties. The United States had used an import ban to require WTO members in other regions to adopt a regulatory programme that was essentially the same as the United States programme, and did not take into consideration the different conditions in these other member states.[35] The Appellate Body stated that discrimination results 'when the application of the measure at issue does not allow for any inquiry into the appropriateness of the regulatory program for the conditions prevailing in those exporting countries'.[36] Within the Americas; however, the United States had engaged in far less coercive treatment of shrimp exporting states.[37] In addition, the regulations amounted to arbitrary discrimination because the US government had applied them in a rigid and inflexible manner that lacked transparency and procedural fairness.[38]

c   *International Dispute Settlement*

When a WTO member considers that another member has violated one of the WTO's agreements (i.e., GATT), the disputing parties may have recourse to the WTO's elaborate and compulsory dispute settlement procedures, which are for the settlement of inter-state disputes (as opposed to disputes between investors and states).[39] The procedures set out in the 1994 DSU are compulsory in that WTO members automatically consent to the

---

[32] WTO, *United States: Import Prohibition of Certain Shrimp and Shrimp Products—Report of the Appellate Body* (12 October 1998) WT/DS58/AB/R.
[33] ibid, para 2.   [34] ibid, para 3.   [35] ibid, paras 161–5   [36] ibid, para 165.   [37] ibid, paras 166–75.
[38] ibid, paras 177–84.   [39] See, generally, Stoll (n 15).

settlement of their disputes through the agreed procedures, as a consequence of membership in the WTO.[40] The WTO's dispute settlement procedures provide for the resolution of disputes in a relatively expeditious manner compared with other international courts and tribunals, as well as the previous dispute settlement system under GATT.[41] In addition, the DSB is responsible for overseeing the enforcement of its decisions – another unusual feature of this dispute settlement system, and a function that other international courts and tribunals do not possess.

Before disputing parties may resort to litigation; however, they must first conduct 'consultations', with a view towards 'reaching a mutually satisfactory solution' through negotiations, which are necessarily less formal and speedier than litigation.[42] Consultations are the preferred solution to dispute settlement within the WTO system, as evidenced by the fact that members are obliged to enter into consultations first, for a fixed period of time, before requesting the establishment of a panel. If consultations are unsuccessful sixty days after the receipt of the request for consultations, then the complaining party may request the DSB to establish a panel.[43] A complaining party has a right to the establishment of a panel by the DSB if consultations have failed.[44]

When requested to establish a panel, the DSB selects panellists from a list of well qualified individuals maintained by the Secretariat of the WTO.[45] Each panel consists of three, or exceptionally five individuals who are meant to have diverse backgrounds and professional experience as trade lawyers or trade policy experts, for example (a legal background is not necessary). Although some panellists are officials of their home governments, they always serve in their individual capacity. The procedures of WTO panels are less formal than those at other international courts and tribunals, as panels allow for input from the parties on drafts of their reports.[46] Panels also operate with relative speed, as they are bound to produce their reports within six months of their appointment.[47] If a panel finds that a trade measure violates an obligation under one of the WTO's agreements, then it will recommend that the measure be brought into compliance with the WTOs rules, and it may also suggest how this could be done. After a panel issues a report, it will automatically be adopted by the DSB, unless the DSB reaches a consensus within sixty days to reject it. Although panels technically 'assist' the DSU in make rulings or recommendations, in practice the DSB simply adopts the panels' reports.[48] Both complainants and respondents may appeal a panel report to the Appellate Body within sixty days after its circulation.[49]

Unlike the panels, which are ad hoc and somewhat resemble arbitration tribunals, the Appellate Body is designed to be a permanent body that consists of seven members who serve fixed terms of four years. Since December 2019, however, the Appellate Body has been non-operational because the United States, over a period of years, blocked appointments to the Appellate Body on account of its objections to the procedural as well as substantive decisions taken by the Appellate Body. It remains to be seen how this crisis will

---

[40] Membership in the UN, in contrast, provides for access to the International Court of Justice, the principal judicial organ of the UN, but membership does not constitute consent to the Court's jurisdiction, which must be given separately. See Chapter 9 of this textbook, concerning International Dispute Settlement.

[41] DSU art 2(3).   [42] DSU art 4(3).   [43] DSU art 4(7).   [44] DSU art 6(1).   [45] DSU art 8.   [46] DSU arts 12, 15.

[47] DSU art 12(8).   [48] DSU art 11.   [49] DSU art 16.

be resolved, and in the meantime, panel reports can no longer be the subject of an appeal to the Appellate Body.[50] According to the DSU, each appeal is meant to be heard by three of the seven members of the Appellate Body.[51] The members of the Appellate Body are individuals with recognized authority and demonstrated expertise in law and international trade, and are broadly representative of the WTO's membership.[52] In practice, the members of the Appellate Body have had academic training in law and/or economics, and have had a range of professional backgrounds as government officials, academics, lawyers in private practice, and lawyers at international organizations. The Appellate Body is limited to re-examining legal issues decided by the panel, as opposed to factual issues or new legal issues, and it may uphold, modify, or reverse the panels' findings and conclusions.[53] In keeping with the WTO's emphasis on the prompt settlement of disputes, the Appellate Body is meant to circulate its reports within sixty days after a disputing party has notified it of its decision to appeal, though appellate proceedings may stretch up to ninety days, and in practice have sometimes required more time.[54] As with panel reports, the reports of the Appellate Body are adopted by the DSB, which would have to reach a negative consensus in order to reject a report.[55]

When a panel or the Appellate Body determines that a member's measure is inconsistent with one of the WTO's covered agreements, then it recommends that the party bring its measure into conformity with the agreement.[56] Panels and the Appellate Body can also go further by specifically suggesting how the WTO member could implement its recommendation by, for example, modifying existing laws, enacting new laws, or changing certain administrative practices.[57] The DSB is then responsible for the monitoring or 'surveillance' of the member's prompt implementation of any recommendations or rulings.[58] The DSB also oversees the process of retaliation by the complaining party when the other party has failed to comply with a recommendation or ruling within a 'reasonable period of time' and the disputing parties have been unable to agree on mutually acceptable compensation. Retaliation by a complaining party must be authorized by the DSB, and may involve the complaining party temporarily suspending concessions or other obligations owed under the covered agreements.[59] A retaliating party could, for example, temporarily raise import duties on products in the same sector as the dispute to levels that exceed agreed limits. Retaliation is not intended to be punitive, or to allow complaining parties to recover losses, but is instead intended to bring about compliance with the recommendations or rulings.

Many aspects of the WTO's dispute settlement system make it unique compared with international adjudication and arbitration more generally. Distinguishing features include provisions for an appellate procedure, the relative speed of litigation at the WTO, and an elaborate system for monitoring implementation and enforcement. In addition, the WTO's rules on retaliation constitute a *lex specialis*, which effectively displaces the law of state responsibility, in particular the rules on counter-measures (see Chapter 5). In responding to

---

[50] Geraldo Vidigal, 'Living Without the Appellate Body: Multilateral, Bilateral and Plurilateral Solutions to the WTO Dispute Settlement Crisis' (2019) 20 Journal of World Trade and Investment 862.
[51] DSU art 17(1).   [52] DSU art 17(3).   [53] DSU art 17(13).   [54] DSU art 17(5).   [55] DSU art 17(14).
[56] DSU art 19(1).   [57] DSU art 19(1).   [58] DSU art 21.   [59] DSU art 22.

wrongful acts that breach the WTO's covered agreements, a complaining party is not free to pursue countermeasures in a unilateral manner under the law of state responsibility, but instead must seek authorization from the DSB and abide by the detailed rules set out in the DSU. The willingness of states to submit themselves to such an elaborate dispute settlement system is a testament to the importance that states attach to the swift and effective settlement of disputes that impact the well-being of economies, both domestic and global.

3 International Investment Law

a Introduction

When investors locate in foreign or 'host' states, international investment law governs the treatment owed by the host state to the foreign investor. Despite the inherent risks that may be involved for multinational corporations pursuing investments outside of their 'home' states, in foreign jurisdictions, locating in another state can be an attractive way for firms to access raw materials, such as oil and gas, increase revenues or cut costs, or both.[60] Moreover, economists have found that the economic development of host states benefits from foreign direct investment – a term that refers to the long-term transfer of capital or other resources into a foreign jurisdiction by an investor who retains some management control, and assumes the risk involved in such a transfer.[61] Host states; therefore, have an incentive to create a favourable investment climate by, for example, protecting the property rights of foreign investors and by providing them with access to a reliable dispute settlement mechanism, in the event that a dispute arises between the foreign investor and the host state.[62] But while host states have an interest in fostering favourable investment climates, they also have an interest in retaining their capacity, as sovereign states, to alter their domestic regulations as they see fit.[63] This creates an inherent tension in the field of international investment law between host states' simultaneous interests in retaining their regulatory freedom, and in creating favourable investment climates.

Controversy about the regulation and treatment of foreign investments may be traced back to at least the nineteenth century, when there was a substantial growth in foreign investment, as investors sought access to raw materials and new markets. Latin American host states maintained that foreign investors were not entitled to any rights or privileges which were not enjoyed by their own nationals.[64] According to the Calvo doctrine (named after the famous Argentinian jurist Carlos Calvo), foreigners were not entitled to pursue their grievances by recourse to dispute settlement methods that were not available to their

---

[60] David Collins, *An Introduction to International Investment Law* (Cambridge University Press 2017) 21.

[61] Herdegen (n 1) 406. A portfolio investment, in contrast, refers to a foreign investor's acquisition of shares, stocks, and bonds in circumstances that do not involve management control or risk. ibid. See also *OECD Benchmark Definition of Foreign Direct Investment* (4th edn, OECD 2008).

[62] Herdegen (n 1) 405–6.

[63] See, for example, Caroline Henckels, *Proportionality and Deference in Investor-State Arbitration: Balancing Investment Protection and Regulatory Autonomy* (Cambridge University Press 2015).

[64] Patrick Juillard, 'Calvo Doctrine/Calvo Clause' in *Max Planck Encyclopedia of Public International Law* (last updated January 2007), paras 1–3.

own nationals, who could only pursue disputes before local authorities. Contracts between foreign investors and host states in Latin America therefore typically included a 'Calvo clause', according to which the foreign investor waived recourse to international remedies, namely diplomatic protection.[65] Diplomatic protection refers to the procedure by which a foreign investor's state of nationality (the 'home' state) secures the protection of its investor abroad and obtains reparation for injuries to the investor.[66] In order for a home state to be able to exercise diplomatic protection, the injured investor must possess its nationality, and must have exhausted domestic remedies in the host state. Diplomatic protection typically takes the form of negotiation, though such disputes can also be the subject of litigation before international courts and tribunals.

While the ideas that motivated the Calvo doctrine have not died out, they have lost a good deal of their practical relevance.[67] Since the late 1950s and early 1960s, states have concluded thousands of bilateral investment treaties (BITs) that provide for the resolution of investment-related disputes by forums other than the national courts of the host state.[68] As a result, even though diplomatic protection still exists today, disputes between foreign investors and home states are now largely regulated by BITs, which give investors direct access to international arbitration, as will be discussed in Section 2(c). In addition, the practice of states has solidified into customary rules concerning the international minimum standard of treatment owed by host states to foreign investors.[69] Under the international minimum standard, states are required to provide a common standard of treatment to foreigners, which may be different from that afforded to nationals. While the exact contours of the international minimum standard have been much debated, the standard is understood to include rules on expropriation, fair and equitable treatment, and full protection and security – rules that will be explored in the following section. The remainder of Section 3 addresses the fundamental rules of international investment law, as well as the main features of dispute settlement in this field.

b   *Fundamental Rules of International Investment Law*

Many of the substantive rules of international investment law have customary origins, such as the rules concerning expropriation, fair and equitable treatment, and full protection and security. These rules of customary international law continue to exist alongside what may now be described as a robust body of treaty law. International investment law is now heavily treaty-based due to the proliferation of nearly 3,000 BITs, which generally contain the same

---

[65] ibid. The ILC's 2006 Articles on Diplomatic Protection, however, do not incorporate the Calvo clause. ILC, 'Draft Articles on Diplomatic Protection with commentaries' (2006) ILC Yearbook Vol II (pt ii) art 14, commentary para 8.

[66] See also Chapter 5 of this textbook on state responsibility.

[67] Echoes of the Calvo doctrine may be found, for instance, in the New International Economic Order and the Charter of Economic Rights and Duties of States. UNGA Res 3201 (1 May 1974); UNGA Res 3281 (XXIX) (12 December 1974) art 2.

[68] Juillard (n 64), para 21; see also Convention on the Settlement of Investment Disputes between States and Nationals of Other States (adopted 18 March 1965, entered into force 14 October 1966) 575 UNTS 159 (Washington Convention) art 26.

[69] Hollin Dickerson, 'Minimum Standards' in *Max Planck Encyclopedia of Public International Law* (last updated October 2010), para 6. Martins Paparinskis, *The International Minimum Standard and Fair and Equitable Treatment* (Oxford University Press 2013).

or similar provisions. In addition, law-making has taken the form of numerous multilateral investment treaties, preferential trade agreements, and treaties that concern specific sectors, such as the Energy Charter Treaty. While customary international law continues to exist, its role is secondary to the BITs and other treaties that currently dominate this field. The following introduces the fundamental rules of international investment law, which can typically be found in any BIT, namely: expropriation and compensation, MFN, national treatment, fair and equitable treatment, and full protection and security.

i   Expropriation and Compensation

Expropriation represents the most extreme type of interference by a host state with a foreign investment.[70] In the context of foreign direct investment, an expropriation involves a host state depriving a foreign investor of its property. In other words, the host state 'takes' the property of a foreign investor. The term 'property' encompasses movable and immovable property[71] as well as 'intangible property' such as intellectual property rights and stocks. Even though expropriations represent the most serious type of interference by a host state with a foreign investment in its territory, they are nevertheless permissible under international investment law, so long as they meet four criteria. First, the host state may only expropriate the property of a foreign investor for a public purpose. Second, a host state's expropriation of the property of a foreign investor must not involve discrimination against foreigners. Third, the expropriation must be in accordance with due process.

Finally, expropriation must be accompanied by compensation, paid by the host state to the foreign investor. Most BITs stipulate that compensation must be 'prompt, adequate, and effective', a standard known as the 'Hull formula' (named after its proponent, Cordell Hull, the US Secretary of State from 1933–44).[72] In practice, 'prompt' means that the host state must provide compensation without delay, and with interest. The term 'adequate' indicates that the amount of compensation should be equivalent to the fair market value of the investment immediately before expropriation. Finally, the term 'effective' means that the compensation must be 'fully realizable' and in 'freely convertible currency', meaning that the payment has to be in recognized, usable currency that can be traded into the investor's currency. While most BITs incorporate the Hull formula, this standard cannot be regarded as a reflection of customary international law because developing states have argued that compensation only needs to be 'appropriate' under the circumstances.[73] The views of developing states are, for instance, reflected in the UN General Assembly's 1973 Resolution on Permanent Sovereignty Over Natural Resources, which provides that 'each State is entitled to determine the amount of possible compensation and the mode of payment'.[74]

---

[70] Collins (n 60) 156.   [71] Land and buildings are 'immovable' while personal property, like factory equipment is 'movable'.
[72] Ursula Kriebaum and August Reinisch, 'Property, Right to, International Protection' in *Max Planck Encyclopedia of Public International Law* (last updated April 2019).
[73] Dickerson (n 69), paras 15–16.   [74] UNGA Res 3171 (XXVIII) (17 December 1973) art 3.

Expropriations take many forms, and debate persists in the field of international investment law about what qualifies as an expropriation. A direct expropriation involves a foreign investor's loss of ownership, which is formally transferred from the foreign investor to the host state. Direct expropriation occurs, for example, when a host state 'nationalizes' or takes control over an entire industry, such as the oil industry, or when the host state confiscates a particular foreign investment.[75] An indirect expropriation; however, involves interference by the host state with the foreign investment that falls short of a transfer of ownership. A host state may, for example, indirectly expropriate a foreign investment through a series of regulatory measures that substantially deprive the investor of his or her property. Indirect expropriations are more common today than direct expropriations, which were widespread in communist states, such as those in Eastern Europe, in the decades after the Second World War.[76]

A well-known case, *Metalclad Corporation v The United Mexican States*, illustrates the range of regulatory acts that may be involved in an indirect expropriation by a host state.[77] In the 1990s, a dispute arose between Mexico and Metalclad, an American company that had invested in Mexico with a view towards building and operating a hazardous waste landfill there.[78] At the time of its decision to invest, Metalclad's right to construct and operate the landfill had already been fully approved and endorsed by the Mexican federal government.[79] But after Metalclad had already constructed the landfill, the local municipality denied Metalclad a local construction permit due partly to concerns about the landfill's adverse environmental effects.[80] The arbitration tribunal that heard this case determined that the municipality's denial of the permit had the effect of preventing Metalclad from operating the landfill. Moreover, the municipality had acted outside of its authority by denying the permit, as the Mexican federal government had the exclusive authority to permit hazardous waste landfills. A further blow to the viability of Metalclad's investment occurred when the governor of the Mexican state of San Luis Potosi (where the landfill was located) issued an Ecological Decree that included the landfill site within an ecological preserve, thereby forever barring the operation of the landfill.[81] The tribunal found that both the municipality's denial of a construction permit and the Ecological Decree amounted to indirect expropriation that was not compensated.[82] This case shows that a range of governmental acts, from the denial of permits to environmental regulation, can result in an indirect expropriation by depriving an investor of the benefits of its property, which the investor reasonably expected to enjoy.[83]

ii   Non-discrimination: National Treatment and MFN

Discrimination in the context of foreign direct investment means that a host state treats a foreign investor worse than others who are in a similar position, namely national investors

---

[75] Kriebaum and Reinisch (n 72), para 10.

[76] Direct expropriations are; however, by no means entirely a thing of the past. Zimbabwe, for example, pursued a land acquisition programme in the 1990s and 2000s, which resulted in the unlawful expropriation of large commercial farms owned by Dutch investors who were not compensated for their losses. *Bernardus Henricus Funnekotter and Others v Republic of Zimbabwe* (22 April 2009) ICSID Case No ARB/05/6, paras 96–107.

[77] This dispute arose under the North American Free Trade Agreement (adopted 17 December 1992, entered into force 1 January 1994) 32 ILM 289 (NAFTA) art 1110.

[78] *Metalclad Corporation v The United Mexican States* (30 August 2000) ISCID Case No ARB(AF)/97/1, para 2.

[79] ibid, paras 104–5.   [80] ibid, paras 50.   [81] ibid, paras 109.   [82] ibid, paras 107, 111–12.   [83] ibid, para 103.

and investors from other foreign states.[84] The rules of national treatment and MFN are geared towards creating competitive conditions among investors by precluding a host state from discriminating against foreign investors through the application of its domestic laws. Unlike the other fundamental rules of international investment law discussed in this section, these two rules of non-discrimination are relative rather than absolute. In other words, they do not provide an absolute standard for treatment of foreign investors, but instead concern the treatment of foreign investors relative to other investors who are similarly situated.

National treatment means that host states must not discriminate against foreign investors and foreign investments, in relation to national investors and investments that are similarly situated. Investment treaties typically include a relatively brief provision indicating, for example, that neither party shall subject investments made by investors of the other party 'to treatment less favourable than that which it accords, in like circumstances,' to investments made by its own, national investors.[85] This rule aims to ensure that foreign and national investors can compete with each other as equals under domestic, host state law. In evaluating whether domestic laws discriminate against foreign investors, tribunals focus not on the intent of the law or regulation, but on its practical impact. Some tribunals have, somewhat controversially, interpreted 'like circumstances' relatively broadly, such that investors in different sectors of the economy may still be considered to be in 'like circumstances'. In *Occidental v Ecuador*, for example, the tribunal determined that Ecuador violated national treatment by granting tax concessions to exporters in sectors, such as flowers, mining, and seafood, but not exporters in the oil sector.[86]

Most treaty provisions limit national treatment's scope of application, so that it covers the host state's treatment of foreign investors only after they have established their investments, with the result that discrimination is allowed before the foreign investor has entered the host state's territory. But in some treaties, the scope of the national treatment rule also extends to the establishment and acquisition of investments by foreigners, as well as their operation, etc.[87] Some investment treaties further limit the scope of national treatment by carving out exceptions for laws that are related to health, national security, public order, or the environment, much like Article XX of GATT, discussed in Section 2(b)(iii) of this chapter.[88]

The related rule of MFN prohibits host states from discriminating against a foreign investor or a foreign investment, in relation to another foreign investor or foreign investment from a different state. This rule; therefore, aims to prevent host states from engaging in

---

[84] Collins (n 60) 105.

[85] Treaties may also indicate that each party shall accord to investors of the other party treatment that is 'no less favourable' than that is accorded to its own, national investors who are 'in like circumstances'. See, for example, NAFTA (n 77) art 1102(1); Canada Foreign Investment Protection and Promotion Agreement (FIPA) Model (2021) (Model BIT) art 5.

[86] *Occidental Exploration and Production Company v The Republic of Ecuador* (1 July 2004) LCIA Case No UN3467, paras 167–79.

[87] See, for example, NAFTA (n 77) art 1102(1); Canada Model BIT 2021 (n 85) art 5.

[88] See, for example, Agreement Between Canada and the Republic of Peru for the Promotion and Protection of Investments (entered into force 20 June 2007) art 10.

favouritism on the basis of the nationality of foreign investors.[89] By requiring equal treatment of foreign investors, this rule aims to promote competitive conditions for investors and their investments, regardless of nationality. As with the national treatment rule, MFN usually applies after an investment has been established, but not before. In addition, MFN clauses in some treaties specifically exclude regional trade agreements and customs unions from the scope of this rule.[90]

In practice, MFN requires tribunals to compare the investment treaty at issue with another treaty, in which the host state has purportedly agreed to provide better treatment. This results in the rather unusual, and somewhat controversial practice of tribunals exporting provisions from other treaties, and applying them to the dispute at hand. But perhaps the greatest controversy surrounding MFN has involved disagreement among tribunals (and commentators) about whether such clauses apply only to substantive benefits (such as rules on expropriation and compensation or fair and equitable treatment), or to procedural benefits as well. In particular, tribunals have reached different, and contradictory decisions about whether MFN clauses allow them to export from another treaty a dispute settlement clause that provides for access to investor–state arbitration.[91]

iii   Fair and Equitable Treatment

Fair and equitable treatment essentially requires host states to treat foreign investments in accordance with the rule of law.[92] In disputes between foreign investors and host states, foreign investors very frequently claim that the host state has violated the rule of fair and equitable treatment, and most successful claims brought by investors are based, in part, on violations of this rule.[93] As a result, fair and equitable treatment can be described as the most important substantive rule in international investment law.[94] Despite the importance of this rule and its basis in both custom and treaty law, its exact contours remain somewhat controversial. The term 'fair and equitable' treatment is, in itself, redundant, as the words 'fair' and 'equitable' are synonymous, and together only serve to emphasize the character of the host state's obligations.[95] Moreover, BITs typically include the requirement of fair and equitable treatment without defining the term itself.

When tribunals consider whether a host state has complied with fair and equitable treatment, they focus not on the content of the host state's domestic laws, but rather on the manner in which the host state applies them.[96] In other words, tribunals focus on the host state's decision-making processes and procedures in relation to the foreign investment,

---

[89] Collins (n 60) 109–10.   [90] See, for example, Netherlands Model Investment Agreement 2019 art 2(5).

[91] See, for example, *Emilio Agustín Maffezini v The Kingdom of Spain* (9 November 2000) ICSID Case No Arb/97/7. See *Plama Consortium Limited v Republic of Bulgaria* (27 August 2008) ICSID Case No ARB/03/24. Zachary Douglas, 'The MFN Clause in Investment Arbitration: Treaty Interpretation Off the Rails' (2011) 2 Journal of International Dispute Settlement 97.

[92] Nicolas Angelet, 'Fair and Equitable Treatment' in *Max Planck Encyclopedia of Public International Law* (last updated March 2011), para 5.

[93] Collins (n 60) 125.

[94] ibid; Christoph Schreuer, 'Investments, International Protection' in *Max Planck Encyclopedia of Public International Law* (last updated June 2013), para 51.

[95] Collins (n 60) 127–8.   [96] ibid 125.

and assess whether they are in accordance with the rule of law. Tribunals look, for instance, at whether the host state applies its laws in a transparent, reasonable, consistent, and unbiased manner that respects the legitimate expectations of foreign investors in a stable legal and business environment.[97] In evaluating claims concerning breaches of fair and equitable treatment, tribunals employ a high threshold, meaning that relatively minor injustices suffered by foreign investors would not qualify. In *Elettronica Sicula*, a diplomatic protection case brought by the United States against Italy before the ICJ, for example, the Court described the appropriate threshold for evaluating arbitrariness as 'a wilful disregard for due process of law, an act which shocks or at least surprises a sense of judicial propriety'.[98]

The fair and equitable treatment standard has been litigated in a series of cases arising out of Argentina's sovereign debt crisis from 1999 to 2002.[99] In 1989 Argentina began reforming its economy through the privatization of important industries and public utilities, including the transportation of gas.[100] As a part of this privatization process, a US-based corporation, CMS Gas Transmission Company (CMS), invested in a state-owned Argentine gas transportation company. At the time that CMS made this investment, the Argentine legal regime provided that tariffs collected by the state-owned company for gas transportation would be calculated in US dollars and adjusted periodically according to a certain formula.[101] But a series of measures taken by the Argentine government during the financial crises effectively dismantled this legal regime, with serious financial implications for CMS.[102] The tribunal in this case looked at whether Argentina had thereby breached fair and equitable treatment by changing the legal and business environment in which CMS decided to make its investment in Argentina.[103] The tribunal determined that Argentina had indeed breached fair and equitable treatment because the guarantees that Argentina had given CMS regarding the calculation and adjustments of tariffs were crucial for CMS's decision to invest in Argentina.[104] The tribunal also noted that 'fair and equitable treatment is inseparable from stability and predictability', thereby emphasizing the role of legitimate expectations in the fair and equitable treatment standard.[105] As illustrated by this case, respect for legitimate business expectations and the stability of the business environment comprise key elements of fair and equitable treatment.

iv   Full Protection and Security

The obligation of full protection and security requires host states to prevent physical harm to foreign investments, such as damage to buildings. This duty is narrower and more discrete than fair and equitable treatment, and in practice it also arises far less frequently. Full protection and security imposes a two-fold obligation on host states, which must not only protect foreign investor's property from damage by private actors, but must also

---

[97] ibid 129–32.
[98] *Case concerning Elettronica Sicula S.p.A (ELSI (United States of America v Italy)* (Judgment) [1989] ICJ Rep 15, para 128.
[99] See, for example, *CMS Gas Transmission Company v The Republic of Argentina* (12 May 2005) ICSID Case No ARB/01/8; *Sempra Energy International v The Argentine Republic* (28 September 2007) ICSID Case No ARB/02/16; *Enron Corporation and Ponderosa Assets LP v The Argentine Republic* (22 May 2007) ICSID Case No ARB/01/3; *LG&E Energy Corp, LG&E Capital Corp, and LG&E International Inc v The Argentine Republic* (25 July 2007) ICSID Case No ARB/02/1.
[100] *CMS Gas Transmission Company v Argentina* case (n 99), para 52.   [101] ibid, para 57.   [102] ibid, para 269.
[103] ibid, paras 266–81.   [104] ibid, para 275, 281.   [105] ibid, para 276.

ensure that their own police or military forces do no harm.[106] The host state's duty of protection represents an obligation of due diligence, meaning that this duty is relative, not absolute.[107] Tribunals will not, for example, hold a host state strictly liable for damage inflicted by private actors when the host state's military or police forces did everything in their power to prevent such harm.

A host state's failure to provide full protection and security need not occur in the context of civil unrest or armed conflict, as exemplified by a case brought by the British company, Wena, against Egypt. The events that gave rise to this dispute arose out of the Egyptian Hotel Company's (EHC) seizure of the Luxor and Nile Hotels, which Wena had agreed to lease from EHC and to develop. At the time of the seizure, EHC was a public sector company wholly owned by the Egyptian government.[108] Disputes between Wena and EHC about their respective obligations under the leases led to EHC's ultimate decision to violently repossess the hotels in April 1991. Both hotels were stormed by more than 100 men wielding rods and cudgels, and some of their employees were physically assaulted.[109] The tribunal determined that the government of Egypt was aware that EHC intended to seize the hotels, yet took no action to prevent it from doing so or to promptly restore Wena's control over the hotels.[110] Moreover, the Kasr El-Nile police, who were located only a few minutes away from the Nile Hotel, did not begin investigating until four hours after the seizure, and the Ministry of Tourism police never responded, though they were also nearby.[111] In this case, Egypt failed to fulfil its due diligence obligation to prevent these hotel seizures, and to provide protection once the seizures were underway.

c   *The Settlement of Disputes Arising out of Foreign Investments*

As mentioned at the beginning of this section, one element of a favourable investment climate entails access to a reliable dispute settlement mechanism. Before the advent of investor–state arbitration, foreign investors had just two options when a host state's treatment gave rise to a dispute concerning the host state's alleged violation of the rules of investment law. They could have recourse to the host state's national court system, or they could turn to their home state for diplomatic protection. Both options were unsatisfactory from the perspective of foreign investors. Foreign investors have long been reluctant or unwilling to pursue their claims in the national courts of the host state due, in part, to concerns about judicial bias against them, whether justified or not. Diplomatic protection does not; however, eliminate the need for foreign investors to have recourse to national courts, as investors must exhaust local remedies before seeking diplomatic protection. In addition, diplomatic protection proved to be an unsatisfactory dispute settlement method for investors because home states exercise diplomatic protection on a discretionary basis, and with relative infrequency. Home states are not obliged to take up the claims of their

---

[106] Collins (n 60) 137–8.   [107] ibid 141–2.
[108] *Wena Hotels Ltd v Arab Republic of Egypt* (8 December 2000) ICSID Case No ARB/98/4, para 17.
[109] ibid, paras 33–50.   [110] ibid, paras 84–5.   [111] ibid, paras 89–90.

injured investors, and may very well be uninterested in doing so due, for example, to concerns about disrupting generally good relations with the host state.

The contemporary system of investor–state arbitration eliminates the need for investors to rely on their home state to take up claims on their behalf, and it also generally removes the role of the national courts of host states in resolving investment-related disputes. Instead, individual investors have the capacity to directly pursue their claims against host states before an international tribunal – a capacity that is quite rare in the international legal field. Bilateral investment treaties, for example, commonly include dispute settlement clauses, by which the two states parties consent to the arbitration of investment disputes that may arise in the future with foreign investors from the other state. Such a clause allows a foreign investor to initiate arbitration proceedings when a dispute arises, without the involvement of its home state. Arbitral proceedings concerning investment disputes are therefore always mixed, meaning that they involve litigation between a foreign investor and a host state (rather than the home and the host states). While in theory either the host state or the investor may initiate proceedings, in practice the investor is always the claimant and the host state is always the respondent in investor–state arbitration.

The preferred forum for the settlement of investment disputes is the International Centre for Settlement of Investment Disputes (ICSID), although a number of other important fora exist.[112] ICSID was established in 1966 by a multilateral treaty, known as the Washington Convention (or the ICSID Convention), which was formulated by the World Bank and currently has 155 states parties.[113] Based in Washington, DC, ICSID provides a framework within which states and investors may settle their investment disputes through ad hoc arbitrations (or through conciliation, an option that investors only very rarely pursue). In other words, ICSID does not settle disputes itself, but instead provides an institutional framework for the constitution of ad hoc tribunals, typically consisting of three arbitrators, who enjoy ICSID's administrative support.[114] In addition, the Washington Convention only gives investors (both natural and legal persons) and host states access to ICSID arbitration. Consent must be given expressly and separately from the Washington Convention, and most often takes the form of a dispute settlement clause in a BIT between the host state and the investor's home state, which may specifically provide for arbitration under the auspices of ICSID.[115] Consent may also, however, take the form of a clause in a contract entered into between a foreign investor and the host state, and a host state may also consent to ICSID arbitration through a clause in its national legislation. These two methods for giving consent do not involve the home state of the investor, unlike BITs, which are concluded between states.

The Washington Convention establishes a system of investor–state arbitration that may be described as 'self-contained' in two respects. First, the Convention precludes any resort to other remedies, namely the national courts of the host state, and diplomatic protection.[116] Second, investors or host states that are unhappy with the outcome of a particular arbitration proceeding

---

[112] See, for example, the Permanent Court of Arbitration, the London Court of International Arbitration, and the International Chamber of Commerce.
[113] Washington Convention (n 68).   [114] Washington Convention art 37(1).   [115] Washington Convention art 25.
[116] Washington Convention arts 26–7.

may not challenge the arbitration award in national courts, or by appealing the award. National courts are, in fact, obliged to recognize and enforce the awards rendered by ICSID arbitration tribunals.[117] The only recourse for dissatisfied litigants is provided by the ICSID system, which allows parties to pursue the annulment of an award before an ICSID annulment committee. But the grounds for annulment are quite limited, and concern only the legitimacy of the arbitration process, rather than the substantive correctness of the arbitration award.[118]

d   The 'Backlash'

Even though ICSID came into existence in the mid-1960s, few cases were arbitrated under the auspices of ICSID until the 1990s, when foreign investors really began to make use of investor–state arbitration as a method for dispute settlement. Since the 1990s, investor–state arbitration has grown into a relatively robust field of practice, with hundreds of awards having been rendered by ICSID tribunals alone. The development of this field has; however, also resulted in what may be described as a 'backlash' against aspects of this system.[119] Investor–state arbitration tribunals, which are always ad hoc or temporary, have for example produced inconsistent decisions on certain substantive and procedural issues, which some states and commentators perceive as undermining the predictability and stability of this system of dispute settlement. In addition, host states, and in particular developing countries, have seen foreign investors challenge their regulatory measures with respect to a range of domestic matters, such as environmental protection, economic emergencies, and taxation. Another point of contention has been the relative lack of transparency in the field of investor–state arbitration. Hearings, for example, are typically closed to the public and awards are not always released, despite the ramifications that many of these investment disputes have for the general public.

Perhaps the most visible signs of this general backlash against investor–state arbitration were the withdrawals from many BITs, and the withdrawals from the Washington Convention by several Latin American states, Bolivia (2007), Ecuador (2009), and Venezuela (2012). These states withdrew or 'denounced' the Washington Convention after they had all faced a significant number of claims by foreign investors, which culminated in unfavourable decisions by arbitration tribunals. Despite these denunciations, and a general 'backlash', the system of investor–state arbitration can hardly be said to be in a state of decline. Instead, the regular use of this method of dispute settlement has prompted reflection among states, civil society, and commentators, about how investor–state arbitration should ideally function.

4   International Monetary Law

When states met at Bretton Woods in 1944, they focused in large part on designing an international monetary system that would help facilitate international trade and foreign

---

[117] Washington Convention arts 53–4.   [118] Washington Convention art 52.
[119] Michael Waibel and others (eds), *The Backlash against Investment Arbitration: Perceptions and Reality* (Kluwer Law International 2010).

investment by fostering competitive economic conditions. International trade and business can, for example, be negatively impacted when a state manipulates its domestic currency so as to put its own economy at a competitive advantage. Through an undervalued exchange rate, a state may boost its own export industries, thereby distorting competitive conditions worldwide. During the interwar period, especially in the 1930s, widespread currency manipulation and protectionist trade policies had severe consequences for the global and domestic economies, as world trade declined dramatically, and living standards and employment fell.[120] The Bretton Woods negotiations were; therefore, partly geared towards preventing another Great Depression by creating a stable international monetary system that would facilitate the exchange of goods, services, and capital among countries and sustain sound economic growth.[121]

The IMF was the product of these negotiations, along with the World Bank. This section on international monetary law focuses on the IMF, which was designed in part to enable international trade and commerce. The IMF became operational in 1947, and now enjoys almost universal membership, with 190 member states. From an institutional law perspective, the IMF has an unusual decision-making structure, because members do not have equal voting power. Instead of each member having one vote, as in the UN General Assembly or the WTO General Council, for instance, the voting power of IMF members is based on their 'quotas', which reflect the relative size and importance of their economy. Each member's quota also determines the financing (or 'subscription') that the member is required to pay to the IMF, as well as the amount of financing that the member can receive from the IMF.[122]

a   *Stable Exchange Rates and Surveillance by the IMF*

One of the IMF's original, key functions as an international monetary institution was to secure the stabilization of exchange rates. The term exchange rate refers to the value of one state's currency compared with other state's currencies. Exchange rates are a matter of concern for the IMF because of their international implications for the global economy, especially when states undervalue their exchange rate, as mentioned at the start of this section. For the first twenty-five years of the IMF's existence, member states were bound by a system of fixed exchange rates, according to which the value of their currencies was tied to the US dollar, which was in turn tied to gold. Under this 'par value system', members could only deviate from the established value of their currency within a certain margin.[123] This system began to collapse in 1971; however, when the United States abandoned the gold standard, which was the basis for this par value system.[124] In 1973, this system of fixed

---

[120] Sabine Schlemmer-Schulte, 'International Monetary Fund (IMF)' in *Max Planck Encyclopedia of Public International Law* (last updated October 2014), para 2.

[121] Articles of Agreement of the IMF (adopted 22 July 1944, entered into force 27 December 1945) 2 UNTS 39 (IMF Articles of Agreement) art IV, s 1.

[122] IMF Articles of Agreement art III; art V(3)(b); art XII(5).

[123] Asif H Qureshi and Andreas R Ziegler, *International Economic Law* (3rd edn, Sweet & Maxwell 2011) 81.

[124] The abandonment of the gold standard by the United States was the result of its own balance of payments problems, which had a range of causes, including the war in Vietnam, and increased imports from Japan. See Schlemmer-Schulte (n 120), para 7.

exchange rates was therefore replaced by a system of flexible exchange rates that are no longer based on the gold standard. Instead, IMF members may, for example, allow their currencies to float, or they may peg their currencies to another currency (such as the US dollar) or a basket of currencies. This change is reflected in Article IV of the IMF's Articles of Agreement (as amended in 1976), which articulates relatively vague and flexible obligations for member states with respect to exchange rates.[125]

After the collapse of the fixed exchange rate system, the IMF was entrusted by its members with a consultative function with respect to members' exchange rate policies. The IMF now oversees member states' compliance with these amended, and more flexible rules on exchange rates by exercising 'surveillance' over their exchange rate policies.[126] Members must, in particular, provide the IMF with information about their policies, and consult with the IMF about its policies if requested. Surveillance also involves the issuance of non-binding guidance by the IMF on exchange rate policies, as well as member states' fiscal and tax policies. Surveillance by the IMF is based on the premise that compliance with the IMF's rules in Article IV will be enhanced by obliging states to report certain information, and subjecting them to peer pressure.[127] Such monitoring of treaty obligations is, of course, by no means limited to international monetary law, and can also be seen in the fields of international human rights law and international environmental law, for example. Even though such treaty monitoring does not entail sanctions for non-compliance, surveillance is nevertheless one method by which the IMF influences the policies of member states.

b   *Balance of Payments Problems and Conditionality*

The IMF also plays an important role as a lender of foreign currency to states facing balance of payments problems or other financial crises.[128] A balance of payments problem may involve a state's inability to buy essential imports due to a shortfall of foreign currency. This might occur, for instance, where the value of a state's imports exceeds the value of its exports, potentially leading to the devaluation of its currency. Causes of balance of payments problems can stem from external reasons, such as global financial problems, or internal reasons, such as economic mismanagement.[129] Short-and medium-term loans by the IMF allow member states to deal with balance of payments problems, and more generally stabilize their economies and restore economic growth. Loans by the World Bank, in contrast, are directed towards financing projects and are typically longer term. The IMF is able to provide liquidity, or credit to member states facing such problems by drawing on a pool of members' currencies. The IMF does not, in other words, generate or issue its own currency (although this idea was discussed during the negotiations at Bretton Woods). Member states with balance of payments problems have certain borrowing rights that are determined on the basis of their quotas, which are used to set the maximum amount

---

[125] IMF Articles of Agreement (n 121) art IV(2). Qureshi and Ziegler (n 123) 183.   [126] IMF Articles of Agreement art IV(3).
[127] Qureshi and Ziegler (n 123) 188.   [128] IMF Articles of Agreement art V(3).   [129] Qureshi and Ziegler (n 123) 243–4.

of financing that a state may obtain from the IMF. The IMF has developed various lending 'facilities' that are designed for different types of balance of payments problems. The Rapid Financing Instrument, for example, allows the IMF to provide financial assistance to member states that face balance of payments problems due to natural disasters, post-conflict situations, and most recently, the COVID-19 pandemic.

When a member state borrows from the IMF due to balance of payments problems, it commits to undertaking certain economic reforms in order to prevent such problems in the future. This practice of the IMF is known as 'conditionality' because the IMF conditions the IMF's continued lending to the member state on its acceptance of structural adjustment programs.[130] A borrowing state's failure to fulfil the stipulated conditions can result in the IMF ending or suspending its lending. The term 'Washington Consensus' can refer to a series of reforms imposed by the IMF as well as the World Bank, especially as conditions for lending to Latin American states in the 1990s and 2000s. These conditions include liberalizing and deregulating trade and financial and capital markets as well as privatization of public sectors and fiscal discipline.[131] Such conditionality has been controversial partly because it has allowed the IMF to play a major policy-making role, but also because the conditions imposed by the IMF have proven to be ill-suited to the economic problems faced by some states in the past.[132] During the global financial crisis, however, the IMF reformed its framework for conditionality so that structural conditions would be better tailored to member states' specific situations.[133]

5   Concluding Remarks

Although international trade law, international investment law, and international monetary law represent three distinct areas of international economic law, their histories are intertwined, their goals are interlinked, and they share some fundamental legal principles. States developed these three bodies of international economic law at the end of the Second World War, with a view towards preventing another great depression and subsequent world war. Their goals are interlinked insofar as international trade, investment, and monetary law are all geared towards enabling economic growth and development. Moreover, the international monetary system exists, in part, for the purpose of facilitating international trade and investment. Finally, international trade and international investment law share some fundamental principles, such as non-discrimination, although MFN, and national treatment take somewhat different forms in the two bodies of law. In the last decades, international trade and international investment law have become increasingly robust bodies of law, as the WTO's panels and Appellate Body, and investor–state arbitration tribunals have deepened our understanding of how the law is applied in practice.

---

[130] IMF, 'Guidelines on Conditionality' (25 September 2002); Cesare Pinelli, 'Conditionality' in *Max Planck Encyclopedia of Public International Law* (last updated November 2013), para 3.

[131] Sabine Schlemmer-Schulte, 'International Monetary Fund, Structural Adjustment Programme (SAP)' in *Max Planck Encyclopedia of Public International Law* (last updated October 2014).

[132] ibid, para 5.

[133] Statement of the IMF Staff, 'Principles Underlying the Guidelines on Conditionality' (revised 9 January 2006).

Recommended Reading

Chester Brown, "Resolving International Investment Disputes" in Natalie Klein (ed), *Litigating International Law Disputes: Weighing the Options* (Cambridge University Press 2014).

David Collins, *An Introduction to International Investment Law* (Cambridge University Press 2017).

Matthias Herdegen, *Principles of International Economic Law* (2nd edn, Oxford University Press 2016).

Mitsuo Matsushita et al, *The World Trade Organization: Law, Practice, and Policy* (3rd edn, Oxford University Press 2015).

15

Law of the Sea

Nico Schrijver

1   Introduction

The seas and oceans cover 71 per cent of the surface area of our planet. Pictures from space depict our earth as the 'blue planet'. For centuries, the uses of these areas were characterized by freedom of the seas, under which everyone could freely navigate, conduct commerce, and fish, as long as the rights of others to do so were not hindered. Traditionally, sovereignty was only recognized with respect to a narrow belt of sea along the coast, consisting of more or less three nautical miles, with either visibility or the range of a cannon from ashore as points of reference.[1]

During the twentieth century, this situation changed dramatically, especially with the adoption of the 1982 United Nations Convention on the Law of the Sea (UNCLOS).[2] The Convention recognizes both territorial sovereignty over adjacent maritime areas (i.e., the territorial sea) and functional sovereign rights over natural resources in more distant maritime areas, such as new maritime areas called the Exclusive Economic Zone (EEZ) and the continental shelf.[3] These new zones found recognition in both treaty law and customary international law during the second half of the twentieth century. The rush of coastal states to claim more of the sea has, nonetheless, been somewhat halted by the principle of the freedom of the high seas, and the development of a special new regime for the deep seabed, which is commonly known as the 'Area', and its resources based on the principle of the common heritage of humankind.

While in the twentieth century states focused their attention on the resources of the seas and oceans (especially fish, oil, and gas), in the twenty-first century attention has partly shifted to the vital ecological functions of the oceans, amidst concerns about the impact of climate change, melting icecaps in polar regions, rising sea levels, and the loss of marine biological diversity. This is reflected in United Nations Sustainable Development Goal 14, entitled 'Life Below Water', which aims to contribute to conserving and sustainably using the oceans, seas, and marine resources, in keeping with sustainable development.[4]

---

[1] The term 'nautical mile' refers to a distance of 1,852 meters.
[2] UNCLOS (adopted 10 December 1982, entered into force 16 November 1994) 1833 UNTS 3.
[3] On the various dimensions of the concept of sovereignty, see NJ Schrijver, 'The Changing Nature of State Sovereignty' (2000) 70 British Yearbook of International Law 65, 69–72.
[4] UNGA Res 70/1 'Transforming Our World: The 2030 Agenda for Sustainable Development' (21 October 2015), 23–4.

After a sketch of the history of the law of the sea and the traditional freedoms of the sea, this chapter discusses the various efforts to codify the law of the sea during the twentieth century, which culminated in the adoption of UNCLOS in 1982 (Section 2). Subsequently, the chapter examines the legal regimes governing the various maritime zones (Section 3), as well as two international areas, the high seas and the Area (Section 4). The chapter then takes up thematic issues in the law of the sea, namely the delimitation of maritime boundaries, the protection of the marine environment, the special interests of developing countries, and the system for the settlement of law of the sea disputes (Section 5). The chapter concludes by noting that despite the relatively comprehensive scope of UNCLOS, a number of new challenges have arisen with respect to the law of the sea, especially as a result of human-driven climate change (Section 6).

2   A History of the Law of the Sea

a   *The Origins of the Law of the Sea*

The notions of both sovereignty and freedom have long occupied a place in the classical law of the sea. The Roman Empire considered that the sea was not susceptible to possession as private property and regarded it as a *commune omnium* (property common to all), albeit for Roman citizens only. They; therefore, sought to establish dominium over the entire Mediterranean Sea under the banner *mare nostrum* ('our sea'). Traditionally, the seas were long plagued by frequent acts of piracy. In addition, with the rise of seafaring nations and competition among them from the fifteenth century onwards, conflicting claims to maritime areas emerged. The Treaty of Tordesillas of 1494,[5] for example, was based on the papal bull (i.e., decree) *Inter caetera* ('among others'), by which Pope Alexander VI divided the world outside of Europe between Spain and Portugal by drawing a vertical line between the north and south poles to designate their spheres of influence.[6] The Treaty of Tordesillas between Spain and Portugal provided for Portugal's exclusive right of navigation in the Indian Ocean and South Atlantic Ocean and for Spain's exclusive right of navigation in the West Atlantic Ocean, the Gulf of Mexico, and the Pacific Ocean. This division was; however, soon challenged by new naval powers, most notably, the Dutch, the English, and the French. In 1603, for example, the Dutch seized the Portuguese vessel *Santa Catarina*, which was loaded with china and precious spices, in the Straits of Malacca near Johore (present day Malaysia). Both Spain and Portugal were ultimately forced to confront the reality that they could not establish a monopoly over the seas and oceans. In 1609, Hugo Grotius (1585–1643), who served as an advocate for the United Dutch East and West Indies Companies, published his famous book *Mare liberum* ('On the Freedom of the Seas').[7]

---

[5] Treaty between Spain and Portugal concluded at Tordesillas (7 June 1494) in Frances Gardiner Davenport (ed), *European Treaties bearing on the History of the United States and its Dependencies* (Carnegie Institution of Washington 1917) vol 1, 84.

[6] Bull *Inter Caetera* by Pope Alexander VI (4 May 1493) in ibid 72.

[7] The full title of the book by Hugo Grotius was *Mare Liberum, sive de iure quod Batavis competit ad Indicana commercia Dissertatio* (Elzevier 1609) (tr: On the Freedom of the Seas or the Right Which Belongs to the Dutch to Take Part in the East India Trade).

Grotius argued that the taking of the *Santa Catarina* as a prize of war was lawful and that the sea is free from individual or state property rights, thus challenging the monopolist pretensions of Spain and Portugal. Hugo Grotius wrote that:

neither a nation nor an individual can establish any right of private ownership over the sea itself (except inlets of the sea), inasmuch as its occupation is not permissible either by nature or on grounds of public utility . . . .

But if the Portuguese call occupying the sea merely to have sailed over it before other people, and to have, as it were, opened the way, could anything in the world be more ridiculous? For, as there is no part of the sea on which some persons have not already sailed, it will necessarily follow that every route of navigation is occupied by someone. Therefore we peoples of today are absolutely excluded. Why will not those men who circumnavigate the globe be justified in saying that they have acquired for themselves the possession of the whole ocean! But there is not a single person in the world who does not know that a ship sailing through the sea leaves behind it no more legal right than it does a track.[8]

Grotius' view contrasted with the position of Great Britain, which held that the waters surrounding the Kingdom of Great Britain were, on historical grounds, 'British Seas'. This prompted a fascinating doctrinal rebuttal by the British legal advisor, John Selden, on behalf of King Charles I. In *Mare clausum* ('The Closed Sea'), Selden defended the excessive British claims to huge areas of the sea (*Oceanus Brittannicus*) surrounding British territories around the world.[9]

The 1648 Treaty of Munster, one of the two major treaties of the Peace of Westphalia, provided that the Dutch, in principle, were free to take any route for shipping purposes and could trade freely. The Grotian concept of *mare liberum* was, thereby endorsed by this treaty, but for the Dutch only. Grotius never claimed that all seas were open to use by all persons. It was; however, generally accepted that coastal states enjoyed the right to regulate certain activities in waters adjacent to their coasts, such as for defence purposes, for immigration control, or for the protection of their fisheries against foreign fishermen. Cornelius van Bynkershoek, another Dutch jurist, was the first to identify the concepts of 'freedom of the high seas' and 'sovereignty' of the coastal state as the twin pillars of the law of the sea.[10] During the nineteenth century, Great Britain pursued, as the leading maritime power, a policy of the freedom of the high seas, which was soon also adhered to by the United States and the Russian Empire (later the Soviet Union), which became new leading maritime powers. The concept of the freedom of the high seas was also reflected in US president Woodrow Wilson's 'Fourteen Points', a statement of principles that he outlined on the eve of the negotiations of the Treaty of Versailles in 1918, at the end of the First World War.[11] Wilson's second point provided for '[a]bsolute freedom of navigation upon the seas, outside territorial waters, alike in peace and in war, except as the seas may be closed in whole or in part by international action for the enforcement of international covenants'.

---

[8] ibid, ch 5.
[9] John Selden, *Mare clausum sive de dominio maris* (Will Stanesbeius 1635) (tr: The Closed Sea or Sovereignty over the Sea).
[10] Cornelius van Bynkershoek, *De dominio maris dissertation* (Hagae Baravorum 1703) (tr: Treatise on Sovereignty over the Sea).
[11] The Avalon Project, 'President Woodrow Wilson's Fourteen Points' <https://avalon.law.yale.edu/20th_century/wilson14.asp>.

b   Codification of the Law of the Sea

For centuries, the law of the sea was mainly based upon customary international law. By the end of the nineteenth century, a relatively consistent state practice and a widely shared *opinio juris* had emerged. In 1924, a Committee of Experts that was established in the context of the League of Nations identified the subject of territorial waters as ripe for codification. At the 1930 Conference for the Codification of International Law in The Hague; however, the delegates failed to reach agreement on both the width of the territorial waters and a contiguous (adjacent) zone for purposes of the control of customs, sanitary regulations, and interference with security by foreign ships.

In subsequent decades strong support emerged in favour of a wider scope of coastal state jurisdiction in maritime areas. Emphasis shifted from the sea as a means of transportation and communication to the sea as an important zone for the exploitation of natural resources. In 1950, the newly established International Law Commission, a subsidiary organ of the United Nations (UN) General Assembly, initiated discussions on the law of the sea with a view towards contributing to its progressive development and codification.[12] In 1958 the UN General Assembly convened a diplomatic conference on the law of the sea, which resulted in the adoption of four conventions in Geneva in 1958:

• The Convention on the Territorial Sea and Contiguous Zone;[13]
• The Convention on the High Seas;[14]
• The Convention on Fishing and Conservation of Living Resources of the High Seas;[15]
• The Convention on the Continental Shelf.[16]

While many parts of these Conventions codified customary international law, the recognition of the inherent right of a coastal state to a continental shelf was new. The continental shelf refers to the natural prolongation of the land beneath the high seas. As with the Hague Codification Conference of 1930; however, the 1958 Conference also failed to reach a majority agreement on a limit of three, six, or twelve nautical miles for the territorial sea. The 1958 conference did; however, build on the significant new trend in state practice following the 'Truman Proclamation' of 28 September 1945, by which US president Harry Truman proclaimed that the natural resources of the continental shelf adjacent to the US coast belonged to the United States. The 1958 conference recognized the right of a coastal state to a continental shelf with a breadth of 200 meters or, beyond that limit, to where exploitation of the natural resources (e.g., oil and gas) would be possible.[17]

In 1960, another conference on the law of the sea was convened to adopt a treaty on the topics that the 1958 conference had left open, but was unsuccessful. A US-Canadian proposal

---

[12] See Charter of the UN (adopted 26 June 1945, entered into force 24 October 1945) 1 UNTS XVI (UN Charter) art 13; Statute of the International Law Commission (adopted 21 November 1947) UNGA Res 174(II), art 15.
[13] Convention on the Territorial Sea and Contiguous Zone (adopted 29 April 1958, entered into force 10 September 1964) 516 UNTS 205.
[14] Convention on the High Seas (adopted 29 April 1958, entered into force 30 September 1962) 450 UNTS 11.
[15] Convention on Fishing and Conservation of Living Resources of the High Seas (adopted 29 April 1958, entered into force 20 March 1966) 559 UNTS 285.
[16] Convention on the Continental Shelf (adopted 29 April 1958, entered into force 10 June 1964) 499 UNTS 311.
[17] See 1958 Convention on the Continental Shelf art 2.

for a six-mile territorial sea plus an additional six-mile fishery zone fell only one vote short of the two-thirds majority required for adoption. The failure of the 1958 and 1960 conferences to reach an agreement on the maximum width of the territorial sea and the establishment of an exclusive fishery zone, resulted in a proliferation of divergent state practice. While most Western states continued to observe the three-mile limit, Latin American and newly independent African states began to claim much wider territorial seas.[18] Coastal developing countries considered it to be necessary to halt the large-scale exploitation of what they perceived as their fishery resources by foreign fishing fleets, mainly those of their former colonial powers. Often these claims did not just pertain to the territorial sea in the sense of the 1958 Convention, but also entailed more extensive claims to sovereign rights to resources, such as fisheries, beyond the territorial seas.

Other significant political, technological, and environmental developments further strained the mostly centuries-old law of the sea, as codified in 1958. For example, many developing countries, which gained independence only in the 1960s, had not participated in formulating the law of the sea and wanted their special needs and interests to be considered. Furthermore, great technological advances allowed for the exploitation of the continental shelf at increasingly greater depths, such as for oil and gas. States further anticipated future exploitation of the deep seabed in mining operations for polymetallic nodules, which are a potential source of rare metals. Moreover, overfishing and exhaustion of fish stocks became a real threat, despite the Fishing Convention of 1958, which called for conservation through establishing 'optimum sustainable yields' of fish.[19]

During the 1960s these developments prompted a number of coastal states, in particular Iceland and Latin American states, to claim not only broader territorial seas but also increasingly extensive areas beyond their territorial seas as their own fishing zones. It became clear that the entire law of the sea needed to be revisited. For this purpose, a third conference was convened by the UN in 1973, which ultimately resulted in the adoption of a substantially new and comprehensive law of the sea convention in 1982.[20]

c   *UNCLOS: The World Constitution of the Oceans*

The 1982 UNCLOS lays down rules for virtually all possible uses of the sea, including shipping, fishing, the laying of cables and pipelines, overflight, and marine scientific research. The Convention also delimits the five maritime zones, namely internal waters, the territorial sea, archipelagic waters, the EEZ, and the high seas.[21] In addition, the Convention regulates the rights and duties of states in the contiguous zone, international straits, and the Area. Furthermore, Parts XII–XV deal with thematic issues, namely the protection of the marine environment, marine scientific research, and the peaceful

---

[18] Karin Hjertonsson, *The New Law of the Sea: Influence of the Latin American States on Recent Developments of the Law of the Sea* (Sijthoff 1973); Naslia S Rembe, *Africa and the International Law of the Sea: A Study of the Contribution of African States to the Third Conference on the Law of the Sea* (Sijthoff and Noordhoff 1980).

[19] 1958 Convention on Fishing and Conservation of Living Resources of the High Seas art 2.

[20] UNGA Res 3067 (XXVIII) (16 November 1973). The first conference was in 1958, and the second conference was in 1960.

[21] UNCLOS art 86.

settlement of disputes. Three new institutions were created as a result of UNCLOS: the International Seabed Authority (ISA), the International Tribunal for the Law of the Sea (ITLOS), and the Commission on the Limits of the Continental Shelf (CLCS).[22] The approach pursued through the nine years of negotiations, which ran from 1973 to 1982, was a package deal on all issues. Rather uniquely, the negotiators succeeded in adopting a single convention by which they sought to emphasize the unity of the law of the sea. No reservations were permitted to the Convention.[23] Due to its comprehensive scope and the near universal participation, this Convention has also been referred to as the 'Constitution of the Oceans'.[24]

When UNCLOS was opened for signature on 10 December 1982 at Montego Bay, Jamaica, some controversies remained, especially with regard to the modalities of the regime for deep seabed mining under Part XI of the Convention. It became obvious that the United States and most industrialized states would not become parties to the Convention on account of these controversies. New negotiations therefore began in the late 1980s to resolve these issues. A new agreement relating to the implementation of Part XI of UNCLOS was concluded in 1994, which purported to meet the objections of industrialized states with respect to the regime for the deep seabed.[25] As a result of this '1994 Implementing Agreement', UNCLOS finally entered into force on 16 November 1994. The United States; however, still did not become a party to the Convention, although it accepts much of UNCLOS as reflecting customary international law, and has relied on it in many instances. In 1995 the Straddling Fish Stocks Agreement was also concluded in order to elaborate upon and supplement the rules in UNCLOS concerning the conservation and sustainable management of fish stocks.[26] Currently, UNCLOS has 168 parties, for whom UNCLOS prevails over the 1958 Geneva Conventions.[27]

3   Maritime Areas

In the contemporary law of the sea, the seas have been divided into various maritime zones, over which states may exercise either national sovereignty or more limited sovereign rights or jurisdictional rights falling short of full sovereignty (Figure 15.1). Sovereignty extends to the belt of water immediately off a state's coast, known as the territorial sea. Sovereignty

---

[22] See Robin R Churchill, 'The 1982 United Nations Convention on the Law of the Sea' in Donald R Rothwell et al (eds), *The Oxford Handbook of the Law of the Sea* (Oxford University Press 2015).

[23] UNCLOS art 309.

[24] 'A Constitution for the Oceans', remarks by Tommy TB Koh, President of the 3rd UN Conference on the Law of the Sea (6 and 11 December 1982) <www.un.org/depts/los/convention_agreements/texts/koh_english.pdf>; See also Yoshifumi Tanaka, *International Law of the Sea* (3rd edn, Cambridge University Press 2019) 39 ('Reflecting the package-deal approach, the balance of rights and duties as well as overall equitableness are essential elements of the Convention').

[25] UNGA Res 48/263 (17 August 1994); Agreement relating to the implementation of Part XI of the UNCLOS of 10 December 1982 (adopted 28 July 1994, entered into force 28 July 1996) 1836 UNTS 3 (1994 Implementation Agreement).

[26] Agreement for the Implementation of the Provisions of the UNCLOS of 10 December 1982 relating to the Conservation and Management of Straddling Fish Stocks and Highly Migratory Fish Stocks (adopted 4 August 1995, entered into force 11 December 2001) 2167 UNTS 3 (1995 Straddling Fish Stocks Agreement).

[27] UNCLOS art 311(1). The parties consist of 167 states parties and the European Union.

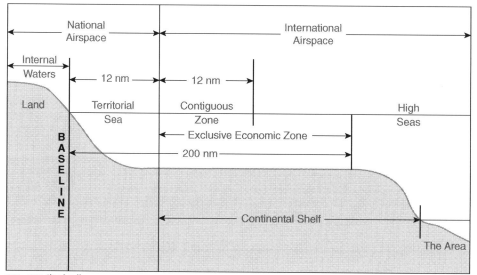

nm - nautical miles

Figure 15.1 Legal boundaries of the oceans and airspace. Graphic courtesy of Law of the Sea Primer Project, The Fletcher School of Law and Diplomacy, Trustees of Tufts College. Copyright 2017 by the Trustees of Tufts College.

also encompasses a state's internal waters and, in the case of an archipelagic state, archipelagic waters. Such areas are considered to be part of a state's territory, and thus, within its sovereignty. Beyond the territorial sea, coastal states possess limited enforcement jurisdiction in the contiguous zone. In the EEZ and the continental shelf, which lies below the sea, states possess certain sovereign rights with respect to resources as well as certain other resource-related jurisdictional rights. States do not possess any sovereignty over the high seas and the deep seabed area, nor do they exercise any sovereign rights or jurisdiction in these zones. The determination of where one maritime area ends and the next begins is based on the fundamental concept that the 'land dominates the sea', meaning that the shape of the coastline, along which the baseline runs, determines the extent of these maritime zones.

Baselines are the imaginary lines along which the sea meets the land at low tide.[28] The low water line, known as the 'normal baseline', is generally used to determine the breadth of maritime zones, but other methodologies to identify the baseline exist.[29] The main alternative to the normal baselines is a straight baseline, which does not follow the natural shape of the coast, but instead connects points on a coast that is deeply indented. As early as 1951, the International Court of Justice (ICJ) recognized in its judgment in the *Anglo-Norwegian Fisheries* case that Norway was entitled to use straight baselines because it has a deeply indented coastline. Both the 1958 and 1982 Conventions allow the use of straight baselines where a coastline is deeply indented.[30] They also recognize special economic

---

[28] UNCLOS arts 3, 5.   [29] UNCLOS art 5.
[30] 1958 Convention on the Territorial Sea and Contiguous Zone art 4; UNCLOS art 7.

interests 'if their reality and importance is clearly evidenced by long usage'.[31] Straight baselines have particular relevance for bays, which are well-marked indentations of the coast.[32] Where the mouth of a bay exceeds twenty-four nautical miles, a straight baseline of twenty-four nautical miles will be drawn within the bay in order to enclose as much water as possible within a line of that length.[33] The waters of a bay that fall on the landward side of such a twenty-four-nautical-mile baseline are considered internal waters that fall within the full sovereignty of the coastal state.[34]

a   *Territorial Sea and Contiguous Zone*

Under UNCLOS, every coastal state has the right to establish a territorial sea of a maximum of twelve nautical miles, as measured from its baselines. The term 'territorial sea' refers not only to the water itself (i.e., the 'water column'), but also to the airspace above and the seabed below.[35] The recognition of the twelve-nautical-mile territorial sea has brought considerable maritime space under territorial sovereignty. A state has the same jurisdiction over its territorial sea that it has on land, which means that the coastal state has the right to regulate activities that take place in the territorial sea, and has exclusive rights to its natural resources, such as fish.[36] A coastal state must; however, allow the ships of other states the right of innocent passage in its territorial sea. A foreign ship may lawfully navigate through a state's territorial sea, so long as the passage is 'continuous and expeditious' and 'innocent', meaning 'not prejudicial to the peace, good order or security of the coastal State'.[37] While the coastal state has broad legislative powers with respect to the territorial sea, it has a limited capacity to exercise enforcement jurisdiction, such as by stopping and boarding a ship involved in drug trafficking and making an arrest.[38]

A coastal state also possesses limited enforcement jurisdiction in the maritime area adjacent to its territorial waters, known as the contiguous zone, which extends up to twenty-four nautical miles from the coast.[39] These jurisdictional rights are limited to preventing or punishing violations of a limited set of domestic laws, namely, customs, fiscal, immigration, and sanitary laws. In contrast to the full territorial sovereignty that the coastal state exercises in its internal waters and the territorial sea, the coastal state only enjoys limited enforcement jurisdiction in the contiguous zone, and no right to exercise legislative jurisdiction over conduct in the contiguous zone.[40] Instead, a coastal state may punish violations by out-bound ships that have violated laws in the state's territory or territorial sea, and it may also prevent future violations by in-bound ships of domestic laws in the territory or territorial sea. A coastal state could, for example, intercept a vessel that has violated a law

---

[31] UNCLOS art 7(5).   [32] UNCLOS art 10(2).   [33] UNCLOS art 10(5).
[34] UNCLOS art 10(4); the waters of a bay qualify as internal waters where the distance between the low-water marks of the natural entrance points of a bay does not exceed twenty-four nautical miles.
[35] UNCLOS art 2(2).   [36] UNCLOS art 2(1).
[37] UNCLOS arts 18–19; see eg, *The Corfu Channel Case* (Merits) [1949] ICJ Rep 4, 28.   [38] UNCLOS arts 27–8.
[39] UNCLOS art 33(2).
[40] UNCLOS art 33(1). A coastal state may, however, exercise legislative jurisdiction with respect to the removal of archaeological and historical objects from the seabed of its contiguous zone. UNCLOS art 303.

against people smuggling in its territorial sea and has moved seaward, towards the high seas, in order to avoid arrest.

b   *Continental Shelf*

The importance of the continental shelf in the law of the sea derives from its potential as a source of oil and gas. Claims to exclusive national jurisdiction over the resources of the continental shelf were first made in 1945 when US president Harry Truman proclaimed that:[41]

Having concern for the urgency of conserving and prudently using its natural resources, the United States regards the natural resources of the subsoil and sea-bed of the continental shelf beneath the high seas but contiguous to the coasts of the United States as appertaining to the United States, subject to its jurisdiction and control.

President Truman notably proclaimed sovereign rights only with respect to the natural resources of the continental shelf, not the seabed and the subsoil as such. The rights of coastal states to the continental shelf were subsequently codified by the aforementioned 1958 Convention on the Continental Shelf, which explicitly states that the waters above the continental shelf retain their character as the high seas. The continental shelf became part of customary international law remarkably quickly. In its landmark judgment in the *North Sea Continental Shelf* case in 1969, the ICJ determined that coastal states have an inherent right to the area of the continental shelf 'that constitutes a natural prolongation of its land territory into and under the sea'. The ICJ further stated that this right exists by virtue of the coastal state's sovereignty over the land, and represents an extension of its sovereign rights for the purpose of exploring the seabed and exploiting its natural resources, and does not depend on actual use or occupation.

The UNCLOS maintains the essential features of the 1958 regime, under which coastal states have sovereign rights for the purpose of exploring the shelf and exploiting its natural resources, including not only mineral and other non-living resources, but also living organisms belonging to sedentary species.[42] The Convention; however, introduced new rules with respect to the breadth of the continental shelf and the delimitation of the continental shelf between states with opposite or adjacent coasts. Article 76 of UNCLOS provides that every coastal state has a 200-nautical-mile continental shelf, even if the geological edge of the continental margin does not extend this far. The term 'continental margin' refers to the physical extension of the coastal state's landmass, down to, but not including the deep ocean floor (i.e., the Area).[43] Only coastal states with a geographically broad continental shelf (such as Brazil, Canada, and Russia) can extend their continental

---

[41] 'United States: Proclamation by the President with Respect to the Natural Resources of the Subsoil and Sea Bed of the Continental Shelf' (1946) 40 American Journal of International Law 45.

[42] These are defined as 'organisms which, at the harvestable stage, either are immobile on or under the sea-bed or are unable to move except in constant physical contact with the sea-bed or its subsoil'. UNCLOS art 77(4); see also the nearly identical art 2(4) of the 1958 Convention on the Continental Shelf.

[43] UNCLOS art 76(3).

margins beyond 200 nautical miles from their coasts, though within specified limits.[44] The outer limits of the continental shelf beyond 200 nautical miles, also known as the outer continental shelf, may be determined with the assistance of the CLCS.[45] On the basis of material submitted to it by the coastal state, the Commission makes recommendations to the submitting state on the outer limit of the continental margin. The coastal state; however, ultimately determines the outer limit of its continental shelf, on the basis of the Commission's recommendation, and deposits that information with the UN Secretary-General.[46]

c.   *The EEZ*

The UNCLOS further provides for an EEZ that begins where the territorial sea ends, and extends to a maximum breadth of 200 nautical miles, as measured from the baseline of the coastal state.[47] The EEZ, thereby overlaps with the contiguous zone. In the EEZ coastal states possess exclusive sovereign rights to the exploitation of natural resources, both living (i.e., fish) and non-living (e.g., oil and gas). Coastal states have, for example, legislative jurisdiction with respect to the exploitation of fisheries in their EEZ, as well as enforcement jurisdiction with respect to foreign vessels suspected of violating these laws.[48] In addition, coastal states possess certain jurisdictional rights in the EEZ, such as the right to establish and use artificial islands, installations, and structures; marine scientific research; and the protection and preservation of the marine environment.[49] While a coastal state may exercise these enumerated sovereign and jurisdictional rights in the EEZ, the freedoms of the high seas otherwise apply in the EEZ. Such freedoms include navigation and overflight and the laying of submarine cables and pipelines.

Like the continental shelf, the concept of the EEZ rapidly became a part of customary international law. The concept was first proposed by Kenya in 1972, and by 1982, while UNCLOS negotiations were still underway, the ICJ referred to the EEZ as a 'new accepted trend' that 'may be regarded as part of modern international law'.[50] In 1985, in its judgment on the *Continental Shelf (Libya/Malta)*, the Court stated that the practice of states demonstrated that the institution of the EEZ had become part of customary international law and that it could extend up to 200 nautical miles from the baseline.[51] Many states have incorporated the EEZ provisions of UNCLOS into their national legislation.[52]

The *Arctic Sunrise* case between the Netherlands and Russia shows how the EEZ represents a maritime zone in which the freedoms of the high seas coexist, to an extent, with the rights of the coastal state.[53] In September 2013, the non-governmental organization Greenpeace used the Dutch-flagged vessel, *Arctic Sunrise*, to stage a protest at an

---

[44] UNCLOS art 76. Strictly defined criteria provide that this can be up to a maximum of 350 nautical miles from the territorial baselines or 100 nautical miles from the 2,500 meters isobath (the line connecting points with a depth of 2,500 meters).
[45] UNCLOS art 76(8).   [46] UNCLOS art 76(9).   [47] UNCLOS art 57.   [48] UNCLOS arts 61, 62, 73.
[49] UNCLOS art 56(1).
[50] *Case concerning the Continental Shelf (Tunisia v Libyan Arab Jamahiriya)* (Judgment) [1982] ICJ Rep 18, para 100.
[51] *Case concerning the Continental Shelf (Libyan Arab Jamahiriya v Malta)* (Judgment) [1985] ICJ Rep 13, paras 34–5, 39.
[52] See Massimo Lando, *Maritime Delimitation as a Judicial Process* (Cambridge University Press 2019), Appendix 1.
[53] *The Arctic Sunrise Arbitration (Netherlands v Russian Federation)* (Merits) (2015) PCA Case 2014–02.

offshore oil platform in Russia's EEZ, in the Barents Sea.[54] Greenpeace was protesting against the potentially harmful environmental impacts of such offshore oil drilling. Russian authorities responded by boarding the *Arctic Sunrise*, seizing it, and towing it to the port of Murmansk. Russian authorities also arrested, charged, and imprisoned the thirty persons on board the *Arctic Sunrise*. Russia was within its rights to construct an oil platform in its EEZ, as UNCLOS specifically permits such installations.[55] The legal issue in this case was instead whether Russia had a legal basis for its response to the protest actions in its EEZ, in particular, the enforcement actions taken against the vessel and its crew. The Netherlands possessed flag state jurisdiction over the *Arctic Sunrise*, which was enjoying freedom of navigation in Russia's EEZ.

The arbitration tribunal that heard this dispute examined many possible legal bases for Russia's enforcement action, including 'hot pursuit', which was the most plausible legal basis.[56] Along with piracy, hot pursuit constitutes one of several exceptions to the general rule that a coastal state may only exercise enforcement jurisdiction over a ship in its EEZ with the prior consent of the flag state, which the Netherlands had not given in this case. Hot pursuit allows a coastal state to pursue a foreign ship outside of its territorial waters or contiguous zone when the coastal state authorities have good reason to believe that the foreign ship has violated its laws or regulations. In this case, the applicable regulation was Russia's prohibition on navigation in a narrow safety zone surrounding the oil platform. The conditions for hot pursuit were nevertheless not met, as the pursuit must be continuous, which was not the case in this instance.[57] As a result, Russia's response to the protest actions was unlawful, and it bore state responsibility for this internationally wrongful act. Though the rights of the flag state and the rights of the coastal state coexist in the EEZ, this case demonstrates the extent to which the coastal state's enforcement jurisdiction is limited, with the result that the law of the sea tends to favour freedom of navigation in the EEZ.

d   Islands

Under UNCLOS, islands are significant because they also generate maritime zones, in addition to the mainland. Islands are defined as 'a naturally formed area of land, surrounded by water, which is above water at high tide'.[58] All islands, regardless of their size, generate a territorial sea of up to twelve nautical miles. Artificial islands, which are not naturally formed, do not generate territorial seas. An island also generates an EEZ and a continental shelf, but only if the island does not qualify as a rock, which is a sub-category of islands.[59] UNCLOS defines a rock as a feature which 'cannot sustain human habitation or economic life' of its own.[60] Neither rocks nor artificial islands generate an EEZ or continental shelf (though rocks may generate a territorial sea).

---

[54] ibid, para 3.   [55] UNCLOS art 56(1).   [56] UNCLOS art 111.   [57] *Arctic Sunrise* case (n 53), para 272.
[58] UNCLOS art 121.
[59] See UNCLOS art 121. See also Sean D Murphy, 'International Law relating to Islands' (2017) 386 Collected Courses of the Hague Academy of International Law.
[60] UNCLOS art 121(3).

States that consist of a group of islands benefit from the concept of archipelagic states, which was introduced by UNCLOS.[61] Such states now have the right to draw archipelagic baselines around the outer edges or fringes of their outermost islands and to consider the water within these baselines as archipelagic waters. Beyond these baselines, archipelagic states may claim a territorial sea and other maritime zones. As a result, vast ocean spaces and the marine natural resources therein, which formerly belonged to the high seas, are now enclosed by archipelagic baselines and governed as part of the territory of archipelagic states. Indonesia, the Philippines, and a number of South Pacific island states are the chief beneficiaries of this new archipelagic regime.

4   Areas beyond National Jurisdiction

a   *The High Seas*

The high seas belong to no state, and represent a maritime space where various freedoms may be exercised by all states.[62] Historically, the high seas began where the narrow belt of the territorial sea ended, but under UNCLOS, the geographical scope of the high seas is more limited due to the existence of other maritime zones under national jurisdiction beyond the territorial sea. The spatial extent of the high seas is defined by UNCLOS in a negative manner as all parts of the sea that are not included in the EEZ, the territorial sea, internal waters, or the archipelagic waters of an archipelagic state.[63] The high seas lie beyond these maritime zones, and are not subject to the sovereignty or jurisdiction of any state. They remain global seas and a kind of *res communis* (common good), which is reserved for peaceful purposes.[64] Every state, whether coastal or landlocked, may exercise certain freedoms of the high seas, under both customary international law and UNCLOS. These freedoms include not only freedom of navigation, but also freedom of overflight, the laying of submarine cables and pipelines, the construction of artificial islands and other installations, fishing, and scientific research.[65] The regime of the high seas applies, in good part, to the EEZ, by virtue of Article 58(1) of UNCLOS, which provides that states enjoy the high seas freedoms of navigation, overflight, and the laying of submarine cables and pipelines in the EEZ.[66]

Although the high seas lie beyond the sovereignty and jurisdiction of all states, ships sailing on the high seas do not operate in a legal vacuum, in which no rules apply. Instead, each ship has a nationality, represented by its flag, and is bound by the rules prescribed by its flag state.[67] Flag states are, in fact, obliged under UNCLOS to regulate ships flying their flag, partly in order to ensure safety at sea.[68] Subject to some exceptions, ships sailing on the high seas are under the 'exclusive jurisdiction' of their flag states. This means that foreign, government owned or authorized ships, such as warships or coastguard ships, may not

---

[61] UNCLOS, Part IV.   [62] UNCLOS arts 87, 89.   [63] UNCLOS art 86.   [64] UNCLOS art 88.   [65] UNCLOS art 87(1).
[66] In addition, art 58(2) provides that the other general provisions of UNCLOS concerning the high seas also apply to the EEZ, to the extent that they are not incompatible with the provisions of Part V, which governs the EEZ.
[67] UNCLOS arts 91–2, 94.   [68] UNCLOS art 94.

board a ship flying the flag of another state, unless certain exceptions apply. Under UNCLOS, the right to board (also referred to as a 'right of visit') may arise, for example, where there are reasonable grounds for suspecting that the ship is engaged in piracy or slave trade, among other exceptional circumstances.[69]

In addition to these grounds for interference with the freedom of the high seas and the exclusive jurisdiction of flag states, these freedoms are also subject to some limitations that relate to the communal character of the high seas. States must show 'due regard for the interests of other states', meaning that each state must take the reasonable interests of other states into consideration.[70] According to this general principle, one state's exercise of its freedoms on the high seas, such as marine scientific research, must not interfere with another state's enjoyment of its rights. In addition, the freedoms of the high seas are limited insofar as states may not endlessly exploit the living resources of the high seas. UNCLOS and other more specific treaties require flag states to regulate the fishing activities of their ships, with a view towards conserving and managing the living resources of the high seas.[71]

b   The Area

The traditionally recognized freedoms of the high seas did not encompass deep seabed exploitation. The regulation of the deep seabed became an issue in the 1960s; however, following the discovery of polymetallic nodules in the deep seabed, and expectations that commercial nodule mining would become a profitable reality. The law of the sea in this respect was fundamentally updated by UNCLOS, by creating a new legal status for the deep seabed, based upon the principle of the 'common heritage of humankind', which means that the resources of the deep seabed 'are vested in mankind as a whole'.[72] According to Part XI of UNCLOS, the deep seabed area and its resources represent the common heritage of mankind.[73] The deep seabed begins where the outer limits of the continental shelf end and is beyond national jurisdictions.[74] In addition, its resources do not belong to any state(s). 'Resources' are defined in UNCLOS as 'all solid, liquid or gaseous mineral resources *in situ* in the Area at or beneath the seabed, including poly-metallic nodules'.[75]

Part XI provides for a detailed international framework for deep sea mining, including the establishment of the aforementioned ISA that manages the exploitation of the seabed on behalf of all mankind.[76] The authority is an international organization that oversees the activities of the parties to UNCLOS that relate to the seabed in areas outside national jurisdictions. This includes the administration of natural resources and the issuing of permits for their exploitation. In recent years the question of who is liable for the environmental consequences that may result from deep seabed exploitation has

---

[69] UNCLOS art 110(1)(a), (b).   [70] UNCLOS art 87(2).
[71] UNCLOS arts 116–20; Agreement to Promote Compliance with International Conservation and Management Measures by Fishing Vessels on the High Seas (adopted 24 November 1993, entered into force 24 April 2003) 2221 UNTS 91; 1995 Straddling Fish Stocks Agreement (n 26).
[72] UNCLOS art 137(2).   [73] UNCLOS art 136.   [74] UNCLOS art 137.   [75] UNCLOS art 133(a).
[76] 1994 Implementation Agreement (n 25).

arisen.[77] Despite the legal machinery in place to govern exploitation of the deep seabed, such exploitation has remained largely theoretical due to the enormously high costs involved in it, and the relatively low prices of the minerals on the world market.

5   Thematic Topics in the Law of the Sea

a   Delimitation of Maritime Boundaries

Section 3 of this chapter described maritime zones that may extend a certain number of nautical miles from the baselines of the coastal state – twelve nautical miles in the case of the territorial sea, for example, and 200 nautical miles in the case of the EEZ. In practice; however, coastal states often may not be able to assert rights to maritime zones to the fullest extent possible, in particular where the maritime entitlements of other coastal states overlap with their own entitlements. It is not uncommon for coastal states that are adjacent or opposite one another to have overlapping maritime entitlements. Where adjacent or opposite states have overlapping entitlements or otherwise disagree about the exact contours of each other's maritime zones, delimitation represents the path towards resolving such disputes. Maritime delimitation disputes have often been litigated, especially at the ICJ, which has developed a long and influential line of judgments on the delimitation of maritime boundaries.[78] States have also resolved such disputes through other means, such as arbitration and negotiations.

In order for coastal states to be able to settle a maritime delimitation dispute they must first resolve any related land disputes, as maritime entitlements are measured from baselines, whether normal or straight. In practice, the ICJ and arbitral tribunals have sometimes had to resolve disputes about where the land boundary ends, which state possesses sovereignty over islands, and whether maritime features actually qualify as islands that can sustain human habitation or economic life.[79]

The rules and jurisprudence concerning maritime delimitation have long reflected a tension between states' interests in ensuring predictability and also maintaining an appropriate degree of flexibility in the establishment of maritime boundaries.[80] Two approaches to maritime delimitation could be discerned in the jurisprudence of the ICJ and during the negotiations of UNCLOS. The first, more predictable and formulaic approach involved drawing an equidistance line between points along the baselines of the coastal states. The second, more flexible approach involved a delimitation based on equity

---

[77] The first advisory opinion given by ITLOS dealt with the question of the legal responsibilities and obligations of states parties that sponsor activities in the Area. *Responsibilities and obligations of states sponsoring persons and entities with respect to activities in the Area* (Advisory Opinion) (1 February 2011) ITLOS Reports 2011, 10.

[78] See, generally, Lando (n 52).

[79] Under UNCLOS art 121(3), rocks cannot generate an EEZ or a continental shelf. Low-tide elevations can only be used as baselines when situated in the territorial sea. UNCLOS art 13.

[80] Malcolm Evans, 'Maritime Boundary Delimitation' in Rothwell and others (eds) (n 22). 1958 Geneva Convention on the Continental Shelf art 6; *North Sea Continental Shelf Cases (Federal Republic of Germany v Denmark; Federal Republic of Germany v Netherlands)* (Judgment) [1969] ICJ Rep 3.

(i.e., fairness). The equidistance line is adopted by UNCLOS as the method for delimitating the territorial sea, though it allows for variations due to 'historic title or other special circumstances'.[81] With respect to the EEZ and the continental shelf; however, UNCLOS leaves the issue unresolved, as a result of which the jurisprudence of the ICJ has been especially important. Articles 74 and 83 of UNCLOS, which respectively concern the delimitation of the EEZ and the continental shelf, simply state that 'delimitation . . . shall be effected by agreements on the basis of international law, as referred to in Article 38 of the Statute of the International Court of Justice, in order to achieve an equitable solution'.

The ICJ has developed a three-stage methodology for maritime delimitation, to give practical application to these vague UNCLOS provisions. Step one begins with drawing a provisional equidistance line, unless 'compelling reasons' make this 'unfeasible'.[82] Step two involves any necessary adjustments of the provisional equidistance line due to relevant circumstances, in order to achieve an equitable result.[83] The lengths of their respective coastlines, the presence of islands or issues concerning navigability could, for example, represent relevant circumstances. Step three involves verification that the equidistance line, which may have been adjusted to account for relevant circumstances, does not lead to a disproportionate outcome.[84] In practice, the application of this three-part methodology has involved some oscillation between relatively rigid adherence to the equidistance principle, and more flexible approaches to maritime delimitation.[85]

b   *Protection of the Marine Environment*

States and other actors widely acknowledge that a healthy marine environment is essential for the sustainability of the planet as a whole.[86] The protection of the marine environment is an interest shared by the international community. International law concerning the protection of the marine environment has; however, developed slowly over time, and in a reactive and piecemeal fashion. The first international instrument adopted on this subject was the 1954 International Convention for the Prevention of Pollution of the Sea by Oil.[87] This Convention had a limited impact, however, because it focused solely on preventing the pollution of the sea through the discharge of oil from ships.

Subsequent international legal efforts to address marine pollution were prompted by a number of major environmental disasters, including the oil spills caused by the *Torrey Canyon* incident in 1967, the *Amoco Cadiz* incident in 1978, and the *Exxon Valdez* incident in 1989. The Torrey Canyon incident occurred when an oil tanker, the *Torrey Canyon*, ran aground when it was entering the English Channel, thereby spilling its cargo of 120,000 tons of crude oil into the sea. This incident, which at the time represented the most

---

[81] UNCLOS art 15.
[82] *Maritime Delimitation in the Black Sea (Romania v Ukraine)* (Judgment) [2009] ICJ Rep 61, para 116.   [83] ibid, para 117.
[84] ibid, para 122.
[85] Evans (n 80) 278. The ICJ, for example, departed considerably from the equidistance principle in *Territorial and Maritime Dispute (Nicaragua v Colombia)* (Judgment) [2012] ICJ Rep 624.
[86] Independent World Commission on the Oceans, *The Ocean: Our Future* (ed Mario Soares, Cambridge University Press 1998).
[87] International Convention for the Prevention of Pollution of the Sea by Oil (adopted 12 May 1954, entered into force 26 July 1958) 327 UNTS 4.

significant oil pollution incident ever recorded, resulted in the drafting and adoption of the 1969 International Convention on the High Seas in Case of Oil Pollution Casualties[88] and the 1969 International Convention on Civil Liability for Oil Pollution Damage.[89] An even larger oil spill occurred in 1978; however, when another oil tanker, the *Amoco Cadiz*, ran aground off the coast of Brittany, France during a storm, and then broke apart and sank, spilling its cargo of approximately 220,000 tons of oil. This accident led France and other states to push for stronger provisions in what became UNCLOS, in order to allow coastal states to take measures to protect their coastlines in situations involving maritime casualties beyond their territorial sea.[90] Finally, the worst oil spill in terms of damage to the marine environment took place in 1989, when the *Exxon Valdez* oil tanker struck a reef off of the coast of Alaska. This incident led the United States to take unilateral, domestic action by enacting the US Oil Pollution Act of 1990, which introduced the use of a 'double-hull' design for tankers, by requiring an extra layer between the oil tanks and the ocean and thereby reducing the likelihood of oil spills.[91] The US legislation has since been incorporated into the international legal regime on maritime safety.[92]

The International Maritime Organization (IMO) has emerged as the central international organization responsible for protecting the marine environment from pollution caused by human activities.[93] Under the auspices of the IMO, states have concluded the 1972 Convention on the Prevention of Maritime Pollution by Dumping Wastes and Other Matter (London Convention), its 1996 Protocol,[94] and the 1973 International Convention for the Prevention of Pollution from Ships (known as MARPOL) and its 1978 Protocol.[95] MARPOL now constitutes the most important and comprehensive instrument that regulates and prevents marine pollution by ships. It addresses not only accidental and operational oil pollution, but also pollution by chemicals, plastics, sewage, garbage, and air pollution. There have been regular updates and amendments to MARPOL through the years, through a series of complex and detailed annexes to the Convention. It has been praised as being effective in combatting marine pollution, as evidenced by substantial decreases in the amount of oil and other pollutants entering the sea. Another major achievement was the 1972 London Convention and its 1996 Protocol.[96] The Protocol now prohibits all dumping

[88] International Convention relating to intervention on the High Seas in Cases of Oil Pollution Casualties (adopted 29 November 1969, entered into force 6 May 1975) 970 UNTS 211.

[89] International Convention on Civil Liability for Oil Pollution Damage (adopted 29 November 1969, entered into force 19 June 1975) 973 UNTS 3.

[90] UNCLOS art 221.   [91] 33 US Code s 2701 ff.

[92] See, for example, MARPOL (adopted 2 November 1973, absorbed by its Protocol and entered into force 2 October 1983) 1340 UNTS 62 (MARPOL); Regulation (EC) 417/2002 of the European Parliament and of the Council of 18 February 2002 on the accelerated phasing-in of double hull or equivalent design requirements for single hull oil tanker and repealing of Council Regulation (EC) No 2978/94 [2002] OJ L64/1.

[93] See James Harrison, *Saving the Oceans Through Law: The International Legal Framework for the Protection of the Marine Environment* (Oxford University Press 2017).

[94] Convention on the Prevention of Maritime Pollution by Dumping Wastes and Other Matter (adopted 29 December 1972, entered into force 30 August 1975) 1046 UNTS 138 (London Convention); 1996 Protocol to the Convention on the Prevention of Marine Pollution by Dumping of Wastes and Other Matter (adopted 7 November 1996, entered into force 24 March 2006) 91 ILM 415.

[95] MARPOL (n 92); Protocol of 1978 relating to the MARPOL (Adopted 17 February 1978, entered into force 2 October 1983) 1340 UNTS 62.

[96] London Convention and Protocol (n 94).

at sea, with the exception of an approved list that includes dredged material, fish waste, vessels and platforms, material of natural origin, and carbon dioxide streams.

In addition to these international instruments, numerous regional treaties govern marine pollution in particular regions. The relatively successful Regional Seas Programme, which was introduced by the UN Environment Programme in 1974, for example, provides a framework for addressing the degradation of the oceans and seas at the regional level. The Mediterranean Programme is the earliest and largest of these regional initiatives, and has produced the 1976 Barcelona Convention for the Protection of the Marine Environment and the Coastal Region of Mediterranean, which aims to prevent and abate pollution in the Mediterranean region.[97]

Against this backdrop of thematic and regional conventions, Part XII of UNCLOS seeks to regulate the protection and preservation of the marine environment on a general level. This part of UNCLOS reflects concerns about marine pollution originating from a range of sources, including land-based pollution, vessel-source pollution, dumping, pollution result-ing from seabed activities, and pollution from the atmosphere. Part XII begins with Article 192, which provides broadly that 'States have the obligation to protect and preserve the marine environment'. This obligation extends to all maritime zones and relates both to protection from future harm and preservation in the sense of protecting or improving current conditions. Article 194(1) further obliges states to take all measures that are necessary to prevent, reduce and control pollution of the marine environment from all sources of pollu-tion, in contrast with the 1954 Convention, which addresses only one source of marine pollution, namely oil. Part XII not only sets out a series of anti-pollution rules with respect to both transboundary pollution and national pollution, but it also imposes on states a general duty to co-operate to prevent and reduce marine pollution. To this end, states are obliged to co-operate on a global basis and, as appropriate, on a regional basis, directly or through competent international organizations.[98] States are, for example, obliged to co-operate with respect to the physical inspection of foreign vessels.[99] Along with UNCLOS, the thematic and regional treaties incorporate aspects of international environmental law, including the precautionary approach, environmental impact assessments, and monitoring (see chapter 16).

c   *Developing Countries and the Law of the Sea*

Many of the states that gained independence during the process of decolonization in the 1950s and 1960s had not participated in the formulation of the four 1958 Geneva Conventions on the law of the sea. These Conventions permitted foreign fleets to fish in what coastal developing countries considered to be 'their' waters and they allowed for the exploitation of the minerals of the seabed on a 'first come, first served' basis. Newly independent developing states favoured the progressive development of the law of the

---

[97] Convention for the Protection of the Mediterranean Sea against Pollution (adopted 16 February 1976, entered into force 12 February 1978) 1102 UNTS 27 (amended and renamed in 1995: Convention for the Protection of the Marine Environment and the Coastal Region of the Mediterranean (adopted 10 June 1995, entered into force 9 July 2004).
[98] UNCLOS art 197.   [99] UNCLOS art 226.

sea because of their interests in controlling the resources off of their coasts and benefitting from the exploitation of resources in the deep seabed. In 1967, an early and significant initiative was led by the Maltese ambassador to the UN, Arvid Pardo, who ensured that the General Assembly took up the subject of the deep seabed, and the use of its resources for the interests of mankind.[100] The Group of 77, which represents the coalition of nearly all developing countries at the UN, supported this initiative. Developing countries viewed the internationalization of the seabed area as an optimal solution that would allow them to benefit from resources that would otherwise have been accessible only to developed states with the technology and the capital needed to extract deep seabed resources.

Pardo's initiative culminated in the UN General Assembly's adoption in 1970 of a declaration that proclaimed that 'the sea-bed and ocean floor, and the subsoil thereof, beyond the limits of national jurisdiction, as well as the resources of the area, are the common heritage of mankind'. The declaration further proclaimed that 'the exploration of the area and the exploitation of its resources shall be carried out for the benefit of mankind as a whole, irrespective of the geographical location of states, whether land-locked or coastal'.[101] The provisions ultimately included in UNCLOS provide that coastal states are, in principle, under an obligation to make payments or contributions with respect to the non-living resources of their continental shelves beyond 200 miles. Such contributions – in fact a kind of international tax – are to be made to the ISA, which is responsible for distribution to state parties to the Convention 'on the basis of equitable sharing criteria, taking into account the interests and needs of developing States, particularly the least-developed and the land-locked among them'.[102] In practice; however, this redistribution system has not yet been very effective, due in part to the near absence of continental shelf exploitation beyond 200 nautical miles.

Many newly independent developing coastal states also sought to consolidate their claims to the fisheries and other natural resources off their coasts. In various parts of the world, developing states declared their 'permanent sovereignty' over marine resources and some even declared extensive fisheries zones or extended their territorial seas to preserve their rights. These developments took place within the context of the New International Economic Order, which was a movement established in the 1970s to bring about economic equality and prosperity for developing countries, including permanent sovereignty over natural resources.[103] During the Third UN Conference on the Law of the Sea, from 1973 to 1982,[104] the Kenyan representative, Frank X. Njenga, introduced the concept of the EEZ, which immediately attracted the support of nearly all developing countries.[105] The

---

[100] See Declaration on the Establishment of a New International Economic Order, UNGA Res 3201 (S-VI) (1 May 1974) (adopted by 'consensus'); see also Charter of Economic Rights and Duties of States, UNGA Res 3281 (XXIX) (12 December 1974) (adopted with 120 votes for, 6 against and 10 abstentions).

[101] UNGA Res 2749 (XXV) 'Declaration of Principles Governing the Sea-Bed and Ocean Floor, and the Subsoil Thereof, Beyond the Limits of National Jurisdiction' (17 December 1970).

[102] UNCLOS art 82.

[103] See also Robert F Meagher, *An International Redistribution of Wealth and Power: A Study of the Charter of Economic Rights and Duties of States* (Pergamon Press 1979); Wil D. Verwey, 'The New Law of the Sea and the Establishment of a New International Economic Order: The Role of the Exclusive Economic Zone', (1981) 21 Indian Journal of International Law 387.

[104] UNGA Res 3067 (XXVIII) (16 November 1973).

[105] Njenga initially introduced the concept in the UN Seabed Committee in 1972 and at the preparatory meeting of the Asian-African Legal Consultative Committee and subsequently at the first substantive session of the Conference in Caracas in 1974.

provisions that UNCLOS included on the EEZ are geared towards promoting the economic development of developing countries, such that UNCLOS can be seen as an example of a treaty that promotes not only economic development but also cooperation between states. First, UNCLOS allows developing states to protect their rights by extending their jurisdiction over a wider adjacent maritime zone than permitted under the 1958 Geneva Conventions. In addition, UNCLOS provides for the sharing of the living resources in the EEZs of coastal states with neighbouring land-locked, or otherwise geographically land-locked developing states under certain conditions, such as the existence of a surplus.[106]

d *A Sea of Troubles: The Peaceful Settlement of Maritime Disputes*

Seas and oceans and their natural resources have long proved to be sources of disputes between states, or between states and companies, especially foreign companies. The proliferation of uses of the seas and the fragility of marine ecosystems in recent times has increased the likelihood and intensity of disputes. Maritime disputes have, for example, concerned questions of delimitation and questions of functional sovereignty over the natural resources of the sea, seabed, and subsoil. In addition, disputes have also arisen with respect to the use of the seas and oceans, especially interference with certain freedoms and rights such as traditional fishing rights, innocent passage and freedom of overflight. The use and management of shared natural resources, such as oil and gas fields or fish stocks that expand or migrate over two EEZs have also been the subject of disputes. Finally, disputes have arisen with respect to the conservation and preservation of the marine environment as well as the exploitation of the natural resources of the high seas and the deep seabed.

The drafters of the four 1958 Geneva Conventions anticipated such disagreements, and therefore adopted an Optional Protocol of Signature concerning the Compulsory Settlement of Disputes, which accompanies the Conventions.[107] The Protocol obliged parties to refer disputes to the ICJ, but this instrument only attracted thirty-seven parties, which is perhaps unsurprising given that states do not easily surrender their freedom of choice with respect to peaceful means for dispute resolution. Nevertheless, in the years following the entry into force of the 1958 Geneva Conventions and the Protocol, the ICJ dealt with an impressive series of cases concerning the law of the sea. In a series of cases concerning fisheries, for example, the Court recognised trends in the modern law of the sea and contributed to the development of rules for the limits of national economic jurisdiction and the delimitation of maritime areas, including an exclusive fishing zone and traditional fishing rights of other states. Even more significant for the development of the modern law of the sea have been the ICJ's judgments in cases concerning the delimitation of continental shelves.[108]

---

[106] UNCLOS arts 69–70.

[107] Optional Protocol of Signature concerning the Compulsory Settlement of Disputes (adopted 29 April 1958, entered into force 30 September 1962) 40 UNTS 169.

[108] See, for example, *North Sea Continental Shelf* cases (1969) (n 80); *Continental Shelf* case *(Tunisia v Libya)* (1982) (n 50); *Continental Shelf* case *(Libya v Malta)* (1985) (n 51); *Case concerning Delimitation of the Maritime Boundary in the Gulf of Maine Area (Canada v United States of America)* (Judgment) [1984] ICJ Rep 246; *Case concerning Maritime Delimitation in the Area between Greenland and Jan Mayen (Denmark v Norway)* (Judgment [1993] ICJ Rep 38.

The drafters of UNCLOS developed an elaborate scheme for the settlement of international disputes arising from the interpretation or implementation of the Convention. One of the Convention's objectives is 'to promote the peaceful uses of the seas and oceans', a goal that is served by numerous sections of the Convention, which together comprise nearly 100 articles related to dispute settlement.[109] This scheme gave rise to the establishment of the ITLOS, a separate judicial institution based in Hamburg, Germany.[110] The states parties to UNCLOS are responsible for various aspects of the tribunal's operations, including the election of its twenty-one judges and the approval of its budget. In addition to settling contentious disputes between states, ITLOS and its Seabed Disputes Chamber may also render advisory opinions.[111]

Part XV of UNCLOS contains the Convention's main dispute settlement provisions. Section 1, which sets out general provisions, is anchored in basic principles of the UN Charter concerning the peaceful settlement of disputes, through a free choice of means.[112] In other words, states can decide how they want to settle their maritime disputes, as long as they do so peacefully, rather than through the use of force. According to UNCLOS, if states have previously agreed to use other settlement procedures, then such agreements take priority.[113] When the parties cannot resolve their dispute through agreed procedures, then UNCLOS directs them towards procedures that do not entail binding decisions by a third party, such as negotiation or mediation.[114] In addition, one party may invite the other party to submit the dispute voluntarily to conciliation. Conciliation is a form of non-binding dispute settlement in which a third party examines all aspects of a dispute, both legal and factual, and makes recommendations that the parties can accept or reject (see Chapter 9). Despite its merits as a non-binding form of dispute settlement that allows for a holistic and even non-legal approach to dispute settlement, states have rarely resorted to conciliation to settle their maritime (or other) disputes. If the other party does not accept the invitation to pursue conciliation, if the parties cannot agree on a procedure, or if the recommendations of the report resulting from the conciliation are rejected by the parties, then the conciliation procedure is deemed to be terminated.[115]

When resort to non-binding dispute settlement methods fails, then parties to a dispute may turn to the 'compulsory procedures entailing binding decisions', set out in Section 2 of Part XV. By virtue of becoming a party to UNCLOS, states consent to the settlement of disputes by judicial or arbitral institutions, in the event that non-binding methods, such as negotiations or conciliation, should fail. The dispute settlement system set out in UNCLOS is; therefore, mandatory and integral to the Convention, whereas the 1958 Conventions on the law of the sea only benefited from an optional protocol on dispute settlement, which parties could decide to ratify or not. At the same time; however, the provisions in UNCLOS

---

[109] UNCLOS, Part XV, Annexes V–VIII; Part XI, s 5.   [110] UNCLOS, Annex VI.

[111] See Massimo Lando, 'The Advisory Jurisdiction of the International Tribunal for the Law of the Sea: Comments on the Request for an Advisory Opinion Submitted by the Sub-Regional Fisheries Commission' (2016) 29 Leiden Journal of International Law 441.

[112] UN Charter arts 2(3), 33; UNCLOS arts 279–80.   [113] UNCLOS arts 280–1.   [114] UNCLOS art 283.

[115] UNCLOS art 284(3); Annex V art 8.

on compulsory dispute settlement give the parties a degree of flexibility with respect to the choice of method (e.g. arbitration or adjudication) and the institutional setting. Parties may indicate by declaration that they prefer to litigate disputes before ITLOS; the ICJ; an ad hoc arbitral tribunal regulated by Annex VII of UNCLOS (Annex VII arbitral tribunal); or a 'special arbitral tribunal' regulated by Annex VIII of UNCLOS. A special arbitral tribunal is exclusively mandated to deal with disputes concerning sensitive topics such as fisheries, environmental protection, marine scientific research, or navigation. Annex VII arbitral tribunals represent the 'default option' under UNCLOS in cases where a party has not indicated a preference or the parties to a dispute have selected different fora.

The application of this compulsory dispute settlement system is subject to a number of 'limitations and exceptions'. Section 3 of Part XV excludes certain types of disputes from the compulsory settlement scheme set out in UNCLOS, namely disputes concerning marine scientific research in the EEZ or on the continental shelf of a coastal state and the sovereign rights of a coastal state with respect to fisheries in the EEZ.[116] States parties remain free to opt out of the compulsory litigation of such disputes. In addition, states parties may opt out of the compulsory dispute settlement system with respect to politically sensitive disputes, such as those concerning maritime boundary delimitation, military and law enforcement activities, and disputes in which the UN Security Council is exercising its functions.[117] The exclusion of disputes concerning maritime boundary delimitation partly reflects the open-ended character of delimitation criteria under the law of the sea. Coastal states may declare that they do not accept any or all compulsory settlement procedures concerning the boundaries of their territorial sea, continental shelf, EEZ, or historic bays. If, however, no agreement is reached within a 'reasonable' time, then one party may request the submission of the dispute to compulsory conciliation. In 2016, the long-standing boundary delimitation dispute between Timor Leste and Australia was submitted to compulsory conciliation, at the request of Timor Leste. This conciliation represents the first time that parties to UNCLOS have resorted to compulsory conciliation.

This elaborate international dispute settlement system is very much part and parcel of UNCLOS. No reservations to it are permitted, apart from the exceptions set out in Section 3 of Part XV. The drafters of UNCLOS took great care to maintain the parties' freedom of choice with respect to methods of dispute settlement. The Convention allows parties to resort to binding as well as non-binding methods of dispute settlement, as well as a range of arbitral and judicial bodies, including ITLOS as well as the ICJ.

6 Concluding Remarks

Following the conclusion of UNCLOS in 1982 and the supplementary agreements on deep seabed mining and fisheries in 1994 and 1995, respectively, the prevailing view among states and scholars was that the codification of the law of the sea was complete. The

---

[116] UNCLOS art 297.   [117] UNCLOS art 298.

provisions of UNCLOS covered the alpha and omega of the modern international law of the sea (with the exception of arms control arrangements, which are regulated by other instruments).[118] The twenty-first century has; however, brought new challenges associated with fundamental changes, most prominently climate change.[119] Increases in global average air and water temperatures, the widespread melting of snow and ice, and a slow but steady rise of global average sea levels are now unmistakable. These changes are having profound consequences for marine ecosystems, and will impact how the law of the sea operates and evolves. Rising sea levels, for example, will impact existing maritime boundaries, as receding coastlines affect the course of normal baselines, and the extent of maritime entitlements. More extreme situations, involving the submergence of one or more islands, may give rise to further legal changes. As islands disappear, states may lose entitlements to large maritime expanses, as the territorial seas and EEZs that were generated by such islands may revert back to the status of the high seas. Exceptionally and most dramatically, the disappearance of an entire island could also affect the very statehood of a small island state.

Global concerns about climate change and rising sea levels have prompted the international community to consider innovative ways of using maritime spaces in order to mitigate climate change and adapt to it. Seas and oceans may harbour many untapped opportunities for the generation of renewable energy, not just wind and solar energy but also new methods such as ocean thermal energy conversion. In addition, attention has shifted to reducing greenhouse gas emissions caused by the shipping industry, and to carrying out offshore oil and gas extraction in a manner that is as environmentally and economically responsible as possible. Studies are also being undertaken on how to maximize the opportunities to use the oceans for the absorption as well as stockpiling of greenhouse gases. The proliferation and intensification of the usages of the seas and oceans has also given rise to an emerging practice of establishing Marine Protected Areas for protecting and preserving aquaculture and special species of marine fauna and flora, including coral reefs. This has led to an initiative to draft a new Convention on the Protection and Conservation of Marine Biological Diversity. Another challenge to the law of the sea is the protection of underwater cultural heritage. These and other developments demonstrate that the international law of the sea is very much a living branch of international law, which has evolved with the centuries to respond to the new challenges that the world faces.[120]

The law of the sea is in many ways symbolic for contemporary international law in general. Next to many classical issues there are a host of novel topics in this dynamic field as well. The nature of the law of the sea is notably marked by both State sovereignty (in its various manifestations) and international co-operation, by duties as well as rights, by spatial

[118] See, for example, Treaty on the Prohibition of the Emplacement of Nuclear Weapons and other Weapons of Mass Destruction on the Sea-Bed and the Ocean Floor and in the Subsoil Thereof (adopted 11 February 1971, entered into force 18 May 1972) 955 UNTS 115. See also Treaty Banning Nuclear Weapon Tests in the Atmosphere, in Outer Space and under Water (adopted 5 August 1963, entered into force 10 October 1963) 480 UNTS 43; Treaty on the Prohibition of Nuclear Weapons (adopted 7 July 2017, entered into force 22 January 2021).

[119] Elise Johansen, Signe Veierud Busch, and Ingvild Ulrikke Jakobsen (eds.), *The Law of the Sea and Climate Change: Solutions and Constraints* (CUP 2021).

[120] Tomas Heidar (ed.), *New Knowledge and Changing Circumstances in the Law of the Sea* (Brill/Nijhoff 2020).

distribution among States as well as widely recognized international areas and *res communes* (now also labelled as 'global commons'). They all co-exist and interact in the law of the sea. Legal evolution of the law of the sea is not limited to treaty law, but rather operates through a variety of sources in which, next to treaty law as the principal source, customary international law and interpretations by international courts and tribunals continue to play an essential role. In these interpretations, developments in other branches of international law, e.g. international environmental law or human rights law, are taken into account. Furthermore, the preamble of UNCLOS affirms that 'matters not regulated by this Convention continue to be governed by the rules and principles of general international law.' Obviously, the law of the sea does not operate in a vacuum. Similarly, progressive development of the law of the sea is often sparked by non-binding instruments (declarations, guidelines, programmes of action) adopted in response to new challenges in a variety of fields and coming from states and their international organisations as well as from non-state entities, such as civil society organisations and the business sector. These non-binding instruments often seek to advance the community interests in the law of the sea and call for an integrated management of the seas and the oceans, building on the finding in the preamble of UNCLOS that 'problems of ocean space are closely interrelated and need to be considered as a whole'.

Recommended Reading

Thomas Cottier, *Equitable Principles of Maritime Boundary Delimitation. The Quest for Distributive Justice in International Law* (Cambridge University Press 2015).

James Harrison, *Saving the Oceans Through Law: The International Legal Framework for the Protection of the Marine Environment* (Oxford University Press 2017).

Kate Purcell, *Geographical Change and the Law of the Sea* (Oxford University Press 2020).

Donald R Rothwell et al (eds), *The Oxford Handbook of the Law of the Sea* (Oxford University Press 2015).

Donald R Rothwell and Tim Stephens, *The International Law of the Sea* (2nd edn, Hart Publishing 2016).

Yoshifumi Tanaka, *The International Law of the Sea* (3rd edn, Cambridge University Press 2019).

16

International Environmental Law

Daniëlla Dam-de Jong

1   Introduction

This chapter explores international law relating to the protection of the environment, a relatively new field of international law that covers a broad range of concerns. The pollution of the oceans and the seas, the extinction of animal species, deforestation, and climate change: these are all concerns addressed by international environmental law. What is evident from these examples is that there is no such thing as *the* environment. The environment essentially comprises the vital ecological functions that sustain life on earth (the climate system, the ozone layer, etc.) as well as the different ecological systems that are part of it (rivers, seas, forests, mountains, etc.). In other words, the environment covers everything around us, including the water we drink and the air we breathe. Or, in the words of the International Court of Justice (ICJ): 'the environment is not an abstraction but represents the living space, the quality of life and the very health of human beings, including generations unborn'.[1]

International environmental law aims to preserve the conditions for life on earth by focusing on specific concerns that threaten these conditions. Since it would be impossible to set up one single regime for the protection of the environment as a whole, international environmental law consists of specialized regimes in which states cooperate through treaties and other instruments to address particular aspects of environmental protection. Some of these address more localized concerns, such as the pollution of a river or the degradation of a nature reserve, while others address truly global concerns, such as climate change or damage to the ozone layer.

This chapter begins by providing a brief overview of the evolution of international environmental law and explains the principal characteristics of this field of international law. It further considers the interrelationship with the concept of sustainable development, which is central to modern approaches towards protecting the environment. It then explores two of the principal concerns addressed by international environmental law: first, the conservation of flora and fauna and second, the prevention of pollution and related environmental harm. Furthermore, the chapter discusses compliance and enforcement mechanisms. Lastly, because environmental protection measures often have implications

---

[1] *Legality of the Threat or Use of Nuclear Weapons* (Advisory Opinion) [1996] ICJ Rep 226, para 29.

for international trade, it briefly deals with the interrelationship between international environmental law and trade law.

2 International Environmental Law as a Field of International Law

This part examines the evolution of key principles of international environmental law and the institutional architecture for environmental protection. It further examines the principal characteristics of this field of international law.

a *The Evolution of International Environmental Law*

International law pertaining to the protection of the environment emerged principally as a reaction to specific concerns, involving states with a particular interest in the matter. This ad hoc approach to environmental regulation persisted until the 1970s. Confronted with the effects of large-scale environmental degradation, such as industrial pollution, deforestation and the depletion of the ozone layer, states started to engage in more systemic development of international environmental law, principally by formulating general principles for environmental regulation and by adopting multilateral conventions to regulate generic concerns.

The United Nations (UN) Conference on the Human Environment, held in Stockholm in 1972, is usually seen as the catalyst for the development of international environmental law.[2] It produced an important Declaration on the Human Environment, which sets out twenty-six principles aimed at the 'preservation and enhancement of the human environment'.[3] Another important step in shaping the contours of modern international environmental law was the UN Conference on Environment and Development, held twenty years later in 1992 in Rio de Janeiro. Its principal outcomes include a Declaration on Environment and Development and an action programme for the twenty-first century, called 'Agenda 21'. The Rio Declaration contains twenty-seven principles aimed at establishing 'a new and equitable global partnership for sustainable development'. These declarations are not legally binding. Yet, they formulate the core principles on which modern international environmental law is built.

Some of the principles included in the Stockholm and Rio Declarations restate existing international law. The 'no harm' principle discussed in this section is an example. The declarations also formulate new principles, which have since found their way into treaties or have become part of customary international law. The current section outlines some of the principles that were instrumental in shaping modern international environmental law. In addition, it discusses in more detail the contribution of the major environmental

---

[2] See Peter H Sand, 'Origin and History', in Lavanya Rajamani and Jacqueline Peel (eds), *The Oxford Handbook of International Environmental Law* (2nd edn, Oxford University Press 2021) 56.

[3] UN Environment Programme, 'Declaration of the United Nations Conference on the Human Environment' (16 June 1972), preamble.

conferences, including the 2012 Rio+20 Conference on Sustainable Development, in developing an institutional framework for international environmental law.

As a first principle, the 'no harm' principle, as included in Principle 21 of the 1972 Stockholm Declaration and Principle 2 of the 1992 Rio Declaration, articulates a right for states to exploit their natural resources 'pursuant to their own environmental [and developmental] policies', but also an obligation to balance this with the responsibility 'to ensure that activities within their jurisdiction or control do not cause damage to the environment of other States or of areas beyond the limits of national jurisdiction'. This principle can be traced back to the 1941 *Trail Smelter Arbitration*,[4] relating to a dispute between the United States and Canada over the release of harmful fumes into American territory by a smelter in Canada close to the US border. The arbitral tribunal dealing with the dispute formulated a principle that has become one of the cornerstones of international environmental law. It held that 'no state has the right to use or permit the use of its territory in such a manner as to cause injury by fumes in or to the territory of another'.[5] The tribunal, thereby imposed an obligation on states to prevent, reduce, and control transboundary environmental harm. The importance of this judgment is that it imposed limits on the freedom of states to use their territory in any way deemed fit by them, for the purpose of protecting the environment of other states.

The Stockholm and Rio Declarations added an important element to the principle as introduced by the arbitral tribunal in the *Trail Smelter* dispute. Whereas the tribunal referred exclusively to environmental harm caused to the territory of other states, Principle 21 of the Stockholm Declaration and Principle 2 of the Rio Declaration extended the responsibility of states to harm caused 'in areas beyond the limits of national jurisdiction', referring to areas such as the high seas and outer space, which do not belong to any state in particular. The declarations, thereby departed from a purely jurisdictional approach, which focuses on individual state interests, and introduced a more comprehensive obligation for states to protect the environment against harm.[6] This approach is exemplary for modern international environmental law, which aims to protect the environment as a whole, irrespective of whether individual states have suffered injuries.

The 1992 Rio Declaration also formulated several other principles that develop the 'no harm' principle. It introduced the 'polluter pays' principle (Principle 16), which requires polluters to pay for the damage caused by their activities. It also formulated the principle of timely notification and consultation for states carrying out (industrial) activities that may have a significant adverse transboundary environmental effect (Principle 19). This principle requires states carrying out risky activities to notify, inform, and consult potentially affected states of the risks to their environment. Section 3 of this chapter will elaborate on the meaning and contents of the 'no harm' and related principles in the context of the prevention of pollution and environmental harm more generally.

---

[4] *Trail Smelter Case (United States v Canada)* (1941) III RIAA 1905.   [5] ibid 1965.
[6] See Alan Boyle and Catherine Redgwell, Birnie, Boyle and Redgwell's International Law and the Environment (4th edn Oxford University Press 2021) 161–162.

An essential innovation of the 1992 Rio Declaration is that it embraces the principle of sustainable development as a way to balance two potentially competing priorities, namely economic development and environmental protection. The Rio Declaration does not provide a definition of sustainable development, but emphasizes in its Principle 4 that 'in order to achieve sustainable development, environmental protection shall constitute an integral part of the development process and cannot be considered in isolation from it'. The idea that economic development should be balanced with environmental protection is not new. Hugo Grotius in his book on the freedom of the seas recognized already in the early seventeenth century that the environment imposes limits on economic growth, in the sense that the exploitation of species, once it reaches a certain level, requires some form of control to prevent over-exploitation.[7] Furthermore, the origin of the contemporary regulation of fisheries can be traced back to the nineteenth century, when states started to conclude treaties to regulate fisheries.[8] The objective of these conventions was however not so much to ensure the survival of the fish species in the long run, but rather to equitably share fish stocks among interested states. These conventions aimed to secure access for the states concerned to the natural resources needed for their economic development, mostly by establishing exclusive fishing zones.[9]

Around the same time, the United States brought a ground-breaking case before an arbitral tribunal. The 1893 *Pacific Fur Seal Arbitration* related to a dispute between the United States and the United Kingdom over the hunting of fur seals in the Bering Sea.[10] One of the questions which the arbitral tribunal was called upon to decide was whether the right of the United States to protect the fur seals in US territorial waters also extended to parts of the sea that were beyond its national jurisdiction. The arbitral tribunal answered this question in the negative, concluding that coastal states do not have the right to extra-territorially impose restrictions on other states' use of natural resources (*in casu* seals). It also; however, provided recommendations for a legal regime to protect the fur seals, as requested by the parties. These recommendations resulted in the conclusion of the 1911 Convention on Bering Sea Fur Seals. This Convention was the first international legal regime (Japan and Russia were also parties in addition to the United States and the United Kingdom) that had as its objective the conservation of an animal species. It, thereby sought to balance the economic interests of the state parties in hunting seals with the need to ensure the long-term survival of the seal population.[11] As such, it was one of the first conventions to adopt a sustainable development approach.

---

[7] Hugo Grotius, *The Freedom of the Seas or the Right Which Belongs to the Dutch to Take Part in the East India Trade* (first published 1609, Ralph van Deman Magoffin tr and James Brown Scott ed, Oxford University Press 1916), quoted in ibid 706.

[8] An example is the International Convention for regulating the police of the North Sea fisheries outside territorial waters (adopted 6 May 1882, entered into force 15 May 1884) Trb 1963, 135, concluded between Belgium, Denmark, France, Germany, the Netherlands, and the United Kingdom.

[9] Richard Barnes, *Property Rights and Natural Resources* (Hart 2009) 184–190.

[10] *Award between the United States and the United Kingdom Relating to the Rights of Jurisdiction of United States in the Bering's Sea and the Preservation of Fur Seals* (1893) XXVIII RIAA 263.

[11] The idea behind the convention was to ensure the protection of seals for the benefit of mankind, including future generations. This can be derived from the arguments put forward by the United States in the *Pacific Fur Seal Arbitration* case. See John Bassett Moore, *History and Digest of the Arbitrations to Which the United States Has Been a Party* (US Government Publishing Office 1898) 811–14, 834–6.

The term sustainable development itself was coined in 1987 by the World Commission on Environment and Development in its report *Our Common Future* as 'development that meets the needs of the present without compromising the ability of future generations to meet their own needs'.[12] The ICJ also provided an authoritative definition of sustainable development in its 1997 judgment in the *Gabčíkovo-Nagymaros* case, regarding a dispute between Hungary and Slovakia over the construction and operation of a major dam in the Danube river, between the Slovakian city Gabčíkovo and the Hungarian city Nagymaros, as well as power plants on the territories of both states. Hungary sought to abandon the project, because of potential threats to the aquatic environment of the Danube river. In its judgment, the Court instructed the parties to 'look afresh at the effects on the environment of the operation of the *Gabčíkovo* power plant' in light of 'new norms and standards' that had been developed since the start of the project.[13] The Court expressly referred to the 'concept' of sustainable development and defined it as 'the need to reconcile economic development with protection of the environment'.[14]

Today, sustainable development has evolved into one of the basic aims or 'organizing principles' of international environmental law.[15] Most modern international environmental conventions, including the 1992 Conventions on Biological Diversity and Climate Change, adopt a sustainable development approach to environmental protection.[16] This means that protection of the environment is not considered as an end in itself, but is embedded in a broader strategy to enable current and future generations of human beings to benefit from a healthy environment that satisfies their needs. These conventions embrace notions such as sustainable use, requiring states not to use the resources that nature produces (such as fish, timber, etc.) beyond their capacity to reproduce; intergenerational equity, which places an obligation on the present generation to safeguard the earth's natural wealth for the benefit of future generations; and the principle of integration, which seeks to ensure that states include the three 'pillars' of sustainable development[17] – economic development, social development, and environmental protection – in all their developmental and environmental policies.

A last key principle introduced by the 1992 Rio Declaration is the precautionary principle (Principle 15), which requires states to take measures to prevent serious or irreversible damage to the environment, even in the absence of sufficient scientific evidence indicating that such damage will occur. In other words, the precautionary principle prescribes states to remain on the cautious side when the harm that may result from their activities would be of a serious nature. The precautionary principle – also referred to as 'approach' by states preferring more flexibility[18] – calls for the careful management of

---

[12] World Commission on Environment and Development, *Our Common Future* (Oxford University Press 1987) 8.

[13] *Case concerning the Gabčíkovo-Nagymaros Project (Hungary v Slovakia)* (Judgment) [1997] ICJ Rep 7, para 140.

[14] ibid.   [15] Jorge Vinuales, 'Sustainable Development', in Rajamani and Peel (n 2) 285.

[16] Convention on Biological Diversity (adopted 5 June 1992, entered into force 29 December 1993) 1760 UNTS 79; UN Framework Convention on Climate Change (adopted 9 May 1992, entered into force 21 March 1994) 1771 UNTS 107.

[17] See the UN World Summit on Sustainable Development 'Johannesburg Declaration on Sustainable Development' (2002) UN Doc A/CONF.199/20, ch 1, Res 1.

[18] See Nico Schrijver, 'The Status of the Precautionary Principle in International Law and Its Application and Interpretation in International Litigation' in *Liber Amicorum Jean-Pierre Cot: Le Procès International* (Bruylant 2009) 243.

risks, for example by undertaking studies to assess the environmental impact of economic activities. This principle is discussed in more detail in Section 3 of this chapter.

In addition to formulating principles of international environmental law, the world conferences were also instrumental in establishing a basic institutional structure for the protection of the environment. The 1972 Stockholm Conference marked the birth of an agency devoted to international environmental governance within the UN: the United Nations Environment Programme (UNEP). Its establishment as a subsidiary organ of the UN General Assembly brought environmental concerns within the UN system.[19] The Rio+20 Conference on Sustainable Development, organized in 2012 to review the progress of the international community in implementing the sustainable development agenda, strengthened the role of UNEP as the 'leading global environmental authority'.[20] One of the most significant changes is that UNEP's 'engagement in key UN coordination bodies' is strengthened and that UNEP is empowered 'to lead efforts to formulate UN system-wide strategies on the environment'.[21] Even though it remains to be seen whether the expansion of UNEP will compensate for the absence of a true World Environment Organization comparable with the World Trade Organization (WTO),[22] it is an important step forward.

Furthermore, a UN Commission on Sustainable Development was established in February 1993 as a follow-up to the 1992 Rio Conference.[23] The Commission's principal responsibilities included reviewing states' progress in the implementation of the documents adopted at the Rio Conference and providing policy guidance to states. It also served as an important platform for dialogue between states and other actors, including non-governmental organizations (NGOs) and the private sector.[24] The role of these other actors and notably the private sector was strengthened as a result of the 2002 Johannesburg Summit. This summit introduced the idea of public–private partnerships for sustainable development, thereby promoting active participation by the private sector in projects aimed at realizing sustainable development.[25] Examples include projects to promote clean energy and access to water.

As a follow-up to the 2012 Rio+20 Conference, the Commission on Sustainable Development has been replaced by an inter-governmental High-Level Political Forum on Sustainable Development. The responsibilities of this body include encouraging system-wide cooperation to promote sustainable development and advancing the post-2015 sustainable development agenda.[26] This agenda includes – very importantly – the implementation of the 'sustainable development goals'.[27] These action-oriented goals are a means to stimulate

---

[19] Nico Schrijver, 'The Evolution of Sustainable Development in International Law: Inception, Meaning and Status' (2007) 329 Collected Courses of the Hague Academy of International Law 221, 246. See UNGA Res 2997 (XXVII) (15 December 1972).

[20] See the Outcome Document of the 2012 Rio Conference on Sustainable Development: UNGA Res 66/288 'The Future We Want' (2012), para 88.

[21] ibid.

[22] Frank Biermann and Steffen Bauer, *A World Environment Organization: Solution or Threat for Effective International Environmental Governance?* (Ashgate 2005).

[23] See UN Economic and Social Council Res 1993/207 (12 February 1993).

[24] See UNGA Res 47/191 (29 January 1993) for the commission's original mandate.

[25] See Johannesburg Declaration on Sustainable Development (n 17) 7–77.

[26] See UNGA Res 66/288 (n 20), para 85 for the forum's mandate.

[27] See UNGA Res 70/1, 'Transforming our world: the 2030 Agenda for Sustainable Development' (2015) 14–27.

concrete action by the international community to achieve sustainable development, including in relation to combating climate change and the conservation of terrestrial and marine ecosystems.

b   ***Principal Characteristics of International Environmental Law***

This section examines the principal characteristics of international environmental law as a field of international law. These have developed as a consequence of the difficulties of fostering agreement in international environmental law. There are various reasons explaining these difficulties. A first is related to the question of state sovereignty. States have been very reluctant to agree on measures that would give other states a stake in protecting 'their' environment. This explains, for example, why there is as of today still no multilateral treaty regulating the protection of forests. A second reason is related to finances. Environmental protection may be costly and imposes limits on economic growth. States are not inclined to spend money on environmental protection if the threats to the environment seem remote or do not affect them directly. International environmental law has developed various strategies to deal with these problems. The current section highlights the principal strategies used to this effect. These are the conclusion of non-binding instruments, a system of gradual norm creation, national implementation and the use of special designations for parts of the environment to balance state sovereignty with internationalization.

A first characteristic of international law is related to the contribution of non-binding instruments to the development of rules in the field of international environmental law. Even though these non-binding instruments are not capable of creating legally binding obligations, they play an important role in the process of law-making. The 1972 Stockholm and 1992 Rio Declarations are important examples of non-binding instruments that have had a great impact on the development of international environmental law. Many of the principles expressed in the declarations subsequently found their way into international treaties or have crystallised into norms of customary international law. Other examples of non-binding instruments that have stimulated the development of international environmental law include (non-binding) decisions taken by the principal decision making bodies established by international environmental conventions, the conferences of the parties (COP).[28] Although COP decisions are generally concerned with the implementation of treaty obligations, some have also substantively and progressively developed the treaty obligations concerned.[29] One of the most far-reaching examples concerns the 2015 Paris Agreement to the UN Climate Change Convention, which formulates concrete obligations for states to combat climate change for the period after the year 2020. This agreement was adopted as a COP decision and subsequently submitted directly to the state parties to the Climate Change Convention for ratification. In addition, UN organs, such as UNEP and (increasingly) the International Law Commission (ILC), as well as NGOs such as the

---

[28] More information on the functions of convention bodies is provided later in this section.
[29] See Ellen Hey, 'International Institutions', in Rajamani and Peel (n 2) 638.

International Law Association (ILA), have formulated important guidelines for states relating, for example, to the management of shared natural resources (international rivers, transboundary forests, etc.) and principles relating to sustainable development.[30]

A second important characteristic of international environmental law is the gradual development of obligations through the negotiation of framework conventions, complemented by protocols that supplement the convention. Framework conventions set out general principles and commitments for cooperation between states to address a generic concern. These often include procedural obligations, such as obligations to develop national strategies, plans, and programs, to monitor the effects of activities on the environment, to cooperate with other states by providing information, by notifying them of specific threats or by consulting them, and to identify and designate specific objects for protection. More concrete obligations, such as agreement on specific targets, are separately negotiated as protocols. An example is the 1985 Vienna Convention for the Protection of the Ozone Layer, which sets out a general framework for cooperation to protect the ozone layer.[31] More concrete actions to control substances that deplete the ozone layer are included in the 1987 Montreal Protocol on Substances that Deplete the Ozone Layer. A major strength of this system of gradual norm creation is that basic agreement on cooperation to address specific environmental concerns can be relatively easily reached, while the more thorny issues can be negotiated separately. This system ensures the broadest possible participation by states in treaty regimes, leaving these states free to decide which additional obligations they are willing to take on by becoming parties to separate protocols. This can also be considered a weakness, since it allows states to refrain from taking on commitments that require them to make economic sacrifices, which are often necessary to ensure effective environmental protection. This is especially so if one considers that framework conventions often contain open-ended procedural obligations.

Furthermore, international environmental law is characterized by a large degree of institutionalization. Most international environmental conventions create an institutional structure for cooperation. The two principal bodies that are usually established are a COP or meeting of the parties and a secretariat. The COP functions as the convention's principal decision-making body and consists of all the state parties to the convention. This body regularly meets to discuss issues relating to implementation and compliance. The secretariat provides administrative support to the COP, organizes COP meetings, and may prepare documents and decisions for those meetings. In addition to these bodies, several environmental conventions have established executive and subsidiary bodies, including standing

---

[30] See the UNEP Draft Principles of Conduct in the Field of the Environment for the Guidance of States in the Conservation and Harmonious Utilization of Natural Resources Shared by Two or More States (1978) 17 ILM 1097 and the ILA New Delhi Declaration of Principles of International Law Relating to Sustainable Development in the ILA Report of the 70th Conference (New Delhi, 2002). More recently, the ILA adopted the 2020 Guidelines on the Role of International Law in Sustainable Natural Resources Management for Development, as annexed to ILA Draft Resolution 4/2020 (79th Kyoto Conference, 2020). Relevant contributions by the ILC include the 'Draft articles on Prevention of Transboundary Harm from Hazardous Activities' (2001) UN Doc A/56/10 and the 'Draft articles for the Protection of the Atmosphere' (work in progress).
[31] Vienna Convention for the Protection of the Ozone Layer (adopted 22 March 1985, entered into force 22 September 1988) 1513 UNTS 239.

committees that can take decisions between COP meetings on urgent matters, or scientific and technical committees, which can advise the COP on scientific, technical or technological issues. Sometimes expertise is also provided by an external body, such as the Intergovernmental Panel on Climate Change (IPCC), which assesses science in relation to climate change policy and provides important input for the implementation of the Climate Change Convention. Another example concerns the International Maritime Organization, which is the principal point of reference for several provisions in the UN Convention on the Law of the Sea (UNCLOS) dealing with the setting of standards, for example for the prevention and control of marine pollution from vessels.[32] Accurate scientific and technical information is key to the proper functioning of international environmental regimes, since decision-making on environmental matters, including in relation to assessing risks, often depends on scientific data. The measures that states need to take pursuant to the 2015 Paris Agreement on Climate Change, for example, are based on a calculation by the IPCC that determines that global warming should stay below 2°C. The integrity of scientific information is therefore essential for the functioning of the system. Lastly, some international environmental conventions have established financial mechanisms to give effect to treaty provisions on financial assistance to developing countries to assist these countries in the implementation of their obligations under the relevant convention.

A fourth characteristic of international environmental law is the emphasis placed by environmental conventions on national implementation. Most international environmental conventions require states to develop national programs and/or to adopt domestic legislation to give effect to the commitments set out in the convention. This method ensures that states retain a maximum of discretion in giving effect to their obligations under environmental conventions. In addition, national implementation aims to ensure that domestic actors, most notably companies, also comply with environmental rules.

A final characteristic of international environmental law is that it assigns a special status to parts of the environment that are of interest to all states. For example, the 1972 UNESCO Convention for the Protection of World Heritage designates parts of the environment within the territory of states as 'natural world heritage', when these parts are of 'outstanding universal value' to mankind.[33] State parties bear a shared responsibility to assist the territorial state in protecting sites designated as world heritage.[34] Also, the deep seabed and the ocean floor underlying the high seas are designated as 'common heritage of mankind', which means that these areas and their natural resources are not subject to appropriation by individual states and should be managed for the benefit of humanity as a whole.[35] In addition, certain environmental processes such as climate change and the loss of biological diversity have been proclaimed a 'common concern of humankind' to denote

---

[32] UNCLOS (adopted 10 December 1982, entered into force 16 November 1994) 1833 UNTS 3 (UNCLOS), see, for example, art 211.
[33] UNESCO Convention for the Protection of the World Cultural and Natural Heritage (adopted 16 November 1972, entered into force 17 December 1975) 1037 UNTS 151, art 2.
[34] UNESCO Convention art 6.   [35] UNCLOS arts 136 and 137.

a shared interest by the state parties in addressing these concerns, based on their respective capacities.[36]

3   Concerns Addressed by International Environmental Law

This part examines two specific goals of international environmental law, namely the conservation of flora and fauna and the prevention of pollution and environmental harm caused by industrial activities. International environmental law does not address these concerns in isolation from each other. The conservation of whales may, for example, require taking measures to protect the natural surroundings of these species against the effects of pollution. Conversely, the protection of particular ecosystems, such as forests, may be part of a broader strategy to address pollution (given that forests act as sinks for the storage of CO_2 gases, an issue addressed by the UN Convention on Climate Change). This section focuses on the rules and principles that have been developed to address these different concerns to the environment.

a   Conservation of Flora and Fauna

The variety of animal and plant species that live on this planet is enormous. While 1.2 million species have currently been classified to date, the total number is estimated to reach almost 9 million.[37] A plethora of conventions has been developed on the bilateral, regional, and multilateral levels to protect these species. Some conventions protect a single species, such as the 1973 Agreement on the Conservation of Polar Bears, while others cover particular categories of species, such as the 1979 Bonn Convention on the Conservation of Migratory Species of Wild Animals.[38] In addition, different regimes exist for species present within a single territory and species that travel from one territory to another. In light of the sovereignty debate referred to in the previous section, it will come as no surprise that most of the existing conventions focus on the conservation of migratory species or of species living in areas beyond national jurisdiction, notably the high seas.

Early conservation efforts focused primarily on preventing the over-exploitation of specific species from the effects of hunting, notably of those that represented an economic value to man. The nineteenth century fisheries conventions mentioned in the previous section are one example. Another early example is the 1946 Whaling Convention, which has undergone a major transformation in the seventy years of its existence, mostly through changes in its schedule that establishes catch limits for whales.[39] Originally, the Convention aimed to protect whales for the purpose of 'the proper conservation of whale stocks and thus

---

[36] Convention on Biological Diversity, preamble; UN Framework Convention on Climate Change, preamble.
[37] Camilo Mora et al, 'How Many Species Are There on Earth and in the Ocean?' (2011) 9(8) PLOS Biology.
[38] Convention on the Conservation of Migratory Species of Wild Animals (adopted 23 June 1979, entered into force 1 November 983) 1651 UNTS 333.
[39] International Convention for the Regulation of Whaling (adopted 2 December 1946, entered into force 10 November 1948) 161 UNTS 72.

[to] make possible the orderly development of the whaling industry'.[40] At the time, the whaling industry was an important and highly competitive economic sector, hence explaining the need for a convention to stop the rapid decline in whale stocks, leading ultimately to the adoption of a moratorium on whaling in 1986. This moratorium, which bans the hunting of whales for commercial ends, is still in force today, even though some species of whales have since recovered. States have held on to the moratorium due to a change in the perception of whales by states. Many states, including former whaling nations such as the Netherlands, recognize whales as highly intelligent animals that should not be captured or killed.[41] This means that the Whaling Convention has effectively shifted from a 'conservation' regime, which allows for the sustainable use of whales and thus for whaling, to a 'preservation' regime, which bans all exploitation of whales, except for scientific research. This change in objective of the Convention is not shared by all states parties. A dispute over this issue was brought to the ICJ by Australia (with New Zealand intervening) against Japan, a pro-whaling nation that was accused of pursuing commercial whaling under the guise of scientific research. The ICJ judged in 2014 that Japan's scientific whaling programme did not satisfy the Convention's requirements for scientific research and that Japan therefore had to abandon its programme.[42] Although considered a victory for anti-whaling nations, the more fundamental issue underlying the dispute, namely whether a complete ban on whaling is justified in light of the object and purpose of the Convention, has not been resolved.

The preservationist approach adopted by the (majority of the) parties to the Whaling Convention is rather exceptional. Most conventions protecting species adopt a conservationist approach to their management, which means that they allow for 'sustainable use' of these species. The 1979 Bonn Convention on the Conservation of Migratory Species of Wild Animals (Bonn Convention), for example, states in its preamble that 'each generation of man holds the resources of the earth for future generations and has an obligation to ensure that this legacy is conserved and, where utilized, is used wisely'. Article 1 of the Convention further provides a list of indicators for states to determine whether or not the conservation status of a species is favourable and whether particular measures, including the conclusion of agreements, should be taken to protect particular species. For several highly endangered species, 'range states' – states that the animals cross on their migration route – have concluded more specific agreements to protect the animals.[43]

Another example of a convention that promotes sustainable use of nature and species is the 1971 Ramsar Convention on the Protection of Wetlands, which aims to protect wetlands like marshes and fens primarily because of their value as a habitat for animals such as birds. This Convention requires a 'wise use' of wetlands and migratory stocks of waterfowl.[44]

---

[40] International Convention for the Regulation of Whaling, preamble.

[41] See Malgosia Fitzmaurice, *Whaling and International Law* (Cambridge University Press 2015) 70.

[42] *Whaling in the Antarctic (Australia v Japan: New Zealand intervening)* (Judgment) [2014] ICJ Rep 226.

[43] See Michael Bowman, Peter Davies, and Catherine Redgwell, *Lyster's International Wildlife Law* (2nd edn, Cambridge University Press 2010) 535–83.

[44] Convention on Wetlands of International Importance especially as Waterfowl Habitat (adopted 2 February 1971, entered into force 21 December 1975) 996 UNTS 245, arts 1, 2(6), 3. Emphasis added.

Wise or sustainable use is also the rationale behind the Convention on International Trade in Endangered Species of Wild Fauna and Flora (CITES). Unlike the Bonn Convention, which focuses on threats to the survival of species related to habitat loss, CITES addresses trade as a factor impacting upon the survival of animal and plant species. Commercial trade in species that are listed in one of the Convention's appendices is restricted or even prohibited, depending on the degree to which these species are endangered. Whereas the Convention does not include terms like sustainable or wise use, its preamble states that 'international co-operation is essential for the protection of certain species of wild fauna and flora against over-exploitation through international trade'.

International fisheries law promotes sustainable use through concepts such as 'maximum sustainable yield' and 'optimum utilization'. The principle of maximum sustainable yield refers to the maximum catch to be allowed without depleting the stocks in the long term. It has become the governing principle for fisheries, as set out in the 1982 UNCLOS. This Convention contains detailed provisions for the conservation and the utilisation of the living resources of the sea, such as fish. States are first of all under an obligation to take proper conservation and management measures so as to prevent over-exploitation of the living resources in their Exclusive Economic Zone as well as in the high seas. These measures are to be designed 'to maintain or restore populations of harvested species at levels that can produce the *maximum sustainable yield*, as qualified by environmental and economic factors'.[45] The 1995 UN Straddling Fish Stocks Agreement, which was adopted to implement the provisions of UNCLOS relating to the conservation and management of straddling fish stocks and highly migratory fish stocks, places more emphasis on environmental considerations.[46] The agreement requires states to 'adopt measures to ensure long-term *sustainability* of straddling fish stocks and highly migratory fish stocks and promote the objective of their *optimum utilization*'.[47] It furthermore requires states to adopt a precautionary approach, as explained in the previous section, and to adopt measures aimed at the conservation of other species, for example those that belong to the same ecosystem or that are dependent on the target species.

The only convention that explicitly defines 'sustainable use' is the 1992 Convention on Biological Diversity. Unlike the other conventions discussed in this section, the Convention on Biological Diversity does not protect species or ecosystems directly. To the contrary, it aims to protect 'the variability among living organisms from all sources including, inter alia, terrestrial, marine and other aquatic ecosystems and the ecological complexes of which they are part'.[48] It therefore aims to safeguard the balance in nature, ensuring sufficient variety between species and ecosystems as well as (genetic) diversity within species and ecosystems. This approach is reflected in the Convention's definition of sustainable use, which is as follows: 'the use of components of biological diversity [i.e. animal and plant

---

[45] UNCLOS arts 61 and 119.   [46] See Boyle, and Redgwell (n 6) 750.

[47] UN Agreement for the Implementation of the Provisions of the UNCLOS of 10 December 1982 relating to the Conservation and Management of Straddling Fish Stocks and Highly Migratory Fish Stocks (adopted 4 August 1995, entered into force 11 December 2001) 2167 UNTS 88, art 5. Emphasis added.

[48] Convention on Biological Diversity art 2.

species] in a way and at a rate that does not lead to the long-term decline of biological diversity, thereby maintaining its potential to meet the needs and aspirations of present and future generations'.[49] This definition provides the essence of sustainable use.

In terms of methods, many conservation treaties resort to listing particular species or ecosystems to ensure their protection. Under the Ramsar Convention on the Protection of Wetlands, states are to designate suitable areas in their territory for inclusion in a list of protected wetlands. The Netherlands has done so for part of the Wadden Sea, mostly because it is home to several marine species and birds and because it plays an important role in flood regulation, shoreline stabilization, and sediment trapping.[50] The UNESCO World Heritage Convention, which aims to protect the world's cultural and natural heritage, also depends on listing. A special committee decides whether a site satisfies the Convention's requirements for inclusion in the list. Some of the sites that have been listed include the Australian Great Barrier Reef and parts of the Amazon. The Bonn Convention and CITES use a different type of listing. Species that need protection are included in separate appendices that reflect the level of protection that is granted to these species. Lastly, the Convention on Biological Diversity does not use a listing system, but requires state parties to establish a system of protected areas and to establish areas where special measures need to be taken to protect (endangered) species (*in situ* conservation). In addition, states must adopt measures for the conservation of species outside their natural surroundings (*ex situ* conservation), for example through breeding programs in zoos.

b   *Prevention of Pollution and Related Environmental Harm*

The obligation on states to prevent harm to the environment of other states and of areas beyond national jurisdiction (the 'no harm' principle) can be regarded as one of the fundamental principles of international environmental law.[51] It is based on the general rule articulated in the *Corfu Channel* case that states have an obligation not to use their territory in a way contrary to the rights of other states.[52] The obligation to prevent harm to the environment of other states and beyond national jurisdiction sets limits on the sovereignty of a state regarding the use of its territory in order to protect the sovereignty of other states.

The obligation was formulated for the first time in the 1941 *Trail Smelter Arbitration* case discussed in the previous section and was included in Principle 21 of the Stockholm Declaration and Principle 2 of the Rio Declaration. This 'Principle 21 obligation', as it is often referred to in the literature, has since been incorporated in several international conventions, including the conventions on climate change and biodiversity and UNCLOS. In addition, the existence of the obligation as a matter of customary international law was affirmed in the case law of several international courts, including the ICJ. In its

---

[49] Convention on Biological Diversity art 2.

[50] For more information on the Wadden Sea as Ramsar Site, see <https://rsis.ramsar.org/ris/289>.

[51] See Jutta Brunnée, 'Harm Prevention', in Rajamani and Peel (n 2) 269.

[52] *The Corfu Channel Case (United Kingdom v Albania)* (Merits) [1949] ICJ Rep 4, 22.

Advisory Opinion on the Legality of the Threat or Use of Nuclear Weapons, the ICJ expressly affirmed 'the existence of a general obligation of states to ensure that activities within their jurisdiction and control respect the environment of other states or of areas beyond national control' and stated that this obligation 'is now part of the corpus of international law relating to the environment'.[53]

The obligation on states to prevent transboundary environmental harm does not imply a complete prohibition on engaging in activities that cause such harm. First, the obligation only concerns the prevention of harm that exceeds a certain minimum threshold.[54] This threshold is usually considered to be damage that may be designated as 'significant', defined as 'something more than "detectable", but [below] the level of "serious" or "substantial"'.[55] Second, the obligation should be interpreted as implying an obligation of care, also referred to as an obligation of 'due diligence'.[56] This type of obligation is very common in international environmental law. It implies that states are to use all the means at their disposal and to take all appropriate measures to prevent transboundary harm. As long as states have taken all reasonable measures to prevent such harm, they are not liable when it actually occurs.

States are furthermore under an obligation to conduct an environmental impact assessment (EIA) to evaluate the effects of their proposed activities on the environment. As set out in Principle 17 of the 1992 Rio Declaration, an EIA 'as a national instrument' should be undertaken for 'proposed activities that are likely to have a significant adverse impact on the environment'. The ICJ, in its judgment in the *Pulp Mills* case,[57] elaborated on this obligation in the context of transboundary pollution caused by a pulp manufacturing facility established by Uruguay on the border with Argentina.[58] The pulp factory was situated on the Uruguayan side of the Uruguay River, which forms the natural boundary between the two states. At the time Argentina brought the case to court, it could not demonstrate that actual environmental harm had occurred. According to the Court, Uruguay therefore had not violated its substantive obligations under the bilateral cooperation treaty concluded by the two states to protect and preserve the aquatic environment of the river. Nevertheless, the Court found that Uruguay had violated some of its procedural obligations, most notably the obligation to inform and consult Argentina on the construction of the pulp mills.[59] Most importantly, the Court noted that the obligation to consult included an obligation for Uruguay to provide Argentina with the results of an EIA prior to the authorization of the project.[60]

Since the parties also disagreed on the content and scope of the obligation to conduct an EIA, the Court took the opportunity to elaborate on this issue. It stated that:

---

[53] *Legality of the Threat or Use of Nuclear Weapons* advisory opinion (n 1), para 29.
[54] See Arie Trouwborst, *Precautionary Rights and Duties of States* (Martinus Nijhoff 2006) 44.
[55] ILC, 'Draft articles on Prevention of Transboundary Harm from Hazardous Activities, with commentaries' (2001) ILC Yearbook II (pt II) 152.
[56] See Boyle, and Redgwell (n 6) 163.
[57] *Case concerning Pulp Mills on the River Uruguay (Argentina v Uruguay)* (Judgment) [2010] ICJ Rep 14.
[58] The Court confirmed the conclusions reached in the *Pulp Mills* case in a 2015 judgment regarding a border dispute between Costa Rica and Nicaragua. *Certain Activities carried out by Nicaragua in the Border Area (Costa Rica v Nicaragua)* and *Construction of a Road in Costa Rica along the San Juan River (Nicaragua v Costa Rica)* (Merits) [2015] ICJ Rep 665.
[59] *Pulp Mills* case (n 57), paras 111 and 122.   [60] ibid, para 121.

the obligation to protect and preserve [the aquatic environment] has to be interpreted in accordance with a practice, which in recent years has gained so much acceptance among States that it may now be considered a requirement under general international law to undertake an environmental impact assessment where there is a risk that the proposed industrial activity may have a significant adverse impact in a transboundary context, in particular, on a shared resource.[61]

The Court, thereby confirmed that the obligation to conduct an EIA has become part of customary international law, which means that the obligation exists independently from any particular treaty regime. In addition, the Court linked the obligation to conduct an EIA to states' 'due diligence' obligation. It emphasized that 'due diligence, and the duty of vigilance and prevention which it implies, would not be considered to have been exercised, if a party planning works liable to affect the régime of the river or the quality of its waters did not undertake an environmental impact assessment on the potential effects of such works'.[62] Conducting an EIA is therefore one of the measures that states must take to give effect to their obligation of care.

This obligation of care also determines the scope and content of an EIA. Even though states retain considerable discretion in this respect, the Court determined that they do need to take into account 'the nature and magnitude of the proposed development and its likely impact on the environment'.[63] Furthermore, the Court made clear that the obligation to conduct an EIA is a continuous obligation; states need to monitor the effects of the project on the environment throughout the project's life cycle.[64]

The obligation to conduct an EIA is ultimately just a means for states to give effect to their obligation to take all appropriate measures to prevent environmental harm. However, does this mean that states need to undertake an EIA for all development projects? In other words, what is the trigger mechanism for this obligation to arise? In *Pulp Mills*, the Court indicated that the obligation to conduct an EIA arises 'where there is a *risk* that the proposed industrial activity may have a significant adverse impact'.[65] In a subsequent judgment on a dispute between Nicaragua and Costa Rica regarding dredging activities in a shared river, the Court clarified that 'a State must, before embarking on an activity *having the potential* adversely to affect the environment of another State, ascertain *if there is a risk* of significant transboundary harm, which would trigger the requirement to carry out an environmental impact assessment'.[66] In other words, a state must conduct a preliminary assessment for all activities that may have transboundary effects. When this assessment confirms that the activity poses a risk to the environment of other states, the state is under an obligation to conduct an EIA. However, the principal question remains unanswered, which is: what qualifies as a risk, triggering the obligation to conduct an EIA? This is not only relevant for the obligation to conduct an EIA, but also for the more general obligation to take measures to prevent environmental harm. More particularly, do states need to take measures only when environmental harm is likely to occur or should they also do so when the risk is more remote or when there is no scientific consensus regarding the risks involved?

[61] ibid, para 204.   [62] ibid.   [63] ibid, para 205.   [64] ibid.   [65] ibid, para 204. Emphasis added.
[66] *Certain Activities Carried Out by Nicaragua in the Border Area* and *Construction of a Road in Costa Rica along the San Juan River* case (n 58), para 104. Emphasis added.

These questions relate to the debate on the role of the precautionary principle, as introduced in the preceding section. When particular activities or policies could cause severe environmental harm, the precautionary principle requires states to take measures to prevent the harm, even if the available scientific evidence does not make it possible to identify the precise risks involved. Precautionary considerations underlie several international environmental regimes and require states to take action. The prime example is the 1992 Climate Change Convention, which notes in its preamble 'that there are many uncertainties in predictions of climate change'. Article 3(3) provides that 'Parties should take precautionary measures to anticipate, prevent or minimize the causes of climate change and mitigate its adverse effects. Where there are threats of serious or irreversible damage, lack of full scientific certainty should not be used as a reason for postponing such measures'.

The 'better safe than sorry' approach[67] adopted by the Climate Change Convention has, however, also led to a heated debate on the measures that need to be taken to combat climate change. The effects of global warming are undeniable. The melting of the polar ice caps, rising sea levels as well as the increase in droughts and wildfires in other parts of the world are all related to the phenomenon of climate change. It is also undeniable that human activities, such as the burning of fossil fuels, the clearing of forests for farm land, and the emission of methane gases due to intensive agriculture, contribute to climate change, which is caused by rising levels of greenhouse gases in the atmosphere. There is, however, considerable disagreement on the precise impact of human activities on global warming. This is recognized by the Climate Change Convention itself, which states in its preamble that increases in the atmospheric concentration of greenhouse gases caused by human activities 'enhance the natural greenhouse effect', indicating that this is partly a natural phenomenon.

The uncertainties surrounding the human impact on climate change have made it difficult for states to agree on decisive action to achieve the ultimate objective of the Climate Change Convention, which is to stabilize 'greenhouse gas concentrations in the atmosphere at a level that would prevent dangerous anthropogenic [i.e. human] interference with the climate system'.[68] A related factor that has made it difficult to achieve consensus on measures that need to be taken to mitigate climate change is the question of who should bear the costs. The climate change regime is based on the principle of common but differentiated responsibilities, which means that states have a shared responsibility to address climate change, but that some states, because of their historical contribution to causing climate change and their more advanced financial and technological capabilities, have a responsibility to take the lead in tackling the problem. This principle proved to be a major bone of contention during subsequent negotiations on concrete measures that states needed to take to tackle the problem. The 1997 Kyoto Protocol, for example, contained emission reduction targets for developed countries for the year 2012 while exempting

---

[67] Jonathan Wiener, 'Precaution' in Daniel Bodansky, Jutta Brunnée, and Ellen Hey (eds), The Oxford Handbook of International Environmental Law (1st ed, Oxford University Press 2007).
[68] UN Framework Convention on Climate Change art 2.

developing countries from this obligation. States with important economies such as the United States never joined the Protocol, while Canada, the Russian Federation, and Japan withdrew from it after the decision to extend the Protocol to 2020. This was a major set-back, since the Protocol was the only legal instrument to impose concrete reduction targets on states.

In December 2015, after years of unsuccessful negotiations, states parties to the Climate Change Convention gathered in Paris to conclude a successor agreement to the Kyoto Protocol. Unlike Kyoto, the Paris Agreement formulates obligations for all state parties to achieve the common aim of the agreement, which is '[h]olding the increase in the global average temperature to well below 2°C above pre-industrial levels and pursuing efforts to limit the temperature increase to 1.5°C above pre-industrial levels'.[69] The principle of common but differentiated responsibilities takes on a secondary role in the Paris Agreement. National capabilities and circumstances continue to determine the extent to which parties contribute to achieving the agreement's aim. However, growing economies, such as China and Brazil, will no longer be exempted from taking concrete measures to reduce their greenhouse gas emissions.

The prevention of pollution and related environmental harm is also an important component of other environmental conventions, especially those protecting particular ecosystems. Article 7 of the 1997 UN Watercourses Convention, which regulates the non-navigational uses of international watercourses, including rivers, lakes and groundwater reserves, provides that 'Watercourse States shall, in utilizing an international watercourse in their territories, take all appropriate measures to prevent the causing of significant harm to other watercourse States'. As indicated by the words 'all appropriate measures', this is an obligation of care (due diligence) rather than an obligation of result. A state will not be liable for causing harm if it has taken 'all appropriate measures' to prevent the occurrence of this harm. Interestingly, the obligation to prevent environmental harm is framed here as an obligation towards other states sharing the watercourse. This would place downstream states (those states situated at the end of the river) at a considerable advantage, since their use of the watercourse would not affect other watercourse states while the harm caused by downstream states would still be detrimental to the environment. This problem is partly remedied by Part IV of the Convention on the protection, preservation, and management of international watercourses. This part sets out a more detailed regime for the prevention and control of environmental harm, including an obligation for watercourse states to protect the ecosystems of international watercourses and to take measures with respect to an international watercourse that are necessary to protect and preserve the marine environment.[70] This is important, since most international rivers flow into the sea.

Harm to the marine environment from land-based sources, such as from (polluted) rivers, is also regulated by UNCLOS. The regime in UNCLOS for the protection of the marine environment is highly developed. In addition to relevant provisions included in the

---

[69] Paris Agreement (adopted 12 December 2015, entered into force 4 November 2016) registration no 54113, art 2.
[70] UN Convention on the Law of the Non-Navigational Uses of International Watercourses (adopted 21 May 1997, entered into force 17 August 2014) 36 ILM 700, arts 20 and 23.

parts that deal with the rights and obligations of states in particular maritime zones, Part XII of UNCLOS is dedicated to the protection and preservation of the marine environment. As a general rule, Article 194(1) of UNCLOS provides that states are under an obligation to take all measures 'that are necessary to prevent, reduce and control pollution of the marine environment from any source'. Similar to the UN Watercourses Convention, UNCLOS therefore formulates an obligation of care rather than an obligation of result. According to Article 194(3), measures should furthermore be designed to 'minimize to the fullest possible extent' pollution from particular sources, including the release of toxic substances from land-based sources, pollution from vessels and from installations and devices. Other relevant obligations include an obligation to notify other states when a state becomes aware of an immediate risk of pollution of the marine environment, to draw up contingency plans, to monitor the risks and effects of pollution and to conduct an environmental impact assessment for planned activities.[71] These general rules are complemented by provisions setting out specific measures that states should take to prevent, reduce, and control pollution from various sources.[72]

4   Compliance and Enforcement

International environmental law is a system that aims to promote rather than to enforce compliance. Several international environmental conventions contain advanced compliance procedures, which function in practice as an alternative to dispute settlement.[73] What makes these procedures especially useful is their incentives-based approach: their emphasis is on assisting states in achieving compliance, while sanctions are only a matter of last resort. In addition, in most cases a convention body takes the initiative to start a procedure. This has the major advantage that the procedure does not depend on complaints issued by other state parties. In some cases, committees established by international environmental conventions to ensure compliance have the authority to issue recommendations that are submitted for consideration to the COP; in other cases, the COP itself issues recommendations, based on information provided by the committees. In all cases, the COP decides on further measures to be taken, including on sanctions.

A typical example of a non-compliance procedure can be found in CITES. The Convention itself contains only a very basic procedure. Article XIII of the Convention determines that the secretariat shall communicate issues of non-compliance to the domestic authorities of the state concerned. The state party must subsequently provide information on the reasons for its non-compliance. This information will be reviewed by the COP, which may issue recommendations to the state party. This non-compliance procedure set out in Article XIII has been developed through COP resolutions, which also provide for

---

[71] UNCLOS arts 198, 199, 204, 206.   [72] UNCLOS arts 207–12.
[73] See Philippe Sands, 'Litigating Environmental Disputes: Courts, Tribunals and the Progressive Development of International Environmental Law' (2007) 37 Environmental Policy and Law 66, 67.

enforcement measures. Most importantly, COP Resolution 14.3 creates the necessary teeth to ensure compliance. It determines that trade in animal and plant species with non-compliant parties may be temporarily suspended to ensure their compliance with the Convention.[74]

Treaty-based compliance procedures are widely used. Nevertheless, states can also resort to a range of dispute settlement mechanisms when other states do not comply with their environmental obligations, including the ICJ, the Permanent Court of Arbitration or specialized tribunals, such as ITLOS. Environmental disputes increasingly end up before international courts and tribunals. However, litigation is not necessarily well suited to the resolution of claims about compliance with environmental law in circumstances where there is no identifiable injured state. Cases before courts and tribunals are generally instituted by injured states (i.e., states that are directly affected by the breach of an environmental obligation by another state, due to the fact that the breach results in environmental harm on their territory). Examples include the *Gabčíkovo-Nagymaros* and *Pulp Mills* cases discussed earlier in this chapter. This does not necessarily mean that states would not have standing to bring a claim before a court if they are not directly affected. Many international environmental conventions contain obligations for state parties that they owe to all other parties to the convention (*erga omnes partes* obligations) and that they could therefore assert before a court. The *Whaling case*, as discussed in Section 3, provides a relevant example. In 2010, Australia instituted proceedings before the ICJ to request compliance by Japan with its obligations under the Whaling Convention, to which Australia is also a party. Australia's interests were not directly affected by Japan's whaling programme. After all, Japan conducted its programme in the high seas and not in Australian waters. Nevertheless, Japan did not contest Australia's standing to bring the dispute before the ICJ. Arguably, this might be interpreted as a silent recognition on Japan's part of Australia's right to bring a claim to protect the common interest of the parties to the Whaling Convention. However, this situation is exceptional. States, generally, tend to refrain from instituting costly and politically sensitive procedures when their interests are not directly affected.

An additional hurdle with respect to litigation of environmental disputes is the consent-based system of international dispute settlement, which requires both states to voluntarily accept the jurisdiction of a court to adjudicate a particular dispute.[75] This poses problems if the state that has caused environmental harm is unwilling to submit the dispute to a court.[76] In the *Whaling case*, consent was not an issue, since both states had deposited an 'optional clause declaration' at the ICJ, which did not contain relevant reservations.[77] However, the circumstances are not always that favourable.

In addition to inter-state litigation, there has also been an increase in cases brought by individuals and public interest groups before human rights bodies and domestic courts. The evolution of international law in the field of sustainable development has enabled

---

[74] See Resolution Conf 14.3 (Rev CoP18) on CITES compliance procedures.

[75] See Chapter 9 on international dispute settlement.

[76] Natalie Klein, 'International Environmental Law Disputes Before International Courts and Tribunals', in Rajamani and Peel (n 2) 1042.

[77] See Chapter 9.

interaction between international environmental law and international human rights law. Today, international environmental law obligations of states are increasingly invoked before global and regional human rights bodies (including courts) as well as before national courts by individuals and public interest groups claiming a right to a decent, healthy, or satisfactory environment, either based on an express legal provision or as part of their rights to life, private life, property, or access to information and justice.[78] The climate cases that have been instituted in several countries, including the Netherlands, Belgium, Peru, and the United States, provide interesting examples of such public interest litigation.[79] These cases are generally instituted against the state by interest groups, claiming that the state concerned does not adequately implement its obligations under the climate change regime as found in international environmental law. One of these cases, instituted by the Foundation Urgenda against the Dutch state, was decided in favour of Urgenda. In an unprecedented ruling, the district court of The Hague ordered the Dutch state to reduce its emissions by at least 25 per cent in 2020 compared with the base year 1990.[80] This number of 25 per cent is based on the Fourth Assessment Report by the IPCC, which states that such a reduction is necessary in order to stay below the critical 2 degrees of global warming. The judgment has been upheld by the Dutch Court of Appeal and the Supreme Court.[81]

5   The Environment and Trade

Several international environmental conventions resort directly or indirectly to trade-related measures to achieve their objectives. The CITES is an example of a convention that relies on trade measures to protect selected animal and plant species against over-exploitation. The states parties to CITES are obliged to issue export and/or import permits for trade in endangered species, and the Convention prohibits commercial trade in some species altogether. These rules also apply indirectly to states that are not parties to this Convention, since trade with non-parties is only allowed if these states issue 'comparable documentation ... which substantially conforms with the requirements of the ... Convention for permits and certificates'.[82]

In addition, states sometimes resort to unilateral trade measures to further the objectives of environmental conventions, even when these conventions do not specifically call for such measures to be taken. The *US Shrimp* case that was brought before the dispute settlement mechanism of the WTO provides a relevant

---

[78] See Sumudu Atapattu and Andrea Schapper, *Human Rights and the Environment: Key Issues* (Routledge 2019).

[79] See UNEP, *Global Climate Litigation Report: 2020 Status Review* (2020).

[80] Rb Den Haag 24 June 2015 (*Urgenda Foundation v The state of the Netherlands*) ECLI:NL:RBDHA:2015: 7196 (The Hague District Court). See Kars J de Graaf and Jan H Jans, 'The Urgenda Decision: Netherlands Liable for Role in Causing Dangerous Global Climate Change' (2015) 27 Journal of Environmental Law 517.

[81] HR 20 December 2019 (*The state of the Netherlands v Urgenda Foundation*) ECLI:NL:HR:2019:2007 (Supreme Court of the Netherlands).

[82] Convention on International Trade in Endangered Species of Wild Fauna and Flora (adopted 3 March 1973, entered into force 1 July 1975) 993 UNTS 243 (CITES) art X.

example.[83] A complaint was launched by four Asian developing countries against the United States for instituting an import ban on shrimp (and shrimp products) that were caught without using a special device in the fishing nets designed to allow incidentally caught sea turtles to escape. The underlying objective of the import ban was to protect sea turtles, which are recognized as endangered animals by CITES and other conventions. However, these conventions do not require states to adopt import bans on products because of harm inflicted on sea turtles.

Measures that restrict free trade are at odds with the basic principles on which international trade law is based, as discussed in Chapter 14. States that are parties to the WTO must provide equal treatment to foreign and domestic products and they are precluded from discriminating between trading partners.[84] In addition, they are not allowed to impose quantitative import or export restrictions on products entering or leaving their territory.[85] The question that can be raised is what the implications of these principles are for states wishing to use trade restrictive measures to advance environmental objectives. Would such measures conflict with their obligations under relevant WTO treaties?

In relation to the trade in goods, the General Agreement on Tariffs and Trade (GATT) allows states to invoke environmental exceptions to the basic rules.[86] These exceptions are listed in Article XX(b) and (g) of GATT. Article XX(b) exempts trade measures that are 'necessary to protect human, animal or plant life or health', which means the measures that constitute the least trade intrusive means available to achieve the particular purpose. Article XX(g) exempts trade measures 'relating to the conservation of exhaustible natural resources', which means that the measures must be reasonably related to the objective of protecting particular species and they must also apply to domestic producers.[87] Furthermore, the measures may not be applied in a manner so as to 'constitute a means of arbitrary or unjustifiable discrimination between countries where the same conditions prevail'.[88] In the *US Shrimp* case, the WTO Appellate Body interpreted this clause as implying that the measures should be sufficiently flexible as to allow other states to choose for themselves how to implement them. In addition to the special device used by the United States, others means to ensure turtles can escape fishing nets must be allowed. In addition, the Appellate Body indicated that the state wishing to protect a particular interest (such as the protection of sea turtles) must make a genuine effort to reach an agreement with other states before enforcing trade measures.[89] In other words, international trade law does accommodate the adoption of trade restrictions for environmental purposes, but preferably by means of international cooperation, most importantly by the adoption of international environmental agreements.

---

[83] WTO, *United States: Import Prohibition of Certain Shrimp and Shrimp Products—Report of the Appellate Body* (12 October 1998) WT/DS58/AB/R.

[84] GATT, Annex 1A to the Marrakesh Agreement establishing the World Trade Organization (WTO Agreement) (adopted 30 October 1947, entered into force 1 January 1948) 1867 UNTS 187 (GATT) arts I and III.

[85] GATT art XI.

[86] See Peter van den Bossche and Werner Zdouc, *The Law and Policy of the World Trade Organization: Text, Cases and Materials* (2nd edn, Cambridge University Press 2017) 544–606.

[87] See GATT art XX(b) and (g).   [88] GATT art XX chapeau.

[89] *Import Prohibition of Certain Shrimp and Shrimp Products* Report of the Appellate Body (n 83), paras 156–76.

6   Concluding Remarks

The protection of the environment is of the essence to sustain human life in the long run. After all, without a healthy environment, life on earth becomes impossible. At the same time, the environment is increasingly put under pressure as a result of a growing world population – from 1 billion to more than 7 billion in just 200 years[90] – and major changes in lifestyle that came with the process of industrialization. There is no easy way to reconcile these competing interests and, to make matters even more difficult, there is also a lack of knowledge regarding the effects of human activities on ecological processes. Important conventions have been adopted to address threats to the environment, often taking a precautionary approach to risks to the environment. Ultimately, the success of these conventions depends on the willingness of states to implement their often open-ended obligations and to make economic sacrifices for this purpose.

On a more positive note, states are increasingly willing to do so. The adoption of the 2015 Paris Agreement on Climate Change after years of failed negotiations attests to this. There is also a growing environmental awareness in international organizations, including in the WTO. Another important development confirming this trend is the readiness that was expressed by the prosecutor of the International Criminal Court in 2016 to prosecute crimes that are committed 'by means of, or that result in', the destruction of the environment.[91] These developments suggest a growing awareness that the environment deserves adequate protection.

Recommended Reading

Alan Boyle and Catherine Redgwell, Birnie, Boyle, and Redgwell's International Law and the Environment (4th edn, Oxford University Press 2021).

Lavanya Rajamani, and Jacqueline Peel (eds), The Oxford Handbook of International Environmental Law (2nd edn, Oxford University Press 2021).

Michael Bowman, Peter Davies, and Catherine Redgwell, *Lyster's International Wildlife Law* (2nd edn, Cambridge University Press 2010).

Pierre-Marie Dupuy and Jorge E Viñuales, *International Environmental Law* (2nd edn, Cambridge University Press 2018).

David Freestone, Richard Barnes, and David Ong (eds), *The Law of the Sea: Progress and Prospect* (Oxford University Press 2006).

Philippe Sands and Jacqueline Peel, *Principles of International Environmental Law* (4th edn, Cambridge University Press 2018).

Nico Schrijver, "The Evolution of Sustainable Development in International Law: Inception, Meaning and Status" (2007) 329 Collected Courses of the Hague Academy of International Law 221.

---

[90] See UN Population Fund 'World population trends' <www.unfpa.org/world-population-trends> (accessed 20 April 2021).
[91] International Criminal Court, Office of the Prosecutor 'Policy Paper on Case Selection and Prioritisation' (15 September 2016), para 41.

Index